WITHDRAWN

THE APOCALYPSE OF ISAIAH
METAPHORICALLY SPEAKING

BIBLIOTHECA EPHEMERIDUM THEOLOGICARUM LOVANIENSIUM

CLI

THE APOCALYPSE OF ISAIAH METAPHORICALLY SPEAKING

A STUDY OF THE USE, FUNCTION AND SIGNIFICANCE OF METAPHORS IN ISAIAH 24-27

BY

BRIAN DOYLE

LEUVEN
UNIVERSITY PRESS

UITGEVERIJ PEETERS
LEUVEN-STERLING, VIRGINIA

2000

ISBN 90 5867 060 0 (Leuven University Press)
D/2000/1869/57
ISBN 90-429-0888-2 (Peeters Leuven)
D/2000/0602/93

Library of Congress Cataloging-in-Publication Data

Doyle, Brian.
 The apocalypse of Isaiah metaphorically speaking : a study of the use, function, and significance of metaphors in Isaiah 24-27 / by Brian Doyle.
    p. cm.
  ISBN 9042908882 (alk. paper)
  1. Bible. O.T. Isaiah XXII-XXVII--Criticism, interpretation, etc. I. Title.

BS1515.2 .D69 2000
224'.1066--dc21

00-055744

*All rights reserved. Except in those cases expressly determined by law,
no part of this publication may be multiplied,
saved in an automated data file or made public in any way whatsoever
without the express prior written consent of the publishers*

Leuven University Press / Presses Universitaires de Louvain
Universitaire Pers Leuven
Blijde Inkomststraat 5, B-3000 Leuven-Louvain (Belgium)

© 2000, Peeters, Bondgenotenlaan 153, B-3000 Leuven (Belgium)

PREFACE

The study of Biblical Hebrew poetry as a literary endeavour has enjoyed something of a revival in recent decades as part of a growing interest in the Hebrew Bible as literature and against the background of related studies in Ugaritic and Akkadian poetry. The ongoing desire to interpret the biblical text in its present condition, assuming that condition to be intentional, has provided the revival with further stimulus. Besides a thorough comprehension of one's chosen segment of Hebrew poetry in all its diachronic dimensions, the analysis of a poem as a poem demands an understanding of the stylistic technique of the poet and how that technique functions in conveying the meaning intended by the ancient author. A fortunate dimension of the revival of interest is the current ability to determine which aspects of the poetic material in question have their roots in its Semitic character and which aspects would appear to be universal (poetic) literary phenomena. The tendency to confine Hebrew poetry within the boundaries of classical poetics has all but disappeared, even if much of the terminology has been maintained.

Scholarly exploration of the use of imagery and figurative language as dimensions of the technique of Hebrew poetry, however, has tended to take second place to the study of the more evidently structural techniques employed by the Hebrew poet (parallelism, metre etc.). At the same time, many biblical commentators seem to treat metaphor – as one among the many figurative uses of language (metonymy, catachresis, synecdoche etc.) – as nothing more than cosmetic decoration, an attractive verbal elaboration without cognitive content. Such an approach tends to lack the conviction that metaphor can express truths, often with respect to abstract concepts which cannot be otherwise expressed. This cognitive dimension frequently holds the key to the meaning of a text. As a result, much of the mystery which often surrounds the use of figurative language and of metaphor in particular remains in place.

The study of metaphor as a particular aspect of figurative language constitutes an ideal point of entry into the analysis of a poetic text because it forces the exegete to examine the final text from a variety of perspectives. How can one discern the presence of metaphorical speech (speech acts rather than individual metaphors)? What are the various types of metaphorical speech available to and employed by the biblical poet? How does the structure of a piece of Hebrew poetry carry its metaphorical dimensions (parallelism // metaphor)? How did the biblical poet make use of these various types of metaphor and to what purpose? Can we ultimately gain access to the poet's meaning? The present study endeavours to provide at least a partial answer to these questions.

A study of the use of metaphor in Biblical Hebrew poetry cannot avoid entering the complex world of linguistics and philosophy with its (over-) abundant literature and often impenetrable argumentation and terminology. In maintaining our focus on the biblical text, however, the present study will endeavour to anchor the abstractions of metaphorical theory with chosen examples. Our primary intention in doing so will be the establishment of a theoretical model for approaching metaphors in biblical texts. The same focus on biblical metaphors inevitably leads the exegete into a perhaps even more complex debate, that of 'God talk'. Can we (does the Bible) speak about God in metaphorical language? Is there any other way of speaking about God? The present study will steer a middle course in this regard, acknowledging the possibility of metaphorical language about God yet denying its exclusivity. One thing clearly emerges from the analysis: metaphor often makes the unspeakable speakable. The Hebrew prophets constitute fertile ground in their use of metaphorical language in that they were often bold enough to speak the unspeakable, especially concerning the relationship between the people and God. The book of the prophet Isaiah and the segment thereof often referred to as the 'Apocalypse of Isaiah' is no exception and as such constitutes the testing ground for the theoretical element of the present study.

The present volume is a revised version of my doctoral dissertation presented at the Catholic University of Leuven (April 1st, 1999) under the direction of Prof. Dr. W.A.M. Beuken. My satisfaction with Wim Beuken as promoter has its roots in my S.T.L. years when he guided me into the world of Biblical Hebrew Poetry and the Psalms and ultimately for my doctoral research to the book of Isaiah. His infectious enthusiasm for the book of Isaiah and youthful curiosity for new exegetical methods has been an inspiration. For his expertise, wisdom and kindness I will be forever in his debt.

A number of individuals and communities of individuals are also due a word of thanks for their support during the preparation of this work. The list is chronological: Justinian McGread and the Passionist Communities of Ireland and Scotland, the Norbertine Communities of Storrington Priory, the Abbeys of Tongerlo, Averbode and Park, Msgr. Padraic Loftus and the community of St Mel's, Woodland Hills, Los Angeles, Msgr. Lloyd Torgerson and the community of St Monica's, Santa Monica, Los Angeles, Mr & Mrs. P. Wright, the staff of the European Centre for Christian Ethics, Prof. Dr. J. Renkema. Thanks are likewise due to Prof. Dr. F. Neirynck for kindly agreeing to publish this work in the BETL series.

A final word of gratitude is due to my parents William and Mary, my brothers Gerard and John and sisters Margaret, Alice and Mary to whom I dedicate this work.

July 7th 1999   Brian Doyle

TABLE OF CONTENTS

Preface VII

Introduction 1

CHAPTER ONE
ISAIAH 24–27: A CONCISE STATUS QUAESTIONIS

I. History of the Redaction of Isa 24–27 11
   1. Fragmentary or Unitary? (13). — 2. The So-Called Prophetic Liturgy (14)
II. The Redactional Process 16
   1. Recapitulations – Themes and Motifs (17). — 2. *Wachstumshypothese* (19). — 3. A Well-Ordered Composition (20). — 4. Isa 24–27's Position in the Redaction History of BI (22). — Conclusion (23)
III. Literary Genre – Temporal Perspective – Date 24
   1. Literary Genre (24). — 2. Temporal Perspective (27). — 3. Date (30). — Conclusion (36)
IV. The Unnamed City (Cities) in Isa 24–27 37
   Conclusion (45)

CHAPTER TWO
AN APPROACH TO METAPHOR

I. Theories and Definitions 51
   1. A Definition of Metaphor (51). — 2. Cognitive Theories of Metaphor (58). — 3. Theories of Metaphor and the Bible (68)
II. Identifying Metaphors (Daniel Bourguet) 77
   1. Formal Indicators (78). — 2. Syntactic Indicators (80). — 3. Semantic Indicators (82). — 4. How Do Metaphors Work? (83)
III. Theological and Biblical Metaphors (Nelly Stienstra) 91
   1. Analogy and Metaphor (92). — 2. Anthropomorphism and Biblical Metaphor (95)
IV. Skills for Approaching Metaphor (Peter W. Macky) 98
   1. Principles and Assumptions – Seven Basic Skills (98). — 2. The Varieties of Metaphor (103). — 3. From Novel to Retired (Dead) Metaphors (107). — 4. Fooled by Hidden Metaphors (110).

— 5. Necessary Metaphor (113). — 6. The Author's Purpose (116). — Conclusion (120)

V. Searching for Metaphors: Notes on Method 123
   1. Metaphor Spotting (123). — 2. Various Types of Metaphor (125). — 3. Author's Purpose (128). — 4. Biblical Talk About God (129). — 5. Hermeneutics of Biblical Metaphors (132). — 6. Methodological Steps: Preliminary Steps; Indicators; Type; Author's Purpose/Interpretation (139). — Conclusion (144)

CHAPTER THREE

ISAIAH 24

Hebrew Colometry & Working Translation 146
Isa 24,1-3 152
   Delimitation of Metaphorical Statement (153). — Indicators (153). — Type (156). — Author's Purpose/Interpretation (158)
Isa 24,4-6 161
   Delimitation of Metaphorical Statement (162). — Indicators (163) — Type (165). — Author's Purpose/Interpretation (168)
Isa 24,7-13 170
   Delimitation of Metaphorical Statement (171). — Indicators (173). — Type (174). — Author's Purpose/Interpretation (177). — V. 13 (179). — Conclusion Isa 24,1-13 (181)
Isa 24, 14-16b & 16c-18d 182
   Delimitation of Metaphorical Statement (183). — Indicators (187). — Type (189). — Author's Purpose/Interpretation (192)
Isa 24,18e-23 195
   Delimitation of Metaphorical Statement (195). — Indicators/Type: I, II, III, IV (198). — Author's Purpose/Interpretation: I, II, III, IV (209). — Author's Purpose/Interpretation of vv. 18e-23 (213). — Concluding Remarks on Isa 24 (214)

CHAPTER FOUR

ISAIAH 25

1. Hebrew Colometry & Working Translation 218
2. Centrality of Zion in Isaiah 222
   Excursus: Jerusalem as Female 223
   Cities as Females; Cities as Daughters; Cities as Wives/Mothers; Cities as Widows; The ברית עולם as a Metaphor for Marriage
3. Delimitation of Metaphorical Statements 231
Isa 25,1-3 & 10b-12 234

Structure, Poetry and the Relationship between Isa 25,1-3 and 10b-12 (236). — Internal vv. 1-3 (237). — Internal vv. 10b-12 (238). — Associations between vv. 1-3 & vv. 10b-12 (239)

Isa 25,4-5 241
Delimitation of Metaphorical Statement (242). — Indicators (243). — Type (246). — Author's Purpose/Interpretation (247). — Type (250). — Author's Purpose/Interpretation (250)

Isa 25,6-8 251
Delimitation of Metaphorical Statement (252). — Indicators (254). — Type (255). — Author's Purpose/Interpretation (256)

Isa 25,9-10a 257
Delimitation of Metaphorical Statement (259). — Indicators/Type (263). — Author's Purpose/Interpretation (271). — Concluding Remarks on Isa 25 (274)

CHAPTER FIVE
ISAIAH 26

1. Hebrew Colometry & Working Translation 276
2. Introduction: Analysis of Isaiah 26 282

Isa 26,1c-6 283
Delimitation of Metaphorical Statement (284). — Indicators (285). — Type (287). — Author's Purpose/Interpretation (288)

Isa 26,7-10 289
Delimitation of Metaphorical Statement (290). — Indicators (291). — Type (293). — Author's Purpose/Interpretation (296)

Isa 26,11-15 298
Delimitation of Metaphorical Statement (299). — Indicators (300). — Excursus: Individual or Civil Resurrection? (304). — Type (305). — Author's Purpose/Interpretation (306)

Isa 26,16-18(19) 308
Delimitation of Metaphorical Statement (310). — Indicators (311). — Type (315). — Author's Purpose/Interpretation (315). — Excursus: A Short Survey of Interpretation (316)

Isa 26,20-27,1 321
Delimitation of Metaphorical Statement (321). — Indicators (323). — Type (326). — Author's Purpose/Interpretation (329). — Concluding Remarks on Isa 26 (331)

CHAPTER SIX
ISAIAH 27

1. Hebrew Colometry & Working Translation 336
Isa 27,2-6 340
   Delimitation of Metaphorical Statement (341). — Excursus: Relationship with Isa 5,1-7 (344). — Indicators (345). — Type (347). — Author's Purpose/Interpretation (348). — Eschatological/Historical Intimations: v. 6 (351)
Isa 27,7-13 253
   Delimitation of Metaphorical Statement (254). — Indicators (357). — Type (363). — Author's Purpose/Interpretation (366). — Historical Intimations: v. 9 (368)

CONCLUDING REMARKS

Redaction 371
Literary Genre/Temporal Perspective 372
Division and Literary Structure 373
The Unnamed City (Cities) 373
Individual or Civil Resurrection? 374
Type of Metaphorical Speech 374

APPENDIX
A TEXT-GRAMMATICAL ANALYSIS
in Dialogue with A. Niccacci

A. Niccacci 379
   History of Research (379). — Methodology / Terminology (382). — Reception (383). — Application to Poetry (384)
Aims of the Present Analysis 386
Clause Hierarchy 390
Commentary 404

ABBREVIATIONS 425
BIBLIOGRAPHY 428
INDEX OF AUTHORS 457
INDEX OF SCRIPTURE REFERENCES 463

INTRODUCTION

In a recent article[1] Adele Berlin laments the fact that biblical poetry as such has been given so little attention by exegetes in recent years. While she admits to the excellent work of those who focus on the linguistic perspectives of poetry and formal aspects such as metre, parallelism, structural devices, repetition etc., she argues that there is a "…need to attend more to biblical poetry *qua* poetry – to give more attention to the *meaning* of a poem and to how a poem achieves its meaning. That is, to develop ways of reading poetry…". According to Berlin, "A good starting-point in the quest for reading strategies is the study of metaphor." While many if not most commentators[2] would tend to view parallelism as the primary guiding force of biblical poetry, Berlin goes on to venture that parallelism and metaphor are two sides of the same coin, both rooted in 'likeness and difference'[3], 'similarities and dissimilarities'[4], 'equivalence and contrast'[5]. For Berlin, then, "The basic form of metaphor is parallelism, in the sense of the contiguous or syntagmatic arrangement of paradigmatic elements such that unlikes become alike. The inevitable conclusion is that both parallelism and metaphor are the defining characteristics of biblical poetry"[6].

P.D. Miscall takes a similar although not identical approach to the poetry of the prophet Isaiah, proposing that in approaching Isaiah we ought to do two things: 1) avoid the historical/theological and emphasise the literary/theological and 2) give priority to metaphor over meaning[7]. He further proposes that tracing an image throughout the entire book of Isaiah will create a labyrinth of corridors into the meaning of the text, thereby implying that as there are many images there are many ways to approach meaning and interpretation of the text. Miscall enters into the

---

1. A. BERLIN, *On Reading Biblical Poetry: The Role of Metaphor*, in J.A. EMERTON (ed.), *Congress Volume, Cambridge 1995*, Leiden, 1997, pp. 25-36.
2. A. BERLIN, *The Dynamics of Biblical Parallelism*, Bloomington, IN, 1985; R. ALTER, *The Art of Biblical Poetry*, New York, NY, 1985; J. KUGEL, *The Idea of Biblical Poetry Parallelism and Its History*, New Haven, CT, 1981 and a host of others.
3. F. LANDY, *Poetics and Parallelism. Some Comments on James Kugel's* The Idea of Biblical Poetry, in *JSOT* 28 (1984), p. 72.
4. J. BRIGGS and R. MONACO, *Metaphor: The Logic of Poetry*, New York, NY, 1990, p. 6.
5. BERLIN, *Dynamics*, pp. 140-141.
6. BERLIN, *The Role of Metaphor*, p. 28.
7. P.D. MISCALL, *Isaiah – Labyrinth of Images*, in *Semeia* 54 (1991) 103-121.

labyrinth of Isaiah via the image of 'light' but soon finds himself in a maze of adjoining corridors which extend and expand and even reverse his original starting point.

Miscall's study has partly provided the inspiration to approach the daunting labyrinth of the book of Isaiah and to enter that labyrinth via the metaphors found in a specific and frequently disputed textual complex, namely the so-called 'Isaiah Apocalypse' (Isa 24–27). Miscall's principles will also help guide us through the text, reminding us that our focus must be literary/theological rather than historical/theological and that attention should be paid "... more to the workings and to the meanings of Isaiah as it stands, not as a mirror of the history of ancient Israel"[8]. Our review of the history of research will reveal that the latter approach has tended to dominate and that a literary approach to the text in which the complex is treated as Hebrew poetry and metaphor is treated as a building block of Hebrew poetry may help us to solve some of the questions left unanswered concerning these chapters of PI, questions concerning literary genre, temporal perspective, date, setting, identification of the 'city' and ultimately, having done so, lead us to primary meaning of the complex as a whole. At the same time, it is our intention to take Berlin's advice also, and to approach metaphor as the other side of the coin to parallelism and its equivalents[9]. Thus, for the most part, it will be through an analysis of the literary shape of the textual units in question that we will endeavour to discern the presence of metaphor and to understand its effect on the meaning of the text. This will be reflected in our methodological approach which, having delimited a unit of poetry within the textual complex of Isa 24–27, will examine that unit for indicators of the use and presence of metaphorical language, broader metaphorical statements rather than individual metaphors. Having discerned the presence of metaphor, our next task will be to determine the type of metaphor being employed, and this will be done on the basis of a number of studies of metaphor as a literary (and cognitive) phenomenon and as a specifically biblical/theological phenomenon. An effort will then be made to uncover the author's intention in using metaphorical language and to work towards an interpretation of the textual units in themselves and the textual complex as a whole.

---

8. *Ibid.*, p. 105.

9. As we shall see, not only parallelism but a variety of structuring and non-structuring poetic devices may be seen to indicate the presence of metaphorical speech, although one might still employ the term parallelism as an umbrella term for the other poetic devices in question since they all ultimately function to bring two or more terms/ideas/images in contact with one another via juxtaposition etc..

A working translation of the text of Isa 24–27 together with the Hebrew text divided according to colometric principles precedes the detailed analysis of each individual chapter of the text complex. Both are based on the diplomatic edition of the Codex Leningradensis (B19A) printed in the *Biblia Hebraica Stuttgartensia* (BHS)[10]. Relevant information gleaned from other diplomatic editions[11], as well as the textual witness of the ancient translations[12] is given due consideration in the context of the text-critical discussion which accompanies the metaphorical analysis of the text. Colometrical divisions together with text-critical remarks are presented and justified *in loco*. A text-grammatical analysis of the material is also provided as an appendix to the present volume.

A number of principles have governed the working translation, colometric division, text-grammar and lay-out of the text of Isa 24–27. In the first instance, an effort has been made to stay close to the word order of the Hebrew text to allow for stylistic patterns to emerge with greater clarity. As a consequence, the English is sometimes a little stultified. Where it has been impossible to avoid a change in the Hebrew word order the translation indicates this with the sigla ∞ at the end of the verse or line in question.

Word repetition in Hebrew has been respected where possible in the English translation, even when more literary English would be obliged to search for synonyms. Repetition is a primary feature of the technique of Biblical poetry and its presence ought not to be ignored. More detail

---

10. K. ELLIGER and W. RUDOLPH et al. (eds.), *Biblia Hebraica Stuttgartensia*, Stuttgart, 1990⁴ (henceforth BHS). Most commentators follow this edition for its completeness and accuracy – cf. J.D.W.WATTS, *Isaiah 1–33* (WBC, 24), Waco, TX, 1985, p. xxxv – if not for its antiquity. A number of principles governing the translation and its presentation are also outlined in the Introduction above.

11. M.H GOSHEN-GOTTSTEIN (ed.), *The Book of Isaiah, Part I and II. The Hebrew University Bible*, Jerusalem, 1975; ID., *The Aleppo Codex* [facsimile edition], Jerusalem, 1976.

12. Septuagint (LXX): A. RAHLFS (ed.), *Septuaginta II*, Stuttgart, 1935⁹; J. ZIEGLER, (ed.) *Isaias. Septuaginta* (Vetus Testamentum Graecum Auctoritate Academiae Scientarium Gottingensis, 14), Göttingen, 1983³; Targum (Tg): A. SPERBER, (ed.), *The Bible in Aramaic. III The Latter Prophets According to Targum Jonathan*, Leiden, 1962; J.F. STENNING (ed. and tr.), *The Targum of Isaiah*, Oxford, 1949; Qumran (IQIsaᵃ and IQIsaᵇ): M. BURROWS (ed.), *The Dead Sea Scrolls of St Mark's Monastery, I The Isaiah Manuscript and the Habbakuk Commentary* (AASOR), New Haven, CT, 1950 (=IQIsaᵃ); ID., *The Dead Sea Scrolls of the Hebrew University*, Jerusalem, 1955 (= IQIsaᵇ); F. GARCIA MARTINEZ and W.G.E. WATSON, *The Dead Sea Scrolls Translated: the Qumran Texts in English*, Leiden, 1994 (= F. GARCIA MARTINEZ, *Textos de Qumran Trotta*, Madrid, 1992); Vulgate: O. WEBER (ed.), *Biblia Sacra iuxta vulgatem versionem II*, Stuttgart, 1969; Other versions: F. FIELD, *Origenis Hexaplorum quae supersunt II*, Oxford, 1875; reprinted 1964.

on the various forms of parallelism (semantic, grammatical, phonetic etc.) and other stylistic features evident in the text will be provided *in loco* in the detailed analysis of Isa 24–27. Text-critical matters with respect to the translation are dealt with in the detailed analysis of each segment of the text. The ambiguous terms ארץ and תבל have been translated 'land' and 'world' respectively throughout. The specific meaning in each case will be discussed in the detailed analysis. This approach to the translation of Isa 24–27, which focuses on the text as a literary datum, does not intend to sidestep problems of a textual nature or leave them unresolved. Nor, indeed, does it intend to leave the division of the text unjustified. It follows the advice of W.G.E. Watson whose methodology for the analysis of Hebrew poetry suggests that translation should be part of the preliminary stage of such analysis because specific difficulties with the text often cannot be solved without a better understanding of the poem's overall structure and the relationship of specific poetic devices within the poem as a whole[13]. An initial, in as far as possible 'unbiased' reading of a poem can allow its poetic features, one of which being metaphor, to emerge with greater clarity before philological complexities begin to cloud the picture. Text-critical choices have indeed been made and are treated, as we noted above, in detail in the close analysis of the text[14]. The reader, however, is invited to suspend his or her desire for detailed substantiation for the time being and to read the translation without prejudice as a literary entity.

The Hebrew colometric division of the text accompanies the English translation, the textual divisions being equivalent. As is the case with the translation, individual textual units (stanzas[15]) are given a separate page. Monocola, bicola and tricola are represented horizontally and are separated by a blank line. Units larger than the tricola are represented vertically. Delimitation of stanzas within a larger work of poetry is no easy task. Indications of opening and closure are frequently few and far between in 'continuous' poetical texts and an element of personal judgement often cannot be avoided. As Watson points out, however, the principle guide in what he refers to as the 'segmentation' of a text is *parallelism*[16] which functions as a highly structuring and highly varied poetic

---

13. W.G.E. WATSON, *Classical Hebrew Poetry, A Guide to its Techniques* (JSOT SS, 26), Sheffield, 1995², p. 17.
14. It will be observed in the detailed analysis of the individual stanzas of Isa 24–27 that serious problems of a text-critical nature are infrequent although not absent.
15. The terminology follows, for the most part, WATSON, *Classical Hebrew Poetry*, pp. 12-15.
16. WATSON, *Classical Hebrew Poetry*, pp. 15, 19.

device both within strophes and between them (at smaller and larger intervals). Besides evident semantic divisions, parallelism has been the primary guide to the colometric segmentation of the present text into smaller[17] and larger[18] units.

An outline presentation and analysis of the text-grammar of these chapters is provided along the same divisions as the translation and the colometry. Where there is an apparent syntactical division within a text which the translation and subsequent detailed analysis treats as a single unit this is indicated by a dotted line in all three locations. It seems evident that the sub-division of poetical texts need not always and necessarily coincide at the semantic/colometric and syntactic levels[19]. Grammatical features also and often provide a further foundation of the division of the text.

Chapter I offers a concise[20] *Status Quaestionis* which intends to survey the history of exegesis of these chapters of Isaiah on the basis of a number of important and recurring (and as yet unanswered) questions relating to the unity (or lack thereof), genre, dating of the complex and the identification of the unnamed city (cities) referred to throughout the piece.

In chapter II we enter the complex world of metaphorical theory assisted by and under the guidance of three recent authors, D. Bourguet[21], N. Stienstra[22] and P. W. Macky[23], each of whom represents a particular understanding of the use and function of metaphor in human speech and literature. Our purpose in this second chapter will be to find an approach to biblical metaphor which will allow us to detect the presence of metaphors in biblical texts, to categorise them according to type and ultimately to try to discover why and to what end a biblical author used a particular metaphor or group of metaphors. This chapter will also

---

17. I.e. monocola, bicola etc. and combinations thereof into strophes.
18. I.e. combinations of strophes into stanzas.
19. On the basis of parallelism, for example, Isa 24,18 is divided into six cola (18af). In terms of clause division, however, the same verse constitutes five distinct yet dependent clauses (18a-e).
20. It would be impossible, and hardly desirable, to attempt an exhaustive survey of the material which has been written on these much disputed chapters of PI. The present survey deals with the most relevant contributions to the field, particularly those which constituted a change of perspective with regard to the exegesis and interpretation of Isa 24–27.
21. D. BOURGUET, *Des métaphores de Jérémie* (EB, 9), Paris, 1987.
22. N. STIENSTRA, *YHWH is the Husband of His People, Analysis of a Biblical Metaphor with Special Reference to Translation*, Kampen, 1993.
23. P.W. MACKY, *The Centrality of Metaphors to Biblical Thought. A Method for Interpreting the Bible* (Studies in the Bible and early Christianity, 19), Lewiston – Queenston – Lampeter, 1990.

have something of the character of a survey, a review of metaphorical theory, which we hope will provide support for the development of a methodology for approaching biblical texts. An effort will be made to expand our understanding of what can be called metaphorical speech, to deal with the question of Hebrew comparative particles and their relationship to metaphor, to focus on metaphorical statements (i.e. on the large and small textual units in which metaphorical speech is employed) rather than on individual metaphors.

Chapters III to VI provide a detailed analysis of the textual complex of Isa 24–27 chapter by chapter. The methodology distilled from the chapter on metaphorical theory is applied in each case, beginning with a delimitation of the 'metaphorical statement' followed by a survey of 'indicators' of the presence of metaphor, an analysis of metaphorical 'type' and concluding with an attempt to discern the 'author's purpose' in using metaphorical speech.

The final segment will draw conclusions from the detailed metaphorical analysis of chapters III to VI with a view to addressing the issues raised in the *Status Quaestionis*. If we view Isa 24–27 'metaphorically speaking' are there answers to be found to the questions which have dogged the history of exegesis of these chapters of PI? Further insights concerning the use and function of metaphor will also be outlined in these concluding pages.

Paul Tillich referred to the opening verses of Isa 24 in his celebrated sermon *The Shaking of the Foundations*: "Behold the Lord maketh the earth empty and maketh it waste, and turneth it upside down and scattereth its inhabitants...towns fall to pieces...gladness has gone from the earth and pleasure is no more. For the earth has been polluted by the dwellers on its face..."[24]. Tillich placed the blame for this destructive intervention on the part of the divinity on human arrogance and pride, the hubris of those who would continually reach beyond themselves and refuse to listen to the voice of the prophets[25]. Tillich's interpretation of these verses was clearly an actualising interpretation related to the destructive horrors of Nazism and Hiroshima[26]. He was convinced, however, that prophetic voices such as that of Isaiah continued to confront

---

24. P. TILLICH, *The Shaking of the Foundations*, London, 1962, p. 16.
25. See M. GRAY, *The Shaking of the Foundations – Again!*, Unpublished lecture delivered at the Feast of St Thomas of Aquinas, Faculty of Theology, KU Leuven, March 7th, 1995.
26. Such an approach lends itself to a non-Apocalyptic interpretation of these verses, a topic to which we will return below.

God's people with the reasons for their experience of collapse and degradation, reasons which have their roots in human relationship with the divine. Tillich's insight provides us with a hint as to the ultimate meaning of the disaster announced in the opening verses of Isa 24. What did the author of these chapters believe to be the reason and purpose for this divine assault? Our analysis of the metaphorical language of these chapters might help us to understand both the character of this Isaian 'shaking of the foundations' and the divine motivation which brought it about.

CHAPTER ONE

ISAIAH 24–27
A CONCISE STATUS QUAESTIONIS

INTRODUCTION

The present chapter's primary aim is to examine a number of unresolved questions arising from the history of research into Isa 24–27 which we will endeavour to answer in and through our study of the presence and use of metaphors in these chapters. Since the present chapter is thus focused, therefore, we must speak of a concise rather than an exhaustive *Status quaestionis*. In the course of the chapter we will endeavour to outline the solutions proposed by commentators ancient and modern in their efforts to understand 'the mysteries of these chapters'[1]. It will be immediately evident that the questions are not mutually exclusive. On the contrary they overlap and influence one another. It will also be evident that the questions move from more 'abstract' to more 'concrete'. Other important, if secondary, questions concerning, for example, the significance of the terms תבל/ארץ (e.g. 24,4), alleged references to the resurrection of the individual (e.g. 26,19) and the meaning of the expression ברית עולם (24,5) and their relationship to the author's use of metaphor will be dealt with *in loco*.

Our first paragraph will deal with the question of the unity (or lack thereof) of Isa 24–27 within the context of the history of redaction of the text. Our second paragraph will focus on the matter of literary genre and the associated questions of temporal perspective and date. The third and final paragraph will be devoted to a survey of the various attempts to identify the city (cities) referred to in the text.

I. HISTORY OF THE REDACTION OF ISAIAH 24–27

While Isa 24–27 has been treated by the majority of commentators as a distinct textual complex (historically, thematically, genre-critically, semantically) within the Book of Isaiah, the degree of consensus is not sufficient to provide a clear and unequivocal answer to the following important questions: Does the redaction of BI as a whole give us reason to treat Isa 24–27 as a distinct unit of material? What are the organising principles which hold the text together and how is it integrated within BI

---

1. W.R. MILLAR, *Isaiah 24–27 and the Origin of Apocalyptic* (HSM, 11), Missoula, MT, 1976, p. 1.

as a whole? Is there evidence of a single redactor? What governed the genesis of this textual complex?

Unlike chapters 1–12 (a core of authentic oracles dealing with Jerusalem and Judah in a heavily redacted context) and 13–23 (primarily oracles against the nations), the remaining chapters of PI do not exhibit the same degree of homogeneity. B. Duhm, for example, viewed chs.36–39 as a bridge between PI and DI, distinguishing, in addition, an apocalypse (24–27), an Assyrian cycle (28–33) and a second apocalypse in the remaining chapters 34–35[2]. L.J. Liebreich, on the other hand, divides PI along partially different lines: 1–12, 13–27, 28–35, 36–39, thus calling the independence of Isa 24–27 as a textual complex into question[3]. P. Redditt is unconvinced by Liebreich's analysis of the redaction of PI and especially his second division which, for a variety of reasons, he maintains 'breaks down' at 24–27[4]. Redditt notes that Liebreich's argumentation in fact supports a division after ch.23[5]. Insisting on the fact that there is apparently no direct connection between chs.24–27 and chs.28–33 and on the distinction with the oracles against the nations in chs.13–23, Redditt argues that chs.24–27 "comprise a separate block of material in the redaction of the book of First Isaiah. This suggests, but does not prove, that they themselves are an edited collection"[6]. Redditt himself offers a number of arguments in support of the edited character of Isa 24–27: the repetition of motifs[7] argues that the text, at the very least, gives evidence of a process of selection; the placing of the expression ביום ההוא[8]; stylistic repetition[9]; extended sentences[10]; frequency of infinitive absolutes; literary technique and theology.

---

2. B. Duhm, *Das Buch Jesaja*, (GHAT), Göttingen, 1968[5], pp. 10-12.
3. L.J. Liebreich, *The Compilation of the Book of Isaiah*, in *JQR* 67 (1956) 236-257.
4. P. Redditt, *Isaiah 24–27: A Form Critical Analysis*, Diss., Vanderbilt University, 1972, p. 151.
5. Based on the fact that there are ten passages in vv. 13-23 each of which begin with משׁא, 'which are surely redactional' (p. 151)
6. Redditt, *Form Critical Analysis*, p. 152.
7. (1) YHWH is going to rise up in punishment: 24,1-6.21-22; 26,21; 27,1; (2) curse language: 24,4-13; 27,10-11a; (3) concentration of material on Jerusalem: 24,13.21-23; 25.6-8.10a; 26,1-6.21; 27,13 (pp. 152-153)
8. 24,21; 25,9; 26,1; 27,1.2.12.13; (27,6). Redditt, in line with P.A. Munch (*The Expression 'Bajjom Hahu': Is It an Eschatological Terminus Technicus?* [Avhandlinger utgett av Det Norske Videnskap-Akademi i Oslo, II Hist.-Filos. Klasse], Oslo, 1936) argues that ביום ההוא functions as a 'temporal redaction phrase' (*Form Critical Analysis*, p. 153). Cf. also S.J. De Vries, *From Old Revelation to New. A Tradition-Historical and Redaction-Critical Study of Temporal Transitions in Prophetic Prediction*, Grand Rapids, MI, 1995.
9. Repetition: 24,16.23; 25,6; 25,9; 26,5-6.15; 27,5.7.
10. Description 'pile-up': 24,13.15.23; 25,1b.6.12; 27,6.9.10-11a.

1. FRAGMENTARY OR UNITARY?

Denying the unity of Isa 24–27, Duhm famously divides the text into a series of songs[11] and apocalyptic passages[12], the latter proclaiming impending global disaster. The apocalyptic content, in Duhm's view, constitutes a continuous series of prophetic announcements which is interrupted by the songs and other intrusions[13]. Leaving the songs aside as secondary, a sort of end-time scenario emerges, describing the immanent destruction of earth and heaven, judgement, messianic banquet, the overthrow of death and the return of the exiles[14]. The insertion of the songs by a redactor is explained by other scholars as follows: 25,1-5 to celebrate the overthrow of the city predicted in 24,10[15]; 25,9-12 refers to both 25,1-5 and 24,10 and is of key significance for the understanding of BI as a whole[16]; 26,1-19 providing the basis for resurrection hope in 25,6-8[17]; 27,2-5 a test prior to the return of the exiles[18]. O. Procksch makes a similar division in the material based, however, on metrical considerations[19]. Since the 'apocalyptic cycle', provides the basic text and the *Weltstadt* cycle a later addition, Procksch clearly has not strayed far from the basic premise of Duhm. Both agree that the 'apocalyptic' material constitutes the older part of the complex. O. Eissfeldt, on the other hand, places the songs first, maintaining that their celebration of the fall of a Moabite city was expanded by apocalyptic material to include world disaster and the immanent arrival of the reign of YHWH[20]. Prior to Duhm, R. Smend argues, finally, that the two types of material arose at the same time, both making reference to the fall of the same

---

11. DUHM, *Jesaja*, p. 172: 25,1-5 (song of thanksgiving); 25,9-11 (mocking song); 26,1-19 (25,12) (song of hope in the resurrection of the righteous); 27,2-5 (song of hope for YHWH's vineyard).
12. 24; 25,6-8; 26,20-27,1; 27,12.13.
13. 27,2-5; 27,7.9-11 (?).
14. REDDITT, *Form Critical Analysis*, p. 159.
15. M.L. HENRY, *Glaubenskrise und Glaubensbewährung in den Dichtungen der Jesaja Apokalypse* (BWANT, 86), Stuttgart, 1967, p. 28-29.
16. E.S. MULDER, *Die Teologie von die Jesaja-Apokalypse. Jesaja 24–27*, Djakarta, 1954, p. 79.
17. HENRY, *Glaubenskrise*, p. 191.
18. G. FOHRER, *Der Aufbau der Apokalypse der Jesajabuchs. Jesaja 24–27*, in *CBQ* 25 (1963) 34-45; = ID., *Entstehung, Komposition und Überlieferung von Jesaja 1–39, Studien zur alttestamentlichen Prophetie* (BZAW, 99), Berlin, 1967, pp. 170-181, esp. p. 39.
19. O. PROCKSCH, *Jesaja I. Erste Hälfte: Kapitel 1–39* (KAT, IX), Leipzig, 1930: Apocalyptic cycle of seven accent lines: 24,1-7.18b-23; 25,6-10a; 26,7-19; 26,20-27,1.6.9a.12-13. *Weltstadt* cycle: 24,8-18a; 25,1-5; 26.1b-6; 27,2b-5.
20. O. EISSFELDT, *The Old Testament: An Introduction Including the Apocrypha and Pseudepigrapha, and also the Works of Similar Type from Qumran; the History of the Formation of the Old Testament* (tr. P.R. ACKROYD), New York, NY, 1966, pp. 326-327.

Moabite city[21]. W. Rudolph offers a highly fragmentary analysis of the textual complex, discerning ten pericopes of unequal size, seven of which he ascribes to the same author[22]. Based on meter and content, E. Sievers offers an equally fragmentary analysis of Isa 24–27, dividing the text into three complexes each of which are further subdivided into groups[23].

The late nineteenth century tendency towards fragmentation seems to have gone unchecked in the years following Duhm's initial division. None of the authors reviewed so far are inclined to ascribe a degree of unity to Isa 24–27 nor to question the process which brought the material together to constitute a final composition in the first place. Evolution in historical-critical methodology, however, brought with it a change of approach to our textual complex and due attention came to be given to the redactional principles which governed the composition of the chapters. The primary authors of this period can be divided into two groups: those ascribing in one way or another to a 'prophetic liturgy' as the organising principle of the text (Hylmö, March, Fohrer and Lindblom) and those who focus exclusively on the history and growth of the material, the relative dating of individual pericopes, the material sources and the theological principles respectively supporting and governing the redactional process (Ludwig, Henry, Plöger).

2. THE SO-CALLED PROPHETIC LITURGY

H. Gunkel had already discussed the hypothetical form of the 'prophetic liturgy' in 1924[24]. Using Isa 33 as an example, he discerned the following three formal elements all of which he considered necessarily present: "(1) a general treasure of thoughts passed along orally from generation to generation, (2) a characteristic alternating speech form, and (3) a definite *Sitz im Leben*"[25]. Concentrating on Isa 25–26, G. Hylmö was the first to suggest the presence of the so-called 'prophetic liturgy' in our textual complex, beginning with a hymn of praise (25,1-5), followed by an oracle (25,6-8) and two further hymns (25,9-12; 26,1-6) and concluding with a *sorgesäng* (complaint and request 26,7-18) and a divine response

---

21. R. SMEND, *Anmerkungen zu Jes. 24–27*, in ZAW 4 (1884) 178-183, 194-195. Cf. also MULDER, *Die Teologie*, pp. 78-79.
22. W. RUDOLPH, *Jesaja 24–27* (BWANT IV, 10), Stuttgart 1933.
23. E. SIEVERS, *Alttestamentliche Miscellen I: Jesajas 24–27* (Verhandlungen der königl. Sachs. Ges. d. Wiss. zu Leipzig, phil. hist. Kl. B 56), Leipzig, 1904, p. 151ff..
24. H. GUNKEL, *Jesaja 33, eine prophetische Liturgie*, in ZAW 1 (1924) 182-183.
25. REDDITT, *Form Critical Analysis*, p. 172.

(26,19-21)[26]. As Redditt has noted, Hylmö takes liturgical/cultic rites as the redactional principle governing the positioning of oracles in these chapters rather than logic[27]. His division of the text, based on changes in meter, as well as his separation of chs.25–26 from the other chapters in the complex are and remain the subject of dispute[28]. W. March solves a number of the problems evident in Hylmö by positing two prophetic liturgies[29]. The first runs from 24,1 to 24,20 (which form an inclusion) and follows the liturgical pattern: announcement, lamentation, assurance. The second begins with 24,21 and runs to 27,1 (also forming an inclusion) and exhibits an alternating pattern of oracles and divine addressations: announcement (24,21-23); song of praise (25,1-5); announcement (25,6-10a); song of praise (26,1-6); prayer of lament (26,7-19) and oracle of assurance (26,20-27,1). The remainder of ch.27 (vv. 2-13) is dismissed as unrelated additions and glosses to the rest of the complex[30]. It is evident from the endeavours of Hylmö and March that the liturgy as a redactional principle cannot account for the entire complex. Fohrer, on the other hand, is more generous in his understanding of what constitutes a prophetic liturgy and is less inclined to excise what does not appear to fit[31]. He discerns three originally independent prophetic liturgies (24,1-20;24,21-25,10a; 27,1-6.12-13) connected together by transitional song texts (26,1-6; 26,7-21)[32]. J. Lindblom later questioned the expression 'prophetic liturgy', preferring to entitle the textual complex a 'cantata'[33], in which alternating singing voices make requests and are given responses[34]. For Lindblom, the complex consists of two interwoven cycles differing from one another on the basis of subject matter: a destroyed city (*Weltstadt*: 24,7-16aα; 25,1-5; 26,1-14, 27,2-11) and eschatological prophecy predicting a future world catastrophe (24,1-6.16aβ-20; 25,6-10a; 26,20-21; 27,12-13)[35].

---

26. G. HYLMÖ, *De s.k. profetishka liturgiernas rytm, stil och komposition* (Lunds Universitets Arsskrift N.F. Avd. 1. Bd. 25. Nr. 5), Lund, 1929.
27. REDDITT, *Form Critical Analysis*, p. 174.
28. Cf. Redditt's critique in ID., *Form Critical Analysis*, pp. 174-177.
29. W. MARCH, *A Study of Two Prophetic Compositions In Isaiah 24:1–27:1*, Diss., Union Theological Seminary, 1966.
30. Cf. Redditt's critique in ID., *Form Critical Analysis*, pp. 177-180.
31. FOHRER, *Der aufbau*. He does exclude 25,10b-11.12; 27,7-11 as either inappropriate to the liturgical context or differing stylistically from the context.
32. Cf. Redditt's critique in ID., *Form Critical Analysis*, pp. 182-183.
33. A 'liturgy', by contrast, consists of alternating spoken voices: God-human person; priest-congregation.
34. J. LINDBLOM, *Die Jesaja Apokalypse: Jesaja 24–27* (Lunds Universitets Arsskrift, N.F. 1, 34, 3.), Lund, 1938.
35. Material is excluded (24,21-23; 25,10b-12; 26,15-19; 27,1) mostly on the grounds that it appears to be prose. Cf. Redditt's critique in ID., *Form Critical Analysis*, pp. 186-188.

II. THE REDACTIONAL PROCESS

While Hylmö, March, Fohrer and Lindblom differ from one another in the details of pericope division and terminology, they share a belief that the same redactional principle governed the present shape of Isa 24–27, namely 'liturgy' in one form or another[36]. Later authors abandoned this principle to focus, as we noted above, on the history and growth of the material, the relative dating of individual pericopes, the material sources and the theological principles respectively supporting and governing the redactional process. O. Ludwig, for example, discerns three distinct collections of material at the basis of the present complex[37]: the *Stadtlieder* (early: 24,7-12; 27,10-11 / later: 25,1-5; 26,1-6; 27,2-4) and two apocalypses (I 24,1-3.4-6.13.18b-20.21-23; 25,6-8 / II 26,20-27,1.12-13. The apocalypses constitute the basis for the redaction of the entire complex, the *Stadtlieder* being interwoven therewith at a later stage together with other material. Dependence on Duhm's apocalypse/ song dichotomy is evident although not total[38]. As Redditt notes, however, Ludwig once again has difficulty in meaningfully accounting for almost half of the verses (27/69). M.-L. Henry takes a different approach to Ludwig and her other predecessors, one which focuses purely on the growth and final redaction of the text of Isa 24–27 on the basis of *überlieferungsgeschichtlich* research. For Henry, the text material stems from a variety of contexts which have been re-worked in order to render the religious conditions of the exilic and post-exilic community. Thus the text has undergone a growth process from what she considers the oldest segments (victory songs: 24,7-12; 25,1-5; 26,4-6[39]) through an optimistic addition (24,14-16aα)[40], additions characterised by disillusionment (24,16aβb; 26,7-19), Day of YHWH material (24,1-6.17-20; 26,20-27,1)[41], and eschatological pericopes (24,21-23; 25,6-8)[42]. The final step in the process is that of redaction whereby the various segments were woven together around the theological themes of YHWH's

---

36. More recently J.D.W. WATTS, *Isaiah 1–33* (WBC, 24), Waco, TX, 1985, esp. pp. 309-351.
37. O. LUDWIG, *Die Stadt in der Jesaja-Apokalypse, Zur Datierung von Jes. 24–27*, Cologne, 1967.
38. Cf. Redditt's critique in ID., *Form Critical Analysis*, pp. 191-192.
39. HENRY, *Glaubenskrise*, p. 14.
40. *Ibid.*, pp. 51-53.
41. *Ibid.*, pp. 61, 74.
42. *Ibid.*, pp. 146-148.

kingship and universalism[43]. Once again, unlike her predecessors, Henry emphasises the final unity of these chapters on the basis of a thematic redaction principle rooted historically in the experience of exile and its aftermath. O. Plöger's study[44] focuses on Isa 24–27 in an attempt to trace the origins of apocalyptic literature and the community which gave birth to it[45]. His analysis of the textual complex, however, inclines him to divide it into three collections based on a redactional principle which alternates songs and oracles. Each of the three collections exhibits a particular theme: 24,1-20 (theme: future); 24,21-26,21 (theme: "…confession of faith of the man on the way to the eschatological millennium"[46]; 27,1-13 (theme: reunification). Inconsistent with the unity of the chapters provided by the evident purposeful redaction which he maintains they have undergone, Plöger rejects passages such as 25,1-5 and 26,1-6 and has difficulties with 25,10b-12 and ch.27 as a whole[47].

1. RECAPITULATIONS – THEMES AND MOTIFS

Redditt notes the lack of consensus on the composition of Isa 24–27 found among his predecessors and insists that this textual complex can be shown to be "…a carefully worked out structure which has remained intact, though the text suffered somewhat in transmission"[48]. He is of the opinion that the text is made up of four sections each of which consists of a number of pericopes[49]. From the redaction critical perspective, however, he is convinced that each section has its own redactional principle and that each section exhibits relational bonds with the rest of the complex, thus constituting a unified composition. There is a conscious effort on the part of the redactor, he notes, to tie each new section to the first, a fact exhibited most clearly in the 'recapitulations' found in 24,21-23, 26,20-21 and 27,1 which hark back to 24,1-20. In addition, each section is tied to the one preceding and the one following[50]. A further redactional

---

43. Her apparent reason for excluding 25,10a-12 and 27,2-11 from the final composition as too nationalistic (p. 17-19). Cf. also Redditt's critique in ID., *Form Critical Analysis*, p. 195.
44. O. PLÖGER, *Theocracy and Eschatology* (tr. S. RUDMAN), Richmond, VA, 1968.
45. As P. HANSON (*The Dawn of Apocalyptic*, Philadelphia, PA, 1975) will later.
46. REDDITT, *Form Critical Analysis*, p. 198.
47. Cf. Redditt's critique in ID., *Form Critical Analysis*, pp. 199-202.
48. REDDITT, *Form Critical Analysis*, p. 204.
49. See his detailed discussion of the organisation and arrangement of these sections and their constituent pericopes in *Form Critical Analysis*, pp. 204-228.
50. REDDITT, *Form Critical Analysis*, p. 229.

feature is evident in what he refers to as the expansion of the "holy" land from Jerusalem/Mount Zion (24,21-23) to Judah (26,1a) to all Israel (27,6). Common themes also unify the textual complex in Redditt's mind: judgement (e.g. 24,1-3; 26,21); curse motifs (e.g. 24,4-6.7-13; 27,10-11a); the future of Jerusalem (the most frequent: 24,13.23; 25,6-8.9-10a; 26,1b-3.21; 27,13). The redactor's overall redactional principle was "to relate the urgent message to unenlightened Israel (24,14-16; 27,11b) that Yahweh was about to strike out against the world in judgement. Israel's salvation would be dependent upon her purification of her worship (27,9), without which the present situation could not be improved. It was God's desire to spare his people from the coming disaster (26,20); but even her future blessing would depend on her fidelity (27,4-5), concerning which the redactor was optimistic (27,6)."[51]

After providing an analysis of the text and prosody of Isa 24–27, W.R. Millar endeavours to establish the structuring presence of thematic patterns in the text and whether these patterns can be established elsewhere in the Ancient Near Eastern tradition[52]. Millar draws thematic connections between our text and the Ugaritic epic of Ba'al and Anat in both of which he discerns the presence of four themes: Threat, War, Victory and Feast[53]. This leads him to suggest that Isa 24–27 is constructed around the familiar pattern of the Divine Warrior Hymn[54] found in the theology of many of the psalms of YHWH's kingship[55] and throughout DI[56]. He concludes that a substantial part of our textual complex (24,1-16a; 24,16b-25,9; 26,1-8) formed the 'apocalyptic' basis of the text and was composed in Jerusalem following the destruction of 587 BCE by a disciple of the Isaiah school around the thematic pattern of the Divine Warrior Hymn. Later additions include 26,11-27,6 and

---

51. *Ibid.*, p. 230.
52. MILLAR, *Origin of Apocalyptic*. Millar's title reveals the primary purpose of his study. He supports the theory of P. Hanson that Isa 24–27 represents early apocalyptic literature from the last half of the sixth century. Refining Plöger, Hanson argues that a struggle between two religious factions – a visionary group in Israel aligned with DI and a realistic group in Babylon aligned with Ezekiel – gave rise to this material. The weaker group of visionaries were forced by tensions with the stronger group of realists to fantasize about the future, thus giving rise to apocalyptic literature. More recent authors have likewise focused on the literary structure of the text: for example, D.J. LEWIS, *A Rhetorical Critical Analysis of Isaiah 24–27*, Diss. The Southern Baptist Theological Seminary, 1985; H.G.M. WILLIAMSON, *Sound, Sense and Language in Isaiah 24–27*, in *JJS* 66 (1995) 1-9; R. ITOH, *Literary and Linguistic Approach to Isaiah 24–27*, Diss. Trinity International University, 1995.
53. MILLAR, *Origin of Apocalyptic*, p. 65-71.
54. *Ibid.*, p. 101-102.
55. *Ibid.*, p. 90-94. Cf. his analysis of Ps 132.
56. *Ibid.*, p. 96-102; examples include: Isa 40,2-3; 42,9-13; 51,9-11; 52,7-8.

27,12-13[57]. Thus while ultimately arguing that the apocalyptic movement has its roots in literary patterns from Ugarit, Millar simultaneously provides a coherent outline of the history of the text's redaction and the redaction principle – apocalypse – which governed its completion. Both his prosodic analysis and his understanding of the structure of the text tend to support a more unified understanding of the material.

2. WACHSTUMSHYPOTHESE

Wildberger begins his analysis by stating "Jedenfalls steht undiskutabel fest, daß die Kapitel... im Ganzen des Jesajabuches einen klar abgegrenzten Teil für sich bilden"[58]. He notes that the collection of oracles against the nations concludes with ch.23 and an unrelated section of the book begins with ch.28 (Isaiah as speaker) thus isolating our complex. The absence of the term משא (verdict) in association with the oracles in chs.24–27 further distinguishes them from the preceding oracles against the nations where it is frequently present as a sort of superscription. This is supported by the fact that, with the exception of Moab (25,10b) no enemy is mentioned in the entire textual complex, only Jacob/Israel. Wildberger maintains, therefore, that the material gathered here was intended to give a universal, eschatological-apocalyptic perspective to the oracles against the nations[59]. Thus Isa 24–27 is inserted here "um diese (Fremdvölkerworte) in ihren eigenen eschatologischen Horizont hineinzustellen"[60]. Wildberger is clear on the fact that in their present form chs.24–27 represent a unified composition. Noting the disparity of the elements which the composition has brought together, however, he insists on the need to continue to search for the process and principles which led to the material now known as the so-called Isaiah Apocalypse. Wildberger follows the suggestions of Kaiser[61] and Vermeylen[62] in this regard, each of whom attempt to delineate layers of once independent material within the text and establish a *Wachstumsprozess*[63]. Kaiser,

---

57. *Ibid.*, p. 104.
58. H. WILDBERGER, *Jesaja 13–27* (BKAT, X/2), Neukirchen –Vluyn, 1978, p. 892.
59. As early as Jerome, CCSL, LXXIII, 316.
60. WILDBERGER, *Jesaja 13–27*, p. 892.
61. O. KAISER, *Isaiah 13–39. A Commentary* (tr. R.A. WILSON) (OTL), London, 1974, pp. 173-179; original German edition: *Der Prophet Jesaja. Kapitel 13–39* (ATD, 18), Göttingen, 1973.
62. J. VERMEYLEN, *La Composition littéraire de l'apocalypse d'Isaïe*, in *ETL* 50 (1974) 5-38.
63. WILDBERGER, *Jesaja 13–27*, p. 895.

Vermeylen and Wildberger thus suggest a layer of original material which attracted additions, expansions and subsequent layers which ultimately developed into the present text. For Kaiser the basic material is 24,1-3.16aβ-20, for Vermeylen 24,2-13.18b-20; 26,8-9*.11-13.16-18.20-21 for Wildberger 24,1-6.14-20; 26,7-21[64]. Wildberger notes further that the complicated process which has given rise to the text is partly responsible for difficulties in establishing its date. Thus, in line with Kaiser, Vermeylen and others, Wildberger proposes his *Wachstumshypothese*, a hypothetical process of expansion and growth. While he admits that it is almost impossible to show how this development took place, he maintains that such a disadvantage need not undermine his hypothesis as a whole. Indeed, if additions and expansions are postulated throughout BI why should the present complex unity be an exception[65]. Basically Wildberger maintains "…daß gerade ein Text, der von der großen bevorstehenden Wende sprach, zu so intensiver Reflexion, Adaption an neue Situationen und darum Neuinterpretation herausgevordert hat"[66]. Thus his understanding of the redactional process as a gradual one, inspired by new situations, does not take away from the fact that he believes the present text to be a unity and to have a purposeful albeit unique place in PI.

3. A WELL-ORDERED COMPOSITION

Authors such as J.N. Oswalt would partly agree with Wildberger at this level. Oswalt notes the redaction-critical approach's tendency to deny the chapters' literary unity except at the thematic level and to focus on the growth of the text from basic strata through additions and expansions to its present form. He likewise notes that such an approach attracts, as we have seen, hardly any degree of consensus[67]. Oswalt's

---

64. Cf. WILDBERGER (*Jesaja 13–27*, p. 904) for a detailed outline of basic material, expansions and additions.
65. Wildberger expressly disagrees with G.A. ANDERSON (*Isaiah XXIV–XXVII Reconsidered*, in *SVT* 9 [1963] 118-126) and H. RINGGREN (*Some Observations on Style and Structure in the Isaiah Apocalypse*, in *ASTI* 9 [1973] 107-115) who maintain that Isa 24–27 were a unified block from the outset (WILDBERGER, *Jesaja 13–27*, p. 896). More recently, Watts has picked up on the cantata or liturgy (even Wildberger calls it a 'symphony' according to Watts) model proposed by Anderson and Ringgren in line with their predecessor Lindblom. For Watts "These chapters comprise a dramatic literary structure… an artistic and complex work of response and interpretation based on the announcement of 24:1-13 which is repeated in 26:21". Cf. WATTS, *Isaiah 1–33*, p. 312.
66. WILDBERGER, *Jesaja 13–27*, p. 897.
67. J.N. OSWALT, *The Book of Isaiah, Chapters 13–39* (NICOT), Grand Rapids, MI, 1986, p. 442.

attention is drawn to the final form of the text: "...it is precisely in its present form that the segment and the book as a whole have their power"[68]. Similarly, D.G. Johnson is critical of his predecessors in their efforts to divide and thereby understand our text[69]. He rather amusingly describes the works of Duhm, Hylmö, Fohrer and March (and presumably their followers) as "procrustean efforts which require either the lopping off of those portions of the composition which do not fit the [their] pattern, or a strained and impossible interpretation of certain pericopae in order to make them accord with the [their] pattern"[70]. While he admits that Kaiser and Wildberger are better placed for their recognition of Wildberger's *Wachstumsprozess* with respect to the growth of Isa 24–27, he has difficulties with the fact that scholars cannot agree on the isolation of units, the order of addition nor the motivation behind it within this alleged process[71]. Indeed, his belief that we are dealing with a well-ordered composition makes it hard for him to accept that the 'choppy' process suggested by Wildberger ever took place. Thus, contra Wildberger, he evidently supports G.A. Anderson's position which maintains the ordered compositional unity of Isa 24–27, albeit from a different perspective[72]. Ultimately, Johnson appears to be correct in saying that "...regardless of how one views the prehistory of these chapters, one may with some confidence speak of the compositional unity of Isa 24–27 in its present form"[73]. He argues, however, that in the midst of great diversity of opinion, there is a degree of consensus on 3 important areas: (1) Isa 24–27 should be dated closer to the exile; (2) there is an emerging consensus with respect to the compositional unity of the chapters; (3) temporal perspective is futuristic rather than apocalyptic[74]. In light of these factors Johnson himself divides the text into three integrated sections: Section A (24,1-20): a lament prior to and announcing the immanent destruction of Jerusalem in 587 rooted in the language of the chaos myth; Section B (24,21–27,1): an announcement of YHWH's victory over the oppressor and the national restoration of Israel; Section C (27,2-13): the concrete elaboration of YHWH's victory in the re-unification of Israel *within* the horizon of history[75].

---

68. *Ibid.*
69. D.G. JOHNSON, *From Chaos to Restoration. An Integrative Reading of Isaiah 24–27* (JSOT SS, 61), Sheffield, 1988, pp. 11-17.
70. *Ibid.* p. 14.
71. *Ibid.* p. 15
72. ANDERSON, *Isaiah XXIV–XXVII Reconsidered*, p. 126.
73. JOHNSON, *Chaos to Restoration*, p. 15.
74. *Ibid.* p. 16. Points 1 and 3 will be discussed in more detail in the paragraphs below.
75. *Ibid.*, pp. 16-17.

4. Isa 24–27's position in the redaction history of BI

In recent years a new line of research has drawn attention to the connections between Isa 24–27 and the rest of BI. R.J. Coggins was the first to devote a particular study to this aspect of the redaction of the text. Coggins argues on the basis of allusions in Isa 24–27 to other texts within BI that "...the book of Isaiah is finally made up of a substantial number of small units, many of them three or four chapters long, each containing a certain basic unity, and each contributing to the complex whole which makes up Isa 1–66. Isa 24–27 will be such a unity"[76]. Coggins was convinced from the outset that there was some link between these chapters and the rest of BI but he was aware at the same time that objective criteria would be difficult to find to establish such a connection. Isa 24–27's present location appears to be far from a haphazard insertion. Sweeney[77] and Skjoldal[78] have continued along the lines set by Coggins, in the search of more objective evidence at the level of so-called 'inner-biblical quotations'. Sweeney identifies seven formal citations from other parts of BI based on their 'high lexical correspondence and thematic correlation"[79] leading him to envisage Isa 24–27 as the youngest segment of BI. The quoted material, he maintains, serves the universalisation of Isaianic themes. For Sweeney, Isa 24–27 were not composed in isolation but were written to order within the Isaianic tradition. As such, Isa 24–27 contribute to the unification of the entire book of Isaiah[80]. Skjoldal considerably limits Sweeney's hypothesis, suggesting that Isa 24–27 are a summary of Isa 5–23. He also maintains that they are by the same author and as such provide evidence that BI as a

---

76. R.J. COGGINS, *The problem of Isaiah 24–27*, in *ExpT* 90 (1979) 328-33.

77. M.A. SWEENEY, *Textual Citations in Isaiah 24–27: Toward an Understanding of the Redactional Function of Chapters 24–27 in the Book of Isaiah*, in *JBL* 107 (1988) 39-52; ID., *New Gleanings from an Old Vineyard: Is 27 Reconsidered*, in C.A. EVANS and W. F. STINESPRING (eds.), *Early Jewish and Christian Exegesis. Studies in Memory of W. H. Brownlee* (Homage Series, 10), Atlanta, GA, 1987, pp. 33-49.

78. N.O. SKJOLDAL, *The Function of Isaiah 24–27. Towards an Understanding of the Redactional Function of Ch. 24–27 in the Book of Isaiah*, in *JETS* 36 (1993) 63-67.

79. SWEENEY (Textual Citations, p. 42: 24,13//17,7; 24,16//21,2; 33,1; 25,4-5//4,5b-6; 32,1-2; 25,11b-12//2,9-17; 26,5//2,6-21; 26,17-18//13,8; 66,7-9; 27,1-13//5,1-7; 11,10-16. H.G.M. WILLIAMSON (*The Book called Isaiah: Deutero-Isaiah's Role in Composition and Redaction*, New York, NY, 1994) argues that evidence of quotation of other biblical texts is equally revealing (pp. 181-182; cf. also J. DAY, *A Case of Inner Scriptural Interpretation*, in *JTS* 31 [1980] 309-19). Williamson ultimately maintains that there is "no evidence at any point in Isaiah 24–27 for detecting the hand of Deutero-Isaiah" (p. 177).

80. See M.A. SWEENEY, *Isaiah 1–4 and the Postexilic Understanding of the Isaianic Tradition* (BZAW, 171), Berlin, 1988, for the methodological background of these proposals.

whole stems from a single author, the 8th century prophet IbA (more about which below). It is clear, in any event, that such studies have revived interest in the position of Isa 24–27 in the redaction history of the book.

Conclusion

Disagreement on general points and frequently on the level of detailed division of the text reveals that little consensus has been reached with regard to the redaction history of Isa 24–27. Nevertheless, a clear progression can be discerned from viewing Isa 24–27 as a unique, highly fragmentary, haphazardly placed collection to a well-integrated, internally unified, albeit still unique complex. This has been evident in the various studies which approach the history of the redaction of these chapters in one way or another. Recent broad consensus on the compositional unity of the text as it now stands, however, has given rise to a variety of studies which focus on the present structure and structural principles of Isa 24–27. P. Redditt, for example, concluded that it was possible to "isolate the literary style of the redactor of Isa 24–27. He writes sentences (often long sentences) which employ extended parallelism and repetition. His style shows him to have been not only collector and editor of diverse materials, but also a writer who made a heavy contribution in terms of the total verses written (thirty out of sixty-nine)"[81]. As we noted above, side by side with a prosodic evaluation of the poetry of Isa 24–27 and an attempt to situate this poetry in the process of breakdown from the 'good Hebrew poetic style' of DI to the prose of later apocalyptic[82], Millar sees a thematic unity in the composition based on patterns found in the divine warrior hymns. Wildberger, while proposing a long process of growth for the text, still maintains its present structural unity, describing the chapters as a 'symphony' and insisting that "Daß sie jetzt, wie sie uns überliefert sind, eine einheitliche Komposition darstellen, die als Zeugnis der kommenden Ereignisse bei der großen bevorstehenden Wende der Geschichte verstanden werden will, ist evident..."[83] Watts, in the more recent past, has discerned a dramatic literary structure in the text[84]. Sweeney's 1996 commentary sees

---

81. REDDITT, *Form Critical Analysis*, p. 395.
82. MILLAR, *Origin of Apocalyptic*, p. 15.
83. WILDBERGER, *Jesaja 13–27*, p. 893.
84. WATTS, *Isaiah 1–33*, p. 311, follows along the same lines as Lindblom, Anderson, Ringgren and Redditt.

two structuring themes in the text: "YHWH's punishment of the earth and its implications" and "YHWH's blessing of the earth and its implications for both the nations and Israel"[85]. Thus, in line with the tradition which would view Isa 24–27 as a unified whole, we continue to be free to treat these chapters as a separate section within PI, focusing on a particular feature which further unites them, namely their use of metaphors. At the same time, however, it is important not to loose sight of the fact that the complex's somewhat uncomfortable location within PI and BI as a whole still has to be explained[86].

In our concluding chapter, therefore, we will endeavour to discern whether the consistent use of certain metaphorical language may have served as a redactional/compositional principle uniting and distinguishing and integrating the final text of Isa 24–27 from and within BI.

III. LITERARY GENRE – TEMPORAL PERSPECTIVE – DATE

1. LITERARY GENRE

Depending on one's position on the unity of the textual complex, one's evaluation of the literary genre(s) of the text may vary (side by side with one's opinion as to the complex's date and general temporal perspective): apocalyptic; pre-exilic prophetic judgement literature; prophetic eschatology; exilic or early post-exilic proto-apocalyptic; early apocalyptic? According to Johnson, the present day *communis opinio* on the matter is that "...the initial transformation of prophetic eschatology into what would eventually become full-blown apocalyptic is to be found in Isaiah 24–27"[87]. Hand in hand with the question of literary genre is that of the temporal perspective of Isaiah 24–27. Does it refer principally to a past (e.g. Duhm) or future event (e.g. Rudolph)? Plöger, Kaiser and Wildberger suggest that the complex is an eschatological document

---

85. SWEENEY, *Isaiah 1–39*, p. 312. Along similar lines, J.A. Motyer (*The Prophecy of Isaiah*, Leicester, 1993) understands the entire composition as a contrast between two cities, the ruined and the strong. Cf. also C.R. SEITZ, (*Isaiah 1–39*, [Interpretation: A Bible Commentary for Teaching and Preaching], Louisville, KY, 1994) who describes these chapters as 'A Tale of Two Cities' (pp. 172-201).

86. R.H. O'CONNELL (*Concentricity and Continuity. The Literary Structure of Isaiah* [JSOT SS, 188], Sheffield, 1994) considers the entire book of Isaiah to comprise "...seven asymmetrically concentric sections, each of which presents a complex frameworking pattern of repetitions among its subunits..." (p. 20). Isa 24–27 he considers to be the 'axis' of one of these sections, namely 13,1-39,8, and to be delineated by the key sevenfold repetition of what he refers to as the eschatological phrase ביום ההוא.

87. JOHNSON, *Chaos to Restoration*, p. 11.

anticipating an imminent epiphany of YHWH and that no particular historical event in the future is envisaged. The text symbolises the destruction of ungodly powers in general. A survey of the history of opinion on the literary genre/temporal perspective of our complex will serve to illustrate the major influences on contemporary approaches to the genre of the text and to provide the foundation upon which our metaphorical analysis might serve in turn to confirm or reject genre-critical perspectives

Redditt is correct in pointing out that the three terms 'apocalypse', 'apocalyptic' and 'eschatological' are often used as virtual synonyms[88]. For the sake of clarity, therefore, it would be useful to briefly determine what exactly is meant by these terms and how we can distinguish the one from the other before we endeavour to survey efforts to apply them to Isa 24–27. Based on the work of Hans Dieter Betz[89], Redditt maintains that the term 'apocalyptic' applies to a group of ideas associated with, but not restricted to, the genre 'apocalypse', the latter being best understood as a literary form or *Gattung*.

Klaus Koch's study of 'apocalypse' distinguishes two primary elements or components, the first taking the form of a speech cycle and combining vision and audition giving a view of history from a particular personal perspective and the second taking a paranetic form, drawing out the consequences and implications of the speech cycle (and its visions) for the end-time and urging the listener to persevere[90]. Redditt adopts Koch's term *Rahmengattung* as a way of describing the literary genre of the apocalypse[91], a rather 'elastic' genre which was wide enough to include a variety of related forms. Literary characteristics thereof include: the presence of an interpreting angel, pseudonymity, coded, secretive speech, symbols taken from myths, number symbolism, a long process of growth, inclusive of minor forms such as blessings, wisdom sayings, hymns, prayers[92]. As for the term 'apocalyptic', a number of characteristic elements have been discerned by scholars as evidence of the apocalyptic mindset: periodisation of history, dualism or fluctuating pessimistic/optimistic world-view[93],

---

88. REDDITT, *Form Critical Analysis*, p. 292. He refers to a paragraph in G.H. BOX, *The Book of Isaiah*, New York, NY, 1909, p. 112.

89. H.D. BETZ, *On the Problem of the Religio-Historical Understanding of Apocalypticism*, in *JTC* 6 (1969) p. 135.

90. K. KOCH, *Ratlos vor der Apokalyptic*, Gütersloh, 1970, pp. 20-22.

91. *Rahmengattung* is a collection of related forms. Cf. REDDITT, *Form Critical Analysis*, p. 294 (cf. K. KOCH, *Was ist Formgeschichte? Methoden der Bibelexegese*, Neukirchen – Vluyn, 1974³, pp. 26-30.

92. REDDITT, *Form Critical Analysis*, p. 297.

93. M. NOTH, *Das Geschichtsverständnis der alttestamentlichen Apokalyptik*, in ID., *Gesammelte Studien zum Alten Testament* (Theologische Bücherei, 6), Munich, 1960, p. 272-273.

imminent divine intervention, strong tendency to universalism, interest in angels, demons and science and the presence of a celestial mediator[94].

Given this distinction, we can agree with Redditt that Isa 24–27 is not an 'apocalypse'. How then should its genre be determined? Redditt points out that the perspective of prophecy changed with the Exile. "When the voice of Second Isaiah was raised, it was not with the harsh tones of a Jeremiah or the scathing, vulgar allegories of an Ezekiel. Rather, it was a voice of comfort and good news"[95]. An end was proclaimed to the days of evil which would be replaced by a new day, a day of salvation. Thus prophecy's key perspective became eschatological in the post exilic period. While it is possible to understand the term eschatological as referring to the absolute end of this world, a broader view of the term has been adopted by a number of Old Testament scholars which includes any prophecy which predicts significant, if not total change[96]. Post-exilic prophets preach new hope but the people are also called into action prior to the inauguration of the new day to build the temple (Hag 2,15–19), remove idols (Isa 27,9) and remain faithful to the law, statutes and ordinances (Mal 4,4). After these actions are achieved five elements inevitably follow: the destruction of world kingdoms; redemption of Israel assembled in Jerusalem; paradise for the community; a new ruler (YHWH or Messiah); conversion of the nations[97]. Other elements begin to emerge, however, within post-exilic eschatological prophecy which we have noted to be characteristic of the 'apocalypse' genre outlined above:

---

94. REDDITT, *Form Critical Analysis*, pp. 299-300.
95. *Ibid.*, p. 302.
96. Redditt (*Form Critical Analysis*, p. 304) adopts Lindblom's definition: "Als eschatologisch sind nun... solche Aussagen zu bezeichnen, die auf eine Zukunft hindeuten, wo die Verhältnisse der Geschichte, bzw. der welt, so verändert werden, dass men wirklich von einem neuen Zustand der Dinge, von etwas 'ganz anderem' reden kann". Cf. J. LINDBLOM, *Gibt es eine Eschatologie bei den alttestamentlichen Propheten*, in *StT* 6 (1952) 79-114, p. 81; cf. also TH.C. VRIEZEN, *Prophecy and Eschatology* (SVT, 1), Leiden, 1953, pp. 201-202; E. JENNI, *Eschatology of the Old Testament*, in G.A. BUTTRICK (ed.), *IDB*. Vol. 2, New York, NY 1962, p. 126. G. von Rad's understanding of the concept remains both accurate and relevant: "The prophetic teaching is only eschatological when the prophets expelled Israel from the safety of the old saving actions and suddenly shifted the basis of salvation to a future action of God. [...] The reason for this change in outlook is to be found primarily in history, which had begun to move again in a quite unprecedented way". Cf G. VON RAD, *Old Testament Theology. Vol, II, The Theology of Israel's Prophetic Traditions* (tr. D.M.G. STALKER), Edinburgh – London, 1965, pp. 99-125, esp. 118. Cf. W. BRUEGGEMANN, *Theology of the Old Testament*, Minneapolis, MN, 1997, pp. 646-648, who takes a similar line to that of von Rad. Cf. also J.J. COLLINS, *The Expectation of the End, from Hebrew Prophets to the End of the First Century*, in ID. (ed.), *The Encyclopedia of Apocalypticism*. Vol. 1, New York, NY, 1998.
97. Cf. G. FOHRER, *Die Struktur der alttestamentlichen Eschatologie*, in *ThLZ* 85 (1960) 401-420, esp. 408.

vision/audition and paranesis (Zecheriah); apocalyptic view of history as oscillating between good and bad periods (Isa 24–27 and Isa 65).

On the other hand, Plöger has noted the differences between post-exilic eschatological prophecy and apocalypse: apocalypse stems from distinct, 'separatist' groups (Daniel: the wise among Israel); revelation of YHWH's plans to all becomes revelation of eschatological secrets to a few (4th Ezra 14,45-47); anonymity becomes pseudonymity (providing authority)[98]. Thus there is a clear distinction to be made between eschatological prophecy and the apocalypse genre. Redditt maintains, therefore, that the "distinctions...between eschatological prophecy and apocalyptic apply to Isa 24–27"[99]. In other words, Isa 24–27 focuses on the nation as a redeemed community (esch.), does not speak of secrets (apoc.) and is anonymous (esch.) rather than pseudonymous (apoc.).

While Redditt rightly places these chapters among the post-exilic eschatological prophecies, he notes that there is still an unexplained relationship with apocalyptic literature. How, indeed, do we explain the influence of these chapters on later indisputably apocalyptic material? In answer to this question, F.M. Cross designates Isa 24–27 as 'proto-apocalyptic'[100]. Such elements as the cataclysmic overthrow of the existing world order, the dualistic distinction of the end of this age and history (ch.24), the punishment of celestial beings (24,21-22) and the expected imminent end of the time of evil (26,20-21) all support this designation.

2. TEMPORAL PERSPECTIVE

Brief reference needs to be made at this point to the temporal perspective expressed in Isa 24–27 and its association with the genre-critical terminology applied to the text. Duhm, who, as we noted above, divided the text into songs and oracles was of the opinion that the songs referred to a past event[101]. Lindblom similarly maintained that the songs referred to the more recent past, celebrating the destruction of a hostile city[102]. Rudolph, in contrast, maintained that the songs as well as the eschatological oracles were future oriented, referring to a future event[103].

---

98. Cf. PLÖGER, *Theocracy and Eschatology*, p. 50.
99. REDDITT, *Form Critical Analysis*, p. 309.
100. F.M. CROSS, *New Directions in the Study of Apocalyptic*, in *JTC* 6 (1969) 157-165, p. 159, n. 3; cf. also HANSON, *Dawn*, p. 27: "early apocalyptic".
101. Cf. JOHNSON, *Chaos to Restoration*, p. 15.
102. LINDBLOM, *Die Jesaja Apokalypse*, pp. 42, 53.
103. RUDOLPH, *Jesaja 24–27*, pp. 34-35.

In more recent years, Plöger[104], Kaiser and Wildberger[105] have all maintained that the text of Isa 24–27 is eschatological and refers to a future event, although the latter insists that no particular historical event is intended. Thus while 'the future' appears to enjoy a degree of consensus, the question remains as to whether the author intended the temporal perspective of the complex to go beyond history or remain within it. Johnson is of the belief, and we concur, that the reference is future oriented (including the songs) but remains within history as such. As we noted above, he divides the text into three sections. From a temporal perspective, Section A (24,1-20) refers to the imminent future destruction of Jerusalem[106], Section B (24,21-27,1) to YHWH's (historically) imminent victory and the future destruction of Babylon which would lead to national resurrection and the inauguration of the eschatological age, and Section C (27,2-23) in which YHWH's intervention brings about the reunification of Israel. Thus in terms of temporal perspective Isa 24–27 would appear to have a future orientation, speaking of the inauguration of a new age. The fact that the term 'eschatological' can refer to writings enjoying just such a temporal orientation while remaining within history (historical event inaugurating eschatological age) makes it the most appropriate designation for our textual complex. We shall see in our analysis below whether the use of metaphors tends to confirm or deny this perspective on the text.

Having established some clarity with respect to the significance of the terms 'apocalypse', 'apocalyptic' and 'eschatological', as well as the temporal perspective they imply, we can now proceed to briefly survey the main lines of opinion on the genre of Isa 24–27. Convinced of the apocalyptic character of Isa 24–27, Rudolph Smend was among the first to isolate apocalyptic themes and motifs from later works such as the book of Daniel and attempt to locate the same themes in Isa 24–27. The description of the destruction of the earth (24,18-20), the banquet on Zion (25,8), the alleged reference to personal resurrection (26,19), the blowing of the 'great shofar' (27,13) and the reference to the beasts (27,1) all inclined Smend to characterise the genre of the piece as an apocalypse and to date it between 500 and 300 BCE[107]. Based on similar principles,

---

104. Plöger excludes the songs from this future orientation, maintaining that they are later additions (*Theocracy and Eschatology*, pp. 69-70).

105. KAISER, *Isaiah 13–39*, p. 177; WILDBERGER, *Jesaja 13–27*, p. 957.

106. The destruction of Jerusalem in 587 BCE was so devastating it warranted imagery from the chaos myth.

107. R. SMEND, *Anmerkungen*, pp. 210-211. What Smend believed to be a reference to personal resurrection in 26,19 had to be later than the reference to national resurrection in Ezek 37.

Duhm insisted that one must consider the original body of material to be an 'apocalyptic oracle'[108] with later additional song material[109]. Duhm dated the apocalyptic oracle to 129 BCE during the siege of Jerusalem by Antiochus Sidetes. Rudolph, on the other hand, argued that the chapters were eschatological rather than apocalyptic in perspective[110]. This was underlined by the primary theme of the judgement of the world and the contrast between YHWH's power and that of the world. Ultimately, faithful Israel would survive the judgement of the world and enter into a new era of salvation. Lindblom likewise considered Isa 24–27 to be eschatological rather than apocalyptic[111]. He considered the eschatological segments of the text, however, to be expansions of historical events, and insisted that prophetic language referring to the future often served to renew the present rather than predict an impending new age. Thus for Lindblom, the material is closer to prophetic literature than apocalyptic literature, an Isaianic "Festival Cantata" celebrating an historical event[112]. O. Plöger returned to the search for apocalyptic origins for our chapters in the context of his study of the history of the prophetic movement in Israel as a whole. After the fall of Jerusalem, Plöger maintains, the prophetic spirit was forced into hiding, only to re-surface in the religiosity witnessed in the book of Daniel. Given Daniel's apocalyptic eschatological character, Plöger set out to trace the occurrence of similar material in the prophets, listing three major eschatological texts: Isa 24–27; Zech 12–14 and Joel. Eschatology, for Plöger, constituted the transition between prophecy and apocalyptic[113]. Paul Hanson[114] took Plöger's thesis further, identifying a post-exilic historical situation in which an Isaianic group of visionaries struggled with a Zadokite group of realists and gave vent to their frustrations in the uneven struggle by fantasising about a new age in which matters would be put to rights. According to Hanson this was the birth place of the early apocalyptic material which he discerns in Isa 24–27. Kissane, based on his conviction that Isa 24–27 should be attributed to the 8th century IbA, has argued that these chapters have little to do with eschatology or apocalyptic and everything to do with God's intervention in history[115]. Yehezkiel Kaufmann has

---

108. Cf. DUHM, *Jesaja*, pp. 172-194: 24;25,6-8; 26,20-27,1.12-13.
109. 25,1-5; 25,9-11 26,1-9 (25,12); 27,2-5.
110. RUDOLPH, *Jesaja 24–27*, pp. 34, 35.
111. LINDELOM, *Die Jesaja Apokalypse*, pp. 101-110.
112. *Ibid.*, pp. 80-84. The destruction of a foreign city by YHWH would usher in a new era which would in turn be the beginning of the eschaton, the end of history.
113. PLÖGER, *Theocracy and Eschatology*, p. 96.
114. HANSON, *Dawn, passim*.
115. E.J. KISSANE, *The Book of Isaiah*. 2 vols., Dublin, 1941 (Revised Edition, 1960), p. 267.

likewise argued that the features which typify the apocalypse genre are absent from Isa 24–27 which is prophecy in the true sense and a reference to this-worldly events[116]. While frequently, and often confusingly, maintaining the designation 'Isaiah Apocalypse' more recent scholarship has tended to follow the non-apocalyptic line. Wildberger, for example, is equally aware that Isa 24–27 does not fit the apocalyptic mould and should be thus far removed from any alleged associations with the book of Daniel. While admitting that Plöger's identification of apocalyptic themes is significant, however, he maintains that these topics expand on ideas "die man auch in Prophetismus registrieren kann"[117]. Thus for Wildberger, the designation 'apocalypse' is inappropriate. Watts likewise finds the material "... prophetic and liturgical in style. Only by stretching the definition and the dating of "apocalyptic" can it be called that"[118].

3. Date

The date and historical setting of the complex continue to be the object of dispute. While it is true that commentators' opinions on the dating of the material often go hand in hand with their identification of the anonymous city, it seems more appropriate for our purposes to approach both questions separately. Opinions on the date of Isa 24–27 vary considerably and are best dealt with according to the century proposed rather than in authorial chronological order.

---

116. Y. KAUFMANN, *The Religion of Israel* (tr. M. GREENBERG), Chicago, 1960, pp. 348, 384-385.
117. WILDBERGER, *Jesaja 13–27*, p. 909.
118. WATTS, *Isaiah 13–39*, p. 310. Cf. also OSWALT, *The Book of Isaiah*, p. 440; MOTYER, *The Prophecy of Isaiah*, p. 194 n.1; SWEENEY, *Isaiah 1–39*, pp. 314-315. It is interesting to note here that in the introduction to a recent article – which has an otherwise unrelated focus – T. Thatcher has noted that the use of what he calls 'empty' metaphors is typical of ancient Jewish apocalyptic. He defines 'empty' metaphors as those in which the tenor is 'empty' and the audience is expected to supply the missing referent by 'intertexting' i.e. referring to the preceding context. This would appear to be in line with the possible absence of the *métaphorisant* (cf. chapter II), further examples of which can be found in our textual complex. "Compelled to fill this void or surrender the metaphor to meaninglessness,...[the] reader must create a stabilizing intertext. The empty apocalyptic metaphor invites the reader to textualize some aspect of history or of her own world or experience and make this information the referent that stabilizes the play of the psychological contents. In the latter case the reader does not disregard the "content" of the text; rather, the reader is the content of many apocalyptic metaphors"; cf. T. THATCHER, *Empty Metaphors and Apocalyptic Rhetoric*, in *JAAR* 66 (1998) 549-570, esp. p. 554.

8th Century

Although abandoned in recent years (except by extremely 'conservative' commentators[119]), the authenticity of these chapters, and thus an 8th century dating thereof, has received a small but significant degree of support throughout the history of their exegesis. Beek, for example, associates the chaos portrayed here as reflecting the earthquake mentioned in Amos 1,1 and Zechariah 14,5 which can be dated around 750 BCE[120]. Other authors have suggested the fall of Samaria[121] as the historical setting, others still Sennacherib's siege of Jerusalem[122]. The majority of the supporters of authenticity, however, are unable to apply a specific date to the composition of the chapters by Isaiah[123]. Isa 27,1 is used as the principle segment of our text in support of an 8th century setting, the mythical images of Leviathan and the Sea Monster being interpreted as Assyria, Babylon and Egypt. In the early sixties, J. Mauchline argued for the essential authenticity of the chapters while admitting that certain pericopes may have been added later. Mauchline maintains, for example, that 25,1-5 and 27,10-11 are later additions portraying Jerusalem in the 6th century and that 25,6-8 reflects the deliverance of Jerusalem in 701.

7th Century

F. Bleek, and H. Grätz[124] have ascribed a 7th century date to our complex, maintaining that it was written by a disciple of Isaiah during the reign of Josiah at a time when the supremacy of Assyria was on the wane. Bleek, who incidentally considers Isa 24–27 to be 'probably' a cohesive prophecy, suggests that it was not written by Isaiah himself but by a disciple during the time of the Assyrian destruction when Judah

---

119. Perhaps most recently by J.H. HAYES and S.A. IRVINE, *Isaiah. The Eighth-century Prophet*, Nashville, TN, 1987, pp. 295-320. We use the term 'conservative' as descriptive of a tendency within biblical exegesis. No qualitative judgement is intended thereby.

120. M.A. BEEK, *Ein Erdbeben wird zum prophetischen Erleben*, in Archiv Orientální 17 (1949) 31-40, esp. p. 31.

121. For example, G.R. ROBINSON, *The Book of Isaiah*, New York, NY, 1910, p. 52.

122. For example, C.W.E. NÄGELSBACH, *The Prophet Isaiah* (tr. S.T. LOWRIE and D. MOORE), Edinburgh, 1878, p. 9.

123. Cf., for example, Alexander, Delitzsch, Kaminka, Kaufmann, Kissane, Lagrange, Leupold, Lowth, von Orelli, Zöckler, Young, van Zyl (chronological order).

124. F. BLEEK, *Introduction to the Old Testament* (tr. G.H. Venables), London, 1869, p. 57; H. GRÄTZ, *Die Auslegung und der historische Hintergrund der Weissagung in Jesaja Kap. 24–27*, in Monatschrift für Geschichte und Wissenschaft des Judenthums 25 (1886)1-23, esp pp. 2, 22-23. Cf. also J. WELLHAUSEN, *Einleitung in das Alte Testament*, Berlin, 1878, p. 352, who espouses a similar date.

suffered a great deal under Egypt. He dates the composition to the time of King Josiah or immediately thereafter[125]. Grätz maintains that the city references point to the immanent downfall of Nineveh. He interprets the city reference in 26,1 as suggesting that there was literally no physical wall around the city (YHWH himself being its wall) and that this pointed to the destruction of the wall by Psammeticus[126].

6th Century

A 6th century dating has a considerable following among scholars. Supporters of a pre-exilic dating include F. Hitzig and S.R. Driver[127] while E.W.E. Reuss and W.E. March[128] place the composition of the piece during the early part of the exile. Reading the material as making reference to the destruction of Jerusalem, they arrive at an approximate date of 575-560 BCE. Supporters of a late-exilic dating include W. Gesenius, W.M.L. de Wette, G.A. Smith and E. König[129], all of whom maintain that the images of 27,1 refer to Assyria, Babylon and Egypt. Henry maintains that the songs of 24,7-12, 25,1-5 and 26,4-6 are the earliest segments of Isa 24–27 and that they describe the overthrow of Babylon by Cyrus[130]. Commentators such as Dillmann (539-529) and Kittel (525)[131] date the chapters before or during Cambyses' invasion of Egypt (525). In more recent years, F.M. Cross and two of his pupils, P.D. Hanson and W.R. Millar[132], have favoured a 6th century dating of the complex, almost contemporaneous with DI, for reasons based on the genre-critical designation of the text as 'early apocalyptic' and the belief that the destroyed city is Jerusalem[133]. A number of other scholars attribute the chapters to the post-exilic

---

125. BLEEK, *Introduction*, p. 293.
126. GRÄTZ, *Jesaja Kap. 24–27*, pp. 22-23.
127. F. HITZIG, *Der Prophet Jesaja*, Heidelberg, 1833, pp. 293, 297, 304, 320; S.R. DRIVER, *Isaiah, His Life and Times, and the Writings Which Bear His Name*, New York, NY, 1888, pp. 119-125.
128. E.W.E. REUSS, *Die Geschichte des heiligen Schriften Alten Testaments*, Braunschweig, 1890, pp. 327-330; MARCH, *Two Prophetic Compositions*, pp. 271ff..
129. W. GESENIUS, *Der Prophet Jesaja*, Leipzig, 1829; W.M.L. DE WETTE, *Critical and Historical Introduction to the Canonical Scriptures of the Old Testament* (tr. T. PARKER), Boston, MA, 1867; G. A. SMITH, *The Book of Isaiah*, New York, NY, 1927.
130. HENRY, *Glaubenskrise*, pp. 28-31.
131. A. DILLMANN, *Der Prophet Jesaja* (KHAT, 5), Leipzig, 1890; 1898² (edited by R. KITTEL).
132. F.M. CROSS, *Cananite Myth and Hebrew Epic*, Cambridge, MA, 1973, p. 345; HANSON, *Dawn* pp. 313-314; MILLAR, *Origin of Apocalyptic*, p. 120.
133. More recent scholars such as SWEENEY (*Isaiah 1–39*, p. 317-318) also subscribe to a 6th century date.

period in general without endeavouring to date the material more precisely[134].

5th Century

As Redditt points out, the 5th century provides a turning point for the question of the apocalyptic nature of Isaiah 24–27[135]. Those who date the text around this period are generally convinced that it is not apocalyptic. Lindblom, for example, who refers to the complex as a 'cantata' rather than apocalyptic, draws up a list of apocalyptic features which he maintains are absent from Isa 24–27[136]. Lindblom's 5th century dating of the complex is based on his conviction that the 'world city' which faced destruction was Babylon, destroyed by Xerxes in 485. In addition, the difference in interpretation of the word between Chronicles and Isa 24–27 suggests that the latter should be dated earlier than the former. Finally, the reference to the city wall in 26,1b alludes to the partially rebuilt city wall, completed with the permission of Xerxes. Ringgren and Anderson explicitly follow Lindblom's 5th century dating of the composition[137]. Georg Fohrer can also be counted among those who favour a 5th century dating[138] although he has been reluctant to date the composition with any more precision than this[139]. As we noted above, Fohrer has staunchly defended the non-apocalyptic nature of these chapters and pleads especially for a non-personal interpretation of apparent reference to resurrection in 26,19[140].

4th Century

Several mostly older scholars maintain a 4th century date for the complex[141], among them Rudolf Smend[142] and T.K. Cheyne[143]. Smend

134. Cf., for example, O. KAISER, *Einleitung in das Alte Testament*, Gütersloh, 1969, A. WEISER, *Einleitung in das Alte Testament*, Göttingen, 1966⁶.
135. REDDITT, *Form Critical Analysis*, p. 247.
136. Transcendence, mythology, cosmological orientation, pessimistic view of history, dualism, periodisation of history, doctrine of the two aeons, preoccupation with numbers. While Lindblom did consider the apparent reference to resurrection in 26,19 to allude to personal resurrection, he also considered 26,15-19 a late addition (cf. LINDBLOM, *Die Jesaja Apokalypse*, pp. 102-103).
137. H. RINGGREN, *Die Religionen der Menschheit. Vol. XXVI: Israelitische Religion*, Stuttgart, 1963, pp. 301-303; ANDERSON, *Isaiah xxiv–xxvii Reconsidered*, p. 125.
138. G. FOHRER, *Der Aufbau*, p. 43.
139. ID., *Das Buch Jesaja*, 3 vols. (ZBK), Zürich, 1960-1964, p. 1.
140. *Ibid.*, pp. 30-32.
141. For example, W.I. BAUMGARTNER, *Auferstehungsglaube im Alten Orient*, in *ZMR* 68 (1933) p. 193; A. KUENEN, *The Religion of Israel to the Fall of the Jewish State* (tr. A. H. MAY), London – Edinburgh, 1874, p. 42.
142. R. SMEND, *Anmerkungen*, pp. 210-211.
143. T.K. CHEYNE, *Introduction to the Book of Isaiah*, London, 1895.

maintains that the reference to Moab is highly significant where dating the material is concerned. Upholding the predictive nature of the complex – the fall of Moab being dated around 200 – and insisting on the absence of anti-Moabite sentiment in the 3rd century, Smend proposes a 4th century date for the complex, supporting his argument with the further suggestion that the material exhibits the legalism of Ezra and Nehemiah. In addition to this, Smend argues that the period of Persian weakness (410-344) seems an appropriate setting for the chapters, particularly around the time prior to Alexander the Great's invasion of the Persian Empire (mid-4th century). Smend, like many who support a 4th century dating, maintains that Isa 24–27 is apocalyptic in nature, replete with fantasy (24,18-20; 25,8; 26,19; 27,1.13) and a wish for individual resurrection (26,19). T.K. Cheyne and his disciples, on the other hand, directly associate Isa 24–27 with Alexander's moves against the Persians. Not surprisingly, Cheyne maintained the apocalyptic character of the complex[144] and endeavoured to date the pericopes which were most evidently apocalyptic in nature. Past events such as the repeated abuse of Jerusalem by the Persian army on their way to Egypt in the mid-4th century and Artaxerxes III Ochus' suppression of a Palestinian uprising now give way to a better future in which Alexander's invasion of the Persian Empire plays a significant role. For Cheyne, the enigmatic question of 27,7-11 favourably compares YHWH's punishment of Israel with Alexander's expeditions against the Persians.

3rd Century

O. Procksch, who divides the complex into an older cycle and a later cycle, maintains that the former can be dated between the division of the Macedonian empire and the rise of Rome in 200 BCE[145]. In his opinion, 27,1 refers symbolically to the fall of this empire. The later cycle, and its reference to the fall of a mighty western city which he believes to refer to Carthage, provides him with a date of 146 BCE. E.S. Mulder[146] focuses on the mention of Moab in 25,10b, proposing that it refers to a Moabite city. Based on his discernment of word-play in 24,10 (מדמן/מדמנה [Jer 48,2]), Mulder suggests that we are probably dealing with the Moabite city of Medeba, otherwise known as

---

144. Apocalyptic elements include: world convulsions, nations ascending to Zion, awakening of the dead, imprisoning of the host of the heights, the mythical designation of the three world powers, the mighty sword of YHWH and the blowing of the great shofar (cf. CHEYNE, *Introduction to the Book of Isaia*, pp. 150, 155).
145. PROCKSCH, *Jesaja I*. pp. 343-346.
146. MULDER, *Die Teologie*, pp. 78-93.

Dibon. For Mulder, the overthrow of this city goes hand in hand with the emergence of God's kingdom. The city itself, he maintains, probably fell to the Nabataeans in the first half of the 3rd century. He finally suggests ± 270 as the date of origin of our complex. S.B. Frost strongly defends the apocalyptic character of Isa 24–27[147] which he further designates as "the mythologizing of eschatology"[148]. Based on canon-critical assumptions (Qumran) and the conviction that the author of Isa 24–27 was the same as the final redactor of BI he opts for a mid-3rd century date. Otto Plöger, whose conviction that Isa 24–27 arose from post-exilic divisions within Judaism and set the foundations of apocalyptic literature we outlined above, defends an even later 3rd century dating[149]. Discerning references to universal cosmic judgement and the resurrection of the dead, Plöger appeals for a date closer to the time of Daniel (±225-200 BCE), and the upheaval caused by Antiochus the Great.

2nd Century

Duhm is perhaps the most significant representative of a 2nd century date for our complex[150]. He maintains that 27,1 refers to the Parthians, the Syrians and the Egyptians, that chapter 24 as a whole speaks of the siege of Jerusalem by Antiochus Sidetes, and the hymn of 25,1-5 refers to the destruction of Samaria by John Hyrcanus between 113 and 105 BCE. The powerful western city is, in Duhm's opinion, Rome. The doctrine of resurrection mentioned in ch.26 also reflects this period[151]. Based on his conviction that the city mentioned in Isa 24–27 must be Jerusalem, Ludwig maintains that the events described in these chapters can only refer to the Maccabean period and the devastation of Jerusalem by Antiochus Epiphanes in 168-167 BCE[152].

---

147. Discerning characteristic features in the text such as monotheism, pessimism about the present life, determinism, hope in a golden age, theodicy, nationalism, anonymity and pseudonymity, mythology, symbolism, angels and demons, judgement and resurrection. Cf. S.B. FROST, *Old Testament Apocalyptic: Its Origin and Growth*, London, 1952, p. 17.

148. *Ibid.* p. 32-33.

149. PLÖGER, *Theocracy and Eschatology*, pp. 96-97.

150. DUHM, *Jesaja*, p. 172.

151. It should be noted that J. VAN GILSE (*Jesaja XXIV–XXVII*, in *NedTT* 3 (1914) 167-93) has argued for an even later date for Isa 24–27, namely, if surprisingly, during the Christian period (±119 CE). Few appear to have taken his suggestions seriously.

152. O. LUDWIG, *Die Stadt in der Jesaja-Apokalypse, Zur Datierung von Jes. 24–27*, Cologne, 1967, pp. 59-66.

Undecided

More recent scholarship, such as that of O. Kaiser[153] and H. Wildberger[154], has tended to avoid the dating issue, mainly because of the complexity (if not impossibility) involved in attempting to identify the city of Isa 24–27. Both Kaiser and Wildberger see the composition as thoroughly eschatological in nature and without reference to an historical event nor an historical city. Kaiser concludes that the passage underwent a process of development between the 4th and the 2nd centuries BCE[155]. Wildberger, as we have already noted, also subscribes to the growth process hypothesis but tends to date the complex earlier between 500 and 400 BCE[156]. He bases himself on the evidence of word usage, alleged apocalyptic references and evidence of dependency on earlier prophetic writings[157].

Conclusion

As Johnson has pointed out, there is a clear tendency in more recent years to date Isa 24–27 much earlier than older commentators had tended to do[158]. The period between the 6th and 5th centuries BCE appears to have achieved a degree of consensus, reducing the time-span of possible dates from 650 years to 200 years[159]. Redditt, among others, offers a detailed set of arguments partly agreeing with but mostly criticising the various dating hypotheses we have outlined above and concludes that our complex was probably written between 515 and 380, although he does not 'insist' on this[160]. It is clear that dating is based on two distinct if complementary lines of argumentation: historical allusions and the development of religious/political ideas. Redditt takes the latter approach basing his arguments on the presence or absence of certain ideas and their relevance for the date of the passage (e.g. apocalyptic, eschatological, historical? individual/national resurrection? national

---

153. KAISER, *Isaiah 13–39*, pp. 177, 181.
154. WILDBERGER, *Jesaja 13–27*, p. 911.
155. KAISER, *Isaiah 13–39*, p. 179.
156. WILDBERGER, *Jesaja 13–27*, p. 911.
157. Based on statistical vocabulary analysis of LINDBLOM (*Die Jesaja Apokalypse*, p. 111ff.) and MULDER (*Die Teologie*, pp. 67-77) which associate Isa 24–27 with the rest of BI, apocalyptic references and apparent dependency on other prophetic writings (e.g. Hosea). Cf. WILDBERGER, *Jesaja 13–27*, pp. 908-911.
158. JOHNSON, *Chaos to Restoration*, p. 14; cf. also ANDERSON, *Isaiah XXIV–XXVII Reconsidered*, p. 126; RINGGREN, *Some Observations*, p. 114; B. OTZEN, *Traditions and Structures of Isaiah XXIV–XXVII*, in *VT* 24 (1974) 196-206, esp. p. 206.
159. If one excludes van Gilse (see n. 151)!
160. REDDITT, *Form Critical Analysis*, pp. 269-283.

reunification? incense altars in 27,9? Noachic covenant = eternal covenant? evidence of Priestly ideas). While admitting that such ideas do not necessarily develop in an unbroken line "which is uniform for the whole Israelite community"[161], he nevertheless sets the *terminus a quo* as the exile which he believes is clearly mentioned in 27,8 and the *terminus ad quem* as the period of the ascendancy of the Seleucid kings, i.e. the turn of the 2nd century.

Thus, while disagreement still exists as to the detailed assignation of literary genres to our text, general consensus appears to have been reached concerning temporal orientation and overall genre. A question posed by Millar, however, is significant for our analysis of the text from the perspective of metaphor: "How was the imagery used? Did the language serve to enhance the significance of God's action in an historical event or had the internal power of the themes themselves broken loose from their mooring in historical event drawing the reader more and more into the realm of fantasy?"[162] In other words, does the author's use of (often apparently apocalyptic) images throughout the complex ground it in an apocalyptic world view or does he simply but skilfully use metaphor to focus attention on God's actions in history and how they should be understood by his reader(s). At the same time, what, if anything, does the author's use of metaphors have to say concerning the date and historical setting of the complex? Does the use of metaphors take us beyond and away from history, confirming the understanding commentators such as Kaiser and Wildberger? Or does it focus us on YHWH's relationship with his city (land and people) and its historical failures? We will return below to the question of the identification of the city mentioned in our complex, recognising, along with Redditt, that attempts to identify historical references in the text seem to ignore the fact that it has a future orientation, it expects YHWH's intervention in history to be an event in the future. The many scholars who have assumed this material to be 'prophecy' after the event, are rarely in agreement on the event itself.

IV. THE UNNAMED CITY (CITIES) IN ISA 24–27

Millar has remarked that "In any historical reconstruction of the events underlying Isaiah 24–27, sooner or later one must discuss the

---

161. *Ibid.*, pp. 271-272.
162. MILLAR, *Origin of Apocalyptic* p. 9.

"destroyed city"[163]. Along with Millar we will limit ourselves to the three main proposals (with the strongest evidence) with regard to the identity of the city, since the bewildering variety of 'scholarly' hypotheses on the question has led some to think that any search for an historical city is futile and, in the final analysis, misguided, the composition being too eschatological in character to lend itself to such an identification[164]. In addition, however, we will examine the proposals of those who consider the text to refer to more than one city or to have no interest in a real, historical city at all. References to a city are to be found in 24,7-12; 25,1-15; 26,5-6; 27,10-11.

MOAB OR AN UNKNOWN CITY THEREIN?

The reference to Moab in 25,10b and the so-called 'Moab pericope' constitutes the only apparently historical reference in the entire textual complex. The fact that the text is also found almost word for word in Jer 48,43-44 has led some to support Moab, or a city in Moab, as the unknown city of Isa 24–27. Smend, for example, who sets the historical scene during the expeditions of Alexander the Great into Palestine, held that the rejoicing of 24,14-16 would be instigated by Alexander and would have its ultimate focus in the impending fall of Israel's dreaded enemy Moab[165]. According to him, the two themes of the complex – restoration of the faithful and the destruction of Moab – were combined in the Moab pericope and were the object of song and celebration in 27,2-13. Otto Eissfeldt[166], who was likewise attracted to the reference to Moab in 25,10, challenged the various Babylonian hypotheses on the grounds that the reference to the feet of the poor (i.e. of the Jews) trampling the city in 26,6 implied a city in the region of Judah[167]. Similarities with the oracle concerning Moab in Isa 16 further supported his hypothesis[168]. E.S. Mulder, moves away from the city of Moab to a city in

163. *Ibid.*, p. 15.
164. Cf., for example, KAISER, *Isaiah 13–39*, pp. 177, 181. Other options not discussed here include Nineveh (F. HITZIG, *Der Prophet Jesaja, übersetzt und ausgelegt*, Heidelberg, 1833, pp. 292-298), Carthage which was destroyed by the Romans in 146 (PROCKSCH, *Jesaja I*, pp. 342-346); Samaria which fell to John Hyrcanus in 110 (DUHM, *Jesaja*, pp. 147-148)
165. SMEND, *Anmerkungen*, pp. 193-195, 215-224.
166. O. EISSFELDT, *The Old Testament. An Introduction*.
167. *Ibid*, p. 326.
168. Wine: 16,7-10 // 24,7-11; hatred of Moab: 16,16 // 25,10; Zion as refuge: 16,1-5 // 25,6-8. Cf. EISSFELDT, *The Old Testament. An Introduction*, p. 326-327.

Moab, namely Dibon¹⁶⁹. Insisting that the walls of Jerusalem must have been rebuilt when Isa 24–27 was written and that the ideas expressed in the complex appear to be more in line with later developments, he dates the complex around 270 BCE following the Nabataean invasion of Moab. Other commentators have endeavoured to excise the Moab problem by emending the reference¹⁷⁰, deleting the oracle¹⁷¹, or interpreting the reference as symbolic¹⁷². Millar maintains that although the language is specific, "...its place in the Apocalypse goes back to the theme of New Conquest revived by Second Isaiah. Moab and Edom are symbolic of the resistance met in the Transjordan area during the first conquest"¹⁷³. Johnson has pointed out most recently that "...most scholars have recognised the Moab pericope (25.10b-12) as a polemical intrusion into the text which has nothing to do with its context and is uncharacteristic of the rest of the composition"¹⁷⁴. As we shall see below, our own preference will be to identify the city throughout the complex as Jerusalem. Nevertheless, the reference to Moab need not be excised if one accepts, in line with Mulder, that the term symbolises resistance. It is Jerusalem's 'pride' which will be destroyed while Jerusalem herself will be redeemed (YHWH's hand will rest on Zion [25,10a])¹⁷⁵.

BABYLON?

A number of scholars, have identified our mysterious city as Babylon, based, for the most part, on the deep hatred felt towards this city for destroying Jerusalem and deporting its population into exile¹⁷⁶. Only the destruction of such a world power and its capital could elicit the joy expressed in 24,14-16. The city of Babylon was 'taken over' on three

169. MULDER, *Die Teologie*, pp. 91-93. He partly bases this on an apparent word-play between מדמנה in Isa 24,10 and מדמן in Jer 48,2, the latter being another name for the Moabite city Dibon (cf. Isa 15,2).
170. אויב to מואב; cf. C.C. TORREY, *Armageddon*, in *HThR*, 31 (1938) p. 246.
171. LINDBLOM, *Die Jesaja Apokalypse*, pp. 38-40; MARCH, *Two Prophetic Compositions*, pp. 103-104; JOHNSON, *Chaos to Restoration*, p. 12.
172. MILLAR, *Origins of Apocalyptic*, p. 18.
173. *Ibid.*
174. JOHNSON, *Chaos to Restoration*, p. 12.
175. As Watts notes, the significance of 'the city' in BI is an endeavour to "uncover the role of Jerusalem from chap. 1 through chap. 66... Other cities are emphasised... it is not the cities themselves which are important here, but what they stand for (WATTS, *Isaiah 1–33*, pp. 138-139)."
176. RUDOLPH (*Isaiah 24–27*, pp. 61-64), LINDBLOM (*Die Jesaja Apokalypse*, pp. 72-84), ANDERSON (*Isaiah XXIV–XXVII Reconsidered*, pp. 118-126), HENRY (*Glaubenskrise*, pp. 20-34), OTZEN (*Traditions*, p. 206), SWEENEY (*Isaiah 1–39*, p. 318).

occasions in 539 BCE (Cyrus), 485 BCE (Xerxes I) and 331 BCE (Alexander the Great). Rudolph's belief that the destruction of this city would have world-wide implications led him to focus on Babylon. Given the fact that Cyrus' overthrow of Babylon did not destroy the city he opted for Alexander the Great's devastation of the city in 331 BCE. Lindblom, who was equally convinced that the city of chaos had to be Babylon, ascribed its destruction portrayed in Isa 24–27 to the invasion of Xerxes I in 485 BCE.

Henry took the religious and psychological ideas of DI as a point of departure and insisted that the author of Isa 24–27 had been moved to write from a sense of religious hope initiated in the exilic community by the fall of Babylon. The author had in fact interpreted a particular historical event (the end of the Babylonian exile and the ultimate fall of the city) as a divine intervention in history towards the fulfilment of God's universal purpose. Henry considers the description of the destruction of the city stylised, a fact which she interprets as a sign of typicality or universal validity.

Otzen notes that only two world powers could possibly be identified with the destroyed city of Isa 24–27, Nineveh[177] and Babylon. He bases his choice of Babylon on the following: (i) Babylon plays a more dominant role in Israel than any other hostile city; (ii) Babylon had taken on symbolic significance; (iii) there are evident similarities between the oracles against Babylon (Isa 13; 21,1-10; Jer 50–51) and the Isa 24–27. Indeed Isa 13 contains the same "...strange connection between eschatological descriptions of the imminent world-catastrophe and the fall of the city of the world-power"[178].

Perhaps the most recent commentator to ascribe to the Babylon hypothesis is Sweeney. Sweeney begins by noting that while Isa 24–27 focuses primarily on YHWH's actions against the entire earth, the destruction of the anonymous 'city of chaos' plays a central role in the process of divine intervention. He goes on to dismiss the other candidates for identification on the basis of the fact that they did not represent a sufficient threat to Israel as that posed by Nineveh and Babylon. Based on apparent citations in Isa 24–27 of earlier prophetic literature (including Jer 48,43-44a//Isa 24,17-18a) in which Babylon posed a major threat he is further able to dismiss Nineveh as a candidate for identification. On the positive side, he offers a number of arguments to support his position, among them the following: (i) the reference to the 'city of chaos'

---

177. HITZIG, *Der Prophet Jesaja*, pp. 292-298.
178. OTZEN, *Traditions*, p. 206.

in 24,10 is a deliberate pun on the name of the dragon goddess of the sea Tiamat who represented cosmic chaos and who was defeated by the Babylonian city god Marduk. Thus the destruction of the 'city of chaos' calls the role of Babylon as a world-power into question; (ii) the expressions 'fortified city', 'exalted city' and 'place of aliens' are reminiscent of Nebuchadnezar's fortification of Babylon in the 6th century which so contributed to its reputation as a magnificent yet fear-inspiring metropolis; (iv) the terminology associated with the downfall of the city in 26,5-6[179] is similar to that used of the fall of Babylon in 13,1-22.

JERUSALEM AND VARIATIONS?

The third major option for the identification of the city is Jerusalem itself. W.E. March has argued that Isa 24,1-20 refers to YHWH's punishment of his people for breaking the covenant and that their rejoicing in 24,5-15 is somewhat premature, at least in the mind of the prophet who sees only continued and more severe punishment[180]. Isa 24,21–27,1 (he excludes vv. 2-13) reveals a change of mood[181], however, where the city remains Jerusalem but is identified as Zion, the cities of 25,2 and 26,5 referring to YHWH's enemies in general[182]. Ludwig likewise suggests that Jerusalem is the city referred to in our complex although he maintains that the references need not all reflect the same historical background. He remains undecided as to whether 24,8-12 and 27,10-11 refers to the conquest of Jerusalem by Nebuchadnezar (587) or by Antiochus Epiphanes (168/167). At the same time, however, he maintains that 25,1-5 and 26,1-6 refer to Jerusalem's conquest of Acra[183] in 141 under the Maccabean Simon. Thus he remains undecided with respect to dating the complex as a whole[184]. P. Hanson also identifies the city as Jerusalem but is more confident with respect to the date of the composition: "...if the city of chaos, the destruction of which is celebrated by the apocalypse, is the Jerusalem controlled and defiled (in the eyes of the visionaries) by the hierocratic party, then the composition could stem from a point fairly late in the sixth century, perhaps from the period of

---

179. Also the terminology referring to the fall of the earth in 24,1-13 and the pangs of childbirth in 26,17-18.
180. MARCH, *Two Prophetic Compositions*, pp. 267-268
181. March explains this change of mood on the basis of his proposed date, 560 BCE.
182. MARCH, *Two Prophetic Compositions*, p. 93.
183. Wildberger suggests that קריה is a play on the word Acra (*Jesaja 13–27*, p. 906)
184. LUDWIG, *Die Stadt*, pp. 64, 74f..

the temple controversy, ca. 520"[185]. Strongly influenced by Hanson, W.R. Millar, likewise based on prosodic analysis, also opts for Jerusalem: "The reference to the destroyed city of aliens, never to be rebuilt, the city trampled by the faithful, could be elements introduced into the earlier poems as the tensions between contending parties in post-exilic Israel increased. The Jerusalem of reality and the Zion of faith, for the visionaries, remained apart. As it became defiled by oppressive leaders, it deserved YHWH's continued wrath. The hope was held out, however, for that day when Israel would truly be restored"[186]. Thus the Jerusalem of reality constitutes the 'city of chaos', confronted by YHWH's punishing intervention and the Zion of faith is the city which will ultimately enjoy YHWH's benediction and restoration. Johnson opposes this view in part, arguing that "it is highly doubtful that any Jewish writer would rejoice over the destruction of Jerusalem as portrayed in 25.1-5 and 26,5.6. This is especially true of sixth-century Israel. Even during the highly divisive period when the second temple was destroyed in 70 CE..."[187] Nonetheless, he goes on to argue that the first segment of the composition (24,1-20) refers to the destruction of Jerusalem and not to universal destruction (and its apocalyptic overtones) as has often been assumed. References to the overthrow of an evil city (25,1-2; 26,5.6) point, he believes, to Babylon: "In the aftermath of 587, it would have been evident to any survivor that the hated city was Babylon and not some supra-historical entity"[188].

Thus, there would appear to be three primary variations on the Jerusalem hypothesis[189]: the real Jerusalem, the real Jerusalem and the Zion of faith, the real Jerusalem and the real Babylon. While we will endeavour to defend the Jerusalem hypothesis in the coming chapters, it will be part of our task to discern whether the author's use of metaphors can help us select between the variations.

---

185. HANSON, *Dawn*, p. 314.
186. MILLAR, *Origin of Apocalyptic*, p. 119.
187. JOHNSON, *Chaos to Restoration*, pp. 13-14.
188. JOHNSON, *Chaos to Restoration*, p. 99; cf. his more detailed argumentation on pp. 29-35; cf. also as early as W. GESENIUS, *Der Prophet Jesaia: übersetzt und mit einem vollständigen philologisch-kritischen und historischen Commentar begleitet*, Leipzig, 1821, p. 757; more recently also C.R SEITZ, *Isaiah 1–39*, pp. 172-175.
189. One further, if less significant, suggestion comes from Hayes and Irvine who propose that the reference is to a hated part of the city of Jerusalem which they refer to as the 'Assyrian citadel' which garrisoned troops from throughout the territory who were responsible for good order in Jerusalem and Judah. Thus, for Hayes and Irvine, the terms 'city' and 'town' can also refer to walled enclosures within larger metropolitan entities (cf. *Isaiah the Eighth Century Prophet*, pp. 296-297).

No Specific City?

Based primarily on their understanding of the redactional history of Isa 24–27, a number of authors have maintained that there is no need to identify a specific city or exact historical situation. Plöger, for example, suggests that reference to the city in 24,10 should be interpreted as a reference to 'the city life of contemporary civilisation in general' which Yahweh's destructive activity will not by-pass'[190]. He further maintains that other city references either have nothing to do with the interpretation of the complex (25,2; 26,5.6) or are later additions (27,10)[191]. Kaiser's conviction that the entire composition is eschatological in character likewise leads him to lose interest in the identification of an historical city and in the identification of historical evidence within the text: "...the question of the previous history of individual sections is of no significance for the understanding of the composition as we possess it, for in every case they are given a fresh significance within it"[192]. While Johnson agrees with Kaiser's view that the references to the city in Isa 24–27 are 'pure prophecy'[193] he is unwilling to accept that the author thereof had no particular city in mind. Johnson considers the author to be almost obsessed with the city and its evil character and thus cannot imagine that he did not have somewhere specific as his model[194]. As we have noted above, however, Johnson does not identify all the city references with the same actual city.

The City as Typos? Symbol? Paradigm?

Plöger's and Kaiser's disinclination to identify the city with an historical location has led later author's to take the 'no city' hypothesis a step further. Hanhart, for example, considers the 'jahwefeindliche Stadt' to be a 'typos der Zerstörung menschlicher Gemeinschaft'[195]. While he thus relativises the sigificance of the city in Isa 24–27, he insists that Israel as such is first in line for YHWH's destructive intervention, primarily on

---

190. Plöger, *Theocracy and Eschatology*, p. 56.
191. Plöger, *Theocracy and Eschatology*, pp. 69, 75-78.
192. Kaiser, *Isaiah 13–39*, pp. 177 (27,10), 181 (24,10), 197 (25,1-5), 206 (26,1-6).
193. *Ibid.*, p. 177.
194. Johnson, *Chaos to Restoration*, p. 13.
195. R. Hanhart, *Die jahwefeindliche Stadt*, in H. Donner et al. (eds.), *Beiträge zur alttestamentlichen Theologie: Festschrift für Walther Zimmerli zum 70. Geburtstag*, Göttingen, 1977, p. 152. In this sense he is similar to Plöger. Cf. also, Oswalt, *The Book of Isaiah*, p. 411.

account of her own godlessness: "Darum ist Israel selbst zuerst jener Gottlose, dem Jahwe nicht gnädig ist, und dessen er sich nicht erbarmt (24,11b), weil er, wenn ihm jetzt Gnade widerführe und nicht das Gericht, die Gerechtigkeit nicht lernen, die Herrlichkeit Jahwes nicht erkennen könnte (26,10). Das irdische Israel ist – diese innere Beziehung zwischen den Aussagen von 27,11 und 26,20 ist offenkundig – als das Volk der Erkentnislosigkeit zuerst der Repräsentant jener Gottlosigkeit der ganzen Schöpfung..."[196] One might argue, however, that Israel as representative of the godlessness of creation is herself represented by Jerusalem/Zion which undergoes YHWH's hostility. Thus, while Hanhart abstracts from the historical city of Jerusalem at a specific moment in her history, he seems to remain with Jerusalem as the explanation of the city references in Isa 24–27 albeit as a 'typos'. Wildberger similarly speaks of the city as 'Symbol der grossen Gegenmacht Jahwes'[197] For him, the aspects of the complex which are 'timeless and typical' are more important than those which refer to a specific situation; "Richtig ist aber, daß solche Verkündigung des Zeitlos-Typischen wichtiger wird als der konkrete Bezug in seiner Einmaligkeit"[198]. While this may be true to a degree, we can agree with Johnson that such representativeness can only have applied to Jerusalem[199].

Based on a study of the I-Psalms, M.R. Hauge's recent monograph provides a useful link between the identification of the city in Isa 24–27 and a metaphorical reading of the text. For Hauge, "...language (of the I-Psalms) seems to refer to itself as a religious language, expressing an interpretative symbol system of conceptual character. This seems to be connected with the basic motifs and concepts as expressions of a paradigm of religious reality... In the religious description of humanity being related to God, humanity is set in a sacred topography of contrast localities connected to the idea of movement between the contrast localities"[200]. Thus, for Hauge, one's personal place in the localities of 'Temple' or 'Sheol' and 'way' (cf. 26,7), for example, is illustrative of one's relationship with YHWH. Perhaps, in light of this, the same can be said of the people in relation to YHWH and not only the individual, and that the locations of Jerusalem and the land

---

196. HANHART, *Die jahwefeindliche Stadt*, p. 162.
197. WILDBERGER, *Jesaja 13–27*, p. 957.
198. WILDBERGER, *Jesaja 13–27*, p. 906. A few years before Wildberger, Habets argued on the basis of the LXX translation *pasa polis* that no specific city was intended (cf. G. N. M. HABETS, *Die grosse Jesaja-Apokalypse (Jes 24–27). Ein Beitrag zur Theologie des Alten Testaments*, Diss. Bonn, 1974, pp. 63-64.
199. JOHNSON, *Chaos to Restoration*, p. 30
200. M.R. HAUGE, *Between Sheol and Temple. Motif Structure and Function in the I-Psalms* (JSOT SS, 178), Sheffield, 1995.

and the people's place therein (cf. 26,2 – entering the gate; 27,12-13 – return to Jerusalem) can be understood to constitute paradigmatic metaphors illustrating the relationship between YHWH and his people. Thus the biographical (and historical) character is forcefully lessened and one is free to interpret the city as a paradigm for relationship. Being 'within' and 'without' are clearly important notions in such an approach to the meaning of the city: only the righteous can be 'within' (26,2), the rest are scattered (24,1) or have fled (24,18).

Conclusion

Perhaps one of the advantages of the lack of scholarly consensus on the primary questions discussed here, as well as the secondary questions to which we will return in our analysis of each chapter, is the fact that it encourages us to focus on the literary meaning of the complex and indeed the literary meaning of the city rather than the historical significance and identification thereof[201]. Thus, while we can agree with Johnson, who has maintained that scholars agree for the most part on the compositional unity of the complex, an earlier rather than a later dating and a future rather than apocalyptic orientation, the present study intends to focus on Isa 24–27 as we now have it in order to discern its metaphorical content and the significance thereof. Perhaps, if one approaches Isa 24–27 'metaphorically speaking', there is some chance that diachronic considerations of the sort mentioned in this opening survey may be addressed, that the compositional divisions of the complex can be established and that the significance of the city and other obscurities might emerge.

This study thus proposes to seek answers to unsettled questions (chapter I) concerning these highly disputed chapters of the book of Isaiah in the author's use of metaphors. Chapter II will then turn to the complexities of the theory of metaphor and endeavour to distil an approach to the text which will help us to discern and interpret the presence and use of metaphors in the complex. Each chapter of our complex will constitute its own chapter (III-VI) of the present study. The concluding pages of this work will offer a reflection on the success of the endeavour.

---

201. Cf. WATTS, *Isaiah 1–33*, p. 319

CHAPTER TWO
AN APPROACH TO METAPHOR

INTRODUCTION[1]

The purpose of the present chapter is to examine a number of theories of metaphor and assess their applicability to biblical texts in general. Our final intention will be to draw up some notes on methodology on the basis of which we can attempt to isolate, inventorise and interpret the metaphors used or created by the author(s) of Isa 24–27. As a means to this end we will use the work of Daniel Bourguet *Des métaphores de Jérémie*[2] as our point of departure. Bourguet states clearly in the introduction to his book that his work is restricted to the metaphors employed by the author of the book of Jeremiah[3]. The same introduction, however,

---

1. Since our purpose here is to establish a methodology with respect to metaphor which can be confidently employed with respect to biblical texts, our approach to metaphor will, of necessity, have to be guided by a selection of secondary literature which offers an analysis of the principle and most influential theories on the topic. An exhaustive study of metaphor in its literary-historical and linguistic context would constitute a major work in itself and would take us far beyond the intention of this chapter. Fairly recent bibliographical publications devoted exclusively to studies on metaphor are illustrative of the vastness of the topic: W.A. SHIBLES, *Metaphor: An Annotated Bibliography and History*, Whitewater, WI, 1971; J.P. VAN NOPPEN et al. (eds.), *Metaphor: a Bibliography of Post-1970 Publications*, Amsterdam, 1985; J.-P. VAN NOPPEN AND E. HOLS (eds.), *Metaphor II: A Classified Bibliography of Publications 1985-1990*, Amsterdam, 1990;

2. D. BOURGUET, *Des métaphores de Jérémie* (EB, 9), Paris, 1987.

3. Besides Bourguet, a number of books and articles have appeared in recent years dealing with metaphors on a similar book-specific basis: for example, A.J. BJØRNDALEN, *Untersuchungen zur allegorischen Rede der Propheten Amos und Jesaja*, Berlin – New York, 1986 (cf. esp. pp. 7-103); H. JAUSS, *Tor der Hoffnung. Vergleichnisformen und ihre Funktion in der Sprache der Psalmen* (Europäische Hochschulschriften, 23: Theologie, 412), Frankfurt am Main, 1991; H.-P. MÜLLER, *Vergleich und Metapher im Hohenlied*, Göttingen, 1984; F. LANDY, *In the Wilderness of Speech: Problems of Metaphor in Hosea*, in *Biblical Interpretation* 3 (1995) 35-59; B. SEIFERT, *Metaphorisches Reden von Gott im Hoseabuch*, Göttingen, 1996; G. EIDEVALL, *Grapes in the Desert. Metaphors, Models and Themes in Hosea 4–14* (CB, 43), Stockholm, 1996; J. MCINLAY, *Bringing the Unspeakable to Speech in Hosea*, in *Pacifica* 9 (1996) 121-134. Others focus on a particular metaphor and its application in various biblical texts: for example, M. BRETTLER, *God is King. Understanding an Israelite Metaphor* (JSOT SS, 76), Sheffield, 1989; ID., *Images of YHWH the Warrior in Psalms*, in *Semeia* 61 (1993) 135-65; M.C.A. KORPEL, *A Rift in the Clouds. Ugaritic and Hebrew Descriptions of the Divine*, Münster, 1990; N. STIENSTRA, *YHWH is the Husband of His People, Analysis of a Biblical Metaphor with Special Reference to Translation*, Kampen, 1993. Others still focus on a single metaphor within a specific biblical text: for example, K. NIELSEN, *There is Hope for a Tree. The Tree as Metaphor in Isaiah* (JSOT SS, 65), Sheffield, 1989; K. HAYES, *"The Earth Mourns" : Earth as Actor in a Prophetic Metaphor*, Diss. (UMI), Catholic University of America, 1997 (esp. pp. 187-259); Two valuable approaches to metaphor as an element

provides us with a basic analysis of the notion of metaphor beginning with classical definitions but moving quickly to the perspective of modern linguistics, especially the definition of Paul Ricœur in *La métaphore vive*[4]. Bourguet's approach is useful in that he nuances the definitions of metaphor which come from the study of linguistics for application to the biblical text in general. The fact that a vast amount of literature exists with respect to metaphor, approaching the notion from a variety of perspectives, forces us to confine ourselves to a limited number of authors. In parallel with Bourguet's analysis, therefore, we will examine the work of Nelly Stienstra in her recent publication *YHWH is the Husband of His People. Analysis of a Biblical Metaphor with Special Reference to Translation*[5] together with that of Peter W. Macky in *The Centrality of Metaphors to Biblical Thought. A Method for Interpreting the Bible*[6]. Other authors will be consulted along the way but the primary authors mentioned here have been selected because they each attempt to extract a theory of metaphor applicable to biblical texts from the wide variety of theories available in the world of literature, philosophy and linguistics. While they lead us thankfully through the first labyrinth, they also represent different yet often converging perspectives on metaphor and its function.

---

of Hebrew poetry are: L. ALONSO SCHÖKEL, *A Manual of Hebrew Poetics* (Subsidia Biblica, 11), Rome,1988, p. 108f.; W.G.E. WATSON, *Classical Hebrew Poetry, A Guide to Its Techniques* (JSOT SS, 26), Sheffield 1995², pp. 263-272. Other studies focus on the use and significance of particular (often obscure) images in the OT in light of Ancient Near Eastern iconography without any systematic reference to the theory of metaphor: e.g. M. LURKER, *Wörterbuch biblischer Bilder und Symbole*, München, 1973; O. KEEL, *Deine Blicke sind Tauben. Zur Metaphorik des Hohen Liedes* (SBS, 114/115), Stuttgart, 1984; ID., *De wereld van de oud-oosterse beeldsymboliek en het Oude Testament toegelicht aan de hand van de Psalmen*, Kampen, 1984. A small number of monographs and articles exist with reference to the images and metaphors employed in Isaiah as such: e.g. R. LACK, *La symbolique du livre d'Isaïe. Essai sur l'image littéraire comme élément de structuration* (AnBib, 59), Rome, 1973; K. NIELSEN, *op. cit.*; P.D. MISCALL, *Isaiah: The Labyrinth of Images*, in Semeia 54 (1991) 103-121; Y. GITAY, *Why Metaphors? A Study of the Texture of Isaiah*, in C.C. BROYLES and C.A. EVANS (eds.), *Writing and Reading the Scroll of Isaiah. Studies of an Interpretative Tradition*, Leiden, 1997, pp. 57-65.

4. P. RICŒUR, *La métaphore vive*, Paris, 1975; = ID., *The Rule of Metaphor* (tr. R. CZERNY), London, 1978.

5. N. STIENSTRA, *YHWH is the Husband of His People. Analysis of a Biblical Metaphor with Special Reference to Translation*, Kampen, 1993.

6. P.W. MACKY, *The Centrality of Metaphors to Biblical Thought. A Method for Interpreting the Bible* (Studies in the Bible and early Christianity, 19), Lewiston – Queenston – Lampeter, 1990.

I. Theories and Definitions

1. A Definition of Metaphor

Noting that the ancient Hebrews unlike the Greeks did not have a word which signified metaphor, and thus had not conceptualised the notion as a figure of speech, Bourguet begins his analysis with a definition of metaphor from the world of Greek rhetoric taken from Aristotle: "Metaphor consists in giving the thing a name that belongs to something else; the transference being either from genus to species, or from species to genus, or from species to species, or on grounds of analogy"[7]. Such a definition was at the centre of classical rhetorics until its decline in the last century. We will briefly focus on some intervening positions below when we examine Stienstra and Macky. It is evident, however, that a new rhetorics has emerged in the present century rooted in modern linguistics and with a perspective on metaphor which goes beyond that of Aristotle. In his epoch making book *La métaphore vive*, Paul Ricœur presents and analyses the findings of modern linguistics with respect to metaphor and although his approach is not specifically oriented towards biblical texts it nevertheless provides Bourguet with a starting point for a new definition: "*le fait de décrire intentionnellement, de manière médiate ou immédiate, une chose dans les termes d'une autre qui lui ressemble et qui appartient à une autre isotopie*"[8]. In going on to explain certain aspects of his definition Bourguet endeavours to refine and focus the approach of Ricœur for application to biblical texts. It will be evident from the outset, however, that in contrast to our other authors, Bourguet espouses a primarily rhetorical understanding of metaphor. In line with Ricœur, however, he would insist that it is not only rhetorical but also creative of new meaning[9].

"décrire"

Although Ricœur frequently talks of metaphor in terms of 'speaking', Bourguet rightly points out that such an approach is limited to the oral

---

7. Translation cf. R. McKeon (ed.), *The Basic Works of Aristotle* [Poetics], New York, NY, 1941, 1457b, 6-9. Cf. for Greek edition, I. Bekker (ed.) *Aristotelis Opera*, Berlin, 1960, 1457b, 6-9: μεταφορὰ δ' ἐστὶν ὀνόματος ἀλλοτρίου ἐπιφορὰ ἢ ἀπὸ τοῦ γένους ἐπὶ εἶδος, ἢ ἀπὸ τοῦ εἴδους ἐπὶ γένος, ἢ ἀπὸ τοῦ εἴδους ἐπὶ εἶδος, ἢ κατὰ τὸ ἀνάλογον. For a more detailed discussion of Aristotle on metaphor cf. P. Ricœur, *La métaphore vive* pp. 13-61; = *The Rule of Metaphor*, p. 9-43.
8. Bourguet, *Des métaphores*, p. 10.
9. P. Ricœur, *Stellung und Funktion der Metapher in der biblischen Sprache*, in P. Ricœur and E. Jüngel (eds.), *Metapher. Zur Hermeneutik religiöser Sprache*, Munich, 1974, p. 45.

dimension of metaphor and does not properly apply to written metaphors as we find them in the bible. He opts, therefore, for the more inclusive term *décrire* 'to describe', a term which we will use freely throughout this text. He admits that certain biblical texts reveal traces of an oral phase in which a particular metaphor may have been accompanied by a gesture or an obvious change in intonation which would have been of profound significance for the sense or meaning of the metaphor in question. Since we are limited to the written text, however, such elements are for the most part lost to us. Nevertheless, we should prudently pay attention, Bourguet notes, to the punctuation found in the MT, which, although almost a millennium later than the biblical texts themselves, might still provide clues to intonation. The same, I believe, might be said of Hebrew syntax and the use of poetic devices. Biblical metaphors are written metaphors, whatever their oral history may be. With their 'orality' in mind, however, our definition can best proceed, according to Bourguet, with the more neutral term *décrire*.

"une chose... une autre"

As Bourguet points out, the term *chose* 'thing' can be used in the widest of senses to describe an object or an animal or a person or even God. Bourguet makes an important distinction in this regard, however, referring to the thing described as the '*métaphorisé*' *a*nd that with which the thing is described as the '*métaphorisant*'[10]. He thereby nuances his definition in the following way: "*décrire intentionellement, de manière médiate ou immédiate, un métaphorisé dans les termes d'un métaphorisant qui lui ressemble et qui appartient à une autre isotopie*". Since the familiar terms 'tenor' and 'vehicle' can also be used with respect to simple comparison and are not unique to metaphor, Bourguet prefers the terms *métaphorisé* and *métaphorisant* which can also be found in Ricœur[11] and are similar to Westermann's 'Das Vergleichende' and 'Das Verglichene'[12].

---

10. We will continue to use the French terms. The English translational equivalents 'metaphorised' and 'metaphorising' are too clumsy. These terms are equivalent to 'subject' and 'symbol' or 'tenor' and 'vehicle' (etc.) as we shall see below.
11. Although he does not state where!
12. C. WESTERMANN, *Vergleiche und Gleichnisse im Alten und Neuen Testament* (Calwer Theologische Monographien, 14), Stuttgart, 1984, p. 12. Westermann, incidentally treats in brief the major comparisons in the various biblical books. When it comes to Isaiah, however, he rather oddly states: "Die weitaus meisten Vergleiche in Jes 1–39 (ohne 24–27) begegnen im Zusammenhang der Gerichtsankündigung und deren Begründung in der Anklage" (p. 34). Although his basic statement might indeed be true, the 'ohne 24–27' is left unexplained.

"qui appartient à une autre isotopie"

Bourguet uses the term *'isotopie'* to refer to a sector of vocabulary surrounding a particular subject. A metaphor, therefore, employs two isotopes, that of the *métaphorisé* and that of the *métaphorisant*. A distinction in isotope is an essential dimension of a metaphor, indeed *the* essential dimension of metaphor. Where the isotopes are not distinct one cannot speak of metaphor (more 'simple comparison').

"de manière médiate ou immédiate"

For Bourguet, mediate and immediate refer to metaphors which use or do not use a particle of comparison. He points out in this regard that for Aristotle and classical rhetorics there were no particles of comparison where metaphors were concerned. The particle, in fact, constituted a point of distinction between comparisons and metaphors. As we noted above, however, metaphors and comparisons differ from one another primarily at the level of isotopic distinction, a fact which has been recognised by modern rhetorics. It is possible, therefore, for a metaphor to employ a particle of comparison as long as there is a clear distinction between the isotopes used. Bourguet notes that classical rhetoric points to the provocative dimension of a metaphor without a comparative particle in order to distinguish it from the comparison, e.g. 'Achilles is a lion' as opposed to 'Achilles is like a lion'. He prefers, however, to maintain the closeness of the comparison and the metaphor in modern rhetorics and speaks of a *short metaphor* when there is no particle of comparison and a *long metaphor* when there is. Since the modern metaphor can have something of a comparison about it, its distinguishing feature is no longer formal (lack of comparative particle) but rather isotopic.

"qui lui ressemble"

Resemblance also constitutes an essential element in the relationship between the *métaphorisé* and the *métaphorisant*. Bourguet calls it the *foyer* (seat or heart) of the metaphor. The *foyer* of a metaphor consists in a certain level of repetition, sometimes literal, sometimes implied, but always and necessarily present if one intends to speak of metaphor. Bourguet's understanding of resemblance in relation to metaphor is borrowed from Aristotle's concept of analogy (*rapport d'analogie*) upon which the latter bases the most reliable source of metaphor[13]. The

---

13. Aristotle, *Rhetorics* 1411a 1-2. Bourguet (*Des métaphores*, p. 16) maintains that where Aristotle refers to four different kinds of metaphor only that based on analogy is truly metaphor, the others being more akin to metonymy.

degree of resemblance between the *métaphorisé* and the *métaphorisant* is further elaborated in Bourguet's *Typologie des foyers* (1987:59-64), the most important of which are rooted in explicit repetition (*repetitio*) of terms, paranomasia (also explicit: repetition of terms from the same Hebrew root), and implied resemblance where the repetition is not explicit but rather implied. Such are perhaps the most common of the biblical *foyers*[14]. Resemblance based on Hebrew word-play is considered by Bourguet as rare yet significant. The degree of repetition in such cases – and we will return to this in our analysis of Isa 24–27 below – has to do with proximity of sound or phonological resemblance[15] between the *métaphorisé* and the *métaphorisant*. Although Bourguet does not mention it, it seems reasonable to include orthographic resemblance under the category of word-play between two Hebrew terms which exhibit neither semantic nor grammatical similarity[16].

Bourguet notes that the resemblance dimension of metaphor allows us to distinguish it from metonymy[17] which is to be found among the figures of classical rhetoric. Unlike a metaphor, however, the substitution of words involved in metonymy is based on attribution or relationship and not on resemblance. To 'drink a glass' substitutes 'glass' for the 'contents' (wine) of the 'glass'. 'Glass' and 'contents' do not resemble one another although there may be contiguity at the isotopic level. The use of metonymy in the Hebrew bible, however, is not uncommon[18]. Likewise, in the case of the related term synecdoche[19] the substitution is based on contiguity not

---

14. Resemblance or repetition rooted in the use of synonymous terms taken from completely different Hebrew roots are also significant in biblical usage (*Des métaphores*, p. 60).

15. C.F. WATSON, *Classical Hebrew Poetry*, pasim.

16. In modifying Ricœur's definition of metaphor Bourguet notes: ""Parler" est un terme adéquat, mais trop limité pour être repris ici, dans un travail qui porte sur des métaphores écrits" (*Des métaphores*, p. 10)

17. E.W. Bullinger (*Figures of Speech Used in the Bible*, Grand Rapids, MI, 1993, p. 539ff.) describes metonymy as "a figure by which one name or noun is used instead of another, to which it stands in a certain relation". He notes further, however, that metonymy is not founded on resemblance, as is at least part of the case with respect to metaphor, but on relation. Cf. Also E. König (*Stilistik, Rhetorik, Poetik in Bezug auf die biblische Litteratur*, Leipzig, 1900, p. 15ff.) who deals with metaphor along with comparison and allegory under the heading 'Verdeutlichung durch Parallelen' (*ibid.*, p. 77ff.).

18. A list of examples from Jeremiah and elsewhere in the Hebrew bible can be found in Bourguet (*Des métaphores*, p. 15).

19. Bullinger (*Figures*, p. 614ff.) describes synecdoche as "a figure by which one word receives something from another which is internally associated with it by the connection of two ideas: as when part of a thing is put by a kind of Metonymy for the whole of it, or the whole for a part". Cf. also KÖNIG (*Stilistik*, p. 50ff.).

resemblance. It is our contention that the isotopic resemblance between the *métaphorisé* and the *métaphorisant* in Isa 25,7 is rooted in word-play.

"dans les termes (du métaphorisant)"

Bourguet stresses the fact that the *métaphorisant* is not always constituted by one single word. This leads him to make a distinction between the *sujet métaphorisant* or the name of that to which the *métaphorisé* is compared and the *énoncé* (expression, setting out) *métaphorisant* or the group of terms which apply to the *métaphorisant* and which go to make up the metaphor. The *sujet métaphorisant* applied to YHWH's arrival in Jer 4,13 is constituted by the single word 'clouds' whereas the *énoncé métaphorisant* includes the 'whirlwind' and even the 'chariots' and 'swift horses' also referred to in the verse. Similarly, the *sujet métaphorisant* being applied to Jeremiah in Jer 11,19 is (gentle) 'lamb' (being led to the slaughter) whereas the bracketed words represent the *énoncé métaphorisant*. Sometimes the *sujet métaphorisant* is insufficient for the metaphor to be correctly understood, in which case the *énoncé métaphorisant* becomes a necessity. In addition to this it is possible to establish a metaphor without the presence of a *sujet métaphorisant* when the vocabulary used clearly comes from the isotope of the metaphor in question. Bourguet gives the example of Jer 25,30 "The Lord will roar from on high, and from his holy habitation utter his voice; he will roar mightily against his fold..."[20]. Clearly the metaphor of the 'lion', which is the *sujet métaphorisant*, is intended but the term itself is never mentioned. Bourguet points out that problems can arise for the exegete with respect to delimitation of the *énoncé métaphorisant*. In such cases it is important to establish the terms which belong to the isotope of the metaphor (e.g. terms related to the isotope of 'lion'). The same distinction between *sujet* and *énoncé* also applies to the *métaphorisé*; e.g. in Jer 50,17 the *sujet métaphorisé* is Israel which is described as a 'hunted sheep' while in Jer 11,16-17 it is clear from the context that Israel is once again the *sujet métaphorisé* although this is expressed in a fuller manner in the *énoncé métaphorisé*: 'A green olive tree, fair with goodly fruit'

"intentionnellement"

As Bourguet points out, it is quite possible to inadvertently describe a thing using a term or terms which do not belong to the same isotope.

---

20. With the exception of Isa 24–27 and unless stated otherwise, all English Scripture quotations are taken from the NRSV.

The importance of intentionallity with respect to metaphor he maintains, however, has to do with the fact that there are both 'living' and 'dead' metaphors[21]. For Ricœur a 'living' metaphor comes from the world of invention, an intentional creation on the part of an author at a particular moment of inspiration. The problem arises when a 'living' metaphor is used time and again. In such cases there is ultimately no need to mention the *métaphorisé* because it is already known. The metaphor is dead because it has become 'part of the vocabulary' through frequent use. Bourguet offers the example of the Hebrew term רֹעֶה 'shepherd' as a 'dead' biblical metaphor. While it was initially used with reference to a king or chief it lost its 'flavour' through overuse and finally 'died' when it became no longer necessary to mention the *métaphorisé* (cf., for example, Jer 2,8: 'the shepherds (i.e. rulers) transgressed against me'). For the study of biblical texts it is important to recognise whether a metaphor is 'living' or 'dead' at the time of writing/redaction. Bourguet offers the example of Isa 5,7 where the 'living' vine metaphor is used to designate Israel compared to the 'dead' vine metaphor in Ps 80,9ff. where it is not necessary to mention the *métaphorisé* (Israel) because it is already known.

The problem with 'dead' metaphors is the fact that they tend to influence their non-intentional use. We will return to this problem below when we examine Macky's notion of 'hidden metaphors' and their influence. It is possible, however, to re-animate 'dead' metaphors[22] by using different words or terms from the same isotope or by placing the 'dead' metaphor in an unusual context. Once again more will be said on this notion of re-animation in the pages which follow. Macky prefers the term 'retired metaphors' which permits the metaphor the possibility of 'making a comeback'.

Intentional use of distinct isotopes can raise difficulties with respect to metaphors for the divine. It can happen, for example, that a word used to

---

21. RICŒUR, *La métaphore vive*, p. 368ff.. With reference to what he refers to as *lexicalisation*, a process we will discuss in further detail below, Ricœur is inclined to consider what he calls 'dead metaphors' to no longer be metaphors: "Cette analyse incline à penser que les métaphores mortes ne sont plus des métaphores, mais qu'elles s'adjoignent à la signification littérale pour en étendre la polysémie" (p. 368).

22. *Ibid.*, p. 370. Ricœur is of the opinion that one can re-animate a dead metaphor but he equates this to a conscious process of de-lexicalisation which he considers equivalent to the production of a new metaphor. Macky would follow this to a degree and speaks of retired metaphors implying that they can be 'brought out of retirement' (see below). This will be important for our study of metaphors in Isa 24–27 where certain 'lexicalised' metaphors (retired/dead?) may have been given new life (re-animated/resurrected/de-lexicalised?).

describe an unknown and mysterious subject such as God must be borrowed from another isotope because of a lacuna in the author's vocabulary surrounding that subject. Strictly speaking, therefore, the term borrowed and applied to the divine is an abuse. In a certain sense all language used to discribe God is borrowed in this way because the isotope of the divine is ultimately empty: "on peut considérer l'isotopie divine comme vide des mots qui lui sont propres"[23]. While such usage may be intentional it is better described as catachresis[24] and not metaphor. Bourguet points out the significance of this distinction when vocabulary is used to describe God. Some would argue together with Caird, for example, that "We have no other language besides metaphor with which to speak about God"[25]. Given that all vocabulary used to describe God is borrowed (via catachresis) from another isotope (not proper to the divine), all such words are ultimately inadequate. Bourguet points out, however, that since there are strictly speaking no words available to us which properly belong to the isotope 'divine', descriptive vocabulary for God must be borrowed for the purpose from other isotopes (not proper to the divine) in order to fill the lacuna in our vocabulary. If metaphor requires the intentional choice of terminology from two distinct isotopes then we must agree that much language about God is catachresic rather than metaphoric. Such a position, he maintains, does not exclude the possibility of speaking of God in metaphorical terms. How then do we distinguish between catachresis and metaphor with respect to the divinity? Bourguet points out that our language about God is a sort of 'patchwork' of words taken from a variety of isotopes and turned into vehicles of description by way of catachresis. With use, however, this 'patchwork' began to achieve a certain unity and fill the once empty isotope of the divine. This is due to the fact that the intentional borrowing of terms from other isotopes (catachresis) was done with the sole purpose of designating a single object: God[26]. Theological language thus emerged, in a sense, thanks to catachresis. Over time, the catachresic character of the borrowed terms disappeared. Vocabulary referring to God has its roots, therefore, in what Bourguet calls 'dead' catachresis based on the analogy with 'dead' metaphors which have lost

---

23. BOURGUET, *Des métaphores*, p. 21.
24. Bullinger (*Figures*, p. 675ff.) describes catachresis as "a figure by which one word is changed for another and this against or contrary to the ordinary usage and meaning of it. The word that is changed is transferred from its strict and usual signification to another that is only remotely connected with it. Hence by the Latins ABUSIO, abuse."
25. G.B. CAIRD, *The Language and Imagery of the Bible*, London, 1980, p. 174.
26. BOURGUET, *Des métaphores*, p. 21.

their metaphorical character through time and extensive usage. Faced with a 'created' isotope of the divine it becomes possible once again to speak about God using metaphorical language. The possibility of creating metaphors for God can function, according to Bourguet, in two different ways: one can chose a new term or expression related to the traditional (created) isotope of the divine and underline its character as an image or one can revive a catachresic term, the image character of which has become blurred with usage or has even disappeared, and revive it by underlining its character as an image. In the first instance, Bourguet offers the example of Jer 2,13: "for my people have committed two evils: they have forsaken me, the *fountain of living water*, and dug out cisterns for themselves, cracked cisterns that can hold no water". Jeremiah describes God here as a 'fountain of living water' using an expression which was new for his time. While the designation of the divine as 'water', however, may indeed be catachresic, the prophet's free and intentional extension of the image whereby its relationship to 'cisterns' is underlined is metaphorical. An example of the second instance is related to the catachresic term 'potter' (יוֹצֵר) as a designation for God related to the Hebrew verb 'to form, give shape to' (יצר). In Ps 74,17, however, God is described as having 'made (יצר) the summer and the winter'. 'Potter' is hardly an appropriate term to apply to God as 'author' of the seasons. Clearly the traditional image carried by the verb and established as part of the isotope of the divine has disappeared in this case and the author of the psalm has been free to exploit its character as an image once again. It is equally clear that the context in which a designation for God is intentionally placed is of great importance in determining its catachresic or metaphorical significance.

2. Cognitive Theories of Metaphor

Nelly Stienstra's work on the biblical metaphor of YHWH as the husband of his people focuses more closely at the outset on the topic of metaphor with the hope of establishing a modern cognitive theory of metaphor as a means 'to unravel this delicate network'[27] which biblical metaphor presents. Her approach from the beginning is one which sees metaphors in a text as part of a concept or system and not as isolated figures of speech or idioms. As such her work cannot stand alone but requires the additional material supplied by our other authors. Her

---

27. STIENSTRA, *Husband*, p. 7.

approach is threefold: (i) establish a theory of metaphor to allow one to analyse metaphors in texts; (ii) show that this approach is significant for interpreting the (biblical) metaphors in question especially with respect to the culture and society from which they emerged; (iii) show that the approach has significance for the translation of metaphor. Fortunately for our purposes Stienstra recognises the need to first consider what metaphor is as such. She is of the conviction that metaphor is primarily a cognitive phenomenon rather than an exclusively rhetorical one and that recent study of metaphor from this perspective has forced a change in our understanding of the function and role of the phenomenon. Although our examination of Stienstra's work will focus primarily on the first two parts (i & ii), her thoughts on whether or not a metaphor is translatable[28] are significant for our study of the metaphors in Isa 24–27 and will not be passed over. Stienstra takes the metaphor of YHWH as the husband of his people as what she calls a 'titular metaphor'[29] in order to make a systematic analysis. The existence of such titular metaphors and their presence in Isa 24–27 will also be of significance for our study. Part two of her approach requires an analysis of the concrete reality of marriage[30] as such in the Old Testament[31] and since she notes that important metaphors tend to evolve and change over time the element of the dating of texts will be significant for her study and indeed for our analysis of the metaphors in Isa 24–27[32].

Stienstra begins her approach to the theory of metaphor by underlining the fact that the 'cognitive contribution' of the phenomenon is seen

---

28. Based on the argument between a relativist linguistic theory of language which would insist that all human concepts are bound to language and culture and cannot therefore be adequately translated and the alternative universalist approach which argues that human concepts are universal and as such are open to human persons of all times and cultures by virtue of the fact that they are human persons and are therefore translatable for every age. Cf. STIENSTRA, *Husband*, p. 196-215. Cf. also P. NEWMARK, *The Translation of Metaphor*, in W. PAPROTTÉ AND R. DIRVEN (eds.), *The Ubiquity of Metaphor*, Amsterdam, 1985, pp. 295-326.

29. She also refers to this as a 'metaphorical concept' (p. 9, n.1) which we might understand as a kind of umbrella metaphor upon which other metaphors are based.

30. Cf. S. KOZIOL, *Symbolika malzenska...La symbolique matrimoniale et familiale dans les oracles prophétiques*, Diss. Lublin, 1992.

31. This approach is similar to Bourguet's analysis of the *métaphorisé*. The need for an examination of the isotopes involved in a metaphor is clearly essential in order to understand their cultural significance.

32. It remains a question whether the history of a metaphor can be reconstructed from its first and most novel use to its later, perhaps more conventional and even lexicalised usages.

today as more important than 'its affective and rhetorical efficacy'[33]. In other words metaphor is not simply a decorative device, rather, it expresses truths often with respect to abstract concepts which cannot be otherwise expressed. A brief introduction presents some aspects of the historical development of theories of metaphor moving from Aristotle[34] through Greek[35] and Roman[36] rhetoric or 'the art of speaking well', Christian preachers such as Augustine and Gregory of Nazianzen, the medieval *exemplum* or illustrative story and the gradual disavowal of rhetorical devices beginning with Thomas Aquinas and ending with their complete denunciation in John Locke's *Essay Concerning Human Understanding*[37] as unable to 'inform and instruct' or pass on truth and knowledge – in other words as completely non-cognitive[38].

Max Black[39], acknowledging his debt to I.A. Richards[40], distinguishes between three types of metaphor based on three views of the phenomenon: substitution[41], comparison[42] and interaction[43]. The substitution view holds that metaphor is merely a figure of speech, a decorative way of saying something that might otherwise have been said literally, e.g. 'The chairman ploughed through the discussion' where the word

---

33. Cf. E.F. KITTAY, *Metaphor. Its Cognitive Force and Linguistic Structure*, Oxford, 1987, p. 2. Kittay talks of a 'Perspectival' theory of metaphor similar to Black's (and Richards') 'Interaction' theory. She employs the new term because, she notes: "To call our theory perspectival is to name it for the function metaphor serves: to provide a perspective from which to gain an understanding of that which is metaphorically portrayed. This is a distinctively cognitive role" (pp. 13-14). Clearly Kittay places herself within in the 'cognitive' camp.
34. *Poetics*.
35. Plato's *Gorgias* and *Phaedrus* which attacked rhetoric as an insincere art form that was open to abuse
36. Quintilian and Cicero championed rhetoric and even produced their own manuals. Cf. QUINTILIAN, *Institutio Oratoria* (tr. H.E. Butler), London, 1921.
37. J. LOCKE, *Essay Concerning Human Understanding*, Oxford, 1894; first published in 1690.
38. Stienstra underlines the fact that she does not wish to devalue the metaphor as a rhetorical device but only to concentrate on its cognitive aspects (*Husband*, p. 21).
39. M. BLACK, *Metaphor*, in M. BLACK (ed.), *Models and Metaphors: Studies in Language and Philosophy*, Ithaca, NY, 1962, pp. 25-47; originally published in *Proceedings of the Aristotelian Society* 55 (1954) 273-94
40. I.A. RICHARDS, *The Philosophy of Rhetoric*, Oxford, 1936. Richards viewed metaphor as the "omnipresent principle of language".
41. BLACK, *Metaphor*, pp. 33-34. Cf. also M.S. KJÄRGAARD, *Metaphor and Parable. A Systematic Analysis of the Specific Structure and Cognitive Function of the Synoptic Similes and Parables Qua Metaphor*, Leiden, 1986, p. 59ff..
42. BLACK, *Metaphor*, pp. 35-37. Cf. also KJÄRGAARD, *Metaphor and Parable*, p. 65ff..
43. BLACK, *Metaphor*, pp. 38-44. Cf. also KJÄRGAARD, *Metaphor and Parable*, p. 85ff..

'ploughed' is used as a substitute for 'some other literal expression which would have expressed the same meaning, had it been used instead[44]. Those who support the comparison view of metaphor would claim that the metaphor as such consists of the presentation of an underlying similarity or analogy and that the metaphor in question can ultimately be reduced to a simile or in fact replaced by a simile, e.g. 'Achilles is a lion' can be replaced with 'Achilles is like a lion'[45]. Where the interaction view is concerned, two thoughts or concepts interact with one another and produce a significance which goes beyond anything a literal statement might effect. The metaphor, in this case, forces the reader or listener to connect two concepts which he would otherwise never have thought of. Black uses the illustration 'man is a wolf', designating 'man' as the principal subject and 'wolf' as the subsidiary subject[46]. In the context of the substitution view, the expression 'man is a wolf' would imply that the term 'wolf' could equally well be replaced with a literal expression without loss of meaning (purely rhetorical). In a comparison view, the expression would suggest that there is some analogous relationship between the man and the wolf (close perhaps to Bourguet). The interaction view, on the other hand, suggests that the thoughts we have about man and wolf are brought into active interaction with one another to produce a 'new meaning' for 'man' which is not quite equivalent to its literal meaning. The listener/reader needs to understand both subjects[47] in order to interpret the metaphor. In addition, in the example 'man is a wolf' the metaphor can only become clear if its audience shares what Black calls a *system of associated commonplaces*, or the general knowledge of someone raised in the language in which the metaphor is expressed, with the one who 'produced' the metaphor. The characteristics of 'wolf', whether negative or positive, are called up by this metaphor and applied to 'man'. "It is the associated commonplaces[48] which call up a complex of ideas and thus help us to structure our idea of a man in terms of a wolf."[49] For Black, the only type of metaphor worthy of attention are those based in interaction. Such metaphors do not, however, organise our view of the principal subject in a complete or balanced way. Only those traits of the principal subject which can be expressed in terms of the subsidiary subject will be highlighted.

---

44. BLACK, *Metaphor*, p. 68.
45. *Ibid.*, p. 71.
46. Bourguet's *métaphorisant* and *métaphorisé*.
47. Bourguet's *isotopies*.
48. Bourguet's cross-referencing resemblance?
49. STIENSTRA, *Husband*, p. 23.

Other aspects will be missing in the interaction. When we say 'man is a wolf' we highlight the evil side of human nature and not human altruism. At the same time certain aspects of the subsidiary subject will be irrelevant to the principal subject. When we use the same metaphor we do not imply that human beings have four legs as a wolf does. Interaction metaphors organise our concept of the principal subject in terms of the subsidiary subject and as such this organisation must remain a partial one.

In addition to a metaphor saying something about the principle subject, Black notes that it can influence the listener's/reader's view of the subsidiary subject. The subsidiary subject 'wolf' can take on human characteristics in light of the metaphor 'man is a wolf'[50]. This mutuality of interaction, Stienstra notes, has been largely ignored in modern day discussion of metaphor[51].

In a later paper, written in 1972[52], Black focuses on the cognitive dimension of metaphors in order to ascertain their power to provide insight into 'how things are'[53]. Once again he categorises metaphors into three groups, only on this occasion with respect to their creativity: extinct, dormant and active[54]. Extinct metaphors would not be recognised by the average listener/reader because they would not recognise the etymology of the term used (e.g. 'a muscle as a little mouse, *musculus*'[55]). A dormant metaphor from Black's perspective is one which is not readily recognised as such but becomes intelligible when explained (e.g. 'obligation as involving some kind of bondage')[56]. An active metaphor would be readily recognisable as such by the listener/reader. Black distinguishes two aspects therein: *emphasis* and *resonance*. An active metaphor is emphatic when it functions as a genuine interaction metaphor in which the receiver is given 'food for thought' and must co-operate "... in perceiving what lies *behind* the words"[57]. The way a receiver interprets a metaphor is important here and not only the intention of the producer thereof. When an active metaphor is clearly rich in interpretative implications Black refers to it as resonant. Metaphors which are both 'emphatic' and 'resonant' he calls 'strong' metaphors.

---

50. BLACK, *Metaphor*, p. 44.
51. STIENSTRA, *Husband*, p. 24.
52. M. BLACK, *More about Metaphor*, in A. ORTONY (ed.), *Metaphor and Thought*, Cambridge, 1972, 1984, pp. 19-43.
53. *Ibid.*, p. 21. He agrees with Ricœur that a dead metaphor 'is not a metaphor at all'.
54. *Ibid.*, p. 25.
55. *Ibid.*
56. *Ibid.*
57. *Ibid.*, p. 26 (italics his).

Although he revises his terminology, referring to the principle subject as the primary subject and the subsidiary subject as the secondary subject, Black abides by his interaction theory in his later essay which he restates as follows: "In the context of a particular metaphorical statement, the two subjects 'interact' in the following ways: (a) the presence of the primary subject incites the hearer to select some of the secondary subject's properties, and (b) invites him [sic] to construct a parallel implication-complex that can fit the primary subject, and (c) reciprocally induces parallel changes in the secondary subject"[58]. For Black, therefore, metaphors do function at a cognitive level in that they reveal an aspect of reality, or generate insight into reality, which would not otherwise have been so clear.

Stienstra has insisted from the beginning that human language is fundamentally metaphorical when it is confronted with abstract concepts[59]. Lakoff and Johnson[60] take matters a step further by insisting that the entire human conceptual system is metaphorical in nature[61]. At the essence of metaphor is the fact that human persons not only understand one kind of thing in terms of another but actually experience it as such. Metaphorical concepts structure our perception of reality which ultimately emerges in the form of metaphorical language. They use the examples of the metaphorical concepts 'argument is war' and 'time is money' to illustrate their point although they admit that such concepts are culture-dependent. Stienstra points out the need, however, to distinguish between such culture-dependant metaphorical concepts and others which are what she refers to as 'culture-exceeding'[62]. The importance and quantifiability of time, she notes, makes it a 'valuable commodity' in any culture and need not imply that a culture which lacks the actual use of such a metaphor is so different in its approach to certain concepts from a culture in which such metaphorical concepts do occur[63].

Lakoff and Johnson distinguish three distinct categories of metaphor: structural[64], orientational[65] and ontological[66]. The metaphorical concepts

---

58. *Ibid.*, p. 28.
59. STIENSTRA, *Husband*, p. 9.
60. G. LAKOFF and M. JOHNSON, *Metaphors We Live By*, Chicago, IL, 1980.
61. "Our conceptual system, in terms of which we both think and act, is fundamentally metaphorical in nature. [...] Our concepts structure what we perceive, how we get around in the world, and how we relate to other people" (cf. LAKOFF and JOHNSON, *Metaphors*, p. 3).
62. Although not insisting on the claim to universality (cf. STIENSTRA, *Husband*, p. 27).
63. Stienstra offers Mt 20,1-16, the parable of the labourers in the vineyard, as an 'early' and non-western illustration of the quantifiability of time in terms of money.
64. LAKOFF and JOHNSON, *Metaphors*, pp. 3-6.
65. *Ibid.*, pp. 14-21.
66. *Ibid.*, pp. 25-32.

'argument is war' and 'time is money' fall under the first category in that the initial concepts 'argument' and 'time' are structured in terms of the latter concepts 'war' and money' respectively. Orientational metaphors, on the other hand, organise systems of concepts with respect to each other[67]. Such metaphors, according to Lakoff and Johnson, are inescapably rooted in our physical and cultural experience. Our perception of a thing being 'up' or 'down' or 'inside' or 'outside' illustrates the point of orientation metaphors. Ontological metaphors, finally, have to do with the way we encounter physical objects as, for example, quantifiable, and then view non-physical concepts such as an emotion or an idea in the same way, e.g. 'a lot of pain' or 'a lack of inspiration'. Clearly the first or 'structural' category[68] is most appropriate to Stienstra's study and perhaps most appropriate to our study of biblical metaphors as a whole and those in Isa 24–27 in particular. Lakoff and Johnson add that structuring one concept in terms of another is always partial, with some aspects of the concept being obscured and others highlighted. At the same time, however, such inadequate metaphorical concepts can be extended to include new metaphors created on the basis of the structuring metaphor. This will be very much the case with respect to metaphors for the divine as we shall see.

A number of other important notions with respect to metaphor are determined in Lakoff and Johnson. *Coherence*, for example, implies that a number of metaphors might fit together although they might not be *consistent* in forming one single image[69]. Stienstra uses her 'titular metaphor' as an illustration: YHWH as husband, father and king of his people are three metaphors which fit together in a *coherent* way if we take the basic metaphor to be YHWH as the natural, lawful, loving protector of his people. The three metaphors are not *consistent*, however, in that they do not form one *single* image of YHWH[70]. *Entailment* is related to coherence and determines how a metaphor is structured. If we analyse the concept 'husband', in the metaphor 'YHWH is husband', the various aspects *entailed* in the term 'husband' will structure our concept of YHWH.

---

67. *Ibid.*, p. 14.
68. Cf. Black's interaction theory. Other elements of overlap between Black and Lakoff and Johnson will become apparent below.
69. M. Dahood refers to the text-critical principle that a metaphor be considered consistent until the contrary has been demonstrated. Such a principle, he continues, can be useful in poetic verses comprised of bicola where the metaphor of one colon is clear while the other is obscure. Such a principle will be useful in our analysis and interpretation of the metaphors in Isa 24–27 (cf. M. Dahood, *Congruity of Metaphors*, in J. Barr et al. (eds.), *Hebräische Wortforschung. Festschrift zum 80. Geburtstag von Walter Baumgartner* (SVT, 16), Leiden, 1967, pp. 40-49.
70. Stienstra, *Husband*, p. 29.

Stienstra correctly relates this notion to the semantic field approach presented in the essay of Kittay and Lehrer (see below)[71]. Another important concept with respect to Lakoff and Johnson's approach to metaphor is that of *grounding*. Orientational metaphors are generally *grounded* in physical experience whereas other metaphors are *grounded* almost exclusively in culture. All experience, they insist, is cultural 'through and through' but they point out that there are natural kinds of experience which form what they call 'basic domains' of experience and which are defined and conceptualised in terms of other basic domains of experience[72]. Lakoff and Johnson also talk of 'conventional' and 'new' metaphorical concepts. Conventional metaphorical concepts (e.g. 'time is money') have what Stienstra calls 'a whole trail of conventional metaphors that actually occur and are regarded as true'. New metaphors (e.g. 'love is a collaborative work of art'[73]) can also be accepted and their entailments be accepted as true. It is important to note that Lakoff and Johnson see truth as "... a function of our conceptual system. It is because many of our concepts are metaphorical in nature, and because we understand situations in terms of those concepts, that metaphors can be true or false"[74]. Stienstra offers an illustration of a metaphor (together with its entailments) in the Old Testament which would have been regarded as untrue, namely: 'YHWH is the enemy of his people'.

For Kittay and Lehrer the unit of a metaphor is not a word or a phrase but a semantic field: "... in metaphor two otherwise unrelated conceptual domains are brought into contact in a manner specifiable through the use of the linguistic notion of a semantic field"[75]. A semantic field is described as a "set of lexemes which cover a certain conceptual domain and which bear certain specifiable semantic relations [paradigmatic or syntagmatic] to one another"[76]. In the context of metaphor, when one transfers a lexeme from one semantic field to another, the relations that lexeme originally possessed within its own semantic field are transferred with it. Stienstra uses the example of 'faithfulness' from the semantic field of marriage which, when transferred to the semantic field of

---

71. E.F. KITTAY and A. LEHRER, *Semantic Fields and the Structure of Metaphor*, in Studies in Language 5 (1981) 31-63. Cf. also E. KITTAY, *Metaphor. Its Cognitive Force and Linguistic Structure*, Oxford, 1987, pp. 214-257: "Semantic Field Theory".
72. LAKOFF and JOHNSON, *Metaphors*, p. 117.
73. *Ibid.*, p 318
74. *Ibid.*, p. 179.
75. E.F. KITTAY and A. LEHRER, *Semantic Fields and the Structure of Metaphor*, p. 31.
76. *Ibid.*, p. 32. Once again I believe we are coming very close to Bourguet's analysis of the isotope, the essential element of 'difference' between the isotopes involved being suggested by the 'otherwise unrelated' aspect of the conceptual domains.

YHWH's relationship with his people, still maintains the idea of keeping covenant and not turning to other gods. Black's primary subject is referred to by Kittay and Lehrer as the recipient field[77] while his secondary subject is referred to as the donor field[78]. For Kittay and Lehrer metaphors move across semantic fields or cross from one conceptual domain to another. Where concrete metaphorical concepts are concerned it is fairly simple to see how a concrete concept from a donor field can structure our conception of a concrete concept in a recipient field. Problems arise, however, where more abstract concepts in a recipient field are structured in terms of concrete concepts from the donor field. Once again Stienstra turns to her 'titular metaphor' (YHWH as husband of his people) for an illustration. The donor field is that of the husband relationship in a marriage. This can be fairly concretely filled in if we have studied something of marital relationships in the Old Testament. The recipient field (YHWH), however, is much more abstract and it is not surprising that in order to fill it in people have necessarily resorted to the use of metaphor. In such circumstances the recipient field tends not to develop[79] a great deal over time while the donor field does.

In the framework of Kittay and Lehrer, the notion of consistency raised by Lakoff and Johnson would appear to apply to metaphors based on the same semantic field (the same donor field). Coherent metaphors might similarly be described as deriving from related semantic fields. Stienstra notes that the problem of delimiting one's semantic field is not an easy one. In Kittay and Lehrer's framework one might broaden the semantic field of 'husbanding' to included all kinds of family relationships. In this event, certain elements within the broader semantic field (e.g. husband/father/sibling) might end up being inconsistent (although coherent) with one another while being found within the same semantic field. Caution is necessary, therefore, in delimiting one's semantic field to allow for consistency.

Stienstra notes that in later works[80], Lakoff comes close to combining his (& Johnson's) theory with that of Kittay and Lehrer. "Each metaphor has a source domain, a target domain and a source-to-target mapping"[81]. Clearly we are not far from the notions of recipient and donor semantic

---

77. Bourguet's *métaphorisé*
78. Bourguet's *métaphorisant*.
79. In terms of its entailments.
80. G. LAKOFF, *Women, Fire and Dangerous Things. What Categories Reveal about the Mind*, Chicago, IL, 1987; G. LAKOFF, and M. TURNER, *More than Cool Reason. A Field Guide to Poetic Metaphor*, Chicago, IL, 1989.
81. LAKOFF, *Women*, p. 276.

fields. Stienstra considers both notions to be of great importance in understanding metaphor.[82]

Most theoreticians of metaphor tend to focus on metaphorical concepts of the type A is B (e.g. man is a wolf). While metaphors of this type are in fact quite rare, their surface structure has lent itself to establishment of the idea that metaphor involves two terms often referred to as the *tenor* or the subject of the metaphor and the *vehicle* or the way the subject is being expressed. Black also speaks of metaphors in similar terms as is clear from our outline of his theory presented above[83]. Janet Soskice emphatically rejects such an assumption with respect to the structure of metaphors, noting that both terms frequently are not and need not be present in order to establish a metaphorical statement[84]. Soskice herself borrows Richards'[85] inter-animation theory using the terms *tenor* and *vehicle* and insisting that the *tenor* need not always be explicitly stated.

Stienstra is somewhat critical of Soskice and insists that when it comes to basic metaphorical concepts all are of the type A is B. She agrees that other surface structures do exist but that these are generally speaking derived metaphorical statements which can be further reduced to a basic metaphorical concept of the type A is B[86]. She illustrates her point on the basis of a metaphor proposed by Soskice as an example of those which lack the presence of a tenor: "rosy-fingered dawn". For Stienstra such a metaphor is ultimately derived from the metaphorical

---

82. A word ought to be said concerning the distinction often made between metaphors as semantic (cf. L.J. COHEN, *The Semantics of Metaphor*, in A. ORTONY [ed.], *Metaphor and Thought*, Cambridge, 1993², pp. 58-70) and metaphors as pragmatic (J. SEARLE, *Metaphor*, in A. ORTONY, *op.cit.*, pp. 83-111). The semantic view would claim that a metaphor is determined by the meaning of the words making up the metaphorical statement ('metaphorical meaning inheres in sentences' [COHEN, p. 59]). The pragmatic view would claim that it is the utterance ("Strictly speaking, whenever we talk about the metaphorical meaning of a word, expression, or sentence, we are talking about what a speaker might utter it to mean..." [SEARLE, p. 84]) which makes the metaphor a metaphor. Stienstra follows the compromise between the two offered by Black who insists that some metaphors are always such (can never have a literal meaning) while other metaphors require context to be understood as such (can have a literal meaning). In this sense it is clear that there can be no sharp division between semantic and pragmatic views of metaphor.

83. Cf. also Bourguet's *métaphorisé* and *métaphorisant*.

84. J.M. SOSKICE, *Metaphor and Religious Language*, Oxford, 1985, esp. p. 20

85. "In the simplest formulation, when we use a metaphor we have two thoughts of differet things active together and supported by a single word, or phrase, whose meaning is a resultant of their interaction" (cf. I.A. RICHARDS, *The Philosophy of Rhetoric*, Oxford – New York, 1936, p. 93).

86. Stienstra accepts that this proposal may require modification "extending the A is B format to A V[erb] B for a restricted number of verbs" (*Husband*, p. 38).

concept 'dawn is a person'. Another example taken from Ezek 16,16 refers to Jerusalem as 'playing the whore' which is a metaphor derived from the metaphor 'Jerusalem is a woman' and ultimately from her titular metaphorical concept 'YHWH is the husband of his people'. Basic metaphors for Stienstra, therefore, are expressed in the most basic fashion: Subject is Predicate.

3. THEORIES OF METAPHOR AND THE BIBLE

Peter W. Macky's *The Centrality of Metaphors to Biblical Thought* is an endeavour to distil the vast amount of literature on the topic of metaphor from the particular reference point of philosophy and linguistics in order to assist biblical scholars plumb the depths of biblical metaphor, work their way through some of the contested aspects of the study of metaphor and make the necessary distinctions between the various types of metaphor as found in the biblical text. His own initial approach to the definition of metaphor repeats much of what we have seen so far but his critique of the common positions and his own theoretical perspective on metaphor, with its associated terminology and typology, is extremely relevant and enlightening for our exploration of the field, particularly for its continuous focus on the biblical text. In combination with Bourguet and Stienstra, therefore, Macky's analysis will provide the final stage in the groundwork of our own efforts to establish an adequate theoretical approach to metaphor appropriate to the analysis and interpretation of biblical metaphors which we will take with us into the next chapter.

Macky presents the various principles and assumptions behind his approach in the first chapter. He emphasises the fact that biblical authors did not only set out to communicate ideas but that they also had a rhetorical purpose, a desire to move and change their reader/listeners. For this reason they appealed first to the imagination in order to bring the reader to existential depth, to the place where profound metaphors, as opposed to superficial metaphors[87], challenge the reader to unite his or her own

---

87. This is an important distinction. Profound metaphors can be distinguished by the way we understand the metaphorical speech act. How much of the meaning can be expressed in 'literal' speech? When our 'paraphrasing' is easily able to more or less restate all of the content of the metaphor then we are dealing with superficial metaphors (e.g. 'Buy truth and do not sell it' [Prov 23,23] = 'Seek the truth diligently until you find it, and then do not forget it' [MACKY, *Centrality*, p. 3]). When the same paraphrasing misses the powerful depths of the metaphor in question then we are probably dealing with profound metaphors (e.g. 'Take my yoke upon you... for my yoke is easy and my burden

experience with the picture presented in the metaphorical speech act created or given new life by the author. Macky also points to the need to examine the significance of metaphorical speech acts and come to the most appropriate definition thereof with respect to biblical texts. He examines a number of what he calls 'broad' and 'narrow' definitions, some of which we have seen before, in order to arrive at a position from which one is able to identify, describe and analyse metaphorical speech acts in the bible. Once he has reached this stage he examines the various different types of metaphor used in the bible and their role in biblical metaphorical speech acts and endeavours to establish how they achieve the author's purpose. After examining the question of re-expression of metaphors in literal speech acts he looks at the question of the imaginative/intellectual process which is most appropriate for the purpose of exploring the depths of profound metaphors. He concludes his introductory chapter by providing a sort of glossary of terms, assumptions and basic principles which he will follow, including seven basic skills necessary for approaching metaphor. We will return to Macky's seven basic skills below.

In the process of mentally reconstructing as accurate a replica as possible of the speaker's (author's) meaning, a hearer (reader) must choose from among the various possible ways of meaning which the speaker may be employing, e.g. literal, ironical, symbolical, metaphorical etc.. Since the way of meaning, like the meaning itself, is hidden, it is necessary and important for the hearer to try to deduce the particular way of meaning employed by the author from the context of the speech act. It is obvious, however, that before being able to make a judgement about the way of meaning employed by the speaker, the hearer must be able to distinguish between the minimum possibilities of literal and one or other of the figurative ways of meaning (one of which being metaphor). We will investigate this distinction along with Macky. When it comes to his analysis of the various types of figurative ways of meaning we will encounter some repetition of what we found in Bourguet. As will become evident, however, Macky's analysis is more nuanced than that of Bourguet and of more value in our approach to biblical metaphors. At the same time, Macky is more critical of the cognitive theories of metaphor to which Stienstra and many others subscribe, especially where the bible is concerned. His evaluation thereof is of value to us at this point and will assist us in broadening our approach to the theory of

---

is light' (Matt 11,29-30 [cf. MACKY, *Centrality*, p. 3]). According to Macky there can be no adequate substitute for profound metaphors. We are close here to Stienstra's understanding of metaphorical concepts.

metaphor as a whole and our own methodological approach to the analysis of the biblical text in particular.

1. *Literal/Figurative as Independent/Dependent?*

Macky refers to the work of Earl R. MacCormac[88] as representative of this particular understanding of the literal use of language. MacCormac defines 'literal' as the use of language to express 'concrete' objects and events, 'concrete' meaning 'publicly perceptible'[89]. Macky is correct in noting, however, that such a definition is too narrow since we often refer to inner states – which cannot be publicly perceived – with literal intent, e.g. "I feel tired" or "I am confused".

Perhaps the most common approach to defining literal speech is to describe it as established/conventional use. Authors such as Roland Bartel[90], Paul Ricœur[91] and Janet Soskice[92] all fall into this camp, defining literal language respectively as 'definitions found in dictionaries... standardised meanings', 'current, usual' and 'accustomed usage'. While this type of definition probably covers most cases of literal speech it is still, according to Macky, inadequate. He argues, in the first place, that if literal simply means conventional, then the distinction literal/figurative becomes redundant to be replaced by conventional/ unconventional. As the huge variety of conventional yet figurative[93] uses we find in our language attests, there is clearly more to literal use than simply convention. In this case the equating of literal with conventional is too broad. Where neologisms are concerned, on the other hand, the equation is too narrow. Neologisms, such as 'motel', tend to be used quite literally long before they become conventional. Macky concludes, therefore, that the definition which equates literal speech with established/conventional speech is at once too narrow and too broad and ultimately not precise enough for his purposes.

Independent uses of a word are those which can be understood directly and without allusion to some other meaning of the same word. Macky's example 'to run away' from a fight – i.e. in the physical sense

---

88. E.R. MacCormac, *A Cognitive Theory of Metaphor*, Cambridge, MA, 1985, esp. pp. 53-78.

89. *Ibid.*, p. 73.

90. R. Bartel, *Metaphors and Symbols: Forays into Language*, Urbana, IL, 1983, p. 10.

91. P. Ricœur, *The Rule of Metaphor: Multi-Disciplinary Studies of the Creation of Meaning in Language*, Toronto, 1977, p. 291.

92. Soskice, *Metaphor and Religious Language*, p. 69.

93. Such as the statement "he is always late", in which 'always' is understood hyperbolically.

– can be understood independently while the dependent phrase 'to run away' from one's problems – i.e. in the psychological sense – requires that we have some knowledge of the physical sense before we can adequately grasp its psychological implications. Independent words, Macky adds, tend to have the quality of a label about them which can be applied to some physical thing. Dependent use requires that we understand some other use before we can grasp its dependent use. As we noted above (see note 93), 'he is always late' usually has a hyperbolic meaning yet it can have a literal one. We need to understand the literal possibility before we can grasp the significance of the hyperbolic usage.

Macky draws the line between literal and figurative speech as the same line as that between independent and dependent. All clearly figurative uses of words, he notes, are dependent on some other sense of the same word(s). Metaphoric use of a word or ironic use is always dependent on our knowledge of the literal sense of the word, e.g. the term 'cold' can only be understood psychologically if we have already grasped the meaning of physical 'cold'.

Macky also addresses the problem of private language in which people create terms to designate a particular inner experience, for example, which they can apply directly to that experience. After frequent use such a term can become conventional for that person's reference to the experience in question. The problem arises when one attempts to communicate the term. A further nuance to the equation of 'literal' with 'independent', therefore, is the dimension of communicability. When one is asked to explain a particular term in one's private language which one's 'audience' cannot understand we tend to do so by way of metaphors, but this simply makes the term itself dependent for our listener, dependent on our explanation and its metaphors. Certain inner experiences such a 'tiredness', 'pain' etc. are communicable because they tend to be shared by the listener and not simply part of the private language of the speaker. For Macky, therefore, the best definition of 'literal speech' is 'communicable independent use', the communicability dimension only coming into play when the problem of private languages arises.

2. *Figurative Ways of Meaning*

Macky expands our list of figurative ways of meaning beyond those pointed out by Bourguet[94]: metonymy, ellipsis, hyperbole, irony, joking,

---

94. See footnotes 13, 15, 20.

symbol saying and, of course, metaphor[95]. What is important for Macky, and for us, is the major distinction which he offers between literal speech and figurative speech: "*literal usage is (communicable) independent usage* and *figurative usage is dependant usage*"[96]. All figurative ways of meaning are dependent on other uses, particularly the literal use. Since metaphor is one particular figurative way of meaning, according to Macky it is therefore a dependent way of meaning, a fundamental fact, and perhaps a fundamental problem, which we must bear in mind in our exploration of biblical metaphors. A brief survey of definitions provided by Macky will occupy us in greater detail presently[97].

The varied approaches to the understanding and definition of metaphor are determined by the perspectives and concerns of those involved in their study. Macky usefully focuses on the phenomenon of metaphor from the perspective and concerns of biblical interpretation. Such an approach, to a degree, governs the way he will define the central terms involved in the analysis. He goes to great lengths, however, to stay within the mainstream of definitions of metaphor in order not to alienate the reader or establish too esoteric an approach to the phenomenon. His primary purpose, together with our own, is to determine which definitions are most appropriate for the analysis and interpretation of biblical metaphors.

As we noted above, Macky insists that the basic characteristic of figurative speech is its *dependence* on (in particular) literal use. He uses this fundamental yardstick as a tool for criticising and approving the definitions of metaphor he treats. Many authors[98], Macky notes, tend to define metaphorical speech as something opposite to literal speech, using terms such as 'new', 'uncustomary' or 'anomalous'. While he admits that such terms do have something to say about metaphorical speech he points out their limitation with respect to biblical texts and the metaphors contained therein which may indeed be quite standard metaphors. He considers, therefore, that definitions rooted in such a premise must be considered too narrow.

---

95. More detailed examination of these terms need not occupy us here since our primary focus is on the use of metaphor as a way of meaning.

96. MACKY, *Centrality*, p. 42.

97. Some definitions have been dealt with already and will not be repeated in any detail here. Our main focus will be on Macky's own distillation of the varieties of definition together with his set of 'working definitions' which will contribute to our own methodological approach to the analysis of metaphors in Isa 24–27.

98. C.M. BACHE, *The Logic of Religious Metaphor*, Diss. (UMI), Brown University, 1978; BARTEL, *Metaphors and Symbols*; MACCORMAC, *Cognitive Theory*.

3. Off Target and On Target Theories of Metaphor

The closest we come to a definition of metaphor in I.A Richards' work is contained in the following statement: "In the simplest formulation, when we use metaphor we have two thoughts of different things active together and supported by a single word, or phrase, whose meaning is resultant of their interaction."[99] Macky offers the illustrative example 'God is light' with 'God as the tenor (*métaphorisé*, speaker's subject) and 'light' as the vehicle (*métaphorisant*, symbol used to communicate the subject). He notes, in addition, that the tenor and the vehicle need not be explicit but are often only implied via reference to one or more of their characteristics (e.g. 'God illuminates the darkness'). Macky finds Richards approach too ambiguous. He finds the notion of the metaphor being 'supported by a single word, or phrase' to be unclear and cannot understand why he did not include clauses and sentences as well as words and phrases.

Max Black, as we noted above, acknowledged his debt to Richards. Although we have already examined Black's position, his succinct 'definition' in three assertions may be usefully re-stated here for the purpose of critique: "(1) A metaphorical statement has two distinct subjects – a 'principal' subject and a 'subsidiary one'. (2) These subjects are often best regarded as 'systems of things' rather than things. (3) The metaphor works by applying to the principal subject a system of 'associated implications' characteristic of the subsidiary subject..."[100]. Although Black later revised some aspects of his definition its principle weakness lies in the 'two subjects' aspect by way of which he implied that both underwent change in the metaphorical interaction. Macky argues, however, that such language is unhelpful given the existence of what he calls 'one-way metaphors'. He accepts, however, that there are occasions when the relationship between the subject and the symbol (*métaphorisé* and *métaphorisant*) can be best thought of in terms of a dialogue between two persons in which both are changed (dual-direction metaphors).

Once again, we have already examined the essential elements in the work of Lakoff and Johnson. Their 1980 opus *Metaphors We Live By* proposed that we consider metaphor as "understanding and experiencing one kind of thing in terms of another"[101]. Macky criticises their position as too inspecific to differentiate metaphorical use of language from

---

99. RICHARDS, *The Philosophy of Rhetoric*, p. 93.
100. BLACK, *Models and Metaphors*, p. 44.
101. LAKOFF and JOHNSON, *Metaphors We Live By*, p. 5

other, perhaps figurative, uses. Lakoff and Johnson's definition, although too broad, clearly recognises the roots of metaphor as cognitive. Macky insists, however, that there is a need to connect our cognitive process with our speech (acts) since metaphors are most commonly expressed in speech (written, spoken, painted...).

Macky proceeds at this point to very briefly review three authors whose work he believes comes close to 'Hitting the Target'[102].

From W.P. Alston's *Philosophy of Language*, written in 1964, Macky gleans the following points with regard to metaphor which he believes provide a good basis for approaching the phenomenon: "extension is on the basis of *similarity*"[103]; metaphor, furthermore, gives us something as "a *model* for something else"[104]; there is a *spectrum* of types of metaphor running from novel or innovative metaphors through standard metaphors to those which have found their way into dictionary definitions (lexicalised metaphors, such as the term 'cold' as a description of a person's temperament).

In his *The Rule of Metaphor*, P. Ricœur states: "Metaphor consists in speaking of one thing in terms of another [elsewhere referred to as '*symbol*'] that *resembles* it"[105]. For Ricœur, the dimension of resemblance is most important and can be rooted in the characteristics shared by the 'one thing' and 'the other' or in their common effects or in attitudes taken towards them[106].

Macky provides a useful summary of the important aspects of J. Soskice's *Metaphor in Religious Language* which she in turn has combined from what is valuable in the earlier views she surveys: (1) metaphor is a figurative type of *language use* (i.e. it is not primarily a cognitive phenomenon); (2) there is only *one subject* in a metaphorical speech act; (3) the subject may be *named* or *implied* by references to one or more of its characteristics; (4) the subject or *tenor* is described in terms of the *vehicle* which usually applies to a different reality; (5) associations surrounding both tenor and vehicle interact in an '*inter-animation*' of terms in which the vehicle serves as a symbol; (6) metaphor is a *speech act* in which the subject or tenor is spoken of in terms of the symbol or vehicle[107].

---

102. MACKY, *Centrality*, p. 46.
103. ALSTON, *Philosophy of Language*, p. 97 (italics mine). Cf. also A. ORTONY, *The Role of Similarity in Similes and Metaphors*, in A. ORTONY (ed.), *Metaphor and Thought*, Cambridge, 1993, pp. 342-356.
104. ALSTON, *Philosophy of Language*, p. 102 (italics mine).
105. RICŒUR, *Rule*, p. 53 (italics mine).
106. *Ibid.*, pp. 81-82.
107. SOSKICE, *Metaphors and Religious Language*, pp. 48-49.

Clearly Soskice follows a line different from that of Lakoff and Johnson (and incidentally Stienstra). For her, metaphor is a linguistic phenomenon rather than a cognitive one[108]. In considering her among the 'on target' authors Macky clearly sides with those who would insist on the relevance of a non-cognitive approach to metaphor but to say that this is where he remains would be to narrow Macky's position unjustifiably. In the last analysis, Macky's study of these authors concludes that they are not far removed from each other in their approach to the topic. He ultimately agrees and, indeed, insists that *"all use of language has a mental component"*[109] and proceeds to a working definition which includes both the cognitive and the linguistic dimensions.

4. Working Definitions

Metaphor

Macky defines metaphor as follows: *"Metaphor is that figurative way of speaking (and meaning) in which one reality, the Subject, is depicted in terms that are more commonly associated with a different reality, the Symbol, which is related to it by Analogy"*[110]. He adds that the metaphor as such is couched within a whole speech act and that both the subject and the symbol need not be directly named but can be implied via other characteristics. The analogical relationship between the subject and the symbol can be positive (similarities), negative (differences) or neutral (both positive and negative). To avoid the terminological imprecision which plagues the literature on this topic Macky proposes a further explanation of key terms found in or related to his definition.

Analogy

(a) Analogy is the middle ground between 'identity' and 'radical difference', implying that two realities have points in common while differing on others. The value of the term 'analogy' over 'resemblance' or 'similarity' is rooted in the positive, negative and neutral dimensions which analogy can imply and which allow us to better explore the particular analogical relationship of a particular metaphor; (b) Mathematical (or Proportional) Analogies permit the point of similarity found in the analogy to be precisely stated. This type of analogy has little bearing on the mostly imprecise and hidden dimensions of metaphors; (c) Linguistic

---

108. *Ibid.*, pp. 54-66.
109. MACKY, *Centrality*, p. 49.
110. *Ibid.*

Analogy (as opposed to analogy between non-linguistic realities) implies awareness of a variety of distinctions not often made with clarity. Soskice speaks of analogical extension being effected by stretching a concept to include new applications[111]. This analogical extension is of the *literal use* of a term and not its metaphorical use. Macky points out, however, that there are at least two more kinds of analogical extension. Firstly, analogical extension can take place by adding a *new sense* of a term to the language. Macky offers the term 'to run' as an example of a word which originally was limited to the physical act of running but was analogically extended to include 'running for office' or 'running a business'. Secondly, there is a type of analogical extension which is *dependent analogical use*, relying on our original understanding of the term in question. St Paul's use of the term 'running' in I Cor 9,24-27 and elsewhere is of this variety. As Macky points out, Paul uses the term to point to the way we live our lives, describing life as if it were a race in which we run in order to achieve a goal. Such a dependent analogical use of the term 'running' is the equivalent of a metaphorical use. Thus we have three different senses of the same term, not a single concept which has been stretched, which are analogically related. Over time such uses have become independent and are available for independent use in literal speech without reference to the original literal meaning. Macky concludes that extension of language by analogy does not only stretch a term to include new applications nor even new senses which ultimately become independent. Analogical extension can produce metaphorical use. It is important, therefore, that we learn to distinguish between all three possible instances in our analysis of metaphor.

Symbol

'Symbol' is the term used by Macky for the 'vehicle' or 'subsidiary subject' or 'model' (or *métaphorisant*) used in other definitions. For Macky it is close to Soskice's use of the term 'model' which he prefers to reserve for standardised symbols. The term 'symbol' is used in a variety of senses. Macky follows Edwin Bevan's distinction between 'conventional symbols' and 'insight symbols'[112]. 'Conventional symbols' are "visible objects or sounds which stand for something of which we already have direct knowledge" such as flags or the letters of written language. Such symbols are representative of a reality but do not tell us anything about that reality. 'Insight symbols' on the other hand, convey

---

111. SOSKICE, *Metaphors and Religious Language*, pp. 64-65.
112. E. BEVAN, *Symbolism and Belief*, London, 1938, p. 9-11.

something about the realities they symbolise, thus making resemblance a necessary aspect of the relationship between the symbol and the subject which is not the case with 'conventional symbols'. Macky's use of the term is exclusively confined to 'insight symbols'. *"By a 'symbol' we mean 'one (usually common) reality that stands for, or represents, and gives analogical insight into, more mysterious realities"*[113]. In this sense, every metaphor refers to a 'symbol'.

Model

Macky defines 'model' as follows: *"A model is a symbol that is established enough in its use with a particular subject (e.g. father with God) for some of the parallels to have been worked out and become conventional"*[114]. The metaphorical use of 'God is our father' illustrates his point. This metaphor speaks of the subject of God's relationship to humanity in terms of the symbol of a 'conventional' father-child relationship. The symbol can be seen as 'established' because certain dimensions of the positive analogical relationship between the God-humanity relationship (subject) and the father-child relationship (symbol) have become established or conventionalised within certain areas of the religious community. Models, indeed, have 'establishment in a community' as one of their main characteristics.

Macky's definition of metaphor and explanation of the terminology used therein will contribute to our own methodology in analysing the metaphorical usage in Isa 24–27. He continues his preparatory material, however, with a survey of the varieties of metaphor, making further useful distinctions (see below).

II. IDENTIFYING METAPHORS (DANIEL BOURGUET)

Having established his definition of metaphor, Bourguet goes on to examine some of the signs which allow us to spot the presence of metaphor in a biblical text. In a certain sense Bourguet is unique in offering an outline of what he believes to be textual indicators of the presence of metaphor. Neither Stienstra nor Macky offer explicit reference to this aspect of the analysis.

One of the most characteristic aspects of a metaphor is that it elicits a certain shock in that it leads to the 'insertion' of a term from one particular

---

113. MACKY, *Centrality*, p. 54 (italics his).
114. *Ibid.*, p. 55 (italics his).

isotope into another isotope where it does not, strictly speaking, belong[115]. Such 'shocks', Bourguet notes, are either immediate (*short* – without particle of comparison; cf. below for examples) or mediate (*long* – with particle of comparison; cf. below for examples). Mediating Hebrew particles which accompany 'long metaphors' constitute a formal indication of a metaphor and are, for Bourguet, extremely important for recognising a metaphor in a given text. Other non-formal indications, however, also help us to spot a metaphor. Although Bourguet only examines the use of non-formal indications as they are found in Jeremiah, the two main types he presents are recognisable in other biblical texts: *syntactic* indications and *semantic* indications. It is Bourguet's conviction that metaphors, by their very shocking character, do not seek to hide or conceal themselves, unlike the 'enigma' and the 'allegory' which do. Where the latter two figures are concerned the isotope from which the descriptive terminology is borrowed raises the text to a point where the reality described is occult or hidden. The metaphor, on the other hand does not seek concealment and we can assume, therefore, that there are indications which allow it to 'stand up and be counted'[116].

1. FORMAL INDICATORS

Once again Bourguet focuses only on formal indications of metaphor in Jeremiah. His inventory remains enlightening, however, and can be supplemented later where necessary with references to further formal indicators in Isaiah.

---

115. E.A. MACCORMAC, *Metaphor and Myth in Science and Religion*, Durham, NC, 1976, p. xi: "... a metaphor can be best characterised by the 'tension' or surprise it causes in the hearer by means of its absurdity" (= the so-called 'tension theory of metaphor'). Cf. Also P. WHEELWRIGHT, *Metaphor and Reality*, Bloomington, IN, 1962: "Even in the simplest forms of poetic language some semantic tension can be discerned and felt, for without at least a flicker of tensive life the language would be semantically dead..." (p. 48). In addition, M. Beardsley in his analysis of what is peculiar to metaphors suggets that a twist of meaning is forced "... by inherent tensions, or oppositions, within the metaphor itself" which he terms the 'Verbal-Opposition Theory'; cf. M. BEARDSLEY, *The Metaphorical Twist*, in *Philosophy and Phenomenological Research* 22 (1962) 293-307 (esp. p. 294); It should be noted, in line with Landy, that metaphors have both integrative and disintegrative aspects (cf. F. LANDY, *In the Wilderness of Speech*, p. 35),

116. Macky would probably not agree!

Perhaps the most common formal indicators are the following: the preposition כ[117] (as proclitic כ or as separate form כמו), the preposition מן[118], the adverbs כן[119], אכן[120], כה[121] and ככה[122], and the conjunction כאשר[123]. In each case the term in question in the context of a metaphor

    117. (כ) It should be noted with respect to כ that the particle is polysemic and is not only to be found in relation to metaphors. Since the particle in question has a comparative value, it is used just as often with comparisons (without isotopic distinction) as with metaphors (with isotopic distinction). Certainly the presence of כ is neither a necessary nor a sufficient indicator of the presence of a metaphor and is sometimes even a source of confusion. Since there is no syntactical difference between כ which indicates a metaphor and a different usage thereof, it becomes difficult to distinguish between the two types. It is worth noting, however, that where a metaphor is concerned the כ always precedes the *métaphorisant*. Examples of metaphorical usage: Jer 10,7; 4,13; 18,6; 20,16; 48,6 etc. (cf. BOURGUET, *Des métaphores*, pp. 25-29).
    118. (מן) As with the other particles מן is employed in a variety of different ways (J–M §133e – separation, provenance, partition; J–M §170i – cause; J–M §132d – cause or agent of an action) and as such it is neither necessary nor sufficient to indicate the presence of a metaphor. מן is frequently used for the comparison of superiority but such comparisons also require a change of isotope in order to indicate the presence of metaphor. As with the other particles, מן always precedes the *métaphorisant*. Examples of metaphorical usage: Jer 4,13; 5,3; 15,3; 46,23 (cf. BOURGUET, *Des métaphores*, pp. 30-31).
    119. (כ followed by כן) Such combinations of particles occur with relative infrequency in the bible and when they do they are frequently accompanied by a change of isotope (cf., for example, J–M §166m where כ introduces a comparison between the times of two actions and does not formally indicate the presence of a metaphor). כ is usually followed by a noun with a predicate while כן introduces the apodosis and sometimes precedes a verb which takes up a root found in the protasis. At the same time, כן can be followed by nominal apodosis. There are no syntactical differences to indicate whether we are dealing with a metaphorical usage or not. כ always precedes the *métaphorisant* and כן the *métaphorisé*. Examples of mataphorical usage: Jer 2,26; 5,27; 6,7; 18,6; 24,5.8 (cf. BOURGUET, *Des métaphores*, pp. 31-32).
    120. (אכן followed by כן) This combination occurs uniquely in Jer 3,20 in the context of a metaphor. Without other, non-metaphorical examples it is impossible to determine its significance for identifying metaphors (cf. BOURGUET, *Des métaphores*, p. 33).
    121. (כה followed by כ) According to Bourguet, this combination only occurs twice in the Old Testament (Jer 23,29 and Isa 24,13 [cf. ch. III] both being metaphorical usage) and as such it is difficult to generalise its significance for indicating metaphors. In both cases the כה precedes a common *métaphorisé* which is followed by two different *métaphorisants* each preceded by כ (cf. BOURGUET, *Des métaphores*, pp. 32-33).
    122. (ככה) The particle ככה means 'so', 'thus' and does not have a strong comparative sense. It can be used, according to Bourguet, at the end of a discourse, after an action with which a comparison is established. Once again, however, the presence of the particle is neither necessary nor sufficient to indicate the presence of a metaphor since it occurs in comparisons which are non-metaphoric. The change of isotope becomes the necessary distinguishing element. ככה is always situated before the *métaphorisé*. Examples of metaphorical usage: Jer 19,10-11 (cf. BOURGUET, *Des métaphores*, p. 31).
    123. (כאשר) As with כ above, כאשר is neither necessary nor sufficient to indicate the presence of a metaphor. It can introduce comparative propositions (J–M §174a), temporal propositions (J–M §166n) or causal propositions (J–M §170k). Where the comparative proposition is concerned, a change of isotope is also necessary before one can speak of a metaphor. As for the syntax of כאשר, Bourguet has noted that a repetition of the principle verb can occur where כאשר is used but this applies equally to metaphorical use as well as

does not belong to either of the two distinct isotopes but serves instead to link or relate them. Other formal indicators such as to make something 'compare to' or 'resemble' something else as English renditions of נתן ל and נתן כ[124] are less obvious but can still, according to Bourguet, be considered formal indicators of the presence of metaphor. The particles mentioned are not always used in the same fashion. As indicators of metaphor, for example, כה, כן and אכן are used with another particle, מן and ככה are always used alone and כ and כאשר can appear alone or with another particle.

It would appear that for all the formal indicators of this type, however, the situation has been more or less the same: they are neither necessary nor sufficient indication of the presence of metaphor. In every case they simply accompany an isotopic distinction which they tend to underline.

2. Syntactic Indicators

Surcharge

Bourguet talks of a *'surcharge'* at the clause level, most frequently a simple apposition, as a syntactic indicator of the presence of metaphor. He provides a list of examples, a couple of which might assist us in understanding what he intends by syntactic indicators.

Jer 11,4 – "... when I brought [your ancestors] out of the land of Egypt, from the iron-smelter". In this verse, the same object is mentioned twice, the first time in real terms (the land of Egypt) the second time in metaphorical terms (iron-smelter). Both designations function at the same level in terms of the syntax of the phrase, thereby placing the

---

simple comparison (He offers Jer 43,12 as an example: "and he shall *pick clean* the land of Egypt, as a shepherd *picks* his cloak *clean* of vermin". Note the isotopic change here). As with כ, כאשר always precedes the *métaphorisant*. Examples of metaphorical usage: Jer 13,11, 19,11, 43,12. (כאשר followed by כן) This combination is also not unique to metaphors and its metaphorical use does not differ syntactically from other usages. כאשר usually introduces the protasis and כן the apodosis. כאשר always precedes the *métaphorisant* and כן the *métaphorisé*. Examples of metaphorical usage: Jer 13,11, 19,11-12 (cf. Bourguet, *Des métaphores*, pp. 29-30, 32).

124. A number of figures of speech exist in Hebrew which might be described as formal indicators of the presence of metaphor: e.g. דמה ל, דמה אל 'to be like', 'to resemble'; expressions using שוה 'to be like, comparable' or the *niphal/hiphil/hithpael* of משל; נתן + accusative + ל 'to make X into...'; נתן + accusative + כ 'to make X like unto...'; נתן + accusative + accusative. Since Jeremiah only provides examples of figures using נתן, Bourguet restricts his further analysis to these. He concludes, however, that as with the particles, such formal indicators are neither necessary nor sufficient indicators of the presence of metaphors (cf. Bourguet, *Des métaphores*, pp. 34-37).

métaphorisé and the *métaphorisant* in (asyndetic) apposition. Isotopic distinction is also evident.

Jer 17,3 – In similar fashion to 11,4, only this time in reverse, the *métaphorisant* and the *métaphorisé* are placed in (asyndetic) apposition: "...for they have forsaken the fountain of living water, the Lord." Once again both designations function at the same syntactical level while the apposition underlines the distinction of isotope.

Bourguet notes that such indicators can be divided into two groups: those in which the *métaphorisant* comes first and those in which the *métaphorisé* comes first. Where examples of the former are concerned the *métaphorisé* is sometimes considered a gloss (cf. BHS) introduced by an editor to explain the metaphor which was at risk of becoming too obscure. In this case we are dealing with a formal indicator (syntactic apposition) which is part of the second stage of the transmission of the metaphor and not due to the author himself. If the *métaphorisé* in these examples is not a gloss then the apposition is a constitutive part of the metaphor and can be described as a formal indicator thereof. Where the *métaphorisé* comes first there is less suspicion of glosses and more inclination to see the apposition as a literary procedure used to signal the presence of a metaphor.

The shock aspect of isotopic distinction essential of the metaphor is maintained by this type of indicator, especially since there is no particle of comparison nor co-ordinating ו present. At the semantic level one can speak of a certain repetition between the *métaphorisant/métaphorisé* which, although they are simply placed side by side as designations of the same reality, the very repetition as such underlines the isotopic change. This aspect of repetitive emphasis, given syntactic expression via simple asyndetic apposition, is what Bourguet means by 'surcharge'.

Since apposition is common in Hebrew and does not always indicate the presence of metaphor it must join the ranks of the other indicators we have examined so far as neither necessary nor sufficient but serving to underline the change of isotope which itself is necessary.

Parallelism

A more complex form of juxtaposition, in which descriptive propositions are placed in parallel, can also constitute an indication of the presence of metaphor. Once again parallelism is not specific to metaphor but metaphor certainly makes use of it (cf., for example, Jer 50,23). The characteristic features of this type of indicator are as follows: parallel juxtaposition of syntagms related to two different isotopes in order to compare them, non-use of particles or other figures of comparison. The possibility of such juxtaposition is rooted in the fact that Hebrew parallelism can be synonymous and is given its metaphorical perspective by way of a change of isotope. Of course, not every parallelism in Hebrew implies the use of a metaphor since many, if not most, maintain the same isotope in each of the parallel lines. For this reason parallelism can never be seen as a necessary or sufficient condition for the presence of metaphor. In common with all the other indicators we have seen so far, it supports the isotopic distinction.

3. SEMANTIC INDICATORS

Semantic incoherence

Perhaps the most frequent type of metaphorical indicators are those which do not have a formal or syntactic basis but which emerge out of the intermingling of two distinct isotopes in the course of a phrase or sentence. In such cases there is no 'surcharge' nor repetition nor comparative particle nor comparative figure. In each case, however, there is a sudden emergence of something strange at the semantic level, what Bourguet calls '*semantic incoherence*' or an element of incoherence at the level of the sense of the phrase or sentence (e.g. Jer 12,2). Since such semantic peculiarities are not unique to the metaphor they cannot constitute sufficient grounds for designating the presence thereof. Once again the change of isotope is necessary.

Word-play

Certain metaphors only emerge as such thanks to the use of word-play between the *métaphorisant* and the *métaphorisé*. Bourguet offers the example of Jer 1,11-12 where a play on the root שקד turns שָׁקֵד (almond tree) into the *métaphorisant* of שֹׁקֵד ([God who] watches). Such word-plays are often difficult for us to detect today although Bourguet is without doubt that they were evident to their ancient audience. In any event, word-play is neither sufficient nor necessary for indicating the presence of metaphor. Once again it requires the presence of a change of isotope.

A glance at all the indicators outlined above reveals that none of them is unique to metaphor, nor are they necessary or sufficient indicators of the presence of metaphor. They simply accompany and underline a change of isotope which in itself is a necessary indictor but not a sufficient one in that it requires an accompanying indicator. In effect, the combination of isotopic change plus one or other of the indicators mentioned above allows us to detect the use of metaphor.

4. How Do Metaphors Work?

Bourguet attempts an analysis of the function of the various different elements which are set in motion with respect to the use of metaphor. He begins by examining metaphors which use two different particles of comparison (the 'longest' metaphors) because such metaphors are the most conspicuous and the most loquacious and thereby lend themselves to an examination into the way the various elements function.

Metaphors with two different comparative particles

We noted above how the use of comparative particles serves to distinguish between the *métaphorisant* (כ, כאשר, אשר and אכן always precede the *métaphorisé*) and the *métaphorisé* (כן and כה always precede the *métaphorisant*). At the same time there is juxtaposition between the *métaphorisant* and the *métaphorisé*. In any event, for Bourguet, the particles tend to constitute the most reliable outer boundaries of a metaphor. Another frequent occurrence is the resumption of a word or root between the *métaphorisé* and the *métaphorisant*. Repetition of a root within a metaphor implies that it belongs to two different isotopes between which a kind of 'cross-reference' takes place. If one examines this isotopic 'cross-reference' more closely one can see that it corresponds to the point of resemblance upon which the metaphor is based, the seat or core of the metaphor. Without such isotopic cross-reference (resemblance) there would be no point to the repetition, the core of the metaphor would be inexplicable and the metaphor would probably not exist. It is apparent, therefore, that isotopic cross-reference is essential since it is through this mechanism that we have access to the core of the metaphor. Metaphors which utilise two different comparative particles, therefore, share two characteristics: juxtaposition of the *métaphorisé* and the *métaphorisant* and isotopic cross-reference or resemblance. Such cross-referencing can be either explicit[125] or implicit[126].

125. Bourguet (*Des métaphores*, p. 47) offers several examples but we will restrict ourselves here to those in PI: Isa 26,17-18.
126. Isa 29,8; 31,4; 31,5; 38,13; 38,14.

Metaphors with one comparative particle

Besides metaphors with כ and מן, the other metaphors with one comparative particle function in the same way as we described above: the core of the metaphor corresponds to and is revealed by the explicit or implicit isotopic cross-reference. Metaphors with כ and מן, however, require closer examination. Although such metaphors never contain the necessary repetition to allow for the explicitation of the isotopic cross-reference (which is always implicit), Bourguet does not think that they function in a different way. For him, such metaphors do exhibit isotopic cross-reference which remains bound to the core of the metaphor. The necessary repetition in each case is implied in either the *métaphorisant* (mostly) or the *métaphorisé* (less frequently). He offers some examples from Jeremiah to illustrate his point:

Jer 31,10: (with כ)"[the Lord] will keep Israel as a shepherd [keeps] a flock." Clearly it would be difficult to imagine any other term than 'to keep/guard' implied in the *métaphorisant*.

Jer 46,23: (with מן – the implied repetition is always in the *métaphorisant*) "...they are more numerous than the locusts [are less numerous]".

Such metaphors function, therefore, in the same way as metaphors utilising two comparative particles (see above).

Instead of having an implied verb in the *métaphorisant* or the *métaphorisé*, certain metaphors use one verb with respect to which it is impossible to discern at the grammatical level whether it belongs to the *métaphorisant* or the *métaphorisé*. What is different in such cases is the lack of juxtaposition and the presence of a sort of middle zone between the *énoncé*[127] *métaphorisé* and the *énoncé métaphorisant* where the cross-reference of *énoncés* is to be found. The isotopic cross-reference is reflected in the cross-reference of the *énoncés* and carries it, so to speak. Bourguet offers several examples to illustrate his point here, the least complicated of which we will attempt to outline below:

Jer 46,21: "Even her [Egypt's] mercenaries in her midst are like fatted calves; for they too have turned and fled together, they did not stand; for the day of their calamity has come upon them, the time of their punishment." In this text, Egypt's mercenaries (the *métaphorisé*) are compared to calves (the *métaphorisant*). It is impossible, however, to ascribe one subject to the verbs which follow in this verse (turn, flee, not stand etc.); both 'mercenaries' and 'calves' fit the description. There is

---

127. Once again we stick with Bourguet's terminology. A literal translation in English sounds very clumsy: 'metaphorised expression' and 'metaphorising expression'!

clearly a middle ground in the *énoncés* in which the isotopic cross-reference is reflected.

There are two possibilities, therefore, for the *énoncé métaphorisant* and the *énoncé métaphorisé*: either they are juxtaposed (where the isotopic cross-reference is either explicit or implied) or they cross-reference one another at the same time as the isotopic cross-reference. If the isotopic cross-reference can carry the cross-reference of the *énoncés* then it is important that we clearly distinguish in our analysis of metaphors between what is relevant to the *métaphorisant* and what is relevant to the *métaphorisé* and what is ultimately relevant to both.

The middle ground noted above can be constituted by one single term, one expression or several expressions.

Another important aspect of metaphors with one particle is that while the cross-reference of the *énoncés* may be significant it never affects the *sujet métaphorisé* or the *sujet métaphorisant*. The presence of the comparative particle prevents such an eventuality.

The core of the metaphor, therefore, is to be found in the isotopic cross-reference where the *métaphorisé* and *métaphorisant* are juxtaposed. At the same time it is possible that the core of the metaphor is carried by the cross-reference between the *énoncé métaphorisé* and the *énoncé métaphorisant* but such a cross-reference never includes the *sujet métaphorisé* or the *sujet métaphorisant*.

Metaphors without particles

Although rare, in Bourguet's view, explicit and implicit isotopic cross-reference exists with such metaphors in the same way as it does with metaphors using two or one particle of comparison. In addition, examples can be found which illustrate cross-reference between the *énoncés métaphorisant* and *métaphorisé*[128]. Up to this point, therefore, it would seem that metaphors without particles function in the same way as those with particles. Bourguet's analysis of the function of metaphor has been based on concision, which expresses itself in the progressive disappearance of particles of comparison. The passage from two particles to one revealed the possibility of there being cross-reference or middle-ground at the level of the *énoncés* which signifies concision. When we move from one particle to the absence of particles a new phenomenon emerges which Bourguet calls 'eclipse'. The 'eclipse' does not take a middle or common ground nor does it affect the *énoncés*; it is employed in place of either the *sujet métaphorisé* or the *sujet*

---

128. Cf. BOURGUET, *Des métaphores*, p. 52, for examples taken from Jeremiah.

métaphorisant. Once again an example from Jeremiah serves to illustrate his point:

Jer 47,2-3: "Thus says the Lord: See, waters are rising out of the north and shall become an overflowing torrent; they shall flow over the land and all that fills it, the city and those who live in it. People shall cry out, and all the inhabitants of the land shall wail. At the noise of the stamping of the hoofs of his stallions, at the clutter of his chariots, at the rumbling of their wheels...". The masculine singular suffixes of v. 3 refer back grammatically to the 'torrent' in v. 2 but semantically they point in a different direction, to an 'army' which constitutes the *sujet métaphorisé*. In this instance there is a sort of anonymous *sujet métaphorisé* 'army' which is confused with the named *sujet métaphorisant* 'torrent'. The *sujet métaphorisé* is 'eclipsed' by the *sujet métaphorisant* (or vice versa).

It would appear then that the various forms of metaphor all work in the same way. The phenomenon of 'eclipse' is used abundantly where there are no particles present. In this event one of the metaphorical *sujets* is substituted for the other.

Isotopic cross-reference

Isotopic cross-reference is common to metaphors of every type, with or without particles. It is in fact constitutive of the metaphorical 'event' because it is here that we find the point of resemblance between the *métaphorisé* and the *métaphorisant*, the core (*foyer*) of the metaphor. How does the isotopic cross-reference function?

Isotopic cross-reference exists when a term, expression or group of terms are common to two isotopes, one or some of which, not all, are used to express the point of resemblance between the *métaphorisé* and the *métaphorisant*. The author of a metaphor selects his term or expression from various terms or expressions present in the common zone between two isotopes. This selected term or expression is what Bourguet calls the isotopic cross-reference. As constitutive of metaphor, the isotopic cross-reference is rooted in the repetition (either explicit or implicit) of a common term or expression in the *métaphorisé* and the *métaphorisant*. It is true that most terms and expressions are polysemic and have different connotations depending on the context in which they are used. The same word, therefore, which might be common to two different isotopes can have different connotations in each isotope. If the isotopic cross-reference relies on 'sameness' what happens when this sameness makes way for 'difference'? Once again an example from Jeremiah:

Jer 13,11: "For as the loincloth clings to one's loins, so I made the whole house of Israel and the whole house of Judah cling to me...". The isotopic cross-reference here is based in the repetition of the 'same' term דבק 'to cling'. By using two different conjugations (*Qal* form the first *Hiphil* for the second), however, the author of the metaphor already provides a clue that there is sameness and difference involved in this repetition of terms. The verb דבק used on its own usually refers to a more existential form of attachment similar to a loving relationship. The same verb used with אל, however, denotes physical attachment similar to a girdle tied round a man's waist to hold him in check. Both senses are included in the term דבק. The metaphor, therefore, clearly turns on one word which has different semantic content. There is a certain rupture present in the description of things. To say that God is attached to his people is different from saying that God is attached to his people as a girdle around a man's waist. Thanks to the metaphor, the semantic content of דבק in the *métaphorisant* is added to the semantic content of the same verb in the *métaphorisé* in such a way that the metaphor says something extra, something new. The rupture provides the occasion for the creation of meaning. It is thanks to this rupture that the metaphor is able to be creative and 'poetic'. In our example, the prophet Jeremiah has said something new about the 'attachment' between God and his people.

We noted Aristotle's definition at the beginning of this chapter: "Metaphor consists in giving a thing a name that belongs to something else". Bourguet points out that in speaking of 'transference' Aristotle is saying something essential about metaphors although he remains on the surface, on the level of words. 'Transference', however, also takes place at the level of meaning, within the rupture at the core level of a metaphor. 'Transference' of the meaning of a word in one isotope (the *métaphorisant*) onto the meaning of the same term in the other isotope (the *métaphorisé*). The transference of a name at the level of the subjects brings about a transference of meaning at the core level of the metaphor.

Bourguet concludes that all metaphors are rooted in an isotopic cross-reference which admits of a certain rupture which in turn allows the metaphor to be highly creative and to say something new. This rupture/cross-reference is present in the core (*foyer*) of the metaphor.

5. CLASSIFICATION OF FOYERS[129]

Of the various types of metaphorical core, according to Bourguet, the most frequent are verbal, although a foyer can also consist of an adjective or a noun and even a whole expression as we shall see.

Split core

Such are the most evident type of metaphorical core because of the explicit repetition between the *métaphorisé* and the *métaphorisant*, i.e. one single core repeated in the *métaphorisé* and the *métaphorisant* (e.g. the verb דבק in Jer 13,11: Judah *clings* to YHWH as a loincloth *clings* to the loins). A variant of the same type, which Bourguet calls the paranomastic core, involves two words derived from the same root (e.g. בוש and בשת in Jer 2,26). At the same time the splitting of the core can occur in inverse form, i.e. with a positive use and a negative use of the same term (e.g. ידע in Jer 8,7: the birds *know* but my people do not *know*).

Simple core

Such are the most frequent type of metaphorical core, involving implicit repetition instead of explicit repetition (e.g. Jer 31,10: He who scattered Israel will *gather* him and will *keep* him as a Shepherd [*gathers* and *keeps*] a flock). The core can be explicit in the *métaphorisé* and implicit in the *métaphorisant* as in the above example or vice versa as in Jer 20,9: the word of the Lord [*burns*] is in my heart like a *burning fire*. The foyer can also rest in the 'middle ground' between the *énoncé métaphorisé* and the *énoncé métaphorisant*.

Synonymous core

Instead of being constituted by the same term, the core is sometimes constituted by two synonymous terms derived from different roots, one in the *métaphorisé* and the other in the *métaphorisant* (cf. Jer 18,14-15: synonyms עזב leave/abandon and שכח forget). The synonymous terms can also be found in the *énoncé métaphorisé* and the *énoncé métaphorisant*. Given the inclination towards synonymous parallelism in Hebrew

---

129. Foyer = core. Once again this list is based on examples taken found by Bourgeut in Jeremiah. Our analysis of the metaphors in Isa 24–27 (chs. III-VI) will reveal whether there are types of metaphorical core which are typical of Isaiah and whether there are types of *foyer* which extend beyond this list.

poetry it is not surprising that we frequently find such technique at the level of the metaphorical core.

Word-play core

In the rare examples of this type the metaphorical core is not found in a form of isotopic cross-reference or repetition but, for example, in the phonetic similarity between two terms employed by the author to construct the metaphor (e.g. Jer 1,13-14: נפח boiling pot [from the north] and פתח disaster [from the north]).

Secondary core

There are metaphors in which the primary core is clearly underlined but which also contain a second core (e.g. Jer 13,12-14: primary core = מלא to fill [wine jars/people]; secondary core = נפץ to dash [people/wine jars]. While the secondary core is new and differs from the primary core, it still maintains a certain rapport with the primary core which allows us to speak of a sort of 'follow-up' to the metaphor. In examples where the *sujet métaphorisé* or the *sujet métaphorisant* are made more precise by an extra related term this extra term can also be described as a secondary core.

Multiple core

Certain metaphors possess more than one core without one being principle and the other secondary. Jer 10,5 illustrates the point: "Their idols are like scarecrows in a cucumber field, and they cannot speak; they have to be carried, for they cannot walk. Do not be afraid of them, for they cannot do evil, nor is it in them to do good." While the *métaphorisé* is clearly 'their idols' and the *métaphorisant* clearly 'scarecrows', in the enumeration of points of resemblances between the two which follows each is of equal importance to the core. One might speak here also of a primary core and several secondary cores.

Successive core

While the order of the cores in the previous type might be open to rearrangement, there are metaphors with multiple cores which follow in a logical succession which cannot be disrupted. In Jer 21,12 YHWH's anger (*métaphorisé*) is portrayed metaphorically as a fire which *goes forth* and which *burns* and which remains *unquenched*. The order of the *métaphorisants* is clearly logical and cannot be rearranged.

Diffuse core

Where certain metaphors are concerned it would appear that the core is illusive and difficult to grasp. In Jer 2,23-24, for example, Israel (*métaphorisé*) is described as a 'restive young camel... a wild ass... in her heat sniffing the wind! Who can restrain her lust? None who seek her need weary themselves; in her month they will find her'. In such cases the core tends to be evoked by the entire metaphorical expression, being spread throughout it without any particular proposition taking precedence as the primary core. Although Bourguet does not say so explicitly it would appear that such diffuse metaphorical cores also enjoy a degree of prevalence in the bible.

Absent core

In certain instances the core of the metaphor is not explicit and would appear to be absent altogether. The foyer in Jer 9,22, for example, there are two successive foyers – נפל fall and אסף be gathered. In Jer 8,2 and 25,33, however, allusion is clearly being made via the use of אסף to the metaphor in 9,22 without there being explicit mention of the foyer נפל. Thus familiarity with the book of Jeremiah is necessary in order to supply the absent foyer. In such cases the core of the metaphor does exist but is expressed in a variety of different ways: (i) it can be implied in circumstances where reference is made to a passage where the same metaphor appeared with an explicit core (as in the above example); (ii) the core might be contained in the *sujet métaphorisé* or the *sujet métaphorisant* (Jer 10,7 among the *wise* of the nations there is no one as *wise* as YHWH is *wise*'; (iii) the core may be that of the preceding metaphor (e.g. Jer 4,13).

Dead core

With respect to such metaphors the death of the core implies the non-existence of the core and where 'core death' has been established then the metaphor itself must be pronounced dead. Where there is no longer isotopic cross-reference there is no longer a core and where there is no longer a core there is no longer a (living) metaphor. In Jer 2,8, for example, the Israelites are described as 'shepherds (who) revolted against me'. The verb פשע 'to revolt' has its place in the isotope of politics and not in the pastoral isotope of the shepherd. The verb therefore does not constitute common ground between the two isotopes and cannot function as a foyer. It refers exclusively to Israel's leaders and not to the shepherds.

Classification of Metaphors/Method of Analysis

Bourguet points out that there are different approaches to the classification of metaphors. We need not follow him in his choice of classifying the metaphors in Jeremiah first according to the *sujet métaphorisant* then according to the metaphorical core. He notes the possibility that one can avoid classification altogether and simply study the metaphors as they appear in the order of reading the text. Since our four chapters of Isaiah constitutes a much smaller field of study than Bourguet's entire book of Jeremiah we can opt for the latter approach without risking confusion. A glimpse at his method of analysis reveals a useful step by step approach to the study of each metaphor which will constitute a part of our methodological approach in the concluding pages of the present chapter.

III. Theological and Biblical Metaphors (Nelly Stienstra)

The second chapter of Stienstra's work focuses on questions surrounding theological and biblical metaphors, finding and using comparisons for God and contriving images with which he can be described[130]. While admitting the vastness of the issue she focuses her attention on a number of attempted solutions to the problem which will assist us in the ultimate formulation of a methodological approach to biblical metaphor and those employed by the author of Isa 24–27 in particular.

Logical positivists like A.J. Ayer maintain that metaphorical language about God or any other metaphysical proposition for that matter, is simply nonsense because the propositions themselves cannot be empirically verified[131]. It is true, Stienstra notes, that logical positivism has had its

---

130. Bourguet only touches briefly on this issue.
131. A.J. Ayer, *Language, Truth and Logic*, London, 1971; [first published 1936; T. Binkley, in an article entitled *On the Truth and Probity of Metaphor* (in M. Johnson [ed.], *Philosophical Perspectives on Metaphor*, Minneapolis, MI, 1981, pp. 136-153) points out that metaphors in the past have been simply taken to be false or meaningless unless they are 'translated' into literal language which can be understood as true or false. He rightly argues that metaphors need not be assumed to be false or nonsensical uses of language, that they can be used to state true propositions and that we can discern the truth value of a metaphorical claim in the same way as we would with a literal claim (pp. 136-137). He warns, however, that it is important that we bear in mind the distinction between establishing the truth of an expression and establishing its meaning. Literal and metaphorical expressions differ at the level of meaning but both can make claims that can be established as true or false (p. 150). As N. Goodman points out: "The oddity is that metaphorical truth is compatible with literal falsity; a sentence which is false when taken literally may be true when taken metaphorically, as in the case of "The joint is jumping"

heyday and that philosophers have gone beyond its limited confines with respect to language and its meaning. A problem still remains, however, where the investigation of biblical metaphors is concerned. If we agree that metaphor has a cognitive function, is it possible to extend such an affirmation to biblical metaphors? How can we speak of God and, if we can, what are the implications of such talk? Stienstra examines the positions of a number of scholars on the matter[132].

1. ON ANALOGY AND METAPHOR

Aquinas states in the *Summa Theologica*[133]: "(Since) we come to know God from creatures and (since) this is how we come to refer to him"[134]. Clearly he is aware that the only way we can speak about God is in terms related to our earthly experience, and we do so, as Thomas says, by analogy. Thomas first distinguishes between univocity and equivocity in language. Univocal words refer to a single concept which may or may not also be an umbrella concept for objects which are quite different from each other yet still related. The word 'monarchy', for example, refers to kings, queens, emperors etc. who are quite different yet related in their monarchic condition. An equivocal statement uses a common phonological term to refer to more than one concept, e.g. story (as narrative) and story (as building level). For Thomas, however, neither

---

or "The lake is sapphire"." (cf. N. GOODMAN, *Metaphor as Moonlighting*, in S. SACKS (ed.), *On Metaphor*, Chicago, IL, 1979, p. 175 [80]). In focusing on the meaning of metaphors as rooted only in what the words employed mean in their most literal sense, Davidson denies that a metaphor can have another sense or meaning besides its literal meaning which is absurd and can thereby have no cognitive content (cf. D. DAVIDSON, *What Metaphors Mean*, in S. SACKS (ed.), *On Metaphor*, Chicago, IL, 1979, pp. 200-220.

132. KORPEL offers an analysis of a number of authors across the centuries in their approach to the use of metaphors for the divine: Aquinas, Martin Luther, John Calvin, Herman Bavinck, Karl Barth, Ian Ramsey, Harry Kuitert, J.J. van Es (used by Stienstra as the basis for her analysis of Aquinas on analogy), Herman Heering, Janet Soskice (*A Rift in the Clouds*, pp. 4-26) She concludes: "...although the metaphorical nature of human utterances about God has long been recognised, there still exists considerable difference of opinion with regard to the cognitive content of such metaphors' (*A Rift in the Clouds*, p. 32). She attempts to further clarify the concept of metaphor in the light of new developments in the philosophy of language which brings her into a discussion of the variety of theories of metaphor (*A Rift in the Clouds*, pp. 35-54) which we discuss both above and below. The elements of her definition of metaphor (*A Rift in the Clouds*, pp. 69-70) have already been dealt with in our own analysis. I suspect Macky would not find her approach very much different from his own.

133. THOMAS AQUINAS, *Summa Theologiae, Latin Text and English translation, Introduction, Notes, Appendices and Glossaries*, London, 1964.

134. Cf. AQUINAS, *Summa Theologica* I q. 13,1, ad 2.,

way of speaking is appropriate to God. He, therefore, distinguishes a third type of language, analogical language, in which a word may be used in more than one sense, with the relationship between the various senses being evident. Stienstra follows J.J. van Es'[135] analysis of Thomas' 'theory of analogy' as a useful systematisation of the scattered and unsystematic references made in Thomas' works to the notion of analogy and we can also benefit from the clarity of his analysis.

Van Es distinguishes four types of analogy in Thomas: 'sanus', 'visus', 'leo', and 'bonus'. In the 'sanus' type a word is used in a sense closely related to its main sense. Thomas refers to the relationship between the notions of 'healthy medicine' and 'healthy urine' as mediated by the main sense of the term 'healthy': 'healthy person'[136]. The 'visus' type of analogy is very similar to what we would call polysemy today. When people say 'I see what you mean', for example, they use the verb 'see' in an analogous way, meaning 'see' with the mind rather than the eyes[137]. The 'leo' type of analogy is closest to what we would describe as a metaphor and can be expressed in the A is B structure: 'Hercules is a lion'. The 'bonus' type of analogy, according to Van Es, distinguishes between the meanings of the term 'good' when referred to different objects. A 'good book', for example, does not mean the same as a 'good meal'.

The only concept Stienstra can find belonging to the 'sanus' type which can be appropriately referred to God is expressed by the term 'holy'. Where the main sense of 'healthy' applied to human persons and to other things only in a derived way, the main sense of 'holy' applies to God and other things are described as holy in an analogous manner derived from the primary sense which is God's holiness. 'Visus' type analogy in the biblical context, Stienstra notes, might be 'seen' as metaphorical as such. The term ראה, for example, is used for both God's 'seeing' and human 'seeing'. She continues, however, by pointing out the fact that such use of the term ראה is derived from the metaphorical concept 'YHWH is human with respect to perception', which is an inevitable consequence of the use of anthropomorphic metaphors in the bible. Although we noted that the 'leo' type is closest to what we[138] would understand as fundamentally metaphorical, Thomas himself is

---

135. J.J. VAN ES, *Spreken over God: letterlijk of figuurlijk? Analogie en metafoor in het spreken over God*, Amsterdam, 1979, pp. 7-39.

136. Cf. AQUINAS, *Summa Theologica* I q 13,5.

137. Stienstra notes that this example may be a true, although dormant, metaphor in that we can reduce it to the statement 'understanding is seeing' (A is B).

138. Or at least Stienstra.

dissatisfied with it in that it appears to attribute characteristics to God which cannot really be his. Such metaphors, for Thomas, require to be "more expressly explained elsewhere"[139]. Given his conviction that we can only talk of God in creaturely terms, any further unpacking of this type of metaphor can only be done using further metaphors. It is important to remember, therefore, that while biblical metaphors do tell us something about God they also imply things that are not true and things that are incomplete. It is equally important that we respect the fact that metaphors only organise "part of the concept they structure"[140].

For Thomas, the most appropriate type of language for God falls under the 'bonus' type. What is unique about this type of analogous speech is that it does not say anything untrue about the subject of which it is predicated. As Stienstra notes, "If 'good' means 'good as X', X being the subject of which 'good' is predicated, then 'good' may also be applied to God."[141] Thomas distinguishes five basic universal concepts of this type: 'being', 'one', 'true', 'good' and 'beautiful'. When we apply such terms to God we do not leave behind our earthly understanding of what they mean but, in any event, we do not say anything about him that is untrue since the subject determines at least part of what we mean by the predicate. Other predicates can be added to the list such as 'living' or 'wise'. We do not know exactly what we are saying when we predicate any of these terms of God but at least we can say that the statements which include such predicates are true. Soskice claims that such 'bonus'-type analogous speech is non-metaphorical language[142]. Stienstra is of the opinion, however, that since all the concepts involved in such language are first learned in their human context when we apply them to God we do so metaphorically.

Stienstra brings the theoretical approach of Lakoff and Johnson into a level of dialogue with Thomas' ideas on metaphor and analogy. Lakoff and Johnson noted that a metaphorical concept structured another concept although it was equally possible to say something literal about that concept as well. Where God is concerned, however, the only recourse we have is to metaphorical/analogical language since we can say nothing literal about him (or can we?). Metaphorical structuring, as we noted above, is only partial and the metaphors in the bible provide abundant examples of such partial structuring.

---

139. Cf. AQUINAS, *Summa Theologica* I q 1,9, ad 2.
140. STIENSTRA, *Husband*, p. 48.
141. *Ibid.*, p. 49.
142. SOSKICE, *Metaphor and Religious Language*, pp. 64-66.

Thomas distinguishes three types of concepts which can be applied to God: absolute, relative and negative. 'Absolute' concepts, included among which are his five basic universals, can say something substantial about God, about his very being. 'Relative' concepts denote relationship between God and someone or something, e.g. 'God is creator', 'God is father' etc. Negative concepts tell as something about what God is not, such as 'not finite' or 'not material'. For Thomas, however, the latter two types of concept cannot be applied to God essentially, only the first or absolute type can signify something that God really is, albeit incompletely[143]. Stienstra's 'titular metaphor' – 'YHWH is the husband of his people' – clearly falls under the second or 'relative' category and is concrete rather than abstract. In the last analysis it can only say something partially true about God.

2. On Anthropomorphism and Biblical Metaphor

Stienstra makes the important distinction between anthropomorphism as such and anthropomorphic metaphors. Her titular metaphor 'YHWH is the husband of his people' clearly has an anthropomorphic dimension in that what she refers to as the donor field (*métaphorisant*, secondary subject) refers to the human institution of marriage. Theological language-use tends to be highly anthropomorphic for obvious reasons although some have shown themselves to be uncomfortable with this fact. Nevertheless, anthropomorphic metaphors referring to God or to inanimate objects have been recognised as common for many centuries. Caird notes, in fact, that "anthropomorphism in all its variety is the commonest source of metaphor"[144]. While none of this will come as much of a surprise it remains important to recognise the significance of Stienstra's distinction before we move on to any analysis of biblical texts. As she notes, not all biblical anthropomorphism is metaphoric. She illustrates her point with an example from the book of Genesis in which God is described as walking in the garden and as one who speaks and can be hidden from (Gen 3,8-10). Stienstra describes such talk as real anthropomorphism, allegorical perhaps, but nevertheless describing the deity in purely human and non-metaphorical terms. She notes that it is impossible to boil this and similar stories[145] down to a metaphorical concept

---

143. Cf. Aquinas, *Summa Theologica* I q. 13,2.
144. Caird, *Language and Imagery*, p. 173. Caird, it should be noted, grants both an expressive and a cognitive function to our metaphorical language about God.
145. Gen 18,20-21.

and reminds us of the fact that they are presented as narratives of events which were considered to have really happened. In contrast, the description of YHWH's anger at Jerusalem's (marital) infidelity in Ezek 16 is clearly both anthropomorphic and metaphorical. The metaphorical concept at the root of such material is Stienstra's titular metaphor 'YHWH is husband'.

Literal anthropomorphism, according to Stienstra, tends to be restricted to Genesis and Exodus. The story of Jacob wrestling with God in Gen 32[146], for example, is mentioned later in Hos 12,4-5 at a time when metaphor had largely taken over from literal anthropomorphism. Hosea tones down the literal anthropomorphism by placing YHWH on a par with the angel of YHWH which was clearly an acceptable procedure at his time of writing. Later appearances of YHWH in the OT, however, tend to be more veiled, presented in the form of dreams or visions, presented in fact as anthropomorphic metaphors. One aspect missing from Stienstra's analysis is the use of human limbs[147] (and face) to describe YHWH. The analysis of Isa 24–27 will reveal that such usage can also be classified under anthropological metaphor and is not intended to be literal anthropomorphism.

The attribution of human emotions to YHWH is a more complex though equally important question. Stienstra points out the borderline phenomenon of anthropopathism in which the deity is described as having human senses and emotions and 'changing his mind'. Since the so-called higher senses of 'seeing' and 'hearing' are most frequently attributed to God she reminds us of the metaphorical concept upon which such statements are based, namely 'YHWH is human with respect to perception'. Where there are examples of God being attributed with a sense of smell (e.g. Gen 8,21; Ex 29,18.25.41; 30,34-37; Lev 1,9.13.17; 2,2.9 etc.; 1 Sam 15,22) this is most often in the context of sacrificial offerings. In such contexts, YHWH's evident pleasure at the smell of an offering is actually a reference to his approval of the person making the offering or sacrifice. For Stienstra this is in fact a dormant metaphor given the fact that there is an apparent absence of extension. Sensual perception as a metaphor for the deity is more or less limited to aural and visual perception[148]. Stienstra notes, however, that such statements in biblical texts need to be evaluated in their contexts.

---

146. Exegetes and biblical translators have struggled with this story and tried to tone down the anthropomorphic element.
147. Particularly 'hands' and 'feet'; cf., however, KORPEL, *A Rift in the Clouds*, pp. 108-116.
148. STIENSTRA, *Husband*, pp. 60-62.

In pre-exilic texts (specifically in Genesis and Exodus) in which God actually appears as a man (literal anthropomorphism) the emotional dimension can also be interpreted within this literal framework. Anthropomorphic metaphors, however, tend to absorb the human emotions into the metaphor as such. Thus YHWH is not angry or jealous as YHWH but only within the metaphorical concept of YHWH as father or husband. The inclusive notion of the metaphorical concept, as Stienstra describes it, provides a sort of umbrella metaphor which absorbs the variety of anthropomorphic utterances about the deity[149].

Stienstra devotes a section of her second chapter to the problems resulting from the fact that certain biblical metaphors have influenced the ways in which we interpret religious concepts. Authors such as Elizabeth Schüssler Fiorenza[150], Phyllis Trible[151] and Sally McFague[152] have objected to the repressive dimension of preponderantly 'male' biblical metaphors and the fact that they tend to obscure female metaphors for the deity. Stienstra disagrees in particular with Sally McFague's dismissal of metaphors such as 'God is father' as patriarchal and intended to repress women, to be replaced with metaphors based on the notion of God's body which provides models for speaking about God such as 'God is mother', 'God is lover' and 'God is friend'. McFague, Stienstra notes, is convinced that metaphors structure a concept[153]. Stienstra argues, however, that if we attempt to change a metaphor we are equally likely to structure the concept differently. Her conviction that the bible as such needs to be interpreted and translated but not changed is enough reason for her to part company with theologians such as McFague. I agree with many of the arguments presented by feminist theologians with respect to the metaphors employed by the biblical authors but I also agree with Stienstra's critique of McFague and others and her insistence on the need to respect the integrity of the biblical text. At the same time, however, I believe my analysis of the metaphors in Isa 24–27 will not

---

149. Her description of Kittay and Lehrer's notion of semantic field would appear to function in a similar fashion. "Semantic fields are constituted by content domains that have been articulated by lexical fields" (E. KITTAY, *Metaphor*, p. 229), content domains being recognised in virtue of the fact that we can locate a number of terms which appear to be semantically related (p. 226).

150. E. SCHÜSSLER FIORENZA, *In Memory of Her. A Feminist Theological Reconstruction of Christian Origins*, London, 1983.

151. P. TRIBLE, *God and the Rhetoric of Sexuality*, Philadelphia, PA, 1976.

152. S. MCFAGUE, *Speaking in Parables. A Study in Metaphor and Theology*, Philadelphia, PA, 1975; ID., *Metaphorical Theology. Models of God in Religious Language*, London, 1982.

153. Cf. McFague's notion of 'Radical Metaphors' in *Speaking in Parables*, pp. 50-56.

obscure the clearly feminine metaphors for YHWH evidently present within these chapters[154].

IV. SKILLS FOR APPROACHING METAPHOR (PETER W. MACKY)

Macky points out early on in his work that as certain tools/skills are necessray for every kind of endeavour then we can assume that there will be tools/skills necessary for the exploration of biblical texts in the search for the use of metaphor and the ultimate interpretation thereof. He outlines seven basic skills which can assist our analysis, admitting that arguments still rage with respect to almost all of the areas he represents. Macky also admits that he has bypassed the debate on biblical hermeneutics by focussing entirely on the speaker's meaning and placing the notion of user significance in the background. The same will be true for the analysis of Isa 24–27 which follows, although the topic will recurr in the latter part of the present chapter.

1. PRINCIPLES AND ASSUMPTIONS / SEVEN BASIC SKILLS

Participant knowing

Participant knowing as opposed to spectator knowing[155] is a process whereby we immerse ourselves in a reality, become part of it in order to know it. When dealing with metaphor, we exercise a variety of mental skills which we have learned through participation. Speaking and using

---

154. There is a growing number of authors focusing on biblical metaphors from a feminist perspective: e.g., N. DELBECQUE, *Images and Metaphors in a Feminist Perspective*, in J.-P. VAN NOPPEN (ed.), *Metaphor and Religion. Theolinguistics 2* (Study Series of the Vrije Universiteit Brussel, 12), Brussels 1983, pp. 231-50; C.V. CAMP, *Woman Wisdom as Root Metaphor: A Theological Consideration*, in K.G. HOGLUND et al. (eds.), *The Listening Heart. Essays in Wisdom and the Psalms in Honor of Roland E. Murphy* (JSOT SS, 58), Sheffield, 1987; P. BIRD, *"To Play the Harlot": An Inquiry into an Old Testament Metaphor*, in P.L. DAY (ed.), *Gender and Difference in Ancient Israel*, Minneapolis, MI, 1989, pp. 75-94; R.J. WEEMS, *Gomer: Victim of Violence or Victim of Metaphor?*, in *Semeia* 47 (1989) 87-104; C.V. CAMP, *Metaphor in Feminist Biblical Interpretation: Theoretical Perspectives*, in *Semeia* 61 (1993) 3-36; G.A. YEE, *By the Hand of a Woman: The Metaphor of the Woman Warrior in Judges 4*, in *Semeia* 61 (1993) 99-132; M. BAL, *Metaphors He Lives By*, in *Semeia* 61 (1993) 185-207; F. LANDY, *On Metaphor, Play and Nonsense*, in *Semeia* 61 (1993) 219-237 (a critique especially of C.V. Camp); F. VAN DIJK-HEMMES, *The Metaphorization of Women in Prophetic Speech: An Analysis of Ezekiel 2*, in A. BRENNER (ed.), *A Feminist Companion to the Latter Prophets* (The Feminist Companion to the Bible, 8) Sheffield, 1995, pp. 244-255.

155. Knowing via inference based on observation of external reality.

language (including metaphors), for example, are skills we learn by participation not by following a grammar book and a dictionary. As with our knowledge of God or of profound processes such as love, the metaphorical way of meaning is known in a participant way. Such an approach to metaphor opens up its mysterious dimension and resists reduction to the purely theoretical[156].

Imagining: Creative and Re-creative

Human beings tend to approach reality from two different yet complementary perspectives using either analytical, logical skills which tend to be verbal and linear and considered functions of the left hemisphere of the brain or imaginative, creative skills which are intuitive and spatial and seated in the right hemisphere of the brain. The process of imagining involves applying words to the sensory images received by the brain – a process in which both hemispheres co-operate – but our limited vocabulary means that certain sensory images cannot be verbalised. Imagining, therefore, is often forced to be creative. Re-creative imagining involves an effort to re-create or picture in our own imagination what was being imagined by the speaker or author to which he applied a certain word. According to Macky, the "process of re-creative imagining is at the heart of our processing metaphors we hear or read"[157]. The creator of a metaphor uses a word which he believes his 'audience' will have some direct knowledge of and be able to use as a key to re-create the reality behind the word. Creative imagining involves the 'creation of new realities by the power of imagining'[158]. This is the process of creating metaphors as such.

Concrete and Abstract Speaking and Thinking

Macky defines concrete speech as 'the kind which represents and evokes immediately experienced reality'[159] both at the spectator level of knowing and the participant level of knowing. Abstract speech, on the other hand, is more conceptual and related to definitions of reality rather than immediate experience thereof. Macky rejects extreme positions which insist on the priority of one type of speech/thought over the other

---

156. Cf. J. BAILLIE, *Our Knowledge of God*, New York, NY, 1959; J.H. GILL, *On Knowing God*, Philadelphia, PA, 1981, ch.7, "Knowing Through Participation"; SOSKICE, *Metaphor and Religious Language*, chs. 7 and 8.
157. MACKY, *Centrality*, p. 11.
158. *Ibid.*, p. 12.
159. *Ibid.*, p. 13.

and proposes that we envisage both types in the form of a continuum beginning with that which is immediately experienced and engaging in a process whereby the concrete actuality of the referent is gradually reduced until we arrive at an abstract description of the same referent. Biblical (and other) metaphors tend to employ concrete speech in order to express immediate experience (of God or sin or salvation etc.). Such metaphors are open, for the most part, to interpretation without much abstraction. At the same time, however, Macky's purpose in writing, and a fundamental element of the present dissertation, is to make the depths of biblical metaphors even more accessible by engaging in abstraction, by generalising, defining, identifying metaphors.

The Multiple Purposes of Speaking

Rejecting the extreme view which proposes that there are only two types of speech act (cognitive and emotive), Macky insists on a wide array of speech act purposes and provides an outline of those which are relevant to his study of metaphors. **Presentative**: intended to communicate information or present arguments or conclusions; **Expressive**: intended to verbalise one's feelings but without attempting to affect others; **Evaluative**: intended to express one's judgement of an event or thing; **Performative**: speech acts which have an immediate effect on a situation and are not centred on a linguistic function. (e.g. promises, imperatives, proclamations); **Dynamic**: speech intended to change others at a personal and not exclusively intellectual level. Macky points to three sub-types: *Affective* speech intended to stir emotions; *Pedagogical* speech intended enlighten the recipient; *Transforming* speech intended to change the recipient's attitudes, values etc.; **Exploratory**: the kind of speech which invites its recipients to imaginatively explore their experience in the light of an illustration presented by the speaker; **Relational**: intends to evoke a personal response on behalf of the recipient towards the speaker. The last three types of speech act, Macky notes, are of particular relevance to our understanding of the purpose of biblical metaphorical speech acts.

Meaning: The Hidden Heart of Speaking

Interpreting a speech act demands that we make use of clues provided by the speaker/author and his or her context to endeavour to arrive at the speaker's intention, what he or she meant. Macky, following Black[160],

---

160. M. BLACK, *The Labyrinth of Meaning*, New York, NY, 1968, pp. 207-208., Cf. also W.P. ALSTON, *The Philosophy of Language* (Foundations of Philosophy Series),

rejects referential and ideational theories of meaning as too narrow and opts for a more functional approach, 'thinking of meaning as using a tool'[161], as an instrument for communication etc.. A word, he notes, can have a variety of potential uses or meanings, a 'field of meaning' without a single 'correct meaning'. Different meanings can be related to one another *analogically* – 'to run' a race // 'to run' for office – where the similarities and differences in usage are clear or unequivocal – 'solution' to a problem // chemical 'solution' – where the similarities are almost non-existent. What Macky refers to as the 'speaker's meaning' indicates the move from the potential use of a word to its actual use within the context of a whole speech act[162]. This is particularly important with respect to the meaning of biblical metaphorical speech acts, requiring us to view metaphors in a context and not in isolation. If we acknowledge that speaker's meaning can vary and if we have participant knowledge of the variety of kinds of meaning he or she may be expressing, then we can have access to that meaning to some extent. Macky insists, however, that we must also recognise the mystery of the process of meaning.

Understanding: Reconstructing the Speaker's Meaning

Understanding a speaker's meaning, according to Macky, is frequently expressed in the idea suggested by Michael J. Reddy which he refers to as the 'Conduit Metaphor'[163]. The conduit in question is made up of the words we use into which we place the meaning we wish to communicate to another. These words are received by the other together with the meaning they contain. Reddy accepts the limitations of this 'metaphor' for communication, pointing out that it tends to ignore much of the imaginative, creative work done by the hearer in interpreting and understanding a communication. He offers a more nuanced metaphor for communication in its place: "Language seems rather to help one person to construct out of his [sic] own stock of mental stuff something like a replica, or copy, of someone else's thoughts – a replica which can be

---

Englewood Cliffs, NJ, 1964: "The referential theory identifies the meaning of an expression with that to which it refers or with the referential connection, the ideational theory with the ideas with which it is associated, and the behavioural theory with the stimuli that evoke its utterance and/or the responses that it in turn evokes" (p.11).

161. MACKY, *Centrality*, p. 17.

162. Cf. SOSKICE, *Metaphor and Religious Language*, p. 45: "Meanings are things determined by complete utterances and surrounding contexts, and not by the individual words in isolation".

163. M.J. REDDY, *The Conduit Metaphor*, in A. ORTONY (ed.) *Metaphor and Thought*, Cambridge, 1993³, pp. 164-201.

more or less accurate, depending on many factors."[164] This 'definition' allows for the active and creative element in a communication on the side of the hearer who uses his or her imagination to approximate the speaker's meaning. This process involves a certain amount of being able to stand in the speaker's place and enjoy some knowledge of his or her context. Macky also focuses on the 'receiving' aspect of a communication which involves the hearer in this process of imaginative reconstruction of the speaker's meaning. Receiving is the dimension of understanding the communication before we proceed to make judgements and evaluate it. Understanding for Macky, therefore, is a process of receiving and reconstructing a 'duplicate' of the speaker's meaning. It almost goes without saying that our duplication will only ever be approximate. The greater our knowledge of the context of the speaker (author), however, the more accurate our duplication will be. This dimension is particularly important for understanding biblical 'speech acts' such as metaphors. The importance of our understanding of the broad and narrow context cannot be underestimated.

Explaining the Speaker's Meaning

The next step in the process, after we have achieved as accurate a picture as possible of the speaker's meaning, is to attempt to explain it. Explanation, for Macky, is a process of clearing away obstacles in order to get a clearer perspective on the meaning of a communication. This often involves rendering these obstacles to understanding (difficult words etc.) in simpler, more translucent terms. He offers the following example taken from W.P. Alston[165] by way of illustration: "The meaning of 'procrastinate' is *put things off*". The substitution of a better-known phrase although not an expression of the literal meaning of the word it is replacing allows us nevertheless to grasp something of the meaning of the more difficult term. For Macky this is a good illustration of the fact that the meaning of a word is not simply given and that some dimension of that meaning will always remain hidden in a communication since no explanatory word can be identical with it. At the same time, synonyms must remain only an approximate guide to meaning. The use of synonyms is a common form of explanation although it can never carry the full meaning involved in the original speech act. They simply help us to open what Macky calls 'another

---

164. *Ibid.*, p. 167.
165. ALSTON, *The Philosophy of Language*, p. 11.

window into the hidden meaning'[166] of a speech act. In the case of metaphorical speech acts the dimension of re-expression is often essential. The metaphor itself may not be recognisable, having an implicit subject or allusion which is not detailed enough. The symbol chosen may itself be unknown to the reader (hearer). In the final analysis, however, explanations in the form of literal speech or further metaphors may open another window to the meaning of the original speech act but they can never substitute it completely. Once again Macky returns to the mystery involved in the process of meaning.

The seven skills proposed by Macky are important tools for working with language and particularly with metaphorical speech acts. He admits that while they are not beyond criticism they do allow us some access to the process of understanding a communication, such as a biblical metaphor, and interpreting that speech act as accurately as possible. As with our other authors, Macky now proceeds to examine a number of definitions of metaphor. His critical synthesis thereof is of significant value for his, and our, analysis of biblical metaphors

2. The Varieties of Metaphor

Macky goes beyond the usual limitations in introducing the varieties of metaphor and presents a wide array of types, distinguished from one another on the basis of certain characteristics which will become evident as we examine his survey.

Mysterious Subjects – Physical Symbols

For some authors the very essence of a metaphor is the way it provides insight into a mysterious reality via some better-known reality which it employs as a symbol. For Macky and others, metaphors which evoke physical symbols are the most important and most typical of all metaphorical types. They use physical terms (symbols) to help us conceptualise non-physical (mysterious) subjects. Since the bible is full of non-physical subjects (emotional states, social states [e.g. war, famine], the supernatural realm etc.) such metaphors tend to abound. Macky offers the example of Ps 18,2 by way of illustration: "The Lord is my rock, my fortress..." – a metaphor which allows us insight into the relationship between the human and the divine realm by way of well-known physical symbols.

166. MACKY, *Centrality*, p. 24.

Mysterious Subjects – Non-Physical Symbols

A second type of metaphor which is also typical of biblical usage is that which uses non-observable, non-physical realities as symbols to gain access to mysterious realities: "speaking and thinking of the deep mysteries in terms of some personal experiences that we know better"[167]. Another example taken from the Psalms (106,40) clearly illustrates the point: "Then the anger of the Lord was kindled against his people". Anger kindled against someone is a non-physical, human experience which is employed as a symbol to express something mysterious reality about God and his behaviour[168]. Our knowledge of human anger sheds light on God's behaviour because they are analogically related to one another.

As we noted above, Macky agrees with Janet Soskice's opinion[169] that there is only one subject in a metaphorical speech act. For Macky, metaphors tend to be one-way events and there is little room for mutual modification of both subjects. We normally use well-known and well-delineated realities as our physical symbols, realities which are not affected by the metaphorical speech act in which they are employed – only the subject is affected. Such metaphors Macky terms "one-way". When we employ non-physical realities such as inner human states, however, the situation changes. Since such non-physical realities are not precisely delineated there is room for mutual modification. In Stienstra's 'titular metaphor' – 'YHWH is the husband of his people' – it is possible that the symbol (husband-wife relationship) was modified over time to include other dimensions of the subject (God) which were then incorporated into our standard conception of the symbol. Macky refers to these as 'dual-direction metaphors'.

Well-Known Subjects – Ornamental Metaphors

Macky understands such metaphors as subsidiary to the prototypical biblical metaphors outlined above. Ornamental metaphors, which were once considered the only type of metaphor, are those which substitute more ornamental language for plainer, more literal speech. Given the fact that such metaphors can be translated into more literal language,

---

167. *Ibid.*, p. 59.
168. One might observe, however, that the use of the verb 'to kindle' reveals that behind such words lies a hidden metaphor: 'anger is fire'.
169. Which in turn runs counter to BLACK, *Models and Metaphors*, p. 44; RICŒUR, *Rule*, p. 97; MACCORMAC, *A Cognitive Theory*, p. 10, and McFAGUE, *Metaphorical Theology*, p. 38.

Ricœur considers them to be 'unreal', maintaining that 'real' metaphors cannot be translated, are not ornamental or simply emotive and offer some level of new information about the subject[170]. Macky insists, however, that ornamental metaphors fit his definition of a metaphor and while he accepts that they have a 'subsidiary' character he rejects the 'real' / 'unreal' distinction. One example from the bible (Ps 18,4-5) can serve to illustrate the character and purpose of such metaphors: "The cords of death encompassed me; the torrents of perdition assailed me; the cords of Sheol entangled me; the snares of death confronted me". Put in more literal language, these verses simply state that the psalmist almost died. A literal translation cannot be a complete substitute, however, since the plain text would clearly not have the same emotive effect on the listener/reader nor attract his/her attention in quite the same way.

Well-Known Subjects – Comparative Metaphors

When two well-known realities are combined in a metaphorical speech act, it would seem that the intention is to draw attention to the similarities between them. Of course, it would be easier to simply state the similarities directly but the use of metaphor seems to be called for in order to stimulate the reader/listener to discover the similarities evident to the author and perhaps even new similarities and to draw conclusions therefrom. Although some authors do not include this type under their definition of metaphor, Macky insists that it must have its place if only for the sake of completeness. His example from Prov 19,13 offers a good illustration of this type of metaphor: "... a wife's quarrelling is a continual dripping of rain". Both subject and symbol are well-known realities but the similarities between them are not stated directly, they are simply placed side by side and left for the reader/listener to discover.

Literally True Metaphors (2 types)

Most metaphorical speech acts can be distinguished by the fact that if we took them literally they would be false. 'God is a rock', for example, is not intended to be taken literally but to give insight into the mysterious reality of God via a better-known symbol 'rock' and its various characteristics. Other metaphors, however, can be taken both

---

170. P. Ricœur, *Interpretation Theory: Discourse and the Surplus of Meaning*, Fort Worth, TX, 1976, pp. 52-53.

literally and metaphorically. Macky adopts Ted Cohen's title 'Twice-True'[171] for such metaphors. Prov 4,14 "Do not enter the path of the wicked, and do not walk in the way of evildoers" can be taken both literally and metaphorically and is a good illustration of a 'twice-true' metaphor.

In contrast to Black, Macky insists on including similes under the metaphor 'umbrella'. Black had stated that similes did nothing more than indicate a similarity between two realities but Macky notes that many biblical similes do more than that[172]. Ps 42,1, for example, "As a deer longs for flowing streams so my soul longs for you, O God" is a simile in which allusion may be made to similarity between the two realities involved but the similarity is not stated. What we do have is a subject – the psalmist's longing – illuminated by a symbol – animal thirst. The reader/listener gains insight into a deeper reality by way of the symbol. Such speech acts need to be taken metaphorically. In contrast, however, many other similes overtly state the point of similarity; e.g. Song 7,7 "You are stately as a palm tree" which is meant to be taken literally. Metaphorical similes are quite prevalent in the bible and, as we noted with Bourguet, are frequently marked in a formal way by the use of 'like' or 'as' or a synonym thereof.

---

171. T. COHEN, *Notes on Metaphors*, in *Journal of Aesthetics and Art Criticism* 34 (1975-76) 253-255.

172. K.P. Darr (*Two Unifying Female Images in the Book of Isaiah*, in L.M. HOPFE (ed.), *Uncovering Ancient Stones. Essays in Memory of H. Neil Richardson*, Winona Lake, IN, 1994, pp. 17-30.) notes that simile is often formally distinguished from metaphor on the basis of the presence of comparative particles such as *like* or *as*. Like Macky, however, she herself is unwilling to deny simile the same impact as metaphor in every case. To explain her point she makes use of Janet Soskice's distinction between 'modelling similes' which function in a similar fashion to interactive metaphors using a reasonably well-known subject (*métaphorisant*) in order to explain or structure a state of affairs which is 'beyond our full grasp' and 'illustrative similes' which do nothing more than focus on the similarity between two entities. The former, presumably, can be construed as metaphors while the latter are 'pure' similes employed for the prupose of precision. She adds, in line with W. Booth (*Afterthoughts on Metaphor IV: Ten Literal 'Theses'*, in S. SACKS, *On Metaphor*, Chicago, IL, 1979, pp. 173-174), however, that the distinction between metaphors and similes must ultimately be construed contextually. Darr notes that M.S. Kjärgaard (*Metaphor and Parable*, Leiden, 1986, pp. 84-105) adds a further useful point of distinction to the discussion, namely the presence or absence of secondary predicates. A secondary predicate, she quotes, refers to "the complex of concepts, assumptions and ideas that correctly or incorrectly, but usually, is linked to the secondary subject [*métaphorisant*] and can be derived from it" (KJÄRGAARD, *Metaphor and Parable*, p. 86). Where these secondary predicates are explicit, therefore, one can posit the presence of metaphor and where they are implicit or absent one is more likely to be dealing with simile. Macky's insistence on exploring metaphors in 'metaphorical statements' seems to satisfy both critera. Bourguet's insistence on isotopic distinction between the *métaphorisé* and the *métaphorisant* when speaking of metaphor further underlines the difference between the two figures of speech.

3. From Novel to Retired (Dead) Metaphors

In contrast to many authors who divide metaphors into simply 'living' or 'dead', Macky proposes an expanded spectrum of five major categories which can be summarised as follows:

Novel Metaphors

Novel metaphors are unusual and unfamiliar, tend to elicit our curiosity and often remain quite memorable. The novelty of a phrase such as '[The voice of the Lord] makes Lebanon leap like a calf and Sirion like a young wild ox' (Ps 29,[5]6) remains powerful even today. Macky attributes the longevity of such novel metaphors to the limited nature of the positive analogy between the subject and the symbol. Mary Gerhart and Allan Russel[173] are among those who would limit metaphors to this type alone. In fact they divide this type into those which express consistency with our previous understanding of the terms involved (mere analogy) and those which create analogy where none previously existed, "...which contradict old views, almost forcing people to view the world differently"[174]. Only the latter group are considered to be genuine metaphors. Macky disagrees with this approach, arguing that analogy between two realities exists outside of us and our concepts of those realities. For this reason, he insists, we cannot create similarities between the subject and the symbol but novel metaphors will draw attention to some similarity which may not always have been evident or even contradict former opinions with respect to a reality. What is more common is that they complement our understanding with new insight which accompanies what we already know, although this may ultimately initiate a process which will force us to revise our understanding of the subject and the symbol.

Familiar Metaphors

This type of metaphor is on its way to becoming standard but has not quite reached this stage. An example from the Psalms: "[God] drew me up from the desolate pit, out of the miry bog..." (Ps 40,2). While the novelty value of 'desolate pit' and 'miry bog' as symbols for the depressed/oppressed state of the psalmist may perhaps have disappeared, there are still no standard positive or negative analogies between the

---

173. M. GERHART and A. RUSSELL, *Metaphoric Process: The Creation of Scientific and Religious Understanding*, Fort Worth, TX, 1984, pp. 112-114.
174. MACKY, *Centrality*, p. 74.

subject and the symbols for us to treat them as standard metaphors with a more or less fixed meaning. They may not be unique, attention-catching symbols but they still force us to approach the speech act in question metaphorically and explore the image offered by the psalmist. The bible tends to abound in such metaphors.

Standard Metaphors

After much use in a particular speech community, the positive and negative analogies between certain realities tend to be agreed upon. Perhaps Stienstra's titular metaphor 'YHWH is the husband of his people' might be viewed in this way. At any rate, 'God as father' or 'God as king' are certainly standard metaphors, even to the extent that some may not interpret them as metaphors at all. Nevertheless, they still fit Macky's definition of metaphor.

Hidden Metaphors

Hidden metaphors, according to Macky, are those we do not recognise as metaphors, resulting in our inclusion of certain negative analogies which ought to be excluded. Biblical metaphors for God which evoke realities which are not observable, for example, are good examples of such metaphors. To talk of God's love or justice or mercy means to talk on the basis of dependent analogy between divine attributes and human attributes in which the negative dimension is understated.

Retired Metaphors

Macky uses the term 'retired' instead of the usual 'dead' because he insists that such metaphors can be 'reactivated'. Metaphors reach retirement after passing through a process from novelty to familiarity to standardisation. Such metaphors tend to have their meaning included in the dictionary definition of the symbol in question and are taken as literal use (i.e. independent use that is communicable to others) by most speakers. 'Mouth', for example, may have the meaning 'river delta' included in its definition although the usage is metaphorical. Macky suggests the term 'head' (ראש) in the Hebrew bible is a 'retired' metaphor.

Since 'retired' metaphors retire as part of a process it is important to be able to see when the transition from 'standard' to 'retired' actually takes place. Macky offers some useful guidelines on determining the point at which retirement from 'active service' into literal usage occurs. Since it is often difficult to determine whether certain biblical metaphors, especially those about God, have gone through this barrier it would benefit our study to examine Macky's guidelines more closely.

Macky elaborates on Alston's example of the retired metaphor 'fork in the road'. It is hard to determine which came first, the fork in the road or the fork on one's dining table (probably the fork in the road), but the metaphor eventually became distinct and literal usage: (1) because it became commonplace and (2) because later users could observe the similarity and apply the word fork directly to road. The fork on one's dining table upon which the metaphor 'fork in the road' depended disappeared into the background and eventually vanished altogether. Where biblical metaphors are concerned we have a problem with observing how and when a metaphorical use becomes commonplace. Perhaps frequency of use in a fixed meaning in the biblical documents can indicate how a metaphor caught on. It is clear that the term ראש is used frequently throughout the bible meaning 'top' or 'end point' (of a road, river, mountain, person)[175]. Other less frequent usages are also fairly regular for the same term[176]: Ps 7,16, for example, "Their mischief returns upon their own heads, and on their own heads their violence descends". Here the term ראש clearly refers to the whole person. It remains difficult, therefore, to establish whether a reality is used in a commonplace way or is on its way to such a condition because we do not always have enough examples to go by.

The second point in determining 'retirement' is whether one can apply a (once metaphorical and therefore dependent) term in a literal (independent and communicable) way. Clearly the biblical term ראש can be applied directly in this way because we can observe realities such as mountains and towers and walls etc. as having a 'highest point' which the speech community to which we belong calls 'top'. The user no longer has to think of the original referent of ראש (human or animal 'head') in order to understand the meaning of the term in relation to these other realities. It has become independent, literal, and can be applied directly.

Unobservable realities such as 'the head (or beginning) of the year or month' are also largely independent although originally derived from other uses of the same term ראש. Where unobservable realities such as psychological states, feelings etc. are concerned a third requirement for discerning literal use is necessary, namely that we must be able to

---

175. For example, Ezek 16,25.32; 21,19.21; 42,12; Exod 19,20; Num 14,40; Josh 15,8; 1 Sam 26,13; Isa 2,2; Hos 4,13.
176. For example, Joel 3 4.7; Obad 15; Ps. 7,16; Jud 9,57.

communicate our understanding to others 'by means of conventional concomitants'[177].

4. Fooled by Hidden Metaphors

Sometimes, Macky points out, we are fooled into thinking that certain metaphors have retired while in fact they are still only understood by dependent analogy and, while they may have become conventional, they still function as metaphors. The existence of such metaphors, Macky notes, undermines what he calls the Absolute Literalist theory of metaphor which proposes that all metaphors can be restated in literal speech. Such literal speech, however, often fools itself into thinking it is literal whereas it is in fact replete with hidden metaphors. In opposition to Absolute Literalism Macky posits Radicalism which he defines as a view which proposes that the very use of expressions containing hidden metaphors forces us to think metaphorically whether we want to or not. While he insists on the existence of hidden metaphors, neither extreme is suited to Macky's understanding of the function thereof.

Absolute Literalism

Basically, absolute literalism (or the 'Substitution' Theory of Metaphor) maintains that if there is a cognitive dimension to a metaphor that dimension can be expressed with 'substituted' literal speech[178]. By equating the human conceptual system and human language at the level of literality, metaphor is forced into a second rank, deviant and ultimately confusing use of language which only has truth if it can be re-expressed or paraphrased in a literal speech act. At the level of biblical metaphors, which he maintains are clearly meaningful, G.H. Clark is of the opinion that they can be restated in strictly literal and less ambiguous terms[179]. His 'strictly literal' paraphrasing, however, is often not literal at all but exemplifies rather the presence of hidden metaphor. Speaking literally about God, for example, mostly fools itself into thinking it is engaging in literal speech acts when it is in fact using hidden and somewhat permanent metaphors rooted in dependant analogy. The preconditions for

---

177. MACKY, *Centrality*, p. 123.
178. M. JOHNSON, *Introduction: Metaphor in the Philosophical Tradition*, in M. JOHNSON (ed.), *Philosophical Perspectives*, Minneapolis, MN, 1981, p. 12. Johnson outlines the history of thought behind this theory which tends to elevate literal speech to the level of the human norm and depreciate metaphor to the level of a stylistic variation.
179. G.H. CLARKE, *Religion, Reason and Revelation*, Philadelphia, PA, 1961, p. 143.

literal speech are difficult if not impossible to fulfil where God is concerned.

Radicalism

In opposition to the notion that the human conceptual system is basically literal, Lakoff and Johnson assert that our ordinary conceptual system is in fact a thoroughly metaphorical process. Their famous example 'argument is war' is in fact a largely hidden metaphor, elements of which such as winning, losing, defending, attacking all derive from the war metaphor. While Macky agrees with Lakoff and Johnson in principle on this point he parts company with them on their radical assertion that 'argument is war' is a 'conceptual metaphor' in which one cannot avoid conceiving of the notion of 'argument' outwith the 'war' terms associated with it because these are embedded in our culture in which the imagery in question has become standard. Macky argues that it is possible to conceive of arguing by way of a different metaphor 'argument is a friendly tennis match' in which all the 'war' terms can still be used but with a different significance, i.e. not with respect to war but in a friendly exchange which has a less aggressive motivation. Although critical of the radicality of Lakoff and Johnson's assertions, Macky underlines the value of their category of metaphorical concept, especially when our knowledge of a particular subject is entirely metaphorical (e.g. God).

The Existence of Hidden Metaphors[180]

Macky succinctly defines hidden metaphors as follows: "A hidden metaphor is a dependent analogical use of language that is not recognised as such by the user. Its main effect is to tempt users to carry over unwarranted characteristics from the symbol to the subject."[181] Metaphors become hidden over a period of time, even from those who created them, by a process which Turbayne called the 'Principle of Association'[182] When two ideas are associated over an extended period of time they tend to be confused by creator and user alike. The result is that we tend to take the metaphorical usage literally without recognising that it is really rooted in dependant analogy. Macky provides a useful

---

180. Cf. C.M. TURBAYNE, *The Myth of Metaphor*, Columbia, SC, 1962, p. 56ff., D. SCHOEN, *Invention and the Evolution of Ideas*, London, 1967. MacCormac, Lakoff and Johnson similarly argue the case for the existence and functioning of hidden metaphors.
181. MACKY, *Centrality*, p. 142.
182. TURBAYNE, *The Myth of Metaphor*, p. 26.

screening process as a way to discern whether or not we are dealing with hidden metaphors:

The first two elements in the process are already familiar to us from Bourguet and others: namely that in order for a metaphor to be present there are usually two distinct realms of reality, one in which the subject is at home and the other in which the symbol is at home. Also the realm from which the symbol is taken is usually better known to us and simpler than the realm of the subject which it intends to illuminate. Macky presents a number of pairs of realms (symbol/subject) which emerge frequently in biblical use: physical/spiritual; animal/human; inanimate/animate; individual/social; human/divine; temporal/eternal[183]. So far nothing new. In order for a metaphor to be hidden, however, it has to be standardised, conventional usage. We now have three elements of identification: standard, dual realm, with one realm better known than the other. The next step in the process is to focus on other signs which may indicate the presence of hidden metaphors. Frequently, Macky notes, when we focus on our standard expressions surrounding a given reality we find that they are tied together by what he refers to as an 'underlying metaphor'. In this he is very close to Stienstra's 'titular metaphor' and it would seem that such phenomena are not unusual in biblical usage. Words associated with argument, for example, such as winning and losing, attacking and defending etc. are linked together by the underlying metaphor 'argument is war'[184]. Where the bible is concerned a whole slew of terms, such as those surrounding widowhood, marriage, covenant, protection, provision etc., used to express YHWH's relationship with his people can be linked together in the underlying metaphor chosen by Stienstra as the focus of her research, namely 'YHWH is the husband of his people'. For some users such expressions can be hidden metaphors since they have become standard usage and we tend to think we are speaking literally when we employ them. In addition to underlying metaphors we can often uncover the presence of hidden metaphors in the history of a now standard usage, the metaphorical origins of which have simply been forgotten over time. Macky offers the example of the phrase 'three *personae*/three persons' in the Nicene creed as an illustration. The term *'personae'* literally meant 'masks' and was understood when first used as metaphorical. Nowadays, however, the standardised nature of the creeds has led many to forget this background and take the statement 'three persons' quite literally. A third sign to look for when in

---

183. MACKY, *Centrality*, p. 145.
184. LAKOFF and JOHNSON, *Metaphors*, p. 64.

search of hidden metaphors is the certainty with which certain expressions are used, as if they were literal, and a debunking context. Macky offers the biblical example of Job's friends whose understanding of God was more than likely based on a hidden metaphor which related the divine realm to the human. In the human realm when people are punished we usually assume it to be well-deserved. By dependant analogy the same situation is assumed to be the case in the divine realm: God was punishing Job because he was a sinner. The truth of the matter, however, was hidden from Job's friends until his ultimate vindication. The hidden metaphor which equated human and divine approaches to justice sabotaged the thought of Job's friends and lulled them into thinking they were speaking literally and into transferring unwarranted characteristics from the realm of the symbol (human behaviour) to the realm of the subject (divine behaviour).

Our analysis of the biblical text of Isa 24–27 will benefit from an awareness of all these elements, particularly the notion of hidden metaphors and the influence they have on the thought and speech of those who use them.

5. NECESSARY METAPHOR

Macky takes a stand between the positions of Absolute Literalism and Radicalism outlined above, having proven their inadequacy for dealing with the topic of metaphor. He adopts a more moderate approach which he terms 'Critical Metaphoricalism' which would propose that while there are some things we can say which are literal about any reality, where unobservable realities are concerned – such as inner states, emotions, the supernatural – our only means of exploration, understanding and description must be rooted in metaphor. The bible abounds in expressions which endeavour to plumb the depths of unobservable realities, particularly those related to the human condition and to the divine realm. When confronted with such realities the metaphorical way of speaking can accomplish a great deal more than the literal. Of course, it remains possible to speak literally about certain unobservable realities if there is a level of mutual participation (e.g. pain) and an adequate number of concomitants available to the members of the speech community concerned. There is an evident quantitative distinction, however, between informative speech about observable realities, almost all of which can be expressed literally, and the same speech about unobservable realities, very little of which can be given literal expression. Metaphorical speech can also be more effective and more convenient even where observable realities are concerned. In order to be inclusive and accurate, literal speech describing a given action may need to be long and detailed and may in fact miss the point of the action itself. A. Ortony offers the example of a metaphorical speech act which can say more than a lengthy literal description might, referring to the swimmer who 'dived into the icy water like a fearless warrior'[185]. The possibility of literal speech about unobservable realities is very limited; the more we try to describe such realities the more metaphorical we are likely to become. Paraphrasing metaphors in more literal terms is usually not necessary if the metaphor itself is functioning adequately. It is sometimes necessary to do so, however, where some mature listeners or readers fail to understand the usage. Where unobservable realities are concerned, our tendency will more than likely be to heap up metaphor on top of metaphor in our efforts to explain.

Most significant for our study of metaphors is the discussion concerning literal speech about God in the bible, a reality upon which the principles of Critical Metaphoricalism might shed some light.

Related to this is the notion of the 'unspeakable' side of metaphor illustrated by Judith McInlay[186]. McInlay speaks of Mieke Bal's[187] understanding of the process of metaphor as being a struggle out of which 'normal' expressions emerge while others are repressed. 'Winning' expressions, however, continue to bear traces of their 'loser' counterparts. An unwanted and 'unspeakable' residue remains after the metaphorical struggle to make things speakable. Once again, sensitivity to such an 'unspeakable'[188] residue will necessarily constitute a part of our research into the metaphors in Isa 24–27.

Speaking Literally About God[189]

Macky begins with a presentation of the arguments of those who propose that we cannot say anything literal about God, arguments he finds

---

185. A. ORTONY, *Why Metaphors Are Necessary and Not Just Nice*, in *Educational Theory* 25 (1975) 45-52, "What metaphor does is to allow large 'chunks' to be converted or transferred; metaphor constrains and directs particularization" (= The Compactness Thesis, cf. p. 47).
186. J. MCINLAY, *Bringing the Unspeakable to Speech in Hosea*, in *Pacifica* 9 (1996) 121-134.
187. M. BAL, *Metaphors He Lives By*, in *Semeia* 61 (1993) 185-207.
188. In particular to 'female' dimensions of the deity or allusions to non-Yahwist religious practices and divinities.
189. Cf. also G.A. LONG, *Dead or Alive? Literality and God-Metaphors in the Hebrew Bible*, in *JAAR* 62 (1994) 509-537.

unconvincing. W. Hordern[190], for example, suggests that it is in the nature of theological speech that it must begin with analogy and then erode that initial analogy with further qualifications which simply underline the fact that such speech is inaccurate and approximate in the first place as an expression of truth about God. It would appear that the limitations of human speech and thinking and the transcendent and infinite nature of God are incompatible and that we can only speak about God using finite concepts and terms which are derived of necessity from our imperfect human world and applied to God as ultimately 'inadequate' analogous terms[191]. Even when we employ a speech act which describes the divinity in terms of a particular analogy, the very fact that we have to qualify the analogy reminds us that it is inadequate and that there can be no literal speech about God.

H. Palmer[192] points out a number of weaknesses in this position. Firstly, it tends to assume that because the human world is finite and imperfect then our concepts and speech are also finite and imperfect. This is not necessarily the case since, for example, we can think and speak of numbers etc. in a perfect way. Secondly, our speech about the infinite need not be brushed aside as inadequate. There seems to be confusion between comprehending a reality such as infinity and having an adequate concept thereof. The former may be difficult if not impossible for humans but the latter need not be. Thirdly, the argument that proposes that our speech and thought about God must be inadequate tends to confuse the term 'inadequate' with the term 'metaphorical'. There are many simple, observable realities which our human categories are inadequate to describe, but that does not mean that literal speech about such realities is impossible. All our speech is inadequate to the reality it attempts to describe but that does not mean that we are unable to speak literally even to the smallest extent about reality, whether observable or unobservable. It would appear from Palmer's criticism that the idea that all speech about God must be metaphorical and not literal is inaccurate as a universal theory.

Literal Speech About God: Positive and Negative Pairs of Concepts

Macky employs the arguments of C. Hartshorne[193] whose position allows us to come close to the notion of literal speech about God.

---

190. W. HORDERN, *Speaking of God: The Nature and Purpose of Theological Language*, New York, NY, 1964, p. 125ff..
191. Cf. Stienstra's (van Es') outline of Aquinas' thought on analogy above: *Summa Theologica* 1a.13.3
192. H. PALMER, *Analogy: A Study of Qualification and Argument in Theology*, New York, NY, 1973, p. 26ff..
193. C. HARTSHORNE, *Creative Synthesis and Philosophic Method*, Lanham, MD, 1983, p. 152ff..

Hartshorne proposed that of universally applicable positive/negative pairs of concepts one or the other can be applied literally. With respect to conceptual pairs such as relative/absolute, mortal/immortal, finite/infinite etc., everything is either one or the other – if not one then the other. When speaking of God, then, we can say that if he is not literally finite, relative and mortal then God must be literally infinite, absolute and immortal. The procedure, therefore, is to find a positive/negative pair at least one of which is applicable to the subject and we are looking at literal speech. Where both apply to the subject we may be dealing with metaphor but the context will help us decide which is being used literally (best fitting the context) and which not. Macky goes on to argue on the basis of Hartshorne's axiom that it is plausible that the biblical writers were speaking literally when they made certain assertions about God. His analysis need not delay us here. Suffice to say that his arguments affirm the possibility of speaking literally about God (literal anthropomorphism) and that it is necessary to distinguish this usage from metaphorical speech.

6. THE AUTHOR'S PURPOSE

Up to now we have been examining metaphor for the most part from the point of view of 'presentative speech', when the author's purpose was to communicate information or argue for a particular conclusion. Macky turns his attention at this point to the analysis of other types of speech in line with the seven categories outlined earlier in his work: presentative, expressive, evaluative, performative, exploratory, dynamic and relational. All of these are purposes which can and have been accomplished metaphorically by biblical authors and metaphors have sometimes been essential to the achievement of that purpose. Where metaphor is not essential, however, its use by the biblical author(s) is often a great deal more interesting. Together with Macky we pass over 'presentative speech' and the metaphors therein which has been the principle subject of his work up to now and begin with 'expressive metaphors'.

Expressive Metaphors

The primary purpose involved in the use of expressive metaphors is the pouring out of emotions, the expression of what is going on in the innermost being of the author. The fact that biblical texts abound in such metaphors is hardly surprising given the complexity of human interior life. Certain interior states can be expressed literally, yet poetic metaphor often accomplishes more than literal terms could. Such metaphors verbalise inner emotions and states using symbols which others can readily understand. Macky gives the example of Job 6,2-3: "O that my vexation were weighed, and all my calamity laid in the balances! For then it would be heavier than the sand of the sea". Another beautiful example of expressive metaphor can be found in Ps 133,1-2 (indeed the whole of the psalm is an expressive metaphor): "How very good and pleasant it is when kindred live together in unity! It is like precious oil on the head, running down upon the beard, on the beard of Aaron, running down over the collar of his robes". A description of how it feels to enjoy harmonious living could have avoided such sensuous images, yet without them a more literal, business-like approach would have fallen short of the powerful effect of the expressive metaphor. Once again, given the uniqueness and complexity of human inner states, such metaphors are often highly original.

Evaluative Metaphors

In evaluative metaphorical usage, a speaker employs a symbol to evaluate a particular subject. The chosen symbol is usually one which the speaker and others have already evaluated and when this is applied to the subject the evaluation transfers. The evaluation 'light is good' is one few people would contradict. When we take the symbol 'light' and apply it the God we transfer the evaluation of light's goodness to God. Such metaphors, particularly in biblical contexts, are usually more than simply evaluative since they carry affective (designed to attract us to God) and even exploratory (evoking a sense of wonder and curiosity in the hearer) dimensions.

Performative Metaphors

Performative speech is intended to 'do' something, to bring about a new situation, to create and change human relationships by way of language. Performatives are often to be taken literally as in judges' sentences or the making of a public vow. Other times performatives are metaphorical such as the proclamation made by God to the king in Ps 2,7 "You are my son; today I have begotten you". God's proclamation changed the relationship between God and the king based on the symbol of a father-son relationship.

The necessary use of metaphor in performative speech acts depends on whether the changed situation/relationship is open to adequate literal description or not. The change in situation and relationship evoked by Ezekiel 37, for example, could only be described in metaphorical terms because for his listeners/readers the change (restoration of life) was unfathomable. Since many performative pronouncements in the bible stem from God, metaphorical performatives are therefore quite common in biblical texts.

Since the primary purpose of the biblical writer was probably to enhance the relationship between God and God's people, the most central and frequently used metaphors to achieve that purpose were exploratory, pedagogical, affective, transforming and relational.

Central Biblical Purposes: Exploratory Metaphors

Exploratory metaphors are those which we use to fathom the depths of mysteries from the perspective of that which is more familiar. Metaphors work, according to Macky, by proposing analogies between a symbol and a subject some of which are negative and some positive. When analogies remain which we cannot categorise as negative or positive then we are drawn into the process of exploration. Novel metaphors by their very nature are most likely to evoke exploration of the symbol to see what it can reveal about the subject. Standard metaphors may also have an element of neutral analogy which encourages questioning of the metaphor and further exploration, especially when placed in an unusual context.

Central Biblical Purposes: Pedagogical Metaphors

Pedagogical metaphors, although they may include an element which involves the supply of information, usually have to do with the "illumination of dark areas of reality"[194], the supply of insight which makes the data already present take shape. In cases where a supersensible subject cannot be described literally to the satisfaction of the listener/reader, a pedagogical metaphor often introduces contradictions which create a new picture and evoke the reaction 'Oh, now I see!' from the recipient. When the data available is puzzling and impenetrable, a symbol is introduced which is familiar to the recipients and which has points of positive analogy with the various contradictory elements of the data. The pedagogical metaphor allows us to see into the puzzle and reconcile it, integrating the contradictory data.

---

194. MACKY, *Centrality*, p. 253.

Under a similar heading, L. Boadt has pointed out that authors such as R. Funk[195] understood the *mashal* or parable as more than just an illustrative or illuminative technique. For Funk certain *meshalim* function in a way similar to that of metaphorical speech: "The hearer is drawn into the parable because it is metaphorical and puts together two fundamentally unlike referents that force the imagination to draw connections. The impact of the two when joined together produces a personal vision which cannot be adequately described by discursive speech alone."[196] Such statements are familiar to us where metaphor is concerned. Modern authors, according to Boadt, tend to stress the 'comparison' or 'likeness' dimension of the *mashal* (cf. משׁל II 'to be like') in biblical and other texts[197]. One might imagine, therefore, that biblical authors may have employed the metaphorical dimension of the *mashal* for pedagogical or performative purposes.

Central Biblical Purposes: Affective Metaphors

Affective metaphors attempt to change listeners/readers by arousing emotion. Of course, one need not employ metaphors in order to arouse emotions – any look at the evening news will assure us of that –, but where the subject is abstract or remote from human experience the use of affective metaphors can be very effective. Macky offers the example of the Pharisees and their behaviour. Given their familiarity with the subject, the Jews of the day were unlikely to be stirred by them or their observant behaviour. Jesus wanted to emphasise their hypocrisy and oppressive behaviour, however, – dimensions of Pharisaism which were not so familiar – so he described them with symbols such as 'whitewashed tombs' (Mt 23,27) and as people 'who tie up heavy burdens and lay them on the shoulders of others...unwilling to lift a finger to move them (Mt 23,4)'. Such metaphors were designed to stir the emotions of his listeners and their affective power is still evident today, even outside the gospel context.

---

195. Cf. R Funk, *Language, Hermeneutic and the Word of God*, New York, NY, 1966, pp. 133-162.
196. L. Boadt, *Understanding the* Mashal *and its Value for the Jewish-Christian Dialogue in a Narrative Theology*, in C. Thoma and M. Wyschogrod (eds.), *Parable and Story in Judaism and Christianity*, Mahwah, NJ, 1986, p. 162.
197. Cf. D.O. Via, *The Parables: Their Literary and Existential Dimension*, Philadelphia, PA, 1967; T. Polk, Paradigms, Parables, and Meshalim: *On Reading the* Mashal *in Scripture*, in *CBQ* 45 (1983) 564-83; M. Greenberg, *Ezekiel 1–20* (AB, 22), New York, NY, 1983, pp. 307-324.

Central Biblical Purposes: Transforming Metaphors

Transforming metaphors combine the effects of both pedagogical (insight) and affective (emotions) metaphors to induce transformation. Transformation implies a change in one's way of life, a turn about usually brought on by a combination of metaphors employed to inform, give insight and arouse those who hear/read them to change their (usually) inner lives.

Central Biblical Purposes: Relational Metaphors

Relational metaphors are perhaps the most significant in biblical texts. The importance of enhancing one's relationship with God and one's relationship with one's neighbour was clearly central to biblical writers. Relational speech is evident in the bible where speaker and hearer are present and central to the communication which takes the form of an address (God may be present addressing the people in the person of the prophet). Relational metaphors introduce a level of invitation into relationship where the relationship cannot be expressed adequately with literal terms, going beyond that which literal speech can do. In addressing God, for example, as 'our father or 'our shield', the people of Israel affirmed their belief in metaphorical terms that God intended to relate to them in this way. They founded their relational metaphorical speech on words addressed to them affirming the way God wished to relate to them: "I will be a father to him…" (2 Sam 7,14) or "I will take you for my wife forever…" (Hos 2,19).

Conclusion

Of the three primary positions we have outlined above each author has approached the topic of metaphor from a different perspective.

Bourguet's approach tends to treat metaphor primarily as a rhetorical device albeit in a more nuanced way than that described by classical rhetorics. His basic definition of metaphor can be found in what he calls the 'new rhetorics' of Ricœur in which metaphor is seen to create new meaning. Fundamental to Bourguet's understanding of the process of metaphor is the presence of two items, the *métaphorisant* and the *métaphorisé* which are taken from two distinct yet similar isotopic ranges whose combination creates something of a shock in the reader or listener. The shock emerges from the explicit or implicit 'cross-reference' which takes place when the terms in question are juxtaposed. This point of cross-reference is what Bourguet calls the *foyer* or core of the metaphor[198] which consists of a variety of types. Isotopic cross-reference as far as Bourguet is concerned is common to metaphors of every type and constitutes the metaphorical event as such since it is here that the core of each metaphor is to be found. Isotopic cross-reference has its roots in either explicit (sometimes employing the same word in both the *métaphorisant* and the *métaphorisé*) or implicit repetition. The process of cross-referencing makes way for the creation of new meaning, indeed for poetry. Borrowing from Aristotle's definition, Bourguet speaks of the 'transference' of meaning from a term in one isotope onto a term in another isotope[199].

Stienstra unashamedly opts for a basically cognitive understanding of metaphor rather than a rhetorical one. She believes that the cognitive contribution of metaphor, its expression of truths, however partial, especially with respect to abstract concepts which cannot be spoken of otherwise, is of greater significance today than rhetorical efficacy. Stienstra presents a number of the most significant cognitive theories beginning with Max Black's 'Interaction Theory' from the 1960's, moving through Lakoff and Johnson's 'Metaphorical Concepts' from the early 1980's and concluding with the 'Semantic Field Theory' proposed by Kittay and Lehrer, also from the early 1980's. Having established the cognitive function of metaphor she goes on to ask whether that function can be transferred to biblical metaphor and to God talk in particular. In attempting to answer this question she brings Aquinas' ideas on analogy into dialogue with those of Lakoff and Johnson on metaphor and concludes that it is possible to speak cognitively about biblical realities such as the divinity although we ought not to forget that such metaphors only tell us about part of the reality they 'organise'. The attribution of anthropomorphic features to YHWH, for example, while not always metaphorical in intention[200], can only inform us about their subject in an incomplete way. Even Thomas' absolute, relative and negative concepts can only tell us something incomplete about God. Where the bible is concerned, however, metaphor is employed with respect to concrete as well as abstract realities and it is important to be aware of the cognitive 'level' which can be attained by each. Ultimately, Stienstra is strongly influenced by the notion of basic metaphorical concepts (in her own terms 'titular metaphors') which constitute a sort of irreducible ground

---

198. This core can also be located in the cross-reference between the *énoncé métaphorisant* and the *énoncé métaphorisé*.
199. The closest Bourguet gets, I believe, to suggesting a cognitive function for metaphor.
200. I.e. they are sometimes literal – e.g. God walking in the garden in Gen 3,8-10.

metaphor often expressed with the formula A is B beyond which further reduction is impossible. In other words, when the bible speaks of YHWH as 'lover' or 'protector' then such metaphorical talk can ultimately be reduced to the ground metaphor 'YHWH is the husband of his people'. In contrast to logical positivists like A.J. Ayer she maintains that the primary function of metaphor is cognitive, intended to inform those who read or hear it about the subject which it 'organises' or 'structures'. Stienstra shares the conviction of Sally McFague that metaphors, however partially, structure a concept, i.e. they function cognitively. This forces her to disagree with the movement within women's studies exegesis which would attempt to re-vision the (patriarchal) metaphorical usage of the bible.

After setting out the various principles and assumptions behind his approach to metaphor, Macky presents a critique of a number of traditional positions (some of which are followed by Bourguet and Stienstra), emphasising that where biblical metaphors are concerned we must be inclusive of both the cognitive and the rhetorical aspects of the phenomenon. Thus he appears to take a middle ground in terms of his understanding of the purpose and function of metaphor. As a matter of fact, however, his examination of the wide variety of purposes an author(s) might have in employing metaphor forces us beyond this limited bi-polar (cognitive-rhetorical) understanding of how metaphor works, at least with respect to the bible[201]. In addition, he offers an explanatory glossary of seven basic skills which he considers necessary for approaching and ultimately understanding the use of metaphor in a given textual context[202]. After examining the notions of literal and figurative speech, the latter of which he defines as 'dependant' on literal speech thus providing the basic foundation for his definition of metaphor, Macky goes on to examine, criticise and approve some definitions of metaphor beginning with Richards, through Black, Lakoff and Johnson, Alston, Ricœur and concluding with Soskice. He concludes that although it might appear that the authors in question are far removed from one another in their approach to the topic, the ultimate distance between the rhetorical and the cognitive dimensions is not as great as we might imagine and that the 'gulf' between them is filled with a great many more dimensions. Accordingly, Macky's ultimate definition of metaphor is not far from that subscribed to by Bourguet (basically rhetorical) and Stienstra (unashamedly cognitive), in fact it is inclusive of both.

---

201. Presentative, Expressive, Evaluative, Performative, Dynamic, Exploratory, Relational. See definitions above.

202. Participative knowing, re-creative imagining, concrete and abstract speaking and thinking, purposes of speaking (cf. previous note), meaning, understanding as reconstructing the speaker's meaning, explaining the speaker's meaning.

The inclusive nature of Macky's approach to the topic of biblical metaphor will constitute the basis for our own understanding of the way metaphors function within a text. His examination of the biblical author(s)' purpose in using metaphor seems to demand that we include both purely cognitive and purely rhetorical intentions while recognising a variety of other intentions as well.

V. Searching for Metaphors: Notes on Method

1. Metaphor Spotting[203]

Bourguet is alone among our three authors in offering a specific examination of some of the signs both formal and informal one might look for in an effort to spot or identify metaphors in a text. We will outline his steps of identification here although we must also extend them to our methodology below. Bourguet's conviction (contra Macky, at least in part) that metaphors, unlike 'enigmas' and 'allegories', do not seek to conceal themselves leads, him to assume that there are indications which allow them to stand up and be counted. A primary characteristic of the use of metaphor is, therefore, its 'shock' dimension brought about by the juxtaposition of two apparently unrelated terms taken from distinct isotopes.

Bourguet divides his indicators into three types: Formal, Syntactic and Semantic. Formal indicators include the use of one or more Hebrew comparative particles (long-metaphors – long shock) and figures of comparison (using a formal indicator other than a comparative particle = short metaphors – short shock). Syntactic indicators include 'surcharge' at the clause level in the form, for example, of a simple apposition or juxtaposition at the line level in the form of various kinds of parallelism (also including 'isotopic shock'). We will see in our analysis that the restriction of this informal indicator of metaphor to the line level misunderstands, in a certain sense, the function of poetic parallelism which Berlin, as we noted, considers to be the other side of the coin to metaphor. Parallelism functions both at the line level and beyond it.

---

203. Cf. E. KITTAY, *Metaphor*, Oxford, 1987 pp. 40-95; I. LOEWENBERG, *Identifying Metaphors*, in M. JOHNSON (ed.), *Philosophical Perspectives on Metaphor*, Minneapolis, MN, 1981, pp. 154-181. J.J.A. MOOIJ, *A Study of Metaphors* (North-Holland Linguistic Series, 27), Amsterdam – New York – Oxford, 1976, pp. 18-28. All of the authors mentioned here speak in terms of 'deviance', 'surprise', 'foreignness', 'incongruity', 'first-order meaning' and 'second-order meaning' etc. within a given context.

Semantic indicators include 'semantic incoherence' and word-play. As will be evident, the 'shock' elicited by the distinction of isotope between the *métaphorisant* and the *métaphorisé* is a necessary indicator accompanying all three of Bourguet's categories.

Stienstra's main contribution here is focused on the types of language we use for God and is partly in line with the 'theory of analogy' of Thomas Aquinas[204]. She offers no direct or formal indicators in a text which would show that we are dealing with metaphorical language as such. Language concerning God, she believes, is metaphorical by necessity[205] and tends strongly towards anthropomorphism. She suggests that there is a need to search (hidden metaphors?) within a biblical text referring to the deity for metaphorical concepts which can be reduced to the A is B type. Besides the attribution of (human) physical characteristics to the deity (YHWH having limbs, eyes etc.) one should also be on the look out for the attribution of human emotions (anthropopathism) which tend to be absorbed, she notes, within the (anthropological) metaphor itself.

Macky's approach to biblical metaphor suggests that we must first distinguish between literal and figurative usage and between independent and dependent usage in order to distinguish what is metaphor and what is not. He is of the opinion that the biblical authors made frequent use of what he calls 'profound metaphors' as opposed to 'superficial metaphors', metaphors which cannot be easily reduced to literal speech.

We noted above that Macky distinguished two types of literal use of language: 'empirical' – which he considers too narrow and 'established/conventional' – which he considers too broad. Macky himself prefers to speak of literal speech as independent, i.e. understood directly without allusion to some other meaning or word. Dependent speech implies that we understand some other use of the term or terms in question before we can properly grasp its/their present, dependant use[206]. If literal implies independent then dependant implies figurative. In approaching the biblical texts, therefore, we must be on the look out for dependant/figurative speech acts, especially those with a significant content which cannot be restated in literal/independent terms (profound metaphors)[207].

Once we have discerned a figurative speech act we must determine which 'horizontal' type of figurative speech act is being employed: metonymy, ellipsis, hyperbole, irony, joking, symbol saying, metaphor

---

204. See 'Various Types of Metaphor' below.
205. Although she does make reference to literal speech about God as we shall see below.
206. Bourguet's 'cross-reference'?
207. See Stienstra's 'metaphorical concepts'.

etc.. Although Macky does not mention it, certain distinct types of figurative speech need not exclude one another. A biblical author might readily employ a metaphor at the same time as another rhetorical/stylistic device. It will be necessary, therefore, to make a distinction between the different 'vertical' levels of a figurative speech act employed by an author, in order to establish which is the primary use of figurative language.

While it is unnecessary to repeat Macky's definition of metaphor here it is important to remember when we are searching a text for metaphors that they are couched in whole speech acts. At the same time the 'subject' and the 'symbol'[208] need not always be directly mentioned but can be otherwise implied in the context. In addition we need to be aware that the analogical relationship implied by a metaphor has positive (similarity), negative (difference) and neutral (both) dimensions. Most importantly, we need to be on the look out for dependent analogical use (as distinct from adding a new sense of a term to the language and analogical extension of a term's literal uses) which is ultimately metaphorical.

Symbols, which for Macky constitute the 'vehicle' or 'subsidiary subject' (*métaphorisant*) of a metaphorical speech, need to be separated into two types 'conventional symbols' and 'insight symbols'. Conventional symbols require no level of resemblance to what they refer and are not metaphors as such. Insight symbols, on the other hand, give analogical insight into more mysterious realities.

2. Various types of Metaphor

Bourguet concludes that every type of metaphor has its roots in an isotopic cross-reference (analogous point of contact) which, he maintains, constitutes the core or *foyer* of the metaphor – *Les foyers métaphoriques* – the various types of which he lists for us. We provided a summary of this list above which we do not need to repeat here[209]. They are roughly equivalent to the different types of metaphorical speech act we might expect to find in a biblical text[210]. It will be necessary in our analysis of the text of Isa 24–27, therefore, to ascertain which type of core/cross-reference is at work in the metaphorical speech acts we encounter.

In her search for a cognitive definition of metaphor, Stienstra affirms a number of positions, namely those of Black, Lakoff and Johnson, and

---

208. Bourguet's *métaphorisé* and *métaphorisant*.
209. Split core, simple core, synonymous core, word-play core, secondary core, multiple core, successive core, diffuse core, absent core, dead core.
210. At least those analysed by Bourguet.

Kittay and Lehrer, within which she discerns a number of different types of metaphor.

Black, she notes, speaks of metaphors primarily in terms of interaction. Accordingly, he categorises metaphors according to the creativity of their interaction, their ability to provide insight into reality: *extinct*, *dormant* and *active*, the latter being further divided into *emphatic-active* and *resonant-active*. We have already provided an overview of the implications behind these metaphorical types. They are also presented in more detail by Macky.

Stienstra speaks of 'titular metaphors' which she also refers to as 'metaphorical concepts', a kind of umbrella type of metaphor, usually of the A is B type, beyond which a metaphorical speech act cannot be further reduced. She bases herself here on the work of Lakoff and Johnson who maintain that the human conceptual system is metaphorical by its very nature and that there are metaphorical concepts which structure our perception of reality[211]. In addition, Stienstra makes the important distinction between what she calls '*culture-dependent*' and '*culture exceeding*' metaphorical concepts. Also in line with Lakoff and Johnson, Stienstra proposes three distinct categories of metaphor: *structural*, *orientational* and *ontological*[212].

In her discussion of the ways we speak about God, Stienstra examines Thomas Aquinas' approach to the concept of analogy of which he distinguishes four types '*sanus*', '*visus*', '*leo*' and '*bonus*', which are roughly equivalent to four distinct types of metaphorical speech act. We offered a brief description of each type at the beginning of the present chapter. Once again, it will be of value to discern which of the types (if any) we are dealing with in our analysis of Isa 24–27. When speaking of God, Thomas favours the '*bonus*' type of analogy, within which he distinguishes five basic universal concepts which can be applied to God: '*being*', '*one*', '*true*', '*good*' and '*beautiful*'. These five concepts are among the '*absolute*' ways of speaking about God. We can also speak about God in '*relative*' and in '*negative*' terms. Each of these concepts will be significant when we come to categorise the metaphorical types employed in Isa 24–27.

Finally, Stienstra notes that most metaphors for God are anthropological and anthropopathic, all of which, to paraphrase Stienstra, can ultimately be boiled down to the metaphorical concept 'God is human with respect to physicality and emotion/perception' (=A is B).

---

211. Most important for her being the 'titular metaphor' by which she understands our concept of God to be structured: 'God is the husband of his people'.
212. Lakoff and Johnson also speak of the *coherence*, *consistence* and *entailment* of the various categories of metaphor.

Macky's presentation of the variety of metaphorical types is of value both for its detail and for the fact that it focuses exclusively on biblical texts. He focuses first on what he considers the most common type of metaphor which he divides into two categories: those with *mysterious subjects* and those with *well-known subjects*. The former combine with *physical-symbols* to constitute *one-way metaphors* and with *non-physical* symbols to constitute what can be *dual-direction metaphors*. The latter type constitute what Macky calls *ornamental metaphors* and/or *comparative metaphors*.

Macky goes on to distinguish a further category of metaphor, of which there are two types, which he refers to as literally true. He terms the first type '*twice-true metaphors*' in that they can be taken both metaphorically and literally. By including the idea of simile under the metaphor 'umbrella', Macky distinguishes a further type of metaphor, namely the metaphorical simile (as opposed to the literal simile) which, he points out, are frequent in biblical texts.

Instead of the usual categories which commonly only distinguish between 'living' and 'dead' metaphors, Macky proposes a process giving rise to five distinct metaphorical types: *novel metaphors, familiar metaphors, standard metaphors, hidden metaphors* and *retired metaphors*. Hidden metaphors are of particular interest. Unlike Bourguet who insists that metaphors by their very nature do not seek to conceal themselves, Macky points out that, over time and frequent usage, both creator and audience of a particular metaphor tend to take it more literally and forget that it is originally based on dependent analogy. A close reading of the text in line with Macky's proposed method for screening out such hidden metaphors will be necessary, therefore, if we are to spot this type of metaphorical speech act at work. Hidden metaphors are primarily associated with standardisation through history and with 'underlying metaphors'[213] which readers/audience can easily miss.

On the question of God talk, Macky adopts a position between Absolute Literalism and Radicalism – both of which he regards as over-ambitious –, which he styles 'Critical Metaphoricalism'. Critical metaphoricalism maintains that it is sometimes possible to speak literally about unobservable realities such as God. In such instances, however, metaphorical speech tends to hold sway and where the metaphor is still adequately functioning there is little need to reduce to literal speech.

A further list of metaphorical types emerges from Macky's analysis of the seven categories of speech type we outlined above. Among such

---

213. Metaphorical concepts – titular metaphors?

metaphors, therefore, we can include *expressive metaphors, evaluative metaphors, performative metaphors, exploratory metaphors, pedagogical metaphors, affective metaphors, transforming metaphors* and *relational metaphors*[214]. These categories are also directly related to the question of the author's purpose. For what reason did the author of a biblical text employ metaphor?

3. Author's Purpose

Is the author's purpose ultimately cognitive or rhetorical? This has been the predominant question in the literature dealing with metaphor. Before we can answer this question, however, it is important that we establish whether we can we gain access to the author's purpose in the first place. Of our three 'experts' in the world of metaphor and bible only Macky speaks of gaining access to the purpose of the author. He proposes, as we noted, that we need *seven basic skills* in order to fruitfully approach the metaphors of the bible and understand them. Macky insists, first of all, that the reader cannot be a spectator but must immerse him/herself in the biblical text in order to know it. Being attune to the use of metaphor is a skill learned through participation. At the same time, it is important that the reader be capable of creative and re-creative imagining, a skill which involves the re-creation in our own imagination of what was being imagined by the author when he or she employed certain words and combinations of words. The skill of concrete and abstract thinking and speaking is also essential to the quest for metaphorical language in the biblical text. What is important here is the ability to move between the two forms of speaking and thinking, from concrete experience to the abstract description thereof, without adopting either extreme. The reader must also be attune to the multiple purposes of speech. If one cannot discern the purpose of an author's words then one cannot hope to gain access to his use of metaphors. The ability to read the clues left by an author is essential to the exploration of the meaning of a text. Can we get to the specific meaning or 'author's/speaker's meaning' via his or her choices with respect to the multiple meanings of the words at his or her disposal? At the same time we must learn the skill of 'receiving', of being able to receive and reconstruct an approximate 'duplicate' of the author's meaning, building on our knowledge of the context. Finally

---

214. Once again, more detail on each type can be found above pp. 116-120.

we must have the ability to explain the author's meaning, however incompletely. This may imply the use of literal speech or synonyms or further metaphors in order to open a window into the hidden meaning of the text. Ultimately we must insist along with Macky that biblical authors can and have accomplished a great deal more than the two purposes focused on in the literature. The final part of our methodology, therefore, will explore the various purposes or combinations thereof the author of Isa 24–27 may have achieved by the use of metaphor.

4. BIBLICAL TALK ABOUT GOD

Opinion among our three authors on the topic of God-talk in the bible is representative of a general sense of unease apparent among exegetes and theologians on the question. Some of those who maintain that all language about God is ultimately metaphorical suggest that we should view God-talk in general as broadly metaphorical (frequently anthropomorphisms/anthropopathisms: God 'walks', for example, or God 'sees') with specific or narrower metaphorical language being of greater significance for the study of human perception of the divine (God is a 'rock', for example, or God is 'husband'). This may seem somewhat evident to the modern day exegete/commentator, whose knowledge of the process of metaphorisation is healthy and critical. Can the same be said for the biblical author(s) or redactor(s)? A number of associated questions arise at this point. Can we genuinely gain access to the author's intention? Can we accept that intention is a necessary prerequisite for the use of metaphor as metaphor? What do we understand by metaphorical, catachresic and literal language about God? Is all anthropomorphic language metaphorical? Is there such a notion as literal anthropomorphism as opposed to metaphorical anthropomorphism? Finally, does *the bible* speak literally about God?

While we can agree with Korpel who warns against imagining that we can fully understand the speaker's meaning or intention and insists that we might ultimately be wrong in our interpretation of a text, it remains a fundamental part of the exegetical endeavour that we strive to read the 'set of signs'[215] in the literary product we have at our disposal and offer our interpretation thereof, however inadequate. To insist that we are unable to access the speaker's meaning/intention is to insist that the

---

215. KORPEL, *A Rift in the Clouds*, p. 62. Cf. also E. WINNER & H. GARDNER, *Metaphor and Irony: Two Levels of Understanding*, in A. ORTONY (ed.), *Metaphor and Thought*, Cambridge, 1993[2], pp. 425-443.

exegetical endeavour is to all intents and purposes a waste of time. Once again, Macky's seven basic skills for approaching metaphor in biblical texts are appropriate here: participant knowing as opposed to spectator knowing; imagining both creative and re-creative; concrete and abstract speaking and thinking; an awareness of the multiple purposes of speaking (presentative, expressive, evaluative, performative, dynamic, exploratory, relational); the ability to understand the speaker's meaning (his or her specific use of a term or phrase taken from the potential uses thereof and placed in a context; the capacity to reconstruct the speaker's meaning imaginatively, and based on an informed knowledge of the speaker's context; the capacity to explain the speaker's meaning, admitting that we are only opening a 'window onto the text'.

We noted in our analysis of Bourguet's theory of metaphor that 'intentionality' was an essential element in the equation when it comes to an author's use of metaphorical language. Those who would argue that all God talk, including all biblical God talk, must be metaphorical tend not to take into account the fact that it is possible to make non-intentional use of metaphors, especially those so-called 'dead' or 'retired' metaphors or those which have become hidden behind centuries of use. It might be argued, therefore, that if one can agree that it is possible to access the speaker's intention in a literary context, one can likewise discern whether the author intended to speak metaphorically or not. At the same time, while searching for words to describe the indescribable, the biblical author was forced to intentionally borrow from other isotopes on every occasion, the isotope of the divine being 'empty', as it were. This need not necessarily imply, however, that he or she always intended to speak metaphorically. Bourguet himself is convinced that much of the language about God in the bible is catachresic rather than metaphorical, vocabulary improperly used or applied to a thing which it does not properly denote. Bourguet is equally correct in saying, however, that 'dead' catachresis has filled the once empty isotope of the divine, allowing us to speak about God in metaphorical terms based on a 'created' but nonetheless no longer 'empty' isotope. The fact remains however, that catachresis, while still figurative, is not metaphorical.

Once again, those who would argue that God talk is exclusively metaphorical tend to be unaware of the distinction between metaphorical anthropomorphism, the human isotope being the primary source for metaphors about God, and literal anthropomorphism. Stienstra offers the example of Gen 3,8-10 in which God is described as 'walking' in the garden of Eden. Such language she maintains, is literal anthropomorphism, allegorical perhaps, but nothing more than a description of the deity in purely human terms. Such language is closer to catachresis than to metaphor. As we have already noted, where metaphor is concerned there has to be intention. It remains debatable that the author or redactor intended such language to be metaphorical. Is it not more likely that narratives of this kind spoke of events which were believed to have really happened. It is perhaps understandable that the 20th century bible scholar might complain that such language is evidently figurative but the same cannot be said for the biblical author who does not enjoy the benefits of our literary critical perception. Furthermore, it is impossible to reduce such language to a metaphorical concept. The description of God's anger at Jerusalem's marital infidelity in Ezek 16, on the other hand, is both anthropomorphic (anthropopathic) and metaphorical since it can clearly be reduced to the metaphorical concept 'YHWH is husband'. Further difficulties with the idea of literal anthropomorphism are related to the religio-historical development of YHWHism. Once again Stienstra points out that the literal dimensions of the story of Jacob wrestling with God in Gen 32 were later toned down by Hosea (12,4-5) who 'substituted' an angel for the divinity. On the other hand, Macky warns against being fooled by hidden metaphors into thinking we are speaking literally about a thing. It is necessary to ask, with respect to God for example, if the apparently literal statement can be reduced to a metaphorical statement. We have already insisted that this is not always the case.

Macky uses the expression 'critical metaphoricalism' to describe his approach to the use of metaphors. Critical metaphoricalism maintains that while we can say some things which are literal about any reality, including the divinity, we must resort to metaphor to explore, understand and describe realities such as the human condition or the divine. Metaphorical language clearly accomplishes more in this regard than literal language could ever hope for. Counter to Hordern[216] who maintains that there can be no literal speech about God, Palmer insists, among other things, that all our speech is inadequate in its description of reality whether observable or unobservable[217]. At the same time, however, this does not mean that we cannot speak literally about anything at all. Even the very idea that our speech about God is inadequate and thus metaphorical tends to wrongly equate the two terms. C. Hartshorne, cited by Macky, insists on the possibility of literal speech about God[218]. He suggests that we look for positive and negative pairs of concepts, one of which can ultimately be used liter-

216. See above, note 190.
217. See above, note 192.
218. See above, note 193.

ally. If we say that God, for example, is not literally finite then we can affirm that he is literally infinite. At the same time, if we insist that God is not literally mortal we can affirm that he is literally immortal.

Does the bible speak literally about God? While the question is a stubborn one, it would appear that our three authors are able to affirm the possibility where the *bible* is concerned. It would appear to be necessary, however, that we make a distinction between our own God talk and biblical God talk. The biblical author was free to speak both metaphorically and literally about God but his/her present day interpreter is obliged to see things differently because she/he is aware of the mechanism which creates hidden metaphors and keeps them hidden.

5. Hermeneutics of Biblical Metaphors

Having outlined an approach to metaphor – which we will methodologically refine below – based on the three authors we originally chose to guide us through the complexities of metaphorical theory we now need to situate our emerging model within contemporary biblical hermeneutical debate. Authors such as Paul Ricœur, Eberhard Jüngel, Northrop Frye, Hans Weder and Jean-Pierre van Noppen, among others, although themselves not exegetes, have reflected on metaphor in the context of religious language, particularly language about God. It seems self-evident that the Bible as a written religious document contains language about God and is thus a primary source of religious language, one which feeds theological deliberation[219]. It will emerge, I hope, that a degree of overlap, if not outright consensus, exists among these authors and Bourguet, Stienstra and Macky.

Like Macky, Paul Ricœur[220] speaks of the hermeneutics of metaphor as the analysis of speech and especially as the analysis of biblical speech. For Ricœur, and I would venture for most recent writers on the topic including our three 'guides', metaphor is not only a rhetorical style figure which does not introduce semantic innovation. Like Black and many others, therefore, Ricœur rejects theories of substitution with

---

219. J.-P. van Noppen, *Metapher und Religion*, in Id. (ed.), *Erinnern, um Neues zu sagen. Die Bedeutung der Metapher für die religiöse Sprache*, Frankfurt am Main, 1988, p. 13: "Ein Merkmal christlichen Diskurses ist seine Abhängigkeit von Andeutungen und Aussagen, die in einer Anzahl von Texten schriftlich belegt sind, d. h. in der Heiligen Schrift ....".

220. Paul Ricœur, *Stellung und Funktion der Metapher in der biblischen Sprache*, in P. Ricœur and E. Jüngel, *Metapher. Sur Hermeneutik religiöser Sprache. Mit einer Einführung von Pierre Gisel*, Munich, 1974.

regard to the phenomenon, maintaining that metaphor can be and is creative of new information[221]. Ricœur understands metaphor to function by way of a "metaphorical twist"[222] or "category mistake"[223]. According to Ricœur, therefore, "die metaphorische Auslegung besteht darin, einen sinnwidrigen (nonsensical) Widerspruch (contradiction) in einen sinvollen Widerspruch zu verwandeln"[224]. Bourguet's insistence on the 'shock' element involved in the apposition or juxtaposition of distinct isotopes clearly falls together with Ricœur's understanding of the function of metaphor. Bourguet's emphasis on the core or *foyer* of the metaphor in which distinct isotopes encounter one another at a point of similarity, however, further explains Ricœur in this regard.

Ricœur speaks of "Sinnausweitung", an expansion of the meaning or semantic content of a word (or in our case phrase or word complex). He replaces the Theory of Substitution for a Theory of Tension which results in the creation of meaning (*Sinn-Schöpfung*)[225]. Understood as such, however, Ricœur insists that metaphor only lasts a moment and does not belong to the established meaning of words or expressions. It exists, he maintains, "nur in der inkonsistenten Attribution eines ungewohnten Prädikats"[226]. In order to understand a metaphor, therefore, we must engage in the "Auflösung einer semantischen Dissonanz"[227]. This obviously has significance for translation. How does one continue 'the moment' into another language and culture? Stienstra partly addresses this issue in distinguishing between culture-dependant and culture-exceeding metaphors. It is clear from each of our three guides, however, that while they may subscribe to one or other form of a 'tension' theory of metaphor they would not limit the function of metaphor to 'the moment'. Indeed, while Ricœur is thus obliged to speak of dead metaphors which would appear to have enjoyed a very short life, Macky and others would insist that many metaphorical statements continue to provide insight and that one should even speak of metaphors 'retiring' rather than 'dying' in a long process of lexicalisation.

For Ricœur, metaphor does not only create new meaning it also has the ability to portray reality which he speaks of as "metaphorischen Wahrheit"[228] Thus the tension between literal meaning and metaphorical

---

221. *Ibid.*, p. 45.
222. Cf. M.C. BEARDSLEY, *The Metaphorical Twist*, in *Philosophy and Phenomenological Research* 22 (1962), 293-307.
223. G. RYLE, *The Theory of Meaning*, London, 1957.
224. RICŒUR, *Stellung*, p. 47.
225. *Ibid.*
226. *Ibid.*
227. *Ibid.*
228. *Ibid.*, p. 45.

meaning of a statement gives rise to "eine neue Vision der Wirklichkeit"[229]. "Die Ontologie der metaphorischen Aussage ist ganz und gar in dieser Spannung zwischen dem "ist nicht" und dem "ist wie" enthalten. Die Zweideutigkeit, die Verdopplung weitet sich auf das *ist* der metaphorischen Wahrheit"[230]. Understood as such, therefore, Ricœur would appear to side with those who view metaphor as a cognitive phenomenon and, by extension, a phenomenon which can inform us about God. Ultimately, I believe, all our three guides would accept such a statement without insisting that the function of metaphor be restricted to this dimension.

Hans Weder's important study of the *Gleichnisse Jesu*[231] stands in the same line as Ricœur in many ways. Such comparisons, he maintains from the outset, should be understood as metaphors, both being "*analoge Sprachphänomene*"(cf. also Bourguet and Macky). Biblical imagery, and comparisons in particular, therefore, belong in the context of metaphor. For Ricœur, Weder notes[232], metaphor has to do with the semantics of sentences rather than single words (cf. also Macky)[233]. Metaphor creates meaning in statements. It is a phenomenon of predication. Traditionally, Metaphor was seen as a rhetorical style figure, words of embellishment. Jüngel recalls in contrast that "Es gehört zur Eigenart der Metapher, daß sie zwei Sinnhorizonte zu einander in Beziehung setzt"[234]. Weder notes, therefore, that "Die *sprachliche Grundfrom* der Metapher ist also die eines *Satzes*, der mindestens die Teile Subjekt (S), Prädikat (P) und Kopula (K) hat; S – K – P. Die Metapher macht eine *Aussage*, indem sie einem S ein P prädiziert, zB "Achill ist ein Löwe.""[235]. As such, he maintains, the comparisons of Jesus are unmistakably metaphorical. With regard to biblical texts, we noted along with Stienstra that metaphorical statements can often be reduced to the A is B type. According to Weder, the "is" of such statements is used in a relational way (Relationalität der Kopula) and not in a real way (realer Gebrauch der Kopula). By insisting, however, that the "is" of the metaphor

---

229. *Ibid.* p. 51.
230. *Ibid.* p. 54.
231. H. WEDER, *Die Gleichnisse Jesu als Metaphern. Traditions- und redaktionsgeschichtliche Analysen und Interpretationen*, Göttingen, 1978.
232. *Ibid.*, p. 59.
233. RICŒUR, *Stellung*, p. 54.
234. E. JÜNGEL, *Metaphorische Wahrheit. Erwägungen zur theologischen Relevanz der Metapher als Beitrag zur Hermeneutik einer narrativen Theologie*, in P. RICŒUR and E. JÜNGEL (eds.), *Metapher. Zur Hermeneutik religiöser Sprache*, Munich, 1974, p. 112
235. WEDER, *Die Gleichnisse Jesu*, p. 60.

describes the subject in a new way but does not determine the subject, it would seem that Weder is not at home among those who would insist on a cognitive dimension for metaphorical speech. For Weder, 'is' constitutes a literal 'is not' and a metaphorical 'is' – clearly Achilles is not literally a lion! I believe all three of our guides would have difficulty with Weder in this regard. Macky would argue that metaphors can be both literally true and metaphorically true[236] while Stienstra would clearly be uncomfortable with the consequences of such a statement with respect to the cognitive dimension of metaphor. Bourguet, I believe, would drop the literal/metaphorical distinction and insist that 'A is/is not B' function together in the difference yet similarity which exists between the *métaphorisé* and the *métaphorisant*. Weder also recognises the tension between analogous aspects and differences between metaphor and comparison. At the same time, and in line once again with Ricœur, metaphors are said to work at the level of sentences as tension between words. Comparisons, Weder maintains, work at the level of entire compositions. His belief that metaphors are instantaneous, enduring only as long as the semantic clash between the words in question is observed, raises questions with respect to our access to metaphors in the bible. Comparisons have a degree of endurance which metaphors do not. Weder distinguishes between two types of metaphor: "gewöhnlicher Metapher" which remains inner-worldly and "theologischer Metapher" which elaborates the tension between God and world[237]. The latter type evidently raises questions concerning the truth of biblical metaphor. Although Weder sees metaphor as *sinnstiftend*[238], creative of new meaning, he also insists[239] on the difference between *Wirklichkeit* (reality) and *Wahrheit* (truth) where metaphor is concerned. The truth dimension of a metaphor is related to the fact that it touches on the reality dimension. Familiarity with the literal dimension of both S und P is essential[240]. This works for 'normal metaphors' but not apparently for theological metaphors. God has to be made known first, has to be made familiar for metaphors to create meaning. While Bourguet suggests that we subscribe to a relatively established divine isotope – filled by catachresis – rooted in both revelation and theological tradition, for Weder the fact that we can only know God through metaphors means that we are

---

236. 'Twice-True metaphors', an expression borrowed by Macky from T. COHEN, *Notes on Metaphors*, in *Journal of Aesthetics and Art Criticism* 34 (1975-76), 253-255.
237. WEDER, *Die Gleichnisse Jesu*, p. 62.
238. In line with Ricœur and Jüngel; WEDER, *Die Gleichnisse Jesu*, p. 63
239. *Ibid.*, p. 81.
240. *Ibid.*, p. 82.

confronted with a vicious circle. In his view we can only break the circle by God making himself known to the world. It would seem, therefore, that all theological metaphors, at least for Weder, must be mediated by revealed knowledge of Jesus the Christ[241].

Northrop Frye's *The Great Code. The Bible and Literature* offers an accessible reflection on metaphor in biblical texts, stating from the outset that "...the Bible is contemporary with a metaphorical phase of language where many aspects of verbal meaning cannot be conveyed except through metaphorical and poetic means. Frye, like Berlin, almost comes to identify poetry and metaphor. At the very least, he maintains, the bible – both in its poetry and in its prose – is full of associative and figured speech of verse[242]. As with our three guides, Frye is likewise aware that "... the Bible is full of explicit metaphors of the A-is-B type. Such metaphors are profoundly illogical (in that) they assert that two things are the same while remaining two different things"[243]. His use of the term 'explicit' here distances him from Stienstra, Macky and many others who would maintain that metaphorical concepts of the A is B type often lurk behind metaphorical statements. At the same time, however, Frye argues, that the use of metaphor in the bible is a frequent phenomenon which appears to have been intended as serious and not as merely poetic (sic). Indeed, metaphor is one of the bible's controlling modes of thought. Again much in line with Berlin, in her association of metaphor and biblical parallelism, and with Macky's seven basic skills for gaining access to the biblical author's intention in using metaphorical speech, Frye envisages metaphor as "... the use of a concrete paradox that enlightens the mind by paralyzing discursive reason"[244].

Frye goes on to distinguish between implicit metaphor (without predication) and explicit metaphor (with predication). He would appear, however, to subscribe to the idea that implicit metaphor permeates human language and thus the biblical texts are examples thereof because words are juxtaposed[245]. For Frye, the hermeneutics of the bible implies "bringing out the "hidden" meanings involved in pure juxtaposition"[246]. In this sense he is close to Macky. At the level of determining whether metaphors express truth, however, Frye appears to insist that the bible is

---

241. *Ibid.*, p. 83ff..
242. N. FRYE, *The Great Code. The Bible and Literature*, London, 1982, p. 51.
243. *Ibid.*, p. 54.
244. *Ibid.*, p. 55.
245. *Ibid.*, p. 59.
246. *Ibid.*

a literary document, "a structure of universalized or poetic meaning that can sustain a number of discursive theological interpretations"[247]. As such, therefore, he would appear not to favour a strongly cognitive understanding of metaphor: "In looking at it (the Bible) as metaphor, or a metaphor complex, we come up against the word "revelation," a word that does imply knowledge of a sort, even though it may not be knowledge of history or nature"[248].

Along similar lines, Eberhard Jüngel maintains that "Gott ist ein sinnvolles Wort nur im Zusammenhang metaphorischer Rede"[249]. For Jüngel, "Es gehört zur Eigenart der Metapher, daß sie zwei Sinnhorizonte zueinander in Beziehung setzt, die innerhalb einer Aussage durch zwei Wörter vertreten sind"[250]. Thus metaphors are not words but rather statements containing two (and usually more) words. This need not imply that metaphors resist reduction to the A is B typology, especially when one considers that such reductions are ultimately abstractions.

Between these two *Sinnhorizonte* there is a fundamental difference upon which a hermeneutical tension is established which initiates a linguistic communication between both. By uniting evidently different concepts, metaphor establishes a tension out of which something new emerges. Metaphor makes more precise, clarifies. Metaphor only works, however, if we are familiar with both *Sinnhorizonte*. As such, therefore, "Metaphern rufen in Erinnerung, indem sie Neues sagen"[251]. Metaphorical speech about God, therefore, requires us to have an initial familiarity with God. The problem remains, of course, that we can only get to know God via metaphor. We are in a vicious circle. For Jüngel, however, metaphor allows us to discover God. Metaphor makes precise, further defines. It works with familiarity and estrangement, extending the former and condensing the latter. Metaphors extend the horizon of understanding. As such, Jüngel would appear to be close to Ricœur (and thus Bourguet) in his approach to metaphor although this gradual process whereby metaphorical language allows us to 'discover God' goes beyond Ricœur's insistence on the instant-bound character of metaphor and Weder's dependence on revelation. Macky, I suspect, would also subscribe to Jüngel's understanding of metaphor in general

247. *Ibid.*, p. 65.
248. *Ibid.*, p. 67.
249. E. JÜNGEL, *Thesen zur theologischen Metaphorologie*, in J.-P. VAN NOPPEN (ed.), *Erinnern, um Neues zu sagen. Die Bedeutung der Metapher für die religiöse Sprache*, Frankfurt am Main, 1988, pp. 52-67, esp. p. 52.
250. *Ibid.*, p. 54.
251. *Ibid.*, p. 55.

as clarifying and making more precise. Macky's distinction between familiar (well-known) and un-familiar (mysterious) subjects, however, better explains the problem which emerges from an insistence on familiarity with both *Sinnhorizonte* in a metaphorical speech act. In Macky's view, it is our dependence on the concrete/familiar which allows metaphor to function and expand our knowledge of the unfamiliar. Metaphorical speech is essentially dependent speech.

The inexpressibility of God, for J.-P. Van Noppen, is limited to direct, literal, complete and appropriate language about God, or in other words: "der normalen Sprache"[252]. Such normal speech is thus incapable of speaking meaningfully about God. What other ways are there to speak about God, then, and what value do they have in redressing the problem of God-talk's arguable lack of significance? The classical definition of the relationship between divine reality and human language is that it is analogical. Van Noppen follows F. Ferré in this regard[253] and views "…die analoge Beziehung als eine"formale"Sprechweise beibehalten, die Regeln für den Gebrauch bestimmter Worte, die eigentlich anderen Bereich beheimatet sind, in der Sprache über Gott festlegt"[254]. On the metaphorical event in general van Noppen seems to adhere to Max Black's interaction theory although he notices that the theory would appear to give metaphor the capacity to create new meaning, meaning which ultimately does not belong to the components which make up the metaphorical statement. Thus it would appear that metaphor exercises a creative/cognitive function in discourse. What is the cognitive content and degree of truth associated with religious metaphor? Van Noppen notes that for Black, metaphor functions at a conceptual level, allowing the user to gain access to concepts which are often difficult to access. The interaction involved in the metaphorical process offers a new way of looking at a reality. The metaphorical process is thus instrumental, offering new perspective on the otherwise obscure. This clearly has relevance with respect to religious metaphor which frequently deals with the obscure. For Van Noppen, "… den Interaktionstheorien die Metapher nicht als verzichtbares Ornament betrachtet wird, sondern als eigenständiges Mittel, mit dem sich die Quellen der verfügbaren menschlichen Sprache erweitern lassen, eine Brücke zwischen dem Bekannten und dem

---

252. J.-P. VAN NOPPEN, *Metapher und Religion*, in ID. (ed.), *Erinnern, um Neues zu sagen. Die Bedeutung der Metapher für die religiöse Sprache*, Frankfurt am Main, 1988, p. 9.
253. F. FERRÉ, *Language, Logic and God*, London, 1962, pp. 76-77.
254. VAN NOPPEN, *Metapher und Religion*, p. 11.

Unbekannten, zwischen dem Ausdrückbaren und dem Unaussprechlichen geschlagen wird, dan gestattet die Menschen über Realitäten zu sprechen, die in eideutiger Weise nicht angemessen diskutiert werden können, und doch verstanden zu werden."[255] Ultimately, van Noppen maintains the cognitive claims of metaphor with respect to religious discourse may be real but must remain modest. Clearly the bridge to the inaccessible God established by religious metaphorical language is a narrow one.

It seems reasonable to suggest that each of our authors would support van Noppen's claims for metaphor, especially with regard to the modesty thereof. Where religious metaphor is concerned, then such 'cognitive modesty' seems most appropriate. Black himself was aware of the limits of the interaction process and Bourguet, Stienstra and Macky maintain a similar reserve. It is perhaps significant that Aquinas viewed analogical God talk as only partially informing us about the divinity. Even his five basic universals – God is being, one, true, good, beautiful –, which he includes among the 'absolute' concepts which can be applied to God, can never be complete in signifying the divinity. There is always a gap to be filled in the incomprehensible God. It is small wonder then that the bible, the source of most of our metaphorical God talk, is so varied in its employment of metaphorical concepts in relation to God. Such concepts, although often reducible to the A is B type, are always in need of further unpacking, further elaboration and further metaphorisation. The 'cognitive modesty' called for by van Noppen will, I hope, characterise the analysis of Isa 24–27 which we will undertake in the following chapters. At the same time, however, we can proceed with our interpretation of the metaphorical language of the bible – and of Isaiah in particular – with some degree of confidence. In line with Ricœur, Jüngel, Frye, van Noppen and many others we recognise that the bible is full of metaphorical language, that most of it constitutes an endeavour to say something significant about God and, although some might disagree, we can gain access to that something albeit in a limited and modest way.

6. METHODOLOGICAL STEPS

Our methodology will focus directly on those dimensions of metaphor which should concern us in examining a biblical text. Rather than present

---

255. *Ibid.*, p. 34.

the individual contribution of each of our authors once again, it seems more appropriate to the concrete investigation of the Hebrew text that we confront it with a number of important questions garnered from our research so far in order to discern the presence, type and intention of the metaphorical usage. After some preliminary points we can more systematically group these question under three headings:

Preliminary Steps[256]

(i) Establish the text from a text-critical perspective (see chs. III–VI). Textual criticism is necessary for establishing the text we intend to subject to analysis in our search for metaphorical language. It should be obvious that the determination of the presence of metaphorical language depends significantly on a text which has more or less resolved its textual problems. At the same time, given that the study of metaphor constitutes an element of the poetic analysis of a text it may in turn contribute to the determination of the text as such. An awareness of the fact that repetition, for example, is a primary feature of biblical Hebrew poetry, and that such poetic features often assist in providing the formal context for metaphorical speech, will help us avoid uncalled-for textual emendation. In the following chapters, however, text-critical discussion of the text of Isa 24–27 will be confined to the footnotes.

(ii) Establish syntactical shape of the text (see Appendix). The discussion surrounding the syntax of poetical texts is a complicated one and we have confined our treatment thereof to an appendix. Nevertheless, an awareness of the syntactical shape of a biblical text, its clausal hierarchy, the type of discourse involved together with the orientation of its speech constitutes a necessary preliminary to our search for metaphorical language. As Bourguet has noted, unusual syntax can often indicate the presence of metaphors.

(iii) Establish translation and colometry to allow for parallelism and other poetical features which might indicate the presence of metaphors to emerge (see chs. III–VI). Other textual and philological problems may come to light at this stage which require resolution. The primary aspect of the analysis at this stage, however, is to discern the presence of other

---

256. Considerable reference is made here to W.G.E. WATSON, *Classical Hebrew Poetry. A Guide to its Techniques* (JSOT SS, 26), Sheffield, 1995², pp. 12-44.

poetic features in the text which may provide the supporting structure for metaphorical language.

(iv) Delimit the metaphorical statements within determined poetical units on the basis of semantics, syntax and stylistics. What are its outer limits (see chs. III–VI)? What might be the signs of opening and closure? How do poetical units, once established, relate to one another?

Once these preliminaries have been completed to our satisfaction, the text should then be subject to a process of data gathering based on the following questionnaires. The questions focus on three main analytical themes which have emerged from our research into metaphor as a literary and biblical phenomenon. Once we have confronted the text with these questions we must then endeavour to interpret the data they make available to us.

Indicators

(i) Are there formal indicators in the form of Hebrew comparative particles: long metaphors – 'long shock' (i.e. with one or more comparative particles) or short metaphors – 'short shock' (without comparative particles)?

(ii) Are there informal indicators of metaphor: Syntactic surcharge via apposition or juxtaposition? One or other form of parallelism? Are there other poetic/stylistic features which might indicate the use of metaphor?

(iii) What are the semantic indicators of metaphor? Is there evident semantic incoherence, word-play?

(iv) What is the *métaphorisant* and what is the *métaphorisé*? Are both present?

(v) Are the isotopes which constitute the term(s) of the *métaphorisé* and *métaphorisant* distinct? In what way and to what degree?

(vi) Is the *métaphorisé* a corporeal reality? Is it the divinity? Is the *métaphorisant* a corporeal reality?

(vii) If we are dealing with non-corporeal reality such as God, can the metaphor be reduced to the A is B type, i.e. God is...?

(viii) Is this literal (independent of our familiarity with the terms involved) or figurative (dependent on our familiarity with the terms involved) speech?

(ix) Is there another type of 'horizontal' speech at work (metonymy, ellipsis, hyperbole, irony, joking, symbol saying etc.) employed by the author at the same level? Are there different 'vertical' levels in the speech act (i.e. which of the 'horizontal' features of the speech act enjoys 'vertical' priority)?

Type

(i) What type of metaphorical core/cross-reference is at work between the *métaphorisant* and the *métaphorisé*? At what level can we detect a degree of similarity between the two? Can we propose an analogical relationship between the *métaphorisant* and the *métaphorisé*? Is it positive, negative or neutral?

(ii) Is there more than one metaphorical core/cross-reference? Is there a secondary level of association between the *métaphorisant* and the *métaphorisé*?

(iii) Is the metaphor in question extinct (dead), dormant (retired) or active? Where on the scale between novel, familiar, standard, hidden (metaphorical concepts) or retired metaphors can we locate the metaphorical statement under analysis? Can we establish when a now retired metaphor may once have been novel?

(iv) Is the metaphor emphatic-active or resonant-active or both?

(v) Is there a metaphorical concept ('hidden'/'titular' metaphor) behind these and other metaphors in our text? Is there a metaphor of the 'A is B' type present in the text?[257] Do metaphors 'subsidiary' to the same metaphorical concept tend to cluster in a specific textual complex? Are they author specific?

(vi) Are we dealing with structural, orientational or ontological metaphors?

(vii) Is the metaphorical language culture-dependant or culture-exceeding?

(viii) Where the *métaphorisé* is the divinity, is the allegorical speech involved of the 'sanus', 'visus', 'leo' or 'bonus' type? Is the text expressing something absolute, relative or negative about the divinity?

(ix) Is the *métaphorisé* mysterious or well-known? Is the *métaphorisant* physical or non-physical? Is the metaphorical speech act 'one-way' or 'dual'? Are the metaphors ornamental and/or comparative?

(x) Are we dealing with 'Twice True' (both literally and metaphorically true) metaphors? Is there metaphorical simile (as opposed to literal simile) at work?

---

257. Eidevall seems to come close to the notion of metaphorical concept in his short discussion on 'themes' (repeated components throughout a text such as specific literary motifs, single lexemes, phrases, groups of related lexemes) which he suggests may have a structuring function as well as a metaphorical potential. Thus a theme running through a particular discourse may function as a 'vehicle field' (*Grapes in the Desert*, pp. 40-41).

(xi) Is the *métaphorisant* of the conventional or the insight type? How much of the metaphorical statement can be reduced to literal speech (is this a superficial or profound metaphor)?

(xii) Can we categorise the metaphor in question under a specific speech type: presentative, expressive, evaluative, performative, exploratory, pedagogical, affective, transforming or relational?

Author's Purpose/Interpretation

(i) Is the author intending to communicate information or present arguments or conclusions (presentative = ± cognitive)?

(ii) Is the author simply verbalising his/her own experience (expressive).

(iii) Is the author expressing his/her judgement on a particular event (evaluative)?

(iv) Does the author intend to change his/her audience(s) in some not exclusively intellectual way (dynamic)?

(v) Is the author intending to stir the audience(s)' emotions (affective)?[258]

(vi) Is the author intending to enlighten his/her recipient(s) in some way (pedagogical)?

(vii) Is it the author's intention to change the recipient(s)' attitudes, values etc. (transformative)?

(viii) Does the author's use of language invite his/her audience(s) to imaginatively explore their relationships (especially with God) in the light of what he/she says (relational)?

(ix) Does the author intend to evoke a personal response on behalf of his/her recipient(s) towards the speaker?

(x) Has the author rendered something unspeakable speakable by his/her use of metaphor?

Ultimately we are confronted with the question of meaning which, like any exegetical endeavour, will require a critical evaluation of the results not only of our search for metaphors but of all other levels of exegetical inquiry. Some preliminary steps in the direction of interpreting the meaning of the text, however, can be taken by confronting the information we have gleaned so far with the following questions:

---

258. According to Macky, the use of metaphor for affective, pedagogical, transformative, exploratory and relational intentions are of central concern to the biblical author.

(xi) Can we gain access to the speaker/author's meaning from the context?

(xii) Can we understand and re-construct the speaker/author's meaning?

(xiii) Can we explain the speaker/author's meaning, admitting that some of that meaning must and will remain hidden from us, but hoping that in so doing we will at least open a window into that meaning?

CONCLUSION

Having examined the basic principles governing the different approaches of our three authors, situated them in the broader context of the hermeneutical analysis of biblical texts and God talk in general, and devised a methodology for confronting the biblical text in search of metaphors, we can now proceed to analyse the text of Isa 24–27 armed with our 'questionnaire' and in the hope that our identification of metaphors, their type and intention, may provide us with a 'window' into the meaning of these sometimes obscure verses. This task will occupy us in the following chapters (III-VI). Our ultimate purpose is to ascertain whether this window might also shed some light on the questions raised by the history of exegesis of these chapters (chapter I). Equipped with new tools and with new windows onto the text, we will return to these questions in our final conclusion.

We noted in the general introduction that A. Berlin suggests that parallelism (in the broadest sense of the term) is the flip side of the coin to metaphor and that metaphor is the ultimate key to understanding the meaning of poetry *qua* poetry. This accounts for the first phase of our methodology, namely that of sifting the text for indicators of the presence of metaphorical speech. We noted further that P.D. Miscall proposes that in approaching the poetry of Isaiah we ought to do two things: 1) avoid the historical/theological and emphasise the literary/theological and 2) give priority to metaphor over meaning. His portrayal of the book of Isaiah as a labyrinth of metaphors, windows into the meaning of the text, accounts for the second and third phases of our methodology, namely those of identifying metaphorical type and ultimately endeavouring to enter the open window and interpret the metaphor and allow it to lead us meaningfully through the labyrinth.

CHAPTER THREE
ISAIAH 24

CHAPTER THREE

HEBREW COLOMETRY

24,1 הִנֵּ֨ה יְהוָ֜ה בּוֹקֵ֤ק הָאָ֙רֶץ֙ וּבֽוֹלְקָ֔הּ   וְעִוָּ֣ה פָנֶ֔יהָ וְהֵפִ֖יץ יֹשְׁבֶֽיהָ

2 וְהָיָ֤ה כָעָם֙ כַּכֹּהֵ֔ן

כַּעֶ֙בֶד֙ כַּֽאדֹנָ֔יו   כַּשִּׁפְחָ֖ה כַּגְּבִרְתָּ֑הּ

כַּקּוֹנֶה֙ כַּמּוֹכֵ֔ר   כַּמַּלְוֶה֙ כַּלֹּוֶ֔ה   כַּנֹּשֶׁ֕ה כַּאֲשֶׁ֖ר נֹשֶׁ֥א בֽוֹ

3 הִבּ֧וֹק ׀ תִּבּ֛וֹק הָאָ֖רֶץ   וְהִבּ֣וֹז ׀ תִּבּ֑וֹז

כִּ֣י יְהוָ֔ה דִּבֶּ֖ר אֶת־הַדָּבָ֥ר הַזֶּֽה

4 אָבְלָ֤ה נָֽבְלָה֙ הָאָ֔רֶץ   אֻמְלְלָ֥ה נָבְלָ֖ה תֵּבֵ֑ל

אֻמְלָ֖לוּ מְר֥וֹם עַם־הָאָֽרֶץ   5 וְהָאָ֥רֶץ חָנְפָ֖ה תַּ֣חַת יֹשְׁבֶ֑יהָ

כִּֽי־עָבְר֤וּ תוֹרֹת֙ חָ֣לְפוּ חֹ֔ק   הֵפֵ֖רוּ בְּרִ֥ית עוֹלָֽם

6 עַל־כֵּ֗ן אָלָה֙ אָ֣כְלָה אֶ֔רֶץ   וַֽיֶּאְשְׁמ֖וּ יֹ֣שְׁבֵי בָ֑הּ

עַל־כֵּ֗ן חָ֚רוּ יֹ֣שְׁבֵי אֶ֔רֶץ   וְנִשְׁאַ֥ר אֱנ֖וֹשׁ מִזְעָֽר

WORKING TRANSLATION

1   Behold, YHWH, he is about to depopulate the land and destroy her,
      and he will twist her surface and scatter her inhabitants.

2   And it shall be, so with the people, so with the priest;

      so with the servant, so with his master;
      so with the maid, so with her mistress;

      so with the buyer, so with the seller;
      so with the lender, so with the borrower;
      so with the creditor, so with the one who is given credit by him.

3   [She] shall be completely depopulated, the land.
      [She] shall be utterly despoiled.

      For, YHWH has spoken this word. ∞

4   She wails, she withers, the land.
      She is weak, she withers, world.

      They are weak, the high place[s], the people of the land.
5   And the land is polluted under her inhabitants.

      For, they have transgressed laws, by-passed precept[s],
      [for] they have broken the covenant everlasting.

6   Therefore, a curse consumes land,
      and they are held guilty, those who dwell in her.

      Therefore, they diminish, those who dwell in land,
      and what remains is a single man, a mere few.

7	אָבַל תִּירוֹשׁ אֻמְלְלָה־גָפֶן	נֶאֶנְחוּ כָּל־שִׂמְחֵי־לֵב
8	שָׁבַת מְשׂוֹשׂ תֻּפִּים	חָדַל שְׁאוֹן עַלִּיזִים שָׁבַת מְשׂוֹשׂ כִּנּוֹר
9	בַּשִּׁיר לֹא יִשְׁתּוּ־יָיִן	יֵמַר שֵׁכָר לְשֹׁתָיו
10	נִשְׁבְּרָה קִרְיַת־תֹּהוּ	סֻגַּר כָּל־בַּיִת מִבּוֹא
11	צְוָחָה עַל־הַיַּיִן בַּחוּצוֹת	עָרְבָה כָּל־שִׂמְחָה גָּלָה מְשׂוֹשׂ הָאָרֶץ
12	נִשְׁאַר בָּעִיר שַׁמָּה	וּשְׁאִיָּה יֻכַּת־שָׁעַר
13	כִּי כֹה יִהְיֶה בְּקֶרֶב הָאָרֶץ בְּתוֹךְ הָעַמִּים	כְּנֹקֶף זַיִת כְּעוֹלֵלֹת אִם־כָּלָה בָצִיר
14	הֵמָּה יִשְׂאוּ קוֹלָם	יָרֹנּוּ בִּגְאוֹן יְהוָה צָהֲלוּ מִיָּם
15	עַל־כֵּן בָּאֻרִים כַּבְּדוּ יְהוָה	בְּאִיֵּי הַיָּם שֵׁם יְהוָה אֱלֹהֵי יִשְׂרָאֵל
16a	מִכְּנַף הָאָרֶץ זְמִרֹת שָׁמַעְנוּ 16b	צְבִי לַצַּדִּיק

7   It wails, the new wine, it is weak, the vine.
    They groan, all the joyful-hearted.

8   It rests, the gaiety of timbrels.
    It ceases, the uproar of the exultant.
    It rests, the gaiety of the lyre.

9   With song no longer, do they drink wine.
    It is bitter, strong drink, to those who drink it.

10 She is broken, the town of chaos.
    It is barred, every house, from entering in.

11 A shriek of distress for wine is in the streets.
    It descends into darkness, all joy.
    It is banished, the gaiety of the land.

12 What remains in the city is gloom.
    [Into] a ruin is crushed the gate.

13 Indeed, thus shall it be within the land,
    among the peoples.
    Like the striking of the olive-tree,
    like the gleanings when the vintage is complete.

14 They, they raise their voice,
    they cry aloud over the majesty of YHWH,
    they shout from the West.

15 Therefore, in the East give glory to YHWH,
    in the islands of the West,
    [to] the name of YHWH, the God of Israel.

16a From the edges of the land praise songs we hear,
16b [praise songs] of beauty to the Righteous One.

16c	וָאֹמַר רָזִי־לִי רָזִי־לִי	אוֹי לִי
	בֹּגְדִים בָּגָדוּ	וּבֶגֶד בּוֹגְדִים בָּגָדוּ
7	פַּחַד וָפַחַת וָפָח	עָלֶיךָ יוֹשֵׁב הָאָרֶץ
18	וְהָיָה הַנָּס מִקּוֹל הַפַּחַד	יִפֹּל אֶל־הַפַּחַת
	וְהָעוֹלֶה מִתּוֹךְ הַפַּחַת	יִלָּכֵד בַּפָּח

18e	כִּי־אֲרֻבּוֹת מִמָּרוֹם נִפְתָּחוּ	וַיִּרְעֲשׁוּ מוֹסְדֵי אָרֶץ
19	רֹעָה הִתְרֹעֲעָה הָאָרֶץ מוֹט הִתְמוֹטְטָה אָרֶץ	פּוֹר הִתְפּוֹרְרָה אֶרֶץ
20	נוֹעַ תָּנוּעַ אֶרֶץ כַּשִּׁכּוֹר	וְהִתְנוֹדְדָה כַּמְּלוּנָה
	וְכָבַד עָלֶיהָ פִּשְׁעָהּ	וְנָפְלָה וְלֹא־תֹסִיף קוּם

21	וְהָיָה בַּיּוֹם הַהוּא	יִפְקֹד יְהוָה עַל־צְבָא הַמָּרוֹם בַּמָּרוֹם וְעַל־מַלְכֵי הָאֲדָמָה עַל־הָאֲדָמָה
22	וְאֻסְּפוּ אֲסֵפָה אַסִּיר עַל־בּוֹר	וְסֻגְּרוּ עַל־מַסְגֵּר וּמֵרֹב יָמִים יִפָּקֵדוּ
23	וְחָפְרָה הַלְּבָנָה	וּבוֹשָׁה הַחַמָּה
	כִּי־מָלַךְ יְהוָה צְבָאוֹת	בְּהַר צִיּוֹן וּבִירוּשָׁלַ͏ִם וְנֶגֶד זְקֵנָיו כָּבוֹד

16c But I say, "Emaciation is to me! Emaciation is to me!
Woe to me.

The treacherous deal treacherously.
[With] treachery the treacherous deal treacherously.

17 Terror and tomb and trap
are upon you, dweller of the land."

18 And it shall be, the one who flees from the sound of terror,
shall fall into the tomb,

and the one who climbs from the tomb,
shall be seized by the trap.

18e Indeed, the floodgates of the height are open.
They tremble, the foundations of land.

19 Torn, torn asunder is the land.
Split, split apart is land.
Shaken, shaken senseless is land

20 She staggers all over, land, like a drunkard.
She sways like a hut.

It is heavy upon her, her transgression.
She falls and she shall never again rise.

21 And it shall be on that day:
he will bring punishment, YHWH, on the army of the height in the
height,
[he will bring punishment, YHWH,] on the kings of the earth on
the earth.

22 And they will be herded [as] a herd of captives into a well,
and they will be confined to a cell,
and after many days they will be punished.

23 It will blush, the moon,
it will be ashamed, the sun.

For he reigns, YHWH Ts^{e}ba'ot,
on the mountain of Zion and in Jerusalem,
and before its elders [in] glory.

ANALYSIS OF ISAIAH 24

We begin our analysis with this first distinct segment (24,1-3) of the first major division (24,1-13)[1] of Isa 24–27. Our purpose as noted in the introduction will be to examine the text for indicators of the presence of metaphors, move on to characterise the metaphorical usage according to type and finally endeavour to establish the author's purpose on the basis of the clues provided by text and context with the aim of interpreting their metaphorical use. As we shall see, many commentators establish the primary major division differently but then demarcate vv. 1-3 as the initial sub-unit of their division. It is important for our analysis of the metaphors in these chapters, however, to be able to view the complex as a whole. Division into shorter segments will ultimately allow us to focus on metaphorical statements, delimited contexts in which metaphors are used by an author for a variety of purposes. Beyond this, however, it is of vital importance that the metaphorical statements of Isa 24–27 can be seen as a whole, and that these chapters, in the last analysis, constitute one metaphorical statement.

Isa 24,1-3

a   Behold, YHWH, he is about to depopulate the land and destroy her,
b   and he will twist her surface and scatter her inhabitants.

2a   And it shall be, so with the people, so with the priest;

b   so with the servant, so with his master;
c   so with the maid, so with her mistress;

---

1. Note the summarising tone of v. 13 and the shift from lament to expressions of joy in v. 14 (cf. D.G. JOHNSON, *From Chaos to Restoration. An Integrative Reading of Is 24–27* (JSOT SS, 61), Sheffield, 1988, p. 19). G.B. GRAY and A.S. PEAKE, *A Critical and Exegetical Commentary on the Book of Isaiah I–XXVII* (ICC), New York, NY, 1912, p. 408-14; E.J. KISSANE, *The Book of Isaiah*. 2 vols., Dublin, 1941; revised edition, 1960, p. 281; H. WILDBERGER, *Jesaja 13–27* (BKAT, X/2), Neukirchen – Vluyn, 1978, p. 912ff.; O. KAISER, *Isaiah 13–39* (tr. A.WILSON) (OTL), Philadelphia, PA, 1983², p. 181; J.D.W. WATTS, *Isaiah 1–33* (WBC, 24), Waco, TX, 1985, p. 313ff.; P. HÖFFKEN, *Das Buch Jesaja Kapitel 1–39* (NSKAT, 18/1), Stuttgart, 1993, p. 177; M.A. SWEENEY, *Isaiah 1–39 with an Introduction to Prophetic Literature* (FOTL, 16), Grand Rapids, MI, 1996, p. 325ff. all extend the first section through to v. 13 although their sub-divisioning may vary.

d   so with the buyer, so with the seller;
e   so with the lender, so with the borrower;
f   so with the creditor, so with the one who is given credit by him.

3a [She] shall be completely depopulated, the land.
b   [She] shall be utterly despoiled.

c   For, YHWH has spoken this word. ∞

Delimitation of Metaphorical Statement

Commentators establish the boundaries of the first pericope of Isa 24 in a huge variety of places, for example: vv. 1-20[2]; vv. 1-12[3]; vv. 1-7[4]; vv. 1-6[5]; vv. 1-5[6]; vv. 1-4[7]; vv. 1-2[8]. I take vv. 1-3 to be the first stanza of an announcement of judgement which extends from 24,1-13[9]. While the description of imminent calamity extends beyond these first three verses, the unit consisting of vv. 1-3 is clearly demarcated by verbal inclusions (ארץ/יהוה/בקק), has YHWH as subject throughout (the 'wailing earth'/ 'devouring curse' take over in vv. 4-6), and is focused on total devastation at both the natural and human levels which is expressed with succinct completeness by way of the hyperbolic v. 2 and the infinitive absolutes in v. 3. The framing formula in v. 3c also serves to conclude the unit, introducing retrieved, background information with *qatal* and grounding the prophetic communication in the divinity, YHWH.

Indicators

It is evident in this first section that there are no formal indicators of the type proposed by Bourguet[10] although it is equally clear that the

---

2. L.A. SNIJDERS, *Jesaja*. Deel I (POT), Nijkerk, 1969, p. 234ff.
3. E. KÖNIG, *Das Buch Jesaja eingeleitet, übersetzt und erklärt*, Gütersloh, 1926, p. 228
4. O. PROCKSCH, *Jesaia I. Erste Hälfte: Kapitel 1–39* (KAT, IX), Leipzig, 1930, p. 343.
5. A. CONDAMIN, *Le Livre d'Isaïe: Traduction critique avec notes et commentaire* (EB), Paris, 1905, p. 165; J. LINDBLOM, *Die Jesaja-Apokalypse: Jesaja 24–27* (Lunds Universitets Arsskrift, N.F. 1, 34, 3.), Lund, 1938, p. 13; L. ALONSO SCHÖKEL and J.L. SICRE DIAZ, *Profetas I, Isaias & Jeremias* (Nueva Biblia Española, Comentario), Madrid, 1980, p. 204.
6. C.J. BREDENKAMP, *Der Prophet Jesaja*, Erlangen, 1887, p. 147
7. F. HITZIG, *Der Prophet Jesaja, übersetzt und ausgelegt*, Heidelberg, 1833, pp. 291-293.
8. SWEENEY, *Isaiah 1–39*, P. 327
9. F. DELITZSCH, *Biblical Commentary on The Prophecies of Isaiah* (tr. J. Martin), Edinburgh, 1875, p. 421; H. WILDBERGER, *Jesaja 13–27*, pp. 912-930; WATTS, *Isaiah 1–33*, pp. 315-317
10. Comparative particles and comparative phrases; cf. D. BOURGUET, *Des métaphores de Jérémie* (EB NS, 9), Paris, 1987, pp. 24-37.

author is presenting us with three rather distinct isotopes: the divine, the enemy/hostility, earthly/human creation, which together serve to further delimit the metaphorical statement. The initial 'short shock'[11] is to be found in v. 1 with the juxtaposition of YHWH, the isotope of the divine, and the isotope of hostile enemy in the context of creation. The presentative הנה followed by a number of participles with YHWH as subject is offering a negative image of YHWH as destroyer, intent on despoiling and depopulating the land. We are immediately confronted with a *métaphorisé* (the divine – YHWH)) and an *énoncé métaphorisant* (hostility [participial forms] – and its consequences for creation both human and earthly). The concatenation of verbs of enemy hostility[12] is presented in an [a]bb'a' parallel structure with YHWH placed at its head in an emphatic position, all of which appears to be a literary procedure signalling the presence of metaphor. In a sense, the entire parallel expression constitutes the *énoncé métaphorisant*, [a] having a human focus and [b] an earthly focus, juxtaposed to the *métaphorisé*. The *métaphorisé* is clearly a non-corporeal reality which perhaps allows us to reduce our metaphorical statement to an A is B type[13], i.e. YHWH is the enemy, the latter being represented by the *énoncé métaphorisant* which consists of corporeal realities, both earthly and human, inclusive of an extended idiom (כ ... כ) focusing on the human dimension and its magnitude. It is perhaps here that we can point out a further non-formal indicator of the presence of metaphor, namely the semantic incoherence inherent in such a statement. Although YHWH is frequently described in hostile terms, such references would always have carried a semantic tension within them in the light of

---

11. Metaphorical 'twist' without comparative particle (cf. BOURGUET, *Des métaphores*, p. 13).
12. Cf., among others, D.J. LEWIS, *A Rhetorical Critical Analysis of Isaiah 24–27*, Diss. (UMI), The Southern Baptist Theological Seminary, 1985, pp. 48-49. בקק (NBDB 1238; DCH II 250; HALOT 150; NIDOTTE 1327 [KONKEL]) suggests the notion of 'emptying'/ 'devastating' the land; בלק (NBDB 1110; DCH II 182; HALOT 135; NIDOTTE 1191 [VAN DAM]) suggests the idea of 'laying waste', 'devastation'; עוה (NBDB 5753; HALOT 796; NIDOTTE 6390 [VAN ROOY]) implies 'twisting' / 'distorting' (used in 1 Sam 20,30) to describe Jonathan's mother as a perverse and rebellious woman; פוץ (NBDB 6327; TWAT VI 544 [RINGGREN]; NIDOTTE 7048 [CARROLL]); בזז (NBDB 962; DCH II 133; HALOT 188; NIDOTTE 1024 [DOMERIS]) means to 'plunder'/ 'despoil'. Although YHWH is the subject of the verb forms in 24,1, the parallel relationship with v. 3 'despoil' / 'plunder', which is clearly an enemy activity, suggests that both YHWH and the enemy have to be considered together, i.e. both engage in these hostile activities (positive analogy). The choice of the translation 'depopulate' for בלק is based on the internal parallelism with פוץ 'to scatter'. It is interesting to note along with Ringgren that the *hiphil* form of פוץ usually refers to the scattering of 'lightweight things'.
13. Cf. N. STIENSTRA, *YHWH is the Husband of His People. Analysis of a Biblical Metaphor with Special Reference to Translation*, Kampen, 1993, p. 38.

Israel's expectations[14]. The present verses (1-3) make this semantic tension even more apparent by way of the *énoncé métaphorisant* which contains a set of polar similes treating of various classes of people in three distinct steps: people & priest (religious life – monocolon); master & servant (household world – bicolon); buyer/seller & lender/borrower (economic world – tricolon). Clearly the author wishes to drive his metaphor home with some force.

A further indicator of the presence of metaphor here is the fact that the *métaphorisé* – YHWH – is used in a dependant and therefore figurative/metaphorical manner. Some might insist that any statement with regard to the actions of the divinity must of necessity be dependent or figurative, given that the 'isotope' of the divine is more or less 'empty' and that descriptive statements of the divine must therefore rely on other isotopes, most frequently that of the human[15]. Others insist that there are places where God is spoken of literally[16], yet the obvious presence of hyperbole in the present statement (esp. in vv. 2-3) suggests we should lean towards metaphorical (dependant) use rather than literal (independent) use. If we are moving in a world of apocalyptic or even eschatological scenarios then it might be possible to understand these statements 'literally'. Recent scholarship on these passages, however, while acknowledging that Isa 24–27 may lie at the origins of apocalyptic[17] or have eschatological inclinations[18], has tended to avoid such scenarios and focus on real and 'present' or at least 'imminent' events[19].

Stienstra notes that the metaphor 'YHWH is the enemy of his people' together with its entailments would have been regarded as untrue within the conceptual system of the Old Testament, thus making the 'metaphorical twist' even more tensive[20]. True or not, the use of the metaphorical concept[21] 'YHWH is the enemy' seems to bring together two evidently

---

14. See, for example, the great many expressions of contrast between the Israel's expectations of YHWH and their actual experience of him throughout the book of Lamentations. Cf. J. RENKEMA, *Klaagliederen* (COT), Kampen, 1993, esp. p. 149ff..
15. Cf. G. CAIRD, *The Language and Imagery of the Bible*, London, 1980-1988, p. 174; BOURGUET, *Des métaphores*, pp. 19-21; P. MACKY, *Centrality of Metaphors to Biblical Thought. A Method for Interpreting the Bible*, Lewiston – Queenston – Lampeter, 1990, pp. 229-241.
16. Cf. MACKY, *Centrality*, p. 189; cf. also Stienstra's suggestion of literal anthropomorphism in Gen 18,20-21, for example (*Husband*, p. 56).
17. This too, according to Johnson, is 'purely speculative' (*Chaos to Restoration*, p. 11).
18. KAISER, *Isaiah 13–39*, p. 177; WILDBERGER, *Jesaja 13–27*, pp. 957, 977.
19. Cf., for example, WATTS, *Isaiah 1–33*, p. 315, the reference being to 'a defined territory'; JOHNSON, *Chaos to Restoration*, p. 16.
20. STIENSTRA, *Husband*, p. 30.
21. *Ibid.*, pp. 35-40.

distinct isotopes. Notions of 'the divine' and 'the enemy', however, are related by way of analogy at both positive (similarity – YHWH is powerful; YHWH also engages in 'depopulation' / 'destruction' / 'twisting' / 'scattering') and negative (difference – YHWH is [usually] not hostile to his people; YHWH never 'plunders' his land) levels. The presence of both makes the 'tension' aspect of the metaphor all the more evident. Finally, it is clear that the *énoncé métaphorisant* is of the 'insight' type[22] in that it provides analogical insight into *métaphorisé* which is a more mysterious reality.

Type

It is evident in these verses that the semantic content of the *énoncé métaphorisant* (enemy/hostility) is being 'added' to the *métaphorisé* (YHWH) by way of a metaphorical speech act. This creates what Bourguet calls a 'rupture' at the core level (isotopic cross-reference[23]) of the metaphor – which I interpret to be the interjection of tension into the metaphorical statement – which ultimately allows for the creation of 'new meaning'. According to Bourguet's classification, it would appear that the primary core (*foyer*) in the present verses is a 'simple core'[24] rooted in implicit repetition which is explicit with respect to the *énoncé métaphorisant*, i.e. 'hostility' but implicit with respect to the *métaphorisé*, i.e. YHWH. There also appears to be a secondary core which is absorbed into the metaphorical concept 'YHWH is enemy', namely that 'YHWH is angry'. We noted above that according to Stienstra the attribution of emotions to the deity tends to fall within the framework of anthropomorphic metaphorical statements about YHWH which would include the metaphor 'YHWH is the enemy'[25]. In this sense YHWH is not angry as YHWH but as enemy. In any event, the metaphor clearly adds to the tension already established by the syntax (the nuance of events 'about to happen'[26]). YHWH is not only about to act, but his deeds will not be in line with covenant expectations, rather they will be in line with what the population of the land would have expected from a hostile force.

One can classify the metaphor employed here according to Black's categories[27] as 'active' since it would be readily recognisable as a metaphor

---

22. MACKY, *Centrality*, p. 54.
23. BOURGUET, *Des métaphores*, pp. 56-59.
24. *Ibid.*, p. 60.
25. STIENSTRA, *Husband*, p. 62.
26. WILDBERGER, *Jesaja 13–27*, p. 917; A. SCHOORS, *Jesaja* (BOT, IX), Roermond, 1972, p. 145 'futurum instans'.
27. Extinct, dormant or active; cf. M. BLACK, *More about Metaphor*, in A. ORTONY (ed.), *Metaphor and Thought*, Cambridge, 1979, p. 25.

by the reader/listener. As such, and in line with Black's further categories, the present metaphor is 'active-emphatic' in that it is a genuine interaction metaphor which gives the reader/listener 'food for thought', forcing him or her to reflect on what lies behind the words. The metaphor's evident richness in interpretative implications also classifies it as 'active-resonant'. According to Lakoff and Johnson's categories, the present metaphor would appear to be of the 'structural' type in that the isotope of hostility and destruction at least partially 'structures' our understanding of the isotope of the divine. We will return below to the notion of structuring as a dimension of the cognitive aspect of metaphors when we focus on author's purpose and intention. Stienstra's distinction between 'culture-dependant' and 'culture-exceeding' metaphors has its place with respect to the present metaphor. Arguments could be made for categorising 'YHWH is enemy' in both camps: 'culture-dependant' in that the images themselves speak primarily to those – past and present – who are familiar with 'biblical religion'; 'culture-exceeding' in that the notion of a protector (divine or otherwise) turning nasty would more than likely resonate as universally terrifying. I am inclined, therefore, not to make any option in this case.

In line with Van Es' analysis of Aquinas, we would have to place the present metaphor under the 'Leo' type of analogical speech. As we noted above, Thomas himself was not satisfied with the 'Leo' type because it appeared to attribute characteristics to God which would not have been normally associated with the divinity. In the present context the attribution of the content of the isotope of enemy hostility would appear to be an inappropriate way of speaking about God. In line with Thomas, however, it remains for such 'negative' metaphors to be further unpacked on the basis of other metaphors which can place the metaphor of a hostile divinity in its broader context. Such metaphors are abundant in Isa 24–27 and throughout the bible. While the present metaphor must be understood as a metaphorical concept which structures our understanding of the divine, it remains a relative concept on two levels: it expresses something about the *relationship* between the divinity and humanity (Thomas) and, at the same time, it is *relative* to our understanding of the broader context in which it is uttered.

Clearly our *métaphorisé* can be categorised as 'mysterious' while the *métaphorisant* (*éncncé métaphorisant*) is a *more* physical reality. Macky notes that such metaphorical types abound in the bible and this is hardly surprising, the physical subject giving insight into the more mysterious reality. Macky and others[28] point out that there is only one subject

---

28. MACKY, *Centrality*, p. 60; J. SOSKICE, *Metaphor and Religious Language*, Oxford, 1985-87, p. 49.

(*métaphorisé*) in a metaphorical speech act and that metaphors with physical symbols (*métaphorisant*) tend to be particularly 'one-way' in this regard, i.e. only insight into the *métaphorisé* is provided by the metaphorical statement and not vice versa. It is important here to note that the same is not true for non-physical symbols and this may be partly the case in the present context. The reduction of our metaphor to the A is B type leaves us with a metaphorical statement of the order 'YHWH is the enemy' the *métaphorisant* being a quite physical reality. It is possible, however, that over a period of time and in certain contexts the notion of 'enemy' was affected by its association with the divine and thereby took on 'supernatural' dimensions (and descriptions of such are not infrequent). Such metaphors Macky refers to as 'dual-direction' in which our understanding of the *métaphorisant* (symbol) is partly structured by the *métaphorisé* (subject).

We have already mentioned the possibility of the bible speaking literally about God. The present metaphor seems to allow for the possibility of making a literal as well as metaphorical statement about YHWH in that the events it predicts are not to be understood as imaginary but as very real indeed (if exaggerated by hyperbole). Macky would refer to such a metaphor as 'Twice-True': metaphorically true and literally true.

The metaphor employed by the author here must be considered 'novel' in the spectrum proposed by Macky. The limited nature of positive analogy between the *métaphorisant* and the *métaphorisé* supports such a categorisation as does the fact that it forces the contradiction of old views and institutes a new way of looking at reality. The metaphorical statement 'YHWH is the enemy' certainly draws attention to a level of similarity between the *métaphorisé* and the *métaphorisant* leading us to deeper insight into both.

We can categorise the metaphor in Isa 24,1-3 as 'performative' in that the author intends to tell us something about YHWH and thereby 'do' something, to bring about a new situation, to create and change human relationships by way of language, 'pedagogical' in that the author wishes to illuminate a 'dark' area of Israel's reality by way of a familiar *métaphorisant*, 'affective' in that it attempts to elicit an emotional response, 'transformational' in that it clearly employs both emotion and pedagogical insight for a rhetorical purpose, and 'relational' in that it says something about Israel's relationship with God and visa versa.

Author's Purpose/Interpretation

It is clear that the author is employing a metaphorical concept 'YHWH is enemy' in order to communicate information to his audience about

YHWH although his ultimate intention is more than merely informative. He is presenting an image of YHWH as a hostile enemy lying in wait or lining up his forces, ready to invade and destroy the land and scatter its population. Such an image is neither an expression of his own emotive state nor is it an evaluation of his present situation. His intention is clearly to change his audience in some way beyond that of providing intellectual information. The metaphor in question bears a partly pedagogical and partly transformative edge, but this is only made clear by the fact that the author's use of language constitutes an invitation to his audience to imaginatively explore their 'relational' experience with God in light of what he is saying. His intention is not to elicit a personal change of attitude among his recipients towards himself, but rather towards God. Perhaps in the midst of this metaphor there is an 'unspoken' dimension which somehow relates YHWH to the hostility of non-Yahwistic deities. It is clear that the dominant or 'winning' image in the metaphorical struggle[29] relates YHWH to a human enemy but there may still be a subliminal residue of a less palatable 'losing' image of YHWH as a hostile 'foreign' deity[30].

What, in the last analysis, does the author mean by his use of the metaphor 'YHWH is the enemy'? Macky informs us that we can gain access to the author/speaker's meaning via the clues he leaves in his use of terminology. Each word has a field of potential meanings from which the speaker selects (an) actual meaning(s) for his context. It was particularly the author's use of verb forms in these verses which led us into the isotope of enemy hostility. The evident verbal inclusion between v. 1 and v. 3 serves to underline this choice as does the author's use of hyperbole in the idiomatic expression of v. 2 and the infinitive absolutes in v. 3. The prophetic context, together with the framing formula in v. 3c, suggests we are in the presence of an announcement of impending judgement but we must be cautious at this point since our knowledge of the broader context of these verses is still limited and already chosen options among commentators might prejudice the outcome of our research. It is partly possible for us to reconstruct the author/speaker's meaning on the basis of what we already know since we can stand to a

---

29. M. BAL, *Metaphors He Lives By*, in *Semeia* 61 (1993) 185-207. Cf. also S. GRÄTZ, *Der strafende Wettergott, Erwägungen zur Traditionsgeschichte des Adad-Fluchs im Alten Orient und im Alten Testament* (BBB, 114), Leipzig – Bodenheim, 1998, who discusses Isa 24,1-6 (p. 144-146) and Isa 27,4 (p. 222-224), among other texts, from the perspective of Ancient Near Eastern weather deities and the imagery surrounding them.

30. Cf. M. GERHART, J.P. HEALEY and A.M. RUSSEL, *Sublimination of the Goddess in the Deitic Metaphor of Moses*, in *Semeia* 61 (1993) 167-182.

certain extent in the author's place, aware of the general, if unspecified, context of an impending disaster which will have 'supernatural' proportions. As we continue our analysis of these texts our knowledge of the broader context will grow and allow us to return to this initial metaphor and be more specific about the author's meaning. By reducing the entire metaphorical statement contained in these verses to the metaphorical concept 'YHWH is the enemy', however, we do at least open a window into the author's meaning. In the last analysis, we can agree to an extent with Long: "... what modern readers call metaphor among the writers of the Hebrew Bible for their God is testimony that through such figuration God, the Other, was comprehensible."[31] The biblical author must at least partly have intended to help his audience understand their God in all his dimensions.

A further question remains to be briefly discussed at this point, namely the significance of term ארץ (and its parallel synonyms: תבל & אדמה) for the author of these verses and the verses which follow. According to Watts[32], ארץ should be translated 'land' in the sense of 'civilised territory' (unlike תהו) while אדמה focuses more on the cultivable soil and תבל on the 'world' within the horizons of Ancient Israel's day. Such distinctions, however, are more limited than they might suggest today. For Watts they simply designate different dimensions of the same geographical territory which was Israel's 'world': Palestine, Syria, Mesopotamia and Egypt. As early as 1834, Bishop Lowth stated "The world is the same with the land; that is, the kingdoms of Judah and Israel; orbis Israeliticus"[33]. While maintaining that the terminology employed here must be understood as 'cosmic in nature', Johnson[34] argues along similar lines to Watts but arrives at a different conclusion. He translates the term ארץ consistently as 'earth' and argues that it constitutes the kind of hyperbolic language characteristic of theophany. Both authors are in agreement that the immanent destruction of הארץ (even when paralleled with תבל in 24,4) need not imply a world-wide or universal catastrophe. Together with W.E. March[35], Johnson proposes that we read the term 'figuratively' instead of 'literally',

---

31. G.A. LONG, *Dead or Alive? Literality and God-Metaphors in the Hebrew Bible*, in *JAAR* 62 (1994) 522.
32. WATTS, *Isaiah 1–33*, pp. 316-317.
33. R. LOWTH, *Isaiah: A New Translation*, London, 1834[10]; first edition, 1779, p. 263.
34. JOHNSON, *Chaos to Restoration*, pp. 25-26.
35. W.E. MARCH, *A Study of Two Prophetic Compositions In Isaiah 24:1–27:1*, Diss. (UMI), Union Theological Seminary, 1966, pp. 27-28.

i.e. that it does not designate a geographical territory (neither universal nor local) but as a figure for the 'unity of creation', 'the realm of nature'. I am more inclined to follow Watts on the matter and consider 'earth' – and its parallels – to be a geographical designation viewed from a variety of perspectives. The metaphorical statement in 24,1-3, however, tends to focus on the isotopes of 'the hostile' and 'the divine', while הארץ has a somewhat passive role. In the following verses תבל/ארץ take centre stage in the metaphorical statement as the *métaphorisé*, and, as we shall see, does express something of the idea of unified creation in relating earthly and human realities. In the last analysis, it is important that the term ארץ and its equivalents be read in context, a fact which can influence our understanding and indeed translation thereof

Isa 24,4-6

4a She wails, she withers, the land.
b   She is weak, she withers, world.

c   They are weak, the high place[s], the people[36] of the land.
5a And the land is polluted under her inhabitants.

b   For, they have transgressed laws, by-passed precept[s],
c   [for] they have broken the covenant everlasting.

6a Therefore, a curse consumes land,
b   and they are held guilty, those who dwell in her.

---

36. According to D. Barthélemy (*Critique textuelle de l'Ancien Testament, 2. Isaïe, Jérémie, Lamentations* [OBO, 50/2], Göttingen, 1986, pp. 172-174), the variety of readings of this expression are based on the fact the MT has a plural verb followed by a singular subject which consists of two nouns in the construct state, the second of which has a collective significance. This, he maintains, constitutes a *lectio difficilior* which has led to harmonisations and contradictory interpretations on the part of the witnesses and later translations, and in some cases to the omission of the term עם (1QIsa^a, Pesh.). While following the MT, Barthélemy and his team ultimately opt for the association of the term עם with מרום, leaving the reference to 'people' explicit and translating the expression as a reference to the élite of the land. Objections to this perspective maintain, however, that the whole population is affected by the calamity and not just the élite. The parallelism is inclusive of people/inhabitants and land. I interpret the term as 'high place', which, according to NIDOTTE (8123 [SMITH/HAMILTON]) occurs with some frequency in BI (16x). The notion of 'high place' might suggest that both Jerusalem and the surrounding land are included in this weakening and withering.

c   Therefore, they diminish, those who dwell in land,
d   and what remains is a single man, a mere few.

Delimitation of Metaphorical Statement

Several commentators establish vv. 4-6 as the following sub-division of vv. 1-13[37]. As we noted above with respect to vv. 1-3, the subject changes in the present verses from YHWH to 'wailing earth'/'inhabitants'. Thus the metaphorical statement in vv. 4-6 moves its focus from the isotope of the divine to the isotope of 'earth'/ 'world' and its 'inhabitants'/'dwellers' which constitute the *énoncé métaphorisé* while the isotope of 'wailing' / 'withering' / 'being weak' / 'polluted' / 'consumed' / 'held guilty'/'diminished'/'a remainder' constitutes the *énoncé métaphorisant*. The entire image in these verses, while alternating between earth and inhabitants as in vv. 1-3, dwells more on the earth and what is happening to it as a result of human failure and transgression than on the inhabitants and what is happening to them as a result of earth's destruction (vv. 1-3). Syntactically speaking the use of asyndetic *qatals* (cf. *Indicators* below) demarcates the unit from what precedes it ($w^e qatals$) as does the change of actant in v. 7 ('earth' / 'inhabitants' to 'wine' / 'joy' / 'mirth'). From a structural/colometric perspective vv. 4-6 also constitute a concentric pattern of bicola ($^{abcb'a'}$) turning around v. 5bc which is a quite 'literal' language not intended to be part of the metaphorical statement (^{a}: 4ab; ^{b}: 4c-5a; ^{c}: 5bc; $^{b'}$: 6ab; $^{a'}$: 6cd). The concentric shape of the metaphorical statement is based on the interplay between the *énoncé métaphorisé* and the *énoncé métaphorisant*. Thus the structural pattern leads us to view certain terms metaphorically because of their parallel relationship with other more clearly figurative language (see *Indicators* below). The central place of v. 5bc suggests that we envisage these words as the primary focus of the unit even although it appears to be unrelated to the metaphorical statement as such. The double על־כן in v. 6 "... acts as an effective device of conclusion"[38].

---

37. KISSANE, *The Book of Isaiah*, p. 273; P. REDDITT, *Isaiah 24–27: A Form Critical Analysis,* Diss. (UMI), Vanderbilt University, 1972, p. 73ff.; SCHOORS, *Jesaja*, p. 144 (sub-division of vv. 1-6) WILDBERGER, *Jesaja 13–27*, p. 912; LEWIS, *A Rhetorical-Critical Analysis*, p. 49ff. (vv. 4-6 constitute the first of three strophes dividing up vv. 4-13); JOHNSON, *Chaos to Restoration*, p. 21 (vv. 4-6 are a distinct pericope but they share vocabulary and tone with vv. 7-12); HÖFFKEN, *Das Buch Jesaja*, p. 177; P. MOTYER, *The Prophecy of Isaiah*, Leicester, 1993, p. 198 (a sub-division of vv. 1-20). Authors arrive at their divisions on a variety of different textual bases (genre, structure, syntax, semantics etc.).

38. LEWIS, *A Rhetorical-Critical Analysis*, p. 50.

Indicators

It is clear once again that the metaphorical statement in vv. 4-6 has no formal indicators in the form of comparative particles (and their equivalents) and is thus, in Bourguet's terminology, a 'short' metaphor presenting a 'short shock'. The *métaphorisé* is 'earth'/'world' and its 'inhabitants' which featured also in vv. 1-3. The alternation between earth and inhabitants continues here while the structure of the unit places the inhabitants of earth in a central position as was also the case in vv. 1-3. It is interesting to note that the tripartite categorisation of the land's population in v. 2 is reflected here in the triple causative of v. 5bc. In both the first unit and the present unit these statements do not appear to constitute metaphorical language although they are 'sandwiched' within an evidently metaphorical statement. The 'dwellers of the earth' in the present metaphorical statement are only presented in relation to 'earth' and not independently. While 'inhabitants' may be considered part of the *énoncé métaphorisé*, the primary focus thereof is clearly 'earth'. The *énoncé métaphorisant* is spread out over a number of verb forms in these verses and includes 'wailing', 'withering', 'being weak', 'polluted', 'consumed by curse' [indirectly also 'being held guilty', 'diminishment', 'remaining few'], all of which are part of the isotope of 'mourning' / 'sin' as well as that of 'desolation'[39]. Evidently, therefore, both *métaphorisé*

---

39. אבל is used for external acts of mourning or mourning customs (cf. Gen 37,34; 2 Sam 13,31-37) and not usually for the inner feelings associated therewith although this is not excluded. Elsewhere it refers to the devastation of nature and vegetation due to drought (cf. Isa 33,9; Jer 4,28; 12,4.11; 23,10; Hos 4,3) where it is often paralleled with יבש 'to dry up' (Jer 12,4; 23,10). It can also mean 'to be desolate' when paralleled with שמם (Jer 12,11) (cf. TDOT I 45-47 [BAUMANN]; DCH I 106-109; NIDOTTE 61 [OLIVER]); אמל likewise can refer to both humans and natural phenomena and can imply both emotional feebleness (Ezek 16,30) as well as 'being dried up' (parallel יבש Joel 1,12; Isa 16,8; 33,9; cf. DCH I 314; HALOT 63; NIDOTTE 581 [HAYDEN/TOMASINO]). Like אבל, אמל also has a secondary connection to the notion of 'shame' (respectively Isa 33,9; Jer 15,9) which surely has relevance in the present context. The notion of 'diminishment', or 'dwindling' is likewise part of the semantic field of this term (cf. 1 Sam 2,5; Isa 19,8; Jer 18,9; Hos 4,3); נבל has the general meaning of 'to sink' / 'to drop down' and can apply, once again, to humans (from 'exhaustion' Ex 18,18; from 'discouragement' 2 Sam 22,46; figuratively: of 'a good man' Ps 1,3; of 'Israel' Jer 8,13; of 'the wicked' Ps 37,2). The usual subjects are natural, such as trees (Isa 1,30; Ezek 47,12), leaves etc. (cf. NBDB 5034; NIDOTTE 5570 [HAYDEN]); חנף means 'to make godless' / 'to profane' and can be applied to persons (Jer 23,11) and (passively) to earth (Jer 3,1; Ps 106,38; cf. NBDB 2610; HALOT 335; NIDOTTE 2866 [AVERBECK]); אכל basically means 'to eat' and frequently occurs together with שתה ('to drink') as a sign of human well-being and happiness (Isa 21,5; Jer 15,16). Its negative side suggests the notion of being 'destroyed' or 'devoured' and is frequently used with 'locusts' as subject as they desolate and destroy the land (Ex 10,5.12.15; Joel 1,4; 2,5; Am 4,9; 7,2; Ps 105,35) and its natural produce (grass: Gen 3,18; Ex 10 12.15; Am 7,2; Ps 105,35) or with 'fire' / 'flame' which burns up and destroys the earth (Isa 1,7) or human persons in one form of another (Dt 7,16; Zech 12,6;

and *métaphorisant* are both present. The isotope of 'earth' / 'world' is clearly distinct from that of 'sin' / 'mourning', the former being solid, corporeal, inanimate reality (no matter how far it extends), the latter turning around negative concepts ('withering', 'being weak', 'polluted', 'consumed', 'guilty' [also 'diminished', 'remaining']) and expressed negative emotion ('wailing') more usually associated with sentient, human reality. The lack of formal indicators is certainly made up for by the abundance of informal indicators of the presence of metaphor. Syntactic surcharge is evident via the simple (asyndetic) juxtaposition of terms from both isotopes while consistent parallelism between the cola contributes to the confrontation of the terms in question with one another (both within the isotope and outside it) and heightens the metaphorical 'tension'. As we noted above, the concentric structure of this unit, focusing on v. 5bc, tends to lead us to search for the core of the metaphorical statement in this bicolon. The *énoncé métaphorisant* is also marked by stylistic features such as rhyme, alliteration, onomatopoeia etc. which serve to provide cohesion to the metaphorical statement.

Based on what we have noted already it is apparent that the metaphorical statement as such extends to v. 6. In vv. 7-13, a new *métaphorisé* is introduced ('wine'/ 'joyful noise' which itself constitutes an *énoncé métaphorisant* with YHWH as the unspoken *métaphorisé* as we shall see) and the entire metaphorical statement takes a different turn. It is also evident that we are dealing here with dependant and therefore figurative speech. All of the verb forms of the *énoncé métaphorisant* can only apply to the *métaphorisé* (earth) because of their already established connection with human persons and their psychological/physical states.

Ps 14,4; Hab 3,14; Prov 30,14 etc.; cf. DCH I 240-248; TDOT I 236-241 [OTTOSSON]; NIDOTTE 430 [O'CONNELL]). אשם in its *qal* form basically means 'to be guilty' and mostly refers to human persons (Ezek 6,6; Hos 10,2 etc.). It can also refer to a country (Judah Hos 4,15; Ephraim Hos 5,15; Samaria Hos 14,1 – signifying both territory and nation; cf. DCH I 414-415; NIDOTTE 870 [CARPENTER/GRISANTI]). In Ezek 6,6, אשם is parallel with חרב, which usually suggests 'to be dried up' (of 'waters'/'rivers': Gen 8,13; Isa 19,5; Ps 106,9; Jer 51,36 etc.) or (חרב II) to be laid waste, depopulated ('sanctuaries' Am 7,9; 'cities' Jer 26,9; Ezek 6,6; 'nations' / 'lands' Isa 37,18; 42,15; cf. NBDB 2717). Like אמל and אבל there is also as secondary association with sin (parallel חטא Lev 4,22) and 'being unclean' / 'shame' (parallel טמא, referring to Jerusalem); חרר (NDBD 2787 I; NIDOTTE 3081 [WAKELY]) basically means 'to be scorched' / 'to burn' which can apply to human beings ('burn with fever' Job 30,30) or to nature ('the vine' Ezek 15,4.5); nominal form signifies a 'parched place' (Jer 17,6 where it is parallel to עבר and figurative for the life of the godless); שאר has developed theological connotations which tend to shroud its original more neutral meaning, namely 'to be left over/alive' from a larger group (of people) or natural condition (land) after famine, plague or other disaster (human bodies and lands Gen 47,18; the land Ex 10,15; Josh 13,1ff., cities Jer 34,7; people Gen 7,23; Ezek 9,8 etc.; cf. TWAT VII 935ff. [CLEMENTS]; NBDB 7604 I; NIDOTTE 8636 [PARK]).

In light of the double meaning associated with the terms involved in the *énoncé métaphorisant* it is possible to envisage much of the present metaphorical statement in more literal terms, viewing it as a statement of the dry and empty earth in time of drought. Oddly enough, however, the two terms ארץ/תבל, according to the scheme proposed by Watts (see above), tend to refer more to the civilised world than the cultivable soil (cf. אדמה) which one would associate with the effects of drought. In this light, therefore, it becomes more difficult to reduce to literal speech and we must regard the metaphor of languishing wailing earth as 'profound' rather than 'superficial'.

At the horizontal level we appear to be in the presence of metaphorical language, at least in vv. 4-5a. Vv. 5b-6d appear to be non-figurative although, as we noted above, the concentric structure embraces them in the metaphorical statement to the extent that the terms involved can be included in the *énoncé métaphorisant*. In any event, the author does not appear to be employing other vertical levels of figurative speech simultaneously.

The analogical relationship between the *métaphorisé* and the *métaphorisant* appears to be 'neutral' in that it has both 'positive' and 'negative' dimensions. Both similarity and difference between the *métaphorisé* and the *métaphorisant* are rooted in the possibility of interpreting the isotope of the *énoncé métaphorisant* in both physical (non-human) and psychological (and thus human) terms. As with the focal metaphor in vv. 1-3, the level of analogical resemblance/difference is what allows the *métaphorisant* to provide insight into the *métaphorisé*.

Type

The primary core of the metaphorical statement in these verses appears to be located in the isotopic cross-reference contained within the terms of the *métaphorisant* ('wailing', 'withering', 'being weak', 'polluted', 'consumed by curse': terms from the isotope of 'mourning' / 'sin' as well as that of 'desolation'), in the ambiguity of the 'lamenting' (psychological) and 'parched' (physical) earth. K.M. Hayes[40] is correct (and not alone[41]) in pointing out that some of the roots involved in our metaphorical statement have a double meaning (overlapping isotopes) which has found its way into the dictionaries (i.e. it has been lexicalised): the physical/earthly (e.g. 'to dry up') and psychological/human

---

40. K.M. HAYES, *"The Earth Mourns": Earth as Actor in a Prophetic Metaphor*, Diss. (UMI), Catholic University of America, 1997, pp. 14-24, 187ff.
41. Cf. MARCH, *Two Prophetic Compositions*, p. 27.

'to mourn' (ritually as well as interiorly). It is within this ambiguity that we must search for the primary isotopic cross-reference between the *métaphorisant* and the *métaphorisé*. The ambiguity as such, however, makes the metaphor quite complex and, I believe, 'dual direction', the *métaphorisé* ('earth'/'world' and its 'inhabitants') and the *métaphorisant* in part informing one another. The primary core or isotopic cross-reference is evidently 'absent' in that it does not rest in the so-called 'middle ground' of resemblance between the *métaphorisant* and the *métaphorisé* but is contained or 'hidden' within the ambiguity of *métaphorisant* itself. It is thus the ambiguity established by the terms of the two overlapping isotopes (the *métaphorisant*: mourning/desolation) that makes it possible to view this as a metaphorical statement concerning earth and its inhabitants (the *métaphorisé*). While not specifically a 'word-play' core as it is defined by Bourguet, the isotopic cross-reference hidden within the terms of the *métaphorisant* is clearly supported and underlined by their phonetic similarity (esp. אמל, אבל).

Hayes has suggested that we are dealing here with a 'dead' metaphor, originally derived from observations that ritual actions of a mourner mimic the state of the earth in periods of drought[42]. If one were to accept that the metaphor in question is 'dead', however, then one would have to accept, along with Ricœur[43], that it no longer functions as a metaphor and this is far from the case in the present text. According to Black[44], the reader/listener would not recognise the etymology of the term(s) employed in the *énoncé métaphorisé* where 'dead' metaphors are concerned (he calls them 'extinct'). The very fact that the ambiguity of the terms involved here has been lexicalised suggests that the listener reader would be well aware of their dual significance and quite aware that they were being employed metaphorically. In Black's terms this would make our metaphor 'active' and both 'emphatic' (a genuine interaction metaphor) and resonant (rich in interpretative implications).

It may be possible to discern a metaphor of the A is B type in the present text, namely 'earth is mortal'. It is also possible to turn the entire concept around and suggest that 'mortals are earthly'. The link between 'earth' and 'people' is established in the primary metaphorical core and in the structure of the text: what the people do has an effect on the earth (pollution) – the earth's condition has an effect on the people ('guilt', 'burned up'). In this sense the metaphor works in two directions and

---

42. HAYES, *The Earth Mourns*, p. 20.
43. P. RICŒUR, *La métaphore vive*, Paris, 1975, p. 370.
44. BLACK, *More about Metaphor*, p. 25.

thus serves to underline the intimacy of the relationship between people and earth (or people and land). The fact that the *métaphorisé* is a well-known reality and the *métaphorisant* both physical and non-physical (emotional) at the same time allows for further possibilities in interpreting the metaphorical statement.

In terms of Lakoff and Johnson's categories of metaphorical concepts, the metaphorical statement in vv. 4-6 would appear to be 'structural' in that it encourages us to structure our understanding of earth/world (and its population) in terms of mourning ritual/pollution/sin. The presence of ambiguity in the *métaphorisant* also allows for the possibility of the metaphor being 'Twice True', i.e. both a literal statement about the earth (it is devastated, dried up) and a metaphorical one (it is in mourning). Stienstra's observation that certain metaphors are culture-dependant and others culture-exceeding also seems relevant here. Since the core of the metaphor is locked or hidden in the terms of the *énoncé métaphorisant* it is evident that modern readers, unfamiliar with mourning rituals of the Ancient Near East, would only partly understand the full extent of the metaphor (perhaps more as 'humans are earthly' than as 'earth is mortal'). To this extent the metaphor is predominantly culture-dependant.

We noted above that Hayes was of the opinion that the metaphorical of the 'mourning earth' has its roots in a 'dead' metaphor. Macky's broader set of categories which sets metaphorical usage on a continuum running from 'novel' to 'retired' obviates the need for a 'dead' or 'alive' debate. The analogy between mourning patterns/rituals and the parched earth may at one time have been more evident than it is today. In a certain sense, the modern reader would probably be inclined to see the metaphor as 'novel' since it draws our attention to a similarity which we did not already know. At the same time, the fact that the ambiguity in the *métaphorisant* has, to a certain extent, been lexicalised, suggests that even the modern reader would ultimately be able to find his/her way into the metaphor without too much difficulty. The 'dual direction' of the metaphor might even lead the modern reader into establishing analogies at a 'novel' psychological level (e.g. parched/scorched earth as metaphor for traumatised human psyche). For the author and his first 'audience', however, the content of the metaphorical statement in vv. 4-6 was probably quite evident, the metaphor thus being 'familiar' according to Macky's categories. As he notes, however, the positive and negative analogy between the *métaphorisé* and the *métaphorisant* was still enough to invite the reader/listener to approach this speech act as metaphorical and thereby explore the image offered by the author. In this sense the metaphor in these verses is not 'ornamental' but 'comparative' in that it invites its audience to explore the analogy (+ and -) between *métaphorisé* and *métaphorisant*. Macky also points out that such 'familiar' metaphors abound in the OT. We can certainly go along with Hayes in part in that the core of our metaphorical statement here seems to have been well on its way to 'retirement', i.e. to independent, literal use.

Author's Purpose/Interpretation

For what type of speech has the author employed a metaphorical statement? Clearly the metaphor is evocative of human emotion associated with mourning and the speech act might be described, thus, as 'expressive'. As we have already noted, however, the emotional dimension of the metaphor seems to take a secondary position to expression of mourning in ritual form. It would appear that the present metaphor is pedagogical in that it intends to illuminate the consequences of sin/transgressing with regard to ancient laws, precepts and covenant. At the same time the author may have employed this particular metaphor for the purpose of stimulating a sense of mourning in his audience related to a new awareness (transformation) of their misdeeds. In this way, one might categorise the speech act as affective as well as pedagogical and, thus, ultimately transformative. There also seems to be an element of 'relational' purpose involved in the metaphor in that the triangular relationship between earth/people/inhabitants is understood to be open to change (for good or bad) by the deeds of any one of the parties involved[45].

Given the concentric structure of the present unit it seems reasonable to assume that the author has employed a rather elaborate metaphorical statement to shed light on a 'real' (if primarily theological) situation of transgression and its consequences. The metaphor ultimately continues on from the announcement of judgement begun in vv. 1-3 in which the metaphor of 'YHWH as enemy' took centre stage. To a certain degree, therefore, vv. 4-6 (esp. 5bc and 6a) present the audience with a particular argument or communicate information (transgress and you will suffer the consequences) but this 'presentative' (or 'cognitive') dimension of the text remains secondary. The primary focus of the author is on the results of the judgement announced in vv. 1-3 which turn around the inharmonious triangular relationship between earth (including its 'high places' which we take to mean 'heavens'[46]), inhabitants and God who ultimately brings about judgement. Although not directly mentioned in

---

45. MACKY, *Centrality*, p. 17
46. Cf. SNIJDERS, *Jesaja*, pp. 235-236; SCHOORS, *Jesaja*, p. 145.

these verses, God is present in the person of the prophet as well as in the various allusions to breaking covenant. We can also agree with Motyer[47] on this point: "Every covenant dispensation had its regulatory aspect, however undeveloped it may have been in comparison with the normative Mosaic system. This may be why Isaiah used the plural *laws*, so as to cover every period and aspect of covenant law-giving. (...) In essence, the annulling of the covenant was the refusal to live in the fellowship which God opened"[48]. The relationship between God and humans is disturbed, and this reveals itself in the relationship between humans and earth insinuated by the metaphor. Earth dries up (natural phenomenon) and mourns (human phenomenon). Humans pollute the earth instead of cultivating it and as a consequence they too are diminished, dried up, scorched; they too wail along with the earth[49]. While the author is clearly offering a judgement of the situation, evaluating what he sees, and inviting his audience to reflect on what he says and ultimately change their ways, his primary purpose here seems to be relational. He invites his audience to explore their relationship with earth and with God, cunningly establishing a triangular relationship between them: between humans and earth via the metaphorical statement and between God and humans/earth via the allusions to broken covenant.

As with vv. 1-3, the author has provided us with a sufficiency of signs, permitting us to gain access to the 'speaker's meaning'. From the field of potential meanings surrounding the terms of the *énoncé métaphorisant*, the author has selected a double focus, encouraging his audience to view the earth/world in human terms and, by extension, to view humans in earthly terms. By employing these metaphorical terms in the context of a central statement about the transgression of laws and the breaking of covenants (5bc), the author sets up a two-way image of dysfunctional relationship: between God and his people (humanity?) and between the people and the earth (and visa versa). Since the significance of the terms involved is partly accessible to the modern reader, even beyond the cultural gap which separates us from these texts, it

---

47. Motyer notes that the expression 'everlasting covenant' is "...used of the Noahic covenant (Gen 9,16; cf. also I. FISCHER, *Tora für die Israel – Tora für die Völker: Das Konzept des Jesajabuches* [SBS, 164], Stuttgart, 1995, who understands the transgression here to be against the Noahic covenant [Gen 9,5-6.16] which calls for cosmic, flood-like consequences for the earth), the Lord's covenant dispensation reaching back to Abraham (Ps 105,10), the Sabbath within the Mosaic covenant (Lev 24,8) and the Davidic covenant (2 Sam 23,5)..." (p. 199).
48. MOTYER, *Prophecy of Isaiah*, p. 199.
49. Note the inclusive effects of v. 4ab (withering earth) and v. 6cd (burned up, diminished humans).

remains possible for audiences of any age to have participant knowledge of the author's/speaker's meaning and gain (limited) access thereto. In line with Macky's approach to the imaginative re-construction of the speaker's meaning, it is possible, to a degree, to stand in the author's place and understand his statement before evaluating it and interpreting it. The statement and its terminology is not obscure and, at the same time, the author employs his stylistic skills to call our attention to the essentials of his speech act. While acknowledging the mystery involved in the process of meaning, it seems possible and is perhaps even essential, at least in these verses, to restate the entire metaphorical statement in a way which explicitly unlocks the ambiguous content of the *énoncé métaphorisant*. Knowing that these terms have an earthly and a human referent has in fact led us to reduce the metaphorical statement to the A is B type (see above). Taking all the factors into consideration we can now nuance that statement: for God, earth is mortal – for God, humans are earthy, both earth and its inhabitants are mutually destructive when their relationship with God is severed.

Since it has been one of our principles to view metaphors in the context of speech acts and broader metaphorical statements, we will have to reserve judgement on the full and primary message contained in the speaker's meaning until we have completed our analysis of the larger unit vv. 1-13. So far, however, we have opened two windows into that meaning.

Isa 24,7-13

7   It wails, the new wine, it is weak, the vine.
    They groan, all the joyful-hearted.

8   It rests, the gaiety of timbrels.
    It ceases, the uproar of the exultant.
    It rests, the gaiety of the lyre.

9   With song no longer, do they drink wine.
    It is bitter, strong drink, to those who drink it.

10 She is broken, the town of chaos.
    It is barred, every house, from entering in.

11 A shriek of distress for wine is in the streets.
    It descends into darkness, all joy.
    It is banished, the gaiety of the land.

12   What remains in the city is gloom.
     [Into] a ruin is crushed the gate.

13   Indeed, thus shall it be within the land,
     among the peoples.
     Like the striking of the olive-tree,
     like the gleanings when the vintage is complete.

Delimitation of Metaphorical Statement

Along with most modern commentators[50], we understand the present unit to begin with v. 7 and to end with v. 12. V. 13 is frequently considered to be a (redactional) summary conclusion, referring back to both the previous unit and the present one[51]. In itself it extends the metaphorical statement in an explanatory manner (cf. the formal indicators). Lewis suggests that we are dealing with two independent strophes: vv. 7-9 and 10-13[52] but, as we shall see below, it is clear from the complex parallel structure of the unit taken from vv. 7-12 that what appears to be a thematically different second strophe (dealing with the town of *tohû*) has to be read together with vv. 7-9 (lack of joy and mourning wine).

It might appear at first sight that the only strictly metaphorical language in this unit is to be found in v. 7a since all the other affirmations can be taken literally. If we accept the colometric shape of the unit (2-3-2 // 2-3-2), however, we can see how external parallelism brings terms into contact with one another further extending and substantiating the metaphorical statement beyond single verses. Thus v. 7 (bicolon) has to be read alongside v. 10 (bicolon), v. 8 (tricolon) alongside v. 11 (tricolon) and v. 9 (bicolon) alongside v. 12 (bicolon).

At both the syntactical and semantic level, the introduction of new actants indicates a new beginning and a new unit in v. 7. While the actants are indeed new they do not lose their connection with the previous unit(s), 'wine' being the fruit of ארץ and 'joy' the emotion of its inhabitants. When both are present it is clear that the three-way relationship between YHWH, earth and human persons is in balance. Once again,

---

50. SCHOORS, *Jesaja*, p. 147; ALONSO SCHÖKEL and SICRE DIAZ, *Profetas I*, p. 204; J.N. OSWALT, *The Book of Isaiah, Chapters 13–39* (NICOT), Grand Rapids, MI, 1986, p. 443; HÖFFKEN, *Das Buch Jesaja*, p. 177; MOTYER, *Prophecy of Isaiah*, p. 200ff.; SWEENEY, *Isaiah 1–39*, p. 326; HAYES, *The Earth Mourns*, p. 193ff. etc..

51. HÖFFKEN, *Das Buch Jesaja*, p. 177; LEWIS, *Rhetorical-Critical Analysis*, p. 63; cf. also WILDBERGER *Jesaja 13–27*, pp. 928-929; SCHOORS, *Jesaja*, p. 147, etc..

52. LEWIS, *Rhetorical-Critical Analysis*, p. 63ff.; cf. also WILDBERGER, *Jesaja 13–27*, pp. 925-928.

however, the author of these verses is employing a complex metaphorical statement to suggest that the opposite is also true. Thus YHWH is also 'present' in the metaphorical statement by YHWH's absence. A portion of the terminology employed in the previous unit is also carried over into the present one, suggesting that they should not be read in strict isolation. The wine/vine 'wails' (אבל) and is 'weak' (אמל) and the 'joy' of ארץ's inhabitants is diminished. We can agree with Hayes, therefore, that while the psychological dimension of these terms seems to predominate in the present unit, the physical dimension of drought is not absent, the suggestion of a failed harvest being stated over-abundantly in the frequently repeated negation of the joy and celebration usually associated therewith[53]. The blend of terminology open to psychological and natural/physical interpretation continues in שבת and חדל[54]. We can likewise agree with Hayes' suggestion[55] that the terminology in vv. 10-12 which centres around the 'town of *tohû*' (more on which below), leaves the impression of military invasion and defeat linking up with the metaphorical statement in 24,1-3 in which it was evident that YHWH was the enemy[56]. The connection between emotional states and actual, physical devastation, however, is far from absent. It has simply moved from the fields into the city. The multiple significance of the verbal roots שבר, סגר, שאר, גלה, ערב and כתת further supports this proposal[57]. Thematically,

53. HAYES, *The Earth Mourns*, p. 206.
54. While שבת basically means 'to cease', 'to come to an end', its positive associations with the Sabbath rest in Exod 34,21 and the notion of the rest of the land in the 7th year in Lev 26,34.35 cannot be overlooked. To employ such a term with 'the gaiety of the timbrel/lyre' as subject would certain have been considered an ironic statement (cf. TWAT VII 1041-1046 [HAAG]; NBDB 7673; NIDOTTE IV, p. 1157 [BOSMAN]). חדל, on the other hand, has the basic meaning 'to cease' performing a particular activity it can also mean 'to withdraw' in the face of hostility (1 Sam 23,13; Jer 41,8; 51,30). Elsewhere it carries the nuance of being rejected or forsaken (1 Sam 9,5; 10,2). Interestingly enough it is used of Sarah in Gen 18,1 to refer to the end of her menstruation, i.e. she was no longer fruitful (cf. TDOT IV 216-221 [FREEDMAN/LUNDBOM]; NIDOTTE 2532 [HILL]).
55. Following B. DUHM, *Das Buch Jesaia übersetzt und erklärt*, Göttingen, 1902², p. 146) & GRAY, *A Critical and Exegetical Commentary on the Book of Isaiah I–XXVII*, p. 413.
56. HAYES, *The Earth Mourns*, p. 209.
57. The basic meaning of שבר is 'to break into pieces' (cf. Judg 7,20; Lev 11,33; Jer 49,35). It can also stand for the deliverance implied in the breaking of a siege or similar (e.g. Jer 28,2.4.11; 38,8). Most importantly for our purpose, however, the *niphal* can be used to suggest a 'broken heart' (cf. NBDB 7665; TWAT VII 1027-1040 [KNIPPING]; NIDOTTE 8689 [HAMILTON]). The *qal* of סגר basically means 'to shut in' and the *pual* 'to be shut up'. A further meaning of the *qal*, however, speaks of the closing of the womb (1 Sam 1,6), a sign of infertility related also to v. 8b (cf. NBDB 5462; HALOT 743; NIDOTTE 6037 [ARNOLD]). ערב V is related to sundown and the oncoming of darkness. As such it is used metaphorically here for the transformation of joy into misery. There may also be the hint of a reference to ערב IV from which the term ערבה 'desert place' is derived (cf. NBDB

therefore, the entire metaphorical statement is related to the previous unit, moving from the wider concepts of the earth and its inhabitants through the vineyards on the outskirts of the city and into the city itself. Everywhere it is the same: chaos and devastation and gloom.

Indicators

There appear to be no formal indicators of the presence of metaphor in this text although a (partly) new *énoncé métaphorisé* is clearly introduced in vv. 7-12 [13] ('wine'/'joyful noise'/ 'gaiety'/'uproar' = festival). Thus the metaphorical statement takes a different turn which partly contributes to its delimitation. The isotope of the *énoncé métaphorisant* is constituted by a complex of words each with a negative significance and many with both a human/psychological orientation and natural/earthly orientation, continuing yet augmenting the *métaphorisant* of the previous unit: 'wailing'/'groaning'/'resting'/'ceasing'/'bitterness'/'brokenness'/'inaccessibility'/'shrieking'/'darkening'/'banishment'/'remaining'/'crushing'. As we already noted, many of these terms have to do with waning nature (both earthly and human). Thus the isotope of the *métaphorisant* continues to carry the ambiguity we noted with regard to the preceding unit. The isotope of the *métaphorisé* is taken from the world of festival with its dimensions of joyous celebration, singing, dancing and imbibing the fruits of the harvest. Once again it is clear that the entire metaphorical statement places these two distinct isotopes together and in the encounter the *énoncé métaphorisé* is changed. Festival is banished, turned into mourning, drowned by darkness. In a certain sense, terms such as 'wine'/'joyful noise' themselves constitute an *énoncé métaphorisant* with YHWH as the unspoken *métaphorisé*. YHWH's absence, withdrawal, is the reason for this state of affairs.

Apart from the lexicographic/semantic evidence of the presence and extent of the metaphorical statement in vv. 7-12, both are underlined by the parallel structure of the unit. The unit constitutes a diptych in which the centre of each panel presents a statement of the metaphor in the clear

---

6150, 6160; HALOT 877; NIDOTTE 1332 [KONKEL]. גלה basically means 'to remove' or (trans.) 'to depart'. It clearly has strong connotations with the idea of depopulation and exile (cf. 2 Kgs 17,23; Isa 5,13; Jer 1,3 etc.; cf. also Isa 24,1-3). While it usually refers to human beings and here refers to the 'joy of the earth' it can also refer to the disappearance of such natural things as, for example, 'grass' (cf. Prov 27,25). Both ארץ (Judg 18,30) and Jerusalem (Jer 1,3) can be its subject (cf NBDB 1540; HALOT 191; NIDOTTE 1655 [HOWARD]). For the meaning of שאר see footnote 39. כתת in the *qal* means 'to beat or crush' and is basically the same in the *hophal* (only passive) 'to be crushed'. The term can be used figuratively, however, to refer to persons (frail human person – Job 4,20; NIDOTTE 4198 [VAN DAM])

juxtaposition of elements from each isotope (8b & 11b). It is primarily the strong parallel between 8a-c and 11a-c which unites both panels. Internal parallelism unites what are more evidently metaphorical expressions with what can be taken as quite literal expressions, thus drawing them into the wider metaphorical statement. In v. 7, the 'joyful hearted' are paralleled with the 'new wine' and both 'wail' and 'groan'. In v. 9 the absence of 'song' is paralleled with the absence of 'wine', the people involved being forced to drink 'strong drink' which does not bring joy but rather bitterness. In v. 10, the 'town of *tohû*' is presented/personified as being broken. The terminology suggests both physical and emotional brokenness (broken heart) which relates it by external supplementary parallelism with v. 7. The 'town of *tohû*'s' internal parallel is 'every house' which is presented as boarded up and barred as if the population had abandoned the city. In v. 12, the city is paralleled with gate as the focal point of its social existence. By external parallelism, the gloom of the city is associated with the brokenness of the 'town of *tohû*'. At the same time as the entry to 'every house' is barred – with its suggestion of the absence of family life –, so the main entrance to the city is a ruin – suggesting the absence of social life as a whole. Thus literal (independent) speech and figurative (dependent) speech are intertwined in a complex parallel structure.

A further indicator of the presence of metaphor is evident in the semantic incoherence involved in such expressions as 'It wails, the new wine, it is weak, the vine' (v. 7a) or 'It descends into darkness, all joy' (v. 11b). At the same time, the incessant hammering repetition of the negative terminology of the *énoncé métaphorisant* intensifies it to the extent that the *énoncé métaphorisé* (wine/joy/festival) is almost completely swamped by it.

It is difficult in the present unit to determine whether the *métaphorisé* and the *métaphorisant* are either corporeal or non-corporeal. The metaphorical statement is too complex to permit such a distinction. At the same time, it is evident in the use of ambiguous terminology that both emotional states and physical states are present in the metaphorical statement.

The elements of *métaphorisant* are clearly of the 'insight' type in that they juxtapose familiar yet ambiguous terminology of destruction and diminishment with the emotional state of the human persons and their social existence ('town of *tohû*') and the 'emotional state' of ארץ and its produce ('wine/vine').

Type

The isotopic cross-reference between the *métaphorisé* and the *métaphorisant* is similar to that of the preceding unit, indeed a number of terms from the preceding *métaphorisé* are explicitly repeated. The joyful emotional state of festival revellers, who normally celebrate the new wine (produce of ארץ) with song, dance, music and gaiety of every kind, is placed side by side with a variety of terms from the word-field or isotope of mourning, cessation, devastation and banishment. In line with the preceding metaphorical statement, therefore, we can conclude that the core is 'absent', lying hidden in the ambiguity (both psychological and physical) of the terminology of the *métaphorisant* rather than in any similarity between the *métaphorisé* and the *métaphorisant*. In addition, an examination of Bourguet's categories might also suggest that we are dealing here with a 'diffuse' metaphorical core, one which tends to be evoked by the entire metaphorical expression rather than specific points of cross-reference between individual terms.

Also in line with the previous unit, YHWH (or his absence), although not explicitly present in the metaphorical statement, appears to be part of the scene, constituting a *métaphorisé* with wine/joy/civil and family life (cosmos: or its absence) as the *métaphorisant*. In this dimension of the metaphorical speech act, therefore, the *métaphorisé* (YHWH) itself would appear to be absent, only made implicitly present in the semantic content of the terms of the *métaphorisant* (cosmos). In this context we are dealing with a 'simple' core, resting in the semantic middle ground or point of cross-reference between the *métaphorisé* (YHWH) and the *métaphorisant* (cosmos). As with the preceding unit, therefore, the metaphorical statement at work here is complex, multi-directional and exhibiting more than one core.

Ultimately, therefore, we are confronted here with a two-dimensional metaphorical statement, both aspects inextricably linked with one another: 'wine/joy/cosmos as mourning, devastated, darkened, banished' and 'YHWH as (the absence of) wine[58]/joy/cosmos'. According to Black's categories the first dimension would be both 'active-emphatic', providing its audience with much food for thought and 'active-resonant' in that it is rich in interpretative connotations and would be readily recognisable as a metaphor to its readers/listeners. At the same time one might be able to discern a metaphor of the A is B

---

58. It is interesting to note here in passing that יין, גפן, and תירוש are used throughout the bible as a symbol/metaphor for God's generosity / abundance / blessing / *Segensgabe* (cf. TDOT VI 64 [DOMMERHAUSEN]; TDOT III 53-61 [HENTSCHKE]; TWAT VIII 647 [FLEISCHER]). At the same time, the lexica also point out the other side of these terms as 'punishment', 'cup of wrath'. One might be tempted to translate v. 11a as irony or as a pun: the longing for the wine of blessing and the actual presence of the 'cup of wrath'.

type in the continuation of the previous (vv. 4-6) notion of 'earth is mortal' being extended to the 'town/city is mortal'. While the metaphorical statement in the present verses extends its initial connotations in 'mourning ritual', it now focuses less on the 'earthly' and more on the human dimension at the personal, liturgical, family and civil levels. Everything is engulfed in darkness and the almost palpable silence is only occasionally pierced with a shriek of distress from one of the city's inhabitants. Once again the metaphor here is of the 'structural' type in that it encourages its audiences to structure their understanding of each level of their environment in terms of cessation, barrenness, absence all of which are locked into the ambiguity of the terminology of the *métaphorisé* thus making the metaphor less accessible to cultures unfamiliar with the language and once again primarily culture-dependant. The awareness that חדל, for example, has associations with the cessation of menstruation and, therefore, with the end of human fertility (and this has links throughout the text complex Isa 24–27) would not have been wasted on its Hebrew audience. Ultimately the continuation of a mix of both well-known realities and less tangible, emotional states further allows the metaphorical statement its richness. Once again the presence of ambiguity in the *métaphorisant* allows for the possibility of a 'Twice True' metaphor – both a literal and a metaphorical statement being involved in the speech act. As with the previous metaphorical statement, the semantic content of the terminology involved was probably quite evident to its Hebrew audience, making the metaphor 'familiar' according to Macky's categories. The positive and negative analogy between the *métaphorisant* and the *métaphorisé* would have been sufficient still to invite the audience to explore the analogy ('comparative' as opposed to 'ornamental') and ultimately to approach these verses as metaphorical. Finally, with regard to the type of speech for which the author has employed metaphor it would appear that the primary focus is 'expressive', focusing on human emotion. Rooted in the connection between this and the preceding metaphorical statement we might also be able to discern a pedagogical purpose here – all of this devastation being the further result of sin and transgression (cf. v. 5bc). In light of the second dimension of the metaphor, however, namely that in which the *métaphorisé* YHWH is absent, I am more inclined to see the author's ultimate purpose as relational – all of the devastation is the result of YHWH's withdrawal from his people.

The second dimension of the metaphorical statement – YHWH is wine/joy/cosmos – expresses, once again, something relative about God, ultimately something negative: YHWH is not present. The failure of the wine harvest, the silencing/cessation of all joy and the return of '*tohû*' to town, darkness to city and ruin to the gate together constitute a metaphorical statement in which the *métaphorisé* is absent. We already noted that wine was considered a symbol of God's abundance and generosity as well as of Israel's fruitfulness. In addition, the evident reversal of cosmic creation in the use of the term '*tohû*' (also the sense of 'emptiness' associated with the term)[59] as well as the strongly theological dimension of the terminology surrounding human rejoicing[60] all serve to point to a severance in the relationship between God and his people, an absence which is expressed in metaphorical terms perhaps because such a statement would have been almost unthinkable in literal terms.

The isotopic cross-reference or core of the metaphor would appear, therefore, to be rooted in the theological associations attached to the *métaphorisant*. The literal fact of the absence of wine/joy cosmos has further metaphorical connotations in the divine absence it ultimately signifies. In terms of core type this metaphorical statement is secondary to the primary core outlined above. At the same time the core is 'absent' in that it seems to be contained in the *métaphorisant* as such. There is little doubt that such a metaphorical statement would have been active, resonant, structural, and culture-exceeding yet familiar. Most importantly, however, the statement, in line with much of the metaphorical usage in these chapters is ultimately relational. It states, once again, that the relationship between YHWH and his people/his creation has been disrupted and YHWH has withdrawn.

Author's Purpose/Interpretation

As we noted in our delimitation of the present unit, vv. 7-13 need to be read together: v. 7 in light of v. 10; v. 8 in light of v. 11 and v. 9 in light of v. 12. We also noted that v. 13 is an interpolated redactional

---

59. Cf. Gen 1,2; Jer 4,23 (of land reduced to primeval chaos); Isa 34,11; 45,18. 'Emptiness': cf. 1 Sam 12,21; Isa 29,21; 40,17.23 etc. (cf. NBDB 8414).; cf. also TWAT VIII 555-563 (GÖRG). The relationship between v. 10a and vv. 1 and 3-6 is also significant here.

60. VANONI notes that the term שמחה (TWAT VII 808-822; NIDOTTE 8523 [GRISANTI]) is rarely found in a profane context and that the majority of its uses are theological: cultic (Hos 9,1); table joy (Isa 22,13); in response to YHWH's help/justice: Ps 5,12; 16,9; 21,2; 58,11; 97,10; 1 Sam 2,1; Isa 25,9; in Ezek 7,12, it is interesting to note that the 'end of joy' is a sign of YHWH's judgement. משוש is also frequently used in theological contexts (cf. YHWH rejoicing in humans: Deut 28,63; 30,9; Jer 32,41; Isa 62,5; humans rejoicing in YHWH: Ps 35,9; 70,5; 119,17 etc.; cf. NBDB 7797) as is עליז (cf. Isa 13,3; but also presumption and pride before God: Isa 22,2; 23,7; 32,13 etc.; cf. HALOT 833)

summary rounding off the unit and we will return to this point below. We likewise noted above how more literal statements about human persons and their emotional 'fruits' together with earth/city and its physical 'fruits' are combined in a complex interweave of both internal and external parallelism, linking the two panels (7-9 & 10-12) of our unit and thereby constituting a wider metaphorical statement.

The two central statements of each panel (8b & 11b) would appear to constitute the authors primary purpose: to convey his evaluation of events as a sign of divine withdrawal couched in terms of the cessation of festival joy both in the countryside and in the city. In this sense his purpose was both evaluative and relational. By extension, then, both earthly and human 'fruitlessness' are a result of this withdrawal. Wine and joy are the earthly and human response to a harmonious relationship with each other and with YHWH. The absence of either implies that ארץ, city/town, and home are all without YHWH (the creator of cosmos) and thus in a state of chaos. The 'town of *tohû*', therefore, appears to be a focal metaphor – idea of 'chaos' as opposed to a town (civil cosmos) – in the metaphorical statement, shedding light on the wider situation. Everything is in a state of chaos, there is darkness over the earth[61]. It is interesting to note Hayes' suggestion that תהו itself can mean 'desert place' which further underlines the continuity of imagery[62]. The 'crushed' gate (v. 12b)[63] implies lack of civil/social life (justice is impossible) while the 'barred' houses (v. 10b) imply the absence of home/family life (there is no security). Clearly there is an invitation here to explore inter-personal and divine-human relationships in the light of this situation. Indeed, the author has rendered the unspeakable speakable by way of metaphor: YHWH has abandoned his people. At the same time, the incessant hammering of the negative terminology of the *énoncé métaphorisant* intensifies the sense of YHWH's absence and the disharmony between humanity and nature which that absence brings about. Surrounding this, the author also seems to have the purpose of communicating his own experience. It is almost as if he is a first hand observer of these events.

While we must admit that the speaker's meaning, as Macky would describe it, is impossible to reconstruct and interpret in its fullest sense,

---

61. Cf. the parallelism in v. 11: a//b – a'//b' – a''//b'', linking darkness to earth.
62. HAYES, *The Earth Mourns*, pp. 222-223.
63. Elder may also be correct in pointing out that the 'gate' was often used as a cultic metonym for the city: cf. Ps 24,7.9; 69,12; 87,2; 122,2; Isa 14,31; 45,1; 60,11.18; cf. W. ELDER, *A Theological-Historical Study of Isaiah 24–27*, Diss. (UMI), Baylor University, 1974, p. 136.

the author does appear to have left us enough clues in his choice of terminology to allow us some access to his intentions. Having introduced YHWH as the enemy in vv. 1-3, the author confronts us throughout the remainder of this first part of Isa 24 with ambiguous terminology which can be used of humans and earth to express the degradation of both. Of particular interest are the potential meanings of סגר and חדל outlined above (end of menstruation/closing of the womb). If one stresses the personification of the city/town as a woman then what appear to be literal terms might also be understood metaphorically as sexual/conjugal terms. I would venture to suggest, even at this early stage, that an even more inclusive metaphorical statement is present within the entire complex Isa 24–27, one which will have implications for the identification of the unnamed city. It is possible that the author's primary intention is to suggest that the relationship between Israel (Jerusalem constituting its focus both in terms of the land and the population thereof) and YHWH ought to be understood as a conjugal relationship. In this sense the language of mourning (of a widow) has its place in a broader scheme of things, as does the language of annihilation and infertility both of land and population. 'Earth'/'city'/'inhabitants' are in mourning because they have lost their 'husband'. We shall see below (esp. with respect to 25,10a) that the notion of widowhood and its restoration and the ultimate reversal of infertility are central to this textual complex, helping to explain some of its apparent mysteries.

V. 13

Although the 'distressed nature' images continue in v. 13 and are placed in parallel once again with ארץ and its population (foreshadowing perhaps a more complete identification elsewhere), the use of formal comparative particles which have so far been absent throughout the text suggests that we are in the presence of simile rather than metaphorical expression. Bourguet would propose that such particles are among the indicators of metaphor (long shock) and the essential element of isotopic distinction does not seem to be missing here. Macky also speaks of 'metaphorical similes' as those which say more than mere comparison of subject and symbol. Black, in contrast, would insist that simile is quite distinct from metaphor in that it simply points out the similarity between two realities and nothing more. Indeed, in the present example one might argue that the comparison being made is to some extent insightful and as such may have some metaphorical implications. Closer examination reveals, however, that the comparison is really quite a simple one – ארץ and its inhabitants are like stripped branches[64]. If this were another metaphorical statement it would come as something of an anticlimax and stylistic let-down after the complex and quite creative metaphorical statements which precede it. At the same time, the very summary aspect of this verse suggests it is a redactional conclusion[65], offering an elaboration on the intervening verses: there will only be a few left alive. After hostile destruction and withdrawal of YHWH from his people, ארץ and its inhabitants are compared to the all but bare branches of the olive tree and the vine.

Wildberger points out the similarity between v. 6 which concluded our preceding unit (vv. 4-6) and v. 12 here[66]. He further suggests, therefore: "Ein Leser fühlte sich an 17:6 erinnert und wollte bezeugen, daß jene jesajanische Weissagung nun zur Erfülling kommen werde."[67] The quotation of Isa 17,6 (the reduction of Jacob to 'a few berries on a branch') in v. 13b might be intended to broaden our perspective and focuses our attention on the ultimately universal reduction of human persons[68] within the inhabited earth. Others would argue, however, that reference to Isa 17,6 and the parallel statement בתוך העמים // בקרב הארץ might represent the idea that "Jerusalem was the centre of the world, the 'navel' of the earth"[69] and that we have an indication here that the text is dealing primarily with Jerusalem and Judah.

In stylistic terms the verse is an indication of closure[70]. It also constitutes an inclusion with the future oriented prophetic predictions in vv. 1-3[71]. Other authors take v. 13 with the following pericope, the 'rest' being the subject of the songs of praise heard in the following unit[72]. The concluding,

---

64. Even D.N. Lord distinguishes between the comparisons in this verse and the metaphorical language preceding it; cf. D.N. LORD, *A Designation and Exposition of the Figures of Isaiah Chapter XXIV*, in *Theological and Literary Journal* (1853-1854) 321-329 (p. 325).

65. SCHOORS, *Jesaja*, p. 147. He notes, in addition, that authors such as Fohrer and Feldmann consider v. 13 to be a later addition, inserted to show how complete YHWH's judgement is among the nations.

66. WILDBERGER, *Jesaja 13–27*, pp. 897-898: נשאר בעיר שמה // ונשאר אוב מזער.

67. *Ibid.*, p. 898.

68. HÖFFKEN, *Das Buch Jesaja*, p. 177; J.H. HAYES and S.A. IRVINE, *Isaiah: The 8th Century Prophet: His Times and His Preaching*, Nashville, TN, 1988, p. 301f..

69. Cf. MARCH, *Two Prophetic Compositions*, p. 45, following LINDBLOM, *Die Jesaja-Apokalypse*, pp. 20-21; cf. also KISSANE, *The Book of Isaiah*, p. 281; SNIJDERS, *Jesaja*, p. 239.

70. LEWIS, *Rhetorical-Critical Analysis*, pp. 66-68; W.R. MILLAR, *Isaiah 24–27 and the Origin of Apocalyptic* (HSMS, 11), Missoula, MT, 1976, p. 30, sees this tricolon as a 'nice example of climactic parallelism'; cf. also REDDITT, *Form Critical Analysis*, p. 81.

71. JOHNSON, *Chaos to Restoration*, p. 21.

72. BREDENKAMP, *Der Prophet Jesaja*, p. 147; W. RUDOLPH, *Jesaja 24–27* (BWANT IV, 10), Stuttgart, 1933, p. 32; E.S. MULDER, *Die Teologie van die Jesaja-Apokalypse*.

summary character of the verse, the inclusion with the prophetic predictions of vv. 1-3 and the contrast between the cessation of joy in vv. 7-12 and the 'resumption of joy' in vv. 14-16 would seem to preclude such a possibility.

Conclusion Isa 24,1-13

We can agree with Hayes when she states that although many authors[73] "... consider vv. 7-13 either an addition or an independent unit, these verses fit almost seamlessly into the context of the devastation of the earth established in vv. 1-6. Apparent inconsistencies between the imagery of vv. 1-6 and that of vv. 7-13 may simply represent the characteristic juxtaposition of motifs found in many biblical poetic passages."[74]

Initial analysis of these verses seems to reveal a clustering of primarily relational metaphors surrounding 'YHWH', 'the earth' and its 'inhabitants', all of which are profoundly negative: hostility, depopulation, mourning/drought, exile of joy/music, lack of wine, desolation. If we enter the 'labyrinth' via any one of these metaphors we find ourselves linked up with all of the others and more. All the metaphors surround the notion of YHWH's judgement as an ongoing act of hostility and alienation from his people. As we already noted above, the entire unit, from v. 1 to v. 13, turns around the central relationship between 'YHWH', ארץ and its 'inhabitants'. Distortion at any level within this three-way union results in devastation for all – including YHWH[75].

The focal metaphor ultimately related to the earth is that of the 'town of *tohû*', the darkened city with its crushed gate and boarded up homes. While it is not apparent at first sight, the feminine image/personification of the city and ultimately Jerusalem as a woman[76] feeds the metaphorical

---

Jesaja 24–27, Djakarta, 1954, p. 13f.; ALONSO SCHÖKEL and SICRE DIAZ, *Profetas I*, p. 207ff.; MOTYER, *Prophecy of Isaiah*, p. 202;

73. She cites WILDBERGER (*Jesaja 13–27*, pp. 904, 925-929) and O. PLÖGER, *Theokratie und Eschatologie* (WMANT, 2), Neukirchen – Vluyn, 1968³, p. 56.

74. HAYES, *The Earth Mourns*, p. 203.

75. Similarities between the present devastation and that described in the book of Lamentations are difficult to miss. One of the important dimensions of the attitude of the גבר in the face of such devastation is articulated in Lam 3,33: 'It is not according to YHWH's heart'. Ultimately the same may be said of YHWH in the present situation. Cf. RENKEMA, *Klaagliederen*, pp. 293-294.

76. Cf. Lamentations *passim*; RENKEMA, pp. 61-63; M. BIDDLE, *The Figure of Lady Jerusalem: Identification Deification and Personification of Cities in the Ancient Near East*, in B. BATTO, W. HALLO and L. YOUNGER (eds.), *The Canon in Comparative Perspective* (Scripture in Context Series, 4), Lewiston, 1995, pp. 173-187; J. GALAMBUSH, *Jerusalem in the Book of Ezekiel: The City as Yahweh's Wife* (SBL DS, 130), Atlanta, GA, 1992.

statements throughout the text complex Isa 24–27. While we can continue to reserve judgement on the identification of the 'town of *tohû*', many aspects are emerging which tend to portray the mysterious city/town as woman, as alienated from YHWH, and in fact as widowed, all of which might incline the balance in one direction or another. Certainly the metaphor of YHWH as the husband of his people, although not explicitly, is beginning to emerge as significant in this text complex[77]. The barren images at the beginning (24,1-13) and in the middle (26,17-19) of the textual complex are reversed towards the end with abundance of fruit, filling the entire world (27,6). Jerusalem can have no children without her husband.

Isa 24, 14-16b & 16c-18d

14a   They, they raise their voice,
b   they cry aloud over the majesty of YHWH
c   they shout[78] from the West.

15a   Therefore, in the East give glory to YHWH,
b   in the islands of the West,
c   [to] the name of YHWH, the God of Israel.

16a   From the edges of the land praise songs we hear,
b   [praise songs] of beauty to the Righteous One[79].

c   But I say[80], "Emaciation[81] is to me! Emaciation is to me!
d   Woe to me.

---

77. Cf. Isa 24,1-13; 25,6-10a; 26,11-21; 27,6ff..

78. Some commentators and editions (e.g. RUDOLPH, *Jesaja 24–27*, p. 11; LINDBLOM, *Die Jesaja-Apokalypse*, p. 22; MARCH, *Two Prophetic Compositions*, pp. 13-14; BHS) are tempted to deal with the problematic lack of *waw* consecutive (remember this is poetry) with צהלו by emending it to read as an imperative, detaching it from v. 14 and attaching it to the beginning of v. 15 where the verb forms and line of thought are easily paralleled (cf. 1QIsaᵃ). This is not necessary in light of the frequent absence of expected waw throughout the text complex, the triple verbal clause which changes to a series of CNC's after the על־כן as well as the presence על־כן which introduces the direct speech and would otherwise be misplaced (cf. DUHM, *Jesaja*, p. 147).

79. LEWIS, *Rhetorical-Critical Analysis*, p. 80.

80. Beuken proposes that we read the opening ואמר as 'Yes, I have said' by which the prophet refers back to a former prophecy of his found in 21,1-4 which he sees as still operative in the present and which he is about to quote in the present context. The triple joyful acclamation of the preceding verses has a prophecy of doom as its background. Praise of God's majesty is to be followed by the downfall of the treacherous. The

e   the treacherous[82] deal treacherously.
f   [With] treachery the treacherous deal treacherously.

17a   terror and tomb and trap
b   are upon you, dweller of the land."

18a   And it shall be, the one who flees from the sound of terror,
b   shall fall into the tomb,

c   and the one who climbs from the tomb,
d   shall be seized by the trap.

Delimitation of Metaphorical Statement

Hayes notes how some commentators, in assessing the evident distinction between vv. 14-16b and their surroundings – thanksgiving contrasted

---

prophecy of 21,1-4 is the key to understanding the present situation. This, of course, has implications for the identity of the other actants in the unit. Beuken identifies the 'they' group as primarily Israel but not excluding the nations; cf. W.A.M. BEUKEN, *The Prophet Leads the Readers into Praise. Isa 25,1-10 in Connection with Isa 24,14-23 Seen against the Background of Isaiah 12*, Unpublished paper read at the Annual Meeting of the AAR-SBL, Orlando, FL, November, 1998 (to be published in OTS, XLIII, Leiden, 1999). I partly agree with Beuken here, particularly with respect to the identity of the 'I' figure as the prophet and the 'they' figure as a single actant representing primarily the people of Israel but not excluding the nations. As for the temporal aspect of ואמר, I am also inclined to follow Beuken's suggestion of a term introducing a quotation. 'They', however', I prefer to see as adversative, whereby the prophet, referring to his former prophecy, reminds his audience what their present optimism is doing to them. They should be sick with fear rather than singing with joy.

81. The meaning of רזי־לי is disputed. Some suggest it means 'secret' (in line with Syr: 'it is a mystery to me'; V: *secretum meum mihi*, 'my secret is mine'; cf., for example, O. PROCKSCH, *Jesaja I. Erste Hälfte: Kapitel 1–39* (KAT, IX), Leipzig, 1930, p. 812) others 'emptiness', 'weakening', 'Auszherung' – derived from the root רזה which would certainly seem more appropriate to the preceding metaphorical statements: pining away, wasting away (prophet as widowed city?). Note the relationship of this root to barren land in Num 13,20; There may also be a connection between this 'pining' and ritual mourning (perhaps an allusion to מר – mourning cry = NBDE 4797-4798). 'Leanness' & 'emaciation' are clearly more appropriate. For רזון cf. NIDCTTE 8136 (BOSMAN); cf. also GRAY, *Isaiah*, p. 419. 'Secret' is meaningless unless one leans towards an apocalyptic understanding of the textual corpus as a whole (cf. Dan 2,22; 4,6)!! Cf. the discussion in BARTHÉLEMY, *Critique Textuelle*, p. 174ff..

82. Some commentators and editions (notably MULDER, *Die Teologie*, p. 15 following GRAY; LXX T]; cf. also CONDAMIN, *Le Livre d'Isaïe*, p. 167; PROCKSCH, *Jesaja I*, p. 812;) suggest that we read an emended אוי לבגדים as the ideal parallel sequence to the preceding צבי לצדיק. This is an unnecessary emendation as the MT is perfectly understandable as it is. The triple complaint of the prophet is also appropriate in contrast to the triple action of raising their voices, crying aloud and shouting of v. 14 (a further reason for reading the two sections as one).

with judgement –, have tended to consider them a later addition[83]. I agree with her assessment of the situation, however, and see these verses as a stylistic supplement to the negative thrust of the chapter as a whole. Further stylistic associations with the context will become evident as we explore the text.

While the emphatic המה[84] serves to open this new unit, the author clearly establishes a contrast with the 'end of joy' in the preceding unit and the fourfold expression of joy in YHWH here in vv. 14-16b. His purpose in doing so, however, remains somewhat vague until we read further. In addition, according to Sweeney[85] we are evidently faced with a new literary form here, namely a prophetic disputation pattern. Moreover, there is no syntactical relationship with v. 13, and the introduction of new, unidentified actants provides further separation from the preceding unit. The change of perspective in v. 16c to 1st person and to 3rd person in v. 21 are both linked with conjunctive *waw*, suggesting that these verses should be read as one unit. According to Lewis, the raising

---

83. HAYES, *The Earth Mourns*, pp. 194-195; KAISER, *Isaiah 13–39*, p. 178; J. VERMEYLEN, *Du prophète Isaïe à l'Apocalyptique. Isaïe, I – XXXV, miroir d'un demi-millénaire d'expérience religieuse en Israël I-II* (EB) Paris, 1977-1978, p. 356) against WILDBERGER, *Jesaja 13–27*, p. 898). HÖFFKEN, *Das Buch Jesaja*, p. 177) sees vv. 14-16 as an additional section (a lament??) interrupting the flow of events from vv. 13-17ff..

84. Who are these unidentified 'המה'? Three primary suggestions are identifiable in the literature: 'a remnant': KAISER, *Isaiah, 13–39*, pp. 198-199; ALONSO SCHÖKEL and SICRE DIAZ, *Profetas I*, p. 204f.; MOTYER, *The Prophecy of Isaiah*, p. 202); 'Jews in the diaspora': R. SMEND, *Anmerkungen zu Jes 24–27*, in ZAW 4 (1884) 161-224 (pp. 168-169); PROCKSCH, *Jesaja I*, p. 311; SCHOORS, *Jesaja*, p. 147; WILDBERGER, *Jesaja 13–27*, p. 934; a 'sinful' remnant awaiting a 'favourable hearing': MARCH, *Two Prophetic Compositions*, pp. 46-48. Hayes and Irvine see vv. 14-16 as a reference to far flung celebrations at the end of Assyrian domination (both Israel and the nations??), but this depends on their understanding of the historical situation behind these words. They see the 'town of *tohû*' (10a) and the 'city of foreign nations' (25,3) as references to an Assyrian garrison in Jerusalem which had been destroyed in a rebellion against Assyria. I favour Johnson's position on the identity of the המה (cf. *Chaos to Restoration*, pp. 36-41): i.e. those against whom YHWH is moving in judgement are the antecedent of המה in vv. 1-13 – but they do not realise it. He views the context from a historical perspective: rejoicing at Nebuchadnezzar's departure is parallel to that of Sennacherib in Isa 22,(5).12-14. Isaiah rebuked the optimists then as he does here. The prophet knew it was but a temporary reprieve. He is referring here to his former prophecy, therefore we should interpret ואמר as 'I said.' It is impossible to escape the Day of YHWH to come. Cf. also P. AUVRAY, *Isaie 1–39* (SB), Paris, 1972, p. 227) who suggests that the prophet is opposing the incorrect reaction of Israel (and those who respond to her invitation to praise) with his own reaction. The prophet speaks of himself in words which the people, city, earth should be using: emptiness, wasting away and absence of YHWH – the widow is emaciated. WATTS (*Isaiah 1–33*, p. 324, perhaps following REDDITT [*Form Critical Analysis*, p.82]) appears to follow this line of thought also, pointing out that from v. 18 onwards the people are being reminded by the prophet of the curse announced in v. 6 and that it is all consuming: on the people (v. 18); on the land (v. 20) and on the kings (vv. 21-22).

85. SWEENEY, *Isaiah 1–39*, pp. 328-329.

of the voice 'to shout' is a device from Ugaritic poetry used to indicate a shift or break in a poem⁸⁶.

Redditt enumerates the wide variety of opinions with respect to the delimitation of this pericope⁸⁷. While the contrast between 3rd person plural in v. 14 and 1st person singular in v. 16b leads some to split v. 16, Redditt is of the opinion that the very contrast itself is intended, the change of person simply underlining a change of perspective (joyful praise to terrible reality). He leaves v. 16 intact, therefore, and based on its similarity with Jer 48,43-44a, he understands 17-18a to be a separate unit⁸⁸. Since Redditt's primary reason for distinguishing discreet units is the identification of literary genres, his division of the text here is understandable. From a different literary perspective, however, we are entitled to disagree with Redditt's position here as we shall see.

Lewis points out the multiple use of assonance⁸⁹ and the complex parallelism⁹⁰ involved in these verses. His suggestion that we see vv. 14-16/17-18 as two strophes which must be read together – hymn of thanksgiving in vv. 14-17 together with judgement in vv. 17-18 – is insightful and useful in delimiting the metaphorical statement⁹¹. It is in fact vv. 17-18 and the transitional v. 16c which govern the metaphorical statement as a whole, providing the *énoncé métaphorisant*. One should note that metaphor is perhaps not the primary stylistic feature of this pericope. It is hard to avoid interpreting terms such as 'West', 'East', 'islands of the West', 'edges/wings of the earth' in vv. 14-15 as a somewhat standard sort of merism referring to the entirety of the 'civilised/populated world'. This also has a climactic force, moving from one point of the compass to the other and culminating in the inclusive 'wings/edges of the earth'⁹². While the transitional v. 16c brings us back to a central focus in the 1st person of the prophet we expand once again through the second person of v. 17 to the once more inclusive 'the one' of v. 18. Irony certainly governs the first part while word-play governs the second. It is in fact these two stylistic features which bind together the

---

86. Cf. LEWIS, *Rhetorical-Critical Analysis*, p. 73, following MILLAR, *Origin*, p. 31.
87. Cf. REDDITT, *Form Critical Analysis*, p. 89ff..
88. While the text from Jeremiah is directed against Moab the other use of this curse is evidently directed against Jerusalem (and surrounding territory) and its inhabitants cf. Lam 3,47.
89. LEWIS. *Rhetorical-Critical Analysis*, p. 71ff..
90. *Ibid.*, p. 77.
91. Similarly Schoors, who points out that both 14-16a and 16b-18 are by the same author and purposefully underline the contrast between 'they' and 'I'. Cf. also MULDER, *Die Teologie*, p. 14.
92. Lord calls this an 'elliptical metaphor' intended to denote boundaries (*Isaiah Chapter XXIV*, p. 326).

énoncé métaphorisé (irony) and the *énoncé métaphorisant*. We are still faced with a relational content however. The prophet's words underline the absence of YHWH from the picture, making the praise of vv. 14-16b hollow and empty. The reason for YHWH's absence is the treachery reigning in the land, among the people, which is the primary reason for the catastrophe facing ארץ and its inhabitants – this time expressed in terms of 'terror, tomb and trap' and the ultimate impossibility of escape. The prophet speaks of himself in words which the people, the city and the land should be using of themselves: emptiness, wasting away and absence of YHWH – the 'widow' is emaciated[93]. Kilian connects 16c-20 with 1-6, there is no escape from the destruction[94]. This allows us to connect 14-16b with its multiple contrasts to the preceding vv. 7-13: joyful noise, ארץ and inhabitants sing (noise is insisted upon as opposed to silence). Thus YHWH is made 'present' in various ways in these verses but this is a rhetorical device, a 'straw man' set up for the prophet's ultimate purpose. The intensity of this 'false' praise is underlined in the vv. 14-16b by the repetition of the divine name YHWH. The intensity of the speaker's pain is underlined by the multiple repetitions of roots for treachery and the alliterative words for the trap.

ואמר is the transitional word between vv. 14-16b and 16c-18d. Note that it introduces the prophet's personal involvement. There is an evident progression from 'they' –» 'we' –» 'I' –» 'you', all of whom are only vaguely identified except for the prophet. Indeed, the prophet is central. His sickly anguish is not a present reality but a reminder of a previous warning which the people have ignored. Their praise is empty indeed and cannot save them. In fact, their praise amounts to treachery! Who are the treacherous (v. 16de)? Mulder suggests the reference is to robbers/looters still present in the city making the praise song premature[95]. I am inclined to see it as the treacherous among the people themselves whose 'false/empty' praise is ultimately only a symptom of an attitude towards YHWH which itself lies at the origin of this disaster. Reading the two units together suggests that praise and glory (vv. 14-16b) are parallel with treachery (vv. 16c-18d). Note how repeated praise (which can take all sorts of verbal forms: כבדו, צהלו, ירנו, ישאו קולם, even זמרת שמענו) is paralleled to repeated treachery [for which there is only one word: בגד]).

---

93. Elder (*Theological-Historical Study*, pp. 105-106) thinks this 'song of praise' part is inappropriate, sandwiched as it is between two blocks of judgement. Irony explains its presence. He believes it can only be appropriate if the addressees of 16b-18 are some other enemy and not Israel.
94. R. KILIAN, *Jesaja II: 13–39* (NEchB, 32), Würzburg, 1994, p. 145.
95. MULDER, *Die Teologie*, p. 15.

There is a certain similarity between vv. 18 & 13. Both are introduced by 'והיה(ו)' and both are more prosaic extrapolations of the metaphors which precede them: devastation/depopulation & terror, tomb and trap. The imagery in the present case is taken from 'the hunt'[96], although the curse itself (v. 17) is 'proverbial'[97].

For a variety of reasons outlined above, therefore, we opt to delimit the present unit to 24,14a-18d as the next location in our efforts to identify metaphorical language in the text complex Isa 24–27.

Indicators

Since there are clearly no formal indicators of metaphor in the present unit we must look elsewhere for evidence of metaphorical usage.

V. 16c constitutes a key verse in the unit, a focal metaphor in which the prophet identifies himself with the effects of devastation contrasting powerfully with the rejoicing and praise of the preceding verses (14-16b). In so doing he refers back to a prophecy in Isa 21,1-4[98] which is now about to be fulfilled for the inhabitants of ארץ[99]. At the level of metaphor, indicators include syntactic surcharge via juxtaposition, repetition (triple SNC = very sparing and very direct) and semantic incoherence (via the possible meanings of the verb and their identification with speaker). Hayes is correct in noting that the similar syntactic patterning between רזי־לי רזי־לי and אוי לי[100] places רזה in a 'figurative context' in which physical wasting away stands side by side with mourning and lament[101]. The *métaphorisé* is the 'I' figure, i.e. the speaker (the prophet) made present in the form of the first person suffix. The *métaphorisant* is derived from the verb רזה which has a number of associations which link it up with other metaphorical themes in the surrounding verses. In the transitive sense it usually means 'to allow to dwindle, to vanish' and can refer to people, gods, the land etc.[102]. As we noted elsewhere, there may

---

96. Cf. RENKEMA, *Klaagliederen*, p. 314 with respect to Lam 3,47.52.
97. Cf. LEWIS, *Rhetorical-Critical Analysis*, p. 83; a more or less identical formula is to be found in Jer 48,43.
98. For the multiple levels of relationship between the present text and Isa 21,1-4, cf. BEUKEN, *The Prophet Leads the Readers into Praise*, pp. 3-4.
99. For ואמר as a past tense cf. ALEXANDER, KÖNIG, PROCKSCH, KISSANE, KAISER, WILDBERGER, BEUKEN.
100. Perhaps the absence of *maqqeph* with אוי לי suggests a slowing down, consistent with the idea of pining/mourning; cf. MOTYER, *The Prophecy of Isaiah*, p. 203. The minimal expression here might also suggest a climax.
101. HAYES, *The Earth Mourns*, p. 213.
102. Cf. HALOT 1029: *qal*: Zeph 2,11 (gods of the earth); *niphal*: Isa 17,4 (Jacob – interesting that 17,6 is quoted in 24,13); adjective = 'thin/gaunt': refers to ארץ in Num 13,20; noun: Isa 10,16 (God's warriors), Ps 106,15 (people in the wilderness).

be an allusion to the term מרזח which is used to refer to a cultic celebration with much revelry in Amos 6,7 as well as to a funeral meal/mourning ritual in Jer 16,5[103]. Clearly, therefore, we have distinct isotopes. Other stylistic features which one might include as indicators of metaphor include the centralisation or hinge character of the expression in 16c which functions in the establishment of two parallel panels vv. 14-16b & vv. 16d-18d. In addition, the speaker in v. 16c is focused upon via the transition from 'they' to 'we' to 'I' to 'you' to the indefinite 'one' in v. 18. The *métaphorisé* is a corporeal reality while the *métaphorisant* contains the possibility of being both corporeal (referring to human persons and the land) and emotional (funeral lament/revelry of cultic celebration). It thus joins the ranks of the verbs used so far to express this ambiguity. It would seem possible to envisage the metaphorical statement here in v. 16c as of the A is B type in that the prophet identifies himself with land/city/inhabitants via a term which could be applied to them all. Ultimately, the prophet is the focus of these verses in that he brings the entire metaphorical statement into himself: the premature revelry of 14-16b should continue to be the mourning of 7-13 and the consequences of his earlier prophecy have not yet fully unfolded either for individuals (both high and low), the land herself or the cosmic forces (cf. vv. 18e-23).

This central metaphorical statement constitutes the key to the identification and understanding of the larger metaphorical statement. While emaciation 'is' the prophet, treachery and its consequences (cf. transgression and its consequences in 24,4-6) 'is' the people's praise of YHWH. Once again, stylistic features such as repetition, word-play and a variety of parallel associations join the two panels. We already noted that the variety of words for praise and the various inclusivising references (East-West, edges of the earth) are paralleled with the repeated word for treachery (בגד: 'their' praise is singularly treacherous) and the inescapability of punishment: 'they' may try to escape to the edges of the earth but their fate is inevitable. V. 17 bluntly states the punishment due to the 'dweller on the land' with a SNC followed by a triple predicate built on consonance, assonance and alliteration, thereby focusing our attention on the 'punishment' of 'terror, tomb and trap'. V. 18 takes up each dimension of the punishment but places the unidentified 'one' who must undergo it within two X + *yiqtol* clauses (CNC), drawing our attention to the individuals being punished who cannot escape their fate. The 'Righteous One' of v. 16b is also paralleled antithetically with the treachery of

---

103. Cf. HALOT 634.

v. 16d where CNC's once again draw our attention to the X element, i.e. to the perpetrators of this treachery. The latter bicolon is also related to v. 14 via its 3rd person plural verbal suffixes.

On the surface the descriptive speech is apparently literal, a simple account of people praising YHWH, followed by a direct speech prophetic condemnation of the treacherous 'dweller on the earth'. By way of the use of irony mentioned above together with the central metaphorical key of v. 16c, however, which is itself dependant speech – dependant upon the audience's awareness of the earlier metaphorical statements in the chapter leading us to identify city/land and inhabitants with the speaker (via the various possible meanings of רזה) –, we are invited to juxtapose the two surrounding panels. Thus the larger metaphorical statement becomes dependant speech. We are led to read the 'praise' and 'universality' of vv. 14-16c in light of the negative accusations of treachery and the 'inevitability' of ongoing punishment in vv. 16d-18d.

In the key metaphor of v. 16c there is some positive analogy since רזה can be applied to human persons and therefore to the speaker. There is also negative analogy in that the term can also be applied to 'gods' and the land (which is perhaps the strongest association being made in the light of the other metaphorical statements in the chapter). We remain in the realm of relational metaphors as we shall see below. The larger metaphorical statement places human praise of YHWH as *métaphorisé* in a metaphorical relationship with the negativity of prophetic judgement expressed in terms of 'the hunt' as *métaphorisant*[104]. The quite profound isotopic distinction between words of praise and words of accusation and of the hunt underline the absence of positive analogy between the *métaphorisé* and the *métaphorisant* suggesting that the latter is of the insight type, telling us something about the 'praise' which is not immediately apparent. As such the metaphorical statement would have been quite shocking to it's audience as would the irony which under-girds it.

Type

Having established the presence of two distinct isotopes in both the key metaphor in v. 16c and the wider metaphorical statement surrounding it (vv. 14-16b // vv. 16d-18d) we must now try to establish the area of cross-reference between the two, i.e. the level of similarity between

---

104. Cf. KAISER, *Isaiah 13–39*, p. 190; Lewis notes along with NBDB (809) that 'פחת (pit) refers to the hunter's pit which is dug for the capture of large animals, and the פח (trap) is the snare used for the capture of small game birds'(cf. *Rhetorical-Critical Analysis*, p. 82).

the two isotopes. V. 16c would seem to be an example of a 'simple core' (implicit repetition between the *métaphorisé* [the prophet] and the *métaphorisant* [emaciation]) which is more explicit in the *métaphorisant* than in the *métaphorisé*. In this sense there is a transference of meaning between the *métaphorisant* (emaciation) and the *métaphorisé* (the prophet). The wider metaphorical statement constitutes a secondary core (maintaining a certain semantic connection with the primary core). Bourguet lack's terminology for the type of core which appears to be functioning here although on might ascribe it to what he refers to as a 'diffuse core', i.e. one which is illusive and difficult to grasp. The distinction between the isotopes is so great that one would almost have to describe the core as structural/syntactic (these being the main elements which establish connection between the *métaphorisé* [praise/song] and the *métaphorisant* [treachery] or antithetical/semantic (since the significance of the terminology in the *métaphorisé* and the *métaphorisant* is so different).

Neither metaphorical statement could be described as 'extinct/dead' or 'dormant/retired'. In Black's terminology both are clearly 'active' metaphors and as such would have been recognised as metaphorical language by their audience leading to genuine interaction between *métaphorisé* and *métaphorisant*. At the same time Black's category of 'resonant-active' might be appropriately applied here given that each metaphorical statement would certainly have invited, indeed, demanded the interpretative reflections of those who heard it.

At a first level of reduction it might be possible to postulate an A is B type metaphor: prophet is empty/praise is treachery[105]. While not explicitly so, however, the present metaphors, in context with the surrounding metaphors of the entire chapter, might reasonably be reduced to an ultimately relational metaphor of the A is B type: YHWH is absent. The almost exaggerated insistence on his presence in vv. 14-16b, the turning point of v. 16c which might be understood as a statement of the prophet's 'emptiness/emaciation' as a result of alienation from YHWH and his true assessment of the situation in vv. 16d-18d as one of treachery and its

---

105. Perhaps one must also allow one metaphorical statement 'prophet is empty' to structure the other 'praise is treachery'. If the prophet constitutes a sign embodying the condition of city/ארץ/inhabitants which ultimately connects us to the other metaphorical statements we have seen so far and with the relational metaphor YHWH is absent then it would not be inappropriate to suggest that its key position is intended to invite us to structure our understanding of vv. 14-16b and vv. 16d-18c in the same way. Thus praise of YHWH, no matter how 'universal' it becomes is inescapably treacherous and falls because its object has withdrawn and its practitioners may be fooling themselves but not the prophet.

consequences – panic driven hunt / unprotected 'dweller on the earth' – would certainly support such a conclusion.

According to Lakoff and Johnson's categories, both metaphorical statements in the present unit would be considered 'structural' in that they invite us to structure our understanding of 'praise & rejoicing' in terms of 'treachery and its consequences' as well as to structure our concept of the 'prophet' in terms of 'emptiness', 'emaciation' and ultimately the other 'infertile images' applied to city/land and population throughout this chapter. The final aim of this 'restructuring' appears to be a relational statement – YHWH/land/inhabitants are out of harmony and this is expressed in the key metaphor of the 'prophet as emaciation'! Viewed in this manner it would be reasonable to suggest that the metaphors involved in this unit are culture-exceeding. The terminology of *métaphorisé* and *métaphorisant* would be familiar to every culture/time which has at least some understanding of religious feelings and human hypocrisy.

While the divinity is mentioned in a variety of ways in the *métaphorisé* of the larger metaphorical statement, God does not constitute the *métaphorisé* as such, but is simply the repeated object of 'they' and 'their praise'. In a sense, the *métaphorisants* in both cases ('emaciation'/'treachery') are well-known realities, terms descriptive of familiar states. Popular 'praise and rejoicing' is likewise familiar as the *métaphorisé* of the larger metaphorical statement and its association with 'they' gives it something of a physical quality. The same might be said of the speaker ('me'/the prophet) who constitutes a *métaphorisé* which might have even more intense physical qualities. In neither statement is the speech act 'dual-direction' as Macky would understand it. At the same time it is clear that the metaphorical statements are far from being simply 'ornamental'. Macky points out that the alternative, 'well-known comparative' metaphors, tend to be rare and focus on the similarity between *métaphorisé* and *métaphorisant*. In the present context, however, both metaphorical statements do invite comparison of well-known realities but the primary purpose is to reveal that, no matter how different they are, there is in fact a similarity on which each metaphorical statement must ultimately hinge. Once again this would be easier to understand with respect to the key metaphor in v. 16c if the audience were in fact able to see the prophet in an emaciated state, making the statement 'Twice True' at at least one level (literal observation and metaphorical statement).

It is evident from the limited nature of positive analogy between 'treachery' and 'praise' that the metaphorical statement established by the structural juxtaposition of vv. 14-16b and vv. 16d-18d is quite novel.

Indeed, from Gerhart & Russel's perspective (they only support novel metaphors) this metaphor is a true metaphor since it ultimately forces its audience to look differently at their world. At the very least these verses force us to re-interpret our understanding of what seems out of place as a positive statement of praise in a context of overwhelming negativity. Since the application of the various forms of רוח to human persons is relatively rare in the OT, its novelty value as a metaphor must be insisted upon. The possibility of application of the term to ארץ also opens it up to further interpretations and joins it by implication with the remaining metaphors in the chapter. The possibility of there being a literal statement involved, however, slightly diminishes the metaphorical impact of this verse.

Author's Purpose/Interpretation

A brief glance at Macky's enumeration of authorial purpose in employing metaphor (and other 'horizontal' speech) reveals the incredible richness and depth of these verses. Once again it would appear that the author's primary purpose was to invite his audience into an imaginative exploration of their relationship with God and the land (the prophet himself) and in this sense the images used are subtly integrated into the entire chapter's metaphorical thrust. Yet there are so many other levels at work here. The prophet is certainly verbalising some of his own experience ('expressive' purpose) in v. 16c while at the same time trying to change his audience by juxtaposing the denunciation of their treachery with the proclamation of their praise. As such he is engaging in 'dynamic' as well as 'transformative' speech. In addition, the author's words are 'evaluative' in that they express judgement on a particular event (rejoicing and universal praise) via the metaphorical relationship established between vv. 14-16c and vv. 16d-18d. Ultimately the prophet himself and his emaciated/mourning condition is the catalyst which empowers the larger metaphorical statement. As such the audience's emotive response at the sight of the prophet is drawn a step further into their emotive reaction to the juxtaposition of praise and treachery ('affective' purpose). The author could easily have said 'your praise is a lie' but he chose to say it differently via metaphorical speech and to better effect. One might even say that the idea of 'praise' as 'treachery' would have been considered 'unspeakable', in which event the author would be rendering it 'speakable' via his use of metaphor and other speech techniques.

The author has certainly left us a multitude of clues to interpret his words. In the context of an extended metaphorical speech act, he has employed a number of terms from the isotopes of 'praise' and 'rejoicing' and of 'wasting away'/'mourning' and 'accusation'/'judgement'/'the hunt'. By way of the structure of the text he has invited us to look at these words metaphorically and to understand them together. In so doing, he forces his audience to select a particular interpretation of his words from the range of possible interpretations inherent therein. To a certain degree, therefore, we can have access to the speaker's meaning, admitting, as we noted above, that his intentions were manifold. At the same time, it would appear to be possible to receive and re-construct the 'speaker's meaning' on the basis of the clues he has left us, accepting, of course, that our reconstruction can only ever approximate to accuracy. Our knowledge of the wider context of the present speech act will assist us, however, in the process of re-construction and interpretation.

Awareness of speaker's purpose and with the various clues to the speaker's meaning in view we can now endeavour to explain that meaning, accepting, of course, that we are always in the realm of approximation. The clues as such draw our attention to a wider metaphorical speech act with a narrower metaphorical speech act at its core: the latter, among other things, informing the former and empowering it. In the core metaphor, the speaker identifies himself with the 'drying up'/'wasting away'/'mourning' of the land/city/inhabitants connecting himself to the metaphors employed elsewhere in the chapter. He goes on then to remind his audience that this situation is a consequence of their transgression by way of the wider metaphor which reveals that their 'praise' is ultimately 'treachery' and is thus premature. The judgement continues. The unidentified hunter who constitutes a sort of background actant of v. 18a-d is paralleled with the object of praise, shouting and rejoicing in vv. 14-16b. The general lack of identification of the actants – the only named actant being YHWH – serves to underline the shock value of the metaphor as the audience identify themselves with the figures in the speech act: 'they' becomes 'we' becomes 'you'. At the same time, the irony of vv. 14-16b is bolstered. Such 'universal' praise should receive nothing but commendation from the speaker (the prophet) but in fact it elicits his condemnation. It has its roots in the fact – evident to the speaker at least – that there are those who praise YHWH blind to their own transgression and blind to the fact that they are facing destruction. Parallel repetition of 'praise' and 'treachery' is not only a partial indication of the metaphorical statement, it also inclines us to see the 'transgression' spoken of in 24,5 and later in 24,20 as false, unworthy praise[106]. Bearing all this in

---

106. Who are the subjects of the transgression in each case? Cf. SWEENEY, *Isaiah 1–39*, p. 329

mind it seems reasonable to suggest that the primary purpose of the 'speaker' is to inform his audience that the relationship with YHWH, broken by the 'heavy' transgression of unworthy praise, is not yet mended and that their punishment is not over. At the bottom line, this and each of the metaphors we have seen so far has an ultimately relational purpose. Transgression has alienated YHWH and the prophet points to the ongoing effects thereof in his own person as well as the continuing effects thereof in the one who flees yet falls, who climbs up yet is pulled down. Ultimately, in their affected praise, 'they' betray themselves since their praise cannot make YHWH present.

Many of the commentaries confirm our findings with respect to vv. 14-18d. Sweeney, although dividing the text along different lines, agrees that the prophet is offering a contrastive perspective to the joy being proclaimed throughout ארץ by those who see the situation as favourable but which the prophet knows will 'turn against them'[107]. Johnson refers to these verses as an inappropriate response to Isaiah's earlier prophecy of judgement[108]. The inhabitants of the land's optimism is uncalled for. Kilian hints at the relational dimension of these words: "Nicht nur die Zuverlässigkeit der Erde schwindet dahin, ihr fester Grund und Boden zerbrechen, auch menschliche Zuverlässigkeit schlägt in Treulosigkeit um. Auf nichts und niemanden ist mehr Verlaß."[109] Motyer focuses on the repetition of בגד, pointing out that the author's intention is to show that it is still unchanged (as are its consequences) no matter how much 'praise' is being offered to YHWH[110]. Self-delusion, and its concomitant blindness to YHWH's absence from the relationship established by covenant between YHWH, the earth and its inhabitant's, will not reverse the guilt/disgrace of his people (cf. 25,8 & 27,9, cf. also 26,21).

---

107. SWEENEY, *Isaiah 1–39*, p. 329.
108. JOHNSON, *Chaos to Restoration*, p. 39. He finds parallels with Isa 22. Note also that his identification of 'they' as 'the same people against whom Yahweh is moving in judgement, though they do not realise it' (*ibid.*, p. 40) further underscores the irony of vv. 14-16b. If he is correct then his interpretation of the historical situation which gave rise to this 'praise/rejoicing' (i.e. the departure of Nebuchadnezzar from his siege of Jerusalem in 597) further reinforces the identification of the 'city' as Jerusalem.
109. KILIAN, *Jesaja II*, p. 146. The relational dimension has its roots in the Noahic covenant which the people have transgressed; cf. HÖFFKEN, *Das Buch Jesaja*, p. 178; KILIAN, *Jesaja II*, p. 145; SWEENEY, *Isaiah 1–39*, pp. 328-329: "These verses maintain that the land's inhabitants have violated the terms of the eternal, or world-wide covenant (*berit olam*) that defines the relationship between YHWH and the world... the Noahic covenant"; WILDBERGER, *Jesaja 13–27*, p. 898.
110. MOTYER, *The Prophecy of Isaiah*, pp. 203-204.

Isa 24,18e-23

18e Indeed, the floodgates of the height are open.
f   They tremble, the foundations of land.

19a Torn, torn asunder is the land.
b   Split, split apart is land.
c   Shaken, shaken senseless is land

20a She staggers all over, land, like a drunkard.
b   She sways like a hut.

c   It is heavy upon her, her transgression.
d   She falls and she shall never again rise.

21a And it shall be on that day:
b   he will bring punishment, YHWH, on the army of the height in the height,
c   [he will bring punishment, YHWH,] on the kings of the earth on the earth.

22a And they will be herded [as] a herd of captives into a well,
b   and they will be confined to a cell,
c   and after many days they will be punished.

23a It will blush, the moon,
b   it will be ashamed, the sun.

c   For he reigns, YHWH $Ts^eba'ot$,
d   on the mountain of Zion and in Jerusalem,
e   and before its elders [in] glory.

Delimitation of Metaphorical Statement

From a syntactical perspective we are clearly dealing here with two discreet units. Vv. 18e-20d opens with a change of actants, an asseverative כי and a shift from discursive to descriptive language while vv. 21a-23e are marked off by framing formulae, a further change of actants and a return to discursive speech. The same may also be true from the perspective of colometry[111]. I think Hayes is correct in noting, however, that a new set

---

111. 2-3-2-2 (vv. 18e-20d); 2-3-2-3 (vv. 21a-23e).

of images is introduced in vv. 18e-20d which turn more specifically around the land and provide further (and more active) description of her punishment to be followed by vv. 21a-22c which focus on the inhabitants of the land and what is happening to them[112]. Throughout chapter 24 ארץ and her inhabitants have been treated together as part of a circle of relationship with YHWH, suggesting that at least at one level vv. 18e-20d and vv. 21a-23e are related. Besides this, a number of poetic features of these final verses of chapter 24 serve to establish them as a unit as well as link them, in particular, with the beginning of the chapter (vv. 1-4)[113]. In addition, the author has clearly picked up themes and images from the rest of the chapter as a kind of summary of what has happened and is about to happen to both ארץ and her inhabitants.

ארץ
twist surface	(v. 1)	//	torn, split, shaken (v. 19)
wailing, withering, weak	(vv. 4-5)	//	staggering, swaying (v. 20)
polluted under sinful inhabitants	(v. 5)	//	sin heavy upon her (v. 20)

inhabitants
(והיה) extended simile	(v. 2)	//	(והיה) merism (v. 21)
terror, tomb and trap	(v. 17)	//	well, cell (v. 22)

Two further merisms serve to unite the unit: 'floodgates of the height' / 'foundations of the earth' (v. 18) and 'moon' / 'sun' (v. 23), both of which introduce a cosmic dimension to the text and remind us of the 'high places' / 'land' in vv. 4-5. V. 23c is also reminiscent of v. 3c and similarly constitutes a framing formula, drawing the chapter to a close and concluding the poetic unit. Semantic recapitulation is also abundantly evident as we shall see below. The state of ארץ and the future of her inhabitants turn around a central statement in which punishment at the hands of YHWH is announced. The relational metaphors which have emerged so far in the text are here confirmed.

Thus, the various associative recapitulations between these final verses of chapter 24 suggest that from the perspective of metaphor, we

---

112. HAYES, *The Earth Mourns*, pp. 213-214.
113. Poetic features linking the two units include: devices which underline completeness such as extended simile and infinitive absolutes in vv. 1-3 and merism and infinitive absolutes in vv. 18e-23e; semantic/thematic associations (see text) and a plethora of repetitions, rhymes, alliterations, and onomatopoeias; cf. LEWIS, *Rhetorical-Critical Analysis*, pp. 83-90.

are not dealing with two separate statements but rather a complex return to the metaphorical images and statements we have already seen within the chapter. Indeed, it would seem that we are here provided with a new set of *métaphorisants* which relate to *métaphorisés* located throughout the previous verses.

Commentators differ widely on the delimitation of these verses although most tend to split v. 21ff. from v. 20. Höffken, for example, considers vv. 1-13 and vv. 17-20 of chapter 24 to be a more original unity and proposes that vv. 14-16 should be understood as a lament of later provenance and vv. 21-23 as 'Sonderstück' with its own formal and substantial unity[114]. Kilian sees vv. 18e-20d as a revocation of God's creation and vv. 21-23 as a proclamation of YHWH's manifestation of his glorious reign on Zion with which heavenly and earthly powers will be forced to reckon[115]. Motyer likewise splits vv. 18e-20 and vv. 21-23, the former he views as a description of 'the earth broken up', the latter as an announcement of divine visitation followed by divine reign[116]. Johnson likewise argues that the formula והיה ביום ההוא and the sudden change from ארץ to אדמה argue for ending the unit at v. 20 (he begins in v. 16aβ and sees the whole thing as one announcement of doom)[117]. Lewis sees vv. 21-23 as introductory of new themes and a new style, suggesting that these verses serve better as an introduction to what he describes as an 'enthronement scene' in the following chapter (25)[118]. It remains possible, however, that vv. 21-23 look both backwards and forwards. Fohrer and Lindblom, who limit the unit to v. 20 as the conclusion to an

---

114. HÖFFKEN, *Das Buch Jesaja*, p. 177.
115. KILIAN, *Jesaja II*, p. 146-147.
116. MOTYER, *The Prophecy of Isaiah*, p. 204.
117. JOHNSON, *Chaos to Restoration*, p. 41; cf. also F. DELITZSCH, *Commentar über das Buch Jesaia* (Biblischer Commentar über das Alte Testament, III/I), Leipzig, 1889⁴, pp. 432-436; LINDBLOM, *Die Jesaja-Apokalypse*, pp. 23-24; 62-63; G. FOHRER, *Das Buch Jesaja*. 3 vols. (ZBK), Zürich, 1960-64, p. 3; WILDBERGER, *Jesaja 13-27*, p. 898-899; S.J. DE VRIES (*From Old Revelation to New. A Tradition-Historical & Redaction-Critical Study of Temporal Transitions in Prophetic Prediction*, Grand Rapids, MI 1995) points out that the temporal expression here in 24,21a expresses a transition from one event to another in the remote future (p. 54). This may be acceptable if one is inclined to accept the presence of eschatological/apocalyptic language at this point. As an extension of the metaphors expressed elsewhere in the chapter in which the events described are imminent future it would seem more reasonable to understand v. 21a as an expression of synchrony with the remaining images. The sudden change from ארץ to a synonym thereof is not unusual (cf. v. 4).
118. LEWIS, *Rhetorical-Critical Analysis*, pp. 91-99. Note, however, that together with ALONSO SCHÖKEL and SICRE DIAZ (*Profetas I*, p. 209) we can recognise a particular stylistic approach (repetition, alliteration, assonance, word play) in these verses which is not inconsistent with the style of the rest of the chapter. Watts only takes v. 23 as part of the enthronement scene and lumps vv. 14-22 together as one poem.

'eschatological poem' (beginning in v. 16) followed by an 'eschatological addition' in vv. 21-23 seem to miss the fact that the eschatological nature of the material tends to unify it rather than separate it[119]. March correctly notes that up to v. 20, the poem has been picking up and developing themes found in earlier units but he also insists on a split between v. 20 and v. 21, noting that the climactic character of v. 20, and the new themes, new vocabulary and a change of tone in vv. 21-23 argue for separation[120]. Elder is correct, however, in pointing out that vv. 21-23 form an equally adequate climax to the chapter as a whole and that the alternation of themes found throughout the piece is also reflected in these final verses. Millar interestingly notes that vv. 18e-23 are marked by mixed meter, long lines being interspersed with short lines, purposefully suggesting the turbulence of the 'return to chaos' and moving towards a crescendo. He sees the entire unit as continuing the same alternating pattern (bicolon/tricolon) with the climax in v. 23 which, according to him, constitutes a tricolon with extra long lines[121].

Given the complexity of themes, stylistic features and metaphorical language found in the present chapter, however, and given our emerging awareness of the inter-related nature of humanity, the land and YHWH[122], we can allow redactional and form critical and even syntactical considerations to take second place and explore these verses as one concluding poem in which the themes and metaphors of the rest of the chapter are further unpacked.

Indicators / Type

Since it would appear that the unit running from 24,18e to 24,23d picks up and continues the metaphors of the rest of the chapter, we need not be on the look out for fresh indicators. As we noted above, however, much of the present unit constitutes additional *métaphorisants*, complementing and extending the metaphorical statements already noted throughout the chapter. In this sense, our first task is to establish the *métaphorisants* in these verses and their corresponding *métaphorisés* elsewhere in the chapter. Once this is done we can explore isotopic distinction and cross-reference, whether we are dealing with dependant or independent speech, whether the *métaphorisé* is corporeal or not,

---

119. Cf. ELDER, *Theological-Historical Study*, p. 87.
120. MARCH, *Two Prophetic Compositions*, p. 53-54.
121. MILLAR, *Origin*, p. 36. Procksch is among the few who delineates the unit from vv. 18e-23 (*Jesaja I*, p. 313).
122. The *berit olam*???

whether there are other figurative language types at work, what level of analogy we are dealing with etc.. Clearly what relates these verses to the other metaphorical statements are syntactic/stylistic similarity, semantic parallels, repetitions, word-plays etc., associative components which should become clearer as we proceed.

I – Associations with vv. 1-3

Vv. 18e-19c and 23ab are related to one another in their use of images of de-creation in the context of a merism: heights/foundations and a word-pair: moon/sun. Although using terminology different from that of the creation story in Gen 1 we are, nevertheless, brought into the realm cosmic (de-)creation via these images[123]. The first merism signifies top to bottom (vertical/spatial) inclusion. The images of torn, shaken and split ארץ serve to relate vv. 18e-19c with the opening metaphorical statement (vv. 1-3), continuing its assertions about the relationship between YHWH, ארץ and its inhabitants and extending the destruction and de-creation which inevitably follows upon the breakdown of that relationship to the widest possible spatial extremes. Thus, thematically and metaphorically we return to the same arena as was established in vv. 1-3. The use of infinitive absolutes in v. 3 and v. 19 further associate the two texts. While the principle actant – ארץ – remains the same in both passages, the metaphorical statement in vv. 1-3 turned around YHWH as the *métaphorisé* with 'enemy hostility' expressed in the form of a number of verbs of destruction and their consequences for creation both earthly and human as the *métaphorisant*. The present text (vv. 18e-19) extends the *métaphorisant* with further verbs (this time more descriptive) of destruction[124] focusing primarily on ארץ (in vv. 1-3 the *métaphorisant* had a double focus: ארץ and its inhabitants although the primary focus was ultimately inhabitants). YHWH remains as the unmentioned *métaphorisé* and, while it is unnecessary to repeat what we have already said on this identification, the present verses add an extra dimension by their more explicit reference to de-creation. YHWH is not only

---

123. Cf. Gen 7,11; 8,2 & Ps 93,1; 96,10; Job 38,6.
124. רעש I basically means 'to shake/tremble' (HALOT 1271/2). Interestingly, Childs has recognised here a code word for the primeval chaos; cf. B.S. CHILDS, *The Enemy from the North and the Chaos Tradition*, in *JBL* 78 (1959) 187-198. In light of the main themes of the chapter as a whole there may also be a pun here on רעש II which means 'to be abundant/plentiful'; רעע ii has the basic meaning of 'to smash/shatter' which in the *hithpolel* means 'to burst asunder' (HALOT 1270); פרר also has the primary meaning of 'to be convulsed' although in the *poel* it is used for the stirring up of or even division of the sea (Ps 74,13; HALOT 975); טוט means 'to sway, to be tossed about like a ship in a storm' (Sir 33/36,2; cf. HALOT 555).

'the enemy of his people', inflicting punishment for their transgressions, he is clearly putting creation into reverse. The 'removal' of humanity which was the consequence of YHWH's actions in vv. 1-3 is now complemented with the destruction of ארץ and the return of the chaos waters. We are, once again, reminded of the Noahic covenant here[125], the firmament of the heavens no longer holding back the waters above the heavens (Gen 7,11 – same terminology – וארבת השמים נפתחו). Even the trembling foundations of ארץ might be explained by the bursting forth of the 'great deep' (also in Gen 7,11). Part of the shock of this statement is that it appears that YHWH is going back on his promise (Gen 8,21-22). Once again, therefore, the *métaphorisant* and the *métaphorisé* are related primarily by negative analogy: YHWH does not usually go back on his word. Along with Thomas Aquinas, however, we are also aware that such apparently negative statements about YHWH have to be seen in their metaphorical context. We have already noted the ultimate primacy of relational metaphor within this chapter. The attribution of de-creation and infidelity to YHWH has to be seen in this context which in combination with the other relational metaphors in chapter 24 makes it clear that the true culprits are those who have 'transgressed' and it is they who have broken the '*berit olam*' (v. 5) and brought this 'curse' (v. 6) upon ארץ and themselves.

Thus the isotope of hostile destruction established in vv. 1-3 in contrast with the isotope of the divine is continued here in more cosmic but no less destructive terms. The metaphor of YHWH as enemy is extended to its furthest extremes. This remains dependent speech in that it already assumes a knowledge of the divine 'isotope' with which these images are juxtaposed via the connections between vv. 1-3 and vv. 18e-19c.

Type

As an extension of the metaphorical statement of vv. 1-3, vv. 18e-19c exhibit a 'simple' core. The hostility presented in this new *métaphorisant* (trembling, torn, split and shaken ארץ) constitutes an explicit repetition of the hostility which is present implicitly in the *métaphorisé* (YHWH). These are YHWH's deeds and as with vv. 1-3 they are not in line with covenant expectations, indeed the shock of attributing a return of the chaos waters to YHWH runs counter to his promise to Noah that he would never again allow the flood waters to return and destroy life (Gen 9,14). If there was any suggestion in vv. 1-3, however, that the subject

---

125. Cf. KILIAN, *Jesaja II*, p. 146.

of all this destruction was some hostile human force, this extension of the *métaphorisé* puts paid to it, focusing the metaphor on YHWH who alone can bring about this reversal of his creation. We remain in the presence of an active/emphatic/resonant metaphorical statement here, one which would not only be readily recognisable to its audience but would also invite them into genuine interactive exploration of the richness it contains. It is also a 'structural' metaphor in that it leads us to view the *métaphorisé* (YHWH) in a new way, as a hostile figure who can reverse creation. In line with Aquinas, the present metaphor must be considered an example of the 'Leo' type of allegorical speech in that it continues the attribution of negative characteristics to YHWH found in the first metaphorical statement of the chapter. The attribution of hostility and de-creative activity to YHWH, however, is clearly placed within a context of disturbed relationship between YHWH, ארץ and its inhabitants. We categorised the *métaphorisant* in vv. 1-3 as a physical reality in contrast to the mysterious reality of the *métaphorisé*. In the present verses a mysterious dimension is added to the *métaphorisant* by way of the cosmic introduction. The events depicted by this extension of the *métaphorisant* are clearly to be understood as real events and not imaginary ones. In their association with YHWH they are part of a metaphorical statement but they also constitute a level of literal description thus making the metaphor 'Twice True'. Finally, the limited nature of the positive analogy between the *métaphorisé* (YHWH) and the images contained in these verses (*métaphorisant*) suggests that we are in the presence of a quite novel metaphor according to Macky's spectrum, one which contradicts old views and institutes new ways of envisaging reality, both real and mysterious. In reducing the metaphor of vv. 1-3 to 'YHWH is enemy' we became aware of its focus on a level of similarity between the *métaphorisé* and the *métaphorisant*. The extra 'cosmic' dimension of the present extension thereof makes such positive analogy less obvious and increases the 'shock' of the metaphor as a whole.

II – *Associations with vv. 7a-13e*

The second merism in v. 23a-b signifies temporal (horizontal) inclusion. The sun and moon no longer rule (משׁל I) the day and night (Gen 1,16) and seasons because they have grown dark with shame[126]. Without light and without seasons, ארץ and its fruit are forced to endure an arid, infertile and joyless existence for which they can only weep and wail.

---

126. חפר and בושׁ appear in parallel here and in Isa 1,29. They are synonyms, both meaning 'to be ashamed' (HALOT 341, 116/7).

Thus the de-creation image of v. 23a-b is related to our third metaphorical statement (vv. 7a-13e).

V. 23ab constitutes a small metaphorical statement in itself with the juxtaposition of verbs usually related to human realities (blushing, being ashamed) with cosmic terms of moon and sun[127]. Given that the latter two terms are part of the isotope of 'sources of light', their 'shame' suggests darkening and disability. They no longer function as they should. Interestingly, בוש is employed in Joel 1,12.17 to suggest the ruination of joy, wine (תירוש), grain etc. The entire context of these verses in Joel also includes terminology of ארץ mourning and lamenting using the same words as we find in vv. 4 and 7 (אבל, אמל). The parallel phrase in v. 11b; ערבה כל־שׂמחה, evokes a similar scenario. Thus v. 23ab constitutes a new *métaphorisant* taken from a new isotope: shame/darkening/ruination. Without the light of sun and moon there is no temporal order and ארץ, like the קרית תהו of v. 10, sinks into chaos. The corresponding *métaphorisé* comes from vv. 7a-13e and the isotope of wine, joy, gaiety and festival. All are swept up into the chaos of this image of de-creation. While the lament and ultimate absence of wine (תירוש) is underlined by the ending of the seasons, festival and its associated joy must also come to an end without sun and moon to mark them. The emotional brokenness which is the focus of the metaphorical statement in vv. 7a-13e takes on cosmic dimensions via a new *métaphorisant* and its implications.

The absence of festival which marked the metaphorical statement in vv. 7a-13e is also given a further twist here. If there is no sun and moon to guide them then festivals cannot be celebrated and the temple itself becomes the real focal point and the קרית תהו begins to look like Jerusalem. This is further confirmed by the remainder of v. 23. Human existence in ארץ and Jerusalem with its wine and joy and festivals was once governed (משל) by sun and moon (Gen 1,16-17), but no longer. There is nothing left but chaos, darkness, mourning. Now it is YHWH Ts^{e}ba'ot who reigns (מלך) in Jerusalem, contrasting creation's diminishing light with His glory (כבוד).

Type

The core of the small metaphorical statement in v. 23ab is a 'simple' one, suggesting a multiple (2x) yet implicit repetition of 'disappearance

---

127. Cf. the use of לנבה in Isa 30,26 where it is also related to חמה (cf. NBDB 3842). The metaphor in this latter text constitutes the opposite of what we have here, i.e. brilliant light as opposed to the diminishment of light and its consequences.

of light' from the face of human persons and from the 'face' of cosmic bodies. This 'disappearance' is rooted in the positive analogy made possible in juxtaposing two distinct isotopes: human shame and cosmic light. We are invited to restructure our understanding of sun and moon in terms of the fading glory of human agents who like sun and moon the are descending into chaos. The metaphorical statement itself might be quite novel, given the limited positive analogy between the two isotopes and the rarity of the expressions. There is no doubt that its audience is being invited to explore the richness of the interaction between the two isotopes and as such we can categorise the metaphor as active and emphatic/resonant. As cosmic realities in the Ancient Near East were invested with mystery, it is possible that the metaphor here must remain largely culture-dependant. At the same time, however, as mere sources of light, the idea of their ultimate eclipse and the consequences thereof is an image which extends beyond the cultural boundaries of the ANE.

As a metaphorical statement in itself, v. 23ab constitutes an extension of the *métaphorisant* of vv. 7a-13d where we already noted that the *métaphorisé* YHWH is absent. A long list of the negative results of YHWH's withdrawal from creation is started in vv. 7a-13d and continued here: failure of the wine harvest, cessation of joy, *tohû*, gloom and ruin in the city, now diminishment of the cosmic lights. Thus the semantic association of joy/wine/festival with blushing sun and moon has its roots in the absent *métaphorisé* of vv. 7a-13d. Both isotopes have YHWH at their core, thus, as with the metaphor it extends, v. 23ab is primarily a relational metaphor: the relationship between YHWH and his people/creation has been broken. YHWH is absent. The complexity of images provided by this extension of the *métaphorisant* makes this statement active, resonant and structural. Mere ornament is clearly not intended here but rather an invitation to enter into the speech act and compare its elements.

III – Associations with vv. 4a-6d

V. 20 is related to our second metaphorical statement (vv. 4a-6d). We noted that the *métaphorisé* in vv. 4a-6d alternated between ארץ and its inhabitants although ארץ was its primary focus. Thus ארץ remains the *métaphorisé* in this extension of the metaphorical statement. Once again the *métaphorisant* is spread out over a number of verb forms (נוע, נוד, נפל), adding to the list of verbs from vv. 4a-6d (אמל, נבל, אבל etc.). We noted above that terms such as אמל, נבל, אבל bear an internal ambiguity in that they can be assigned to the isotope of 'mourning' / 'sin' as well as that of physical desolation. The same is true here. ארץ is not only physically devastated, she engages in the movements of lament and mourning, swaying to and fro and falling down. The root נוד in particular can signify the expression of grief and lament over the dead[128]. The other verb forms suggest similar movements[129]. The expression 'like a drunkard' is a metaphorical simile[130] suggesting that ארץ's behaviour is like that of a drunkard swaying[131], tottering and ultimately falling down without the ability to get up again. The expression 'like a hut' functions in a similar fashion, a מלונה being a fragile structure which could be made to sway and collapse without much effort[132]. Both the original metaphorical statement in vv. 4a-6d and the present extension thereof introduce the realm of transgression as the cause of ארץ's current condition. The mention of 'transgression' in v. 20c immediately recalls the triple accusation of v. 5 in which the polluted state of ארץ is blamed on her inhabitants and their ultimate sin of having broken the ברית עולם. The equation of ארץ and her inhabitants is effected by the use of the terms תחת in v. 5a and עלי(ה) in v. 20c, relating 'transgression' to 'pollution' and thus ארץ to her inhabitants[133].

V. 20 primarily extends the metaphorical statement of vv. 4a-6d by introducing additional terminology from the isotope of lament/mourning/sin thereby extending the *métaphorisant*. The *métaphorisé* ארץ is present in v. 20 and is identified with the inhabitants of ארץ via the weight of transgression here and the effects of transgression in v. 5, i.e. pollution. The words and sounds of lament from vv. 4a-6d are extended to include the gestures of lament here in v. 20 and in case there is any doubt as to the negative significance of her actions, they are related by way of simile to those of a drunkard and the fragile/unstable condition of a watchman's hut.

Type

The extension of the *métaphorisant* found in v. 20 primarily focuses on the lament/mourning/sin aspect which was present in the ambiguous

---

128. NBDB 5110. In Jer 15,5 and 16,5 as well as in Isa 51,19, the term is used to signify grief/lament concerning Jerusalem.
129. The phonetic similarity between נפלה and נבלה further connects v. 20 to v. 4.
130. Introduced to underline the metaphor via simple comparison. Macky includes some biblical similes under the umbrella of metaphor.
131. There may be an element of irony involved here given that absence of wine is lamented in v. 11a.
132. Darr points out that the same term is used in Isa 1,8 as part of a series of three similes for Zion; cf. K.P. DARR, *Isaiah's Vision and the Family of God* (Literary Currents in Biblical Interpretation), Louisville, KY, 1994, p. 135-136.
133. Note also the relationship with Gen 8,21 and the Noahic covenant: "I will never again curse the ground because of humankind...".

terminology of vv. 4-6 (אמל, נבל, אבל). The emotional dimension of lamentation and mourning which went side by side with a physical 'drying up' of ארץ is also represented in the terminology of v. 20 (נוע, נוד, נפל: note alliteration) but with the emphasis on a different physical aspect. ארץ staggers and sways and falls to the ground under the weight of her transgression. Once again there is a level of isotopic cross-reference or metaphorical core lying within the terminology of the *métaphorisant*. As with vv. 4-6, the core might therefore be considered 'absent' or 'hidden' in that it does not lie, as Bourguet thinks it should, in the middle ground between the *métaphorisant* and the *métaphorisé*. The *métaphorisé* ארץ is also present in v. 20. The metaphorical similes attached to the description of ארץ's gestures, however, suggests that in the present instance we look for the primary core precisely where Bourguet would have us look, in the middle ground between the *métaphorisant* and the *métaphorisé*. As we already noted, the *métaphorisé* ארץ is portrayed in terminology taken from the isotope of human lament and in particular its physical dimensions. The comparison with drunken behaviour, however, introduces a note of insincerity into the image, implying that ארץ's condition is her own fault and is ultimately due to her own transgressions. The metaphorical core, therefore, would appear to lie in the evident similarity or positive analogy between the land and human persons in mourning. The original metaphor which the present verse extends focuses on more passive similarities such as weakness, pollutedness, withering, consumption, diminishment. Here, perhaps inspired by the images of destruction immediately preceding it, we have more active similarity between ארץ and lamenting humans. The reason for the state of affairs is the same in both cases: transgression. We might describe such a metaphorical core as 'simple', with the aspect of similarity more explicit in the *métaphorisant* than the *métaphorisé*. In any event, the image is what Black would call a genuine interactive metaphor (active emphatic), rich in interpretative implications (resonant). As with the metaphorical statement it extends, v. 20 might also be reduced to the same A is B type metaphor: 'earth is mortal'. At the same time the metaphor provides a link between ארץ and its inhabitants via 'transgression'. V. 5a describes ארץ as polluted 'under' her inhabitants while v. 20c portrays her as bearing the heavy weight of her transgression 'upon' her. Thus 'inhabitant' is identified with 'transgression' and both weigh heavily upon ארץ. Once again, therefore, the metaphor appears to be working in two directions and is underlining the intimacy of the relationship between people and land.

In terms of Lakoff and Johnson's categories the present metaphor would appear to be 'structural' in that it forced us to view ארץ in terms of a lamenting individual who is behaving like a drunkard. The similes of 'drunkard' and 'fragile hut' suggests that the metaphor would be predominantly 'culture exceeding', as Stienstra would describe it. Although readers may be unfamiliar with Ancient Near Eastern mourning rituals, the behaviour of those suffering 'bereavement' is fairly universal and can be readily recognised in the metaphorical expression. Once again, the addition of the similes here adds a novel twist to the metaphorical statement, suggesting that 'staggering, swaying, falling' ארץ in v. 20 would be less familiar an image to its audience than 'withering, wailing, weak' ארץ in vv. 4-6. Evident positive and negative analogy between the *métaphorisé* and the *métaphorisant* would inspire the listener to approach this speech act as metaphorical inviting comparison in the process of exploring the metaphor (comparative metaphor rather than ornamental metaphor).

IV – Associations with vv. 14a-18d

A variety of stylistic, verbal and semantic associations[134] suggest that we refer vv. 21-22 (23cde) to our fourth metaphorical statement in vv. 14a-18d in which we found a core metaphor identifying the first person speaker (the *métaphorisé*: the prophet) with the devastation/emaciation (*métaphorisant*) in ארץ and a broader metaphor in which the people's praise of YHWH (*métaphorisé*) is identified with their treachery and its punishment (*métaphorisant*). Parallel connections between v. 21 and v. 23cde are clear (army // YHWH Ts^{e}ba'ot & kings // YHWH rules) and serve to include this latter part of the final verse into the extension of the metaphorical statement. The primary purpose of the extension appears to be the addition of the image of the 'well'/'cell' to the *métaphorisant* of the main metaphorical statement in vv. 14-18d, i.e. treachery and its consequences expressed in terms of 'the hunt'. Thus praise and glorification of the majesty of YHWH, the primary *métaphorisé* of vv. 14-18d, is being juxtaposed here with a new *métaphorisant*, that of containment in a 'well/cell' as a punishment. This latter image appears to be both literal and metaphorical. As an extension of the primary *métaphorisant* of vv. 14-18d, its significance as a place in which precious water was stored

---

134. Language of the hunt, captivity // to be herded/imprisoned (אסף- ambiguous term can mean gather as animals or as people or to one's grave: cf. DCH I 348); height/land merism // East/West merism; majesty (גאון) of YHWH // YHWH reigns (מלך); glory of YHWH (כבוד) // glory to YHWH (כבד); 'They'/ 'the treacherous' // army of the height and kings on the land; triple alliteration/consonance (אסף, אסיר, סגר // פחד, פחת, פח)

suggests that we not only read it as a place of imprisonment but also as a place of ambiguity with possible negative connotations of panic and drowning. The floodgates of the height might be open but this brings no relief to ארץ or her inhabitants, only destruction (Noahic covenant?). Water which could have brought fertility to parched and wailing ארץ now brings punishment. The image is reminiscent of the situation confronted by the גבר in Lamentations (Lam 3,53-54) who describes himself as being left to die in a cistern (בבור) steadily filling with water, breathlessly waiting for the waters to rise above his head[135]. It is interesting to note that the image of the cistern in Lamentations also follows upon hunting imagery (3,52). After 'terror, tomb and trap' there is ultimate confinement and probable drowning. Having been set in parallel with the isotope of 'the hunt' the isotope of praise/glorification/majesty is now associated with the isotope of imprisonment and inevitable death. The phrase 'after many days' does not appear to imply that having confined his prisoners YHWH will return at a later time to punish them. In the context of the image of the cistern, simply the passage of time would have dealt out punishment to those imprisoned within it. The central metaphor in v. 16c in which the prophet constituted the *métaphorisé* and 'emaciation' the *métaphorisant* does not appear to be extended in these final verses of chapter 24. It is possible to read the prophet's voice, however, in v. 23cde. In the original metaphorical statement of vv. 14-18d the prophet denounced the premature praise of the treacherous by referring to a former prophecy in which he identifies himself with the state of ארץ and its population and pronounces dreadful punishment. Here, as speaker, he extends the images portraying punishment in vv. 21a-22c and concludes with a bold statement of true praise in v. 23cde taking elements from the treacherous praise of his original denunciation (YHWH, glory, majesty), ultimately centering them on Zion and in Jerusalem and perhaps insisting on these locations as the only places of true worship as opposed to 'East and West'.

It is interesting to note the interchange of passive/active participation in these verses. Initially YHWH is the **passive** recipient of **active** praise (vv. 14a-16b) and **active** treachery (v. 16ef) yet his response is **active** punishment (vv. 17a-18d; 21a-22c). Indeed, majesty and glory in the mouths of 'they' (as subject) in v. 14b and 15a constitutes the profoundest treachery. As we noted, the prophet concludes with a strong affirmation of His reigning (majesty 14b) in glory (15a). The prophet is a central, yet **passive** 'I' figure. The anonymous 'one' in v. 18a-d will **actively**

---

135. Cf. RENKEMA, *Klaagliederen*, p. 325.

endeavour to escape terror, tomb and trap (vv. 17a-18d) but without success. In a parallel statement in vv. 21a-22c, 23cde the now identified 'they' are central; 'they' will **passively** endure cell/well/prison. YHWH is '**active**', punishing 'them' (kings and army are now **passive** recipients) in response to treachery. The prophet continues to stand in the middle. The general term 'dweller on the earth' who was the subject of terror, tomb and trap is extended to included army of the height and kings of the land.

Although he considers the temporal expression והיה ביום ההוא to be an introduction to a futuristic expansion of Isa 24–27, S.J. De Vries notes further that it expresses synchronicity with the 'universal judgement' depicted in the preceding verses. Thus the day in which the treacherous are confronted with terror, tomb and trap is synchronous with the day the army of the height and the kings in the land will be herded into the well to meet their punishment[136].

Type

Having established vv. 21a-22c,23cde as an extension of the primary metaphorical statement of vv. 14a-18d we must now establish the latter's relationship with those who will meet their final end, abandoned in a pit, gasping for air as it fills with water. Thus it is the process of de-creation, the opening of the floodgates, which brings death. It might be reasonable to suggest, therefore, that the core of the metaphorical extension is 'antithetical/semantic' as well as 'structural' since all these elements combine to allow us to associate both texts and adjudge the present verses to be a metaphorical extension of vv. 14a-18d. In any event, the association of images of praise and of the pit certainly can be described as a resonant-active metaphor, establishing genuine interaction between the *métaphorisé* and the *métaphorisant* and demanding interpretative reflection in the part of its audience. Together with the metaphorical statements in vv. 14a-18d, the present text further affirms the negative relational nature of the metaphor functioning here. Although YHWH is named as the one 'bringing punishment' he does not function as the subject of v. 22abc. The fate of 'they' is the result of YHWH's withdrawal from the cosmos. In the terminology employed by Lakoff and Johnson it would seem that we are still in the realm of structural metaphor here since the text invites us to structure our understanding of 'praise & rejoicing' in terms of 'treachery and its consequences', i.e. the בור and its implications. If

---

136. De Vries, I believe wrongly, considers Isa 24,1-20 to be directed against the nations and not Israel. This allows him to include the salvific references of Isa 25 in synchronicity with those of judgement via the expression והיה ביום ההוא.

terror, tomb, trap, captivity, cell and drowning are held up against praise and rejoicing then we are forced to restructure our understanding of the latter: 'praise and rejoicing' then take on a negative significance. This is what allows the prophet to use himself, as it were, as a metaphorical statement and introduce the idea of treachery. Unlike the metaphorical statement which they extend, the present verses do not appear to be culture-exceeding. The idea of death as the ultimate punishment for religious hypocrisy does not extend to every time and culture. We are clearly invited to compare two well-known yet distinct realities and search for what relates them. The final cola provide the clue. The prophet's affirmation of YHWH's reign and glory on Mount Zion and in Jerusalem (v. 23cde) serves to underline the fact that while YHWH is present, he is ultimately absent to the praise of the treacherous who must endure the consequences of his absence. The limited positive analogy between the two realities involved in this metaphorical statement and its extension here suggests that we are dealing with a quite novel metaphor. We already noted that the metaphorical statement functioning here forced us to re-interpret the unexpected introduction of a positive expression of praise (vv. 14a.16b) into a broader context of pretty overwhelming negativity (chapter 24 as a whole). The present metaphorical extension serves to confirm this.

Author's Purpose/Interpretation

It would seem that the author's primary purpose in vv. 18e-23e is to extend each of the metaphorical statements by adding new terms and images to their *métaphorisants*, in each case introducing a 'plus' dimension, thereby adding something extra to the original metaphorical statement. Where there is a 'plus' dimension, however, we need to determine in what way this extends the author's original purpose in employing metaphorical language.

I (//vv. 1-3)

We noted above that the metaphorical statement running from vv. 1-3 included a variety of intentions on the part of the author: 'performative' – providing information about YHWH; 'pedagogical' – illuminating a dark area of Israel's reality; 'affective' – encouraging emotional response; 'transformational' – using both emotion and pedagogical insight to persuade his audience. Primarily, however, we concluded that its purpose was ultimately 'relational' – intended to invite the audience to explore their relationship with YHWH in light of what the prophet says and in light of their knowledge of him up to that point. It is this 'relational' dimension which provides the focus of the author's use of metaphorical language. We noted also that there was a hint of the use of metaphor to relate YHWH to a hostile foreign deity. The extension of this metaphorical statement found in v. 18e-19c appears to continue the 'relational' focus of the metaphor, the extra cosmic dimension inviting the audience to include YHWH as creator (as well as the possibility of his withdrawal therefrom) in their reflection. The heights and the foundations are beyond the reach of hostile deities, however, since they constitute the 'boundaries' of YHWH's creation (as opposed to creation's 'surface' and its 'inhabitants' in vv. 1-3). Thus the statement is purified of any possible residual comparison of YHWH to a foreign deity.

In terms of gaining access to, understanding, re-constructing and explaining the speaker's meaning, the same holds true here as it did for the original metaphorical statement. The 'speaker' uses terminology with a variety of potential meanings and, by placing it in a particular context, selects an actual meaning from those potential meanings. Thus it would appear that the *métaphorisant* or focal isotope (actual meaning) of 'hostility' leading to impending disaster with 'supernatural proportions' in vv. 1-3 is extended here in vv. 18e-19a. The author is thus referring to the same disaster, although his terminology is more descriptive, portraying ארץ as she is now. The impending nature of the original metaphorical statement is here placed to one side: the events of vv. 18e-19c are already real. At the same time, the author's initial use of verbs with YHWH as subject is replaced here with verbs which have ארץ as passive subject. Thus, an announcement of impending judgement is fulfilled and has taken on cosmic proportions. In light of the relational aspect of the metaphor in vv. 1-3 and its extension here, our interpretation of these words remains the same: YHWH has withdrawn from his relationship with ארץ and its inhabitants. Only in this light can one explain the return of the chaos waters and the darkening of the cosmic lights (v. 23ab).

II (// vv. 7a-13e)

We noted above that the central statements of diptych structure of vv. 7-13 (8b and 11b) seemed to convey the author's primary purpose: evaluation of events as a sign of divine withdrawal couched in terms of the cessation of festival joy both in countryside and in the city. While this purpose may have been primarily evaluative it remains at base relational. The absence of the 'fruits' of ארץ (wine) and human persons (joy) are a direct result of YHWH's withdrawal and the audience is invited to explore its relationship with YHWH in the light of this return to chaos (תהו). The extension of this metaphorical statement proposed in v. 23ab further underlines the disintegration of festival and harvest via the collapse of time. We also noted above that it was perhaps possible to interpret the terminology employed by the author in vv. 7-13 as conjugal/sexual terms descriptive of an aspect of the relationship between YHWH, ארץ and its inhabitants. The language of mourning takes on the features of a widow's mourning at the loss of her 'husband'. The extension of this metaphorical statement in v. 23ab may also be seen to underline this interpretation of the text, human menstrual seasons collapsing in chaos as the 'husband' of creation (and of the personified, feminine town/city) withdraws and the lights which govern time hide themselves in shame. With the absence of time there is a concomitant absence of menstruation and thus of fertility.

III (// vv. 4a-6d)

The 'emotional' terminology employed in vv. 4-6 established the metaphorical statement therein as having a degree of 'expressive' purpose although the element of lament and mourning may also suggest a 'pedagogical' dimension, teaching its audience about the consequence of transgression. As with the metaphor in vv. 1-3, however, we appear to be focused still on the expression of relationship between YHWH, ארץ and its inhabitants, thus the author's relational purpose for using metaphor appears to be central. The extension of this metaphorical statement here in v. 20 introduces a further terminological ambiguity in that נוע, נוד and נפל can be assigned to the isotope of mourning (psychological desolation) as well as physical desolation. The passive weakness and withering of vv. 4-6 are extended to include more active gestures of mourning supported by similes of fragility and drunkenness. The author appears, therefore, to be continuing his original 'expressive' and 'pedagogical' purpose with the 'relational' purpose never far from his mind. By repeating the element of transgression, v. 20 may also be seen as a 'presentative' in that it is communicating information (transgress and you will suffer the consequences) but as was the case with the metaphorical statement it extends, such a purpose seems to be secondary. While it is clear even here that the author wants to evaluate what he sees and invite his audience to change their ways (transformative purpose) it would seem that the 'relational' aspect of the metaphorical extension in v. 20 must take pride of place. Transgression of relationship (and its results) was focused in vv. 4-6 on the inhabitants of א־ץ. Here it touches on ארץ herself, tainting even her mourning gestures with negative images of drunkenness. All this is the ultimate result of the breakdown in the relationship between YHWH, ארץ and its inhabitants established in (whatever) covenant.

We suggested that the author's intention in vv. 4-6 was to have his audience view earth/world in human terms and humans in earthly terms via a dysfunctional association with YHWH. The extension of the metaphor in v. 20 has the same effect. For YHWH, earth is mortal (staggering/falling like a drunk [v. 20]) and mortals are earthly (weak, withered, polluted [vv. 4-5]). Both are mutually destructive in the context of covenant transgression, when the relationship with YHWH is severed.

IV (// vv. 14a-18d)

We noted the variety of purposes involved in the metaphorical statement found in vv. 14-18d: verbalisation of personal experience ('expressive'), inviting change ('dynamic'/'transformative'), judging the situation ('evaluative'), inviting emotional reaction in his identification with withered ארץ and his juxtaposition of praise and treachery. As with the other metaphorical statements in this chapter, the author's primary purpose seems to have been 'relational', inviting his audience to explore their relationship with YHWH and ארץ (via himself). The extension of this metaphor in vv. 21a-22(23cde) introduced the image of the בור and its implications. Thus those who engage in treacherous praise will not only endure 'the hunt' (terror, tomb and trap) they will have to face death 'at the hands' of precious water which has reverted to chaos waters. The metaphorical extension found in these verses, therefore, seems to highlight the author's 'evaluative' purpose as he announces judgement over what he sees. As elsewhere, however, the 'relational' aspect is far from lost.

We interpreted the metaphorical statement in vv. 14-18d as a relational statement in which the prophet identifies himself with withering ארץ in order to show that her inhabitants' praise is ultimately treacherous and that their assumed relationship with YHWH is false. The present extension continues this by further detailing the consequences of relational 'blindness' for human persons (perhaps specifying particular groups such as armies, and kings): withering and wailing, terror, tomb and trap will finally lead to the בור and inevitable death. Death will be the result of cosmos reversed. YHWH is the active subject of this 'punishment' (v. 21bc), 'they' its passive object (v. 22abc). The temporal phrase 'after many days', however, suggests that the actual subject of punishment is the בור and its contents (the return of the chaos waters; cf. v. 18e). Transgression has led to YHWH's withdrawal and an all round return to pre-cosmic chaos.

Author's Purpose/Interpretation of vv. 18e-23e

The overall thrust of the metaphorical extensions in vv. 18e-23e continues that of the four primary metaphorical statements found in ch. 24 as a whole. The author intends to stir the emotions of his audience ('affective' purpose) and to enlighten them with regard to the events they are experiencing ('pedagogical' purpose). To some extent he continues to make the unspeakable reality of YHWH's hostility towards his people speakable via metaphor. In the last analysis, however, the introduction of a cosmic dimension here in these final verses focuses his attention once again on the relationship, established by covenant, between YHWH, ארץ and its inhabitants[137]. YHWH as a 'hostile enemy' does not attack in the conventional way. His tactic, as it were, is to withdraw from relationship with ארץ and its inhabitants, to withdraw from his creation in response to transgression (treacherous praise). Thus YHWH is not actively destroying his creation, rather it is destroying itself: its transgression pollutes and consumes it and is heavy upon it. The cosmic terms introduced here are simply metaphors for earthly realities of time and space. With meristic dimensions they signal the withdrawal of YHWH and the return of chaos. Chaos in the city is extended to 'the gate' and to ארץ in vv. 7-13; here it extends to all creation both temporal (v. 23ab) and spatial (v. 18ef). Ultimately these final images inform the reader/audience that a process of 'de-creation' which is the inevitable result of the breakdown in relationship between YHWH, ארץ and its inhabitants, has begun. The final, positive statement in v. 23cde seems out of place against this strong confirmation of YHWH's absence. Its purpose emerges on closer inspection, however. Having shockingly portrayed YHWH as a hostile enemy, withdrawn from his covenantal relationship in response to treacherous praise, the author is compelled to affirm his presence in the very place which he said he would not abandon, in his very dwelling place. As we noted earlier, he uses terminology from vv. 14-16 where YHWH's majesty and glory were praised in East and West. Here in v. 23cde he insists that YHWH reigns in glory in Zion and Jerusalem. One suspects, thereby, that he is equating the 'town of

---

137. Note that the 'army' and the 'kings' mentioned in v. 21bc extend the categories of people who will endure this judgement outlined in v. 2: priest/people; master/servant; borrower/lender; now also army/kings.

tohû' with Jerusalem, the centre from which the transgression of treacherous praise has emerged.

The author is evaluating a situation of distress, relating it to already delivered prophecy which has been ignored (cf. Isa 21,1-4), revealing the consequence of transgression as the withdrawal of YHWH and its implications for humans and their environment and underlining, albeit negatively, the importance of right relationships between YHWH, ארץ and its inhabitants.

Concluding Remarks on Isa 24

The author(s) of Isa 24 has(ve) employed a series of intricate metaphorical statements to portray an essentially relational reality. We have already hinted at the more or less active or passive roles engaged in by each of the three relational poles in this reality. K. Hayes sheds further light on these roles. She notes that punishment ultimately takes the form of a devouring curse in Isa 24, one which has disastrous consequences for humans and ארץ alike. The curse[138] is the result of the fact that ארץ lies polluted under the transgression of her inhabitants (cf. v. 5,20c)[139]. In introducing the terminology of transgressed 'laws' and by-passed 'precepts', she notes, the author is focusing on the history of the relationship between YHWH, ארץ and its inhabitants. The twice used expression על־כן in v. 6, however, underscores the primary roles which have engendered this situation: the act of violation/transgression (whether social or cultic) begets its consequence – sin begets punishment. Hayes also confirms the relational focus of ch. 24 in pointing out that social disorder (transgression/absence of joy/breakdown of social intercourse) ultimately leads to natural disorder expressed in images of impending disaster, failure of the harvest and the reversal of creation[140]. YHWH's hostility, therefore, is not an active one, even his 'punishing visitation' in v. 21bc is indirect since it has to do with the fact that He no

---

138. HAYES notes (*The Earth Mourns*, pp. 220-221) that the 'curse' of drought is accompanied here by traditional curse elements found throughout the ANE mentioned in D.R. HILLERS (*Treaty-Curses and Old Testament Prophecy* [BibOr, 16], Rome, 1964, pp. 57-58) and in Hos 2,13; Jer 7,34; 16,9; 25,10; Lam 5,15; Ezek 26,13.

139. She correctly notes that while the ברית עולם in v. 5 is reminiscent of the Noahic covenant of Gen 9,16, the breaking of which is something of a contradiction, the terms תורת and חק which are also part of the act of transgression, allow for possible violation. She points out that WILDBERGER (*Jesaja 13–27*, p. 922) asserts that Isa 24,5 implies a confluence of Noahic (promise based) and Sinaitic (obligation based) covenants.

140. HAYES, *The Earth Mourns*, pp. 218-220.

longer maintains the firmament which keeps out the chaos waters. It is the waters themselves which are the ultimate punishers. His withdrawal from relationship with ארץ and its inhabitants sets in motion a process of de-creation which has its ultimate focus in the 'town of *tohû*' (v. 10a), the state of ארץ before creation and the state to which it returns without YHWH. The reversal of creation is the automatic consequence of transgression.

Hayes also notes that the images and metaphors employed by the author of Isa 24 describe a reaction akin to the traditional response to the 'advent of the divine warrior'. "The quaking of the earth, the drying up of the land, the scorching of its inhabitants, and the rainstorm ensuing from the opening of the heavens are all natural phenomena that manifest the theophany of YHWH."[141] She notes significant similarities between Isa 24 and Jer 4,23-28 in this regard which we need not rehearse here[142]. What makes Isa 24 distinct, however, is the fact that the advent of the divine warrior lacks a specific enemy as its target whereas similar texts (e.g. Nah 1,2-8 and Jer 4,23-28) are not so lacking. This lack of identification of a target nation leads her to interpret Isa 24 as a "culminating manifestation of divine power against all on the earth who oppose it."[143] Clues within the metaphorical structure of the text would appear to suggest otherwise. The meta-metaphor with its relational purpose which dominates the entire chapter, the focus on violation of covenant and unfulfilled obligations, the subsequent breakdown of religious (liturgical), social, political, agricultural and even cosmic order all ultimately converge, in my opinion, on Judah and Jerusalem. Lack of identification of a national/city referent in the text itself seems to me to be intentional, part of a technique to lure the audience into self-accusation. The variety of terms for 'earth' (ארץ, אדמה, תבל) as well as the references to East and West and the meristic images for inhabitants of ארץ function in a similar way. If the metaphors are intended to invite the audience to reflect on their relationship with YHWH and in the light of their present condition and the prophecy of worse, then vagueness of location serves the metaphor. This is not 'everybody's problem', this is 'our problem'. The possibility of reading a level of conjugal imagery within these verses further ties the metaphors to Judah and Jerusalem, the widow of YHWH. Hayes considers the focus on ארץ, the lack of proper names and clear historical allusions side by side with the broad sweep of social

---

141. *Ibid.*, p. 215.
142. *Ibid.*, pp. 215-216
143. *Ibid.*, p. 217.

classes in v. 2 to set the parameters of the disaster portrayed in Isa 24[144]. She suggests that whereas in Jer 4,23-28 the cosmic images of sky and earth focus the vision of disaster on Judah in Isa 24 they suggest boundaries wider than any nation or city. At the same time she reckons that references to תורת, חק, and ברית עולם speak explicitly of covenant between YHWH and Israel which has roots in the covenant between YHWH and all humanity going back to creation itself. Each of her arguments, however, can be seen in reverse: the focus of cosmic allusions in Jeremiah supports a more localised reading of Isa 24; references to תורת, חק, and ברית עולם speak of the history of God's unique relationship with Israel (she already notes that mention of תורת and חק include the notion of a covenant of obligations [Sinai] side by side with the covenant of promise [Noahic]) from creation on, underlining a relationship in which Israel has responsibilities. This aside, Hayes is correct when she points out that the effect of the metaphors and supporting literary techniques in Isa 24 tends to pattern together a variety of images to focus the reader's awareness on the significance of the judgement about to befall ארץ and its inhabitants. That significance I see to be the withdrawal of YHWH from the ברית עולם and the subsequent intervention of 'curse' as the counterpart of the transgression of תורת and חק.

What follows in ch. 25 only serves to confirm the notion that ch. 24 had a more limited audience in mind. While no one can deny that it is possible to interpret both chapters from a universal perspective, the central metaphor of chapter 25 (25,10a) is one which replaces YHWH's absence with his blessing presence. The husband is restored to his people/city/land. The relationship is whole once again and each party thereto will benefit. All the images of false praise, death, want, destruction, absence of festival/wine/joy, are thrown into reverse. What YHWH has done and continues to do for *his people* now becomes the subject of the author's use of metaphors. Domestic images take the place of destructive, violent ones. Those who did not engage in treacherous praise now rejoice that their silence has been rewarded. The repetition of 'On this mountain' (25,6.7.10) suggests that from this central location, from this place of marriage between YHWH, earth and its inhabitants, blessing will spread out to include all nations and all peoples. Lamentation (images of mourning) will not only be banished from Judah and Jerusalem but will be removed from all the nations. Israel will have fulfilled her 'mission' by waiting and enduring until her God returns with salvation. The metaphors of ch.24 are put into reverse in ch. 25 where the focus of the author's attention is much more clearly Jerusalem/Zion.

---

144. *Ibid.*, pp. 216-217.

CHAPTER FOUR

ISAIAH 25

Hebrew Colometry

25,1	יְהוָה אֱלֹהַי אַתָּה	אֲרוֹמִמְךָ אוֹדֶה שִׁמְךָ
	כִּי עָשִׂיתָ פֶּלֶא	עֵצוֹת מֵרָחוֹק אֱמוּנָה אֹמֶן
2	כִּי שַׂמְתָּ מֵעִיר לַגָּל	קִרְיָה בְצוּרָה לְמַפֵּלָה
	אַרְמוֹן זָרִים מֵעִיר	לְעוֹלָם לֹא יִבָּנֶה
3	עַל־כֵּן יְכַבְּדוּךָ עַם־עָז	קִרְיַת גּוֹיִם עָרִיצִים יִירָאוּךָ

4	כִּי־הָיִיתָ מָעוֹז לַדָּל	מָעוֹז לָאֶבְיוֹן בַּצַּר־לוֹ
	מַחְסֶה מִזֶּרֶם	צֵל מֵחֹרֶב
	כִּי רוּחַ עָרִיצִים	כְּזֶרֶם קִיר
5	כְּחֹרֶב בְּצָיוֹן	שְׁאוֹן זָרִים
	תַּכְנִיעַ חֹרֶב בְּצֵל עָב	זְמִיר עָרִיצִים יַעֲנֶה

Working Translation

25,1   YHWH, my God are you.
      I will extol you, I will laud your name.

      Indeed, you have done great wonders,
      plans from long ago, perfectly faithful.

2   Indeed, you have made the city into a heap,
      the town with high walls into a ruin.

      The palace of strangers is a city no more.
      In eternity it will not be [re]built.

3   Therefore, they will glorify you, a nation strong.
      A town of nations violent will revere you.

....

4   Indeed, you have been a refuge for the poor,
      a refuge for the needy in his distress;

      a shelter from the storm,
      a shade from the heat.

      Indeed, the blast of the violent
      is like a storm of hail;

5   like heat in the desert
      the din of strangers.

      You will subdue heat, with the shade of a cloud.
      The song of the violent will be suppressed.

6   וְעָשָׂה֩ יְהוָ֨ה צְבָא֜וֹת   לְכָל־הָֽעַמִּים֙ בָּהָ֣ר הַזֶּ֔ה

     מִשְׁתֵּ֥ה שְׁמָנִ֖ים   מִשְׁתֵּ֖ה שְׁמָרִ֑ים

     שְׁמָנִים֙ מְמֻחָיִ֔ם   שְׁמָרִ֖ים מְזֻקָּקִֽים

7   וּבִלַּע֙ בָּהָ֣ר הַזֶּ֔ה   פְּנֵֽי־הַלּ֖וֹט ׀ הַלּ֣וֹט עַל־כָּל־הָֽעַמִּ֑ים

     וְהַמַּסֵּכָ֥ה הַנְּסוּכָ֖ה עַל־כָּל־הַגּוֹיִֽם   8 בִּלַּ֤ע הַמָּ֙וֶת֙ לָנֶ֔צַח

     וּמָחָ֨ה אֲדֹנָ֧י יְהוִ֛ה דִּמְעָ֖ה מֵעַ֣ל כָּל־פָּנִ֑ים וְחֶרְפַּ֣ת עַמּ֗וֹ יָסִיר֙ מֵעַ֣ל כָּל־הָאָ֔רֶץ

     כִּ֥י יְהוָ֖ה דִּבֵּֽר

9   וְאָמַר֙ בַּיּ֣וֹם הַה֔וּא

     הִנֵּ֨ה אֱלֹהֵ֥ינוּ זֶ֛ה   קִוִּ֥ינוּ ל֖וֹ וְיֽוֹשִׁיעֵ֑נוּ

     זֶ֣ה יְהוָה֙ קִוִּ֣ינוּ ל֔וֹ   נָגִ֥ילָה וְנִשְׂמְחָ֖ה בִּישׁוּעָתֽוֹ

10a כִּֽי־תָנ֥וּחַ יַד־יְהוָ֖ה בָּהָ֣ר הַזֶּ֑ה

     [וְנָ֤דוֹשׁ מוֹאָב֙ תַּחְתָּ֔יו   כְּהִדּ֥וּשׁ מַתְבֵּ֖ן בְּמֵ֥י [בְּמוֹ֥] מַדְמֵנָֽה

11   וּפֵרַ֤שׂ יָדָיו֙ בְּקִרְבּ֔וֹ   כַּאֲשֶׁ֛ר יְפָרֵ֥שׂ הַשֹּׂחֶ֖ה לִשְׂח֑וֹת

     וְהִשְׁפִּיל֙ גַּאֲוָת֔וֹ   עִ֖ם אָרְבּ֥וֹת יָדָֽיו

12   וּמִבְצַ֞ר מִשְׂגַּ֣ב חוֹמֹתֶ֗יךָ הֵשַׁ֧ח הִשְׁפִּ֛יל   הִגִּ֥יעַ לָאָ֖רֶץ עַד־עָפָֽר]

6 And he will prepare, YHWH *Ts^eba'ot*,
for all peoples on this mountain,

  a [drinking] feast of fat dishes,
a feast of fine wines,

  of fat dishes full of marrow,
of fine wines filtered clear.

7 And he will swallow up, on this mountain,
the face of the shroud shrouding all the peoples,

  the web woven over all the nations.
8 He will swallow up death forever.

  And he will wipe away, the Lord YHWH,
tears from every face.

  Then the shame of his people he will remove
from all the land.

  Indeed YHWH has spoken.

9 And a person will say on that day:

  "Behold, our God is this.
We waited for him and he saved us.

  This is YHWH: we waited for him.
Let us rejoice and be glad in his salvation."

10a Truly it rests, the hand of YHWH, on this mountain.

[10b But it will be trodden down, Moab, in its place,
as it is trodden, a heap of straw, into the waters of a dung pit.

11 And it will spread out its hands in the midst of it,
as a swimmer cups [hands] to swim. ∞

  But it will be made humble, its pride,
in spite of the cleverness of its hands.

12 The lofty fortifications of your walls he will make humble, ∞
he will cause [them] to bend, let touch the land, even the dust.]

ANALYSIS OF ISAIAH 25

Chapter 25 takes up elements of the preceding chapter as a sort of memory. We are clearly in a different time perspective (future oriented) and a different mood (positive). The threatened disaster of chapter 24 now appears to be history and the prophet offers praise for what YHWH has done (great wonders) and the effects it will have ('they' will glorify you). A new and clearer focus begins to emerge in which Zion will take centre stage. The heart of the relational metaphors which we discerned in chapter 24 evolves from 'YHWH – ארץ – inhabitants' to 'YHWH – Zion'. Under this heading we shall see that a process of restoration has begun, reversing YHWH's alienation from his people and land and re-establishing his relationship with them via the metaphor of YHWH as husband. This 'root' or 'titular' metaphor is developed via a number of metaphorical statements scattered progressively throughout chapter 25, each dealing with a different aspect of husbanding and culminating in the restoration of the marital relationship between YHWH and Zion. It would be of some value, therefore, to briefly examine the notion of Zion in Isaiah and at the same time give some attention to the concept of the city as female/daughter/mother/widow in the Ancient Near East and in the OT.

CENTRALITY OF ZION IN ISAIAH

K.P. Darr[1] along with B.G. Webb[2], R.J. Clifford[3] and C. Seitz[4] argue that Jerusalem/Zion is the dominant concern throughout BI. According to Seitz, "the second major character alongside God is Zion"[5]. We have picked up the thread of relational metaphors throughout chapter 24. In line with P. Miscall's[6] exploration of what he describes as a labyrinth of recurring metaphors (light, darkness, fire, water) in Isaiah we can use the relational metaphor 'YHWH – Zion' as a point of entry into that labyrinth

---

1. K.P. DARR, *Isaiah's Vision and the Family of God*, Louisville, KY, 1994, p. 19ff..
2. B.G. WEBB, *Zion in Transformation. A Literary Approach to Isaiah*, in D.J.A. CLINES et al. (eds.), *The Bible in Three Dimensions. Essays Celebrating Forty Years of Biblical Studies in the University of Sheffield* (JSOT SS, 87), Sheffield, 1990, pp. 65-84.
3. R.J. CLIFFORD, *The Unity of the Book of Isaiah and Its Cosmogonic Language*, in *CBQ* 55 (1993) 1-17.
4. C. SEITZ, *Isaiah 1–66: Making Sense of the Whole*, in ID. (ed.), *Reading and Preaching the Book of Isaiah*, Philadelphia, PA, 1988, pp. 105-126.
5. SEITZ, *Making Sense of the Whole*, p. 122.
6. P. MISCALL, *Isaiah – Labyrinth of Images*, in *Semeia* 54 (1991) 103-121.

of metaphors. We will return to Miscall's perspective on the metaphors in Isaiah below, particularly when we examine the metaphorical statement in Isa 25,10a. In the meantime we will continue our exploration of the centrality of Zion in BI. As Darr notes,

> Central among the vast array of issues addressed in Isaiah are the nature and status of ongoing relationships among Yahweh, Israel (both narrowly and broadly defined), and Judah's capital city, Jerusalem. Isaiah's authors did not, of course, analyse these relationships – which transcended the human realm and were by their nature mysterious – systematically. Rather, they frequently employed tropes derived from everyday familial roles (husband/wife, parent/child) and experiences (e.g. marriage, labour and delivery, disciplining recalcitrant children) to shed light on the powerful bonds they believed existed between Israel and its God. Such relationships and experiences might not themselves be devoid of mystery (e.g. childbirth), but they were better known, or at least more commonly experienced, than the ties they sought to disclose[7].

Darr's statement is almost a definition of metaphor. As we noted above, it would appear that the present chapter is narrowing the relational field of the metaphors it employs. ארץ fades into the background and the relationship between YHWH and his people, personified in the city of Jerusalem/mountain of Zion, takes pride of place. In what way does the author present this relationship? Our exploration of the metaphors in Isa 24 led us to believe that there was a certain element of the 'marriage/widowhood' metaphor present in the way in which the relationship between YHWH and his people was portrayed. Since further aspects of that type of relationship appear to be present here in chapter 25, it would be of considerable value at this point to explore the notion of Jerusalem/Zion as YHWH's wife/widow in the OT as a whole and in proto-Isaiah in particular

EXCURSUS: JERUSALEM AS FEMALE

In her study of familial metaphors in the OT in general and in Isaiah in particular K. P. Darr outlines the place and function of references to women as females, daughters, wives, mothers and widows[8]. She begins by pointing out that there are few literal references in Isaiah to women in any capacity although she goes on to imply that this is not quite the case at the figurative level. For the most part, she notes, both literal and

---

7. DARR, *Isaiah's Vision*, p. 35.
8. *Ibid.*, pp. 124-134.

figurative references reveal a rather stereotypical OT vision of women and only a few tend to lean towards innovation of any kind[9]. Isaiah in particular divulges a variety of what Darr calls 'complex associations' such as "subordination and dependence; vulnerability; haughtiness and vanity; submissiveness; limited knowledge and competence; familial and conjugal love; fertility and reproduction; maternal devotion, compassion and nurture; bereavement with its rituals of mourning and lament; and women's sexuality as a source of danger and shame (menstrual pollution, prostitution and adultery)."[10] We will return to some of these themes – particularly fertility, compassion and bereavement/lament – as we explore the metaphors in Isa 25–27. Our primary purpose here, however, must be restricted to Isaiah's personification of cities as women and in particular as wives and widows in relation to YHWH. Darr correctly notes that many of Isaiah's personifications draw on the familial (female) sphere with sufficient consistency as to contribute to our reading of Isaiah as a coherent literary work. In contrast to many exegetical approaches, however, she resists the temptation to jump immediately from a female image or metaphor to its more 'literal' implications, thereby taking the poet's choice of terminology, structuring and metaphor seriously.

Cities as Females

Darr points out that there was little innovation involved when the prophets of Israel employed female images for cities. Such usage was common throughout the ANE[11] and may even have had a psychological origin in that the city was evidently a place of protection, nurture and provision[12].

---

9. She rightly insists that the recovery of stereotypical ideas about women in ancient Israelite society is not equivalent to a reconstruction of their actual lives (*ibid.*, p. 86).

10. *Ibid.*

11. Darr lists a number of recent studies including F.W. DOBBS-ALLSOPP, *Weep, O Daughter of Zion: A Study of the City-Lament Genre in the Hebrew Bible* (BibOr, 44), Rome, 1993; A. FITZGERALD, *The Mythological Background for the Presentation of Jerusalem as a Queen and False Worship as Adultery in the OT*, in *CBQ* 34 (1972) 403-416.; ID., *BTWLT and BT as Titles for Capital Cities*, in *CBQ* 37 (1975) 167-183 and E.R. FOLLIS, *The Holy City as Daughter*, in ID. (ed.), *Directions in Biblical Hebrew Poetry* (JSOT SS, 40), Sheffield, 1987, pp. 173-184. Cf., more recently, J.C. SCHMITT, *The City as Woman in Isaiah 1–39*, in C.C. BROYLES and C.A. EVANS (eds.), *Writing and Reading the Scroll of Isaiah. Studies of an Interpretative Tradition*. Vol. 1, Leiden, 1997, pp. 95-119; Schmitt concludes that Isaiah and his editors were quite familiar with the image of the city as a woman and used it to their own ends. Cf also the recent work of P. DEL BRASSEY, *Metaphor and the Incomparable God in Isaiah 40–55*, Diss. (UMI), Harvard Divinity School, 1997, especially his chapter on YHWH as 'kin' (cf. pp. 225-280).

12. Cf. T. FRYMER-KENSKY, *In the Wake of the Goddesses: Women, Culture and the Biblical Transformation of the Pagan Myth*, New York, NY, 1992, p. 172 (cf. DARR, *Isaiah's Vision*, p. 126).

In common with neighbouring cultures, Israelite cities often enjoyed a familial relationship with their God YHWH. In contrast to many other cities of the ANE, which were not (grammatically) construed as female (Accadian word for a city *alu* being masculine and the Sumerian word *URU* neuter), however, the feminine gender of terminology for cities in Hebrew and other Northwest Semitic languages facilitated the development of notion of the Israelite city as having the male God YHWH as 'her' patron. Indeed this developed into a theological device which would replace the tendency towards the deification of cities found amongst her neighbours[13]. Darr agrees that grammatical gender markers do not automatically imply personification but that we should take the associations and contextual functions evoked thereby more seriously[14]. It will become clear that the use of female city metaphors in Isa 24–27 has important significance for our understanding and interpretation of the text and that Darr's advice here should not be ignored.

J. Galambush points out two distinctions between female personified cities among Israel's neighbours and in Israel herself: they are never referred to as goddesses in Israel and they are almost always a negative image[15]. With respect to the metaphor of the city as the wife of its patron deity, Galambush is convinced that among the other cultures of the ANE this was so well established that its metaphorical content had ceased to function, in other words it was a 'dead' metaphor. In Israel, however, the metaphor was "'revived' by its extension to include aspects of marriage that had not previously been active parts of the metaphor"[16].

---

13. M.E. BIDDLE, *The Figure of Lady Jerusalem: Identification, Deification and Personification of Cities in the Ancient Near East*, in K. LAWSON YOUNGER, W.W. HALLO, B.F. BATTO (eds.), *The Biblical Canon in Comparative Perspective* (Scripture in Context, IV), Lewiston – Queenston – Lampeter, 1991, pp. 175-194.

14. DARR, *Isaiah's Vision*, p. 127.

15. In his analysis of the relationship between god(s) and their cities in the ANE, H. Spieckermann introduces a distinction between a 'city god' which was associated with and responsible for one particular city (especially in Egypt and Mesopotamia) and Zion, the City of God in which the presence of YHWH ultimately came to rest – changing the very essence of that city for all time – once his universal power had been recognised. Cf. *Stadtgott und Gottesstadt, Beobachtungen im Alten Orient und im Alten Testament*, in Bib 73 (1992) 1-31.

16. J. GALAMBUSH, *Jerusalem in the Book of Ezekiel. The City as Yahweh's Wife* (SBL DS, 130), Atlanta, GA, 1992, p. 26. It is interesting to note that the identification of cities as women may later have developed associations with the 'apocalypse' genre. Cf. E. MCEWAN HUMPHREY, *The Ladies and the Cities: Transformation and Apocalyptic Identity in Joseph and Aseneth, 4 Ezra, the Apocalypse and the Shepherd of Hermas* (JSOT SS, 17), Sheffield, 1995.

Cities as Daughters

Biblical poetry, Darr notes, contains frequent reference to the terms בתולה/בת in association with a city. Although the specific meaning and thus interpretation of these terms is the subject of some dispute[17], Darr underlines the fact that the metaphor of the city as daughter often functioned "to foreground certain of its associated commonplaces: youth; beauty, sexual ripeness; vulnerability; (potential) fertility; and value, including especially the value of her reproductive capacity."[18] Much of this will be of interest when we come to explore the metaphors in Isa 25 although the specific usage of this chapter would appear to lean towards the city as wife/married woman. It is also interesting to note that Darr contests the idea that 'Daughter Zion', for example, was a 'dead' metaphor. She agrees with E. Follis that the expression carried considerable rhetorical weight[19] and counters Galambush's assertion that the prophets used the expression without further personification or elaboration by correctly insisting that such usage need not imply 'dead' metaphor but simply conventional metaphor which was in fact developed 'in various striking ways', often with the purpose of fore-grounding the association of social vulnerability[20].

Cities as Wives/Mothers

Darr agrees with J. Lewy[21] (followed by A. Fitzgerald[22] and J. Galambush[23]) that cities were sometimes regarded as the (often deified[24]) wives of their divine patrons although she notes that T. Frymer-Kensky[25] insists that there is no evidence for such identification. Her primary concern is the fact that in certain Isaian texts, Jerusalem is depicted as YHWH's wife and as mother of her (his?) children (inhabitants) although she does not appear to concede to the presence of female personifications

---

17. Especially בתולה which may signify a 'maiden' or a young virgin or a young newly-wed or even a women who had never engaged in sexual intercourse. Cf. DARR, *Isaiah's Vision*, pp.128-129.
18. *Ibid.*
19. FOLLIS, *The Holy City as Daughter*, p. 177.
20. DARR, *Isaiah's Vision*, p. 129.
21. J. LEWY, *The Old West Semitic Sun God Hammu*, in *HUCA* 18 (1944) 436-443.
22. A. FITZGERALD, *Jerusalem as Queen*; ID. BTWLT *and* BT.
23. GALAMBUSH, *Jerusalem in the Book of Ezekiel*. pp. 20, 25-59.
24. Galambush is correct in noting that the city in the OT is nowhere referred to as a goddess. The marriage metaphor may, however, have been employed to render such 'deification' speakable. Cf. GALAMBUSH, *Jerusalem in the Book of Ezekiel*, p. 25, esp. n. 1. Cf. also M. BAL, *Metaphors He Lives By*, in *Semeia* 61 (1993) 185-207.
25. FRYMER-KENSKY, *In the Wake of the Goddesses*, p. 269.

in the textual complex Isa 24–27. In any event, the very possibility of personification of this type allowed for the prophets and other biblical authors to develop the marriage metaphor into that of adultery, harlotry and widowhood (as associated commonplaces) and the ultimate restoration of the city to YHWH as his faithful wife with reference to Jerusalem. While Darr may be correct in stating that there is no explicit female personification of Zion in Isa 24–27, our analysis of the metaphors which emerged in Isa 24 and those still to be explored in Isa 25 would seem to point towards a depiction of a period of widowhood for Jerusalem (on account of the sins of her 'children') and the ultimate restoration of the 'marital' relationship between the city and her husband YHWH[26].

Julie Galambush focuses her attention on the specific and distinctive use of the marriage metaphor in Ezekiel which she introduces with an exploration of other texts, prophetic and non-prophetic[27], in which the metaphor is employed. It is her belief that in the vast majority of cases – she can find only one exception (2 Sam 20,19) – the extension of the marriage metaphor found in the OT is related to adultery or infidelity of some kind for which the Israelite city is being punished. We will return to this below but it is worth bearing in mind at this point that if we can establish that the ברית עולם is intended as a metaphor for marriage between YHWH and his people represented by Zion, then the breaking of the ברית עולם presented (climactically: Isa 24,5bc) as the reason for YHWH's hostile actions and ultimate withdrawal from city, ארץ and inhabitants in Isa 24 may imply apostasy as adultery or infidelity. Galambush is unable to detect more than a brief personification of Jerusalem as YHWH's faithful wife in Proto–Isaiah (Isa 1,21[28]), a wife who has become 'whore–like'. Clearly the author(s) is(are) exploiting

---

26. Cf. also J.J. SCHMITT, *The Motherhood of God and Zion as Mother*, in *RB* 92 (1985) 557-569.

27. Galambush proposes five levels of distinction between prophetic and non-prophetic use of the metaphor. Although her work ultimately focuses on the use of the metaphor in Ezekiel her preparatory distinctions apply to prophetic texts in general and thus to Isaiah also: 1. absence of personification of the capital city in non-prophetic texts and its relative prominence in prophetic texts; 2. Use of בת in prophetic texts and its relative absence in non-prophetic texts; 3. the common extra-prophetic determination for cultic infidelity זנה אחרי is rare in the prophets (only Ezek 6,9; 20,30); 4. the term for infidelity (זנה) in non-prophetic works refers exclusively to cultic infidelity whereas in the prophets it can refer to cultic *or* political infidelity; 5. the personified city is punished/shamed by YHWH in the prophets as an unfaithful wife. In so doing the prophets not only expressed their horror at the cuckoldry of the husband-god but also restored the god's honour by shaming the wife/city instead. Cf. GALAMBUSH, *Jerusalem in the Book of Ezekiel*, pp. 35-37.

28. *Ibid.*, pp. 52-59. The marriage metaphor is perhaps most persistent in Hosea (cf. Hos 1–3 etc.).

the 'adulterous wife' extension of the marriage metaphor at this point. It is my belief, however, that a further extension of the city as wife of YHWH is exploited, perhaps less explicitly, via the metaphors in Isa 24–27, namely that of the abandoned/widowed wife who will ultimately have her husband restored to her. It is interesting to note that Deutero-Isaiah deals with a different set of 'extensions' of the marriage metaphor. As Galambush notes:

> Beginning in chap 51, the author announces her restoration by Yahweh. "Daughter Zion" has been punished with bereavement of her children (51,18 [cf. also Isa 26,17-18]), forced drunkenness (51,17.21-22 [cf. also Isa 24,20]), shameful "widowhood" (54,4), and God's anger [cf. Isa 24]. Now her tent will again be pitched in safety (54,2); she is now promised children [cf. also Isa 26,15.19], "lasting love", and "lasting covenant" (51,8.10) from Yahweh[29].

Cities as widows[30]

It is important to note C. Cohen's thesis with respect to widowhood[31] at the outset: the lack of a male provider was sufficient for a city to be seen as a 'widow'. Cohen arrives at his conclusion on the basis of the direct use of 'widow' terminology in Accadian, Hebrew and Egyptian texts. The focus of the metaphor was not, therefore, on the death of the husband but on the widow's need for support and provision. If one applies this metaphor to a city then it is the notion of vassaldom of a once 'provided for' city which is transferred. As Cohen states: "...the 'widowed' city motif seems to refer to a once independent city which has become a vassal of another state"[32]. By restricting himself to the occurrences of the terms אלמנות - אלמנה in association with a city, Cohen finds only 5 texts where the motif occurs (Isa 47,8-9a; 54,4; Jer 51,5; Lam 1,1bc; Stele of Merneptah: 27-28). Our analysis of the use and occurrence of metaphors, however, allows us detect the presence of the 'city as widow' metaphor not only in direct use of the terminology but also in its implied presence in a metaphorical statement (even when the *métaphorisant* may be absent) or in the use of other words from the isotope of widowhood (as we shall see below). We can agree with Cohen, however, that to dwell as a widow was the opposite of dwelling

---

29. *Ibid.*, p. 59.
30. On the notion of widowhood in the bible as such cf. V. H. MATTHEWS and D.C. BENJAMIN, *Social World of Ancient Israel, 1250-587 BCE*, Peabody, MT, 1993, pp. 132-141.
31. C. COHEN, *The Widowed City*, in JANES 5 (1973) 75-81.
32. *Ibid.*, p. 79.

securely³³. The secure dwelling of the city as woman provided for by her husband would appear to be the metaphorical focus of a substantial part of Isa 25. Darr is correct in noting that the "logical transition from 'widowed woman' to 'widowed city' is not as smooth as Cohen suggests"³⁴. She agrees, however, that in both cases it is the negative and precarious position in which the widowed woman/city finds herself, in other words her *vulnerability*, which is placed in the foreground in both literal and metaphorical usage.

P.S. Hiebert³⁵ investigates some of the conventions surrounding the widow in the ANE in order to create a more concrete picture of her social status. Her primary conclusion is relevant to our study:

> The wicked take advantage of the *'almanâ* because they fear no reprisals from outraged family members [thus the enemy can destroy a widowed city without fear of interference from its patron/husband deity]. Yahweh takes special care of the *'almanâ*, supplying the role of the missing male kin who would have been concerned for her well-being and economic support [שלום cf. Isa 26,12]. To wish that an enemy's wife be an *'almanâ* is to wish for her a life of alienation from one of the most basic aspects of existence, namely family and all that kinship means in a traditional society, and a life of destitution that accompanies this alienation³⁶.

Clearly the application of such an image to a city such as Jerusalem has significance for the status of the kinship (or as Darr would describe it 'familial relationship') between YHWH and his city. Hiebert's study thus confirms both Cohen and Darr and provides further background for our analysis of what appear to be widow/widowed city metaphors in Isa 25.

The ברית עולם *as a Metaphor for Marriage*

While it is evident that the meaning of the term/concept ברית in the Old Testament is a point of contention among biblical scholars, even its translation as 'covenant' remains a sticking point, some have proposed that we read the term ברית as a relational metaphor expressing Israel's relationship with YHWH. E.J. Adler has taken this further, suggesting that the notion of covenant is often presented in the OT as a metaphor for

---

33. *Ibid.*
34. DARR, *Isaiah's Vision*, p. 134.
35. P.S. HIEBERT, *Whence Shall Help Come to Me?': The Biblical Widow*, in P.L. DAY (ed.), *Gender and Difference in Ancient Israel*, Minneapolis, MN, 1989, pp. 125-141.
36. HIEBERT, *The Biblical Widow*, p. 137.

marriage³⁷. She notes a number of traits which Israelite marriage had in common with the covenantal relationship between YHWH and his people: they are both legal and artificial relationships; both oblige fidelity from one party in particular (Israel/wife); there is an element of choice or election; terms describing emotional attachment or its absence such as love, jealousy, passion etc., are applicable to both. We noted in the early part of chapter III that the reference to the violation of the ברית עולם, lamented in Isa 24,5, was best understood as a literal statement, parallel to the breaking of 'laws' and 'statutes', an explanatory statement providing background information for the primary metaphorical statement of the passage in question which turned around the relationship between the people and the earth. Given the use elsewhere of the notion of covenant as a metaphor for marriage, albeit for the most part in the context of another metaphor, that of 'prostitution', we might have to reassess our understanding of the violation of the ברית עולם in Isa 24,5, at least potentially, as an expression of abandonment of faith expressed as an 'adulterous' violation providing grounds for abandonment and rejection by YHWH and the feared experience of 'widowhood' which was its consequence. Understood in the broader context of the relational metaphors of the entire textual complex (YHWH is husband), the ברית עולם might be considered a reference to the violation of marital fidelity and as a metaphor for the rupture of the faith relationship between YHWH and his people. In its context in 24,5, however, the dominant metaphor is that of 'wailing earth' and the expression forms part of an explicative statement providing the background thereto.

Adler notes a number of 'associated commonplaces' which function within the metaphor in question and which might be illuminating in the present context. Gender, for example, is significant in that a woman/Israel was to be dominated by her husband/YHWH. At the same time, however, the husband/YHWH had to provide for/protect his wife/people, even although he/YHWH was at liberty to prosecute in case of adultery³⁸. She agrees with Johannes Hempel³⁹ that the metaphor is limited in that it never ventures into sexual intimacy.

---

37. E. J. ADLER, *The Background for the Metaphor of Covenant as Marriage in the Hebrew Bible*, Diss. (UMI), University of California at Berkeley, 1989 (cf. Hos 1–3; Jer 2–3; Ezek 16; 23); G.P. HUGENBERGER, *Marriage as a Covenant. A Study of Biblical Law and Ethics Governing Marriage Developed from the Perspective of Malachi* (SVT, 52), Leiden, 1994 (esp. pp. 8-12); J.S. GRABOWSKI, *Covenant Sexuality*, in *Église et Théologie* 27 (1996) 229-252.

38. E.J. ADLER, *Covenant as Marriage*, pp. 22-26.

39. J.HEMPEL, *Die Grenzen des Anthropomorphismus Jahwes im Alten Testament*, in ZAW 57 (1939) 82-84; ADLER, *Covenant as Marriage*, pp. 26-27.

From what we have been able to understand so far with regard to the textual complex Isa 24–27, the relational metaphors of the city as wife/widow hinted at in chapter 24 are made more explicit here in ch. 25 and ultimately put into reverse. As we shall see, the metaphors in chapter 25 speak of the restoration of YHWH as husband to his widow Jerusalem: the metaphors of the banquet, the removal of mourning shroud, the substitution of husbanding for alienation (resting hand of YHWH = restoration of widowhood), the removal (swallowing up) of death as a metaphor for the restoration of marriage (word-play בעל / בלע) etc. all contribute to this picture.

DELIMITATION OF METAPHORICAL STATEMENTS

Sweeney has noted[40] that ch. 25,1-12 forms a distinct unit within the textual complex Isa 24–27. First of all, 25,1 is unrelated to 24,23 at the level of syntax, differing from what precedes it in the transition from 3rd person singular description of YHWH to 2nd person singular address of YHWH. Sweeney is also of the opinion that the first distinct unit ends in v. 5 since it is from v. 6 onwards that we find a reversion to 3rd person description. Vv. 6-12 are related to what precedes them via the conjunctive ו and, at the level of content, continue to elaborate YHWH's deed proclaimed in vv. 1-5. The opening ביום ההוא in 26,1 indicates a new unit. We can agree with Sweeney's initial division on form critical grounds between vv. 1-5 (Communal Thanksgiving Song for YHWH) and vv. 6-12 (Announcement of YHWH's blessing) yet within this basic structure he distinguishes three causative statements supporting the initial praise of v. 1ab, each introduced by a causative כי. The first of these supporting statements is general in nature and is followed by two further statements which specify the 'reason' for praising YHWH. Whatever the primary form-critical function of כי might be[41], it serves in any event to divide

---

40. SWEENEY, *Isaiah 1–39*, pp. 333-335. Cf. also KILIAN, (*Jesaja II*, pp. 147-148), who along with BREDENKAMP, *Der Prophet Jesaja*, p. 147; RUDOLPH, *Jesaja 24–27*, p. 34; LINDBLOM, *Die Jesaja Apokalypse*, p. 30; SCHOORS, *Jesaja*, pp. 150-151; KAISER, *Isaiah 13–39*, p. 197; VERMEYLEN, *L'Apocalypse*, p. 18; WILDBERGER, *Jesaja 13–27*, p. 899; ALONSO SCHÖKEL and SICRE DIAZ, *Profetas I*, p. 209; LEWIS, *Rhetorical-Critical Analysis*, pp. 99-108 (from a structural perspective); JOHNSON, *Chaos to Restoration*, pp. 57-58; HÖFFKEN, *Das Buch Jesaja*, pp. 181-182; MOTYER, *The Prophecy of Isaiah*, p. 208 etc. also maintains a certain sub-division between vv. 1-3 and 4-5 but insist on viewing the unit as a *Danklied* running from vv. 1-5.

41. Recent form-critical analysis, however, would tend to identify such use of the particle כי as emphatic (acknowledgement of YHWH's deeds, joyful exclamation) rather than causative, underlining the 'contents' of the Thanksgiving Song rather than providing

the text into more or less discrete statements, the first of which in vv. 2-3 and the second in vv. 4-5 will form the basis upon which we will examine the text from the metaphorical perspective. When we come to examine the various elements which indicate the presence of metaphor this division will be clearly confirmed. It will become evident that the metaphorical statement which will govern this chapter has its beginnings in vv. 4-5 and runs through vv. 6-8 and 9-10a. The remaining verses 1-3 and 10b-12 are in many senses related and both are highly structured units employing a variety of poetical devices including somewhat simpler metaphors depicting the ruin of foreign cities as a climactic process of humbling of their prideful attitudes.

Johnson's analysis of the history of exegesis of this unit is instructive, particularly with reference to the identity of the city in v. 2. Johnson's basic position, which I follow, is that Isa 24,1-20(23) is about the destruction of Jerusalem. The latter verse of Isa 24, he notes, implies that "YHWH had *not* been reigning in Jerusalem"[42] up to that point and that the forces of chaos and destruction had been the result of his absence. Now he reigns once again in Zion. This, according to Johnson, confirms his view that we are dealing with Jerusalem in these verses. He concludes that the phrase portraying YHWH's appearance 'before his elders' is an indication that the covenant broken (24,5) has now been restored[43]. It is our contention that this is the principal theme running through the metaphors of chapter 25, expressed in terms of the restoration of widowhood to marital life with Zion as representative of Israel once again knowing a husband to provide for her. Johnson agrees that virtually all[44] commentators see vv. 1-5 of chapter 25 as a *Danklied*. What is more significant, however, is the fact that many authors consider these verses along with 26,1-6 as independent of the rest of the textual complex and referring to the destruction of a fallen city from the past. Wildberger supports this position although he insists that one must interpret the unit in its present context which is predominantly future

---

'reasons' for praising/thanking YHWH. Hence our translation 'Indeed'. Cf. C. WESTERMANN, *The Praise of God in the Psalms*, Richmond, VA, 1965, esp. p. 17ff.; F. CRÜSEMANN, *Studien zur Formgeschichte von Hymnus und Danklied in Israel* (WMANT, 32), Neukirchen – Vluyn, 1969, pp. 32-35; H.-J. KRAUS, *Psalms 1–59*, Minneapolis, MN, 1988, p. 43ff.; J. GERSTENBERGER, *Psalms, with an Introduction to Cultic Poetry* (FOTL, 14), Grand Rapids, MI, 1988, pp. 14-19.

42. JOHNSON, *Chaos to Restoration*, p. 56ff.

43. *Ibid.*, p. 57, supported by KAISER, *Isaiah 1–39*, p. 195.

44. With the exception of Lohmann who sees it as a 'religiöses Siegeslied'. Cf. P. LOHMANN, *Die selbständigen lyrischen Abschnitte in Jes. 24–27*, in *ZAW* 37 (1917) 1-58. Johnson refers readers to the useful discussion of the form of this unit in REDDITT, *Form Critical Analysis*, pp. 106-115.

oriented[45]. The entire discussion has its roots in Duhm's division of the textual complex Isa 24–27 into eschatological prophecies and past oriented songs[46]. Rudolph argues to the contrary, insisting that 25,1-5 were written for their present context based on the evidence that 26,6ff. do not follow on from 24,23 and that 25,1-5 presuppose YHWH's reign on Zion which is established in 24,23[47]. Kaiser adds to this that v. 3 introduces a futuristic note to the pericope[48]. Johnson agrees with Rudolph and Kaiser and believes that this calls for a more comprehensive approach to the textual complex as a whole (contra Duhm etc.), a future oriented interpretation of the city spoken of in 25,1-5 since it is not a description of a past event. He concludes that the author must have seen some connection between a future historical event and the introduction of a new eschatological age which argues for a non-dualistic/apocalyptic interpretation of the text[49].

Johnson offers some further important remarks on the identity of the city mentioned in Isa 25,2. He correctly points out that the crescendo of phrases concerning the demise of this city in v. 2 is an indication of the extent of the prophet's hatred towards it. In light of his belief – and mine – that the city in Isa 24 is Jerusalem, it seems evident, therefore, that another city is intended here, perhaps the city responsible for Jerusalem's destruction: Babylon. In addition, YHWH's defeat of hostile powers in the concluding verse of ch. 24 and the introduction of a new (eschatological) age in Isa 25,6-10a – proclaimed, as we shall see, in terms of the restoration of marriage/widowhood metaphor – suggests that the anti-godly powers embodied by Babylon had to be destroyed for good (in eternity) before the new age could begin. Finally, the destruction of this city would effect all the nations (cf. 25,3). For Johnson, therefore, the only appropriate candidate is Babylon which fits the bill at every level[50]. Johnson disagrees with a number of commentators[51] in insisting that a distinction be made between the city in Isa 24 and the city of Isa 25,2. While the destruction of a city constitutes common ground between the two, the consequences of the destruction differ at a

---

45. WILDBERGER, *Jesaja 13–27*, p. 953.
46. DUHM, *Jesaja*, p 172
47. RUDOLPH, *Jesaja 24–27*, p. 34.
48. KAISER, *Isaiah 1–39*, p. 197.
49. JOHNSON, *Chaos to Restoration*, p. 59.
50. *Ibid.*, p. 60; cf. also RUDOLPH, *Jesaja 24–27*, p. 62, LINDBLOM, *Die Jesaja Apokalypse*, p. 72ff. and M.L. HENRY, *Glaubenskrise und Glaubensbewährung in den Dichtungen der Jesaja Apokalypse* (BWANT, 86), Stuttgart, 1967, pp. 20-34, among others, who also interpret the city in 25,2 as Babylon.
51. Notably LINDBLOM, *Die Jesaja Apokalypse*, pp. 20-34.

variety of levels: (1) the context of lament in Isa 24 \\ the context of joyful song in Isa 25; (2) the reversal of cosmos to chaos and dreadful devastation in Isa 24 \\ good outcome in Isa 25 including the end of chaos and the return to cosmos with YHWH reigning on Mt. Zion. Ultimately, Johnson notes, "...for the Jewish mind, the destruction of Jerusalem alone could lead to a collapse into chaos, while only the destruction of Babylon could initiate the new eschatological age."[52] What is important for our study is that there is no longer any need to view Isa 25,1-3 as a statement, metaphorical or otherwise, about Jerusalem. Similarly, given the description of Moab's punishment in 25,10b-12 it is clear that this latter statement is likewise unrelated to Jerusalem, at least not directly.

Before proceeding, therefore, with the primary metaphorical statements of this chapter, which I believe to be vv. 4-5, vv. 6-8 and vv. 9-10a, we will first examine the shape and unifying features of Isa 25,1-3 and Isa 25,10b-12, including their use of metaphor, and their evident climactic association with one another. At the literary level they form an inclusion around the three main metaphorical statements of chapter 25.

Isa 25,1-3 and 10b-12

1a   YHWH, my god are you.
 b   I will extol you, I will laud your name.

 c   Indeed, you have done great wonders,
 d   plans[53] from long ago[54], perfectly faithful.

2a   Indeed, you have made the city[55] into a heap,
 b   the town with high walls into a ruin.

---

52. JOHNSON, *Chaos to Restoration*, p. 61.
53. Eitan suggests that we read עָצוֹתָ 'you have counselled' here as a perfect form of עוץ. His opinion is based on a perceived need to supply a verb to the context and bolster the parallelism with what precedes it. All of this seems unnecessary to me. Evident consonance between עצות and עשית is enough to establish a level of parallelism between the terms without insisting that both be verb forms. Semantically nothing is gained by the emendation. Syntactically speaking, עצות מרחוק and אמונה אמן are subordinate to and dependant on the initial verb. Cf. I. EITAN, *A Contribution to Isaiah Exegesis*, in *HUCA* 12-13 (1937-1938) 55-88, esp. p. 71.
54. מרחוק 'from afar' has a temporal meaning in the present context: 'from long ago'. Cf. WATTS, *Isaiah 1–33*, p. 328.
55. There is some difficulty involved here in understanding and therefore translating the Hebrew idiom. Emerton notes the primary problems: the verb from שמת appears to have no object while the preposition on מעיר would also seem to be required by קריה which does not have it. Confusion arises from the fact that both parts of the clause appear

c   The palace of strangers[56] is a city no more[57].
d   In eternity it will not be [re]built.

3a   Therefore, they will glorify you, a nation strong.
b   A town of nations[58] violent will revere you.

to be employing a מן ... ל construction which is partially incomplete. This has led to emendation based on LXX (πόλειι), Peshitta (qrjʾ), Vulgate (civitas) and the Targum (קרוי פצחין) which show no signs of the preposition. Other options include emendation to העיר based on graphic confusion between ה and מ (cf. WILDBERGER, *Jesaja 13–27*, pp. 951-952 [following R. LOWTH, *Isaiah: A New Translation*. 2 vols., London, 1834[10]; first edition, 1779; J.C. DÖDERLEIN *Esaias, ex recensione textus Hebraei*, Altsofi, 1789 etc. and BHK]. BFS, in contrast, favours the plural reading of LXX and suggests the emendation ערים, moving the initial מ to a final position. Emerton and Van der Kooij opt for עיר, noting that the plural option of LXX is a translational characteristic with respect to the present textual complex. Cf. J.A. EMERTON, *A Textual Problem in Isaiah 25:2*, in ZAW 89 (1977) 64-73, esp. pp. 66-67. A. VAN DER KOOIJ, *Isaiah 24–27: Text Critical Notes*, in H.J. BOSMAN, H. VAN GROL et al. (eds.), *Studies in Isaiah 24–27: The Isaiah Workshop (De Jesaja Werkplaats)* (OTS, 43), Leiden, 1999, p. 13. Rudolph suggests that the מ should be dropped because it was written under the influence of the second מעיר which is an appropriate and simple negation but I fail to see the logic involved in his argument. Although it makes little difference to the translation we opt (hesitatingly) for the emendation proposed by Van der Kooij and Emerton.

56. Emerton offers a detailed discussion of the text critical problems surrounding this phrase. He insists that there can be no certainty as to whether LXX read זדים instead of the MT זרים (cf. WILDBERGER, *Jesaja 13–27*, p. 952) although he points out that the alternative reading is clearly attested elsewhere. In his opinion there is little difference involved between the two possibilities and he can see no reason why the poet may have described the enemy as both 'arrogant' and 'foreign'. Perhaps one might argue for a pun in the text, given the similarity between the terms. The proximate expression 'high walls' might also figuratively suggest some sense of arrogance. Redditt sees the term זדים as a *terminus technicus* for the anti-godly powers, and the subjugation of such powers as the deed being praised (cf. REDDITT *Form Critical Analysis*, p. 28) and opts for emendation. Together with Emerton (cf. also BARTHÉLEMY, *Critique Textuelle*, p. 178; WATTS, *Isaiah 1–33*, p. 328; MOTYER, *The Prophecy of Isaiah*, p. 208), we see no need for proposing a change to the MT.

57. Emerton argues that it is difficult to say that the 'palace of strangers' is no longer a city (privative מן; cf. Isa 7,8) since in his mind it 'never was a city'. This leads him to seek an alternative interpretation for the second מעיר in v. 2. He opts for an emended reading מְעֹר, the *hophal* participle of ערר: 'the palace of foreigners is destroyed'. The emendation seems unnecessary as the 'palace of strangers' is clearly the climax of two phrases which precede it, both of which refer to a town or city. Perhaps the somewhat vague use of ארמן is influenced by ארוממך in v. 1b. Cf. EMERTON, *A Textual Problem*, pp. 70-73.

58. Although some scholars have problems with this phrase, the ancient textual witnesses support the MT (1QIsa[a], LXX [pl.], Targ, Pesh, Vulg.). Counter to E. LIEBMANN, *Der Text zu Jesaja 24–27*, in ZAW 22 (1902) 285-304; ZAW 23 (1903) 209-86, esp. p. 266, PROCKSCH, *Jesaja I*, p. 316, KAISER, *Isaiah 13–39*, p. 196, BHS, WILDBERGER, *Jesaja 13–27*, pp. 951-952) we consider it unnecessary to omit the קרית, since its singular form may be understood as a collective (reconciling it with the masc. pl. verb). Cf. also REDDITT, *Form Critical Analysis*, p. 29; WATTS, *Isaiah 1–33*, p. 327; MOTYER, *The Prophecy of Isaiah*, p. 206 (although he perhaps wrongly relates it to the קרית תהו of 24,10); SWEENEY, *Isaiah 1–39*, p. 334, who avoids the problem to some extent by translating קרית as 'community of...'). As we shall see, the metaphorical statement evident here also relies on its presence.

[10b But it will be trodden down, Moab[59], in its place,
c   as it is trodden, a heap of straw, into the waters[60] of a dung pit.

11a   And it will spread out its hands in the midst of it,
b   as a swimmer cups [hands] to swim. ∞

c   But it will be made humble, its pride,
d   in spite of the cleverness of its hands.

12a   The lofty fortifications of your walls he will make humble, ∞
b   he will cause [them] to bend, let touch the land, even the dust.]

Structure, Poetry and the Relationship between Isa 25,1-3 and 10b-12.

Sweeney sees vv. 10b-12 as a secondary appendage[61] with a triple statement about the destruction of Moab (it will be 'trodden', it will spread its hands like a swimmer, it will be humbled). Literary associations with the rest of chapter 25, however, would seem to suggest that, if

---

59. Redditt (*Form Critical Analysis*, p. 32) notes the temptation to emend the term מואב to read אויב because the mention of a specific nation seems abrupt and out of place in the overall context of Isa 24–27. He is correct in pointing out, however, that other cities/nations are mentioned elsewhere in the text complex: Jerusalem (24,23 & 27,13), Judah (26,1) and Assyria and Egypt (27,13). Schoors (*Jesaja*, p. 152) sees Moab as a 'type' for the Great Enemy and adds that there is a lack of text-critical evidence to support a change.

60. The $k^e tib$ has במי (the waters of) while the $q^e re$ suggests במו, (simple 'in'). The $k^e tib$ is supported by IQIsa^a, Symmachus and Targum while LXX, Peshitta and Vulgate support the $q^e re$. Commentators (and textual witnesses for that matter) seem fairly evenly divided on this text critical issue. As Van der Kooij points out (*Isaiah 24–27: Text Critical Notes*, p. 14), we can distinguish two interpretations of the text depending on one's choice of the $k^e tib$ or the $q^e re$: (a) a threshing floor using some sort of threshing car which crushes straw under its wheels or (b) the threshing of straw in water and animal dung to make either clay or manure. The context of the image of the swimmer seems to tip the balance towards the $k^e tib$ 'the waters of' although the final image of being forced face down into the dust of the ground might support the $q^e re$. Together with Redditt (*Form Critical Analysis*, p. 32) and Motyer (*The Prophecy of Isaiah*, p. 211, n. 2) etc., I opt for the $k^e tib$ because it fits better with the subsequent image of the swimmer and does not introduce another instrumentality into the punishment of Moab beyond that of YHWH's foot (contra LEWIS, *Rhetorical-Critical Analysis*, p. 117; WATTS, *Isaiah 1–33*, p. 334). Wildberger (*Jesaja 13–27*, pp. 970-971) is convinced that the $q^e re$ is correct but his decision appears to be based for the most part on his understanding of the meaning of מדמנה as a town מדמן in the land of Moab instead of a dunghill. He further points out, however, that מו can also mean 'water' (cf. R. ALTHANN, *Psalm 58,10 in the light of Ebla*, in *Bib* 64 [1983], 122).

61. SWEENEY, *Isaiah 1–39*, p. 335; cf. also PROCKSCH, *Jesaja I*, pp. 318-319; LINDBLOM, *Die Jesaja Apokalypse*, p. 66; FOHRER, *Der Aufbau*, p. 37; MARCH, *Two Prophetic Compositions*, pp. 103-104; KAISER, *Isaiah 13–39*, p. 204;

not original, it is at least well connected to its new context. There appear to be parallels, for example, with the triple ruination of the city in vv. 1-3 (city into a heap, town into a ruin, annihilation of city). Motyer points out the contrast established between the eschatological provision for (the people of) Jerusalem expressed via the metaphor of a banquet which is set opposite the disgusting image of the dunghill which is the lot of (the people of) Moab. Further contrast is evident in the hope filled 'passive' endurance of those who are ultimately to attain the blessings of the divine promise and the pride of Moab expressed in the image of the swimmer 'actively' endeavouring to rise from the waters of the dunghill by the strength of his own hands but being confronted only with the 'foot' of YHWH. Indeed, the interplay of hands and feet with positive and then negative inference helps bind the text to its context. Furthermore, as Motyer notes, "Swimming provides a superb illustration of a go-it-alone policy. But the Lord does not admire Moab's *cleverness*."[62] March deletes vv. 10b-12 as a secondary expansion on the basis of content and style differences[63]. I would maintain that contrast can also be a binding element and need not necessarily imply interpolation.

There is clear internal evidence of literary structuring via a number of poetic devices in the textual units vv. 1-3 and vv. 10b-12 as well as verbal and semantic associations between them.

Internal vv. 1-3

Lewis notes the variety of what he calls 'sound systems' which add to the quality of the poetry in this unit[64]. Clearly the abundant repetition of א and ע sounds (both consonance and alliteration) adds cohesion to the passage as does the repetition of the second person suffix ך. The latter also serves a delineative function which Lewis seems to miss, namely providing for an inclusion between v. 1 and v. 3. The unit is built up of five parallel bicola, the first and second (v. 1a//b; v. 11c//d), fourth and fifth (v. 2c//d; v. 3a//b) being consecutive and the third and central (v. 2a//b) being synthetic. This parallel pattern together with the inclusion noted above focus our attention on the ruination of the city/town with high walls, the central theme of the unit, the identification of

---

62. MOTYER, *The Prophecy of Isaiah*, p. 211. Cf. the parallels here with the oracle against Moab in Isa 16–17.
63. MARCH, *Two Prophetic Compositions*, pp. 103-104, following PROCKSCH, *Jesaja I*, pp. 318-319; LINDBLOM, *Die Jesaja Apokalypse*, p. 66; FOHRER, *Der Aufbau*, p. 37.
64. LEWIS, *Rhetorical-Critical Analysis*, p. 101ff. Lewis points out other sonorous features but in line with the majority of exegetes, he stretches the unit to include vv. 1-5.

which we discussed in the *Status Quaestionis*. At the same time, there is an evident semantic pattern which focuses concentrically on v. 2ab: extol you – laud you (v. 1b) // glorify you – revere you (v. 3ab); (v. 1d) לעולם // מרחוק (v. 2d). Finally, there is an evident evolution in the subjects and objects of the unit: I – you (v. 1ab); you (v. 1cd); you – it/them (v. 2ab); it/them (v. 2cd); it/them – you. From the perspective of metaphor[65], the only possible candidate would seem to be the expression 'town with high walls' which, in conjunction with the final verses of chapter 25 (esp. v. 12), seems to be a metaphor for pride. We will deal with this minor metaphorical statement in the usual fashion below.

Internal vv. 10b-12

Lewis agrees with the delimitation of this last section which he considers a later addition on the grounds of irregular rhythm, having been connected to its present position on the basis of the catch-word principle[66]. There is evident end rhyme and alliteration (דוש and פרש; שפל and שוח respectively), possible word-play (מואב and במי מדמנה) as well as syntactical structuring: passive/Moab (v. 10bc); active/swimmer (v. 11ab); passive/swimmer (v. 11cd); active/YHWH (v. 12ab). This alternation appears to serve a semantic function, suggesting via the metaphorical simile of the swimmer that it is Moab's 'go-it-alone' pride which will be the cause of its ruination and humiliation which is expressed via the metaphor of humbling its pride/fortified walls. A similar expression in v. 2b suggests that this metaphor extends to include both cities/nations (Babylon and Moab) as we shall see below. Lord notes that vv. 10 and 11 contain simple "Comparisons of the mode in which they (Moab) are to be trodden down by the Most High, to the treading of straw on a dunghill; and of their spreading their hands in the prostrate condition, as a swimmer spreads his..."[67]. I would prefer to view these two images as an extended metaphorical simile, the image of the filthy watery pit extending to provide the location for the swimmer to attempt to rise to the surface by his own efforts but being thwarted in his endeavours by

---

65. D.N. Lord (*A Designation and Exposition of the Figures of Isaiah Chapter XXV and XXVI*, in *Theological and Literary Journal* (1853-1854) 479-93, esp. p. 479) sees a metaphor in v. 1 in the terminology of exultation. He notes that the verbal root רום literally means 'to raise someone to a higher place'. We will not follow up this lead as the term רום is lexically well attested in its meaning 'exalt' and as such would no longer seem to function as a metaphor.

66. He limits this to יד־יהוה in v. 10a and the double mention of ידיו in v. 11a and v. 11d but the suggestion of 'feet' implied in the term דוש strikes me as a more deliberate semantic level of association with the context.

67. LORD, *The Figures of Isaiah Chapter XXV*, p. 485.

the relentless treading of YHWH. While for Bourguet the formal evidence of comparative particles (כהדוש and ...כאשר) might suggest metaphor, we can still view these expressions as similes with some metaphorical significance[68] since they go a little bit beyond simply comparing YHWH's treading into water and Moab's efforts to swim back to the surface by its own power. The sense of disgust aroused by the image of the dung pit illuminates our understanding of the relationship between YHWH and Moab while the sense of futility evoked by the swimmer trying to rise by his own efforts suggests an aspect of pride which is stated explicitly in the following colon. We shall see below that a metaphorical statement exists in which the two distinct isotopes of 'humiliation' and the 'tearing down of high walls' are juxtaposed (vv. 2b and 12a) and thereby serve to relate the two passages. A final word deserves to be said on the dynamics of these verses. A veritable struggle is presented between downward thrusts of YHWH (feet) and the upward endeavours of Moab (the swimmer's hands). A certain climactic pattern emerges: downward (v. 10a); downward (v. 10b); upward (v. 11a); upward (v. 11b); downward (v. 11c) upward (v. 11d); downward (v. 12a); downward, downward, downward (v. 12b).

Millar[69] is of the opinion that vv. 10-12 are prosaised poetry and does not offer much hope for getting to the bottom of their poetic background[70]. For some commentators, however, the discernment of poetry would appear to be entirely dominated by considerations related to meter only. It seems clear, however, that the passage in question is riddled with poetical devices which would tend to undermine any suggestion of prose and support both internal cohesion, contextual imbedding and mutual association.

Associations between vv. 1-3 & vv. 10b-12.

As we already noted above both vv. 1-3 and vv. 10b-12 refer to a city/nation and in agreement with Johnson we consider the former to be a reference to Babylon and the latter Moab. The text of ch. 25 between these two textual units is clearly referring to Jerusalem. While we have demonstrated a degree of internal cohesion within each unit there is evidence of relationship between them both with respect to terminology and semantic content. A climactic process is instigated in v. 2ab with references to the

68. Cf. Soskice's 'modelling similes'. Note, however, the lack of what Kjärgaard refers to as 'secondary predicates'.
69. MILLAR, *Origin*, p. 44.
70. Cf. also SCHOORS, *Jesaja*, p. 152.

destruction of a city, its being made into a ruin/heap. This is carried on in the humbling and bending to the ground of v. 11b-13a. The repetition of physical 'humiliation' underscoring the completeness of Moab's ruin semantically parallels the temporal statement with regard to Babylon in v. 2d 'In eternity it will not be [re]built'. Terminological association (word-play/consonance) between מפלה/פלא[71] in v. 2c and שפל in v. 11c and v. 12b suggests that YHWH's greatest wonder and the core of his salvific action is the ruination/humiliation of Moab/Babylon. At the same time, the upward connotations of praise in vv. 1-3 are contrasted with the upward associations of pride presented in the image of the swimmer in vv. 10b-12.

Perhaps the most important association between the two passages is their apparent combined involvement in one metaphorical statement. The expression 'town with high (fortified) walls' (בצורה) in v. 2b taken on its own would appear to be a literal reference to physical destruction. The repetition of the concept 'high (fortified) walls' (מבצר: as *métaphorisé*) in v. 12a, in the context of the humbling of Moab's pride, introduces a metaphor with what one might view as having a double-duty *métaphorisant*, namely the notion of 'humbling' (שפל), which while present in vv. 1-12 (2x) is absent in v. 2b. Terminological repetition (בצר) and word-play (מפלה/פלא and שפל) function to associate the *métaphorisé* in v. 2b with its *métaphorisant* in v. 11-12 establishing a metaphorical statement which applies a concept from the isotope of human demeanour/emotion 'humbling of pride' to an architectural edifice 'city walls' thus implying that the primary shortcoming of the cities in question was their pride, hinted at in the first passage and made more explicit in the second via the simile of the swimmer and the metaphor of 'high (fortified) walls'. The core of the metaphorical statement appears to be locked up in the term שפל which, having the basic meaning 'to lay low', can serve both the physical (felling, laying low) and human/psychological (humbling of pride) isotopes[72]. If pride, however, is the primary transgression of Moab it is not pride which has incurred the wrath of YHWH where Jerusalem is concerned but rather the transgression of the ברית עולם. The relational metaphorical statements with regard to YHWH's own people both here in ch. 25 and in the preceding chapter are thus quite distinct and ultimately far more profound.

We can now turn to the first of the metaphorical statements in chapter 25:

---

71. This term has the basic meaning of 'heap of rubbish' (cf. NBDB s.v נפל 4651; NIDOTTE 5877 [HARMAN]) and may be semantically related to מדמנה 'dung pit' in v. 10c

72. Primarily used in the figurative sense 'to abase', often parallel with שחח as it is here (cf. NBDB 8213; NIDOTTE 8820 [LONG]).

Isa 25,4-5

4a   Indeed, you have been a refuge for the poor,
b   a refuge for the needy in his distress;

c   a shelter from the storm,
d   a shade from the heat.

e   Indeed, the blast of the violent
f   is like a storm of hail[73];

5a   like heat in the desert
b   the din of strangers.

c   ᵃYou will subdue[74] heat, ᵇwith the shade of a cloud[75].
d   ᵇ'The song[76] of the violentᵃ' will be suppressed[77].

73. 1QIsaᵃ, 1QIsaᵇ, Targum, Peshitta and Vulgate support the MT here. Wildberger finds קיר 'wall' impossible and along with BHS suggests we read קור (קֹר) 'winter/cold'. Barthélemy notes that this reading of the text has support among a large number of commentators, among them Knobel, Bredenkamp, Duhm, Liebmann, Condamin, Procksch and Fohrer (cf. also SCHOORS, *Jesaja*, p. 153 VAN DER KOOIJ, *Isaiah 24–27: Text Critical Notes*, p. 14 etc.). The term קר suggests intense cold (HALOT 1128; NIDOTTE 7981 [ARNOLD]) and in the context it is parallel to רוח. The contrasting images of intense heat and intense cold as descriptions of the violent/strangers suggest that the idea of a hail storm' would not be inappropriate here. On the basis of parallel images, therefore, we opt for קר (contra BARTHÉLEMY, *Critique Textuelle*, p. 179).

74. I have moved back the *atnach* here from תכניע to זרים. The ensuing colometry not only makes sense semantically but is supported by a chiastic bicolon in v. 5cd, the b/b' elements of which reflect and elaborate on the comparisons made in the preceding bicola, vv. 4ef and 5ab (blast of the violent is like a storm/ heat in the desert is like the din of strangers). There is also external chiastic parallelism between the bicola vv. 4ef and 5ab. Chiasm functions as a literary expression of reversal of fortunes. The colometry is supported by LOWTH (*Isaiah: A New Translation*, p. 267); BREDENKAMP (*Der Prophet Jesaja*, p. 149ff.); KISSANE (*The Book of Isaiah*, p. 276); MARCH (*Two Prophetic Compositions*, p. 81ff.); ALONSO SCHÖKEL and SICRE DIAZ (*Profetas I*, p. 14ff.); LEWIS (*Rhetorical-Critical Analysis*, p. 100ff.).

75. BHS suggests that we scrap חרב בצל עב since it is absent from LXX. WILDBERGER (*Jesaja 13–27*, p. 952) is convinced it is a gloss. Given that the LXX also does not render the following three words and in light of its less formal approach to the translation of this particular part of Isaiah (i.e. 24–27) Van der Kooij correctly suggests that there is no sound argument for postulating a shorter Hebrew text. The other witnesses, he notes, support MT (*Isaiah 24–27: Text Critical Notes*, p. 14). Repetition, which Redditt notes has been the occasion of many reconstructions for Isa 25,4-5 (cf. REDDITT, *Form Critical Analysis*, pp. 30-31 for a sample), and the parallelism of the verses (cf. LEWIS, *Rhetorical-Critical Analysis*, p. 104) suggests a high degree of literary structuring. Our understanding of the colometry of these verses obviates any emendation of MT. Barthélemy, following a different colometric division, translates 'comme la chaleur sous l'ombre d'un nuage, le péan des violents s'assourdit' (*Critique Textuelle*, p. 180), favouring an additional comparative כ.

76. Wildberger wonders whether the term זמיר should not be read as זמרה 'strong' which he suggests might be more fitting with respect to the verb ענה 'to subdue'. At the

4a[78]	כִּי־הָיִיתָ מָעוֹז לַדָּל
b	מָעוֹז לָאֶבְיוֹן בַּצַּר־לוֹ
c	מַחְסֶה מִזֶּ֫רֶם
d	צֵל מֵחֹרֶב
e	כִּי רוּחַ עָרִיצִים
f	כְּזֶרֶם קִיר׃
5a	כְּחֹרֶב בְּצָיוֹן
b	שְׁאוֹן זָרִים
c	תַּכְנִיעַ חֹרֶב בְּצֵל עָב
d	זְמִיר עָרִיצִים יַעֲנֶה׃

Delimitation of Metaphorical Statement

The present metaphorical unit is distinguished from the rest of ch. 25 primarily on semantic grounds and ultimately also on the basis of the metaphorical statement itself. From the syntactic perspective there is a disjuncture between v. 3 and v. 4. The על־כן of v. 3a referring back in a causal sense to the central statement of vv. 1-3 (v. 2ab) – i.e. the strong/violent nation will offer praise because it has been ruined by YHWH – whereas the כי of v. 4a refers forward to vv. 4-5 and has more of an emphatic nuance. In addition, the opening verbal clause addressed to YHWH in v. 4a, and the series of descriptive sub-clauses which depend on it, is echoed in the final verbal clause of the unit in v. 5c with a move from present perfect nuance (*qatal*) to anticipated information (*yiqtol*). Both verbal clauses surround two nominal clauses in vv. 4ef-5ab. While there may be some evidence for treating vv. 4-5 as syntactically independent they remain part of a larger syntactic unit running from vv. 1-5, marked by an opening vocative and alternating *qatal/yiqtol* verbal forms. Semantically speaking the unit is a well-rounded, static description of YHWH's deeds (being a refuge/shelter/shade) followed by an explanatory comparison detailing YHWH's adversaries followed by an active portrayal

---

same time, however, the idea of זמיר is a better parallel of שאון (*Jesaja 13–27*, p. 952). The interplay of images of powerful storm, relentless heat and the 'din'/ 'song' of strangers is an effective way of suggesting the intensity of the enemy's attack which is, nevertheless, easily overcome by YHWH.

77. *Niphal* repointing of the MT (יַעֲנֶה) obviates any need to postulate a second person verb here in order to parallel תכניע.

78. The Hebrew colometry is provided here for the sake of clarity.

of YHWH's continued protection. Colometrically speaking we have five parallel bicola focusing on a descriptive statement of the enemy in v. 4e-f and v. 5a-b. Verbal agreements are evident between vv. 4 and 5 both in terms of simple repetition (חרב בצל [v. 4d] // חרב [v. 5a] // צל מחרב [v. 5c]) and consonance (זרם [v. 4c,e] // זרים [v. 5a] // זמיר [v. 5d]). The latter appears also to function as a sort of word-play within the unit and can hardly have been lost on its audience, particularly in the similarity between זרם 'storm' (v. 4c,e), זרים 'strangers' (v. 5b) and זמיר 'song' (v. 5d) which further supports the ring construction of the piece[79]. Perhaps most significantly, the central descriptive statement of the enemy in v. 5a כְּחֹרֶב בְּצָיוֹן 'like heat in the desert' must have had punning connotations with כְּחֶרֶב בְּצִיּוֹן 'like a sword in Zion'. This kind of word-play contributes to the evidence for the use of metaphor in the text, serving to juxtapose terms from different isotopes and to introduce by inference absent *métaphorisés* and *métaphorisants*.

Indicators

What appear to be formal indicators of metaphor are present in v. 4f (כזרם) and v. 5a (כחרב) yet the absence of strict isotopic distinction – רוח + זרם being from the same isotope[80] and חרב + שאון being from the same isotope[81] is a clearer indication of simple simile. These comparative

---

79. The presence of the terms זרים and עריצים in v. 2b and in v. 3b // v. 5b and v. 5d respectively serves to suggest that the foreign nation from which YHWH has proved himself a shelter is the same as that described as ruined in 25,1-3.

80. The basic meaning of רוח is 'air in motion' and according to HALOT 1199 it is used in this sense more than 100 times in the OT. Viewed in this way, therefore, it can be seen as part of the isotope of 'storm'. The term also has an extended meaning of 'rage' / 'ill-temper (Qoh 10,4; Judg 8,3; Isa 33,11; cf. NIDOTTE 8120 [VAN PELT/KAISER/BLOCK])). In conjunction with זרם, therefore, it constitutes a qualification of storm – a raging storm. זרם (HALOT 281) has to do with severe weather conditions including heavy rain and thunder (Isa 4,6; 28,2). Worth noting is the similarity with the term זרמה which means 'phallus' (HALOT 282). There may be a connection with possible sexual imagery related to YHWH's 'hand' in v. 10a. It is evident that there is a great deal of other 'horizontal' speech at work in these verses as well as throughout the entire textual complex Isa 24–27.

81. שאון has the basic meaning of 'roar' / 'din' and is commonly associated with the 'roar of water (Isa 17,12; Jer 51,55). More figurative applications include the roar or din created by a battle (Amos 2,2; Hos 10,14; Ps 74,23) with an extra nuance of YHWH as victor over the enemy (Isa 13,4; 66,6; Jer 25,11). It is interesting to note that the term is also used in Isa 24,8b (cf. also Isa 5,14) for the 'uproar of revellers' which was significant in the metaphorical statement in 24,7-13. The absence of the 'uproar of revellers' there is contrasted with the presence of the 'uproar of strangers' here (NBDB 7588). חרב has the basic meaning of 'to lay waste by drying up' (HALOT 349-350) and is used for ארץ (Isa 34,10), עיר (Jer 26,9; Ezek 6,6; 12,20; Sir 16,4) and מקדש (Am 7,9). Both שאון and חרב are isotopically associated via the related though distinct (TDOT IV 151 [Kaiser]) roots חרב I and חרב II, the latter providing the nominal derivative חֶרֶב 'sword' and the verb חרב 'to make war' (cf. 2 Kgs 3.23; Jer 50,21.27). The combination of שאון and חרב (sword)

statements constitute a sort of aside (see syntactical analysis) in which the transition is made from the first metaphor to the second by way of catchwords חרב and זרם. Thus two metaphors appear to be at work in these verses in the context of one single metaphorical statement, the first of which has YHWH as its *métaphorisé*, the second the violent/stranger. As we noted above, syntactically speaking the present verses are still governed by the vocative in v. 1a which allows YHWH to be present in the metaphorical statements of vv. 4-5. Although not directly mentioned, he is represented by the 2nd person addressation at the beginning and end of the unit. The first metaphor is expressed in the isotope of 'protection' which constitutes the *métaphorisant* and is built up of a number of nominal terms and verbal forms: ענה, כנע, צל, מחסה, מעוז[82].

Thus with respect to the first metaphor, the *métaphorisé* is present in the 2nd person suffixes and the *métaphorisant* in the aforementioned nominal and verbal terms. The *métaphorisé* and the *métaphorisant* are clearly distinct from one another, the former the divinity, the latter the isotope of protection. The frequent application of such terms of protection and refuge to the divinity, however, appears to have affected a degree of transference of the attributes they describe to provide an element of content to the isotope of the divine which, as we noted above, is in itself 'empty'. We will return to this below when we discuss the type of metaphor involved in this statement. The absence of formal indicators

---

occurs in Jer 25,31! The combination of רוח, זרם, חרב and שאון suggests the destructive power of extreme weather conditions which can lead to both flood and drought. There are clear associations with the 'drying up' of ארץ in ch.24. Where YHWH is absent there is only chaos.

82. מעוז from the root עוז has the basic meaning of 'mountain stronghold' or 'place of refuge' (Judg 6,26; Isa 17,10; 23,11.14; 27,5) and is used in conjunction with מקדש in Dan 11,31 to refer to the temple (HALOT 610). מחסה literally refers to a place of refuge for animals although it is frequently used in an extended sense as a refuge for human beings (Jer 17,17; Joel 4,16; Ps 14,6; 46,2; 61,4; 62,9; 71,7). The term often occurs in construct with עוז meaning a 'protective shelter' (HALOT 571). צל is perhaps the most significant and most 'loaded' term in the isotope of 'protection'. It basically suggests the idea of shadow or shade and occurs also elsewhere in conjunction with מחרב (Isa 4,6; Sir 14,27). Other meaningful combination include: tree (Jud 9,15; Ezek 17,23; 31,6.12.17; Hos 4,13); vine (Ps 80,11); cloud (Isa 25,5); Rock (Isa 32,2). Some or all of these dimensions are being brought into association with the divinity via the metaphorical statement. The term is already used figuratively of God with the addition of יד (Isa 49,2; 51,16; Hos 14,8) which adds to the 'protective' interpretation of YHWH's hand in 25,10a. Cf. Lam 4,20 where it refers to the protection of the משיח יהוה i.e. the king. The verbal forms in v. 5cd both have to do with the idea of 'humbling' (כנע; ענה; cf. HALOT 485 and 853 respectively) although unrelated to the terms for the same concept found in vv. 10bff.. They constitute the other side, as it were, of YHWH's protective activity, portraying the result thereof for the enemy who were the subject of the comparison in vv. 4de and 5ab and who return here in the terminology repeated from these verses both in terms of their 'heat' and their 'noise'.

of metaphor leads us to look elsewhere in the informal arena. Simple attribution via the verb היה (2nd person singular) of the qualities of protection constitutes the primary indication of metaphor supported by repetition (מעוז), alliteration (מעוז, מעוז, מחסה) and even the syntax which introduces the *métaphorisé* via the verbal clause in v. 4a and follows it up with a climactic series of parallel (supplementary) subordinate clauses ending with the most pregnant of all the terms of the *métaphorisant*, namely צל (see note 82). Where the *métaphorisé* is an incorporeal reality there is always an element of semantic incoherence in that the *métaphorisé* – in this case the divinity – is being described in terms of the physical/corporeal phenomena of 'place of refuge', 'shelter' or 'shadow'. The semantic ambivalence of the terminology from the isotope of protection allows it to be applied in a partially determinative way to the divinity thus establishing the metaphorical statement. Each of the terms in question already has both literal and figurative usages. It would seem possible, therefore, to reduce the metaphor to the A is B type: YHWH is protector (with all the implications this word contains), yet even at this point there seems to be a further step possible, the terms of the *métaphorisant* implying a special kind of protection. It is interesting to note that of the terminology applied to the traditional groups deserving of YHWH's (and the king's)[83] protection, the specific significance of דל and אביון is not easy to determine. The Anchor Bible Dictionary[84] proposes that when both terms are combined a more stylised mode of referring to the poor and the needy is at work[85]. If we follow the suggestion of ABD that דל is more of a reference to the rural poor and that אביון is a more inclusive term for the needy, especially those burdened with insecurity of various kinds including homelessness then there would appear to be a progression in our present text from the field to the city, from the rural poor to the urban poor (reflecting a similar progression throughout ch. 24). Indeed the latter group – אביון – may also hint at the protection of the widow which was also YHWH's special concern[86]. We are certainly in the realm of figurative, dependant speech since the reader must have an awareness of the physical protective qualities of

---

83. God's concern for the poor: Job 5,15; Ps 9,12; 10,12; 34,6; 107,41; 132,15; Isa 49,13, etc.. The king's concern for the poor, cf. esp. Ps 74, also Isa 11,4f.; Prov 29,4. Subject of Mosaic legislation and prophetic exhortation: Ex 23,3; Lev 19,15; Dt 10,17.18; 2 Sam 22,28; Isa 1,23; 25,4; Ezek 22,7; Am 2,6; 4,1; Mic 2,2 (G.A. BUTTRICK [ed.], *IDB*. Vol. III, New York – Nashville, 1962, p. 863. Cf. also TDOT I 27-41 [BOTTERWECK]).
84. D.N. FREEDMAN (ed.), *The Anchor Bible Dictionary*, New York, NY, 1992.
85. ABD V 403ff.
86. Dt 10,18; Jer 49,11; Ps 68,5; 146,9 (cf. IDB IV 842).

the *énoncé métaphorisant* before he or she can attribute the same to the divinity. It would appear that the analogical relationship between the *métaphorisant* and the *métaphorisé* is positive, i.e. affirming something positive of the divine. The terminology of protection taken from the human/animal world is attributed via the metaphor to partially describe the divinity. Clearly the *métaphorisant* is of the insight type in that it tells us something about the divine reality to which it is attributed via the metaphorical statement.

Type

Bourguet concluded that all metaphors are based in isotopic cross-reference (positive analogy) between the *métaphorisé* and the *métaphorisant* which admits of a certain rupture (negative analogy) both of which are to be found in the *foyer* or core of the metaphor. In terms of Bourguet's core classification, the present metaphor would appear to be an example of an 'absent core' which is contained implicitly within the *métaphorisant*, i.e. in the ambiguity of the isotope of protection which allows the terminology involved to be used literally and figuratively. The 'absent' core is synonymous in nature in that the *énoncé métaphorisant* contains a number of synonymous terms from differing roots. There is also a secondary core involved in the second metaphor (see below) which constitutes the other side of the coin with respect to the present metaphor within a single statement. There can be no doubt that the metaphor we are dealing with is still active in that its 'reader' would have recognised the language as figurative speech about YHWH and given the creative possibilities provided by the combination of terminology we are clearly in the presence of what Black would call a strong metaphor, i.e. one which is both active and resonant. We already raised the question as to whether we are dealing with a metaphor of the A is B type. We noted in response that there was perhaps more behind the notion of YHWH (A) is protector (B) in that protection of the poor and the needy (the widow and the orphan and the sojourner) has a variety of interpretative features. The remaining metaphors in ch.25 tend to suggest that behind this metaphor there is an even more fundamental (titular) metaphor upon which it is based, namely 'YHWH is husband'. For Lakoff and Johnson the statement 'YHWH is protector' would constitute a structural metaphor in that our understanding of the terms of the *métaphorisant* structures our understanding of the *métaphorisé*. The terminology of the *métaphorisant* seems to be culture-exceeding to the degree that refuge/shelter from heat/storm (even in the figurative sense as danger/hostility) is a notion which would be understood by every culture. Given that the *métaphorisé* is the divinity we can determine the type of allegorical speech involved to be of the 'bonus' type, as Thomas Aquinas would term it, speech in which the *métaphorisant* at least partly determines what we understand by the *métaphorisé*. Of the three types of metaphorical concepts Thomas maintains can be applied to God, the present metaphor is evidently of the 'relative' type in that it denotes something (always partial) about the relationship between God and someone or something else[87]. According to Macky's analysis, the present metaphor would be typical of the majority of biblical metaphors in that it employs a physical/well-known *métaphorisant* (symbol) to a mysterious (divine) *métaphorisé* (subject) and by so doing it allows us insight into the relationship between the human and the divine. Although he admits of the possibility that in the 'dialogue' between subject and symbol both can undergo 'change' (so-called dual-direction metaphors), this does not seem to be the case here. Nor does there seem to be a question of the metaphor being 'twice-true' (i.e. both literally and metaphorically true). Clearly the authors are speaking metaphorically and do not expect us to understand this speech in a literal sense[88]. Ultimately we might be able to categorise this metaphor as standard given its frequent occurrence throughout the OT and the fact that one can almost dispense with the *métaphorisé*. While it clearly has elements of the expressive (emotive prayer context), evaluative (YHWH is protective), exploratory (elements of neutral analogy which encourage questioning of the metaphor) types of speech, the primary type would seem to be relational, affirming belief that God has and will indeed relate to his people in this protective fashion. We will explore this dimension of our metaphor below when we explore the author's purpose.

Author's Purpose / Interpretation

Our analysis of the first metaphor in the metaphorical statement running from vv. 4-5 suggests that the author's purpose is primarily a relational one, an invitation to his audience(s) to imaginatively explore their relationship with YHWH in the light of the metaphor of YHWH as protector. While there is evidently an evaluative/cognitive/presentative (see the good things the Lord has done for us in the past and will continue to do

---

87. The example he offers from Ps 18,2; "The Lord is my rock, my fortress..." is similar to the present metaphor.
88. Although the reference to the temple as a refuge (Dan 11,31) might introduce a literal element.

in the future) and a degree of affective purpose in that he clearly intends to stir his audience(s) into praise, his primary purpose is relational and he expects to his audience to respond in some way to this positive affirmation of YHWH's protection for his people from hostility.

The terminology of the *métaphorisant* provides a rich source for the author to say what he wants to say about this relationship. In contrast to many of the metaphors in the previous chapter we are now confronted with a God of refuge rather than a hostile God, a God of protection rather than a God of scattering. The multiple terms of the *métaphorisant* certainly allow us a degree of access, therefore, to the author's meaning. Words which imply basic physical refuge (e.g. for animals/people: מעוז and מחסה) suggest YHWH's concern for the physical well-being of his people, that he provides such places of refuge in times of danger. Most importantly, however, is the term צל, the final and climactically most significant protective image of the three in which YHWH is identified with 'shade'. The many associations called to mind by the use of this term suggest that YHWH has all the qualities of those physical objects (cf. note 75) which provide shade/shadow in the desert heat[89]: tree, vine, cloud, rock. The final affirmation of ch. 24,23 – כי־מלך יהוה צבאות – perhaps provides a clue as to the specific image the author had in mind: YHWH – the king – the tree. In his commentary on the book of Lamentations, J. Renkema notes[90] with respect to Lam 4,20b that although there is no mention of a tree, the presence of the phrase בצלו 'in his shadow' clearly indicates that the metaphor of the shadow providing tree is at work. He points to texts referring to the messianic expectation in which the Davidic king is described as a cedar planted by YHWH in the branches of which the birds find shelter and shade from the extreme heat of the desert. Renkema further explains that the image of the protective tree is not confined to Israel and its king[91]. In Egypt, for example, the goddesses Hathor and Nut were presented as tree goddesses, while Sumerian royal hymns portrayed the king as a tree of life which provided shadow and protection to his people. Even the pharaoh is compared to a tree in Ezek 31. In the OT, the metaphor is transferred to the Davidic king (cf. Ps 2) in whose shade God's people will live in safety in the

---

89. Ultimately also a metaphor for hostile forces; see 2nd metaphor.
90. RENKEMA, *Klaagliederen*, p. 400ff..
91. Cf. Judg 9,8ff.; Ezek.17; 31. Renkema refers to O. KEEL, *YHWH-Visionen und Siegelkunst* (SBS, 84/85), Stuttgart, 1977², p. 165ff.; G. WIDENGREN, *The King and the Tree of Life in Ancient Near Eastern Religion* (King and Saviour, IV), Uppsala, 1951, p. 59 as well as TWAT IV 467f. (MULDER) and TWAT VI 293f. [NIELSEN]. The metaphor of the tree in Proto-Isaiah is thoroughly unpacked in K. NIELSEN, *There is Hope for a Tree. The Tree as Metaphor in Isaiah* (JSOT SS, 65), Sheffield, 1989.

midst of the גוים (here זרים / עריצים). Ultimately, however, the protection offered by the king-as-tree is guaranteed by YHWH himself, a fact which Renkema employs to explain the direct references to YHWH himself as a protective tree[92]. Hos 14,8 describes YHWH as a cypress tree which provides fruit for Israel. Thus the image of the protective tree can alternate in the OT between the king and the divinity. Given the parallel destruction of land, city and population (cf. Isa 24) presented in Lamentations it seems reasonable to assume that in the present text the protective obligations have fallen back to YHWH, their basic provider. The king's role as upholder of justice and protector of the poor and the needy (4a-b) devolves upon YHWH in the absence of the king.

It would appear, therefore, that the image of the tree hidden in the *métaphorisant* of refuge/protection/shade opens a window into the author's understanding of the relationship between YHWH and his people, a view which contrasts powerfully with the presentation of that relationship in ch. 24. As protector of the poor and the needy after the fashion of the king, YHWH is obliquely called upon in vv. 4-5 to continue to be a 'tree' for his people, a shade from the heat, as he was in the past. In line with much of OT theology, the memory of YHWH's past deeds moves into an expression of confidence that he will continue to save in the present and in the future.

Further categories of those deserving of protection are dealt with in the metaphorical statements in vv. 6-8 and 9-10a where the primary focus of the metaphor is the widowed city, Jerusalem.

The second metaphor juxtaposes terminology from the isotope of hostile (to humans) weather conditions: storm, hail, heat//sounds: blast, din, song with the 'enemy' which is portrayed via a number of terms from the isotope of 'hostility': 'distress of the needy', the 'violent', 'strangers' in a second metaphorical statement. As we noted above, this second metaphor states the other side of the coin with respect to the first, revealing what YHWH protects *from* in a parallel statement which employs both metaphor and simple comparison. The primary indication of metaphor is found in the repetition of זרים זרם, זמיר) and עריצים (note word-play, assonance and end rhyme) which are juxtaposed in the parallelism of v. 4ef//v. 5ab. with terminology descriptive of storm (זרם) and heat (חרב). We are evidently dealing with distinct isotopes which establish the 'stranger'/'violent' as the *métaphorisé* and 'harsh weather' as the *métaphorisant*, both corporeal realities. The comparison (כ... כ) serves

---

92. Cf. Ps 91,1; TWAT VI 1040 (SCHWAB).

to underline the intensity of the metaphor and functions in a partly explanatory manner[93] which suggests that the metaphor itself may not have been immediately evident to its audience. We are clearly dealing with figurative language, however, since we are dependant on our knowledge of the reality of the *métaphorisant* in order to apply it to the *métaphorisé*. The introduction of a degree of positive analogy between the *métaphorisé* and the *métaphorisant* seems to be part of the function of the comparison in v. 4ef//v. 5ab, introducing the aspect of 'battle din' which is like a blast of wind or a storm. The *métaphorisant* is clearly far from conventional since it tells us something about the reality with which it is associated. As such we can describe this second metaphor as an 'insight' metaphor.

Type

While there is a small degree of isotopic cross-reference between the *métaphorisé* and the *métaphorisant*, its primary core is to be found in the word-play core centring around the terms זרים (זרם, זמיר) and עריצים. As Bourguet notes, such cores are quite rare and are based on phonetic similarity between terms found in both isotopes. Other aspects of type include: resonant-active (rich in interpretative possibilities); structural (structure our understanding of 'the violent' in terms of 'hostile weather'); comparative rather than ornamental (two well-known realities juxtaposed in a metaphorical speech act with the intention of highlighting the similarities between them); novel (limited though underlined positive analogy). The speech type involved here appears to depart from the relational terminology which has governed much of the metaphorical language we have encountered so far. The primary type would seem to be evaluative speech, assessing the intensity and power of 'the violent'/ 'the stranger'.

Author's Purpose / Interpretation

As the 'other side' of the primary metaphor (YHWH is protector) in these verses, it seems evident that the author's purpose is to raise the stakes, as it were, with regard to the hostile powers YHWH is able to suppress so gently and effortlessly[94]. In the last analysis, the author(s) is (are) expressing judgement on the violent and their 'attack' and at the

---

93. Cf. SWEENEY, *Isaiah 1–39*, pp. 333-334.
94. Cf. MOTYER, *The Prophecy of Isaiah*, p. 209 with reference to J. SKINNER, *Isaiah Vols. I & II*, Cambridge, 1905.

same time magnifying YHWH's deeds past, present and future. To the extent that hostile weather conditions may represent alien divinities it is possible that there is an allusion here to some kind of divine battle. In this sense, the author's use of metaphor allows him to speak of matters which had perhaps become unspeakable[95]. Taken together, both the metaphor of 'YHWH as protector' and that of the 'enemy' as 'hostile weather' combine to present a powerful image of YHWH's salvific action (on behalf of the poor and needy) which is still alive in his people's memory and as such provides hope for future acts of salvation/protection. In this sense YHWH stands between his people and their enemies as a barrier against their onslaught.

Isa 25,6-8[96]

6a	And he will prepare, YHWH $Ts^eba'ot$,
b	for all peoples on this mountain,
c	a [drinking] feast of fat dishes,
d	a feast of fine wines,
e	of fat dishes full of marrow,
f	of fine wines filtered clear.
7a	And he will swallow up, on this mountain,
b	the face of the shroud shrouding all the peoples,
c	the web woven over all the nations.
8a	He will swallow up death forever.
b	And he will wipe away, the Lord YHWH,
c	tears from every face.
d	Then the shame of his people he will remove
e	from all the land.
f	Indeed YHWH has spoken.

---

95. Cf. ELDER, *Theological-Historical Study*, p. 155; MARCH, *Two Prophetic Compositions*, pp. 91 (note 1), 94.

96. See WILDBERGER (*Jesaja 13–27*, pp. 959-960) for a text critical review. None of the remarks therein significantly effect our translational options.

Delimitation of Metaphorical Statement

Many commentators view vv. 6-8 as a distinct unit within chapter 25 although Johnson does point out that there is some division on the matter. Those who divide the text after v. 8 tend to do so on the basis of the Isaianic key signature[97] closing formula כי יהוה דבר and the opening formula in v. 9 ויאמר ביום ההוא[98]. Those who extend to verse 10a point to either consistent meter[99] or the inclusion formed by בהר הזה (v6c – v. 10a)[100]. Although Johnson himself tends to extend the unit to v. 10a on the basis the inclusion he does not deny the formal characteristics which mark off vv. 9-10a (see below) and views it as a separate strophe within the larger unit vv. 6-10a. Lewis is of a similar mind, insisting that the primary consideration for determining the extent of the unit must be the inclusion בהר הזה in v. 6b and v. 10a, but again he admits that there are strophic divisions to consider here[101]. While we can agree with Johnson and Lewis to a degree, for our own purposes it seems evident that the (first) metaphorical statement (of vv. 6-10a) extends to v. 8 and that vv. 9-10a introduce a related yet distinct metaphor which functions climactically with regard to what precedes it. Vv. 6-8 describe a feast with the best wines, the best foods and the best gifts, all served by the Lord YHWH // YHWH Ts^{e}ba'ot. At the level of content these verses are quite distinct from what follows in vv. 9-10a since the latter describe the people's reaction/comment to the gifts provided in the former. The verses are thus related yet distinct.

Motyer suggests that the background to this text is the covenant banquet of Ex 24,11 at which not only the elders but all the people will now be able to eat and drink. The covenant in this sense is sealed with a banquet. In light of what we have noted above with respect to covenant, this banquet takes on the dimensions of a wedding banquet. We shall see below that the notion of marriage as covenant also appears to be a functioning metaphor within the text.

Clearly the syntax of the passage also serves to mark the present unit from what precedes it by a change of person (2nd to 3rd) which then

---

97. MOTYER, *The Prophecy of Isaiah*, p. 210.
98. RUDOLPH, *Jesaja 24–27*, p. 35; O. LUDWIG, *Die Stadt in der Jesaja-Apokalypse, Zur Datierung von Jes. 24–27*, Cologne, 1967, pp. 113-115; FOHRER, *Der Aufbau*, p. 43; REDDITT, *Form Critical Analysis*, p. 116; SCHOORS, *Jesaja*, p. 151-152; WILDBERGER, *Jesaja 13–27*, p. 959ff.; ALONSO SCHÖKEL and SICRE DIAZ, *Profetas I*, pp. 210-211; SWEENEY, *Isaiah 1–39*, pp. 334-335; KILIAN, *Jesaja II*, p. 149; etc..
99. PROCKSCH, *Jesaja I*, p. 319.
100. Johnson himself (*Chaos to Restoration*, p. 61); LINDBLOM, *Die Jesaja Apokalypse*, p. 34; MARCH, *Two Prophetic Compositions*, p. 105); etc..
101. LEWIS, *Rhetorical-Critical Analysis*, pp. 108-110.

governs the entire statement through to its repetition in the concluding formula in v. 8f.. The primary actant – YHWH – remains the same as the previous statement, being mentioned twice within the metaphorical statement itself and then again in the concluding formula. The unit is also dominated by w^{e}qatal forms – as opposed to the qatals of vv. 9ff. – (2nd בלע in v. 8 is perhaps due to author's apparent preference for asyndetic forms[102]), indicating three future events all of which serve one single metaphorical statement which centres around the restoration of Zion as wife of YHWH and the ultimate reversal of widowhood.

The structure of the passage is not difficult to determine. Seven bicola with the central focus on v. 7a – 8a which is marked off by the repetition of the act of 'swallowing', perhaps the primary focus of the metaphorical statement found in these verses. Three actions of YHWH are described: עשה 'to make' (followed by what he shall make = 2x feast)[103] // בלע 'to swallow' (followed by what he will swallow = 3x shroud/web/death) // מחה (+ syntactically dependant סור) 'wipe away' (+ 'remove') (followed by what he shall wipe away/remove = 2x tear/shame)[104].

---

102. Sweeney notes that because of the absence of the *waw*-consecutive form v. 8a stands as an appositional explanation of the meaning of vv. 6-7. In this event, according to Motyer, one must understand the second בלע as a participial perfect 'having swallowed up' (*The Prophecy of Isaiah*, p. 209). BHS suggests we read in line with the Peshitta but as Van der Kooij points out (*Isaiah 24–27: Text Critical Notes*, p. 14), the majority of textual witnesses (lQIsa^a, LXX, Theod, Sym, Tg, V) support the MT

103. Note Beuken's suggestion (*The Prophet Leads*, p. 7) that the use of עשה with YHWH as subject in the song of thanksgiving in v. 1ff. (*qatal*) and its use in the prophecy concerning the banquet in v. 6ff. (w^e*qatal*) may suggest two distinct temporal phases, the first suggesting immediate future, the second open future. He adds that the change from 2nd to 3rd person and the additional mention of 'YHWH *Tseb'ot*' as subject further underscore this change in temporal perspective. Although vv. 1-5 and vv. 6-8 belong together from the redactional perspective (*ibid*., pp. 9-11), evident distinction at other levels allows us to treat them as separate units even although they have clearly been attuned to one another.

104. Understood literally, all the verb forms in this unit can be seen as acts of provision which a human agent might perform for another human agent, all with the exception of בלע, that is, which usually has a more destructive sense in the human arena. With YHWH as subject, however, all of these words, including בלע, can also stand for acts of salvation, at least in the figurative sense. With YHWH as subject, עשה is used as a description of what YHWH does in his governance of the world: great things (Ps 71,19); wonders (Ex 3,20; Isa 25,1; Ps 72,18 etc.); righteousness (Ps 103,6); judgement (Ezek 5,10.15; 11,9; 25,11 etc.); annihilation (not of Israel) (Isa 10,23; Jer 30,11 etc.). For the most part, therefore, YHWH's 'doing / making' constitutes an act of salvation, the content of what he does being determined, of course, by the remaining context (TWAT VI 414-432 [RINGGREN]). מחה in the literal sense is used for the act of wiping away (tears). The theological sense usually constitutes a figurative extension an introduces a salvific act on the part of YHWH (cf. TDOT VIII 227-231 [ALONSO SCHÖKEL]). סור in the *hiphil* means 'to cause to turn aside' / 'to remove'. In the *qal* it frequently refers to human 'abweichen' from the way/commandments of YHWH (Dt 17,20; Jos 1,7; 23,7 etc.). With God as subject of a *hiphil* form, however, a complete reversal is established: YHWH removes his people's

Indicators

Semantically speaking, the verbal forms of this unit can all express acts of salvation on the part of YHWH and each can be understood as part of this isotope. In this sense each act is taken from the human realm and applied to YHWH as subject, thus introducing the salvific element. Since there is no strong isotopic distinction between the terms, however, we must look elsewhere for indicators of the use of metaphor. One term, namely בלע, stands out in this unit for a variety of reasons: syntactically distinct from the other verb forms in the unit, repetition (v. 7a, 8a), central parallel placing, distinct meaning with respect to divine subject, contrast to אכל 'a curse devours' in ch. 24[105]. Thus we have a variety of informal indicators suggesting that we focus on this term as the core of the metaphorical statement. In addition, the other actions of this unit can be reduced to literal speech while the act of 'swallowing' death/shroud/web clearly has to be understood in a dependent, figurative sense. As we shall see, it seems clear that we are dealing with a profound metaphor in that the divinity is being portrayed in terms associated with human marriage. At the same time, the divine action of 'swallowing up' death is the reverse of what one would normally expect, i.e. that death would be the subject of the verb and humans its object. It would appear that the author wishes to draw our attention to this term as the primary *métaphorisant* (with YHWH as subject, the *métaphorisant* also has an incorporeal dimensions[106]) of the segment. The *métaphorisé*, however, appears to be absent. Given the context, consonantal similarity between the roots בלע 'to swallow' and בעל 'to marry/ be lord over'[107] suggests the presence of a rare word-play metaphor (more about this type below) in which the

---

guilt. In the human application of סור there are clear semantic connections with the verb forms of 24,5bcd (עבר, חלך, and הפר) (TWAT V 803-810 [SNIJDERS]). בלע literally means to gulp down food and is often use to express a destructive effect. With YHWH as subject, however, it can represent both punitive and salvific acts on his part. Note the parallel with אכל in 24,6a where a 'curse' devours ארץ. One is left with the possibility that the 'curse' should be understood in the light of the then parallel terms 'death/web/shroud' here (TDOT II 136-139 [SCHÜPPHAUS]).

105. As Motyer points out, death is not understood here as the transience of human life but rather as that death which reflects the curse imposed as a consequence of sin (p. 209), 'the devouring curse' of 24,6a. As a consequence of transgression YHWH has become alienated from his people (ultimately focused on Zion) and the breakdown of their relationship is presented as widowhood.

106. As such, it ought to be considered that behind the metaphor employed here there may be a metaphor of the A is B type, namely 'YHWH is husband'. More will be said on this below.

107. Cf. TDOT II 181-200 [DE MOOR / MULDER] for a thorough analysis of the mythical dimensions of the term בעל. The verb form is not unknown to BI: Isa 16,13; 54,1.5; 62,4.5 (cf. HALOT 142).

métaphorisé is understood as בעל and the act of 'swallowing up' death etc. is to be understood as a reference to the restoration of marital status. As the evident focal point of the metaphorical statement, the word-play metaphor בעל // בלע governs the other actions of YHWH in this unit and thereby incorporates them into the act of restoring marital status by way of providing food (banquet), future (swallow up shroud/death), comfort (wipe away tears) and dignity (remove shame[108]) for his people. Thus, if we understand the *métaphorisé* to be בלע and the *métaphorisant* to be בעל, the analogical relationship between the two terms must be seen as positive, i.e. that in 'swallowing up' death YHWH is once again asserting his 'lordship' (marital relationship) with Zion (בהר הזה) and as such we are dealing with an 'insight' metaphor, providing insight into the mysterious reality of God's relationship with his people.

Type

According to Bourguet's classification the present metaphorical statement is governed by a word-play metaphor rooted in the phonetic (consonantal) similarity between בלע and בעל, the former constituting the *métaphorisé*, the latter the *métaphorisant*. As we noted above, such word-plays are often difficult for us to detect today although Bourguet is without doubt that they were evident to their ancient audience. Recognition of a *métaphorisant* from the isotope of marriage would have been supported by the context, especially the removal of 'shame' (חרפה) and the association with 'tears' (דמעה) in the proximate context. Thus the metaphorical statement turns around a 'word-play core' which does not rely on isotopic cross-reference between the *métaphorisé* and the *métaphorisant*. Indeed there is complete isotopic distinction between בלע and בעל. Since they are dependant on the phonetic structure of the language, such metaphors would appear, of necessity, to be culture-dependant. At the same time, however, their function can be discerned outside the culture, through our awareness of the semantic content of the terms employed. Indeed, as we noted above, we appear to be being introduced to the realm of the titular metaphor 'YHWH is husband' once again.

---

108. It is interesting to note that widowhood is also presented as an experience of humiliation in Isa 4,1; 54,4, employing the same term חרפה as here in v. 8d. דמעה, 'tears' are also directly associated with the widowhood of Zion in Lam 1,1-2 (DCH II 453). While there appears to be no direct relationship between the widow and מסכה / לוט, the imagery seems consistent, nevertheless, with that of a woman mourning her lost husband. There is also some possibility that reference is being made with the latter term to the cause of the widow's situation since the term can also refer to idols or molten gods (TDOT VIII 431ff. [DOHMEN]).

Since YHWH is the subject of the *métaphorisé* בלע one can assume he is the subject of the *métaphorisant* בעל. In this sense the metaphorical statement is telling us something about YHWH following the A is B structure ('leo' type of allegorical speech) via a quite novel combination of terms. The metaphor can be classified, therefore, as 'presentative', i.e. intended to communicate information or present arguments or conclusions. The information itself, however, is exploratory in that it endeavours to reveal the depths of a mystery. The mystery in question being the relationship between YHWH and his people. As we noted in the preceding chapter, relational metaphors introduce a level of invitation into relationship where the relationship cannot be expressed adequately with literal terms, going beyond that which literal speech can do. In speaking of God, for example, as the one who 'provides' (עשה) and 'consoles' (דמעה מחה...) and 'dignifies' (וחרפת עמו יסיר) his people, then placing an apparently unrelated term בלע at the heart of this context, the prophets of Israel affirmed their belief in metaphorical terms that God intended to relate to them in this way as a 'husband'. They founded their relational metaphorical speech on words concerning him, affirming the way God wished to relate to them: "I will take you for my wife forever..." (Hos 2,19). It is interesting to note that the confession of 26,13 includes an admission of being 'ruled over' (בעלונו: 'married to') by other lords (אדנים) besides YHWH, the only name acknowledged, however, is 'Your name'.

Author's Purpose / Interpretation

Clearly it is part of the author's purpose here to invite his audience to explore their relationship with YHWH in the light of his words and their metaphorical content. In this sense his purpose is unequivocally relational, as have been the majority of metaphorical statements so far in this textual complex. It will also become clear that the author is asking his audience to view themselves as Jerusalem/Zion and to consider their relationship as a transition from widowhood ('this mountain' alienated from YHWH) to full marital status (YHWH restored to 'this mountain' as husband of Jerusalem and his people'). At a less significant level, it would seem that the author desires to communicate information (presentative/± cognitive purpose) to his audience also, information which he hopes will elicit a personal response on behalf of his audience. This will become clear in the words which follow in 25,9-10a.

One should note the possibility, however, that direct reference to YHWH as husband of Jerusalem may have been 'unspeakable' because of its possible associations with idolatry[109]. The use of the word-play metaphor בעל/בלע at the core of the metaphorical statement in 26,5-8 which draws in images of provision, comfort and restoration of dignity has the effect of rendering the 'unspeakable' 'speakable' via associations with covenant as marriage. Ultimately, the tears and humiliation and 'death' of the widow has been removed by YHWH who is reaffirmed here as husband of his city/people.

In our endeavour to gain access to the speaker's meaning through his use of metaphors we have opened a number of windows onto the text. As we continue the view becomes more focused, allowing us to reconstruct the speaker's meaning and interpret it. We find ourselves in the world of relationship between YHWH and his people/ארץ and the ups and downs that relationship has known. There is a clear movement from alienation and breakdown (with all its consequences for people and ארץ) to restoration and intimacy which will culminate in the image of benediction and restored 'rest' (25,10a), the end of alienation, which we will explore below.

Viewed in this way, it will be clear that the image of YHWH 'swallowing up death for ever' cannot be viewed as a reference to personal resurrection[110]. Indeed, Watts notes that a reference to "'death' *per se* ignores the definite article. A specific 'death' is to be swallowed up. A specific 'disgrace' is to be removed"[111]. Within the metaphorical statements of the entire textual unit, this 'death' and 'disgrace' has to be related to the devastation/curse portrayed in ch. 24. The image of the restored widow provides the focal context for this 'swallowing up'/'removal', for the end of the curse and the restoration of Zion.

Isa 25,9-10a

9a   And a person will say on that day:

b   "Behold, our God is this.
c   We waited for him and he saved us.

---

109. Indeed, the possibility of a direct pun at the core of our metaphor relating YHWH to Ba'al in view of the latter's mythical annual conquest of Mot would not have been lost on the prophet's audience. On rendering the unspeakable speakable through metaphor cf. M. BAL, *Metaphors He Lives By*, in *Semeia* 61 (1993) 185-207.
  110. OSWALT, *Isaiah 1-39*, p. 464; LORD, *Chapter XXV and XXVI*, p. 483.
  111. WATTS, *Isaiah 1-33*, p. 333.

258   CHAPTER FOUR

d   This is YHWH: we waited for him.
e   Let us rejoice and be glad in his salvation."

10a   Truly it rests, the hand of YHWH, on this mountain.

ואמר ביום ההוא	9a
הנה אלהינו זה	b
קוינו לו ויושיענו	c
זה יהוה קוינו לו	d
נגילה ונשמחה בישועתו	e
כי־תנוח יד־יהוה בהר הזה	10a

According to Sweeney's overall division, Isa 24,1-23 constitutes a prophetic announcement of punishment by YHWH and 25,1-12 an expression of YHWH's blessing of ארץ at Zion[112]. Within the latter division there is a statement (25,10a) which can act, in a sense, as the turning point between disintegration and re-integration, a phrase which combines a 'retired' *métaphorisé* ('the *hand* of YHWH') with an unusual *métaphorisant* ('...*rests* on this mountain'), thereby bringing the *métaphorisé* out of retirement to present a particular view of Israel's blessing and restoration This colon is something of a key, therefore, a doorway into the labyrinth[113] of metaphors used/restored/created by the

---

112. *Ibid.*, p. 325, 333.
113. Miscall has noted that most studies on Isaiah tend to subordinate metaphor to meaning, seeing it as a means for conveying meaning (usually with respect to historical processes and figures) and not as a "textual element in its own right" (*Labyrinth*, p. 103). Our own approach here has endeavoured to a degree to follow Miscall's lead and move forward on the basis of his two premises: 1) avoid the historical/theological and emphasise the literary/theological and 2) give priority to metaphor over meaning (i.e. let the meaning emerge from the metaphor). He further proposes that tracing an image throughout the entire book of Isaiah will create a labyrinth of corridors into the meaning of the text, thereby implying that as there are many images there are also many ways to approach meaning and interpretation of the text. We will restrict ourselves to the focal chapters of the present work for the time being (Isa 24–27), although we will return to the broader picture of Isaiah as a whole in our concluding chapter. Miscall enters into the labyrinth of Isaiah via the image of 'light' but soon finds himself in a maze of adjoining corridors which extend and expand and even reverse his original starting point. To an extent we have already entered the labyrinth and discovered an inter-connecting maze of corridors which reveal more and more with respect to YHWH's relationship with his people and his ארץ. The present metaphorical statement provides something of a focus for the rest. Like Miscall, however, it is our intention once inside the labyrinth to look "...

author which allows us to explore the relationship between an apparently angry, destructive deity (ch. 24) who is ultimately restored to his sinful people (ch. 25–27)[114].

Before proceeding to the metaphorical statement contained in these verses as such, let us situate Isa 25,10a in its immediate literary context.

Delimitation of Metaphorical Statement

At the beginning of our analysis of Isa 25 we noted that consensus was lacking among scholars on the exact limits of the pericopes in question and this is equally true of the pericope within which 25,10a is located. Sweeney[115] lists two factors which suggest that 25,1-12 can be envisaged as a distinct unit: (i) 25,1 lacks any syntactical connection with 24,23; (ii) the introductory ביום ההוא in 26,1 indicates the beginning of a new unit. The further division of 25,1-12, however, reveals a considerable variety of opinion[116]. The majority of scholars seem to agree that vv. 1-5 constitute a unity (a 'hymn of thanksgiving') while disagreeing on what to do with the remaining verses. Sweeney basically divides the chapter into two major sections (1-5 & 6-12) with further subdivisions – 6-8 = blessings; 9-10a = response; 10b-12 –, although he notes that all the subdivisions are clearly connected. For the sake of simplicity, therefore,

---

more to the workings and to the meanings of Isaiah as it stands, not as a mirror of the history of ancient Israel" (*Labyrinth*, p. 105). Inside Isaiah's labyrinth of metaphors our endeavours have and will continue to be to allow the 'door' metaphor to be our guide rather than trying to discover our own pathway based on some pre-conceived conceptual notions about history and prophecy. For Miscall, Isaiah is primarily a vision "... in the sense of a text that presents something to be seen and imagined rather than just thought of and conceptualised.. 'vision' in the broader sense of the realm of the imagination... a panorama of God and world and, against this backdrop,... a way of life that is God's way and an ideal community that dwells on God's holy mountain" (cf. P.D. MISCALL, *Isaiah* [Readings: A New Biblical Commentary], Sheffield, 1993, p. 12).

114. Cf. B. DOYLE, *A Literary Analysis of Isaiah 25,10a*, in J. VAN RUITEN and M. VERVENNE (eds.), *Studies in the Book of Isaiah. Festschrift Willem A.M. Beuken* (BETL, 132). Leuven, 1997, pp. 173-193.

115. SWEENEY, *Isaiah 1–39*, pp. 333-334. Watts (*Isaiah 1–33*, p. 327) begins the first pericope with 24:23 and ends it with 25,8.

116. WATTS, *Isaiah 1–33*, p. 327: 24,23 – 25,8.9-12; BREDENKAMP, *Das Buch Jesaja*, p. 151: 1-5; 6-9; 9-12: DELITZSCH, *The Prophecies of Isaiah*, pp. 436-443: 1-8; 9-12; CONDAMIN, *Le Livre d'Isaïe*, pp. 168-170: [1-5 after 26,6] 6-8; 9-12; SCHOORS, *Jesaja*, pp. 150-152; KILIAN, *Jesaja II*, pp. 147-150); HÖFFKEN, *Das Buch Jesaja*, pp. 181-184; WILDBERGER, *Jesaja 13–27*, pp. 942-974; ALONSO SCHÖKEL and SICRE DIAZ, *Profetas I*, p. 204; MOTYER, *The Prophecy of Isaiah*, pp. 207-210: 1-5; 6-8; 9-12; P. AUVRAY, *Isaie 1–39* (SB), Paris, 1972, pp. 229-231: 1-5; 6-26,6; LINDBLOM, *Die Jesaja Apokalypse*, pp. 30-40: 1-5; 6-10a; 10b-12; KISSANE, *The Book of Isaiah*, pp. 284-287: 1-2; 3-5; 6-7; 8-9; 10-12; MILLAR, *Origin*, pp. 38-45: 1-4c; 6-8; 9; 10-12; MARCH, *Two Prophetic Compositions*, pp. 81-105; LEWIS, *Rhetorical-Critical Analysis*, pp. 99-121: 1-5; 6-10a; [10b-12]; SWEENEY, *Isaiah 1–39*, pp. 333-335: 1-5; 6-12; etc..

we will follow Sweeney's calculations here. 25,10a is thus located within subdivision vv. 6-12 which Sweeney describes as an "Announcement of YHWH's blessings of peoples and [Israel's] response"[117]. The statement contained in 25,10a is more precisely situated in the smaller subdivision made up of vv. 9-10a and constitutes a response on Israel's part to her awareness of new blessing after a period of affliction and, more importantly, of divine alienation. In 25,10a Israel confesses that YHWH has been restored to His city and His people[118]. Johnson[119] follows Lindblom[120] in placing a division after v. 10a because of the inclusion formed by the repeated בהר הזה here and in v. 6. Wildberger also draws a line at v. 10a – seeing the colon as a song of thanksgiving – but he is equally aware that the text as we have it links v. 10a with v. 10bff. by way of a conjunctive (perhaps appositional) ו forcing us to read what follows the ו in the light of what precedes it, i.e. to contrast salvation for Zion with downfall for Moab[121]. Certainly from the stylistic perspective it is important to read vv. 9-12 as a piece as a brief glance at the colometry of the unit will reveal

9 And a person will say on that day:

"Behold, our God is this.[a]
We waited[b] for him and he saved us.[c]

This is YHWH[a']: we waited for him.[b']
Let us rejoice and be glad in his salvation."[c']

10a Truly it rests, the hand of YHWH, on this mountain.

[10b But it will be trodden down,[a] Moab,[b] in its place,[c]
as it is trodden,[a'] a heap of straw, [b']into the waters of a dung pit.[c']

---

117. SWEENEY, *Isaiah 1–39*, p. 333.
118. We agree with Johnson (*Chaos to Restoration*, pp. 62-64) here that the particularisation of Zion need not exclude an otherwise universalistic interpretation of the text.
119. *Ibid.*, p. 61.
120. LINDBLOM, *Die Jesaja Apokalypse*, p. 34.
121. WILDBERGER, *Jesaja 13–27*, p. 972. Cf. SCHOORS (*Jesaja*, p. 152) who argues convincingly that v. 10b-12 are probably an interpolation and do not belong to the original text which would then have ended with v. 10a; cf. also MARCH, *Two Prophetic Compositions*, p. 103. Although the poetic elements of these verses may be obscure we cannot agree that they have been completely prosaised as Millar (*Origin*, p. 44) and others would claim. Evidence of poetic features will be presented below.

11   And it will spread out^a its hands in the midst of it,^{b'}
     as a swimmer cups^{a'} [hands] to swim.^{b'} ∞

     But it will be made humble,^a its pride,^b
     in spite of the cleverness^{a'} of its hands.^{b'}

12   The lofty fortifications^b of your walls^{a'} he will make humble,^b ∞
     he will cause [them] to bend,^{b'} let touch the land,^c even the dust.^{c'}]

The unit vv. 9-12 consists of an opening formulaic monocolon followed by a single strophe containing two bicola exhibiting a complex parallel pattern ($^{a\text{-}b\text{-}c}$ // $^{a'\text{-}b'\text{-}c'}$)[122] followed by a climactic monocolon[123] in 25,10a. In a certain sense this climactic monocolon draws the unit to a close, offering an explicative reason for the rejoicing of the previous colon which itself constitutes the climax of the manifold affirmations of God's presence accumulated in preceding bicola. It is within this climactic monocolon that we find the metaphor of 'the hand of YHWH resting'. Clearly its climactic position, affirming salvation from God, indicates its importance to the author of the text. Our examination of the metaphor will further reveal the content of that salvation and how it might be understood within the labyrinth of what appear to be, for the most part, relational metaphors running through the text. Lewis divides the text into word units (as opposed to cola?), some of which are synonymously parallel, but comes up with the same basic pattern as we have suggested[124]. He describes the parallelism of vv. 9-10a as follows:

9a	ואמר ביום ההוא
b	הנה אלהינו זה
c	קוינו לו ויושיענו
d	זה יהוה קוינו לו
e	נגילה ונשמחה בישועתו
10a	כי־תנוח יד־יהוה בהר הזה

---

122. **a** – affirmation of God's presence; ^b - waiting; ^c – salvation // ^{a'} - affirmation of YHWH's presence; ^{b'} – waiting; ^{c'} salvation + rejoicing
123. W.G.E. WATSON, *Classical Hebrew Poetry. A Guide to its Techniques* (JSOT SS, 26), Sheffield, 1984, 1995², p. 170.
124. LEWIS, *Rhetorical-Critical Analysis*, pp. 112-113.

Lewis also notes that v. 10a is longer than the surrounding verses, further affirming our belief that it has a climactic/emphatic function. Johnson, to conclude, points out that the deictic particle כי further strengthens the exhortatory character of the concluding phrase of the pericope[125].

With regard to vv. 10b-12, Lewis points out that the conjunctive ו and the repetition of the term יד are strong reasons to suggest that we need to read these verses in the light of what precedes them. 10bc, therefore, must be seen, according to Lewis, as the consequence of 10a. 10bc, 11ab, 11cd and 12ab all constitute bicola in synthetic parallelism[126].

While it has been noted that practically every word of the text complex Isa 24–27 can be discussed and disputed at a text critical level, nothing of major significance exists with regard to our pericope or, in particular, the specific monocolon which constitutes the focus of our study[127].

Millar has noted that from Isa 24,1-25,9 we have an "excellent example of Hebrew poetry"[128]. From v. 10 onwards, however, he feels that the text has been prosaised to such an extent that poetic features are hard to trace although he does point out some evident residue of poetry. Much of Millar's difficulties lie with the fact that from v. 10 onwards there is metrical imbalance. Notwithstanding the fact that the text may be corrupt at this point[129] one should look further than the much disputed element of meter in order to establish whether a text is poetic or not[130].

---

125. JOHNSON, *Chaos to Restoration*, p. 67.
126. 10b: ^{a}//$^{a'}$ – trodden // trodden; ^{b} // $^{b'}$ - Moab // straw; ^{c} // $^{c'}$ – location // location; 11ab: ^{a} // $^{a'}$ – extending; ^{b} // $^{b'}$ – hands; 11cd: ^{a} // $^{a'}$ – humbled // cleverness negated; ^{b} // $^{b'}$ – pride // hands; 12ab: ^{a} // $^{a'}$ - fortifications // walls, ^{b} // $^{b'}$ - humble // bend; ^{c} // $^{c'}$ – earth // dust.
127. For a detailed text critical analysis of vv. 9-12 cf. WILDBERGER, *Jesaja 13–27*, pp. 970-971. I agree with Wildberger (and most others) with respect to one point, however, and disagree on another, both of which deserve to be noted here if only to defend my English translation of the Hebrew text. In IQIsa^a and Syr., the opening verb of v. 9 (MT ואמר) is in the 2nd person ואמרת. Wildberger (and others) see no referent for the second person and treat the MT as a sort of impersonal third person (German '*man*'), hence our translation 'a person will say…'. For the discussion of במי see note 60 above. A final point relates to the translation of the verb פרש. Most frequently this verb is rendered 'to spread (the hands)' for swimming. In a recent note, however, J. Ellington has pointed out (cf. *A Swimming Lesson*, in *BibTr* 47 [1996] 246-247) the lack of logic involved in such an interpretation, given that swimmers cup/extend their hands for swimming rather than 'spread' them out like a fork. He notes in addition that RSV has opted for the translation of פרש as 'extend/stretch out' in several other places (e.g. Exod 9,29.33; 1 Kgs 8,38; 2 Chron 6,29; Job 11,13; Jer 4,31; Lam 1,10.12). Our translation reflects his recommendations.
128. MILLAR, *Origin*, pp. 43-45.
129. LEWIS, *Rhetorical-Critical Analysis*, p. 119.
130. Cf. WATSON's discussion of the topic in *Classical Hebrew Poetry*, pp. 91-113.

We already noted some of the aspects of parallelism when we established the colometry of our pericope. Further analysis shows that the author used assonance through repetition + anaphora (v. 9 – זה, קוינו לו, בישועתו // ויושיענו; v. 10 – דוש; v. 11 – פרש), consonance alliteration (10c – מתבן במי מדמנה), possible punning (מדמן - being a town in Moab מדמנה a 'dungheap')[131]. Perhaps the most intriguing feature of the text, however, is its sense of movement (or its absence): v. 9cd – waiting (stasis); v. 9e – rejoicing (up); v. 10a – resting hand (stasis); v. 10b – treading foot (down further); v. 11 – swimmer's hands/clever hands/pride (up); v. 12 – humbling to the earth/dust (down as far as you can go!). Contrastive images are everywhere and are supported by this pattern of movements: the person who waits (trustfully קוה) is rewarded with 'a gesture of benediction'[132]; the person who attempts to rise by the cleverness of his own hands is rewarded by being trodden into a dungheap. Moab's hands are paralleled with those of the swimmer in v. 11ab and constitute a metaphor for human pride/cleverness which is further related by external parallelism to the lofty fortifications and walls of v. 12a. Sweeney, perhaps unhappy about the idea of a swimmer 'spreading' his hands, misinterprets the metaphor of the swimmer, suggesting that he is spreading his arms 'to portray Moab's demise'[133]. The context, however, seems to relate the idea of the swimmer's hands to self-sufficient pride (rising to the top by one's own devices) in contrast with patient trust ('waiting' for YHWH)[134]. Thus the hands of Moab and hand of YHWH are also set in contrast. YHWH's hand rests, but his 'feet' appear to be more than active in the contrast between v. 10a and 10b. Finally, v. 12 contains a beautiful extended metaphor taking the *hiphil* forms of שחח, שפל and נגע, normally related to 'bringing down' persons[135], and applying them to inanimate lofty walls/fortifications.

The most powerful poetic device employed in this pericope is the metaphor of 'YHWH's hand resting'. The said metaphor will now constitute the focus of our study.

Indicators / Type

So far we have rather uncritically taken for granted that the expression 'YHWH's hand rests' is a metaphorical statement. Before going on to examine some aspects of the theory and function of metaphor with

131. Cf. WILDBERGER, *Jesaja 13–27*, p. 971.
132. MOTYER, *The Prophecy of Isaiah*, p. 211.
133. SWEENEY, *Isaiah 1–39*, p. 335.
134. Cf. MOTYER, *The Prophecy of Isaiah*, p. 211
135. Cf. BDB 7817; 8213; 5060.

regard to 25,10a as a whole, however, a word or two needs to be said about what indicates the presence of metaphorical speech here. We have discussed the matter of speaking metaphorically about God in the bible elsewhere. A brief review of the primary aspects of this discussion is necessary here, however, before we proceed to a more detailed analysis of Isa 25,10a. First of all we need to ask whether it is possible to speak literally about God? In his discussion on the use of literal and metaphorical speech with regard to unobservable realities – inner states, emotions, the supernatural, the divine –, Macky admits that the possibilities of literal speech in this context are limited and that our only means of exploring, understanding and describing such realities is metaphor[136]. On the question of speaking literally about God, Macky continues, William Hordern[137] suggests that it is in the nature of theological speech that it must begin with analogy and then erode that initial analogy with further qualifications which simply underline the fact that such speech is inaccurate and approximate in the first place as an expression of truth about God. It would appear that the limitations of human speech and thinking and the transcendent and infinite nature of God are incompatible and that we can only speak about God using finite concepts and terms which are derived of necessity from our imperfect human world and applied to God as ultimately 'inadequate' analogous terms. Even when we employ a speech act which describes the divinity in terms of a particular analogy, the very fact that we have to further qualify the analogy reminds us that it is inadequate and that there can be no literal speech about God.

Humphrey Palmer[138] points out a number of weaknesses in this position. Firstly, it tends to assume that because the human world is finite and imperfect then our concepts and speech are also finite and imperfect. This is not necessarily the case since, for example, we can think and speak of numbers etc. in a perfect way. Secondly, our speech about the infinite need not be brushed aside as inadequate[139]. There seems to be confusion between comprehending a reality such as infinity and having an *adequate* concept thereof. The former may be difficult if not impossible for humans but the latter need not be. Thirdly, the argument that proposes that our speech and thought about God must be inadequate tends to confuse the term 'inadequate' with the term 'metaphorical'.

---

136. MACKY, *Centrality*, pp. 163-187.
137. W. HORDERN, *Speaking of God: The Nature and Purpose of Theological Language*, New York, NY, 1964, p. 125f..
138. H. PALMER, *Analogy: A Study of Qualification and Argument in Theology*, New York, NY, 1973, p. 26f..
139. Of course, the assumption is that figurative, dependant, analogous speech is inadequate!!

There are many simple, observable realities which our human categories are inadequate to describe, but that does not mean that literal speech about such realities is impossible. Indeed, all our speech is inadequate to the reality it attempts to describe but that does not mean that we are unable to speak literally even to the smallest extent about reality, whether observable or unobservable. It would appear from Palmer's criticism, therefore, that the idea that all speech about God must be metaphorical and not literal is inaccurate as a universal theory.

Macky employs the arguments of Charles Hartshorne[140] whose position allows us to come close to literal speech about God. Hartshorne proposed that of universally applicable positive/negative pairs of concepts one or the other can be applied literally. With respect to conceptual pairs such as relative/absolute, mortal/immortal, finite/infinite etc., everything is either one or the other – if not one then the other. When speaking of God, then, we can say that if he is not literally finite, relative and mortal then God must be literally infinite, absolute and immortal. The procedure, therefore, is to find a positive/negative pair, at least one of which is applicable to the subject, and we are looking at literal speech. Where both apply to the subject we may be dealing with metaphor but the procedure will help us decide which is being used literally (best fitting the context) and which not. Macky goes on to argue on the basis of Hartshorne's axiom that it is plausible that the biblical writers were speaking literally when they made certain assertions about God. His analysis need not delay us here. Suffice to say that his arguments affirm the possibility of speaking literally about God and that it is necessary to distinguish this usage from metaphorical speech[141].

Stienstra likewise affirms such a possibility, making an important distinction between anthropomorphism as such and anthropomorphic metaphors[142]. The 'titular metaphor' which constitutes the focus of her study 'YHWH is the husband of his people' clearly has an anthropomorphic dimension in that what she calls the donor field (*métaphorisant*, secondary subject) refers to the human institution of marriage. Theological language-use tends to be highly anthropomorphic for obvious reasons although some have shown themselves to be uncomfortable with

---

140. C. HARTSHORNE, *Creative Synthesis and Philosophic Method*, Lanham, MD, 1983, p. 152f..
141. Cf. the summary of the discussion between Lakoff/Johnson and Earl A. MacCormac with regard to the sense of 'literal' and the possibility of a speech act being literal in one sense and non-literal in another in G.A. LONG, *Dead or Alive? Literality and God-Metaphors in the Hebrew Bible*, in *JAAR* 62 (1994) p. 509ff.
142. Cf. STIENSTRA, *Husband*, pp. 60-62.

this fact. Nevertheless, anthropomorphic metaphors referring to God or to inanimate objects have been recognised as common for many centuries. Caird notes, in fact, that "anthropomorphism in all its variety is the commonest source of metaphor"[143]. While none of this will come as much of a surprise it remains important to recognise the significance of Stienstra's distinction before we move on to our analysis of the content of 25,10a As she notes, not all biblical anthropomorphism is metaphorical. She illustrates her point with an example from the book of Genesis in which God is described as 'walking in the garden' and as 'one who speaks and can be hidden from' (Gen 3,8-10). Stienstra describes such talk as real anthropomorphism, allegorical perhaps, but nevertheless describing the deity in purely human, literal and non-metaphorical terms. She notes that it is impossible to boil this and similar stories[144] down to a metaphorical concept and reminds us of the fact that they are presented as narratives of events which were considered to have really happened. One aspect missing from Stienstra's analysis is the use of human limbs[145] (and face) in reference to YHWH. The analysis of Isa 25,10a will reveal that such usage must be classified under anthropological metaphor and is not intended to be a literal anthropomorphism[146].

According to G.A. Long, "the writers of the Hebrew Bible were aware that they used language we today call figurative and, to be more specific, figures of speech we call metaphors"[147]. While it is true that, from the perspective of the modern reader, God is anthropomorphised, anthropopathised, theriomorphised and physiomorphised[148] it seems clear that the same authors intended certain language about God to be understood literally and that it is usually fairly easy to distinguish between the two. It remains somewhat chauvinistic to state that the biblical authors were simply mistaken in *thinking* that they were being literal when

---

143. G.B. CAIRD, *The Language and Imagery of the Bible*, London, 1980, p. 173. Caird, it should be noted, grants both an expressive and a cognitive function to our metaphorical language about God.
144. E.g. Gen 18,20-21.
145. Particularly 'hands' and 'feet'; cf., however, KORPEL, *Rift*, pp. 108-116.
146. Literal anthropomorphism, according to Stienstra, tends to be restricted to Genesis and Exodus. The story of Jacob wrestling with God in Gen 32, for example, a text with which exegetes and biblical translators have struggled in their efforts to tone down the anthropomorphic element, is mentioned later in Hos 12,4-5 at a time when metaphor had largely taken over from literal anthropomorphism. Hosea himself tones down the literal anthropomorphism by placing YHWH on a par with the angel of YHWH which was clearly an acceptable procedure at his time of writing. Later appearances of YHWH in the OT, however, tend to be more veiled, presented in the form of dreams or visions, presented in fact as anthropomorphic metaphors.
147. LONG, *Dead or Alive?*, p. 523.
148. *Ibid.*, p. 521.

speaking about the deity and that we are correct in stating that they were *always* being metaphorical.

Is 'YHWH's hand' a literal anthropomorphism or an anthropomorphic metaphor? The fact that we are dealing with an anthropomorphism is beyond dispute – according to biblical tradition YHWH does not have hands. The question remains: is the expression literal or metaphorical? In order to attempt an answer to this question we need to take a look at the usage of the expression in the bible and in PI.

According to Bourguet's theoretical perspectives[149], we are clearly dealing with metaphor here since we have a simple juxtaposition of two terms stemming from quite distinct isotopes, one divine (the divine name)[150] one human, the cross-reference or metaphorical core of which lies in the positive analogy between divine power and the power/strength of the human hand. Even Macky would have to accept that the expression 'YHWH's hand' is metaphorical or figurative because at the bottom line it is dependant speech, a speech act dependant on our knowledge of the functions of human hands[151].

Besides the ordinary, non-theological and unequivocally literal usage of יד[152] in the OT as a whole[153], the term is frequently[154] employed to express the notion of human/ military power or strength (Gen 31,29; 41,35; 49,24; Dt 28,32; Josh 8,20; Ps 89,26; Dan 8,25; Job 34,20 etc.). Where the divinity is concerned, however, the vast majority of usages appear to be related to power of various kinds both negative and positive: divine power in general: Job 30,21; creative power: Isa 41,20;

149. BOURGUET, *Des métaphores*, p. 7-71, esp. p. 10 & p. 59.
150. Although see also his discussion of the isotope of the divine (*ibid.*, pp. 20-22).
151. MACKY, *Centrality*, p. 36-39.
152. As 'hand', 'wrist' or 'arm' (Gen 24,22 etc.), as 'holding' (Gen 22,6; 40,11; Num 22,23; Josh 8,18; 2 Kgs 11,8; 1 Chron 11,23 etc. [the extended sense of 'having in one's control' (Ex 22,3; 1 Sam 21,4) emerges in a number of texts while the literal sense dominates in others (e.g. Ex 32,4; Prov 6,17)]; for 'gestures of various kinds' (Prov 11,21; Job 17,3; Lev 5,21; Ezek 17,18; Gen 38,28; Ex 6,8; Ps 28,2; 134,2 etc.), cf. TDOT V 393-427 (BERGMAN, VON SODEN, ACKROYD).
153. Cf. also ימין which is similar in meaning and when associated with יד also takes on the figurative implications of power and strength (Ps 74,11; 89,14; 138,7; 139,10; Isa 48,13 etc.). In the theological context, however, it would appear that ימין more than יד is associated with YHWH's positive power, laying foundations/creating (Isa 48,13), protecting/upholding (Ps 63,9; 139,10), supporting (Ps 18,36), a source of righteousness (Ps 48,11); cf. TDOT VI 99-104 (SOGGIN/FABRY).
154. IDB II 520-1 (DENTON) suggests that the majority of uses are thus intended: "Most numerous are those in which it [יד] occurs as a picturesque symbol of 'power'". Other less common metaphorical usage includes 'portion' or 'share' (Gen 47,24; Jer 6,3; 2 Sam 19,44; 'debt' (Neh 10,32); 'monument' (Isa 56,5; 1 Sam 15,12; 1 Chron 18,3); 'sexual'/'genital' references are fairly frequent but may also be related to power and vitality (Dt 23,13; Isa 57,8.10; Song 5,4f. etc.).

45,12; 48,13; 66,2; Ps 95,4; protective power: 1 Kgs 18,36; Ezra 8,22; 1 Chron 4,10; Ps 37,24 with חזק suggesting hostile military power (both positive and negative to Israel): Ex 3,19; 13,3; 15,12; Num 20,20; Isa 9,11 etc.; deliverance from and into alien control: Ex 3,8; Dt 32,39; 7,8; Ps 49,16; 106,10; 107,2; Jer 31,11; Neh 1,10 etc.. A significant number of references point to hostile divine power: with enemy as (God's) agent: Dt 19,12; Josh 2,24;; Jud 2,14; 1 Sam 30,15; with reference to God: Ex 9,3; 14,31; Dt 2,15; Jud 2,15; Ruth 1,13; 1 Sam 17,46; Ps 31,9; 109,27; Isa 8,11; Jer 15,17; 16,21; Ezek 3,14 etc.[155]. Johnson notes that יד יהוה is used frequently in the Isaianic tradition to denote YHWH's power, both in the negative and positive sense. With respect to PI, the expression is found in Isa 1,25 (hostile); 11;11 (deliverance); 11,15 (hostile); 19,16 (hostile); 31,3 (hostile); 34,17 (hostile)[156]. We agree with Johnson that in Isa 25,10a the expression clearly has to do with promised deliverance but what is the content of that deliverance? Is it just a bald statement of YHWH's ability to deliver or does it go deeper than that?

It would appear then that 'YHWH's hand' is a fairly conventional metaphor[157]; one might even call it a lexicalised, 'retired' or even 'dead' metaphor, a notion to which we will return below. Long might call it a conventional literal expression[158]. Given the frequency of occurrences being related to the firmly lexicalised understanding of 'hand of God' as hostile divine power (especially in PI) it would be reasonable to suggest that such usage would, at the very least, not have created much metaphorical tension[159]. In any case, the phrase appears to have shaken off its dependant character and taken on an independence of its own through frequent use and ultimate lexicalisation. For Macky, then, it would have to be viewed as non-figurative. Bourguet would probably confirm such a claim on similar grounds: "La particularité des métaphores morts c'est que leur lexicalisation entraîne leur emploi sans intentionnalité"[160]. On its own, therefore, the biblical authors probably

---

155. TDOT V 393-426 (BERGMAN/VON SODEN/ACKROYD); HALOT 386-388. In some of these cases, certain translations simply render יד as 'power' or 'might' or 'great work': e.g. NRSV – Ex 14,31; Jer 16,21

156. JOHNSON, *Chaos to Restoration*, p. 67; cf. his footnote 97, p. 127.: Isa 1,25; 11,11.15; 19,16; 31,3; 34,17 etc.).

157. Cf. LONG, *Dead or Alive?*, p. 523-524.

158. *Ibid.*, p. 511.

159. E.A. MACCORMAC, *Metaphor and Myth in Science and Religion*, Durham, NC, 1976, p. xi: "... a metaphor can be best characterised by the 'tension' or surprise it causes in the hearer by means of its absurdity" (= the so-called 'tension theory of metaphor').

160. BOURGUET, *Des métaphores*, p. 19. His claim that lexicalisation as an indicator for discerning 'dead' metaphors is only valid for living languages (cf. footnote 14, same

did not intend 'YHWH's hand' to be understood metaphorically. Said authors and their audience simply understood it as 'power' without referring to the notion of human power.

What makes 'YHWH's hand' in Isa 25,10a so interesting as a focus of study, however, is the verb of which it is the subject, namely נוח 'to rest'. Wildberger is among the few to note that the expression 'the hand of YHWH rests on this mountain' is unique in the OT. Watts makes a similar statement, agreeing with Wildberger that the phrase is kin to the Zion Theology of the Psalms[161]. Neither author, however, makes much of the fact that the expression is unique, particularly in the combination of יד and נוח. Ackroyd points out that the phrase as a whole may suggest divine protection[162]. In the same place, however, he points out that Ps 38,3 parallels the combination of נחת and יד with נחת and חץ. His reason for doing so is apparently to suggest that via a possible word-play on נחת and נוח the expression 'the hand of YHWH rests' might be given a hostile interpretation. My suspicion that this suggestion is unconvincing is confirmed by Motyer who points out that the *qal* of נוח never expresses violent action[163]. We will return to the positive meaning of this verb below. Suffice to say that Motyer understands the phrase as a gesture of divine benediction[164] but the question remains: what is the (relational?) content of that benediction?

The unique combination of יד יהוה and נוח suggests a specific kind of protection/security/benediction by 'YHWH's hand' informed by the term נוח at the level of metaphor. Looked at from Bourguet's perspective, a 'new' metaphor is being created here, one in which a familiar expression – YHWH's hand – becomes the *métaphorisé* and the unexpected 'rest' becomes the *métaphorisant*. We are forced to re-interpret our assumptions about the significance of the *métaphorisé* – יד יהוה – in the light of

---

page) might be countered by Macky's assertion that it is still possible to distinguish 'common' (conventional) and 'uncommon' (perhaps metaphorical) usage on the basis of frequency and, of course, a little common sense. He offers the example of the more than 50 uses of the term ראש meaning 'head' or 'high point' to be taken literally (e.g. head of a road: Ezek 16,25.31; 21,19.21; 42,12; top of a mountain: Ex 19,20; Num 14,40; Josh 15,8; 1 Sam 26,13; Isa 2,2; Hos 4,13 etc.) and the few examples where it is probably not meant literally (e.g. Joel 3,7; Obad 15; Ps 7,16; Jud 9,57).

161. WATTS, *Isaiah 1–33*, p. 335; Wildberger actually says the following: "In 10a formuliert der Verfasser eigenständig; daß die Hand Jahwes »auf diesem Berg« ruht, wird sonst so nicht gesagt, entspricht aber durchaus der Zionstheologie. »Hand« ist Symbol für Stärke, Macht; es geht um den absoluten Schutz, den Israel auf dem Gottesberg finden kann". (cf. *Jesaja 13–27*, p. 972).
162. Cf. TDOT V 409 (ACKROYD).
163. MOTYER, *The Prophecy of Isaiah*, p. 710.
164. *Ibid.*, p. 711.

what we know about the *métaphorisant* – נוח. The same is true from Macky's perspective given that 'YHWH's hand' is placed in a dependant relationship with the verb 'rest'[165]. Thus, using Macky's terminology, one reality, namely the Subject (יד יהוה), is depicted in terms that are more commonly associated with a different reality, namely the Symbol (נוח). For both authors, however, the two realities in question have to be related to one another at some level: for Macky by positive or negative analogy; for Bourguet by cross-reference or isotopic intersection.

We have already looked in some detail at the 'content' of the *métaphorisé* or subject of our metaphorical statement. Before we can further unpack the significance of the entire metaphorical statement, however, it is important that we examine the *métaphorisant*. What is the meaning and usage of the verb נוח in OT and PI?

The *qal* of נוח in OT primarily means 'to settle (on)' or 'to rest'. One can divide the (±)35 OT occurrences of the *qal* into three types or categories: (i) more literal – Gen 8,4; Ex 10,14; Num 10,36; 2 Sam 17,12; 21,10; Isa 7,2.19 (ii) more abstract – (wisdom) Prov 14,33; Qoh 7,9; (the spirit of YHWH) Num 11;25f.; 2 Kgs 2,15; Isa 11,2; (iii) fuller/more comprehensive – (being at rest) Isa 14,7; Job 3,13.26; (nuance of death as rest) Job 3,16; Prov 21,16; (rest from one's enemy) Isa 23,12; Est 9,16.22; Neh 9,28[166]. Evidently there is nothing particularly unusual about the usage of the term in the OT as a whole or in PI in particular. As we noted above, however, what makes the expression in Isa 25,10a unique is the combination of terms. If we were to understand the use of נוח in 25,10a as belonging to type (i) then the expression would mean nothing more than it says, YHWH's hand would settle on 'this mountain' like a bird settling on the branch of a tree. Similarly, if we were to place it under category (iii), the reference would focus us on the subject: YHWH's hand would be experiencing rest, be at sleep, be free from its enemies. In line with Stolz, therefore, we understand the significance of נוח in Isa 25,10a to be more abstract, 'like wisdom settling on the hearts of the wise' or like 'the spirit of YHWH resting on the prophets or the king' and entering therein. Such an interpretation allows a clearer insight into the function of the combination of terms at the metaphorical level. What then is the specific meaning of נוח in 25,10a? The full answer to

---

165. Although authors such as Janet Soskice (there can be only one 'subject') disagree with the possibility of what Macky calls 'dual-direction' metaphors, it seems at least possible that the present metaphor can function in the opposite direction: יד יהוה informing our understanding of נוח; cf. SOSKICE, *Metaphor and Religious Language*, p. 49; MACKY, *Centrality*, p. 60.

166. Cf. THAT II 43-46 (STOLZ); HALOT 678-679; TWAT V 298-307 (PREUß).

this question can only emerge if we look at the term in its context, the context of the metaphorical statement: כי־תנוח יד־יהוה בהר הזה.

Author's Purpose / Interpretation

We have already conceded the fact that in speaking about God (and other incorporeal realities) the use of metaphor is often necessary. In the present context we have also noted that part of the metaphorical statement contained in Isa 25,10a is a 'retired' metaphor – the hand of YHWH –, one which through frequent use (and ultimate lexicalisation) has come to mean the 'power of God', often bearing hostile overtones. Seen as a whole, however, it would appear that the metaphorical statement is not confined to the retired metaphor 'YHWH's hand'. The introduction of the notion of 'resting' and its connotations insinuates a new dimension to our understanding of the 'hand of YHWH', one which brings it out of retirement. It is clearly possible to see two distinct isotopes at work in the statement, one powerful and perhaps even hostile, the other gentle and protective, bringing security. Thus our understanding of YHWH's hand is made dependant on our understanding of the content of the term נוח. The uniqueness of this combination of terms in the OT suggests that the author was quite aware that he was reactivating a 'retired' metaphor and that his 'audience' would have been jarred by the unusual character of the combination into reflecting on the profundity of the reality it was attempting to describe, namely that there is salvation for Israel and that said salvation had a specific content which is revealed in the complexity of the 'reactivation'. The author employs his creative skill to transform a retired metaphor into a novel metaphor.

It is at this point that we can enter further into the metaphor (and into the labyrinth)[167] and endeavour to explore some of its depths.

(i) At the first, and perhaps most obvious level, the association of נוח with the hand of YHWH constitutes a cessation of the negative power being meted out by YHWH in the first part of the text complex Isa 24–27. At the same time, the destructive power of YHWH's hand is not only at rest, it is now a source of protection and benediction.

(ii) As we move further into the labyrinth we are confronted with further associations. In his commentary on the book of Lamentations, J. Renkema argues that the phrase לא מצאה מנוח in Lam 1,3 does not

---

167. For Miscall, one creates the labyrinth by entering it. It does not already exist. Its corridors are made up of images, terms, metaphors. It has no single entrance and is not already mapped out. Thus our interpretation of a text will depend on the direction we follow as we enter and explore the labyrinth of Isaiah. Cf. MISCALL, *Labyrinth*, pp. 117-118.

signify Deuteronomistic 'rest' of a safe and peaceful lifestyle in the land of the promise (cf. Dt 3,20; 12,9f.; 25,19; 28,65)[168] but should be associated with the idea of rest and security provided by marriage. The use of the concept in the Book of Ruth helps point us in a direction which fits much more appropriately in the present context. "Naomi is in search of 'rest' for Ruth. As events turn out it would appear that she finds it by urging her daughter-in-law to enter into a new marriage, through which she will be relieved of her widowhood. Naomi had already expressed such a wish in 1,9. A woman finds 'rest', therefore, in the house of her husband who obliges himself to care for her needs and protection. When a woman becomes a widow, however, she forfeits her 'rest'. It is evident from Ruth 1,9 and 3,1 that such 'restlessness' is a fact of widowhood"[169]. The metaphor of widowhood in Lamentations is applied to both Jerusalem (1,1) and Judah (1,3; cf. also 5,3). Both widows sit restlessly: both have lost house and husband. Thus the metaphorical statement of Isa 25,10a can be understood as bringing a term which would be at home in the isotope of widowhood[170] in contact with a retired anthropomorphic metaphor from the isotope of the divine, restoring its vitality. Throughout the book of Lamentations YHWH's hand is turned against Lady Jerusalem and Daughter Zion[171]. Throughout the first part of the text complex Isa 24–27 we are witness to YHWH's hostile dealings and then to his absence (there is no wine?). Perhaps a different branch of the labyrinth might lead us into the theme of the temple in Jerusalem and the ark as the location of 'YHWH's rest' as a metaphor for his active presence among his people and the abundant blessing and provision such a presence brings[172]. Interestingly, the ark narrative in 1 Sam 4-6 portrays the ark as the manifestation of YHWH's power as well as his presence.

---

168. Having said this, he insists that the Deuteronomist's later theological formulations with respect to 'redemptive rest' may already be present here in embryonic form. Indeed, as part of the metaphor, the restlessness of widow Judah corresponds at its deepest level with the rupture in the relationship between YHWH and Judah's inhabitants, which turned out for them to mean loss of house and home, peace and security.

169. RENKEMA, *Klaagliederen, pasim*.

170. The remaining context may be further enlightened by such an association. The banquet (25,6), the removal of the veil (25,7) the swallowing up of death (25,7), the wiping away of tears (25,8), the removal of disgrace (25,8) etc. may all be associated with the notion of widowhood and its restoration. Note also the image of women birthing only 'wind' in Isa 26,16ff. Without her husband, Zion is unable to procreate.

171. For the personification of the city as a woman cf. RENKEMA, *Klaagliederen, pasim*; cf. also C. COHEN, *The Widowed City*, in *JANES* 5 (1973) 75-81; P.L. DAY, *Whence Shall Help Come to Me?: The Biblical Widow*, in P.L. DAY (ed.), *Gender and Difference in Ancient Israel*, Minneapolis, MN, 1989, pp. 125-141.

172. Cf. 1 Chron 28,2; Isa 11,10; esp. Ps 132,8.14; called into question in Isa 66,1; TWAT V 306 (PREUB).

Indeed, in Josh 4,24 the ark is brought out in procession so that the nations will know that YHWH's *hand* is mighty[173]. In the context of Isa 25,10a, however, it would seem that 'YHWH's hand' rests on 'this mountain' is primarily a sign of the restoration of a widow's rest, his hand rests as a husband's hand, he has come back.

(iii) If one ventures even further into the labyrinth, further metaphorical associations emerge. Marjo Korpel describes the idea of the city personified as a woman as a kind of root metaphor upon which others are based, i.e. the city as widow[174]. Here it is Daughter Zion who is seen as a woman and a widow. As such, the restoration of YHWH as husband signifies the presence of what Nelly Stienstra calls a 'titular metaphor' (or a metaphorical concept), namely 'YHWH is the husband of his people'[175]. Although she does not think there are references to YHWH as husband in PI she is clearly mistaken[176]. "YHWH's hand rests on this mountain" can be reduced to metaphorical concept: YHWH is the husband of his people.

(iv) Isa 25,10a is a unique combination of images, a reactivated retired metaphor opening up an entrance to the complex labyrinth of metaphors employed by the author(s) of Isaiah and allowing as to explore the depths of that labyrinth. The 'resting hand of YHWH' can be understood as a symbol of restoration out of chaos[177], the restoration of YHWH to his people as husband and the reversal of 'their' widowhood. In this sense, Isa 25,10a is a unique metaphor for salvation. It invites its 'reader' to imaginatively explore and re-evaluate his or her relationship with God[178]. In the context of Isa 24–27 as a whole it is equal in contrastive power to the many violent words found in these chapters. In former times, YHWH's hand was turned against Israel's enemy and was a source of protection for Zion. After a time of destruction and a period of widowhood, YHWH's hand once again offers protection and thus 'rest' is restored to 'restless' Zion[179]. Read in the light of 26,6 with which בהר הזה constitutes an inclusion, the full expression serves as a climax of blessing, a sign of complete restoration: the table is set and Zion's husband is at home for the feast.

173. ABD I 386-394, s.v. 'ark' (C.L. SEOW).
174. KORPEL, *Rift*, p. 261
175. STIENSTRA, *Husband*, p. 9, footnote 1, p. 12.
176. *Ibid.*, p. 162.
177. Cf. JOHNSON, *Chaos to Restoration*, esp. Chapter 2.
178. MACKY, *Centrality*, pp. 260-263: 'Relational metaphors'.
179. and his foot is turned against the enemy (25,10b).

Concluding Remarks on Isa 25

We noted in the concluding remarks to our analysis of Isa 24 that the author(s) of these verses employed intricate metaphorical statements primarily as a means of imaging the relationship between the incorporeal deity, YHWH, and his very corporeal people/ארץ, a tripolar relationship. In ch. 24, the content of that relationship was almost entirely negative, marked by punishment, curse, drought, restlessness, pollution, absence of joy etc.. In ch.24, the ultimate disgrace was YHWH's evident withdrawal from the relationship, leaving the other two poles, people and ארץ in a state of pre-cosmic chaos. The metaphors of ch. 25 have continued the relational focus of the metaphors of ch. 24, 'conflating' people and ארץ into one single pole represented by Jerusalem/Zion which, in light of ancient traditions which personified the city as a woman, allowed the author(s) to use the metaphor of Jerusalem/Zion as wife (widow) with YHWH as her (alienated) husband. Via a convergence of disaster and distress on Jerusalem/Judah, the metaphors of ch. 24 revealed a situation of alienation between husband and wife which ch. 25 resolves. The central metaphor of ch. 25 (cf. 10a) speaks of restoration of the relationship between YHWH and his widow Zion. The negative images of death and destruction found in the preceding chapter are reversed and cosmos/wholeness is restored, expressed in images of domestic rest and welfare and the return of YHWH's husbanding. The covenant – seen as a metaphor for marriage – is restored upon YHWH's initiative. All his 'wife' had to do was wait and keep faith.

Ch. 26 appears to be a reflection on the experience of punishment/alienation and ultimate restoration and cosmos. The metaphors contained therein, however, continue the relational theme. Exhortation to ongoing trust in YHWH stands side by side with admission of guilt and failed self-sufficiency, the ultimate justification of YHWH's actions side by side with thanksgiving for his gratuitous salvation.

Thus, while the meta-metaphor continues to reflect on Israel's relationship with her God, the individual metaphors in this coming chapter tend to focus on Israel's transgression/infidelity and powerlessness in juxtaposition to YHWH's strength and solidity, chastening yet forgiving.

CHAPTER FIVE
ISAIAH 26

HEBREW COLOMETRY

26,1	בַּיּ֥וֹם הַה֖וּא	יוּשַׁ֥ר הַשִּֽׁיר־הַזֶּ֖ה בְּאֶ֥רֶץ יְהוּדָ֑ה
	עִ֣יר עָז־לָ֑נוּ	יְשׁוּעָ֥ה יָשִׁ֖ית חוֹמ֥וֹת וָחֵֽל
2	פִּתְח֖וּ שְׁעָרִ֑ים	וְיָבֹ֥א גוֹי־צַדִּ֖יק שֹׁמֵ֥ר אֱמֻנִֽים
3	יֵ֣צֶר סָמ֔וּךְ	תִּצֹּ֖ר שָׁל֣וֹם ׀ שָׁל֑וֹם כִּ֥י בְךָ֖ בָּטֽוּחַ
4	בִּטְח֥וּ בַֽיהוָ֖ה עֲדֵי־עַ֑ד	כִּ֚י בְּיָ֣הּ יְהוָ֔ה צ֖וּר עוֹלָמִֽים
5	כִּ֤י הֵשַׁח֙ יֹשְׁבֵ֣י מָר֔וֹם	קִרְיָ֖ה נִשְׂגָּבָ֑ה יַשְׁפִּילֶ֕נָּה
	יַשְׁפִּילָהּ֙ עַד־אֶ֔רֶץ	יַגִּיעֶ֖נָּה עַד־עָפָֽר
6	תִּרְמְסֶ֖נָּה רָ֑גֶל	רַגְלֵ֥י עָנִ֖י פַּעֲמֵ֥י דַלִּֽים
7	אֹ֥רַח לַצַּדִּ֖יק מֵֽישָׁרִ֑ים	יָשָׁ֕ר מַעְגַּ֥ל צַדִּ֖יק תְּפַלֵּֽס
8	אַ֣ף אֹ֧רַח מִשְׁפָּטֶ֛יךָ יְהוָ֖ה קִוִּינ֑וּךָ	לְשִׁמְךָ֥ וּֽלְזִכְרְךָ֖ תַּאֲוַת־נָֽפֶשׁ
9	נַפְשִׁ֤י אִוִּיתִ֙יךָ֙ בַּלַּ֔יְלָה	אַף־רוּחִ֥י בְקִרְבִּ֖י אֲשַֽׁחֲרֶ֑ךָּ
	כִּ֞י כַּאֲשֶׁ֤ר מִשְׁפָּטֶ֙יךָ֙ לָאָ֔רֶץ	צֶ֥דֶק לָמְד֖וּ יֹשְׁבֵ֥י תֵבֵֽל
10	יֻחַ֤ן רָשָׁע֙ בַּל־לָמַ֣ד צֶ֔דֶק	בְּאֶ֥רֶץ נְכֹח֖וֹת יְעַוֵּ֑ל וּבַל־יִרְאֶ֖ה גֵּא֥וּת יְהוָֽה

WORKING TRANSLATION

26,1   On that day,
   it will be heard, this song, in the land of Judah.

   A city strong is ours!
   Salvation he secured, walls and bulwark.

2   Open the gates!
   That it may enter the nation of righteousness,
   which guards fidelity.

3   [One of] a frame of mind constant
   you preserve in peace, peace
   for in you he trusts.

4   Trust in YHWH till eternity.
   For in YH YHWH is a rock everlasting.

5   Indeed, he has brought low the dwellers of the height.
   The town of loftiness he humbles.

   He humbles it to land,
   he causes it to touch even the dust.

6   It tramples down, a foot,
   the feet of the humble,
   the steps of the poor.

7   The way for the righteous is level,
   level the path of the righteous, you smooth.

8   Surely, [in] the way of your judgements, O YHWH, we await you.
   Your name and your memory are the hunger of the soul.

9   As I live I hunger for you in the night.
   Surely, [holding] my breath within me, I search for you.

   Indeed, when your judgements are in the land,
   righteousness they learn, those who dwell in world.

10   [However] if the wicked is shown favour, he does not learn right-
                                                               eousness. ∞

   In a land of uprightness he acts perversely.
   He does not perceive the splendour of YHWH.

11	יְהוָה רָמָה יָדְךָ בַּל־יֶחֱזָיֻן	יֶחֱזוּ וְיֵבֹשׁוּ קִנְאַת־עָם אַף־אֵשׁ צָרֶיךָ תֹאכְלֵם
12	יְהוָה תִּשְׁפֹּת שָׁלוֹם לָנוּ	כִּי גַּם כָּל־מַעֲשֵׂינוּ פָּעַלְתָּ לָּנוּ
13	יְהוָה אֱלֹהֵינוּ בְּעָלוּנוּ אֲדֹנִים זוּלָתֶךָ לְבַד־בְּךָ נַזְכִּיר שְׁמֶךָ
14	מֵתִים בַּל־יִחְיוּ	רְפָאִים בַּל־יָקֻמוּ
	לָכֵן פָּקַדְתָּ וַתַּשְׁמִידֵם	וַתְּאַבֵּד כָּל־זֵכֶר לָמוֹ
15	יָסַפְתָּ לַגּוֹי יְהוָה	יָסַפְתָּ לַגּוֹי נִכְבָּדְתָּ רִחַקְתָּ כָּל־קַצְוֵי־אָרֶץ
16	יְהוָה בַּצַּר פְּקָדוּךָ	צָקוּן לַחַשׁ מוּסָרְךָ לָמוֹ
17	כְּמוֹ הָרָה תַּקְרִיב לָלֶדֶת	תָּחִיל תִּזְעַק בַּחֲבָלֶיהָ
18	כֵּן הָיִינוּ מִפָּנֶיךָ יְהוָה	הָרִינוּ חַלְנוּ כְּמוֹ יָלַדְנוּ רוּחַ
	יְשׁוּעֹת בַּל־נַעֲשֶׂה אֶרֶץ	וּבַל־יִפְּלוּ יֹשְׁבֵי תֵבֵל
19	יִחְיוּ מֵתֶיךָ	נְבֵלָתִי יְקוּמוּן
	הָקִיצוּ וְרַנְּנוּ	שֹׁכְנֵי עָפָר
	כִּי טַל אוֹרֹת טַלֶּךָ	וָאָרֶץ רְפָאִים תַּפִּיל

11 O YHWH, raised high is your hand [but] they do not take notice.
    Let them take notice and let them be shamed at [your] jealousy
                                                  [for your] people.
    Surely, the fire of your adversaries, let it consume them.

12 O YHWH, you provide peace for us
    Indeed, even all our achievements you have done [them] for us.

13 O YHWH, our God, they have ruled us, other lords, besides you.
    [But] only in you have we kept remembrance of your name.

14 The dead do not live!
    The shades do not rise,

    indeed you have punished and have wasted them,
    you have wiped out all remembrance of them.

15 You have increased the nation, O YHWH.
    You have increased the nation, you are glorified.
    You have enlarged all the boundaries of land.

16 O YHWH, in distress they missed you.
    They poured out an incantation [when] your punishment was on
                                                          [him] them.

17 Like a pregnant woman close to birthing,
    she writhes and cries out in her birth pains

    thus were we before you, O YHWH
18 We were pregnant, we writhed.
    [But] like [a pregnant woman] we birthed, [only] wind.

    Deliverance we could not win [on] land,
    and they would not fall [be born], the dwellers of world.

19 They shall live, your dead.
    My corpses shall rise.

    Wake up and shout with joy,
    [you] that abide in the dust.

    For a dew of lights is your dew
    and land shall birth shades. ∞

20	לֵךְ עַמִּי בֹּא בַחֲדָרֶיךָ	וּסְגֹר דְּלָתֶיךָ [דְּלָתְךָ] בַּעֲדֶךָ
	חֲבִי כִמְעַט־רֶגַע	עַד־יַעֲבוֹר [יַעֲבָר־]זָעַם
21	כִּי־הִנֵּה יְהוָה יֹצֵא מִמְּקוֹמוֹ	לִפְקֹד עֲוֺן יֹשֵׁב־הָאָרֶץ עָלָיו
	וְגִלְּתָה הָאָרֶץ אֶת־דָּמֶיהָ	וְלֹא־תְכַסֶּה עוֹד עַל־הֲרוּגֶיהָ

....

27,1	בַּיּוֹם הַהוּא יִפְקֹד יְהוָה	בְּחַרְבּוֹ הַקָּשָׁה	וְהַגְּדוֹלָה וְהַחֲזָקָה
	עַל לִוְיָתָן נָחָשׁ בָּרִחַ	וְעַל לִוְיָתָן נָחָשׁ עֲקַלָּתוֹן	וְהָרַג אֶת־הַתַּנִּין אֲשֶׁר בַּיָּם

20 Go, my people, enter your chambers.
    Shut your doors behind you.

    Hide for a moment,
    until it has passed, the wrath.

21 For behold, YHWH is going forth from his place,
    to punish the iniquity of the dweller on the land (upon them).

    she will disclose, the land, her blood,
    and she will not conceal again her slain.

27,1 On that day, he will bring punishment, YHWH,
    with his fierce sword,
    the great and the strong, ∞

    upon Leviathan, the serpent fleeing,
    and upon Leviathan, the serpent twisting,
    and he will kill the monster which is in the sea.

Analysis of Isaiah 26

The blessings announced in ch. 25 are continued here and focused on the 'strong city' as a further relational metaphor expressing YHWH's salvific action on behalf of his people. The chapter is full of contrasting images: salvation versus humiliation, righteousness versus wickedness, waiting versus prideful self-sufficiency, human powerlessness versus YHWH's powerfulness. Commentators divide the material in a variety of ways, although it would seem that virtually the entire chapter exhibits unifying features[1]. Sweeney adds that the introductory ביום ההוא at the beginning of the chapter and the same formula at the beginning of ch. 27 also serves to demarcate the unit which he sees as a description of the results of YHWH's announced blessings in 25,1-12[2]. Johnson is aware of an overall "sense of homogeneity"[3] yet, in like fashion to many, he is able to establish further sub-divisions in the poem. He sets the first unit as vv. 1-6[4] which he describes as song of trust in YHWH.

Together with Sweeney, Johnson and others, we take v. 1ab to be an introductory announcement of a 'song', 'a superscription'[5] which is not part of the song proper although it sets the entire song in the future. As a further sign of the unity of the entire textual complex, however, the renewal of 'song' in Judah is reminiscent of its declared absence in 24,8-9. Where this, together with the absence of wine/festival, signified the alienation of YHWH from his people, the present opening colon constitutes a proud reversal of that alienation: YHWH has returned. The song itself begins in v. 1c and runs through to v. 6, with its core being a bold exhortation to trust in YHWH the rock, the central metaphor of the song. The resourcelessness of YHWH's people who nevertheless trample their enemy echoes the opening statement of strength in the city: both have been secured by YHWH[6]. Indeed, the ultimate theme of the song is YHWH's victory over a proud 'enemy' and is intended to instill confidence in YHWH in its audience. Johnson offers four reasons for ending

---

1. Johnson (*Chaos to Restoration*, p. 67) notes the frequent use of assonance, wordplay etc. already pointed out by Duhm (*Jesaja*, p. 183). Sweeney adds that 'shifting forms of address' characterise the entire chapter and that the central plea or petition in vv.11-19 gives it the features of a complaint song. Cf. also Watts, *Isaiah 1–33*, p. 335ff., although he further divides the text into a pilgrim song (vv.1b-4), a dialogue among the pilgrims (vv.5-18) and an epiphany (vv.19-21).
2. Sweeney, *Isaiah 1–39*, pp. 338-339.
3. Johnson, *Chaos to Restoration*, p. 67.
4. Cf. Also Wildberger, *Jesaja 13–27*, p. 975; Alonso Schökel and Sicre Diaz, *Profetas I*, p. 211f.; Kilian, *Jesaja II*, p. 151 etc..
5. Johnson, *Chaos to Restoration*, p. 68
6. Cf. Motyer, *The Prophecy of Isaiah*, p. 214.

the first unit after v. 6: Direct address to YHWH begins in v. 7; concatenation begins in v. 7; contrast of strong city and hostile city ends in v. 6; future orientation ends in v. 6[7].

Isa 26,1c-6

[1   On that day,
     it will be heard, this song, in the land of Judah.]

     A city strong is ours!
     Salvation he secured, walls and bulwark.

2   Open the gates!
     That it may enter the nation of righteousness,
     which guards fidelity.

3   [One of] a frame of mind constant
     you preserve in peace, peace
     for in you he trusts.

4   Trust in YHWH till eternity.
     Yes, (in[8]) YH YHWH[9] is a rock everlasting.

5   Indeed, he has brought low the dwellers of the height.
     The town of loftiness he humbles.

     He humbles[10] it to land,
     he causes it to touch even the dust.

---

7. JOHNSON, *Chaos to Restoration*, p. 68.
8. *Beth essentiae*; cf J-M §133c n.3.
9. The expression found in the MT can also be found in Isa 12,2. BHS suggests we delete the first ביה in line with LXX which has ὁ θεὀι. Wildberger (*Jesaja 13–27*, p. 976) proposes that the first ביה be taken up at the end of v.4a but this, according to Watts (p. 338), would tend to overextend the colon. We agree with Van der Kooij (*Isaiah 24–27: Text Critical Notes*, p. 14; cf. also WATTS, *Isaiah 1–33*, p. 338), who states that since LXX frequently renders repetitions by single terms the MT should be allowed to stand as it is. The parallel terrace structure of the entire unit also supports the repetition. Indeed the triple repetition of the name of YHWH calls our attention to the focal role it plays in the metaphorical statement.
10. Move *atnah* forward to include first use of שפל, cf. BARTHÉLEMY, *Critique textuelle*, p. 131. Repetition is due to the evident parallel terrace pattern.

6   It tramples down, a foot,
    the feet of the humble,
    the steps of the poor.

Delimitation of Metaphorical Statement

It seems clear, therefore, that from a form critical perspective, among other things, we can establish our first poetic unit as vv. 1b-6 and as the first locus in Isa 26 in which we can search for indicators of metaphor. Semantic repetition together with literal repetitions mark out the unit. The repetitions as such turn around a triple repetition of YHWH's name in v. 4 which constitutes the core of the unit. After this point contrasting terminology is introduced: security/constancy/fidelity (vv. 1b-4) making way for pride/humiliation/ruin (vv. 5-6). The primary contrast is that of the two towns/cities and their inhabitants in relation to YHWH: the first is secure in YHWH 'the rock', the second is torn down and trampled by those whom YHWH preserves, his faithful people. It is important to note, along with Motyer, that the two cities which are paralleled in our unit, at this stage at least, are contrasting 'idealised cities'[11].

While it seems possible to further divide the unit from the perspective of metaphorical statements, the technique of repetition, and more importantly the extended *parallel terrace pattern* (see fig. 1)[12] it establishes, suggests that we understand the metaphorical statement as continuing from the word field of security and strength, through YHWH the rock and into the contrasting word field of humiliation, bringing low, trampling etc.. The contrast is intended to show that for the proud and self-sufficient YHWH is the opposite of what he is for those who are righteous, who wait (24,9), who guard fidelity and are constant. We can discern three metaphors, therefore, which constitute one metaphorical statement which we will further elaborate below: building terms/emotional and spiritual security; YHWH/rock ('everlasting' cf. ברית עולם 24,5); height terms/pride (absent *métaphorisant*) brought low. The primary and most evident metaphor in the unit stands at the centre: YHWH is a rock[13].

---

11. MOTYER, *The Prophecy of Isaiah*, p. 213, n.1.
12. A simple terrace literally repeats the last part of a line at the beginning of the next line. This is partly evident in the literal repetitions in our unit (שׁפל ;יהוה ;בטח ;שׁלום) but for the most part the repetitions are based on synonymous expressions. Watson suggests that the parallel terrace serves, among other things, the cohesion of a poetic unit (cf. *Classical Hebrew Poetry*, p. 212).
13. Colometry = v.1cd (bicolon 2 + 4); v.2abc (tricolon 2 + 2 + 2); v.3abc (tricolon 2 + 2 + 2); v.4ab (bicolon 3 + 4); v.5ab (bicolon 3 + 3); v.5cd (bicolon 2 + 2); v.6abc (tricolon 2 + 2 + 2).

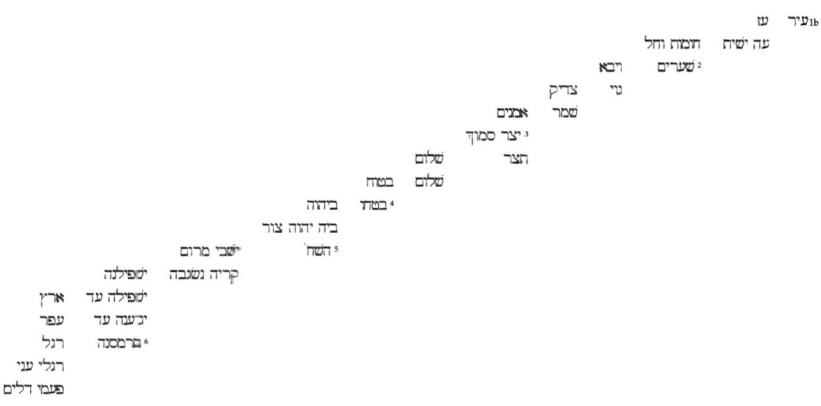

Fig. 1

Indicators

Clearly the most evident metaphor in the unit is to be found in v. 4b which states that YHWH is a rock (everlasting). Without the presence of comparative particles this metaphor has the quality of a 'short shock' although its content may have been quite familiar to its audience. The *métaphorisé*, 'YHWH', and the *métaphorisant*, 'a rock everlasting', are clearly present and clearly stem from distinct isotopic arenas: divine and natural. The nominal clause places YHWH and 'rock' in simple juxtaposition, supplying further informal indication of the presence of metaphor. In addition, the use of the *beth essentiae* serves to underline the fact that the metaphor as such is revealing something of YHWH's essence. Since we are dealing with a non-corporeal *métaphorisé*, we are clearly in the realms of figurative dependant speech here (profound metaphor), it being impossible to reduce the statement to literal, independent, speech. In terms of analogical relationship between the *métaphorisé* and the *métaphorisant* there are clear positive elements, especially in the security of the rock and its associated temporal permanence. Sweeney's comments on the parallel passage Isa 17,10 are enlightening with respect to the outer limits of the metaphor 'YHWH is a rock':

> In the Old Testament 'rock' is not just a broad symbol for divine strength, durability etc. Its link… with salvation, indicates that it is not a static but a dynamic metaphor, taking its origin in biblical use from Exodus 17, the provident rock from which the saving waters flowed. The Lord as Rock is the Lord in his dependable, saving actions, here providing the fortress-like protection which his people need in a menacing world.…fortress is a 'place

of strength', the same word as in 'strong cities' [ערי מעזו] in verse 9. Thus, Isaiah insists that the way of faith is the way of true realism in this world[14].

What is significant here is that the word field of strong, fortified cities with their walls, bulwarks and gates, constitutes an extension of the *métaphorisant* 'rock'. It is thus YHWH who is a 'strong city', and since YHWH is 'ours', the consequences for the life of his people are salvation and realistic physical security with its associated emotional security both of which come together in the repeated term שלום. In contrast, the town of loftiness and its inhabitants are not 'in possession' of YHWH but are the subject of his humiliation. Vv. 5-6 constitute a metaphorical statement in themselves, although by way of contrast, they are clearly dependant on the larger metaphorical statement running from vv. 1c-6. In vv. 5-6, the *métaphorisé* is constituted by the 'town of loftiness' and the 'dwellers of the height' while the *métaphorisant* is built up of the semantically similar terms 'bring low' (שחח), 'cause to fall' (2x שפל) and 'cause to touch' (נגע). The ABBA parallelism of v. 5ab suggests that we identify the 'town' with its 'dwellers' as the *métaphorisant* while the repetition of שפל provides a stylistic signal that the primary significance of the *métaphorisé* is to be found in this term. The notion of 'humbling' is almost exclusively the basic meaning of שפל hiphil. In PI, it refers particularly to the humiliation of the proud[15]. For the righteous who guard fidelity the gates of the strong city (i.e. YHWH) are open. For the proud and self-sufficient 'dwellers of the proud city' there is only complete humiliation from YHWH rounded off by an act of crushing under the

---

14. SWEENEY, *Isaiah 1–39*, p. 159.
15. TWAT VIII 438-444 (ENGELKEN); cf. also Qoh 10,6 which contrasts the proud with the humble (שפל). The term appears to be a favourite of Isaiah: 19 of 69 occurrences. It is used on 7 occasions as a synonym of שחח (also a favourite of Isaiah: 8 out 18 occurrences) which in the *hiphil* means 'to be made to bend low', i.e. to be humbled (cf. TWAT VII 1210-1214 [RUPPERT]; NIDOTTE 8820 [LONG]). Both are usually used of Israel's human enemies, in this case via the metaphor they are used of the idealised 'lofty city', i.e. the proud. Recent discussion has called the root שחח into question, suggesting that it may rather be a *hishtaphel* of the root חוה, meaning 'to prostrate oneself' (reflexive of the ancient causative *shaphel*; cf. Ugaritic *hwy*). Other suggestions as to the etymology of the term include Arabic *hawā*: 'sich zusammenrollen'; Egyptian *hwj*: 'schlagen'. Efforts to find the etymological roots in the verb *hwy/hyw:* 'to live' seem inappropriate in the present semantic context. The root primarily signifies the action of bowing down in worship with one's face to the ground. Perhaps there is some suggestion of false worship in the present context since the usual response to such prostration is not so negative as we find it here (cf. J-M §79t; NIDOTTE 2556 [FRETHEIM]; TDOT IV 248-256 [PREUSS]; J. TROPPER, *Die hebraischen Verbalwurzeln šhh, šhh, šhh*, in *ZAH* 4 [1991], 46-54). When applied to persons, the *niphal* participle of שגב suggests 'pride/haughtiness' (cf. Isa 2,11.12). When applied to the 'town' which is identified with its inhabitants as the *métaphorisé*, physical loftiness and its connotations of security takes on the significance of human haughtiness and pride.

feet of the humble and the poor, further categories (together with the righteous [v. 2b], faithful [v. 2c], constant [v. 3a]) of those who deserve YHWH's protection and for whom the gate to the strong city lies open.

Clearly the *métaphorisant* 'rock' and its extension 'strong city' are of the insight type in that they reveal something of the (divine) reality they metaphorise. YHWH is not only solid and permanent, as an idealised city he is a secure refuge and a place of שלום.

Type

The core of the central metaphorical affirmation 'YHWH is a rock' is clearly a simple core, explicit only in the *métaphorisant*. At the same time, however, there is clearly a secondary core at work, similar to the primary core, in which the *métaphorisant* is the 'city strong' (YHWH remains *métaphorisé*), constituting a follow-up or extension of the primary metaphor. It is evident from the multiplicity of occurrences of the expression – especially in the psalms[16] – that the metaphor 'YHWH is a rock' would have been quite familiar to its audience yet it could hardly be described as an extinct (dead) or even dormant (retired) metaphor. As emphatic, resonant and active, the metaphor (together with its secondary core) invites its audience to explore the richness of 'interpretative implications' it makes possible. In Black's terms such a metaphor would be considered 'strong' and a source of genuine interaction.

The entire metaphorical statement here must be understood as 'structural' in that the *métaphorisant* helps structure the way we understand the *métaphorisé*. In Thomistic terms, the metaphorical statement is of the 'Leo' type (A is B) yet, along with Thomas, it is clear that where the divinity is concerned, such metaphors/analogies only reveal a part of the picture since they also contain a degree of negative analogy (i.e. YHWH is not 'hard' or 'dumb' as a rock). Ultimately, the *métaphorisant* only structures a part of the *métaphorisé* and as such the metaphorical statement only intends to say something relative (and not absolute or negative) about the divinity. The *métaphorisé* is clearly a mysterious reality while the *métaphorisant* constitutes something very physical and well known, thus making the metaphorical speech act one-way. We noted in our chapter on metaphorical theory that Macky used a similar metaphor

---

16. Cf. Ps 18,3.47; 19,15; 28,1; 31,3; 62,3.7.8; 71,3; 73,26; 75,6; 78,35; 89,27; 92,16; 94,22. 95,1; 144,1; cf. also Dt 32,4.15.18; 2 Sam 23,3; Isa 17,10; 30,29. A 'standard' metaphor in Macky's terms. Note also the evident word-play between YHWH as צור in v. 4b and the יצר of v. 3a (cf. also Isa 44,8-9), suggesting further levels of metaphorical expression with respect to the relationship between YHWH and his people.

from Ps 18,2 ("The Lord is my rock, my fortress...") to show that the primary intention of the author was to allow his audience to gain insight into the relationship between the human and the divine realm by way of well-known physical 'symbols' (*métaphorisant*). This is evidently the primary speech type being employed here.

While aspects of presentative speech are evident, the audience being invited to 'trust' in 'the rock/city', the primary invitation is for the audience to explore its relationship with the divinity via the *métaphorisants* of 'rock' and 'city strong' and come to understand that YHWH wishes to relate to his people in this way (and to the proud and haughty in converse fashion).

Author's Purpose / Interpretation

YHWH mediates salvation through security in Zion. He is the city restored (everlasting) which stands open for those who remained faithful, those who waited, those who did not turn to self-reliance. As with the majority of metaphorical statements in these chapters, the author is endeavouring to say something about the quality of the relationship between YHWH and his people. The metaphorical statement extends, therefore, beyond the simple affirmation of YHWH as a rock everlasting. YHWH himself is a strong city with secure walls, a place for the upright, a source of peace. In Isa 2,10.19.21, the audience is invited to 'enter into the rock' (בוא בצור) as a means of security from the 'terror of the Lord'[17]. Thus what was a familiar metaphor speaking of YHWH's permanence and solidity/reliability is given a further twist in that it speaks also of YHWH as a secure place of hiding for the humble. Similarly in Isa 2,11ff., those who are 'haughtiness / pride / high / proud / lifted up / fortified wall' (חומה בצורה, נשא, גאה, רום, גבהות) will be 'humbled / brought low' (שפל)[18]. In the present text, the self-reliant are a contrasting kind of city, a town of loftiness and pride which will ultimately face humiliation. Thus the contrasting cities/towns and the equally contrasting fate they both endure, express the opposite sides of the coin in human/ divine relationships: patient waiting brings security, pride brings humiliation. Two cities, one 'proud' one 'faithful' represent two attitudes to YHWH and YHWH reacts to each with blessing or ruin. The same contrast between the 'righteous' and the wicked is taken up in the following

---

17. This perhaps sheds some light on Isa 26,20ff..
18. Terminological repetition between Isa 2,10ff. and Isa 26, 1-6 is clearly extensive enough to be significant. It is also worth noting that where YHWH alone will be exalted (נשגב יהוה לבדו) 'on that day' in Isa 2,11, it is the town of loftiness (קריה נשגבה) which will be humbled 'on that day' in Isa 26,5.

verses from a variety of different perspectives. Our analysis of these verses as we now have them gives no reason to suggest that two actual towns are being spoken of here, no matter what the historical perspective of the text. The metaphorical statement takes what may have had historical associations and puts them to a new use at a new literary level. While the 'town of loftiness' may be Moab and the 'city strong' Jerusalem / Zion, they now function in the metaphorical statement as contrasting positions with respect to YHWH. While clearly using the metaphor to express relationship with YHWH, the intention of the author would also seem to be transformative, an exhortation to his audience to change their attitudes and avoid self-reliance. This same theme is taken up later by the audience itself in a more 'confessional' way in the birthing metaphor of 26,16-19, in an admission that personal efforts at achieving victory and continued existence are useless (wind) without YHWH. Thus, it appears possible once again to gain access to the speaker's meaning via the clues he has left in the text in the form of a metaphorical statement concerning the relationship between YHWH and his people.

Isa 26,7-10

7a The way for the righteous is level,
b   level[19] the path of the righteous, you smooth.

8a Surely, [in] the way of your judgements, O YHWH, we await you[20].

---

19. As Barthélemy notes (*Critique Textuelle*, pp. 180-181), many translations endeavour to eliminate the repetitions in this text, often forcing an emendation of the syntax indicated by the MT accents. BHS recommends that we drop the term ישר from v.7b. An example of the difficulties surrounding the term is provided by 4Qc, which has a space (5 letters) after the first four letters of the first word (מישרים) with a suspended ו between the ש and the ר perhaps indicating that it understood the term to be מישור. LXX appears to have approached the repetitions systematically and lacks each of them. The Vulgate, Syriac and 1Qa support the MT. Based on the versional support, Barthélemy and his committee prefer to maintain the repetition as it is. It is also evidently a stylistic feature of the piece (cf. also WILDBERGER, *Jesaja 13–27*, p. 982). The term has been interpreted as a vocative (e.g. NRSV) and as an adjective qualifying ארח (WILDBERGER, *Jesaja 13–27*, p. 982). The latter appears to be a better reflection of the internal parallelism of v.7 (cf. WATTS, *Isaiah 1–33*, p. 338).

20. 1QIsa^a, LXX, Syriac and Targum do not have the 2ms suffix and interpret the syntax differently, taking the expression 'your name' with the verb קוינו. This unnecessarily ignores both the text and the accentuation of the MT which Barthélemy thinks has been misunderstood (*Critique Textuelle*, p. 193). The Vulgate makes perfect sense of the syntax of the MT: *in semita iudiciorum tuorum Domine sustinuimus te* (cf. WILDBERGER, *Jesaja 13–27*, p. 983; VAN DER KOOIJ, *Isaiah 24–27: Text Critical Notes*, pp. 14-15).

b   Your name and your memory are the hunger of the soul.

9a As I live I hunger for you in the night.
b   Surely, [holding] my breath within me[21], I search for you.

c   Indeed, when your judgements[22] are in the land,
d   righteousness they learn, those who dwell in world.

10a [However] if the wicked is shown favour, he does not learn righteousness. ∞
b   In a land of uprightness he acts perversely.
c   He does not perceive the splendour of YHWH.

Delimitation of Metaphorical Statement

Along with most commentators[23] we can agree that from a form-critical perspective, vv. 7-19 constitute a Song of Lament, however 'broken apart'[24] it might appear. Further sub-divisions within the lament genre constitute discreet metaphorical statements, the first of which we can establish as vv. 7-10, verses Johnson describes as a 'general statement of belief'[25]. The evident change to more 'abstract' actants – the righteous

---

21. Wildberger and others follow Guthe here in reading the variant בבקר instead of בקרבי (*Jesaja 13–27*, p. 983). While this does make some sense of the parallelism, it seems possible to make equal if not better sense of the MT as it is. I understand the phrase as an expression of excited anticipation 'holding one's breath' (cf. WATTS: 'my spirit within me', *Isaiah 1–33*, p. 336). While apparently opting for a reading with both בבקר and בקרבי, Sweeney (*Isaiah 1–39*, p. 214) offers a more religious interpretation of בקרבי as expressing the 'inwardness of true religion'. I prefer a more literal interpretation.

22. LXX has διότι φῶς τὰ προστάγματά σου ἐπὶ τῆς γῆς ('because your commandments are light upon the earth') and appears to have read כ[אר] instead of כאשר. Wildberger notes that some have insisted that כאשר needs to be followed by a verb which encourages him to conjecture a missing בוא (WILDBERGER, *Jesaja 13–27*, p. 983). The expression כאשר 'as soon as' does not appear to be out of place, however, since it continues the intention of the emphatic כ, suggesting that the righteous need no time to interpret YHWH's judgements and learn from them (cf. BARTHÉLEMY, 'dès que...', *Critique Textuelle*, p. 167).

23. Cf., among others, WILDBERGER, *Jesaja 13–27*, p. 987ff.; JOHNSON, *Chaos to Restoration*, p. 70ff.; SWEENEY, *Isaiah 1–39*, p. 337ff.; Johnson notes that Rudolph (*Jes. 24–27*, pp. 6-8, 42ff.) and Lindblom (*Die Jesaja Apokalypse*, p. 40ff.) are the main two 'older' scholars who disagree with this opinion. His refutation of their arguments is nevertheless convincing.

24. 'stark "*zersetztes*" Klagelied', cf. WILDBERGER, *Jesaja 13–27*, p. 987

25. Johnson regards Wildberger's division of the lament (*Jesaja 13–27*, p. 987) as useful but follows a slightly different arrangement which we largely adopt here: vv.7-10: A general statement of belief; vv.11-15: A plea regarding the specific situation; vv.16-18: The lament proper; v.19: das *Heilsorakel* (*Chaos to Restoration*, pp. 72, 79).

versus the wicked (referred to in singular terms) – introduces and governs the unit up to and including v. 10. V. 11 introduces a more specific situation and specific set of actants – adversaries/them *versus* your people/us (referred to in the plural). Certain stylistic features – mainly chiastic parallelism[26] – also provide cohesion and further support for this initial division[27]:

vv. 9-10

יעול .... כאשר
;ארח משפטיך // מעגל צדיק // מישרים ... ארח :vv. 7-8a
נכחות .... משפטיך
בארץ..לארץ
צדק..צדק
בל־ילמד........................למדו
רשע .... ישבי תבל
יחן

Indicators

Due to the absence of any formal indicators of metaphor, we are obliged to focus our attention on informal elements in our search for the use of metaphor in the present text. It is primarily within the stylistic features of this unit that we can discern the presence of a metaphorical statement, based on two related metaphors[28]. The first metaphor is indicated by the repeated emphatic particle אף followed by two terms/expressions from distinct isotopes which are nonetheless related by consonant parallel word-play, ארח משפטיך (the *métaphorisant*) and רוחי // נפשי (the *métaphorisé*). The term ארח has both a literal (path, way) and figurative significance (way one should go, behaviour)[29]. The 2nd person suffix of משפטיך together with the vocative יהוה which follows it place the term in a theological context where the full expression constitutes a metaphor in itself – albeit a lexicalised metaphor –, signifying a person's life lived "as a movement from a point of beginning to

---

26. As we can see, frequent examples of repetition also characterise this and other passages in the chapter.
27. Cf. LEWIS, *Rhetorical-Critical Analysis*, pp. 129-130 (following W.H. IRWIN, *Syntax and Style in Isaiah 26*, in *CBQ* 41 (1979) 240-61, esp. p. 245). Cf. also WILDBERGER, *Jesaja 13–27*, p. 986.
28. The metaphors are also related to each other via word-play. After a series of bicola, the third colon of the tricolon in v.10 constitutes a degree of emphasis which parallels yet replaces the use of אף elsewhere in the passage. Emphasis is now placed on three consonant terms ארח, רוח and ראה.
29. NIDOTTE 782 (MERRILL)

a goal"[30]. The cognate root meanings of the terms נפשי 'my breath/my life'[31] and רוחי 'my breath'[32] place them in the same isotope: life sustaining respiration. Thus our *métaphorisé* could be categorised – at least in its primary sense – as a corporeal reality 'breath/life' while the *métaphorisant*, in context with משפטיך and יהוה is a non-corporeal reality 'the way of YHWH's judgements'.

Clearly we are dealing with dependent/figurative speech here in that our understanding of the relationship between the *métaphorisant* and the *métaphorisé* depends on our knowledge of the multiple meanings applicable to the terminology concerned. We would also appear to be in the presence of a profound metaphor in that it would seem impossible to reduce the statement 'the way of your judgements is my breath' to literal speech. As we shall see below, the metaphorical association of 'my breath' and 'God's way' suggests a degree of internalisation (בקרבי 'within me' v. 9b) which is set in contrast to the attitude of the wicked. Associated positive affirmations of 'waiting', 'searching', 'hungering' and 'learning' on the part of the righteous further support the metaphor, adding to the sense of interiorisation of 'the way'.

The second metaphor focuses on the intentionally centralised term חנן 'favour' which constitutes the *métaphorisant* to the *métaphorisé* which is גאות יהוה 'the splendour of YHWH' which takes an emphatic position at the end of the segment. Thus both here and in the first metaphor of the segment, stylistic features are the primary indicators of the presence of metaphor. The isotopes are clearly distinct: יחן is a *hophal* form of חנן which primarily means 'to show favour to someone' and is used for generous, unnecessary kindness between human beings. When used with respect to divine-human relationships the one-sided generosity of God tends to be emphasised, "God's grace is finally rooted, not in what people do, but in his disposition to be gracious in ways beyond any human formula or calculation..."[33]. This aspect of the super-generosity of God appears to constitute the heart of the *métaphorisant*. The term גאות is derived from the root גאה which means 'to rise up/be exalted'. In its nominal form the term has to do with 'majesty and pride'[34] and when

---

30. *Ibid.*
31. NIDOTTE 5883 (FREDERICKS) which also insists that we be wary of applying a 'Greek paradigm of psychology' to the term.
32. NIDOTTE 8120 (VAN PELT/KAISER/BLOCK); Gen 6,17; Job 12,10; Isa 38,16; 42,5; Ezek 37,5-14; Mal 2,15-16.
33. NIDOTTE 2858 (FRETHEIM); cf. also HALOT 334-335.
34. It is interesting to note that the notion of YHWH's 'pride' is in contrast to the previous metaphors which focus on YHWH's humiliation of the haughty pride of the 'fortified city'.

used of YHWH it signifies his "gracious acts of salvation, deliverance and preservation."[35] If we follow Lord, therefore, in understanding גאות יהוה as hypocatastasis for the manifestation of YHWH's power in the enactment of his judgements[36] and ultimately as signifying YHWH himself then we arrive at the heart of the *métaphorisé*: the divinity himself. We can therefore reduce the metaphor to an 'A is B statement': 'YHWH is favour/grace', the former being incorporeal reality made concrete in its metaphorical association with the latter reality of human generosity.

Once again dependant speech is at work here in that we can only understand YHWH as generous in the context of our knowledge of human kindness and generosity. The metaphor is profound, therefore, in that it cannot be reduced to literal speech. Indeed we shall see below that the metaphor functions in two directions: 'favour' informing us (however partially) about 'God' and 'God' informing the notion of 'favour' with divine qualities. In contrast to the first metaphor, associated negative affirmations are unequivocal: the wicked 'do not learn' and 'do not perceive' (ראה). Neither YHWH's judgement nor YHWH's favour is sufficient to penetrate their lack of perception/blindness. Thus while the first metaphor centres on the internalisation of 'the way/the judgements of YHWH' (cf. v. 8a), the second emphasises the wicked's inability to internalise the 'favour/ splendour of YHWH' (v. 9cd, v. 10). Note also the consonance between the terms ארח, רוחי and ראה (בל-) which further serves to delimit and unite the two metaphors into one metaphorical statement.

A degree of hyperbolic exaggeration and indeed irony also appear to be at work here, revealing that the author(s) was (were) not confining themselves to metaphor as the only horizontal speech type.

Type

As far as the first metaphor is concerned – 'the way of your (YHWH's) judgements is my breath/soul – we appear to be dealing with a core or foyer set up by the word-play between ארח and רוח. Our examination of the multiple significance of both terms, both literal and figurative, suggests, however, that there is an evident degree of semantic cross-reference

---

35. NIDOTTE 1448 (SMITH/HAMILTON).
36. LORD, *Chapters XXV and XXVI*, p. 488. Hypocatastasis constitutes a declaration of implied comparison or resemblance in which one of the two elements is missing but clearly implied. Bullinger sees this as more acute than a metaphor in which he maintains 'both nouns' are named (not everyone would agree). He gives the following example by way of explanation: 'you are like a beast' (simile); 'you are a beast' (metaphor); 'Beast!' (hypcatastasis). Cf. BULLINGER, *Figures of Speech*, pp. 744-747.

between them, perhaps rooted in the understanding of life as an active journey and life as physical existence sustained by breath. The metaphor as such is clearly active in that it would be recognised as a metaphor by its audience and both emphatic and resonant (and thus 'strong' according to Black) in that it is evidently interactive and at the same time open to a variety of interpretative possibilities. One might also suggest that a 'titular' type of metaphor (and thus perhaps a hidden metaphorical concept) lies behind these words – 'YHWH is my life' – which fits well with the contrasting second metaphor of the passage and subsequent metaphors in the chapter which deal with new life and the dead. As such, the metaphor intends us to structure (Lakoff and Johnson's 'structural metaphor') our understanding of YHWH's judgements, however terrible they may be with respect to Israel, in terms of life and breath, as something to be longed for and sought after instead of feared, as a level path for the righteous instead of an indicator of ignorance and lack of perception on the part of the wicked.

While one can reduce the metaphor to 'YHWH is life' the primary dimension of the *métaphorisant* is not YHWH himself but 'the way of his judgements' (in contrast to 'his favour' in the second metaphor) and as such both the *métaphorisé* and the *métaphorisant* have a physical dimension and a non-physical dimension established in the lexicalised metaphor implied by the term ארח and the multivalent significance of the term רוח. The metaphor itself, however, would appear to function only in one direction, the *métaphorisant* structuring our understanding of the *métaphorisé*. While the reduced form of the metaphor may suggest the presence of a hidden metaphorical concept, the statement 'the way of your judgements is my life' suggests a degree of novelty based on the limited extent of positive analogy between the *métaphorisé* and the *métaphorisant*. At the same time, while there is clearly an expressive level in these words intended to reveal something of the speaker's feelings and emotions together with an evaluative/pedagogical level intended to view YHWH's judgements in a new and positive light and pass on that new understanding to others, the primary speech type involved here would appear, once again, to be relational. This dimension is underlined by the second metaphor which establishes contrast between what is possible in one's relationship with God and what is not.

The dimension of cross-reference at the core of the second metaphor – YHWH is super-generous – would appear to be absent (absent core) and dependant therefore on the core of the preceding metaphor (word-play core). Indeed, there is clearly a degree of phonological consonance[37] between the terms of the *métaphorisé* (יהוה) and the *métaphorisant* (יחן). As such the metaphor must be viewed as resonant-active, functioning in genuine interaction and providing a rich field of interpretation for its audience, inviting them to structure (structural metaphor) their understanding of YHWH according to the full and resonant content of the *métaphorisant*. As with most figurative references to the divine, the present metaphor is 'culture-exceeding' in that it can function outside of Israel's life world and inform readers of every generation about this dimension of the divinity. Clearly the *métaphorisé* is the divinity.

Since the more theological 'super-generosity' implied in the *métaphorisant* יחן is derived from our understanding of human kindness and grace, Thomas would probably describe such allegorical speech about God as conforming to the 'Leo' type – the A is B structure – and thus, for him, in need of further 'unpacking' by way of further metaphors. The metaphorical statement implied in the present verses (vv. 7-10) and throughout the textual complex Isa 24–27 clearly engages further metaphors in its endeavour to communicate and describe God and his relationship with both humanity and planet. At the same time, of the three concepts which Thomas proposes can be applied to God in allegorical speech, the present metaphor falls between the *relative* category in that the expression 'YHWH is favour/grace' says something about the relationship between YHWH and the enemy/his people and the *absolute* category since the expression is not far from the absolute statement 'God is good'.

One can also affirm that such a metaphor works in two directions, the notion of 'favour' not only informing and helping to structure our understanding of the divinity but the grandeur of God in theological contexts also informing and structuring our understanding of favour as 'super-generosity'. According to Macky's metaphorical types, the expression 'YHWH is favour/grace' evokes a reality which is ultimately not observable. To talk of God's grace or favour means to talk on the basis of dependent analogy between divine attributes and human attributes in which the negative dimension is understated. He would therefore categorise such speech as containing a hidden metaphor. In terms of speech type, however, several possibilities are evident and neither need exclude the other. There is a degree of 'presentative' speech present in that the

---

37. Repetition of the same or similar consonants. Cf. BERLIN, *Dynamics*, p. 103. Berlin limits her discussion to phonological parallels (sound-pairs) within parallel lines. We have already noted that this kind or repetition can extend much beyond the line and this would not appear to be excluded by Berlin's limitations.

author intends to communicate information and even educate (pedagogical) with regard to the divinity both in the individual metaphors and in the larger statement running from v. 7 to v. 9. At the same time there is an element of evaluative speech at work in which our positive human evaluation of 'favour' is transferred as it were to God. This also carries with it affective (designed to attract us to God) and even exploratory (evoking a sense of wonder and curiosity in the hearer) dimensions.

Clearly the speech act which these verses (vv. 7-9) encompass exhibits a primarily relational intention: how the wicked relate to YHWH and how the people relate to their God. Combined by the opposing notions of internalisation *versus* lack of learning/perception, both metaphors constitute a single statement with relational significance. While the righteous are able to enter into relationship with God whom they recognise and internalise in his judgements, however terrible, the wicked are unable to enter into relationship with God because they cannot even perceive him in his favours. As a combination of two discrete metaphors – 'the way of your judgements is my breath' and 'YHWH is favour/grace' – the statement invites us to reflect on the divine-human relationship via the categories of judgement and favour.

Author's Purpose / Interpretation

The author continues to contrast the proud and self-reliant with those who wait faithfully, initially expressed in the idealised cities of the first metaphorical statement of the present chapter. It would appear that the author's primary purpose is one of invitation to his audience to explore the relationship between YHWH and his people and YHWH and the wicked. To this end he employs two metaphors which combine into one contrastive metaphorical statement. The first person plural speaker[38] is aware that YHWH's judgements are to be sought after and hungered for as the very breath which sustains life. They are a source of righteousness for those who wait for them and 'internalise' them. While YHWH's people can internalise him in his judgements the wicked cannot even internalise him in his favours. They do not wait or learn when YHWH's favour is 'in the land' but rather they act perversely and demonstrate their inability to perceive his splendour. Together with this invitation to reflect on two possible ways of relating to YHWH, the author also appears

---

38. Note how the change to the singular in v.9 focuses the relational dimension of these verses on personal relationship with YHWH: "There is no such thing as the people of God apart from the individuals composing it; there is no genuine corporate spirituality unless it is true of every member." Cf. MOTYER, *The Prophecy of Isaiah*, p. 215.

to be attempting to both enlighten (pedagogical) his audience and to change their attitude (transformative[39]) towards the disastrous events which they have undergone, to teach them that YHWH is faithful and that they need only wait for and hunger for his name and his memory (his past deeds[40]). As with the majority of the metaphors in these chapters, however, the author's primary purpose in using the present metaphors appears to be to speak of the relationship between YHWH and his people.

Given the immediate context of metaphors of salvation from the preceding verses (and indeed the preceding chapter), access to the speaker's meaning via his use of metaphors seems feasible. These are words which call for a confession of faith and trust in YHWH as opposed to pride and self-reliance. Life is given and sustained by YHWH and 'waiting' for him or indeed following his 'smooth path' brings righteousness. The theme of waiting as opposed to taking the initiative is prevalent in the textual complex of Isa 24–27[41]. The reference to 'night' in v. 9a further underlines the author's intention. In a land fraught with judgement, a land in darkness, those who wait are still able to learn. In a land of favour and uprightness, however, a land in which YHWH's splendour provides a contrast to the darkness of night the wicked can neither see nor learn[42]. In this sense, the author is calling upon his audience to learn from their experience about the correct attitude to have towards YHWH. The wisdom aspects, (the way/path, righteousness, learning/not learning, lack of perception) of these verses are unmistakable: "If one does what is right, blessings are forthcoming (the way is made level, the path smooth). But if one violates the created order by doing what is wrong, then a curse will follow."[43]

---

39. Cf. SWEENEY, *Isaiah 1–39*, p. 340: "The purpose of this subsection is to lay the basis for the petition that follows in vv. 11-19. It proceeds by presenting a progressive series of statements that build confidence in YHWH's righteousness and the experience of the righteous versus those who are wicked."

40. "In the OT, the synonymous terms שׁם, זכר, point to Yahweh's acts of deliverance on behalf of his people." Cf. JOHNSON, *Chaos to Restoration*, p. 73.

41. cf. 25,9-12;

42. Further obviating the need to emend v.9b to read בבקר 'in the morning'. Jer 48,29 is interesting to note here, especially as Moab is singled out for her pridefulness in Isa 25,10f.: 'We have heard of Moab's pride (גאון), her great pride (גאה) and conceit (גבהו), her pride (גאונו) and arrogance (גאותו) and the haughtiness (רום) of her heart.' In other words, the righteous searches for YHWH's גאה and does not rely on his own.

43. *Ibid.*: cf. also KAISER, *Isaiah 13–39*, p. 210; R.E. CLEMENTS, *Isaiah 1–39* (NCBC), Grand Rapids, MI, 1980, p. 213; WILDBERGER, *Jesaja 13–27*, pp. 987-990.

Isa 26,11-15

11a   O YHWH, raised high is your hand [but] they do not take notice.
b   Let them take notice and let them be shamed[44] at [your] jealousy [for your] people.
c   Surely, the fire of your adversaries, let it consume them.

12a   O YHWH, you provide[45] peace[46] for us.
b   Indeed, even all our achievements you have done [them] for us.[47]

13a   O YHWH, our God, they have ruled us, other lords, besides you.
b   [But] only in you have we kept remembrance of your name[48].

44. BHS suggests, without giving any reason, that this first part of v.11b should be deleted. I can find no reason for deleting these words either. In fact the repetition of the verb חזה is in conformity with the style of the entire textual complex (cf. WILDBERGER, *Jesaja 13–27*, p. 983).

45. Wildberger discusses the various interpretations of the root (cf. *Jesaja 13–27*, p. 984) opting for 'to lay down, give' in line with LXX, θ, V. We translate 'to provide' as a means of illustrating the alliteration with 'peace' (שלום/שפת).

46. BHS suggests שִׁלּוּם ('vengeance') instead of שָׁלוֹם and כִּגְמֻל ('as recompense') instead of גַם כָּל. Wildberger notes in this regard that the Syriac basis does not provide sufficient support for these emendations (*Jesaja 13–27*, pp. 983-984). In support of the MT, Johnson (73) refers to H.H. Schmid who has pointed out that violated order (from the preceding verses) must be restored and that this necessary corrective action is now mentioned in v. 12 via the provision of שלום (cf. H.H. SCHMID, *Schöpfung, Gerechtigkeit und Heil, 'Schöpfungstheologie' als Gesamthorizont biblischer Theologie*, in *ZTK* 70 [1973] 1-19).

47. Johnson argues for a different translation: 'Since you have requited all our misdeeds', citing textual support from the Targum, internal literary support from Wildberger (word-play: בעלונו // פעלת לנו) structural support: ABA'B' connecting v.12 with v.16 and contextual support: lament form reflecting a situation of distress brought on by YHWH's chastisement (cf. JOHNSON, *Chaos to Restoration*, p. 76). In the context, however, the idea of YHWH providing and achieving on Israel's behalf becomes central to the contrast between what Israel was able to achieve alone (nothing) and what YHWH has done for her (everything). This is ultimately concretised in the image of birthing and population increase which is taken up more explicitly in the following metaphor (vv.16-19). This seems a more logical path to follow, an intentional turn in Isaiah's labyrinth of metaphors. Indeed, the word-play between פעלת לנו with YHWH as addressee and בעלונו, the lording of other lords (whether deities or humans and their deities) seems to support this contrast more than suggest that YHWH's actions here are 'of a corrective nature'.

48. LXX reads v.13 as follows: κύριε θεὸς ἡμῶν, κτῆσαι ἡμας· κύριε ἐκτὸς σοῦ ἄλλον οὐκ οἴδαμεν, τὸ ὄνομά σου ὀνομάζομεν (Lord, our God, you acquired us. Lord, we have not known others apart from you; we have named your name). The Greek word κτῆσαι might be interpreted as an imperative (aorist middle) of the verb κτάομαι which in some instances in the LXX refers to 'acquiring as a husband acquires a wife'. It is possible that LXX understood the text in this relational, husband/wife way (cf. LEH II, 269). Wildberger (*Jesaja 13–27*, p. 984), however, points out that Hebrew reconstructions of this LXX text do not make it any clearer. While he agrees that there may be some error present he is not convinced of any of the proposed emendations. It is my belief that attention to the chiastic structure of vv.13 and 14 makes perfect sense of the text as it stands.

14a   The dead do not live!
  b   The shades do not rise,

  c   indeed[49] you have punished and have wasted them,
  d   you have wiped out[50] all remembrance of them.

15a   You have increased the nation, O YHWH.
  b   You have increased[51] the nation, you are glorified.
  c   You have enlarged all the boundaries of land.

Delimitation of Metaphorical Statement

From the perspective of syntax, a series of vocatives in first position (excluding v. 15a) followed by verbal clauses (predominantly *qatals* and *wayyiqtols*) marks off the unit which opens and closes with a tricolon (v. 11 and v. 15). As we note in our syntactical analysis, the unit is also marked off by a preponderance of 2ms addressation, placing the addressee YHWH in the foreground. The interplay of we/you and they/you suffixes and addressation suggests once again that we are dealing with relational language intended to highlight the contrast between what YHWH has done and will do for his people and what he has done and will do to the enemy. This perspective is also true of the verses which follow (16-19) but here the semantic focus changes and the contrast is no longer

---

Note also the parallel with Hos 13,4 which, for J. Day, argues in favour of the LXX. His primary point, however, is to suggest that the parallel with Hos 13,4 would lead us to interpret the present expression 'other lords' as a reference to 'other gods', the gods of the nations. I am inclined to follow Day here, especially in his counter argument to those who raise v. 14 (death, shades etc.) in support of a human interpretation of 'lords'. The idea of being ruled by other gods (who can be and are destroyed by YHWH: Isa 24,21–22; Ps 82,6-7) fits well with the other metaphorical statements in the textual complex, especially those which refer to YHWH as husband and the metaphors which follow which refer to the inability to give birth. The metaphor of Israel's idolatry as expressed in the form of adultery is well attested. In context with the surrounding metaphors, therefore, the expressions 'the dead do not live! The shades do not rise' (v.14ab) should be understood as a reference to 'unsuccessful pregnancies', futile liaisons with other 'husbands' who could not 'increase the nation' but created 'only wind'. Only the offspring of YHWH/Israel 'rise' and 'live' (v.19). Cf. J. DAY, *The Dependence of Isaiah 26,13–27,11 on Hosea 13,4–14,10 and its Relevance to Some Theories of the Redaction of the "Isaiah Apocalypse"*, in C.C. BROYLES and C.A. EVANS (eds.), *Writing and Reading the Scroll of Isaiah. Studies of an Interpretive Tradition*, Leiden, 1997, pp. 357-368.

49. Asseverative לכן following WILDBERGER, *Jesaja 13–27*, p. 984, and HALOT 530.
50. 1QIsa[a] has ותאסר but the MT is supported by LXX, Tg and Syr. Wildberger (*Jesaja 13–27*, p. 984) notes further that אבד occurs with זכר in Ps 9,7 and with שם in Ps 41,6.
51. Repetition is clearly part of the style of the text and need not necessitate emendation or deletion.

between the enemy and the people but the people past and present. Exegetes commonly include v. 11 with v. 10 and preceding verses[52] but Sweeney appears to be correct in placing it at the opening of the present unit. From a form-critical perspective, he suggests that we take vv. 7-10 to be the preparation for a petition which follows in vv. 11ff.. Sweeney extends the petition to v. 19 but this is largely based on his understanding of v. 16 which he translates: "O YHWH, as an enemy they have visited you, pour out the spell of your chastisement on them!"[53], clearly the language of petition.

Our interpretation of this verse views it as a reference to the people and not the enemy, a reference followed by a confession of their inability to achieve their own salvation via the metaphor of 'birthing'[54]. Johnson's argumentation in support of delimiting vv. 11-15 as a *Plea Regarding a Specific Situation*[55] is quite convincing. In v. 11 he notes that the author makes a transition from the general to the particular, from the wicked in general to the enemies of YHWH in particular. V. 15 concludes the unit with a statement of restoration, reversing 24,6d 'a mere few remain' and 24,11c 'It is banished, the gaiety of הארץ'. As with v. 11, v. 15 indicates a move from the righteous in general (us/we) to a specific group (the nation) who receive YHWH's favour. V. 16 turns from the specific enemy to focus on Israel's own self-reliant pride which introduces the lament proper (vv. 16-18).

Indicators

In contrast to Isa 25,10a where YHWH's hand was understood as a metaphor for the restoration of widowhood and the 'rest' which accompanies such restoration, the first metaphor in the present statement implies a different perspective on the hand of YHWH[56]. The absence of formal indications of metaphor (short shock) forces us to

---

52. WILDBERGER, *Jesaja 13–27*, pp. 987-988, WATTS, *Isaiah 1–33*, p. 340; MOTYER, *The Prophecy of Isaiah*, p. 216, among others.
53. SWEENEY, *Isaiah 1–39*, p. 340.
54. Clearly much depends on one's translation of the expression בצר. Most commentators and translations tend to understand it as 'in distress' and not 'as an enemy' (cf. WILDBERGER, *Jesaja 13–27*, p. 982; WATTS, *Isaiah 1–33*, p. 337; JOHNSON, *Chaos to Restoration*, 106; NRSV etc.). The term צרר basically conveys the notion of confinement, restriction or binding (cf. NIDOTTE 7674 [BALOIAN]) which seems more appropriate to the language of birthing which dominates the following unit, namely vv.16-19
55. JOHNSON, *Chaos to Restoration*, pp. 75-78.
56. Note the parallel images: YHWH's hand resting on 'this mountain' (25,10a); feet trampling 'proud Moab' (25,10cff.); feet of the poor trampling the lofty (proud) town (26,5-6) and YHWH's hand raised in an act of jealous provision for his people (vv.11-15).

look elsewhere for signs of the presence of metaphor. External parallelism between v. 11 and v. 15 constitutes the expression 'raised high is your (YHWH's) hand' (v. 11a) as the *métaphorisé*. The vocatives, the 2nd person addressation and the actual (11a; 13a,b) or assumed (11d) presence of 2ms suffixes, however, lead us to extend the content of the *métaphorisant* to include YHWH's 'jealousy'/ 'provision of peace' / 'deeds' / 'increase of the nation'. The repetition of יסף 'increase' together with the cognate term רחק 'enlarge' in v. 15 suggests that the focal aspect of YHWH's 'raised hand' is YHWH's 'jealousy for his people' and 'increase of the nation', עם and גוי[57] establishing a synonymous parallel between vv. 11 and 15. This is supported by the colometric structure of the unit, the tricola of vv. 11 and 15 forming the 'bookends' surrounding a portrayal of YHWH's deeds and a confession of guilt (v 13a) spelled out in more detail in the form of four bicola (12ab; 13ab; 14ab; 14cd). The 'raised hand of YHWH' as *métaphorisé* is thus informed by the terminology of the *métaphorisant* which includes קנאת־עם (11b)[58], שפת שלום (12a)[59], פעל לנו (12b)[60], יסף לגוי[61] (15a,b), כבד (15c)[62], רחק (15d)[63].

---

57. Both terms ultimately refer to different aspects of the same thing. עם, for example, frequently stresses blood kinship of a collective while גוי focuses more on the population of a territory seen as a whole. In any event, Israel is גוי in Gen 18,18; Isa 60,22; Ezek 35,10; Ps 106,5. Cf., also, the combination of both terms in Ex 33,13 and Dt 4,6 (HALOT 183).

58. "His [YHWH's] *qin'â* is not directed against the idols, but against the disloyal covenant partner. His *qin'â* is not like that of the deceived husband against his rival, but rather like that of the lord/sovereign who does not tolerate anyone else next to him in the covenant with his subjects, and in that way he claims and maintains the exclusive relationship with his people" (NIDOTTE 939 [PEELS]). Peels reserves the role played by YHWH's *qin'â* in the marriage metaphor to texts in Ezekiel (16,38.42; 23,25) but it seems evident that the term is at home in the isotope of covenant relationship which, as we noted above, has associations with marriage. Several of the metaphorical statements in the textual complex Isa 24–27 would serve to confirm an association here with marital *qin'â*. At the same time YHWH's *qin'â* can be directed against an external threat and constitute a 'punishing fiery wrath against the enemy of Israel'.

59. As Philip Nel notes, the term שלום represents one of the most prominent theological concepts in the OT, one which depends very much on the context for its interpretation. The majority of instances in which YHWH is subject of the verb שלם are related to his retribution or revenge for Israel's sin or the evil deeds of Israel's enemies. As a noun, שלום is used to designate material well-being and bodily health, as well as internal states of satisfaction and fulfilment. According to Nel, it also expresses social or communal relationships between friends, parties and nations. It is used on four occasions with ברית to designate a 'peace covenant' or 'a promissory covenant of God given to his restored people as an eternal blessing and salvation'. שלום in the present text would appear to designate a condition of a renewed relationship with God (cf. NIDOTTE 8966 [NEL]).

60. 17 of the 57 usages of the verb have YHWH as subject, stating a variety of things concerning him and his activities: he has 'prepared' his mountain (Zion) as his own dwelling; he 'brings' deliverance/salvation for his people; he 'bestows' goodness on

The terminology of the *métaphorisant* stems from the isotope of covenant relationship and its further associations with the marital relationship between YHWH and his people and the blessing/increase that relationship involves when Israel is attentive to her husband. L.C. Allen notes that the lifting of a person's hand was a symbolic gesture of power and pride. Analogously, God lifting his hand is to be understood metaphorically as a threatening gesture on the part of the deity, in this case directed towards his enemies[64]. He notes further that such a gesture is frequently depicted thus with respect to ANE deities. As *métaphorisé*, therefore, the 'raised hand of YHWH' clearly stems from the isotope of the divine and constitutes an expression of power with respect to the divinity[65]. The isotope of the *métaphorisant*, however, suggests that the gesture of raising the divine hand indicates more than simply a threat to God's or Israel's enemies and that the content of this expression of power should be understood differently. Thus, as with the 'resting hand of YHWH' in 25,10a, the present reference to YHWH's hand 'raised' has to be interpreted in light of the content of the *métaphorisant*[66]. It would

those who seek refuge in him, thereby fulfilling his covenant promises and blessings (cf. NIDOTTE 7188 [CARPENTER]).

61. The verb יסף primarily means 'to add' and in the *hiphil* 'to increase'. It is also at home in the specific context of covenant, used in specific formulae as a stimulus to obedience to covenant stipulations or as means of calling 'more' covenant curses upon oneself (cf. NIDOTTE 3578 [HILL]). Hill also notes the eschatological overtones of יסף with respect to so-called 'remnant theology', the notion that a Hebrew remnant will flourish in Jerusalem. The 'few' remaining (cf. Isa 24,6) will enjoy increase. Together with the verb רחק, we are being prepared here for the following metaphor of birthing as the concretisation of Israel's increase.

62. Note the parallel between the affirmative use of כבד (YHWH as subject) in v.15b and the negative use of the cognate term גאות in v.10c (construct relationship with YHWH).

63. רחק basically means 'to be distant'. In the *piel* the meaning suggests complete removal and can imply the extension of boundaries as in the present usage. It is used here as a parallel to יסף adding geographical increase to population increase. Once again there are overtones of the blessings of the covenant.

64. NIDOTTE 8123 (ALLEN); for יד יהוה as a metaphor for 'power/might' see the discussion of Isa 25,10a above.

65. Lord sees the gesture as hypocatastasis for analogous acts of inflicting blows of destruction on the enemy (cf. *Chapters XXV and XXVI*, p. 488).

66. According to J. Lust, the alternative expression נשא יד with God as subject can adopt different meanings which mostly appear to refer to an active intervention of God's part rather than the 'swearing of an oath' as some have suggested (cf. J. LUST, *The Raised Hand of the Lord in Deut 32,40 According to* MT, *4QDEUTQ, and* LXX, in *Textus* 18 (1995) 33-45; ID., *For I Lift Up My Hand to Heaven and Swear: Deut 32,40*, in F. GARCÍA MARTÍNEZ et al. (eds.), *Studies in Deuteronomy in Honour of C.J. Labuschagne on the Occasion of his 65th Birthday*, Leiden, 1994, pp. 154-164. The use of רום here instead of נשא is probably intended to contrast with the use of the same root as a reference to the 'high host of heaven/prideful' in 24,21 and as a parallel to the exultation of YHWH's name (cf. 26,13b) in 25,1b.

also seem possible to reduce the metaphorical statement here to the A is B type: YHWH (via the gesture of the 'raised hand') is jealous of, peace provider for, achiever for, 'increaser' of his people. As we shall see below, this might be further reduced to the metaphor 'YHWH is husband of his people'. Clearly, therefore, we are dealing here with dependant speech, a statement concerning the relationship between YHWH and his people which depends on our understanding of human marital relationships.

As with the previous metaphorical statement, the present verses appear to include a metaphor within a metaphor. Vv. 13 and 14ab juxtapose 'the dead'-'the shades' as 'not living'/'not rising' with '(other lords) ruling' via word-play[67] and end-rhyme: בעלונו (v. 13a) // בל־יחיו - בל־קומו (v. 14a,b). Vv. 13 and 14 also contain a literal statement concerning Israel's faithful remembrance of YHWH's name and YHWH's annihilation of the remembrance of 'them' (the other lords who ruled) which surrounds, supports and underlines the metaphor. In this part of the metaphorical statement '(other lords) ruling' constitutes the *métaphorisé* and 'the dead'/'the shades' the *métaphorisant*. If one harks back to the metaphorical statement of 25,7 in which reference was made to YHWH as husband, and one accepts that the reference to 'other lords' here is in fact a reference to 'other gods', then the present metaphor seems to suggest that Israel has engaged in the worship of other gods. This admission is often expressed in the form of the difficult metaphor of adultery[68].

67. Terms with consonants בעל appear to be favourite word-play components of the author: cf. בעל/בלע in 25,7. Echoes of the stories of Ba'al and Anat are present here and elsewhere: cf V.H. MATTHEWS and D.C. BENJAMIN (eds.), *Old Testament Parallels. Laws and Stories from the Ancient Near East*, New York – Mahwah, NJ, 1997, p. 254:

In the seventh year, Mot, the son of El, spoke,
He cried out to Ba'al the almighty:
"Because of you, Ba'al, I have lost face...
Because of you...
"I have been cut up with a sword,
I have been burnt with fire [Isa 26,11c].
I have been ground with a millstone,
I have been winnowed with a sieve.
I have been scattered like seed in the fields,
I have been sown in the sea.
Now give me one of your brothers to eat,
Let us make peace [Isa 26,12a; 27,5bc].
If you do not give me one of your brothers,
I will make the dead devour the living [Isa 26,14]. (*VI*, v, 9-24)

68. Since the verbal root בעל also belongs to the isotope of marriage, the notion of being ruled by other gods can also imply having been married to other gods, or having

Liaisons with other gods, however, were fruitless acts for Israel who, as a widow bereft of her husband YHWH[69], turned to the gods of other nations who themselves turned out to be impotent. Thus the *métaphorisé*, being 'ruled by other gods', is a statement at home in the world/isotope of marital/extra-marital relations[70] while the expression 'the dead do not live! The shades do not rise...' is taken from the isotope of 'life/living'[71] or rather the negation thereof. Extra-marital relations, fruitless relationships and jealous husbands, all provide the background 'speech' upon which this metaphorical statement depends.

Excursus: Individual or Civil Resurrection

The root חיה (v. 14a) for the most part refers to physical life and this appears to be the case here also. Further connotations include the fact that the living (in contrast to the dead) can praise God, an action referred to here in the expression 'keep remembrance of your [YHWH's] name'. Any praise/remembrance of the other gods who once ruled Israel is wiped out by YHWH in his act of jealousy. Brensinger points out, in addition, that the root חיה is used in 'three primary futuristic contexts' in the Latter Prophets: referring to national resurrection (cf. Hos 14,7[8]; Ezek 37,1-14); actual (bodily) resurrection (perhaps Isa 26,14.19; Hos 6,2); eschatological age with lists of the 'living' (e.g. Isa 4,3)[72]. Thus the question as to whether national 'resurrection' as opposed to individual bodily resurrection is being referred to here in 26,14 must be raised here. It is evident that the metaphorical statements running from vv. 11-15 and vv. 16-19 are governed by the image of birthing or the absence thereof. In the context of a textual complex filled with relational metaphors concerning YHWH and his people it seems more reasonable to see the present verses as a reference to national rebirth/resurrection after a time of judgement during which the 'nation' sought unsuccessfully to extend itself with the help of other 'lords' and without YHWH. In this sense, the association between 'personally won victory' and birth/re-inhabitation of the world

---

engaged in sexual relations with other gods which, as the following metaphors suggest, were fruitless engagements. Only YHWH as Israel's true husband can increase the nation. Perhaps the chosen expression 'they ruled us' rather than 'we served them' suggests a degree of reserve on the part of the poets

69. Absence of children/offspring to support her is typical of the image of the widow.

70. "בלע heißt im Alten Testament meist "zur Frau nehmen, heiraten", wobei in Jer 3,14 und 31,32 Übertragung auf Jahwe als Eheherrn Israels vorliegt." (WILDBERGER, *Jesaja 13–27*, p. 991).

71. J.F.A. SAWYER, *Hebrew Words for Resurrection of the Dead*, in *VT* 23 [1973], 218-234.

72. NIDOTTE 2649 (BRENSINGER).

in v. 18 (contrast 24,1b) clearly speaks of national rebirth rather than of resurrection as such. Martens likewise notes that קום in association with חיה signifies some kind of restoration[73]. Together with Brensinger, he points out that J.F.A. Sawyer is of the opinion that these are words for resurrection of the individual from the dead[74]. The analysis of metaphors in this textual complex inclines me to support Clements' position that the metaphor is a reference to the rebirth of the nation (see also 26,19 below)[75]. Redditt may be correct in discerning the deliberate use of personal terminology in these verses. He continues, however, that in spite of this, his belief that the text stands within the context of a communal lament inclines him to opt for national/civil resurrection[76].

Type

The isotopic cross-reference between the *métaphorisé* and the *métaphorisant* of the metaphorical statement in vv. 13-14 is based on word-play, i.e. on the phonological similarity between the isotope of the *métaphorisé* and that of the *métaphorisant*, inviting us to read the marital image of v. 13a 'being ruled by other lords' in light of the negations of life of v. 14ab. Adulterous, extra-marital relations with 'other lords' ultimately leads to the negation of life. It is also possible to speak of an 'absent' core, one which is found elsewhere – in this case in the following metaphor which deals more explicitly with 'phantom pregnancies'. In a certain sense, however, the core of the metaphorical statement found in vv. 11-15 as a whole is diffuse, the cross-reference being spread throughout the terms of the *métaphorisant* in the verses in question. The manifestation of divine power expressed in the gesture of the 'raised hand of YHWH' suggests a deed on YHWH's part, a 'work of his hand'. These works are expressed in the 'provision of peace', the 'achievement of Israel's deeds', the 'increase of the nation' and the 'enlargement of the boundaries'. As we suggested with respect to 25,10a, the image of the 'raised hand of YHWH' is a metaphor in itself (distinct isotopes: human/divine; dependant language: human/divine) which in a sense may be regarded as 'retired' or 'dormant', i.e. no longer readily recognisable as a metaphorical usage. Placed in relationship with the isotope of the *métaphorisant* via the cross-reference 'work/action (of YHWH), it is taken out of retirement and given active/resonant qualities.

---

73. NIDOTTE 7756 (MARTENS).
74. J.F.A. SAWYER, *Hebrew Words*, pasim.
75. CLEMENTS, *Isaiah 1–39*, p. 216.
76. For a full discussion of the topic cf. REDDITT, *Form Critical Analysis*, pp. 283-291.

As we noted above, if it possible to reduce the present metaphorical statement to the A is B type – YHWH is provider/fruitful husband – then it may also be possible to reduce the central metaphor of vv. 13-14 to a similar A is B type assertion, albeit a negative one: 'other lords' are not providers/fruitful husbands. Both metaphors are structural, inviting us to consider YHWH in terms of a jealous provider and 'other lords' in contrast as providers of death/shades. Where YHWH constitutes the *métaphorisé* in vv. 11 and 15, the analogy is clearly of the 'Leo' type, once again coming close to the notion of 'YHWH as husband', and expressing something relative about the divinity rather than absolute or negative. Both metaphors are comparative at base rather than ornamental. As with many metaphors in which the non-physical divinity constitutes the *métaphorisé*, there is an evident dual-direction to the speech act, the concepts of jealousy, provision of peace, population increase being informed by the notion of the divine and vice versa. While both metaphors ought probably to be considered novel, that of vv. 11 and 15 would suggest the use of a 'hidden metaphor', namely 'YHWH is husband'. Once again we are in the presence of relational metaphorical speech, intended to focus on the way YHWH is related to his people as a husband to his wife and the way YHWH's people are related to 'other lords' as an adulteress to her lovers.

Author's Purpose/Interpretation

The combined metaphorical statements of vv. 11-15 suggest that the author(s) used metaphor primarily for pedagogical and relational purposes. In the first place, the text invites its reader to explore his relationships, both with YHWH and with 'other lord'. The contrast inevitably established by such exploration has a pedagogical end: Israel cannot effect its own salvation (restoration/re-population) by turning to others for help. Only YHWH can bring about the necessary 'achievement', the increase of the nation, life instead of death. We noted above that it is possible to locate the core of the second metaphorical statement (vv. 13-14) elsewhere, the dead/shades are not gods but rather the increase of the nation. They are the 'wind' of verse 18b, the absence of life, the lack of increase of the nation when Israel was ruled by other lords/gods who could not 'impregnate' her successfully. This is only possible in the restored relationship with her husband YHWH. Thus, the dead remain dead and the shades remain shades and there is no life in the land unless Israel is at rights in her relationship with YHWH. The 'mere few' remaining in 24,6 will be put into reverse.

Clearly the evidence points to relational language with a pedagogical purpose. In line with the other relational metaphors in the textual complex Isa 24–27, the present verse provides us with a degree of access to the speakers meaning, consistent with our reading of the text so far. In this sense we can reconstruct and attempt to explain the speaker's meaning by interpreting the metaphorical clues he has be gradually setting out. The people (and ארץ) stand in relation to YHWH, a relationship which is necessary for their survival. YHWH is portrayed as a 'husband' who has withdrawn from his 'wife'; his people are left 'widowed', without rest, without peace, without offspring, without wine, without joy, without joy, without increase, without future. Isa 24,5 presented the reason for YHWH's absence and the curse which was diminishing both the people and ארץ: transgression of law, statute, the everlasting covenant. The admission of guilt here in 26,13 suggests that the content of Israel's transgression is related to her endeavours to do (literally) without her husband, to function outside the covenant, to seek the husbanding of other 'lords/gods'[77]. YHWH, however, is a jealous husband, Israel's only true husband, the only husband who can provide, bring forth living offspring. It is *his* offspring who live and rise (26,19).

Isa 26,16-18 (19)

16a O YHWH, in distress they missed you[78].

---

77. Johnson suggests that given the way politics and religion were mixed in the ANE, it would be better to understand v.13 as referring to the rule of other human lords together with their gods (cf. *Chaos to Restoration*, p. 77).

78. Wildberger (*Jesaja 13–27*, p. 993)) suggests emendation to the first person plural here (פְּקַדְנוּךָ) in line with BHS and Lowth (*Isaiah: A New Translation*, p. 270) based on certain Greek MSS, Ethiopic, Arabic and two Hebrew MSS. While there is no doubt that the MT is questionable as it stands, we are inclined to follow the *lectio difficilior* along with, among others, Barthélemy (*Critique Textuelle*, p. 185: 1QIsa^a; V; S; T), Watts (*Isaiah 1-33*, pp. 237-239), Motyer (*The Prophecy of Isaiah*, pp. 217-218); Sweeney (who suggests 'they/we' is a reference back to the distinction between the wicked and the righteous; *Isaiah 1–39*, pp. 340-341). Wildberger also finds the translation 'to seek' of the root פקד somewhat unusual, especially if one is then forced to envisage 'the wicked' seeking YHWH in prayer! I believe a solution can be found in interpreting this difficult verb along with H. Gese (*Vom Sinai zum Zion: alttestamentliche Beiträge zur biblischen Theologie*, Munich, 1974, p. 89, n. 34; KBL) as 'to miss', in the sense of looking for something that one has lost. This certainly fits the context well. Without YHWH, his people are in distress and turn elsewhere for help when his punishment (i.e. his absence) is upon them. There is evidently no need to translate צר as 'enemy' (HALOT, צר II, 1052; cf. SWEENEY, *Isaiah 1–39* p. 340, wrongly claiming support from the RSV).

b   They poured[79] out an incantation[80] [when] your punishment[81] was on [him] them[82].

17a Like a pregnant woman close to birthing,
b   she writhes and cries out in her birth pains,

c   thus were we before you, O YHWH
18a We were pregnant, we writhed.
     [But] like [a pregnant woman][83] we birthed, [only] wind[84].

b   Deliverance we could not win [on] earth,
c   and they would not fall [be born], the dwellers of world.

19a They shall live, your dead.
b   My corpses[85] shall rise.

---

79. LXX, V and Syr have a substantive as opposed to a verb form for this unusual term. Wildberger (*Jesaja 13–27*, p. 984) opts for a verb form, however, noting along with Gesenius and Delitzsch that the term may be understood as a *qal* perfect 3cpl with a paragogic *nun* from the root צוּק II, 'to pour out' (cf. HALOT 1014; NRSV).

80. Wildberger (*Jesaja 13–27*, p. 984) insists that no sense can be made of this sentence without major alteration. Thus he reads the term לחשׁ as מלחץ, 'chastisement' and, having emended the text in two places to read 1st plural he translates: "Yahwe, in der Not suchten wir dich, wir schrien, da deine Züchtigung uns bedrängte" (*Jesaja 13–27*, p. 982). Watts notes that BDB assumes that the preceding verb is to be taken from the root צוּק II but includes a 'magical' dimension, probably in line with the 'magic power'. In combination with לחשׁ as 'incantation', 'conjuring' (NIDOTTE 793 [HORSNELL]; HALOT 527) the sentence seems to me to make perfect sense. At any rate, it would seem that the author intended the idea of prayer, magic, whispering incantation, to be part of the scene here.

81. Since מסור is frequently used as a reference to the exile (Isa 53,5; Jer 7,28; 17,23; 30,14.17; Ezek 5,15; Dt 11,2), this lends support to the identification of 'they/them' as Israel and not the enemy.

82. As with v.16a we maintain the MT (contra WILDBERGER, *Jesaja 13–27*, p. 984 who follows G.R. Driver).

83. Ellipsis, carried by the comparative particle כְּמוֹ; cf. v.17a.

84. Wildberger notes the association between 'wind' and magical incantations in the Akkadian setting Maqlu— VII, 22: "Ihre Hexerei, die ihr gehext habt, möge [zu] Wind [werden]"; VIII, 57; "Ihre Zaubereien seien Wind! Ihre Zaubereien seien Sturmwin[d]!" (*BAfO* 2 [1937] 47, 56) (cf. Wildberger, *Jesaja 13–27*, p. 994). One could almost translate vv.16a-18a as: our incantations/sorceries turned out to be wind! Wildberger does not, however, make any connection between לחשׁ and רוח.

85. Wildberger (*Jesaja 13–27*, p. 985) notes the strangeness of נבלתי 'my corpse' following מתיך 'your dead'. While he maintains that one would expect to find a second singular suffix here, he is able to understand the Syriac *wsldyhwn* – נְבֵלָתָם 'and their corpses' (cf. BHS) nevertheless. In light of the fact that LXX seems to support the deletion of the term March (*Two Prophetic Compositions*, p. 145) adopts the same position as Wildberger and, among others, Liebmann (*Der Text zu Jesaja 24–27*, pp. 285-87) and Lohmann (*Die selbständigen lyrischen Abschnitte in Jes 24–27*, in ZAW 37 [1917-18], 1-58, esp. pp. 53-55). G. Hylmö (*De s.k. profetiska liturgiernas rytm, stil och komposition,*

c   Wake up and shout with joy[86],
d   [you] that abide in the dust.

e   For a dew of lights is your dew[87]
f   and the earth shall birth shades.∞

Delimitation of Metaphorical Statement

The preceding metaphorical statement consisted of an inclusive metaphor referring to God's jealous protection of and expansion of the nation surrounding a metaphor referring to futile liaisons with other gods which produced no fruit, no offspring. The present metaphorical statement takes up and further develops the aspect of birthing. The birthing metaphor in fact governs this and the previous statement, guiding in particular our understanding of expressions in the text which refer to 'death' and 'rising'. Sweeney notes that vv. 16-19 constitute the final and climactic subsection of the petition contained in vv. 11-19[88]. The second

[Lunds Universitets Arsskrift N.F. Avd. 1. Bd. 25. Nr. 5], Lund, 1929, pp. 57-58) reads the term as a plural (we understand singular for collective) and Procksch changes the suffix to a 2ms. I am inclined to agree with Watts (*Isaiah 1-33*, p. 339) here who proposes YHWH as speaker and understands the expression as YHWH's claim to all the righteous. Johnson (*Chaos to Restoration*, p. 80) agrees! The different suffixes (2nd person followed by 1st) simply state that 'the dead' belong both to Israel and to YHWH. They stand in contrast to 'the dead' of v.14. Here YHWH continues the promise of 25,7-8 and the author continues the metaphor: Israel's husband will be restored to her and she will have offspring. Sweeney (*Isaiah 1-39*, p. 341) agrees that figurative language is employed here (implying the absence of a reference to resurrection as we would understand it) but does not elaborate on the significance thereof. Cf. also BARTHÉLEMY (*lectio difficilior*), *Critique textuelle*, p.187.

86. Wildberger (*Jesaja 13-27*, pp. 985-986) finds the first imperative הקיצו 'surprising' and the second רננו 'impossible'. There is substantial textual support for a *wayyiqtol* (Syr) or a *yiqtol* (1QIsaa; LXX) in the first instance and a *wayyiqtol* (1QIsaa) or a *yiqtol* (Aquila) in the second. Both he and Redditt (145) among others support emendation to an imperfect reading. I find the imperatives neither 'surprising' nor 'impossible', however, and retain them along with Lewis (Rhetorical-Critical Analysis, p. 136), Watts (*Isaiah 1-33*, p. 342), Motyer (*The Prophecy of Isaiah*, p. 219) and Sweeney (2ms address forms: *Isaiah 1-39*, p. 341); Cf. also BARTHÉLEMY (*lectio difficilior*), *Critique Textuelle*, p.188.

87. Motyer (*The Prophecy of Isaiah*, p. 219) notes that the term טל 'dew' has a broad metaphorical significance and usage. The term literally means dew or light rain. It is particularly copious during the spring and early summer and plays a significant role in agriculture. Note also that Prov 3,20 contrasts טל as celestial waters from above the firmament with תהום as waters from the deep (cf. also Dt 33,13). According to Futato (NIDOTTE 353), such rainfall was part of the original creation. Likewise, the withholding of טל brings about complete agricultural failure in Hag 1,10. The absence of טל signifies the most severe drought of divine displeasure, the opposite being the epitome of divine blessing on the land. Ps 133,3 speaks of טל settling on the mountains as the abundance of YHWH's blessings on his people living in unity.

88. SWEENEY, *Isaiah 1-39*, pp. 340-341. Cf. also REDDITT, *Form Critical Analysis*, p. 129: complaint/request.

person address and the common plurals of the preceding units are continued here and further identify the unit. He rightly points out that the metaphor of the pregnant woman unable to give birth is a description of the situation of the people and that the author uses figurative language in v. 19 also (the dead rising, the dew of lights: Sweeney) to relate YHWH's reversal thereof[89]. Motyer correctly notes the contrast between the vv. 12-15 and vv. 16-18(19): what YHWH has achieved and what his people have achieved. In contrast to Sweeney, however, he pictures the 'they' of v. 16 and the 'we' of v. 17 as the same group (i.e. Israel) and does not identify 'them' with the enemy.

Wildberger opts for emendation of the text here to bring v. 16 into line with the first person references throughout the remainder of the unit[90]. While this requires minimal textual emendation, it does not appear to be a requirement of sense. One can interpret v. 16 unemended in at least two ways: as a reflection on Israel's past during a moment of penitence[91] or as a reference to what Israel did in the absence of her 'husband', i.e. she poured out an incantation (a whispered charm), she turned to other gods[92]. This latter is in line with the reference in the preceding section to the 'other lords' who ''ruled Israel in YHWH's absence. In this case, which we support here, the use of the third person may imply a degree of psychological distance from the act. Indeed the number of variations found among the translations and the versions suggests a degree of discomfort with the idea of Israel offering incantation to other gods. YHWH's punishment implied barrenness for the people and the land. They missed his presence as husband and turned to other 'lords/gods' for help but to no avail.

The change from the people's appeal to YHWH to YHWH's command to his people to 'enter their chambers' further demarcates the unit, supporting a division between vv. 19 and 20.

---

89. Cf. also Johnson, who relates the birthing metaphor to Isa 49,21; 54,1 and 66,7.8 and applies it to the return of the exiles.

90. WILDBERGER, *Jesaja 13–27*, pp. 993-994; cf. also, among others, KILIAN, *Jesaja II*, p. 154; ALONSO SCHÖKEL AND SICRE DIAZ, *Profetas I*, p. 213. In contrast to this position, the transition from 3rd to 1st person may simply constitute a concretisation (cf. Appendix).

91. REDDITT, *Form Critical Analysis*, p. 129; SCHOORS, *Jesaja*, p. 156; MOTYER, *The Prophecy of Isaiah*, pp. 217-218; cf. the thorough discussion in MARCH, *Two Prophetic Compositions*, pp. 142ff..

92. KAISER, *The Book of Isaiah*, p. 213; WATTS, *Isaiah 1–33*, p. 341;

Indicators

For the first time[93] in the textual complex Isa 24–27 we encounter formal indicators of the presence of metaphor, the comparative particle כְּמוֹ together with the demonstrative particle כֵּן (which is always used together with another comparative) which together introduce what Bourguet would call a 'long shock' or 'long metaphor'. Bourguet also notes the relative frequency of this combination of particles in the Scriptures as formal indicators of metaphor. כְּמוֹ usually introduces the *métaphorisant*, in the present case introducing a collection of terms to do with birthing: נפל, חבל, זעק, חוּל, ילד, הרה while the particle כֵּן usually introduces the *métaphorisé*, in this case the people (we) in relation to (מִפָּנֶיךָ) YHWH. Clearly the isotopes are distinct: 'birthing' and 'the people in relationship to YHWH', i.e. 'the nation'. The structure and syntax of vv. 17-18a also serve to underline and delimit this aspect of the wider metaphorical statement intended by vv. 16-19. The repetition of כְּמוֹ with the elliptic presence of הרה provides an inclusio (containing the *métaphorisant*) around the focal clause introduced by the particle כֵּן (containing the *métaphorisé*). Syntactically speaking two CNC's with comparatives include five VC's. After כֵּן *yiqtols* change to *qatals*. Evidence of dependant speech is also clear, it being necessary to understand the effort involved in the human process of birthing in order to establish what this might mean figuratively with respect to the people's relationship with YHWH, i.e. the struggle of birthing is worthless without a fertile relationship with one's husband. The negative outcome of the metaphorical statement, 'we birthed wind (רוּחַ[94])', is elaborated in more literal (independent) language in v. 18b-c as an explanation of the metaphorical confession. It is impossible to win one's own deliverance on earth, certainly

---

93. The comparative particples in 24,2-3 constitute an extended simile and do not form part of the metaphorical statement.

94. The term רוח can signify "...something unseen in order that the visible effect of this invisible force might be adequately apprehended" (NIDOTTE 8120 [VAN PELT/KAISER/BLOCK]). The term has a 'broad range of meanings' but the present context suggests that it should be understood quite literally as 'wind', not as a force of nature under YHWH's control but as a depiction of 'powerlessness, worthlessness or vanity' (cf. Eccles 1,6.14.17; 2,11.17.26; 4,4.6.16; 6 9). Of primary significance here is the fact that the prophets used the term to '...mock the forged images of idols, referring to their impotence as "wind and confusion" (Isa 41,29).' Once again such an understanding of the term here is consistent with the suggestions throughout the textual complex that in the absence of her husband YHWH, Israel sought increase with the help of other gods. The birthing metaphor here is intended to highlight the futility of such a course of action. Just like the gods themselves, the outcome of any liaison with them can only be 'wind'.

if that deliverance is vested in population increase. By way of word-play (consonance), however, a negative metaphor about Israel's inability to achieve its own salvation by birthing new generations (נפל [בל־יפלו]) is transformed into a positive metaphor that with YHWH as father/husband the nation (which is both YHWH's ['my corpses'] and the people's ['your dead']) will live/rise (נבל [נבלתי יקומון]). The promise is repeated in v. 19cd in the command to 'wake up and shout with joy' which is addressed to the שכני עפר (//תבלי ישבי[95]) in v. 18c). Here we are once again faced with two distinct isotopes: 'living/rising/waking/rejoicing' which constitutes the *métaphorisant* and 'dead/corpses/dwellers in the dust' which constitutes the *métaphorisé*.

Semantic incoherence further supports the evidence of metaphor: how can the dead live? Knowledge of the content of the isotope of 'the living' and that of 'the dead' clearly establish this as dependant speech which ultimately cannot de reduced to a literal statement.

A third metaphor follows which focuses the birthing metaphor on ארץ via the metaphorical expression 'dew of lights'. Clearly there are no formal markings of metaphor here (short shock). The simple juxtaposition (via *status constructus*) of two terms from distinct isotopes establishes the presence of metaphor assisted by semantic incoherence: what is a 'dew of lights'? At the same time, the stylistic repetition of the term טל and the emphatic particle כי serve further to focus our attention on the expression. The *métaphorisé* 'dew' is taken from the *isotope* of fertile agriculture and has associations with creation while the *métaphorisant* 'lights'[96] has strong links with the isotope of cosmic phenomena (cf. cre-

---

95. Note the semantic parallelism between עפר, תבל and ארץ. עפר is used in a variety of ways, one of which (20x/110x; NIDOTTE 6759 [HAYDEN]) refers to dry, loose earth which is consistent with the image of an arid, joyless ארץ/תבל which has been reduced to עפר because of YHWH's absence.

96. Selman notes that, whatever its form, אור has a consistently theological emphasis. Light does not exist independently of God. Even the light which emanates from other light sources is ultimately from Him. The nominal form refers to a divine quality. Light is part of God's essence. This would seem to have its roots in his creation of light in Gen.1. What is of importance here is the fact that the idea that God is light "...is more commonly expressed in terms of covenantal relationships. Individuals ("The LORD is my light,"Ps 27,1; cf. Mic 7,8) and the nation of Israel (the Lord is"the Light of Israel,"Isa 10,17;60,19-20) can rely on God's light for help and salvation, whether as vindication for the oppressed (Mic 7,8-9), the fire of judgement against attackers (Isa 10,17), or a future hope that will outlast the sun and the moon (Isa 60,19-20). Though God saves in many different ways, the emphasis is always on God as light..." (cf. NIDOTTE 239 [SELMAN]). Thus the notion of 'light' includes, first and foremost, a divine quality which is associated with the various aspects of covenant blessing: salvation (Ps 27,1; Isa 49,6); prosperity and peace (Isa 45,7); God's covenant (Isa 42,6); justice and righteousness (Isa 59,9); blessing (Ps 89,15). All of the latter are evident topics of Isa 24–27. The combination with טל focuses the covenant blessings associated with אור on ארץ. אור is also a symbol

ation narrative in Genesis) and may also have background associations with the seasons which govern husbandry. In the first place, however, the term appears to be mostly associated with the divine and with various aspects of covenant blessing. In this sense, the 'dew of lights' becomes a metaphor for the restoration of YHWH to ארץ and to his people. We are clearly dealing with dependent and thus figurative speech here since the significance of the combination of the two natural phenomena (dew and light are both 'physical' realities) is incomprehensible without knowledge of the significance of both phenomena independently, where they meet analogically and where they ultimately encounter the isotope of the divine.

A fourth metaphor is evident in the expression 'the earth shall birth'. The isotope of ארץ is juxtaposed as *métaphorisé* with the isotope of human birthing from the metaphor in vv. 17-18a which thereby constitutes the *métaphorisant*. Likewise, a degree of semantic incoherence arising from the primary meaning of נפל provides further indication of the presence of metaphor: how can ארץ 'drop' or 'let fall'? The third and fourth metaphors are linked together via the synonymous terms רפאים // נבלתי // מתיך and further linked with the first metaphor (vv. 17a-18a) via the explanatory vv. 18b-19d: ילד // נפל. As such, therefore, we can speak of one single metaphorical statement in this verses. This will be further elaborated in the *Interpretation/Author's Purpose* below.

Type

The four metaphors which constitute the present metaphorical statement function together as a combination of metaphorical cores. The first metaphor (vv. 17a-18a) seems to be a simple core with the cross-reference ([in]fertility/[in]fertile relationships) more explicit in the *métaphorisant* (birthing) than in the *métaphorisé* (the nation). The core is supported by a further absent core from the preceding metaphor in which the idea of (in)fertility is introduced in the word-play core of v. 13. The second metaphor (v. 19a-d) has its core in a word-play between נבל and נפל, suggesting, in addition, that its primary core is that of the preceding metaphor ([in]fertility/[in]fertile relationships). The third metaphor (v. 19e) is also governed by a simple metaphorical core, a point of cross-reference (covenant blessing/fertile agriculture) which is implied in both

---

for life, prosperity and salvation, the very elements which widow Israel lacks (cf. TDOT I, 160 [AALEN]; J. HEMPEL *Die Lichtsymbolik im Alten Testament*, in *Studium Generale* 13 [1960], 352-368).

the *métaphorisant* and the *métaphorisé*. The fourth metaphor (v. 19f) appears to be what Bourguet calls a secondary core, stemming from the two preceding metaphors: (in)fertile relationships + covenant blessing/ fertile agriculture. As a sort of follow up to the preceding metaphors the third has its core in the combination of their cores: infertility becomes fertility for ארץ. It would seem that a metaphorical concept (A is B) is at work behind these metaphors, however, namely that which we have found elsewhere: YHWH is husband (absent and restored). The extensive use of this kind of relational metaphor in the textual complex Isa 24–27 suggests that it is emphatic and resonant, i.e. a 'strong' metaphor with rich possibilities of interpretation both with respect to our understanding of ארץ and the people. It is structural in that it invites us to structure our understanding of all three 'poles' in relation to one another. In this sense the present metaphorical statement is almost the reversal of what we encountered in ch. 24. Physical realities dominate the unit yet YHWH is only indirectly absent, his presence implied in the restoration of covenant blessing and its consequent rebirth of nation and ארץ.

We can follow Macky here and propose that the primary metaphor (YHWH is husband) is hidden behind the three secondary metaphors and that while the primary metaphor may be familiar and in relatively frequent use, the metaphors which conceal (and at the same time reveal) it are quite novel, there being only limited positive analogy between the *métaphorisés* and the *métaphorisant* in each case. Ultimately, as with virtually all the metaphorical statements we have encountered so far, the present metaphor(s) can be categorised as relational, designed to affirm the people of Israel's belief in metaphorical terms that God intended to relate to them and to ארץ as a fertile husband. There can be no doubt that this was the insight intended by the speech contained in these verses. There may be a degree of cultural-dependence involved here with respect to the statement contained in v. 19a-d. Discussion of this possibility, however, is best left to out treatment of the author's purpose below.

Interpretation / Author's Purpose

As we have already noted above, it would seem that the author's primary purpose in using metaphor in this textual unit is to invite his audience to imaginatively explore their relationship with YHWH in light of the metaphorical statement running from vv. 17a-19f. Following the first metaphor we noted that a more literal explanatory colon further unwrapped the initial birthing metaphor (vv. 18b-c). In relation to its own context – the failed pregnancy metaphor – and to v. 14 (equivalent terms: dead/shades/corpses) where the dead were the ultimate outcome of futile liaisons with other 'gods', miscarried pregnancies, barren widow Israel is seen to be going it alone, bereft of her husband YHWH[97]. The restoration of the 'dead/corpses/dwellers in the dust' of v. 19a-d must be understood as a metaphor for God's grace, of his intervention as husband. Israel, bereaved of husband and barren, cannot give rise to a new generation unless YHWH intervenes. Thus the dead here are living offspring, the nation's fecundity with YHWH as husband, YHWH's children and those of the nation.

In v. 19 'your dead' represent the unborn of the nation, 'my corpses' (//'my fallen' [נפל נבל]) the increase of the YHWH's people (v. 15), those not born to inhabit the world. As a metaphor for increase of the nation, birthing is explained both literally and in a further metaphor in vv. 18b-19d as something Israel could not do alone or with help from other gods. Without YHWH it was impossible. Only with YHWH as husband, only with a husband's input is it possible to achieve salvation. Ultimately, therefore, birthing is a metaphor for God's grace towards Israel, combining to form a metaphorical statement which puts into reverse the utter devastation of ארץ and populace presented in ch.24. It should be noted that the semantic connection between לחש and רוח may constitute another example of metaphorical language rendering something considered 'unspeakable' 'speakable'. Hints from the preceding metaphorical statement made it clear that Israel had served 'other lords' besides YHWH, although this was couched in passive language. Here, the content of that 'service' is hinted at as the offering of spells/incantations which evolved into 'nothing'/'wind'.

Excursus: A Short Survey of Interpretation

There has been a long standing tendency to interpret the metaphors of these verses otherwise. In 1834, Bishop Lowth stated: "The deliv-

---

97. K.P. Darr does not agree that the text here represents the language of actual birthing either literally or figuratively. Much of her approach to the image (which she refers to as simile although she allows it explicit secondary predicates [gasping and panting/ writhing and crying out]) depends on her interpretation of the passage as a 'lengthy oracle concerning Babylon'. The image, she maintains, is one of distress brought on by the advancing Assyrian threat. It will be evident that the present investigation considers the text in its context (also important for Darr) to be a metaphor for the inability of Israel to achieve its own salvation by turning the other 'lords'. Cf. K.P. DARR, *Two Unifying Images in the Book of Isaiah*, in L.M. HOPFE (ed.), *Uncovering Ancient Stones. Essays in Memory of H. Neil Richardson*, Winona Lake, IN, 1994, pp. 17-30.

erance of the people of God from a state of the lowest depression, is explained by images plainly taken from the resurrection of the dead... And this deliverance is expressed with a manifest opposition to what was said above, ver. 14. of the great lords and tyrants under whom they had groaned: "They are dead, they shall not live; They are deceased tyrants, they shall not rise"... It appears from hence that the doctrine of the resurrection of the dead was at that time a popular and common doctrine: for an image which is assumed in order to express or represent anything in the way of allegory or metaphor, whether poetical or prophetical, must be an image commonly known or understood; otherwise it will not answer the purpose for which it is assumed"[98]. While insisting on the lack of metaphorical speech in v. 19, Lord's analysis (1853/54) of the figures in these chapters is equally unequivocal: "Many commentators suppose that the terms dead and dead bodies are used here by a metaphor, to denote the living Israelites who are then to be in alienation from God, and that the rising to which they are summoned, is a change from sin to obedience. No mistake could be greater. The fancy is not only wholly inconsistent with the laws of the metaphor; but it is forbidden by the apostrophe in which the persons or objects addressed, are always those which the names by which they are designated literally denote.[[99]]... The supposition that they are used representatively of something else, is not only against the principle on which all are conscious they are accustomed to use the figure, but is to render the meaning wholly uncertain. That representative construction of the dead in this passage is confuted, also, by the description of them, which is added, as sleeping in the dust, and as cast out of the earth. They are literally dead, therefore, and 'thy dead', God's dead, the dead bodies of the saints; not his enemies. This shows again decisively that the prophecy relates to the time of Christ's second coming, destruction of the antichristian powers, and resurrection of the holy dead."[100] Such a statement, and such an approach to the text, clearly says more concerning its own position in the *Wirkungsgeschichte* of Isa 24–27 (and of the understanding of metaphor for that matter) than of the intention of the author/redactor of the text itself. A

---

98. LOWTH, *Isaiah: A New Translation*, p. 271.

99. I agree with him that this is not metaphorical speech (there appears to be no isotopic distinction between the terms). I think he misses the point, however, since I believe these words are simply offering a more literal explanation of the metaphor of birthing.

100. LORD, *Chapters XXV and XXVI*, p. 491. We will discuss the development of this interpretation of the text in more detail in our final concluding chapter under the question "Individual resurrection or national restoration?".

substantial list of commentators would tend to support Lowth's position[101].

More recent exegesis has tended, for the most part, to have a different opinion on these verses[102]. The problem seems to lie in reading the verse out of its context and detached from the preceding metaphorical statement[103]. Wildberger is of the opinion, and we concur, that this is an oracle of salvation, "...daß die 'Toten' Israels zugleich Jahwes Leichen sind, d.h. Jahwe steht dem Tod seines Volkes keineswegs unberührt gegenüber... Es kann nicht anders sein, damit kann Israel rechnen: Seine Toten werden leben, werden auferstehen, werden erwachen, und die im Staube wohnen, werden jubeln können."[104] Having interpreted vv. 7-18 as a communal lament arising from a context in which Israel's

---

101. Among them: DELITZSCH, *The Prophecies of Isaiah*, p. 450; DUHM (these verse influenced the doctrine of the resurrection of the dead) *Jesaja*, p. 158; PROCKSCH, *Jesaja I*, p. 330; T.K. CHEYNE, *The Book of the Prophet Isaiah*, New York, NY, 1904⁵, p. 152; LINDBLOM, *Die Jesaja Apokalypse*, p. 50; RUDOLPH, *Jesaja 24-27*, pp. 48-49; MULDER, *Die Teologie*, p. 50; SCHOORS (offers defence of both positions but leans towards the conviction of the one praying that God can raise the dead) *Jesaja*, pp. 157-158; OSWALT, *The Book of Isaiah*, pp. 485-485); KAISER, *Isaiah 13-39*, pp. 216-220; MOTYER (beyond the figurative to the literal), *The Prophecy of Isaiah*, p. 219, all tend to lean towards individual resurrection.

102. Cf., among others, BREDENKAMP, *Der Prophet Jesaja*, pp. 155-158); KISSANE (too literal an interpretation of the text) *The Book of Isaiah*, p. 298; SNIJDERS (a tradition in ancient Israel that a sick person, a prisoner, and an exile were dwellers in the land of the dead, cut off from ordinary life) *Jesaja*, p. 264. n. 34; AUVRAY ("Comme en Ez, il s'agit d'une résurrection symbolique. La nation va revivre..."): *Isaïe 1-39*, p. 237); WATTS, *Isaiah 1-33*, p. 342), SWEENEY, *Isaiah 1-39*, p. 341; G.W. ANDERSON, *Isaiah 24-27 Reconsidered*, p. 126, all of whom would dispute an interpretation of the text along the lines of individual resurrection. Cf. also J. DAY, *Resurrection Imagery from Ba'al to the Book of Daniel*, in J A. EMERTON (ed.), *Congress Volume, Cambridge, 1995* (SVT, 66), Leiden, 1997, pp. 125-133. Day traces the origins of the imagery of resurrection found here through Hos 13,14 and ultimately to images of death and rising of the fertility god Ba'al. He discerns a process of demythologisation of the images beginning with the Ba'al narrative where they constitute a genuine reference to literal resurrection from death through Hosea's use of the images to refer to the destruction and ultimate healing of Israel by YHWH, through Isaiah's reinterpretation of Hosea's images as references to the restoration of the nation, to final remythologisation in Dan 12,2 where there is a return to a literal understanding of life after death, of an 'afterlife'. He partly supports his claim for a national restoration interpretation by referring to Isa 27,8 which he understands to be a reference to the exile; "Isa. xxvii 8, actually speaks of the exile: "By expelling her, by exiling her, you did contend with her; "... Isa. xxvii 8 most naturally refers back to the distress referred to in Isa. xxvi, including xxvi 19." (p. 131). Cf. also ID., *A Case of Inner Scriptural Interpretation: the Dependence of Isaiah xxvi.13–xxvii.11 on Hosea xiii.4–xiv.10 (Eng. 9) and its relevance to some theories of the redaction of the 'Isaiah Apocalypse'*, in *JTS* 31 (1980) 309-319.

103. March notes that it seems possible to read both national and individual resurrection into the text but that taken as a whole one must lean towards national resurrection (*Two Prophetic Compositions*, pp. 165-166).

104. WILDBERGER, *Jesaja 13-27*, p. 995.

very existence was under threat, v. 19 emerges clearly for him as an oracle announcing the reversal of that threat. Every effort to go it alone (or with the help of other lords) failed, turned out to be 'wind', for both the nation and ארץ. Wildberger continues, "Das heißt aber zugleich, daß nicht von der Auferstehung einzelner, sondern metaphorisch von der Wiederaufrichtung Israels die Rede ist."[105] Thus for Wildberger, any talk of resurrection from the dead or the awakening of those who dwell in the dust is metaphorical talk for the restoration of the nation[106]. The cultural context in which these words functioned as a metaphor, however, seems to have been lost in the *Wirkungsgeschichte* thereof. If this is true, therefore, the metaphor must be seen as culturally dependant (*end of excursus*).

If we accept that we are dealing here form-critically with a communal lament, then we must agree with Wildberger that the traditional phraseology found in such songs has been superseded. He notes further, however, that an extraordinary situation calls for extraordinary language of resolution. He agrees that Israel is on the point of believing that there will be actual return to life at some stage, since the metaphorical terms (the isotope of living/rising/waking from sleep) used here imply that such a notion was 'essentially common knowledge'. This does not imply, however, that he would agree with Lowth's pronouncement that resurrection from the dead was a 'popular and common doctrine' at the time. The key, for Wildberger, is the way YHWH makes this impossible thing possible. By employing the phrase טל אורת as having figurative significance for bringing something back to life (cf. the agricultural significance of טל) bringing blessing and salvation (cf. the covenantal/creation significance of אורת) the author is using an explanatory metaphor which states that YHWH has the power to make alive. Wildberger's understanding of the 'dew of lights', therefore, is consistent with our understanding of the metaphor: "lebenspendender, heilbringender, glückschaffender Tau"[107]. In the context of the entire metaphorical statement, however, which has its focus in the birthing metaphor of vv. 16a-18a, the 'rising corpses'[108], the 'living dead' and the 'waking dwellers in the dust' are the offspring of the liaison between YHWH and his people.

Thus while we agree that the terminology of resurrection is metaphorical and is explained in terms of blessing and salvation it hides a more

---

105. *Ibid.*
106. Cf. also Ezek 37 where a similar metaphor is at work.
107. *Ibid.*, p. 998.
108. 'Corpses rising' as opposed to the 'dwellers of the world' literally 'not falling'.

basic metaphor in which YHWH takes on the role of 'only husband', without whom the nation literally cannot survive, but with whom even the most difficult situation can be redeemed.

With respect to these cola, therefore, one might add a secondary pedagogical or perhaps even evaluative purpose to the author's reasons for employing the metaphors he does. Not only did he want his audience to explore its relationship with YHWH in light of these words, he wanted to teach them that his evaluation of the situation was not entirely negative, that there was a future in spite of the past.

Johnson[109] also sees the importance of the context of the birthing metaphor for the interpretation of these words. Judah's inability to give birth in spite of the agony endured in the process of bearing is a figurative description of her ultimate inability to return from the exile by her own devices. He notes further that the imagery surrounding childbirth as related to the exile is well known in the Isaianic tradition and cites three other passages in support of this (Isa 37,5; 49,21; 54,1; 66,7.8)[110]. Convinced that each of these passages uses birthing imagery to 'symbolise Judah's exile and return', Johnson correctly insists that the Isa 26,17 18 must function in the same way. He further supports his argument on the basis of his interpretation of v. 19 as a *Heilsorakel* spoken by YHWH[111]. His arguments in favour of interpreting v. 19 as a reference to national rather than individual resurrection are important here: (1) the greater context being one descriptive of exile (esp. 24,1-20); (2) his dating of Isa 24–27 as 'close to the time of the exile'; (3) the immediate context of national lament which "(a) refers to Yahweh's people en masse over against the enemy (v. 11), (b) affirms the faithfulness of the entire people during the period of foreign oppression (v. 13), (c) depicts Shalom in terms of national well-being (v. 15), (d) notes Yahweh's chastisement of the people as a whole rather than individuals within society (v. 16), (e) employs the language of childbirth, an image well known in the Isaianic tradition as connoting national exile and restoration (vv. 17, 18a), and (f) thinks of deliverance as repopulation of the land (v. 18bff.)."[112] Ultimately it is because of the author of Isa 24–27's understanding of the exile as 'the death of the nation' that he is obliged to use images of

---

109. JOHNSON, *Chaos to Restoration*, pp. 80-81.
110. All from or influenced by (according to Westermann, Isa 66,7.8 is based on Isa 49,20-23) so-called Second Isaiah. Note the significance for the dating of Isa 24–27.
111. JOHNSON, *Chaos to Restoration*, p. 80. Together with Westermann he notes that it is not unusual in the prophetic literature for an 'answer from God' to replace the vow of praise usually associated with the conclusion to a lament of the people (cf. C. WESTERMANN, *Praise and Lament in the Psalms*, Atlanta, GA, 1981, p. 61)
112. *Ibid.*

'rising' and 'awakening' for its restoration. Without an adequate understanding of the background metaphor of birthing, however, there is chance that commentators will take this terminology literally and miss its due reference to the exile.

In v. 19f 'earth will give birth to shades', ארץ in relationship with YHWH will be restored, will be fecund, will be cosmic rather than chaotic. ארץ as a place of shades, as a place of death, will come alive, become fertile because of the 'dew of lights' which the context demands we must interpret as a salvific image for restoration as an adjunct to the salvific image of re-birth for the population. One should also note how the increase in the nation parallels the depopulation of ארץ in 24,1-3 as the devastation of ארץ parallels its restoration here. Depopulated, joyless ארץ\\repopulated, joyful ארץ; arid, fruitless, chaotic ארץ \\ fertile, cosmic ארץ. Similarly, Johnson, following J.Z. Smith, understands the inherent meaning of exile as "to be in a state of chaos, decreation and death; to return from exile is to be re-created and reborn"[113]. We also noted the language and imagery of chaos and de-creation in Isa 24,1-20. The present image turns this chaos on its head for both the people and ארץ. Indeed, terminological and semantic associations (both antithetical and synonymous) with the preceding chapters abound here, especially with chapter 24: ארץ: vv. 1a.3a.4be.5a.6ac.11c.13a.16a. 18ce.19abc. 20a; יושב הארץ: vv. 1d.5a.6bc.17; תבל: v. 4d; ארץ falls (נפל) and will not rise (קום): v. 18cd; נבל: v. 4bd; 'punishment' (פקד): vv. 21bc.22c; lights (חמה/לבנה): v. 23ab; depopulation (בקק); vv. 1a.3a; remnant: (נשאר אנוש מזער) v. 6d \\ re-population; lack of joy (vv. 7-12) \\ restoration of joy; dying ארץ/agriculture/vine (ch.24) \\ dew of lights/fertile ארץ.

Isa 26,20–27:1[114]

20a Go, my people, enter your chambers.
b Shut your doors behind you.

c Hide for a moment,
d until it has passed, the wrath.

---

113. J.Z. SMITH, *Earth and Gods*, in *JR* 49 (1969) 119.
114. There appear to be no significant text-critical problems relevant to these verses.

21a For behold, YHWH is going forth from his place,
b   to punish the iniquity of the dweller on the land (upon them).

c   And she will disclose, the land, her blood,
d   and she will not conceal again her slain.

27,1a On that day, he will bring punishment, YHWH,
b   with his fierce sword,
c   the great and the strong, ∞

d   upon Leviathan, the serpent fleeing,
e   and upon Leviathan, the serpent twisting,
f   and he will kill the monster which is in the sea.

Delimitation of Metaphorical Statement

The delimitation of this unit has been the subject of significant exegetical dispute. Several commentators view Isa 26,8-19 as a communal lament [15] and this will not be disputed here. The problem lies with the proper conclusion to the final element of the lament (divine response) and whether one can offer further arguments for such a conclusion beyond form-critical considerations. A growing majority of authors extend the unit to include the first verse of chapter 27[116]. A brief examination of their various arguments and perspectives seems warranted here.

March has noted that while there is some degree of disagreement as to the beginning of the unit, v. 20 tends to have the majority support. Things are not so evident, however, when we come to the conclusion of

---

115. REDDITT, for example, (*Form Critical Analysis*, pp. 121-133), following DUHM (*Jesaja*, p. 183). He divides the chapter into a song of praise (vv.1-7) followed by a communal lament (vv.8-19) with a divine response (vv.20-21). Duhm, however, apparently includes 27,1 as part of the latter unit.

116. B.W. ANDERSON, *From Creation to New Creation* (Old Testament Perspectives), Minneapolis, MN, 1994, pp. 195-206 (Anderson also agrees with the notion that the slaying of Leviathan is the 'symbolic' equivalent of the destruction of the Israel's עון: see below). Cf. also MILLAR (26,21–27,1) *Origins of Apocalyptic*, p. 54; JOHNSON (26,20–27,1) *Chaos to Restoration*, pp. 81-84; R. ITOH, *Literary and Linguistic Approach to Isaiah 24–27*, Diss. (UMI), Trinity International University, 1995, p. 159ff.; KILIAN, *Jesaja II*, p. 155; LEWIS, *Rhetorical-Critical Analysis*, p. 143ff.; ALONSO SCHÖKEL and SICRE DIAZ, *Profetas I*, pp. 214-215; SCHOORS, *Jesaja*, p. 158ff.; AUVRAY, *Isaïe 1–39*, p. 237ff.; MARCH, *Two Prophetic Compositions*, p. 168ff.; OSWALT, *The Book of Isaiah*, p. 473ff.; KISSANE, *The Book of Isaiah*, pp. 298-299; DUHM, *Jesaja*, p. 159; DELITZSCH, *The Prophecies of Isaiah*, p. 455;

the unit. A number of scholars consider 26,21 as the concluding verse[117] while others still include 27,12-13 with the unit[118]. Argument for such delimitation is based on the amount of ch.27 the scholars in question consider to be secondary. Those who would end the unit with v. 21 consider all of ch.27 to be secondary, while those who include 27,12-13 tend to accept 27,1 and 12-13 and reject vv. 2-11. March responds negatively to supporters of the latter solution by pointing out that vv. 12-13 have a different point of view to that suggested by 26,20-27,1, the former addressing a 'dispersed' audience the latter a 'gathered', waiting audience. At the same time, the assumption that we are dealing with apocalyptic literature in this textual complex leads the same group to include vv. 12-13 on the basis of the mention of the gathering of the dispersed and the blowing of the trumpet. March rightly notes the circular logic involved here. Finally, he correctly notes that if vv. 12-13 are the original conclusion to material beginning in 26,20, one would expect at least some terminological repetition in the said verses but this is not present. For those who conclude the unit with 26,21, March counters that 27,1 constitutes a better conclusion, noting that the material in 27,2ff. bears no relation to anything that has preceded it while 27,1 (he believes) is directly related to 24,21. Secondly, the evident communal lament preceding 26,20 merits some response, a role which 26,20-27,1 adequately fulfils. Thirdly, the content of 26,20-27,1 fits well with that of 24,21-26,19, the former instituting a return to the latter's theme of impending judgement. Fourthly, the recurrence of language and themes in 27,1 from earlier portions of the poem gives witness to a common feature of Hebrew poetry, particularly the climactic treatment of the theme of judgement. Millar includes "vocabulary, scansion, internal parallelism, (and) paranomasia" as further evidence of the antiquity (and I presume 'integrity') of the unit[119].

Lewis agrees with March's apocalyptic circular argument and establishes the conclusion of the unit on strictly rhetorical grounds. The

---

117. March lists CONDAMIN, *Le livre d'Isaïe*, p. 174; HYLMÖ as cited by G.A. ANDERSON, *Isaiah 24–27 Reconsidered*, in *Congress Volume, Bonn* (SVT, 9), Leiden, 1963, p. 120; LINDBLOM (27,1 is an "Eschatologischer Zusatz"), *Die Jesaja Apokalypse*, p. 52; PLÖGER, *Theokratie und Eschatologie*, p. 95. Cf. also KAISER, *Isaiah 13–29*, p. 221ff.; WILDBERGER, *Jesaja 13–27*, pp. 999-1000; CLEMENTS, *Isaiah 1–39*, p. 218; WATTS, *Isaiah 1–33*, pp. 340-345; MOTYER, *The Prophecy of Isaiah*, p. 220 and B. ANDERSON, *From Creation to New Creation* (Old Testament Perspectives), Minneapolis, MN, 1994, pp. 195-206 all maintain that 27,1 stands on its own as a unit.

118. March lists M. LAGRANGE, *L'apocalypse d'Isaïe*, in *RB* 3 (1894) 200-231 (cf. p. 203); BOEHMER, *Zu Jes. 24–27*, in *ZAW* 22 (1902) 333; PROCKSCH, *Jesaja I*, pp. 331-332; RUDOLPH, *Jesaja 24–27*, p. 50; LUDWIG, *Die Stadt*, pp. 129-130.

119. MILLAR, *Origin of Apocalypse*, p. 55.

assonant inclusion between ביום at the beginning of 27,1 and בים at the end of the verse[120] suggests that it functions as a conclusion, the abrupt thematic change between 27,1 and 27,2, the fact that the composition as a whole uses the expression ביום ההוא to conclude a unit as well as begin one and the climactic repetition of 27,1 all contribute further support to the present delimitation[121].

From a form critical perspective, Johnson considers v. 19 to be the divine response to the lament proper, and he takes 26,20-27,1 to be a repetition thereof. At the same time, he refers to De Vries who argues in favour of the retrospective, summarising character of ביום ההוא in 27,1, which De Vries describes as an 'epitome'[122].

Indicators

The absence of what Bourguet defines as formal indicators (comparative particles etc.) implies that we must search for evidence of the use of metaphor among the informal signs employed by the author. The apparent structure of the unit, established primarily on semantic parallelistic considerations supported by other poetic devices including assonance, consonance, word-play, rhyme etc., is once more the primary source of indicators as to the presence of metaphorical speech in our text. Via the said structure, isolated isotopes are brought into contact with one another and one can discern the presence of *métaphorisés* and *métaphorisants*. Antithetical parallelism between 26,20a-d ('enter'/'shut'/'hide') and 26,21c-d ('disclose'/'[not] conceal') together with the juxtaposition of the semantically bound pair ארץ/עם (cf. ch.24) supported by evident consonance/assonance/alliteration (הרוגיה/רגע; עוד/בעדך; גלתה/דלתיך) suggests that we read these cola together as one piece (26,20a-d + 21c-d).

---

120. There is evident poetic assonance/consonance and rhyme throughout the unit. Note also the structural and thematic elements of poetic closure at work here: structural: tricolon in 27,1cde; thematic: reference to death/destruction. Cf. WATSON, *Classical Hebrew Poetry*, pp. 62-65.

121. LEWIS, *Rhetorical-Critical Analysis*, p. 143ff. Lewis also notes that "The effect of rhyme and repetition of similar sounds dominates this final strophe in the pericope of 26,1–27,1" (p. 144).

122. S.J. DE VRIES, *Yesterday, Today and Tomorrow. Time and History in the Old Testament*, Grand Rapids, MI, 1968, pp. 314-323; cf., more recently, ID., *From Old Revelation to New*, p.40: ביום ההוא "... refers to a just-narrated past event... an epitome is a succinct distillation and summation on the part of an authoritative interpreter (the speaker/writer) regarding the central significance of a past event." Cf. also R. ITOH, *A Literary and Linguistic Approach to Isaiah 24–27*, p. 163, who notes that the expression ביום ההוא "apparently indicates anaphoric (backward) movement". He also notes that the repetition of פקד a(26,21 and 27,1) and the central placement of ביום ההוא gives structure to the unit.

Similarly, the same might be said for 26,21a-b + 27,1a-f: repetition (פקד/יהוה) consonance/assonance/end-rhyme (לויתן/עון)[123]. Taking this structure and the associations instigated by the various stylistic devices employed in the text into account, it would appear that we are once again faced with two metaphorical statements, both of which, however, going arm-in-arm, as it were.

The first statement is an extension of the preceding birthing metaphor and is contained in 26,20a-d + 21c-d. The frequently occurring and evidently intimate combination ארץ/עם[124] constitutes its *métaphorisé* and a series of terms from the isotope of birthing – 'chamber'/ 'secure confinement'/ 'disclosing her blood'//'(not) concealing her slain' – constitutes the *métaphorisant*. חדר 'inner chamber' implies a city dwelling and always has a sense of protection about it, a place for sleep[125]. Most importantly for our purposes, however, it is also a place where a man and a woman can be together undisturbed[126]. We are presented then with a double possibility: a bed chamber for YHWH and his people to conceive or a bed chamber for YHWH's people to try to bear with positive outcome. ארץ's blood and slain from v. 21 must be interpreted as offspring which the preceding oracle predicted would 'rise' from the earth. Either functions well within the broader metaphorical statement of this chapter.

On the other hand, חדר used as a figure for the 'chambers of death' (Price) suggests the idea of YHWH's people entering a period of lifelessness, combining both the lack of birthing metaphor and the metaphor of renewed fecundity. Mosis misses the metaphor which he interprets as related to the aspect of protection, a place of safety against YHWH's apocalyptic wrath[127].

חבה primarily means 'to hide' for the sake of protection of one's life[128]. There is also a notion of 'hiding' one's speech, i.e. of being respectfully silent towards a superior individual. Perhaps in the context

---

123. There is abundant evidence of sound related parallelism within each of the bicola/tricola in this unit.

124. "Because the earth is so closely intertwined with the relationship between the personal God and his human personal creation, it is often portrayed in personified terms" (NIDOTTE 824 [WRIGHT]). We already noted with respect to chapter 24 that the disruption of the triangular relationship ארץ – יהוה – עם was the ultimate cause of the chaos (exile) which had befallen Israel and the ultimate context in which one had to interpret YHWH's apparent hostility. In light of chapter 25, however, this relationship has clearly been restored and the triangle ארץ – יהוה – עם is once more cosmic/productive.

125. NIDOTTE 2539 (PRICE).

126. Jgs 15,1; 16,9.12; Song 1,4; 3,4; Joel 2,16. Cf. also Tob 7,15.16; 8,1.4; 2 Sam 13,10.

127. TDOT IV, 223 (MOSIS).

128. TDOT IV, 171 (WAGNER).

one might be free to interpret this as a husband asking his wife to wait in silence. Such an interpretation would fit well with the previous passage in which Israel admits that she 'poured out incantation' at another 'door' in order to win deliverance (metaphorised as birthing)[129]. It seems appropriate that we interpret 'hide' in the extended context of the birthing metaphor as 'go into confinement' or perhaps even 'submit (sexually?) to me (YHWH)'. סגר: סְגֹר דְּלָתֶיךָ 'to shut/close' emphasises the privacy of the situation. גלה דם: 'to disclose blood' may be a euphemism for birthing. Lev 20,18 speaks of 'uncovering the fountain of a woman's blood'[130]. Menstrual blood is a sign of fecundity, the opposite of sterile and infertile widowhood endured by Israel up to now. For ארץ to 'disclose her blood', therefore, is for her to reveal her restored fecundity. כסה הרג: '(not) conceal' (opposite of birth?) can mean 'cover with shame', 'be ashamed'; 'slain' is equivalent of 'dead'/'shades'/ 'corpses' in the preceding metaphorical statement. Thus earth will not be ashamed of her former infertility but will reveal her blood, show herself open and fecund. Here ארץ is no longer a widow. Zion was set free of her widowhood in ch. 25.

The isotope of the *métaphorisé* has its roots in the relationship between YHWH and his people/land, a relationship disrupted by iniquity (breaking the ברית עולם [24,5]). The isotope in question, therefore, contains an implicit divine element which allows us to suggest, once again, that the hidden metaphorical concept 'YHWH is the husband of his people' (A is B) lies behind these words. When the relationship is intact, when YHWH is restored to עם/ארץ, salvation (birthing) is possible once again. Clearly we are dealing here with dependant speech, speech which images positive human relationship with the divine and with ארץ as agricultural and human fecundity.

The metaphorical allusion in 26,21ab + 27,1[131] is based on verbal associations established via word repetition/consonance/assonance: לויתן/פקד/יהוה – עון/פקד/יהוה. The metaphor here brings the isotope of human iniquity towards the divinity – *métaphorisé* עון[132] – into contact with the isotope of chaos represented by the chaos/sea serpent/monster –

---

129. Cf. S.E. BALENTINE, *A Description of the Semantic Field of Hebrew Words for Hide*, in *VT* 30 (1980) 137-153.
130. TDOT II, 479 (ZOBEL).
131. Of course, to speak of YHWH's 'fierce, strong sword' is to make figurative reference to YHWH's power to destroy the chaos monster.
132. The term עון has primarily a religious and ethical function and serves as a 'summary word' for sins against God (NIDOTTE 6411 [LUC]). One should perhaps relate it here to the incantations/service of 'other lords' mentioned in the preceding verses.

métaphorisant תנין//לויתן[133]. As with the preceding metaphorical statement isotopic distinction and dependent[134] speech are evident, speech which images the restoration of cosmos as a show of divine strength before the powers of chaos which fall into retreat and are ultimately destroyed. An incorporeal reality – the *métaphorisé* עון – is concretised by a corporeal reality[135] – *métaphorisant* תנין//לויתן – and what it/they represent(s).

Type

Where the first metaphor of the present textual unit is concerned (land/people = *métaphorisé* / birthing isotope = *métaphorisant*) it would appear that we are dealing with a simple core/foyer, the cross-reference (fecundity/fertility) between the *métaphorisé* (ארץ/עמי) and the *métaphorisant* (language of birthing) being implicit rather than explicit in both. At the same time, however, it would seem possible that the core may be understood as diffuse, the degree of cross-reference (rooted in fecundity or its lack) being spread throughout this and the preceding metaphors. A further possible core identification may suggest an absent core, the cross-reference having its ultimate roots in the metaphorical core of the preceding metaphorical statement, namely, once again, fecundity. The continued suggestion of the birthing metaphor would certainly point in this direction. The metaphor is clearly active rather than dormant in that it would be readily recognisable as a metaphor by the listener/reader. At the same time one might further specify this active metaphor according to Black's terminology as both emphatic and resonant, providing for genuine interaction and offering the receiver 'food for thought' in his or her perception of what lies behind these words. When an active metaphor is clearly rich in interpretative implications Black refers to it as resonant. Metaphors which are both emphatic and resonant he calls strong metaphors. The present metaphor is thus 'strong', in Black's terminology. At the same time one might identify it using Macky's words as an 'insight' metaphor, one which provides us

---

133. The image is taken from the mythology of the ANE. The destruction of the sea monster תנין//לויתן has its parallels in a mythological battle in which the chaos monster is subdued or destroyed by a deity at the time of creation (cf. ANET, 137-138). Associations with the restoration of cosmos and creation would not have been lost on Isaiah's audience (NIDOTTE 4294 [PAUL]). The term תנין can be associated with the great sea creatures which feature in the creation story of Gen 1. Both terms are used elsewhere to represent the powers of evil in general (Isa 51,9; Jer 51,34; cf. NIDOTTE 9492 [PAUL]).

134. None of this can be reduced to literal speech.

135. At least in the mind-set of the author/audience, cf. brief discussion in NIDOTTE 4294 (PAUL).

insight into the deeper reality represented by the statement as a whole. Similarly, one might describe the present metaphor as 'profound' in Mackian terms in that little of it can be reduced to literal speech.

One of Macky's most significant insights was to point out the possibility of hidden metaphorical concepts lying at a deeper level behind many of the statements of the bible, both the overtly metaphorical and apparently literal. This certainly seems to be evident here and it is the same hidden metaphor which has emerged in various guises throughout this textual complex: YHWH is the husband of his people. The language of birthing for humans/his people and fecundity for ארץ clearly points in this direction. Of course, as Aquinas might insist, such language only says something relative about God but there can be no doubt that it simultaneously establishes a situation in which the receiver can reflect on his or her relationship with YHWH (and ארץ) and 'structure' their understanding of that relationship in light of the familiar *métaphorisant* 'husband'. The ultimate typification of such metaphorical speech must continue to be relational although there are evidently presentative, pedagogical and evaluative aspects at work.

The core or point of cross-reference of the second metaphor appears to be rooted in word-play, in the phonological echo between the terms עון and לויתן. J.P. McCreesh calls this echo 'correlation': "...the sounds of the word or words which are key to the meaning are echoed in various ways throughout the verse so as to subtly reinforce the sense... By this means the poet can reiterate his theme while still advancing the thought."[136] While Bourguet considers such word-play cores to be rare, it remains possible, however, to view aspects of parallelism both external and internal in terms of sonority. In this instance the proposals of Berlin[137] would seem to apply, allowing us to view this remote consonantal parallelism as the other side of a 'metaphorical coin'. The repetition of subject (YHWH) and associated verb (פקד) further supports our belief that the terms עון and לויתן have to be read side by side as *métaphorisé* and *métaphorisant*, even although they do not occur in the same colon or adjacent cola. What is being stated here is that one has to structure one's understanding of the more vague term עון[138] in terms of our understanding of the chaos monster לויתן. Since YHWH is clearly part

---

136. Cf. J.P. McCreesh, *Biblical Sound and Sense. Poetic Sound Patterns in Proverbs 10–29* (JSOT SS, 128), Sheffield, 1991, p. 64.

137. See general introduction on parallelism and metaphor: A. Berlin, *On Reading Biblical Poetry: The Role of Metaphor*, in J.A. Emerton (ed.), *Congress Volume, Cambridge, 1995*, Leiden, 1997, pp. 25-36.

138. Note above, however, that the term tends to suggest sins against God.

of the image, it would seem that we are once again in the presence of hidden metaphor, 'YHWH is a warrior' fighting on behalf of his people/ארץ or, perhaps more accurately, 'YHWH is an enemy' punishing his people/ארץ for their infidelity.

Associations with the first metaphorical statement of the entire textual complex are thus not absent. Both terms possess and exhibit a degree of incorporeality: עון having ethical/spiritual connotations and לויתן stemming from the realm of myth. At the same time, however, the perhaps culture-dependant belief that the chaos monster presided over the earth prior to God's creative impulse would seem to lend support to the term having more literal significance, at least in terms of its semantic content: לויתן signifies pre-cosmic chaos. In this sense one can say that the *métaphorisant* is well-know and perhaps even physical while the *métaphorisé* is mysterious and non-physical. It seems clear that we are once again in the presence of an insight metaphor, one which would have opened doors to meaning for those who received it, one which would be difficult to restate in literal speech.

In Macky's terminology, however, it seems quite reasonable to suggest that such a metaphor would have been familiar to those who received it, at least in terms of the *métaphorisant*. In suggesting that 'iniquity is Leviathan', however, such a dormant usage would have been awakened to 'new life'. References to Leviathan would have leaned strongly in the mind-set of the receiver towards association with Babylon and Egypt or the enemy in general[139]. The shock of hearing the term applied to the עון of 'the dwellers on ארץ' would have stimulated much reflection on the content of Israel's iniquity. Once again, therefore, while the metaphor has pedagogical, evaluative and presentative overtones, its roots lie in the challenge to reflect on one's relationship with YHWH in light of his 'visitation' of עון. The statement that YHWH is going to destroy עון as he destroys לויתן is fundamentally a statement of salvation.

Author's Purpose / Interpretation

We have noted on a number of occasions so far that the primary purpose of the author(s) of this textual complex employ metaphor primarily to speak of the relationship between YHWH and his people/his ארץ. The present metaphorical statement is no exception. While there may be a degree of communication of information concerning who YHWH is and what 'iniquity' is (presentative/cognitive) it is the author's desire to have

---

139. Cf. NIDOTTE 4293 (PAUL).

his audience explore their relationship with YHWH in light of what he says about him that takes precedence. One might also suggest a desire on the part of the author to have his audience change (transformative) their values but the value they are invited to change is their trust and fidelity towards their God who always remains faithful. There appear to be sufficient clues in the text to allow us to open a new window into the 'speaker's meaning' and endeavour to understand it within the limits we have already set.

Lord and many others continue to view these verse as references to 'resurrection' in an apocalyptic context. Indeed, with the exception of 27,1, Lord attaches everything to the coming of Christ who takes vengeance upon his enemies[140]. חדריך 'your chambers' in v. 20a has been interpreted by some as 'graves' or 'burial chambers', further supporting the apocalyptic/resurrection interpretation of the text. Interpretation along with Dan 12,13 might suggest such an approach, allowing the idea of individual resurrection to come into play. After some apocalyptic moment the people of YHWH will rise again from the dead and exit their graves. As Wildberger notes, however, the term חדר is never used for this purpose in the OT[141]. He believes that the term should be taken literally as a place of protection from enemy attack in time of war. He ultimately finds the text's background in the flood tradition of Gen 7,1-16, in which those faithful to YHWH were spared punishment in the flood. Johnson disagrees, rooting the text in the Exodus tradition and the Passover experience of Israel in Egypt (Ex 12,23)[142]. Whatever the traditional background of the text it is evident that the metaphorical language used therein speaks of moment of reversal: YHWH moves from punishing his people/ארץ (chaos, dislocation, desolation: ch. 24) to the destruction of chaos/punishment of the iniquity of the 'dwellers on ארץ', and ultimate salvation expressed in terms of human and agricultural fecundity.

Johnson focuses our attention on the primary question at hand in this unit: Who are the 'dwellers on ארץ'? I believe Johnson correctly relates this reference in v. 21 to 24,21. His larger unit, Isa 24,21-27,1, established by the repetition of temporal indicators and the repetition of פקד

---

140. "...for it is they (his slaughtered servants), especially, whom he is to avenge in the destruction of the antichristian hosts, as is shown in the prediction of the overthrow of great Babylon, because in her was found the blood of prophets and saints, and of all that were slain on the earth; she having fostered the evil passions of their enemies, and instigated and encouraged the persecutions and wars in which they were slain".
141. WILDBERGER, *Jesaja 13–27*, p. 998.
142. JOHNSON, *Chaos to Restoration*, p. 82.

with YHWH as subject, speaks of the destruction of an enemy and ultimate victory for YHWH. In connection with ch.24 the enemy in question is identified as an element among the people themselves, those who broke the everlasting covenant. Are we then to believe that the reference ישבי ארץ points to (some among) the people of Jerusalem/Judah or an external enemy? Even within the same pericope, Johnson notes however, a similar phrase 'dwellers on תבל' can have different meanings: e.g. in 26,9 (Judah's enemy) and 26,18 (Judah's offspring). It seems reasonable to suggest, therefore, that the ישבי ארץ and their עון should be associated with those who broke the everlasting covenant (note triple reference) in Isa 24[143]. Now God's people, those who remained faithful, are invited to enter their 'chambers', to wait till the wrath has past. While the idea of 'protection' may be alluded to here, the broader context of the preceding metaphorical statements would seem to suggest that an extension of the birthing metaphor is at work. The announcement of salvation, however, is not only for YHWH's people, it includes his ארץ. The ארץ 'disclosing her blood'/ 'not concealing her slain' seems to extend the isotope of birthing even further, the 'chamber' becomes a 'birthing chamber' or a 'conception chamber'.

In the second part of the metaphorical statement, the necessary prerequisite for restored 'marital' relations between YHWH and his people/ ארץ is explored. YHWH must destroy the chaos brought about by Israel's transgression/iniquity and restore cosmos (שלום-fecundity). The combination of metaphorical references into one statement suggests that the destruction of the chaos monster as a figure for the judgement of Israel's iniquity (and perhaps magical practices[144]) must be read side by side with his salvific act of restoration represented by the figure of fecund ארץ and fecund people. Thus both are salvific metaphors and both speak of restored relationship. As ever, the negative goes together with the positive. Indeed, what links the two metaphors – besides the structural arrangement of these verses – is the notion that the punishment of עון is an act of salvation on YHWH's part and is thus associated with the broader notion of restored fecundity. Mythical terminology certainly does not seem out of place here.

---

143. Note the triple reference to 'transgression' in 24,5 and the triple reference to the chaos monster in 27,1.
144. The metaphor may once again be making the unspeakable speakable (see below).

Concluding Remarks on Isaiah 26

We noted with respect to Isa 24 that the reversal of creation was the automatic consequence of transgression. Isa 26 views matters from the opposite perspective. Reflecting on the content of Israel's transgression – ultimately the service of other 'lord's' and the endeavour to achieve salvation without YHWH – chapter 26 turns the experience of punishment/alienation, and its concomitant lack of fecundity for land and people, into one of restoration of fecundity for Israel and ארץ (the restoration of YHWH to his people) and the return of cosmos presented figuratively in the very final destruction of the chaos monster Leviathan. Thus the devastation of the tripolar relationship of ch.24 (YHWH/his people/ארץ) is restored to harmony in ch.26. If the automatic consequence of transgression was the reversal of chaos, the restoration of cosmos is the automatic consequence of trust, waiting, fidelity and the admission of guilt. In ch. 26 the exhortation to trust, to submit to YHWH, to 'hush' in his presence, stands side by side with the admission that Israel had submitted to others in her endeavour to save herself. Thus while YHWH's acts of devastation are justified by Israel's guilt, we are taken a step further in chapter 26 into the realm of thanksgiving for gratuitous salvation. All Israel has to do is wait for her jealous husband. Once again the evident meta-metaphor of this textual complex continues to reflect on Israel's relationship with her God, the individual metaphors focusing on Israel's transgression/infidelity and her ultimate powerlessness in juxtaposition to YHWH's strength and solidity, chastening yet forgiving.

Semantic and literal associations are apparent between the beginning of ch. 24 and the end of ch.26, especially in the several references to 'those whole dwell upon ארץ' and their transgression in ch. 24 and the iniquity of the same in ch. 26 together with the elaboration of 'YHWH's punishing visitation' in both chapters. Indeed, the final metaphors of ch.26 return to the first metaphors of ch. 24. YHWH is a jealous husband who can appear as an enemy warrior. Yet he is ultimately a 'husband' who desires to provide rest and שלום for his people and fecundity for both his people and his ארץ[145]. The transformation of chaos into cosmos at the end of ch.25 (inc. 27,1) marks the conclusion of a larger unit which includes 24,1-27,1.

Is the עון of 'the dwellers on ארץ' some form of idolatry metaphorised as adultery? The content and context of ch.26 would seem to suggest

---

145. Sweeney notes that the announcement of the destruction of Leviathan here is related to Isa 11,10-16 and as such offers a description of the restoration of Israel to its land (cf. SWEENEY, *Isaiah 1–39*, p. 344-345).

that it is. The relationship between this chapter and ch. 24 might further suggest that the content of the transgression spoken of therein and the subsequent curse which followed it may indeed be the same. We noted above that in contrast to the more general term חטא, the word עון functions as a designative for sin in predominantly religio-ethical contexts. Luc points out that the plural form is sometimes employed as a summary designation for 'all sins against God'[146]. A number of uses of the term in the context of making idols and worshipping other 'gods' would tend to confirm this[147]. The idea of employing metaphors to speak of matters which would otherwise remain 'unspeakable' – such as Israel worshipping/praying to other gods – would seem to confirm Bal's insight in this regard[148].

Wildberger's view of the purpose and thrust of ch. 26 serves for the most part to confirm our understanding of the author's purpose in using metaphors and the interpretation thereof:

> In 26 7–21 ringt der Verfasser mit der Frage nach dem Geschick Israels in der Zeit der unvergleichlichen Katastrophe, die über die Menschheit in Bälde hereinbrechen wird. Wenn die oben durchgeführte Analyse richtig ist, kommt mit diesem Abschnitt der Verfasser der Grundschicht an das Ende seiner Weissagung: Israels Tote werden leben, die Erde wird ihre Schatten wieder gebären. Das ist die große Hoffnung, welche er seinem Volk auf dunklen Pfad durch die Gerichte Gottes mitgibt. Offenbar ist das Wort in eine Situation hineingesprochen, welche Israel in eine schwere Glaubensanfechtung geführt hatte. Der Niedergeschlagenheit, die sich des Volkes bemächtigt hat, nachdem die anfänglich euphorische Stimmung (24 14ff.) in sich zusammengesunken war, setzt er gleich zu Beginn des Abschnittes thetisch die Glaubensgewißheit entgegen, daß Jahwes Wege für den Gerechten gerade sind (V. 7). Und von Anfang an nimmt er das Volk in seine Hoffnung hinein: "Auch auf dem Pfad deiner Gerichte harren wir dein…" (V. 8), ja er legt vor seinen Hörern sein eigen Herz bloß; er hat offenbar die Erfahrung gemacht, daß es Situationen gibt, in denen man der Glaubensanfechtung der anderen nur noch sein persönliches Bekenntnis entgegensetzen kann (V. 9a), in diesem Fall das Bekenntnis, daß Israel mit שלום rechnen darf. Es hat ja in der Geschichte je und dann Jahwes Treue erfahren (12–15). Aber noch einmal und verschärft meldet sich die Stimme des Zweifels: Mag auch Jahwe in Vergangenheit sein Verbundenheit mit Israel under Beweis gestellt haben, jetzt jedenfalls ist die Lage verzweifelt. Man mag sich wie immer auch anstrengen, Heil gibt es nicht (17f.). Aber an dieser Stelle setzt der Dichter der Resignation das Jahwewort entgegen. Israels Not ist zwar unvergleichlich bedrängend geworden, aber unvergleichlich wird erst recht Jahwes Hilfe sein, so über-

---

146. NIDOTTE 6411 (LUC).
147. Cf. especially Ex 20,4-5; 34,9ff..
148. BAL, *Metaphors He Lives By*, passim.

raschend, daß nur das Bild von der Wiederbelebung von Toten das Wunder der göttlichen Treue beschreiben kann. Rettung is Leben aus dem Tod.[149]

---

149. WILDBERGER, *Jesaja 13–27*, pp. 999-1000.

CHAPTER SIX

ISAIAH 27

HEBREW COLOMETRY

27,2	בַּיּ֥וֹם הַה֖וּא		
	כֶּ֥רֶם חֶ֖מֶד עַנּוּ־לָֽהּ		
3	אֲנִ֤י יְהוָה֙ נֹֽצְרָ֔הּ	לִרְגָעִ֖ים אַשְׁקֶ֑נָּה	
	פֶּ֚ן יִפְקֹ֣ד עָלֶ֔יהָ	לַ֥יְלָה וָי֖וֹם אֶצֳּרֶֽנָּה	
4	חֵמָ֖ה אֵ֣ין לִ֑י	מִֽי־יִתְּנֵ֜נִי שָׁמִ֥יר שַׁ֙יִת֙ בַּמִּלְחָמָ֔ה	
	אֶפְשְׂעָ֣ה בָ֔הּ	אֲצִיתֶ֖נָּה יָּֽחַד	
5	א֚וֹ יַחֲזֵ֣ק בְּמָעוּזִּ֔י	יַעֲשֶׂ֥ה שָׁל֖וֹם לִ֑י	שָׁל֖וֹם יַֽעֲשֶׂה־לִּֽי
6	הַבָּאִים֙ יַשְׁרֵ֣שׁ יַֽעֲקֹ֔ב	יָצִ֥יץ וּפָרַ֖ח יִשְׂרָאֵ֑ל	וּמָלְא֥וּ פְנֵי־תֵבֵ֖ל תְּנוּבָֽה
7	הַכְּמַכַּ֥ת מַכֵּ֖הוּ הִכָּ֑הוּ	אִם־כְּהֶ֥רֶג הֲרֻגָ֖יו הֹרָֽג	
8	בְּסַאסְּאָ֖ה בְּשַׁלְחָ֣הּ תְּרִיבֶ֑נָּה	הָגָ֧ה בְּרוּח֛וֹ הַקָּשָׁ֖ה בְּי֥וֹם קָדִֽים	
9	לָכֵ֗ן בְּזֹאת֙ יְכֻפַּ֣ר עֲוֺֽן־יַעֲקֹ֔ב	וְזֶ֕ה כָּל־פְּרִ֖י הָסִ֣ר חַטָּאת֑וֹ	
	בְּשׂוּמ֣וֹ ׀ כָּל־אַבְנֵ֣י מִזְבֵּ֗חַ	כְּאַבְנֵי־גִר֙ מְנֻפָּצ֔וֹת	לֹֽא־יָקֻ֥מוּ אֲשֵׁרִ֖ים וְחַמָּנִֽים
10	כִּ֣י עִ֤יר בְּצוּרָה֙ בָּדָ֔ד	נָוֶ֕ה מְשֻׁלָּ֥ח	וְנֶעֱזָ֖ב כַּמִּדְבָּ֑ר
	שָׁ֣ם יִרְעֶ֥ה עֵ֛גֶל	וְשָׁ֥ם יִרְבָּ֖ץ	וְכִלָּ֥ה סְעִפֶֽיהָ

WORKING TRANSLATION

2   On that day:

       a vineyard fruitful, sing of her!

3   I, YHWH, protect her,
     every moment I water her.

       Lest someone should hurt her,
       night and day I protect her

4   Heat [anger] is not mine
     [But] if he gives me thorn, brier in battle

       I would advance against her
       I would burn her up all at once.

5   Otherwise, let him hold fast to my refuge.
     Let him make peace with me.
     Peace let him make with me.

6   [In] the coming [days], he will strike root, Jacob,
     he shall blossom and bud, Israel,
     and they shall fill the surface of world with [their] fruit.

7   Has he beaten him as with the beating of the one who beat him?
     Or was he slain as his slayers were slain?

8   In shooing her in sending her [away], you contended with her.
     He removed [her] with his harsh wind in a day of East wind.

9   Therefore, with this shall it be forgiven, the guilt of Jacob,
     and this [shall be] the full fruit: the removing of his sin.

       When he makes all the stones of an altar,
       like stones of lime – crushed to pieces.
       They shall not stand upright, sacred poles nor sun-pillars.

10   For the steep city is solitary. ∞
      The dwelling is abandoned
      and deserted as the wilderness.

       There a bull calf grazes, ∞
       there he lies down,
       [there] he strips its branches.

11 בִּיבֹ֤שׁ קְצִירָהּ֙ תִּשָּׁבַ֔רְנָה נָשִׁ֖ים בָּא֣וֹת מְאִיר֣וֹת אוֹתָ֑הּ

כִּ֣י לֹ֤א עַם־בִּינוֹת֙ ה֔וּא

עַל־כֵּן֙ לֹֽא־יְרַחֲמֶ֣נּוּ עֹשֵׂ֔הוּ וְיֹצְר֖וֹ לֹ֥א יְחֻנֶּֽנּוּ

----

12 וְהָיָה֙ בַּיּ֣וֹם הַה֔וּא יַחְבֹּ֧ט יְהוָ֛ה מִשִּׁבֹּ֥לֶת הַנָּהָ֖ר עַד־נַ֣חַל מִצְרָ֑יִם

וְאַתֶּ֧ם תְּלֻקְּט֛וּ לְאַחַ֥ד אֶחָ֖ד בְּנֵ֥י יִשְׂרָאֵֽל

13 וְהָיָ֣ה ׀ בַּיּ֣וֹם הַה֗וּא יִתָּקַע֮ בְּשׁוֹפָ֣ר גָּדוֹל֒

וּבָ֗אוּ הָאֹֽבְדִים֙ בְּאֶ֣רֶץ אַשּׁ֔וּר וְהַנִּדָּחִ֖ים בְּאֶ֣רֶץ מִצְרָ֑יִם

וְהִשְׁתַּחֲו֧וּ לַיהוָ֛ה בְּהַ֥ר הַקֹּ֖דֶשׁ בִּירוּשָׁלִָֽם

11 When they are dry, her twigs, they are dashed.
    Women come and [set] fire to them (to her).

    For, it is not a people with understanding, this!

    Therefore, he will not show them compassion, he who made them
    and he who formed them he will not show them mercy.

    ....

12 And it shall be on that day,
    he will thresh, YHWH, from the spike of the Euphrates
    to the Wadi of Egypt.

13 And it shall be on that day:
    It will be blown (on) the great shofar!

    And they will come, those lost in the land of Assyria,
    and those abandoned in the land of Egypt.

    And they will bow down to YHWH,
    on the holy mountain in Jerusalem.

340   CHAPTER SIX

ANALYSIS OF ISAIAH 27

We can agree with Sweeney's understanding of the structure of the final passage of our text. The metaphorical song of the new vineyard runs from vv. 2-6 and is interpreted in vv. 7-13 'in relation to the return of the exiles to Jerusalem...'[1]. The rhetorical question in v. 7 marks the transition between the two units, each of which concludes with a future reference in v. 6 and vv. 12-13 respectively.

Isa 27,2-6

2   On that day:

     a vineyard fruitful[2], sing of her!

3   I, YHWH, protect her,
     every moment I water her.

---

1. SWEENEY, *Isaiah 1–39*, p. 346. This is based on his understanding that the allegorical use of agricultural imagery, especially that of gleaning, has to do with the return of exiles (cf. M.A. SWEENEY, *New Gleanings from an Old Vineyard: Is 27 reconsidered*, in C.A. EVANS & W. F. STINESPRING (eds.), *Early Jewish and Christian Exegesis. Studies in Memory of W. H. Brownlee* (Homage Series,10), Atlanta, GA, 1987, pp. 54-55). We will briefly discuss some proposals as to the historical setting of this text below.
2. BARTHÉLEMY (*Critique textuelle*, pp. 188-192) notes that the text of BHS, which is intended to be a rendering of the MT of L, does not accurately follow L in this instance, L having חמר, BHS having חמד. Text-critical dispute, therefore, surrounds the reading with ר (MTL,A; 1QIsaᵃ; Peshitta; Vulgate) or the reading with ד (LXX; Targum). Barthélemy and his team ultimately opt for the reading with ד for the following reasons: the expression כרם חמד is not unusual and is found elsewhere (e.g. Amos 5:11); the term כרם is not normally specified by its produce (i.e. wine); the alternative reading may be simply accidental (ר/ד). Together with Barthélemy and the majority of modern translations/commentaries (e.g. NRSV, WILDBERGER, JOHNSON), we follow the reading with ד. Given the possibility noted by Barthélemy that כרם חמד may be the poetic equivalent of גפן יין (an elaboration of 5,1; cf. Dt 32,14)), however, there may be a degree of contrast with the repeated metaphorical use of the absence of wine (and indeed song) in ch. 24 and the copious provision of wine in ch. 25. Motyer (*The Prophecy of Isaiah*, p. 222) notes the possibility of contrast with the undrinkable wine of 5,2.4 (see excursus). Thus the reading with חמר should not be completely dismissed. The 'confusion' may of course be deliberate and part of the metaphor employed in the statement (see *Indicators* below). From the perspective of interpretation, the difference between the two possible readings is minimal. A 'splendid/pleasant' vineyard is hardly likely to be lacking in wine. A good compromise translation, which we follow here, is 'fruitful' (MOTYER, WATTS) which amply carries over the association of fecundity (and its absence) from preceding metaphors.

Lest someone should hurt[3] her,
night and day I protect her

4   Heat [anger][4] is not mine
    [But] if he[5] gives me THorn, BRier in battle

    I would advance against her
    I would burn her up all at once.

5   Otherwise, let him hold fast to my refuge.
    Let him make peace with me.
    Peace let him make with me.

6   [In] the coming [days][6], he will strike root, Jacob,
    he shall blossom and bud, Israel,
    and they shall fill the surface of world with [their] fruit.

Delimitation of Metaphorical Statement

While some scholars treat Isa 27,2-11 as one single unit[7], the main area of dispute tends to surround the question of the ending of the first

---

3. The semantic range of the verb פקד is broad and perplexing (NIDOTTE 7212 [WILLIAMS]). In the context, YHWH is clearly not the subject, leaving the usual negative theological interpretation ('to punish', 'to visit the sins of') out of the question. A more mundane interpretation suggests itself from the context. YHWH protects the vineyard from external attack, from invasion from without which would cause damage to his beloved fruitful vineyard.

4. BARTHÉLEMY notes the distinction between MT ('anger' – חֵמָה [1QIsa^a; Vulgate]) and LXX ('wall' – τὸ τεῖχοι - חֹמָה [Peshitta]). The term 'wall' fits the context of LXX which presents an image of a strong, besieged city in vv. 2-3. It would appear, however, that LXX is a '*construction littéraire aussi libre que cohérente*' (BARTHÉLEMY, *Critique textuelle*, p. 193) and that it would not be correct to take only one element of that construction and place it in a different literary context. Barthélemy also argues that the expression is perhaps key to the present 'second' song of the vineyard and opposite to that of the 'first' (i.e. YHWH's intended aggression in 5,5a). Elsewhere in the textual complex (25,4-5) YHWH 'subdued heat (of aliens)' in an act of providing refuge.

5. The interchange of gender her/him (they) is significant, supporting the identification of the feminine term vineyard with the masculine terms Jacob/Israel.

6. הבאים is supported by 1QIsa^a, LXX, Theodotion, Aquila, Symmachus, Targum, Peshitta, Vulgate, each of which relates 'coming' to 'persons' and not to 'days'. Wildberger summarises the history of exegesis on the interpretation of the expression (*Jesaja 13–27*, p. 1013) but confidently asserts that it is simply to be understood as shorthand for the temporal indicator הימים הבאים. Along with most other modern commentators (e.g., JOHNSON, WATTS) we follow Wildberger. One might venture to suggest that it is related to the preceding 'moment' of making peace with YHWH in which case one could translate it 'in that event'.

7. Lindblom (*Die Jesaja Apokalypse*, p. 53) considers it to be a *Jubellied* similar to 24,7-16aα, 25,1-5, and 26,1-4 celebrating the fall of the enemy city. Henry (*Glaubenskrise*,

unit in these verses, namely v. 5 or v. 6[8]. Redditt[9] offers three reasons for separating v. 6 from vv. 2-5: 1) הבאים in v. 6 is a corrupt form of 'on that day' which he seems to consider exclusively as an introductory formula[10]; 2) v. 6 speaks of the entire nation, north and south, for the first time in the textual complex; 3) v. 6 stipulates no conditions for Israel's 'bright future' whereas vv. 2-5 demand faithfulness in return for YHWH's protection. Wildberger argues in addition that v. 6 no longer deals with the imagery of the vineyard and that the double use of שלום in v. 5 provides a more impressive conclusion to the unit.

Much depends on one's understanding of the first word of v. 6, namely הבאים. While one can agree that it is an abbreviated version of something like 'the coming days'[11], it has already been noted above that such formulae can serve a concluding function[12]. At the same time, the temporal indicators in vv. 2-6 form an inclusio (v. 2 ביום ההוא // v. 6 הבאים) which surrounds the 'song' of the vineyard and simultaneously associates the vineyard with Jacob/Israel. Contra Wildberger, moreover, it is hard to imagine imagery more aligned to that of the vineyard than that provided by v. 6. I imagine any vineyard owner would be anxious that his vine would 'strike root', 'blossom' 'bud', 'fill out' and produce 'fruit'. The fact that such considerations serve to cast doubt on the detachment of v. 6 from vv. 2-5 is supported by a number of more recent authors[13]. Johnson, for example, offers four arguments in favour of determining the end of the unit at v. 6: 1) dramatic change from positive subject matter in vv. 2-6 (protection; refuge; fruitfulness) to negative subject matter in v. 7 (slaying); 2) shift from future perspective in vv. 2-6 to past perspective in v. 7; 3) use of the interrogative in v. 7 as marking a new beginning; 4) since Isa 5,1-7 appears to serve as a model for the second song of the vineyard[14] there is reason to assume they would

---

pp. 192-193) considers it incompatible with the alleged universalism of the other chapters in the textual complex. J. Fischer (*Das Buch Isaias übersetzt und erklärt*, 2 vols. (HSAT), Bonn, 1937-1939, pp. 108-184) also considers vv. 2-11 to be an addition but he takes v. 6 with vv. 7-9 and separates out vv. 10-11 because they refer to a specific city.

8. DELITZSCH, *The Prophecies of Isaiah*, pp. 453-454; DUHM, *Jesaja*, pp. 189-190 (thinks v.6 is a quotation standing on its own); LOHMAN, *Die selbständigen lyrischen Abschnitte in Jes 24–27*, p. 37; REDDITT, *Form-Critical Analysis*, pp. 136-138); KAISER, *Isaiah 13–39*, p. 224; WILDBERGER, *Jesaja 13–27*, pp. 1007, 1012.

9. REDDITT, *Form-Critical Analysis*, pp. 136-137.

10. Cf. also WILDBERGER, *Jesaja 13–27*, p. 1008.

11. Accusative of time; cf. J-M. §126i, Eccl 2,16; cf. Wildberger (*Jesaja 13–27*, p. 1013) for a survey of other possible interpretations most of which follow a similar line of thought.

12. Cf. reference to DE VRIES/ITOH in our chapter on Isa 26, note 122.

13. Ludwig (*Die Stadt*, pp. 31-45) takes v. 6 with v. 5, assuming both to be additions.

14. See excursus below.

both end similarly (mention of Israel and Judah). Motyer likewise sees v. 6 as a development of the implications of the preceding verses, including the entire world into the Lord's vineyard. He further suggests that הבאים ('They are coming') should be understood as exclamatory, "matching the exclamations with which the vineyard song began"[15]. In addition, Motyer claims that the terms 'root', 'bud', 'blossom', 'fruit' are a reference to the 'totality of the vine system'. While he seems to suggest that this reference is to the physical extent of the vine, it would seem more appropriate to see it as a reference to the good functioning of the vine over time[16] (and with divine assistance) in contrast to 5,1-4.

In any event, it seems fair to say that v. 6 constitutes a supportive explanation of the metaphor of the vine, now identified as Israel/Jacob, and how it will respond to YHWH's care and protection if it 'makes peace' (v. 5bc 2x) rather than giving 'thorn and briar' (v. 4b). Sweeney[17] supports this argument, noting that the shift from a 1st person speaker's perspective in vv. 3-5 suggests that the prophet's perspective has returned (from v. 2) to explain the figure. As we shall see below, it would appear that the prophet explains the metaphor with more or less the same metaphor, further suggesting that we take vv. 2-6 as one single metaphorical statement.

Verbal and semantic parallels between v. 2 and v. 6 further establish the unit under question: temporal indicators הבאים // ביום ההוא (note also the temporal references in v. 3 (לילה ויום) and v. 4 (יחד)[18]; חמד // תנובה (note also צוץ and פרח in v. 6)[19]. The colometry is uncomplicated, adding to the cohesiveness of the poetic unit: bicolon (v. 2), 2x bicola (v. 3), 2x bicola (v. 4) tricolon (v. 5), tricolon (v. 6). From a syntactical perspective, the string of *yiqtols* beginning in v. 2 runs over into v. 6 to be rounded of by two *wᵉqatals* suggesting simple succession and anticipated information. At the same time, the conditional clause which runs from v. 4b to v. 5c provides background or circumstantial information to the entire syntactical unit which runs from v. 2a to v. 6d. From almost every perspective, therefore, it seems reasonable to establish vv. 2-6 as the opening unit in chapter 27[20]. The metaphor of the vineyard awaits our analysis.

15. MOTYER, *The Prophecy of Isaiah*, p. 223.
16. Temporal references are abundant in the unit.
17. SWEENEY, *Isaiah 1-39*, pp. 346-347.
18. Even the term או in v. 5 which introduces a 'choice' clause (either/or) may be said to have a temporal nuance.
19. תנובה usually refers to fruit given as a blessing from God (NIDOTTE 3292 [CORNELIUS]) thus the inclusio between v. 2 and v. 6 is underlined: the abundance produced by Israel/Jacob is a result of YHWH's protection of his vineyard.
20. For a detailed analysis of the stylistic features of the pericope cf. LEWIS, *Rhetorical-Critical Analysis*, pp. 153-162.

Excursus: Relationship with Isa 5, 1-7

Associations between what Johnson calls 'the original song of the vineyard'[21] and Isa 27,2-6 are abundant[22]. From a literary perspective, both are clearly songs (עֹנָה//שִׁיר) referring thematically to the fertility of a vineyard[23], a theme which has been treated metaphorically throughout the textual complex. It is here, however, that similarity ends and contrast begins. In 5,5-6 YHWH vents his wrath on his vineyard, removing its (his protection) and commanding the clouds not to provide it with water. Whereas in 27,3-4 he waters it abundantly and constantly, protects it himself and declares emphatically that he has no wrath. Similarly, 'briars and thorns' are the result of YHWH's encouragement (his neglect) in 5,6 whereas they are 'burnt up' (having, presumably been pruned away) in 27,4. Finally, YHWH allows, indeed instigates, the devastation of his vineyard in 5,5-6 because it has produced a useless (wild//no מִשְׁפָּט or צְדָקָה) harvest while the harvest of 27,6 is fruitful (the result of שָׁלוֹם) and so abundant that it 'fills the surface of the world'.

Wildberger is of the opinion that 27,4 (חֵמָה אֵין לִי) may hold the key to both songs of the vineyard[24]. YHWH's evident anger in 5,5-6 has subsided and he no longer desires to indulge his wrath against his people. If we understand the metaphor 'Israel/Judah is a vineyard' to be a vehicle for further relational metaphors illuminating YHWH's relationship with his people and the possible directions this relationship can take, it would appear that Wildberger's intuition makes sense. The first metaphorical statement (24,1-3) in the textual complex portrayed YHWH in terms of an attacking enemy. A further metaphor portrayed the hostile enemy of YHWH's people as 'heat (הָרַב) in the desert' (25,4-5) from which YHWH provided shade (מָעוֹז – 'subdued heat [of aliens]') as a tree provides shade from the heat of the sun. Here in 27,4 YHWH proclaims that he does not have the characteristics of an attacking enemy and that his 'refuge' (מָעוֹז) is still available. Evidently, contrast is the primary characteristic of the relationship between the two songs of the vineyard. The second song, however, while being predominantly positive in outlook, is

---

21. JOHNSON, p. 86.
22. Cf. also in this regard, E. JACOB, *Du premier au deuxième chant de la vigne du prophète Esaïe. Réflexions sur Esaïe 27.2-5*, in J.J. STAMM, E. JENNI, H.J. STOEBE (eds.), *Wort–Gebot–Glaube, Beiträge zur Theologie des Alten Testaments, Walther Eichrodt zum 80. Geburtstag* (AthANT, 59), Zürich, 1970, pp. 325-330; WILDBERGER, *Jesaja 13–27*, pp. 1008-1009.
23. Both vineyards are given an equal chance, being כֶּרֶם ... בְּקֶרֶן בֶּן־שָׁמֶן (vineyard... on a very fertile hill) in 5,1 and כֶּרֶם חֶמֶד (fruitful vineyard) in 27,2.
24. WILDBERGER, *Jesaja 13–27*, p. 1010.

not exclusively so. YHWH's people have a choice. They can respond to his care and concern with thorn and brier or they can make peace and, as a result, produce abundantly. Thus in the second song of the vineyard salvation is not unconditional.

Indicators

Although the presence of metaphorical speech in these verses is rather evident, the author's use thereof is by no means simple. The absence of formal indicators of metaphor suggests that his use of syntax, parallelism and other stylistic features together with semantic considerations should be our search basis for informal indicators of the presence of metaphor.

Syntactically speaking, the *casus pendens* construction draws our attention to the 'fruitful vineyard' (v. 2) as the 'topic' of the unit which will be commented upon in the clauses which follow, primarily via the retrospective 3rd person feminine pronominal suffixes[25]. This is linked by way of the song's circular structure[26] with the final verse of the 'song' (v. 6) via semantic allusions to other (positive) elements from the viniculture isotope. Thus the juxtaposition of the isotope of the vine with Jacob/Israel, terminology from the isotope of the 'people of God', provides the basic structure for our first and most evident metaphor, the *métaphorisé* being God's people and the *métaphorisant* being the isotope of the vine; clearly two distinct isotopes: 'Jacob/Israel is a vineyard' (A is B)[27]. At the same time, YHWH (the isotope of the divine) constitutes a second *métaphorisé* with the terminology of the vineyard continuing as *métaphorisant*: 'YHWH is viticulturist' (also A is B)[28].

---

25. J-M §156.
26. Vv. 2//6: temporal indicators; vine terminology; vv. 3//5: I/me (YHWH) – her/it (vineyard); terminology of protection/refuge; v. 4: A (heat) B (battle) B' (advance against) A' (burn up).
27. Allusion may also be present here to Isa 24 in which the absence of 'wine' and 'song' signified the withdrawal of YHWH's care and protection. Similarly, YHWH's provision of the 'best wines' in Isa 25,6 supported the figure of his restoration of his (marital) relationship with his people. Historical allusions are also suggested here by some commentators who maintain that the direct reference to Jacob/Israel is an effort to include the North within the textual complex which elsewhere refers only to Jerusalem/Judah (cf., for example, JOHNSON, *Chaos to Restoration*, p. 87). The term כרם is used throughout the OT as a figure for 'blessing, wealth, joy, prosperity' (Deut 6,11; 2 Chron 26,10; Isa 5,1-6; 36,17; 61,5; Joel 1,11; cf. NIDOTTE 4142 [CARPENTER/CORNELIUS]).
28. נצר means 'to watch over/guard' and is a synonym of שמר. With YHWH as subject, the object of his 'watching' is mostly related to his people either literally or figuratively (as here). Interestingly, the term is used in Ps 119 (10x) for the observation of YHWH's statutes (119,2.22.129), decrees (119,33.34.145), commands (119,115) and Torah (119.34), the very things that YHWH's people pointedly failed to observe in Isa 24,5

Clearly the broader metaphorical statement employs the vineyard as a means to speak of the relationship between YHWH and his people (more on this below). As we noted above, however, the prospect of YHWH's salvific protection and refuge is not unconditional.

The author introduces a different isotope in v. 4, that of war (battle/advance against)[29], in confrontation with those of the vine (negative: thorn/briar)[30], the divine (I/me)[31] and the people (it)[32]. As Motyer notes, Isaiah is mixing his metaphors here[33]. Sweeney unravels the complexity of the verse[34], pointing out that the metaphor of the vineyard and YHWH's care thereof (YHWH is vine keeper – Jacob/Israel is a vine) has two possible responses which are also expressed metaphorically: negatively, in which case 'God's people' continue to be the *métaphorisé* while 'thorn' and 'briar' (people go into 'battle' – people are potential enemy of YHWH) constitute the *métaphorisant* which induces a negative

---

(cf. NIDOTTE 5915 [SCHOVILLE]). The use of this term here may also constitute a verbal allusion to 'a sprout springing from a root' (cf. Isa 11,1; 14,19; 60,21; cf. NIDOTTE 5917 [WALKER]) together with the many connotations of this expression. שקה in the *pual* contains the notion of making drunk which can be found in Job 21,24 (its only occurrence in this form): "bones drunk with marrow", a synecdoche (*pars pro toto*) symbolising the good health of the one favoured by God. The *hiphil* of שקה suggests 'watering/irrigation' and is widely attested in the OT in regard to the 'planted landscape' (Gen 2,6.10; Dt 11,10; Ps 104,13; Joel 3,18 [4,18]) as well as both animals and humans and is clearly a salvific image. A contrasting image of judgement is found in Jeremiah and elsewhere where the same term is used to portray Israel being forced to drink her own tears (Jer 8,14; Ps 80,5; 102,9; cf. NIDOTTE 9197 [O'CONNELL]).

29. מלחמה is a nominal form from the root לחם II which basically means 'to engage in an act of violence or warfare'. A full survey of the theological significance of the term can be found in NIDOTTE 4309 (LONGMAN). The verb פשע is a *hapax legomenon* here. Its Aramaic, Syriac and Akkadian cognates suggest, however, that it has to do with military/war contexts and that it basically means 'to step/march forth' (NIDOTTE 7314 [HAMILTON]).

30. The synonymous nouns שמיר and שית often occur together (esp. in PI: 5,6; 7,23-25; 9,17; 10,17; 32,13) and have to do with the 'thorny weeds'. In the context of YHWH's judgement of his people (all the Isaianic references) the terms signify Israel's negative response to YHWH's care (NIDOTTE 9031 [YOUNGER]). Note alliteration which, together with other style features, is clearly evident throughout the unit (cf. ITOH, *Literary and Linguistic Approach to Isaiah 24–27*, pp. 161-188).

31. First person references throughout this unit allude to YHWH.

32. Change from feminine suffixes to masculine verb forms may be explained by the fact that כרם is mostly found in masculine forms. In addition, the proximity of the masculine nouns שמיר and שית may also have influenced the gender of the verbs. The pointed and repeated feminine suffixes, however, may be a further hint at the kind of relationship YHWH enjoys with his vineyard, namely that of a husband with his wife. Cf. also ITOH, *Literary and Linguistic Approach to Isaiah 24–27*, p. 171: "While the feminine form for the vineyard is unusual, this alteration of gender is very effective in creating an affection impression for the song, because it is concerned with the intimate relationship between the vineyard and its owner".

33. MOTYER, *The Prophecy of Isaiah*, p. 222.

34. SWEENEY, *Isaiah 1–39*, p. 346-347.

reaction (YHWH 'advances against...' – YHWH is potential enemy of his people); positively, in which case YHWH provides refuge (YHWH is a refuge [cf. hidden tree metaphor: מעוז in relation to 25,4]) and the people are invited to respond by making peace. Dependant speech is evident throughout this unit: knowledge of viniculture being required in order to understand aspects of the divine and unpack the possibilities involved in the relationship between YHWH and his people.

Type

While the metaphorical statement as a whole is somewhat complex, the cross-reference or metaphorical core which exists between the *métaphorisé* and the *métaphorisant* is rather simple. One can reduce the metaphorical statement to the following: YHWH to Israel is (like) a vine keeper to a vine. As a vine keeper protects, nourishes and prunes (burns thorn and briar) so YHWH protects, nourishes and prunes his people. The core of the metaphor basically lies, therefore, in the positive analogy between YHWH and a vine keeper and this is contained in the terminology of protection/nourishment which one can associate both with a vine keeper and with YHWH. The 'repetition' between the *métaphorisé* and the *métaphorisant* is implied, therefore, and not explicit. Bourguet would refer to such a core as 'simple'. The *métaphorisé* 'Israel' and the *métaphorisant* 'the vine' are both governed by the same 'simple' metaphorical core.

It is evident that we are dealing here with an active metaphor in that it would be easily recognised as metaphorical language. At the same time one could further categorise it along with Black as 'emphatic', in that it functions as a genuinely interactive metaphor, giving the audience 'food for thought' and obliging co-operation '...in perceiving what lies *behind* the words'[35]. Continuing with Black's terms, the richness of interpretative possibilities found in the interaction further establishes our metaphor as 'resonant'. A metaphor which is resonant, emphatic and active Black describes as a 'strong' metaphor and that is what we clearly have here. Macky would express this slightly differently with respect to the metaphorical statement in question. I believe he would be inclined to describe the metaphor as 'novel' in that it clearly elicits our curiosity and is and remains quite memorable. At the same time it complements our understanding of the *métaphorisé* with new insight to accompany what we already know (insight metaphor). Ultimately Macky would probably describe the present metaphor as 'profound', i.e. a figurative statement which cannot be reduced

---

35. BLACK, *More about Metaphor*, p. 26 (italics his).

to literal speech. Where the divinity is concerned, however, one is often obliged to employ metaphor since the isotope of the divine – which is filled with metaphors in itself – is relatively empty compared with boundless possibilities from which we can select our *métaphorisées*.

It may also be possible to suggest that a titular metaphor similar to that proposed by Stienstra lies 'hidden' behind the metaphor of YHWH as vine keeper, namely that of 'YHWH as husband'[36]. In any event, the metaphor clearly invites us to structure our understanding of YHWH in terms of our understanding of the vine keeper which, as we shall see below, implies both negative and positive structuring. As with virtually every metaphorical speech act in the bible in which one component is the divinity we are once again in the presence of relational speech.

Author's Purpose / Interpretation

It would appear that the author's use of metaphor in the present metaphorical statement has achieved two purposes: a statement of the restoration of the relationship between YHWH, his people and ארץ and an allusion to the reason why the relationship fell apart in the first place and the reaction on the part of YHWH elicited by Israel's infidelity (and its consequences for ארץ). Thus the author's purpose is primarily relational, an invitation to his audience to imaginatively explore their bonds with YHWH and with ארץ in the light of the metaphors. As with most metaphorical speech, there is a degree of dynamic (designed to change the audience in some non-intellectual way) or affective (designed to stir the audience's 'religious' emotions) purpose involved in the present figure but the primary purpose appears to remain 'relational'. The audience is called upon to view its relationship with YHWH as the same as that of a vine keeper with his vine. The vine keeper waters and protects but at the same time he prunes and burns whatever stands in the way of the good functioning of the vineyard and the possibility of a good harvest. Thus Israel's relationship with YHWH can be positive and negative depending on her response to his salvific acts[37]. The image of the wilting vine in ch. 24 is replaced by an image of a healthy vine in the present verses.

---

36. Stienstra maintains that several related metaphors for the divinity in Israel can be reduced to what she calls a 'titular metaphor' of the A is B type – 'YHWH is husband of his people –, a sort of fundamental metaphor, the associated commonplaces of which were employed as further metaphors for YHWH. Her approach from the beginning is one which sees metaphors in a text as part of a concept or system and not as isolated figures of speech or idioms (cf. *Husband*, esp. p. 9). The, albeit archaic, English term for agricultural activity, husbandry, may have its roots in a similar metaphor: a husband cares for his wife as a farmer (vine keeper) cares for his land (vine).

37. Israel's election is conditional (cf. REDDITT, *Form-Critical Analysis*, p. 226).

Millar describes 27,2-6 as presenting an image of rejuvenated and fertile land, a pastoral metaphor offering serene contrast to the portrayal of the infertile land of ch. 24 which spoke figuratively of broken relationships between YHWH, his people and ארץ. Clearly the present image speaks, once again figuratively, of that tri-partite relationship restored. Millar also detects a thematic pattern throughout the textual complex: threat, war, victory, feast[38], all of which, we have noted, provide the metaphorical humus for a realistic portrayal of YHWH's protectiveness, closeness and concern for his city and his people, as a husband is protective, close to and concerned for his wife.

According to Wildberger, the key to the metaphor and the entire song (as well as Isa 5) is חמה אין לי 'anger is not mine'[39]. I would be inclined to extend it a little further: 'anger is not mine but...'. Israel's history has proved that her infidelity can arouse YHWH's wrath but YHWH does not harbour his wrath for long. Interestingly enough, Wildberger quotes an Arabic proverb which personifies the vine as feminine: "Der Weinstock is eine Dame,...die Olive eine Beduinin, der Feigenbaum eine Bäuerin"[40]. This supports our belief that what ultimately lies 'hidden' behind the pastoral metaphor of YHWH and his vineyard is a marital metaphor – which we have encountered throughout this textual complex – in which YHWH is understood as a husband to his people as he is husband (in the agricultural sense) to his vine. Pruning away and burning the useless and unproductive growth of the vineyard must also be seen, ultimately, as an act of salvation on YHWH's part. By doing so the vine becomes stronger and yields a greater harvest. Nielsen notes that the first song of the vineyard used the imagery of the vine in a song about a man and his faithless wife. The first song/metaphor was thus to be understood as functioning performatively, "to pass sentence on Isaiah's

---

38. Millar applies the basic thematic pattern of Threat-War-Victory-Feast (which he finds in the Baal – 'Anat Epic) to the primary sub-divisions he discerns in the textual complex (cf. *Origin of Apocalyptic*, p. 70):

	24,1-16a	24,16b-25,9	25,10-26,8	26,13-15	26,16-27,6	27,12-13
Threat:		24,16b-18b			26,16-19	
War:	24,1-13	24,18c-23	25,10-12	26,13-14	26,20-27,1b	27,12
Victory:	24,14-16a	25,1-4c	26,1-8	26,15	27,1c	27,13
Feast:		25,6-8			27,2-6 (Rejuvenated Land)	

Millar ultimately believes that thematic pattern forced the author(s) of these verses to transform the hostile intent of Isa 5,1-7 into a vision of peace and feasting.

39. WILDBERGER, *Jesaja 13–27*, p. 1009.
40. AuS IV, p. 311 (cf. WILDBERGER, *Jesaja 13–27*, p. 1010).

contemporaries"[41]. Although Nielsen does not say so, the second song of the vineyard appears to use the imagery of the vine once again in a relational, 'husband and wife' manner but this time with a much more positive prospect. The wrath of the first song is resolved in Isa 27,2-6 but there is still a warning against complacency and a poor response to YHWH's salvific deeds[42]. Word-play (consonance) between חמה and מלחמה in v. 4a and v. 4b suggests that YHWH only responds with judgement when his people indulge their own wrath. Finally, Schoors notes that the terminology of vv. 2-3 is open to erotic interpretation: חמד = 'fruitful'/ 'desirable'; שקה = 'water' / 'kiss'; פקד = 'to visit'. He disagrees with Alonso Schökel, however, that חזק 'to hold fast' should be understood to have an erotic nuance[43]. Schoors even offers an alternative translation for v. 3: "Dikwijls kus ik haar; opdat niemand haar zou opzoeken, houd ik bij haar dag en nacht de wacht"[44].

Motyer, among others, interprets the 'thorn and briar' as a reference to those outside 'vineyard membership' who are now invited to share in YHWH's peace and he considers this reminiscent of the invitation to Moab to seek shelter in Zion[45]. The broader metaphorical context, however, appears to suggest that 'giving thorn and briar' are a response on Israel's part parallel to 'making peace', both of course directed to YHWH. Motyer also considers vv. 3-5 as a whole to be a development towards the extension of God's vineyard into the entire world[46]. He maintains that the invitation to make peace is an invitation to 'every erstwhile enemy'[47], yet it might also be argued that the subtle mixing of metaphors (vine/war & peace) points exclusively to God's people (made explicit in v. 6). It is God's people who have engaged in battle with YHWH and

---

41. K. NIELSEN, *Reinterpretation of Metaphors – Tree Metaphors in Isa 1–39*, in M. AUGUSTIN and K.D. SCHUNK (eds.), *Wünschet Jerusalem Frieden: Collected Communications to the XIIth Congress of the International Organization for the Study of the Old Testament* (Beiträge zur Erforschung des Alten Testaments und des Antiken Judentums, 13), Jerusalem, 1986, pp. 425-429, esp. p. 427.

42. J.P.J. Olivier's article *Rendering ydyd as Benevolent Patron in Isa 5:1* (*JNSL* 22 [1996], 59-65) also affirms the vine metaphor as primarily relational although he interprets the relationship as that of a 'benevolent patron' to his 'clients'.

43. SCHOORS, *Jesaja*, p. 160; L. ALONSO SCHÖKEL, *La Cancion de la viña. Isa 27:2-5*, in *EstEcl* 34 (1960) 767-774.

44. SCHOORS, *Jesaja*, p. 160.

45. MOTYER, *The Prophecy of Isaiah*, p. 223. Watts completely misinterprets the 'symbol' of the thorns and briars as a reference to the 'void in the land left by Israel's evacuation' (*Isaiah 1–33*, p. 350).

46. Watts (*Isaiah 1–33*, p. 350) also follows this line of thought, maintaining that the reference to the cultivation of the vineyard and not of the land implies that Israel will not return to Canaan but rather she will fill the entire world. I believe he is taking the reference to the vineyard here too literally.

47. *Ibid.*

YHWH has advanced against them in judgement[48]. Now they are called upon to make peace with him and accept the refuge he has to offer[49].

Thus the author of these verses presents us with a series of metaphorical references which imply a complete turnabout in Israel's relationship with her God. Fecundity and rootedness take the place of Israel's rootless and fruitless condition after the punishment of her transgression presented in the first part of the textual complex. Once again we are invited to image YHWH's relationship with his people as one of security and fecundity, an image of a husband reconciled with his wife.

As we noted above, Sweeney pointed out explicit references to the future in vv. 6 and 12-13. While they continue the broader use of 'agricultural' images – and this will be our primary approach to them –, these verses have given rise to a great deal of speculation as to their historical setting.

Eschatological/Historical Intimations: v. 6

By introducing the terms Jacob/Israel, v. 6 historicises the metaphorical statement which precedes it. According to Sweeney, the prophet returns to the stage to explain the metaphorical statement in 2-5 in terms of Israel/Jacob, continuing the metaphorical theme of the vine which he applies in a highly positive sense to Jacob/Israel. Given the parallels with the song of the vineyard in 5,7 where the entire house of Israel is the object of the prophecy and of YHWH's judgement, the present song must also contain some reference to both the Northern Kingdom and to Judah. Johnson points out that the notion of reunification, which goes hand in hand with restoration (of YHWH's relationship with his people), is referred to in vv. 12-13. V. 6 also seems to be an attempt to include the North in a textual complex which focuses rather exclusively on Judah/Jerusalem[50]. Johnson goes further, suggesting that since the idea of reunification was well known in the exilic period, one should place the present pericope during the same period and not, as suggested by Wildberger, during the later period of the Samaritan schism[51].

---

48. *Ibid.*
49. According to Wildberger (*Jesaja 13–27*, p. 1011) one need not seek much further than the temple in identifying 'my refuge'.
50. There is pretty wide agreement on this; cf. GRAY, *The Book of Isaiah I–XXVII*, p. 455; KISSANE, *The Book of Isaiah*, p. 302; PLÖGER, *Theokratie und Eschatologie*, p. 73; KAISER, *Isaiah 13–39*, p. 226; WILDBERGER, *Jesaja 13–27*, p. 1018 (although he does not include v.6 in this unit); JOHNSON, *Chaos to Restoration*, p. 87; MOTYER, *The Prophecy of Isaiah*, p. 223 etc..
51. Cf. JOHNSON, *Chaos to Restoration*, p. 87 and note 12. Cf. also Nielsen who believes that the thorns and briars are 'obviously a metaphor for the Samaritans who were

Whatever the historical setting in which these words originated, it is evident that what was perhaps a non-eschatological message has been given a new eschatological focus[52]. Contra Lindblom[53], Rudolph[54], Procksch[55], Plöger[56] (all of whom, following Lindblom, eliminate the introductory ביום ההוא in v. 2 and thereby the text's eschatological tenor) Wildberger and Johnson support an eschatological understanding of the text. As Johnson rightly notes, "When the phrase (ביום ההוא) is retained and the text kept intact, it is clear that the author is looking to the future day when Yahweh will have come from his place (26.20) and will have destroyed Judah's enemies.... This is a view which looks ahead to the restoration of the vineyard which is the whole house of Israel (cf. 5.7a)"[57].

What is of primary importance to us, however, is the fact that the author uses the metaphor of the vineyard together with its other 'associated commonplaces' such as trees (shade/protection), roots, fruit, blossom, bud, watering etc. – surrounding the themes of war and peace – to express YHWH's relationship with his people. Only if one fails to recognise the potentially negative aspects of that relationship is one likely to designate the 'thorn and briar' as some external threat. The present passage has literary associations with the entire textual complex and offers further support to the suggestion YHWH's relationship with his people is like that between a husband and his wife. What is clear is that when that relationship is in a state of שלום, Israel – as a whole, both people and ארץ – will prosper. The destructive, 'enemy' God of the opening verses of ch. 24, the sickly vine, the wailing population, the dried up ארץ, will be turned around. YHWH's חמה does not last forever.

---

considered a menace to future peace and happiness' (*Reinterpretation*, p. 427). Whatever the historical referent, I agree wholeheartedly that the thorns and briars are not a reference to an external threat but rather a metaphorical depiction of one possible response to YHWH's care.

52. "Mit dem Begriff תבל steht deutlich die Eindzeit in Sicht: Wenn Israel wieder in Ordnung ist, dann kommen auch die Dinge in der weiten Welt an ihren Platz" (WILD-BERGER, *Jesaja 13–27*, p. 1018).
53. LINDBLOM, *Die Jesaja Apokalypse*, p. 54.
54. RUDOLPH, *Jesaja 24–27*, p. 52.
55. PROCKSCH, *Jesaja I*, p. 337.
56. PLÖGER, *Theokratie und Eschatologie*, p. 71
57. JOHNSON, *Chaos to Restoration*, p. 86. De Vries considers the temporal expression here to be a transitional marker of a redactional addition, indicating a coming future which is in fact a past/present 'disguised as future'. The phrase, furthermore, anticipates a liturgical response (cf. *From old Revelation to New*, p. 55).

Isa 27,7-13

7a   Was he beaten as the one who beat him was beaten?
 b   Or was he slain as his slayers were slain?[58]

8a   In shooing her[59], in sending her [away][60], you contended with her.
 b   He removed [her] with his harsh wind in a day of East wind.

9a   Therefore, with this shall it be forgiven, the guilt of Jacob,
 b   and this [shall be] the full fruit of removing his sin.

 c   When he makes all the stones of an altar,
 d   like stones of lime – crushed to pieces.
 e   They shall not stand upright, sacred poles nor sun-pillars.

10a   For the steep city is solitary.∞
 b   The dwelling is abandoned
 c   and deserted as the wilderness.

---

58. We follow Johnson's translation here which respects the phonological aspects of the poetry while making some sense of this complex sentence. The author's technical skills are evident here in the alliterative effect of the verse. H. Williamson (*Sound, Sense and Language in Isaiah 24–27*, *JJS* 66 [1995], p. 9) suggests that we follow the Septuagint and the Peshitta (and perhaps 1QIsa^a) here, both of which lean towards an active vocalisation of הרניו (הָרְגָיו as opposed to הֹרְגָיו) but sense can be made of the text as it is. The masculine suffixes refer to Jacob/Israel in the context of a rhetorical question: did Jacob endure the same fate as his enemy? No! His punishment was exile.

59. The reading of בסאסאה without the *mappiq* in the final ה is supported by Th, Aq, Sym, V, and Tg, with the *mappiq* by two MSS of MT and, apparently, by LXX (μαχόμενοι καὶ ὀνειδίζων ἐξαποστελεῖ αὐτούι "fighting and reproaching he will dismiss them"; αὐτούι can refer to 3 other object suffixes). The reading with the *mappiq* is supported by the parallel term in the MT בְּשַׁלְּחָהּ. As is evident from the translation we follow the reading with the *mcppiq*. There is some dispute as to the precise meaning of the expression, however. Th, Aq, Sym, Tg and V understand it to be based on the word סאה meaning 'measure' (בסאסאה 'measure by measure'). LXX understands it to mean 'by warfare'. A more reasonable explanation which respects the repetition within the colon (cf. WILD-BERGER, *Jesaja 13–27*, p. 1014) is suggested by HALAT (738) which proposes that we read the term as a *pilpel* infinitive based on an Arabic root *sa'sa* which onomatopoeically refers to the 'shooing/driving' of donkeys. HALAT also suggests that the term may be derived from *sa*, a sound used for driving goats. Cf., in addition, WATTS, *Isaiah 1–33*, p. 347; BARTHÉLEMY, *Critique textuelle*, p. 195.

60. BHS suggests that the second term in this colon בְּשַׁלְּחָהּ is most likely a gloss but offers no further explanation. While it is not attested in S, it is to be found in 1QIsa^a, LXX, V and Tg. According to Barthélemy, S is a case of '*une simple licence translationnelle*' (*Critique Textuelle*, p. 195). Once again simple poetic repetition supports its presence (WILDBERGER, *Jesaja 13–27*, p. 1014).

d   There a bull-calf grazes,∞
e   there he lies down,
f   [there] he strips her branches.

11a When they are dry, her twigs, they are dashed.
b   Women come, [setting] fire to them [to her].

c   For, it is not a people with understanding, this!

d   Therefore, he will not show them compassion, he who made them
e   and he who formed them he will not show them mercy.

12a But[61] it shall be on that day,
b   he will thresh, YHWH, from the spike of the Euphrates
c   to the Wadi of Egypt.

d   But you, you will be gathered,
e   one by one, O sons of Israel.

13a And it shall be on that day:
b   It will be blown (on) the great shofar!

c   And they will come, those lost in the land of Assyria,
d   and those abandoned in the land of Egypt.

e   And they will bow down to YHWH,
f   on the holy mountain in Jerusalem.

Delimitation of Metaphorical Statement

Scholars have referred to this part of the textual complex as most obscure[62]. The identity of the actants is, for the most part, unclear; there is frequent change from perfect to imperfect tense; there is syntactic disjunction between v. 7 and v. 8 due to the shift of suffix gender; there is an odd juxtaposition of זאת and זה in v. 9; the semantic relationship between vv. 9 and 10 is not evident. Any effort to unravel the mystery of these verses will require that we indulge in a degree of interpretation

---

61. A resoundingly negative situation will ultimately have a positive outcome, thus adversative ו is warranted.
62. Cf., for example, DUHM, *Jesaja*, p. 191; LOHMANN, *Die selbständigen lyrischen Abschnitte in Jes 24–27*, p. 27; RUDOLPH, *Jesaja 24–27*, p. 53; KAISER, *Isaiah 13–39*, p. 226.

and historical situation of the text[63]. For the present, however, we will endeavour to keep this to a minimum, with the assurance that we will return to it in greater detail below when we look at the *Author's Purpose/Interpretation* and the *Eschatological/Historical Intimations*[64]. At the same time, however, our research so far into the presence of metaphors in biblical texts has confirmed that obscurities and semantic/syntactic disjunction should be treated as fertile ground rather than grounds for mere perplexity. Again we will return to this in the following segment: *Indicators*.

Sweeney considers vv. 7-13[65] as interpretative of the preceding allegory of the vine in relation to Israel and Jerusalem's current situation, 'cast in the form of a disputation speech'. By way of the disputation speech, an attempt is made to turn the people's despair at YHWH's rejection around and they are called upon to trust that YHWH's deeds are for their ultimate benefit. The formal elements of the disputation speech, which marks the verses in question as a literary unit, begin with a rhetorical question[66]: are the people as badly off with respect to YHWH as they think? Images of war are taken up from the preceding unit. The rhetorical question is then refuted in vv. 8-13, verses which continue the agricultural imagery of the preceding unit although shifting to a different domain therein (gleaning/wheat/chaff). The basic metaphorical theme is also continued: YHWH may hurt his people but he does so for their own good. The passage is thematically structured in two panels: vv. 8-9 focusing on the situation of the people (East Wind as a metaphor for exile [Sweeney] or Assyria [Johnson]?) and their sin (idolatry: Asherim/Hammanim) which will be removed (positive outcome); vv. 10-13 focusing on Jerusalem's (made explicit by vv. 12-13) desolation which is portrayed metaphorically in terms of vagabond women rummaging in the abandoned ruins looking for twigs (a different dimension of the tree metaphor: twigs = dried up trees/fruitless/infertility?). The people's

---

63. JOHNSON, for example, suggests that the solution to what he refers to as the text's 'editorial problems' depends to a significant extent on the meaning of the text and in particular the identification of the city in v. 10. He follows and adds to J. Vermeylen (*La composition*, pp. 33-35) in this regard, opting, among other things, for Samaria as the 'steep city' after Assyrian capture.

64. Cf. JOHNSON, *Chaos to Restoration*, p. 88.

65. SWEENEY, *Isaiah 1–39*, pp. 347-348. Wildberger treats v. 6 as part of the unit but is forced to admit that it functions as a sort of superscription. He also begins his metrical analysis with v 7 (cf. *Jesaja 13–27*, pp. 1015-1016).

66. Also a stylistic feature for opening a new unit (cf. ITOH, *Literary and Linguistic Approach to Isaiah 24–27*, p. 189 and WATSON, *Classical Hebrew Poetry*, p. 341). Sweeney also recognises the syntactical disjunction (suffixes) between this and v. 8.

'lack of understanding' is the cause of this situation in which their Maker shows them no mercy. A positive outcome is then announced in vv. 12-13, however, both verses being introduced by והיה ביום ההוא. Each verse deals with one theme: v. 12 recovery (ingathering metaphor: God harvests[67]) from exile; v. 13 restoration to Jerusalem/restoration of worship in Jerusalem (blowing of the shofar to intrduce the Jubilee year [Lev 25,8ff.] in which YHWH himself was to provide and guarantee the harvest; shofar also has associateins with worship)[68]. Several scholars end the unit at v. 11[69] but the agricultural terminology of threshing and gathering would suggest that we extend the metaphorical statement as such to include the final two verses of the textual complex. Sweeney's structural analysis outlined above further supports such a conclusion. At the same time, however, it should be noted that the final two verses also serve to conclude the entire textual complex and as such they refer to themes which have an echo in the opening chapter: threshing/gathering (cf. 24,13); restoration of worship (24,7-9); restoration of people – YHWH – ארץ relationship from a state of abandonment and loss to one of harmony (ch. 24).

Seitz is correct in placing historical observations to one side and concentrating on the shift in tone which marks off these verses from those preceding them[70]. From the uplifting vineyard song we are thrown once again into a depiction of judgement and then once again to a positive statement of return and restoration at the end of the chapter. Seitz divides the chapter into four pericopes: 27,1; 27,2-6; 27,7-11; 27,12-13. While we may disagree with his division of the text in this way we can agree that with the apparent exception of vv. 7-11 the other pericopes deal with YHWH's victory over forces hostile to his restorative work. The vision of the 'fortified city' in vv. 7-11, he maintains, need not refer to Samaria nor to Babylon nor any other city for that matter, it is rather a "symbol of strength broken down before the majesty of Israel's God"[71]. In this sense one might suggest that the 'fortified city' and the 'people without understanding' are one and the same, each having undergone a schism in their relationship with YHWH. As elsewhere in the textual complex, the worship of other gods appears to be the source of this schism.

---

67. MOTYER, *The Prophecy of Isaiah*, p. 225
68. JOHNSON, *Chaos to Restoration*, p. 94.
69. Cf., for example, WILDBERGER, *Jesaja 13–27*, p. 1013ff.; JOHNSON, *Chaos to Restoration*, p. 88ff.; MOTYER, *The Prophecy of Isaiah*, p. 223.
70. C.R. SEITZ, *Isaiah 1–39* (Interpretation: A Bible Commentary for Teaching and Preaching), Louisville, KY, 1994, p. 197ff..
71. SEITZ, *Isaiah 1–39*, p. 198.

Indicators

Formal indicators (כְּ) point to simple comparison (lack of isotopic distinction/absence of dependent speech) placed in the context of a rhetorical question: was Jacob's fate like that of his enemy? Did YHWH treat them both in the same way? Is YHWH the same kind of enemy to Jacob (cf. metaphorical statement 24,1-3) as he is to Jacob's enemy? The answer to these questions is ultimately No! Syntactic incoherence in the masculine/feminine suffixes between vv. 8 and 9, however, suggests the presence of metaphor. Terminology from the isotope of 'dismissal/separation' (the terms of the *métaphorisant*: הגה; ריב; שׁלח; סאסא) is applied to YHWH (the *métaphorisé*: isotope of the divine). Each term of the *métaphorisant* repeats the notion of forced separation between YHWH and his people. YHWH 'startles/scares off' (סאסא) his people[72], YHWH 'dismisses/divorces' (*piel* שׁלח) his people[73], YHWH 'contends/goes to court' (ריב) with his people[74], YHWH 'drives away' (הגה) his people[75]. YHWH's 'metaphorical' behaviour is explained in the same verse in the repeated reference to 'his (harsh, East) wind', a fairly standard metaphor for the destruction which has overcome the land and its people (dry, hot wind dries up ארץ) and the ultimate exile of its population[76]. Thus YHWH's apparent hostility is not as serious as it might seem. His punishment is exile, which, like the East wind, is harsh but temporary[77]. The repeated alternation of masculine verb (YHWH as subject) and feminine (ill-defined: blurring of actants?) suffixes suggests that we should also

---

72. HALAT 738.
73. The core meaning of the root שׁלח "involves the subj. [YHWH] inducing the object [his people] to move away from the subj., and often some purpose on the part of the subj. is at least implied". In the *piel* (as here) there is a stronger sense of dismissal implied, with relatively frequent use of the term in divorce contexts (Deut 22,19.29; 24,1.3; Jer 3,1; Mal 2,16: NIDOTTE, 8938 [COLLINS])
74. NIDOTTE 8189 (BRACKE).
75. With a nuance of cleansing/refining; cf. NIDCTTE 2048 (VAN DAM).
76. NIDOTTE 7708 (ROGERS). Wildberger (*Jesaja 13–27*, p. 1019) suggests that the 'harsh wind' may be a reference to the Assyrian invasion of the Northern Kingdom and the subsequent exile of its inhabitants. Historical references aside, however, it is clear that the 'East Wind' is a metaphor for YHWH's punishment. In line with Motyer (*The Prophecy of Isaiah*, p. 224), therefore, it seems more appropriate to interpret the metaphor not as a '...reference to the great exiles (the northern kingdom to Assyria, the southern to Babylon) but to all occasions when enemies invaded and took captives. On every such occasion divine wrath could justly have exacted the full penalty but forbearance intervened, and even when the great exiles came they did so under the promise of return!' Thus while YHWH's 'fierce blast' was indeed destructive it was not endless. Sweeney correctly makes the link between this punishing East wind and the expiation of Israel's sin (idolatry). Cf. also REDDITT, *Form-Critical Analysis*, p. 384.
77. NIDOTTE 7707 (ROGERS).

read YHWH's actions against the background metaphor of the husband and wife relationship which has frequently emerged elsewhere in the textual complex. As YHWH is the husband of his people, exile constitutes a rupture in their relationship, brought about, as we shall see, by idolatry/adultery, grounds indeed for divorce proceedings and ultimate separation[78].

In parallel to the gender interchange between v. 7 and v. 8, v. 9ab interchanges the gender of the demonstratives (זה//זאת), an indication that the metaphor is being continued and extended. The new *métaphorisé*, the forgiveness of guilt/removal of sin, is juxtaposed to a new *métaphorisant*, crushing/destruction of the symbols of idolatry[79]. Read with the preceding metaphor in mind, the text seems to suggest that invasion and exile, will lead to the annihilation of idolatry and the forgiveness and removal of guilt.

The metaphor continues and is extended once again into the following verses. The 'steep city/dwelling' (*métaphorisé*) is completely abandoned (emphatic repetition: solitary/abandoned/deserted/wilderness = *métaphorisant*). Both literal and metaphorical speech is at work here. At the literal level, a real city is portrayed as empty and abandoned, at the metaphorical level, the 'steep city' has been identified elsewhere in the textual complex as a reference to YHWH's people/YHWH's wife/ Jerusalem[80]. Zion is without her husband. The terminology of abandonment is significant here. Each of the four terms of the *métaphorisant* can be understood figuratively to be associated with marriage/separation: בדד signifies Israel's/Jerusalem's separation from God[81]; שלח in the *piel/pual* occurs in the context of divorce[82]; עזר refers to divine assistance/protection but is also used in its nominal form to denote the marital relationship (Gen 2,18.20)[83]; מדבר also has associations with marriage: "In Hos 1–3, and in this precise form only in these chapters, the relationship between Israel and its God is conceived as that between husband and wife. The unfaithful people (the wife) must be subject anew to the wilderness experience so that it may atone for its sins and return in faithfulness to

---

78. See parallels with Isa 17,1-9; VERMEYLEN, *La composition*, p. 33-35; M. SWEENEY, *New Gleanings*, pp. 55-58.

79. MOTYER, *The Prophecy of Isaiah*, p. 224.

80. The 'steep city' is Jerusalem; cf. L. RUPPERT, *Crítica de los dioses en el libro Isaias*, in *Revista Bíblica* 63 (1996), p. 147.

81. NIDOTTE 696 (VAN DAM). Cf. esp., Lam 1,1 and its explanation as a reference to Jerusalem as an abandoned widow (RENKEMA, *Klaagliederen*, pp. 69-70).

82. NIDOTTE 8938 (COLLINS).

83. NIDOTTE, 6468 (HARMAN); cf. also Lam 1,7 (RENKEMA, *Klaagliederen*, pp. 89-93).

God (the husband)"⁸⁴. By way of the repetition of the particle כי, the situation of abandonment is blamed on the people's lack of understanding and the city is identified with its inhabitants (this people: YHWH's people).

The feminine suffixes of vv. 10f and 11ab suggest that the city and its population, 'divorced' in v. 8, is the ongoing location of a further series of obscure yet explanatory images presented here in the description of the steep city's new inhabitants, the bull-calf and the women (and what they do). While it is not impossible that the bull-calf could be found roaming around ruined cities⁸⁵, its presence here is nevertheless somewhat disturbing. The semantic incohesion established by the obscure actions of the bull-calf and the women suggests once again that as actants (the branches/twigs included) they are to be understood metaphorically together with their actions. Thus the actants of v. 10def and v. 11ab together with their actions constitute the *métaphorisé*. J.S. Lu notes that the most significant use of the term עגל, bull-calf, is as an image of the calf-idol⁸⁶. At the same time, the use of the calf also fits in with the various agricultural images which govern the broader metaphorical statement. Ironically, thus, while the calf is frequently represented as peacefully treading the grain on the threshing floor, a pastoral image of settled existence, its location here focuses on its other persona, that of the calf-idol and its disturbing⁸⁷ presence in the city as an image of idolatry which has 'settled in'⁸⁸. The juxtaposition of the isotope of idolatry (v. 9cde) as *métaphorisant* suggests that we read the actions of the women and the bull-calf as speech related to the removal of idolatry. The bull-calf stripped the city's branches, leaving her good for the fire. Once again literal and figurative images are running parallel to one another. The branches/twigs (סעף⁸⁹/קציר⁹⁰) are part of the 'tree' isotope

---

84. TDOT VIII, p. 116-117 (TALMON).
85. "El becerro suele apercer en descripciones pacíficas, si bien aquí el contexto es de destrucción, lo mismo que en Sal 68,31". In the ANE, the calf features in laments concerning abandoned cities. Cf J. GARCIA RECIO, *'La fauna de las ruinas', un topos literario de Isaías*, in *EstBib* 53 (1995) 55-96 (esp. p. 67).
86. 17 out of 36 occurrences; cf. NIDOTTE 6319 (LU). A young bull was also a symbol of divinity in ANE (cf. Ex 32).
87. According to Kissane (*The Book of Isaiah*, p. 301) 'an unnatural picture...'.
88. As subject of the first rupture of the covenant in Ex 32, the golden calf was a symbol of apostasy. The grazing bull-calf appears to have found its way back: the covenant is ruptured once again. The bull-calf and its actions, therefore, appear to be a metaphor for idolatry and breaking of the covenant.
89. Carries an additional notion of duality, two sidedness, division of the heart, inner conflict; cf. NIDOTTE 6188 (HOSTETTER).
90. Etymology uncertain. The term is also found in Job 18,16 and 29,19, the first reference in the context of a description of the death of the wicked as the drying up and withering of roots and branches, the second in the context of a description the phoenix rising after death, watered by dew all night long.

which is used metaphorically throughout Isaiah for both YHWH and the king. We noted in our chapter on Isa 25 that as the tree and its branches provided dwelling and shade for the birds, so both the king and YHWH provided shelter and secure dwelling for his people. Now these branches have been stripped by idolatry, have dried up and are no longer a source of safety. Women gathering firewood within the city seems, semantically at least, somewhat unusual. The continued lack of identity of the actants in question suggests, however, that the women and the twigs should also be seen as part of the *métaphorisé*. Thus the present inhabitants of the abandoned city together with their actions (*métaphorisé*) have to be understood against the background of the isotope of idolatry (*métaphorisant*). The ambiguity of the bull-calf sets up the associative juxtaposition. K. Pfisterer Darr's comments with respect to the women are significant here and deserve quotation:

> "...there is great irony in the juxtaposition of the abolishment of idolatry, women gathering dry branches for firewood, and the immediately following (and syntactically connected) claim,"for this is a people without understanding". They recall yet another Isaian text linking idolatry, the procurement and burning of wood and charges of incomprehension. [...] Like these idol-making men [of Isa 44,9-20], the wood-gathering women – uncomprehending members of an imperceptive people – gather and burn branches from the gardens and trees that both hosted and epitomised Israel's idolatries. Yet they fail to perceive either the folly of their past rituals or the deep irony of gathering as fuel for the fire (cf. 1,31) dry branches from the vegetal settings whence their leaders sought fertility. So construed, the actions of the wood-gathering women are illustrative of, and not simply the result of, the people's lack of understanding"[91].

While it is possible to read independent/literal speech here, our knowledge of the content of the textual complex so far suggests that we read the present speech as dependant/figurative language. The abandoned city – divorced/widowed people – is surrounded (textually) by images of the removal of idolatry (v. 9cde: literal speech) and the residue of idolatry (vv. 10def and v. 11ab). The latter is thus to be read in terms of the former. Ultimately, the people's lack of understanding has allowed idolatry to take root and has led the people to abandonment and solitude.

The structure of v. 11 contributes here to the continuation of the metaphor:

---

91. K. PFISTERER DARR, *Isaiah's Vision and the Family of God* (Literary Currents in Biblical Interpretation), Louisville, KY, 1994, p. 95. Cf. also the women's/people's endeavours to provide offspring to 'other lords' in ch. 25.

11a When they are dry, her twigs^a, they are dashed^b.
 b   Women come^{a'}, [setting] fire to them^{b'} [to her].

 c   For, it is not a people with understanding, this!

 d   Therefore, he will not show them compassion^a, he who made them^b
 e   and he who formed them^{b'} he will not show them mercy.^{a'}

The parallel structure suggests that v. 11de is a response to the preceding statement of idolatrous behaviour and lack of understanding, the women ultimately representing the folly of Israel in running after other gods (v. 11ab). Once again the obscurity of the actants in v. 11de leads us to believe that we are dealing here with metaphorical speech. Although only indirectly present, YHWH clearly constitutes the divine *sujet métaphorisé*. While the verb forms of v. 11de all have strong theological associations (belonging perhaps to the 'artificial' isotope of the divine and perhaps suggesting standard metaphorisation), they are also characteristic of a distinct isotope: making//forming (עשׂה[92]/יצר[93]), compassion//mercy (רחם[94]/חנן[95]), all stemming in varying degrees from the isotope of parenthood. The unmentioned *sujet métaphorisant*, therefore, is clearly a parent. Via a degree of semantic incohesion (male subject//verbs with predominantly maternal associations: an incorporeal *métaphorisé* with a corporeal *métaphorisant*) the author has set up a situation in which YHWH is portrayed as a parent (making/forming) while in the same verse his parental inclinations are denied (no compassion//no mercy). Clearly we are in the presence of dependent speech here and perhaps also in the presence of a metaphor of the A is B type (YHWH is/is not a parent). We will see below that this need not necessarily be interpreted negatively[96]. YHWH's concern for his people is like that of a vine

---

92. While this verb is at home in a huge number of semantic fields, it also has its place in the maternal realm; cf. Ps 139,15 – 'to be made in the womb'.
93. Cf. Jer 1,5; Isa 49,1.5.8.
94. Associations with the nominal form ('womb') of this root are abundant although not always undisputed (cf. NIDOTTE 8163 [BUTTERWORTH]). Suffice to say that the 'compassion' withheld by a mother is perhaps the most painful to experience.
95. The basic meaning of the root חנן is 'undeserved kindness'. The adjective, usually paired with רחום, suggests that the term 'may carry a parental sense' (NIDOTTE 2858 [FRETHEIM]).
96. One might identify here terminology from the isotope of 'the potter' (primarily based on the presence of the root יצר, YHWH forming his people 'with blows' as explanation for his lack of mercy and compassion). The parental isotope appears to dominate, however. Motyer (*The Prophecy of Isaiah*, p. 225) is among the few to recognise the

keeper for his vine (see initial metaphorical statement of this chapter) not that of a parent for his or her child. YHWH's mercy and compassion are conditional unlike those of a parent.

At first sight the opening lines of v. 12 would suggest a distinct metaphorical unit, separated from what precedes it by the introductory phrase ביום ההוא. We have already noted, however, that this phrase can be retrospective in character, pointing back to the moment described in the preceding verses, particularly the parallel expression ביום קדים and the parallel verbs of distancing/separation which are here thrown into reverse ('shoo'/'send'/'remove' in v. 8 v 'thresh'/'gather'/'come' in vv. 12 and 13[97]). The two 'days' and the 'exile' and 'ingathering/harvesting' of the people ultimately have YHWH as their perpetrator. In the present metaphor, YHWH is portrayed as a harvester, one threshing the broadest area (merism[98]: from the spike[99] of the Euphrates to the Wadi of Egypt) and gathering in his crop with care (one by one[100]). According to Motyer, the שופר גדול was blown on the day of atonement, linking this verse with the atonement mentioned in v. 9[101]. The term thus constitutes

metaphor although he also speaks of YHWH as creator/ potter in Gen 2,7. Ultimately the picture is the same, one of personal 'hands on' care similar to that of a mother for her children. Johnson (*Chaos to Restoration*, p. 89 in line with Vermeylen [*La composition littéraire*]) sees a strong relationship between 27,11 and the symbolic name given to Hosea's child (לא רחמה) in Hos 1,6.

97. The verb חבט is part of the action of harvesting. An olive tree is beaten, for example, to get out the olives so that they can be picked up by the farmer. The term is parallel with gathering/gleaning (לקט) in v.12d (cf. NIDOTTE, 2468 [VAN DAM]). There are evident semantic parallels with 24,13: like the beating (כנקף זית) of the olive tree and like the gleaning after the grape harvest (כעוללת אם־שלה בציר), suggesting that we should take cognisance of the latter in our interpretation of the present text. The term also has a harvest background and is not in contrast to the act of threshing. Both terms are simply two different ways of bringing in the harvest. "The pu. is used in Isa 27,12 of God's gathering of his people back into the Promised Land. The word pictures the complete gathering of Israel (individual by individual), back into the land by the covenant-keeping God. See NIDOTTE 4377 (ROGERS/CORNELIUS) and TWAT VI 595 (RINGGREN). For a discussion of the agricultural imagery in these verses see SWEENEY, *New Gleanings*, pp. 54-55; S. TALMON, *Prophetic Rhetoric and Agricultural Metaphors*, in D. GARRONE and F. ISRAEL (eds.), *Storia e tradizioni di Israele. Scritti in onore di J. Alberto Soggin*, Brescia, 1991, pp. 269-270.

98. An 'extent formula' (merism?), NIDOTTE 8673 (GRISANTI); cf. also Wildberger (*Jesaja 13–27*, p. 1023) who describes it as technical terminology for the borders of the Davidic empire, i.e. the ideal borders of the land.

99. The author is evidently punning on the term 'spike' here, שבלת being a 'water course' as well as an 'ear of grain': cf. NIDOTTE 8672/8673 (WEGNER/GRISANTI); cf. also J.J.M. ROBERTS, *Double entendre in First Isaiah*, in *CBQ* 54 (1992) 41-42.

100. Cf. WILDBERGER, *Jesaja 13–27*, p. 1023: "Jahwe vollzieht sein rettendes Sammeln mit ltzter Sorgfalt; keine Mühe ist ihm zu groß, keine einziges Körnchen darf verlorengehen".

101. MOTYER, *The Prophecy of Isaiah*, p. 225. The sounding of the שופר also heralded the Jubilee year and the feast of the New Moon. The agricultural background of Israel's festivals would not have gone unnoticed here in the construction of the metaphor and its

a bridge between the metaphor of YHWH gathering and the restoration of the cult in Zion, an image antithetically parallel to the 'sacred poles' and 'sun-pillars' of v. 9. Thus YHWH himself constitutes the (*sujet*) *métaphorisé* and the (*sujet*) *métaphorisant* is (a farmer) harvesting[102]. His actions are then explained as a return from dispersion and exile, a physical return which has its final result in a return to YHWH in the heart. Thus chapter 27 concludes with the same *sujet métaphorisé* (YHWH) and a similar *métaphorisant* (vine keeper/harvester) as it started. Both metaphorical statements are clearly couched in dependent speech and exhibit distinct isotopes.

Type

A number of related yet individual metaphors go to make up the present broader metaphorical statement. In the first, the *métaphorisant* was constituted by the roots סאסא, שלח, ריב and הגה, all of which, we noted had associations with the isotope of forced separation. As *métaphorisé*, YHWH (or the isotope of the divine) is presented as one who dismisses/divorces. Following Bourguet's classification, the cross-reference or core of this metaphor, while explicit in the *métaphorisant*, is only implied (the metaphor itself activates the implication) in the *métaphorisé* and is thus a 'simple' core. The metaphor appears to be fairly novel, drawing our attention to some similarity between the *métaphorisé* and the *métaphorisant* which may not always have been evident or even contradicting former opinions with respect to a particular reality (YHWH *can* divorce his people), active, rather than dormant or extinct, and emphatic/resonant in that it functions as a genuine interaction metaphor in which the receiver is given 'food for thought' and must co-operate '...in perceiving what lies *behind* the words'[103]. From a Lakoffian perspective, therefore, we are in the presence here of structural metaphor, inviting the reader to (re)structure his or her knowledge of the divinity (an incorporeal reality) in light of the *métaphorisant* (corporeal realities). It remains possible that hidden behind this metaphor, the conceptual metaphor of YHWH as husband is at work. Given the impossibility of reducing these words to literal speech, the present metaphor can be classified as of the 'insight' type and far from 'superficial'. In terms of

---

associated commonplaces. Interestingly, the שופר was also used in military contexts for calling off an attack (2 Sam 2,28; 18,16; 20,1.22): cf. NIDOTTE 8795 (O'CONNELL).

102. According to Watts (*Isaiah 1–33*, p. 351) the author is mixing his metaphors in ch.27: YHWH is a vine keeper and YHWH is a grain harvester. While the metaphors are clearly similar they are also clearly of different significance.

103. BLACK, *More about Metaphor*, p. 26 (italics his).

speech type, the metaphor is ultimately relational. YHWH dismisses/ divorces his people.

The second *métaphorisé*, the forgiveness of guilt/removal of sin, is juxtaposed to a new *métaphorisant*, crushing/destruction of the symbols of idolatry. The *metaphor* invites us to understand Jacob/Israel's guilt as idolatry, and as such it forms a secondary metaphorical core to the preceding metaphor, an explanatory, presentative metaphor in which our understanding of guilt is to be structured in terms of idolatry. Guilt, an incorporeal reality, is made concrete (stone) in the idols which the prophet insists must be crushed to pieces. The juxtaposition of idolatry and guilt suggests a fairly familiar metaphor, one which, given the relationship between idolatry and adultery, can be reduced once again to the conceptual metaphor YHWH is husband, albeit an absent husband. The metaphor is far from extinct or dead, however, since it would readily be recognised as metaphorical by the reader and must thus be considered active.

The 'steep city/dwelling' (*métaphorisé*) is completely abandoned by/separated from (*métaphorisant*) her husband. Zion is a woman alone. Once again the metaphorical core of this statement is secondary to that of the opening metaphor: YHWH dismisses, and ultimately also to the hidden metaphor which may govern the terminology here: YHWH is husband.

The present inhabitants of the abandoned city, the actants of v. 10def and v. 11ab (bull-calf/women) together with their actions (stripping, dashing, burning), constitute a new *métaphorisé* and have to be understood against the background of the isotope of idolatry (*métaphorisant*). The core continues to be secondary to the primary core of the metaphorical statement as a whole, and appears to intend a degree of explanation: the city is alone because it let the bull-calf establish itself.

The unmentioned *sujet métaphorisant*, in the following metaphorical component is 'parent' (corporeal *métaphorisant*) with the divinity as *métaphorisé*. The somewhat shocking negation found here seems to contribute to the 're-animation' of a somewhat standard (albeit subversive) metaphor. Compassion/mercy are clearly shared by both the isotope of the divine and that of parenthood, although at some early stage the connection became well established and even lexicalised. The denial of the metaphor is all the more shocking at this point. Once again the core or point of cross-reference is 'simple': explicit in the *métaphorisant* and implicit in the *métaphorisé*. YHWH is portrayed as a parent (making/ forming) while in the same verse his parental inclinations are denied (no compassion//no mercy). Using a metaphor of the A is B type (YHWH is/is not a parent), the author invites us to re-structure our understanding of the divinity. If YHWH is not a parent, then what is he? Clearly a positive analogy has been slammed into reverse. The characteristics of parenthood go beyond culture and time and as such the metaphor should be understood as culture-exceeding. Once again, it invites its reader to explore his or her relationship with YHWH and to question it in the light of a firmly negated standard metaphor. Is YHWH really like a parent? The answer must be no but there is still no need to panic.

Almost in direct response to the shocking negations of the previous verses, vv. 12-13 affirm YHWH, the (*sujet*) *métaphorisé*, as (a farmer) harvesting, the (*sujet*) *métaphorisant*. YHWH harvests (puts the act of dismissal/divorce into reverse) but only on the condition that the harvest (his wife/people) is ripe (is ready – has abandoned idolatry/adultery). Thus the literal return to Jerusalem, the re-population of the city and the restoration of the liturgy in the temple, is expressed once again in a relational metaphor. YHWH is not a parent, YHWH is a harvester who brings in his people when they are ready. Our knowledge of the farmer harvesting, waiting for the right moment to bring in the crop, is intended to structure our understanding of the divinity. When the day comes he will bring his people in. He will restore his people, Zion. The notion of the farmer as the husband of the land (husbandry) further supports our belief that the metaphor YHWH is the husband of his people is the hidden inspiration behind the present words. The cross-reference between *métaphorisant* and *métaphorisé* is secondary to that of the preceding metaphor, YHWH is not a parent. It evidently constitutes a sort of 'follow-up' to the preceding metaphor. The *sujet métaphorisé*, YHWH, is thus made more precise by the new metaphor.

The structure of the entire metaphorical statement running from vv. 7-13 can be presented schematically as follows:

    A – YHWH dismisses/divorces (sends away)
        B – Destruction of idols is removal of guilt
            C – Zion is desolate widow
        B' – Population are idolaters/without knowledge
    A' – YHWH is not parent/YHWH is harvester (brings back)

Thus a metaphor describing YHWH as one who dismisses and sends away (A) is antithetically parallel to a further metaphor which portrays the divinity as one who brings back (A'). A metaphor concerning the destruction of idols and the removal of guilt (B) is antithetically parallel to a metaphor concerning the presence of idolatry and the absence of knowledge[104]. At the core of the broader metaphorical statement, therefore, we find Zion the desolate widow (C), a metaphor ultimately rooted in the hidden yet influential metaphorical concept 'YHWH is husband of his people'.

Author's Purpose/Interpretation

The opening rhetorical question (v. 7ab) substantially governs the author's use of metaphors in the present textual unit: has YHWH dealt with Israel/Jacob as he did with the other nations? Based on what follows, the answer to the question is clearly No! In line with the preceding metaphorical statement, the author speaks of forgiveness of guilt and the removal of sin (v. 9ab) and ingathering. Jacob's guilt was indeed punished by contention and exile (v. 8ab) and Jerusalem's isolation (v. 10abc) is the result of her idolatry/adultery (v. 10def – v. 11ab). Jacob's guilt will be forgiven (v. 12de: he will be gathered in, one by one), however, when he does away with idolatry (v. 9cde: crushes altars and knocks over pillars and sacred poles). Jerusalem's abandonment had its roots in her own lack of knowledge (v. 11c). Here too idolatry is to be banished (v. 11ab). The author thus poses a rhetorical question and uses metaphors to answer it. Fundamentally, therefore, his purpose is informative, he is trying to communicate information about Jacob/Zion's condition: it was due to his/her sinful 'marriage' to foreign God's. At the bottom line, however, we continue to move here in the world of relational metaphors. The author's primary intention is to invite his audience to reflect on their relationship with YHWH and how they had undermined it with their lack of knowledge and their adulterous behaviour. YHWH 'exiled' Jacob and left his city desolate as a widow. Punishment for Jacob and Israel, however, need not endure for ever. Jacob will be gathered back from wherever he has been scattered and the shofar will sound once again in Zion where YHWH has returned. Once again the widowed city has the presence of her husband restored. As elsewhere, the use of metaphors allows the author to say things which would otherwise be very sensitive: exile and abandonment are the result of idolatry/adultery. In speaking of such matters in metaphorical terms – Israel/Jacob's relationship with YHWH is portrayed as a broken marriage – the author employed familiar experience (widowhood/exile) to confront Israel/Zion with the consequences of her/his behaviour. Thus a personal response also seems to be expected or at least hoped for on the part of the author.

---

104. It is interesting to note that some scholars consider the absence or neglect of the parallel concept דעת אלהים to be related, among other things, to faithlessness and adultery; cf. TDOT V, 476-477.

In terms of general metaphorical structure, the present verses mimic those preceding them (vv. 2-6). Devastation and abandonment had its reasons but YHWH still cares for his people/city and will return to her/gather him back. At the centre of each we have the metaphorical use of 'tree' terminology: 'briars'/'thorns' (v. 4b) // 'branches'/'twigs' (v. 11ab) each signifying idolatry. Surrounding these negative references are further metaphors which speak of YHWH's response to his people's idolatry, a response which is both positive and negative. While he fights back (v. 4cd 'advance against'/'burn up' [YHWH as subject], exiles (v. 8ab) and abandons (v. 10abc) he also 'protects' and 'waters' (v. 3abcd), lets Israel 'blossom', 'prosper' (v. 6ab) and bring forth 'fruit' (v. 6c), 'forgives/removes' sin (v. 9ab [full fruit]), 'gathers' and 'threshes' (v. 12b-d). Ultimately, in each case, the punishment is YHWH's response to the damage done to his relationship with his people by his people. YHWH acts as a vine keeper (vv. 2-6; both positively and negatively) and as a farmer (vv. 7-13; subjecting his 'crop' to a 'harsh east wind' [v. 8b]). In neither case is the fruit/full fruit (v. 6c // v. 9b) of the relationship possible without the struggle ('advance against'/'go to battle' [v. 4bcd] // contention [v. 8a]) required to banish idolatry.

At the same time, the verses round off the entire textual complex by harking back semantically in a number of ways to ch.24: scattering (24,1) \\ gathering (27,12d); city of chaos is desolate (24,11-12) // steep city is deserted (27,10abc); beating of the olive tree/gleaning/grape harvest (24,13) // beating/threshing/gleaning (27,12bcd); lack of joy/music (liturgy: 24,11) \\ blowing of the shofar/restoration of worship (24,13); 'transgression is heavy' (24,20) \\ 'sin will be removed' (27,9). While it is now proclaimed that YHWH is not an enemy (as he was metaphorically portrayed in 24,1-3), he is also not a parent (27,11de). YHWH is a husband (*pasim*)!! While the ruptured marital relationship between YHWH and his people had dire consequences for ארץ (24,1-3; 4-9; 19-20) its restoration also restores ארץ (v. 6 // v. 9b). In several places, agricultural metaphors are used to describe the relationship between YHWH and his people. As it is with the land so it is with the marriage.

The reference in the present text to asheras or standing poles (v. 9cde) confirms our belief that throughout the textual complex, the primary transgression which brought about YHWH's judgement was Israel's infidelity. The fact that idolatry and adultery have strong semantic associations, makes the ideal metaphor for portraying such infidelity that of YHWH as husband. Ultimately we are in the presence of relational metaphors depicting YHWH's hostility towards his people/city in response to his people/city indulging the calf – committing adultery by engaging in idolatry.

Historical Intimations II

A number of significant historical questions can be raised with respect to this text: is the reference to 'Jacob' in v. 9 pointing exclusively to the Northern Kingdom (Israel)?; is the text addressed to the old Northern Kingdom of Isaiah's earlier preaching or does it concern the Jewish-Samaritan conflict of the late post-exilic period?; is the 'steep city' Samaria and if so, in which context: ancient capital of the Northern Kingdom or rival to Jerusalem in the late Hellenistic period?

Johnson offers a detailed analysis of the problems associated with the historical contextualisation of this text and proposes what I consider to be the most satisfying solution. Based on a lexical study published by Vermeylen which compares Isa 27,7-11 and 17,2-11[105], together with his own belief that the author of 27,7-11 was also dependant on Hosea and other passages from Isaiah, Johnson ultimately concludes that theses verses are clearly dealing with "the fate of the erstwhile Northern kingdom, and the city of Samaria. But lest we conclude prematurely that this is all that this pericope is concerned with, due considerations must be given to other evidence, evidence which might suggest that the pericope is dealing with the devastation of Jerusalem in 587 as well."[106] Johnson maintains that the "duplicity of referents" – Samaria and the North and Jerusalem and the South – "is the result of a conflation of two traditions: one relating to the fall of the Northern kingdom and the other to the fall of Judah."[107] Our analysis of the use of metaphorical language in the text, however, forces us to disagree with Johnson's view that problems (syntactical, semantic etc.) with the text can thus be explained as a lack of expertise on behalf of the redactor who tied the two traditions together. Johnson's 'duplicity of referents' almost certainly has to be intentional on the part of the redactor and can hardly have been due to lack of editorial skill on every point. Indeed the expression seems akin to the stylistic technique of the 'blurring of actants' which has been in evidence throughout this textual unit. The author's intention here seems to have been to allow specific referents (Jerusalem/Samaria) to fade into the background so that the text could be applied to a wider audience. The use of this technique appears to both signal the use of metaphor and encourage it.

---

105. For details see, VERMEYLEN, *La composition*, pp. 33-35; JOHNSON, *Chaos to Restoration*, pp. 88-91.
106. JOHNSON, *Chaos to Restoration*, p. 90. Here he offers a detailed survey of references within the text which allude to Jerusalem
107. JOHNSON, *Chaos to Restoration*, p. 91

CONCLUDING REMARKS

THE REDACTION OF ISA 24–27

In a recent article, M.Z. Brettler notes that the DI's efforts to describe the 'incomparable' God often resort to the use of metaphors which are frequently incompatible with one another[1]. In a sense, only incompatible metaphors held the key to successfully 'creating' an image of the incomparability of God. The metaphors employed in Isa 24–27 likewise appear to be incompatible with one another and with the surrounding context. God is portrayed metaphorically as an enemy and as a (albeit jealous) husband, as hostile yet desirous of peace, as rejecting and yet concerned to reclaim, as destroyer and protector at one and the same time. It may be reasonable to suggest that the author(s)/redactor(s) of Isa 24–27 took images from elsewhere in PI (e.g. 5,1-7) and reworked them in line with an understanding of YHWH more current in DI (primarily relational images: parent, husband). The purpose, in line with Brettler's insight, would have been to underline the incomparability of God with images which appear to be contradictory. Perhaps M. Bal makes the same assertion when she speaks of metaphors as making the unspeakable speakable[2]. P. Del Brassey refers to DI as "noteworthy for its extensive development of kinship-based metaphors for YHWH"[3]. Our metaphorical analysis of these chapters has shown that the relational/kinship metaphor of YHWH as the husband of Zion and of Zion as a collective term for Jerusalem, its inhabitants and the people as a whole is likewise strongly represented, in spite of Stienstra's claims to the contrary. DI represents a more positive image of YHWH as a husband in a marital relationship with his people as a wife than is evident in Hosea, Ezekiel and Jeremiah where the image is also to be found although volatility and danger remain[4]. Isa 24–27 is likewise primarily positive in its use of this relational metaphor yet it underlines that the relationship is not unconditional. The relational metaphor of YHWH as husband of his people clearly serves to unify the textual complex and might thus be considered to be a unifying redactional principle allowing us to treat the text as a distinct unit of material within BI. Given the multiple use of the metaphor of YHWH as husband in DI, this further suggests that the metaphorisation of Isa 24–27 as a redactional principle may have been the work of the same

1. M.Z. BRETTLER, *Incompatible Metaphors for YHWH in Isaiah 40–66*, in *JSOT* 78 (1998) 97-120.
2. M. BAL, *Metaphors He Lives By*, in *Semeia* 61 (1993) 185-207
3. P. DEL BRASSEY, *Metaphor and the Incomparable God in Isaiah 40–55*, Diss. (UMI), Harvard Divinity School, 1997, p. 225. Jerusalem/Zion in DI can allude to the geographical city, its inhabitants, and/or the Judaean exiles (cf. p. 234).
4. DEL BRASSEY, *Metaphor and the Incomparable God*, p. 235.

redactor who attuned both segments of BI to one another. Metaphorisation, therefore, might be included in P. Redditt's long list of editorial characteristics[5]. While it is impossible to be certain, the consistency of the use of metaphor in Isa 24–27 might suggest the work of a single redactor. The genesis of the text as we now have it need not be explained in specific historical terms as such. It is clear that the break in the relationship between YHWH and his people stands at its roots and that this is reflected in a catastrophic collapse of 'civilisation' (both field and city). The prophecy can thus be actualised in any similar historical situation.

LITERARY GENRE / TEMPORAL PERSPECTIVE OF ISA 24–27

We noted with D.G. Johnson that the *communis opinio* concerning the genre of this textual complex was that it reflected prophetic eschatology in transformation, a sort of precursor to full-blown apocalyptic[6]. The metaphorical analysis has shown that the primary concern of the so-called 'day of YHWH' is a historical one. The conditional aspects of the metaphorised relationship between YHWH and his city/people/land tend to underline this fact. The text as such does not appear to reflect a past event nor to propose an event in the distant eschatological future. The metaphors speak of immanence, of a belief that YHWH is going to transform things now, that he has punished but now he will deliver. The reasons for YHWH's hostile engagement are rooted in his people's historical infidelity/idolatry which lent itself to metaphorical expression in the husband-wife metaphor. The uprooting of the symbols of infidelity are a sign that the relationship is restored and that widow Jerusalem once more enjoys her husband's protection. From the perspective of metaphor, therefore, the textual complex would not appear to be apocalyptic. From a broader perspective, it seems reasonable to suggest the use of relational metaphors for YHWH provides a sort of 'umbrella' image which can support a variety of relational conditions and temporal perspectives. Past infidelity and its consequences are subsumed into metaphorical statements about forgiveness and renewal.

---

5. Cf Chapter I, notes 7-10. Clearly, however, metaphorisation is far from being a 'surface' level redactional principle.

6. JOHNSON, *From Chaos to Restoration*, p. 11.

The Division and Literary Structure of Isa 24–27

We have seen that proposals on the division and literary structure of the text of Isa 24–27 vary enormously, even to the present day. If one accepts the integrity of the textual complex as a whole, on what basis can one delimit distinct units (poems) within the text and ultimately discern its overall literary structure as a cohesive composition? The metaphorical analysis has tended for the most part to support the major divisions of the text which are based on other structural and formal considerations. Indeed discrete metaphorical statements can, for the most part, be seen as delimiting poetical segments and pericopes.

The Unnamed City (Cities) in Isa 24–27

How does the metaphorical analysis help us in our identification of the city? We have seen that the text is replete with metaphors which speak of the relationship between YHWH and his people (and ארץ, both later more and more identified with Zion). The relationship is ruptured due to idolatry/adultery and ultimately restored as a husband is restored to his abandoned (widowed) wife. It seems clear from the perspective of metaphor, therefore, that hostile, prideful city is Jerusalem personifying the people and the land and personified as a woman married to / widowed from YHWH. The 'unspeakable' rupture of YHWH's relationship with his people/Zion is made 'speakable' by the use of metaphor. This perhaps reflects a developing Zion theology[7] similar to that which gave rise to the book of Lamentations but not yet quite so intense.

In the same context, it seems possible that the ברית עולם of Isa 24,5 might be interpreted as a metaphor for marriage and that its violation might refer to acts of idolatry. It is on these grounds that YHWH has the right to turn against his 'wife', however temporarily. From this perspective, the metaphorical language of the entire textual complex in which the expression ברית עולם is located permits us to step aside from questions concerning the specific identity of the ברית concerned. While examining the statement in 24,5 from a different perspective[8], D.C. Polaski, correctly points out that 'to break' an 'eternal' covenant is something of an oxymoron. Understanding the violation of the עולם

---

7. Cf. RENKEMA, *Klaagliederen*, pp. 40-49.
8. D.C. POLASKI, *Reflections on a Mosaic Covenant: The Eternal Covenant (Isa 24,5) and Intertextuality*, in *JSOT* 77 (1998) 55-73. Polaski finds echoes of the Mosaic covenant found in Deuteronomy (p. 61).

ברית as a breakdown in the faith relationship betwen YHWH and his people expressed in terms of extra-marital adultery seems quite appropriate to the remainder of the metaphorical language employed throughout the complex: Jerusalem/the people have broken their marriage vow by their adulterous/idolatrous behaviour. The vow itself, however, is not thereby automatically annulled. Indeed it remains intact, pending full restoration.

Individual or Civil Resurrection

The husband and wife relationship which governs the metaphorical speech about the relationship between YHWH and Jerusalem/his people supports the idea of national/civil resurrection in the here-and-now rather than individual resurrection from the dead. Childlessness was one of the primary consequences of the people's adultery/idolatry. Their liaisons with other lords were not fruitful. Only in a restored relationship with YHWH as husband can there be increase and a restoration of fecundity, both at the human and at the agricultural levels. The term 'husband' covers both. The nation will increase, children will be born, the land will prosper with YHWH restored as husband to Jerusalem his wife.

Type of Metaphorical Speech

P. Macky outlined a variety of purposes for which an author might employ metaphor. It became clear throughout our analysis of the texts of Isa 24–27 that although the author(s)/redactor(s) employed metaphor for pedagogical, transformational and emotive reasons (etc.), their primary use of metaphor was to allow the reader/audience to explore his/her relationship with God in light of the metaphorical speech in which that relationship was presented. Isa 24–27 ultimately represents a single metaphorical statement portraying YHWH as a jealous yet forgiving husband. It is perhaps fair to say that biblical metaphors about God must by their very nature be relational, if one accepts the premise that the bible is an expression of a community's faith in God at various stages in that community's growth and from a variety of perspectives on the relationship of faith.

The relational metaphors in Isa 24–27 are not simply two-sided affairs. From the beginning of the textual complex we are invited to view the earth and its physiognomy as part of that relationship. Where there is rupture in the relationship between the deity and his people there is similar rupture between the people and the land. Neither is fecund and both lament.

A. Berlin alerted us to the fact that metaphor should be treated as an aspect of the poetry of the Bible, referring to it as the 'other side of the coin' from poetic parallelism. It is in the context of poetic parallelism that distinct isotopes are allowed to meet and interact and 'create' metaphorical language. Given the fact that the technique of biblical Hebrew poetry is based, for the most part, on repetition of one form or another, we were able to take Berlin's insight beyond the confines of strict internal parallelism to include more remote interaction between isotopes served by a variety of poetical devices. Metaphor must thus be seen as a poetic phenomenon served by poetic technique, although not exclusively. The rhetorical/cognitive divide which has dominated research into the function of metaphor must, therefore, shift its focus to the function of poetry. Biblical poets use metaphor for cognitive reasons as well as purely rhetorical reasons.

It might be fair to say, however, that the dominant metaphor in Isa 24–27 – YHWH is the husband of his people – is primarily a cognitive metaphor designed to inform its audience about the mysterious subject of the deity and how he interacts with humans. In his recent and substantial volume on the theology of the Old Testament, W. Brueggemann speaks of 'Testimony of Metaphors' concerning YHWH. While, like many others, he admits that they can never provide a one-to-one match with that to which they refer, he does maintain that metaphorical speech gave Israel access to YHWH to allow her to "respond to the One testified to as judge, king, or father"[9]. Brueggemann divides the metaphors used for YHWH in the Old Testament into two groups: metaphors of governance[10] and metaphors of sustenance[11]. While he does not speak of the metaphor of YHWH as husband, he does point out that there is a degree of incompatibility between the two groups and that they were often used in combination in order to bear witness to the elusiveness of the subject they portray. The metaphor of YHWH as husband as it is presented in Isa 24–27 implies both a metaphor of sustenance (protection, sustenance, fecundity) and a metaphor of governance (punishment, demands of fidelity,

---

9. W. BRUEGGEMANN, *The Theology of the Old Testament*, Minneapolis, MN, 1997, pp. 230ff..
10. YHWH as judge, YHWH as king, YHWH as warrior, YHWH as father.
11. YHWH as artist, YHWH as healer, YHWH as gardener-vinedresser, YHWH as mother, YHWH as shepherd.

conditions on relationship) and constitutes, perhaps a more inclusive and more realistic metaphor for portraying the divinity.

In the last analysis, the poet(s) of Isa 24–27 sought a means to express their faith and that of their community in YHWH. To this end they employed metaphorical language borrowed from their every day world and from the traditions surrounding them which they couched in poetry of the highest quality. In using metaphor, the poet(s) ultimately confess(es) to an incapacity to grasp the deity in language. As such he/she has to admit that the metaphor simultaneously speaks of what/who YHWH *is* and what/who YHWH *is not*. Together with Brueggemann we conclude, therefore, that "Failure to take seriously the 'is not' quality of the noun [as metaphor] is a failure to recognise that the noun is metaphor and cannot draw closer to the Subject [God] than through the practice of metaphor."[12]

---

12. BRUEGGEMANN, *Theology*, p. 231.

APPENDIX
TEXT-GRAMMATICAL ANALYSIS
In Dialogue with Alviero Niccacci

For a variety of reasons, biblical scholars in recent years have experienced the lack of an adequate approach to the syntax of Biblical Hebrew which goes beyond those fashioned by the European, Latin mould with its roots in the middle ages[1]. Among those scholars who have endeavoured to fill this lacuna is Alviero Niccacci whose work, published in English under the title *The Syntax of the Verb in Classical Hebrew Prose*[2] will constitute the basic text for the present approach to the grammar of Isa 24–27. Given that Niccacci's work has not received universal approval, it would seem appropriate at this stage to offer the reader a critical discussion of Niccacci's approach which locates him within the history of research into the topic, discusses his methodology and reviews the reception of his work. At the same time, given the fact that Niccacci, and indeed other grammarians, have focused entirely on prose texts, it will be incumbent on the present writer to explain the viability and value of applying such 'rules' to poetical texts. We will conclude this introduction with a statement of the limited aims of the present analysis.

A. Niccacci and the History of Research

As C.H.J. van der Merwe points out, the problem of Biblical Hebrew turns around its verbal system and the 'oppositions' it entails: *qatal-yiqtol*, *wayyiqtol-w^{e}qatal*, and (w^e)*x-qatal* – (w^e)*x-yiqtol*. Early Jewish grammarians, he notes, simply valued the *qatal-yiqtol* opposition as a tensed 'past-present' opposition. Later grammarians, especially since the mid-19th century have tended to speak of the Hebrew verbal system as aspectual, primarily as expressing 'complete' versus 'incomplete' modes. This latter perspective has continued into many 20th-century grammars. Revisions of traditional grammars such as Joüon-Muraoka[3] have tended to view Hebrew verb forms as expressing both tense and aspect. Such grammars, however, have also been inclined to treat verb forms isolation, rather than in the context of their actual use and function

---

1. A good outline of the restrictive elements of such grammars and the reasons which prompted the renewed approach to the study of the syntax of Biblical Hebrew can be found in C.H.J. van der Merwe, *An Overview of Hebrew Narrative Syntax*, in E. van Wolde (ed.), *Narrative Syntax and the Hebrew Bible. Papers of the Tilburg Conference 1996*, Leiden, 1996, pp. 1-20.

2. A. Niccacci, *The Syntax of the Verb in Classical Hebrew Prose* (JSOT SS, 86), Sheffield, 1990. This volume is a translation of A. Niccacci, *Sintassi del verbo ebraico nella prosa biblica classica* (Studium Biblicum Franciscum Analecta, 23), Jerusalem, 1986.

3. P. Joüon and T. Muraoka, *A Grammar of Biblical Hebrew* (Subsidia Biblica, 14/I-II), Rome, 1991.

in a text. Specific questions concerning the verb forms of Biblical Hebrew as they function within larger texts (beyond the sentence) or the function of Hebrew word order have been the focus of more recent research.

Those who endeavour to address questions related to the function of the Hebrew verbal system have their roots, for the most part, in the theoretical concepts of H. Weinrich[4]. Weinrich's approach makes a distinction, with respect to verb forms, between *discursive* communication which refers to the actual situation of the act of communication and to *narrative* communication which refers to "acts of facts outside the domain shared by the speaker and the listener"[5]. At the same time, a verbal system, for Weinrich, has to distinguish between what van der Merwe translates as 'text relief', namely *background* or *foreground* communication and 'perspective', namely *prior, simultaneous* or *after* the actual communication[6]. Niccacci notes in his foreword[7] that W. Schneider[8] employed Weinrich's 'text linguistic' theoretical model to move away from the traditional syntactical analysis, which treats verb forms in isolation from their context, in order to study verb forms in texts and in relation to their associated linguistic markers. For Schneider, narrative communication is signalled by the use of *wayyiqtol* and discursive communication by the *yiqtol* and *q^{e}tol* forms. Thus he takes his leave of the tense/aspect dispute by relating the use of *wayyiqtol* and *yiqtol* forms to the orientation of the speaker. At the same time, the main line (foreground information) of a narrative is carried by *wayyiqtol* forms and its secondary line (or background information) is carried by *qatal* forms. Background information is frequently given in (*w^e*)*x-qatal* clauses which Schneider refers to as 'compound nominal clauses' since they tend to describe situations rather than actions. Where discursive communication is concerned, the foreground tends to be carried by *yiqtol* and *q^{e}tol* forms and the background by *qatal* and *w^{e}qatal* forms. Shifts of speaker orientation in a text, for Schneider, are marked by a shift of tense.

It is against this background that we can locate A. Niccacci's own approach to Hebrew syntax. Niccacci likewise distinguishes between two

---

4. H. WEINRICH, *Tempus: besprochene und erzählte Welt* (Sprache und Literatur, 16), Stuttgart, 1964.
5. E. TALSTRA, *Text Grammar and Biblical Hebrew: The Viewpoint of Wolfgang Schneider*, in *Journal of Translation and Textlinguistics* 5 (1992), 269-287, esp. p. 271.
6. VAN DER MERWE, *An Overview*, p. 10.
7. NICCACCI, *The Syntax of the Verb*, pp. 9-12.
8. W. SCHNEIDER, *Grammatik des biblischen Hebräisch*, Munich, 1982[5].

orientations on the part of the speaker (linguistic attitude: *Sprechhaltung*): narration (facts in progress) and discourse or direct speech (comment, facts in the past). Foreground (emphasis, *Reliefgebung*, main line of) communication in narrative is carried by *wayyiqtol* forms and background (subsidiary line of) communication by (w^e)*x-qatal*, (w^e)*x-yiqtol*, *w^{e}qatal* and simple nominal clauses. In discourse, foreground is indicated by *w^{e}qatal* and background by (w^e)*x-yiqtol*, on the axis of the future (or anticipated information). Both foreground and background are represented by a simple nominal clause on the axis of the present (or degree zero). On the axis of the past (or recovered information) כי אשר etc. + *qatal* and (w^e)*x-qatal* represent background information in both narrative and discourse[9]. According to van der Merwe, however, Niccacci also speaks of tenses and aspect in Biblical Hebrew[10]. Perhaps the most controversial aspect of Niccacci's syntax is his use of the expression 'compound noun clause' to designate clauses in which the verb does not occupy first position, i.e. (w^e)*x-qatal* and (w^e)*x-yiqtol* clauses. He maintains that such word order, at the sentence level, imposes a degree of emphasis on the *x* element of the clause, making it the predicate. At the same time, at the wider level of the text, such clauses indicate a degree of subordination or dependence between one sentence/clause and another.

Niccacci's intention is to examine the function (syntax) of verb forms (morphology) in the context of texts. His approach is that associated with text linguistics, going beyond the sentence to examine verbs and their order in a textual unit, independently of everything else such as conjugation, date, genre etc.. His study is purely synchronic because he believes there is a need to examine verbs in texts and not in isolation from texts (i.e. the diachronic growth of verb forms and their functions). Thus the verb needs to be studied in connection with all the linguistic signs present in the text. Verb forms for Niccacci are not only reflective of changes in aspect (complete/incomplete) and changes in tense although they include these dimensions.

It will be clear by now that in spite of its shortcomings (see *Reception* below), Niccacci's work is much in line with that of Schneider although it does not exclude reference to more traditional grammatical categories such as tense and aspect. At the same time, it will be equally clear that Niccacci's approach endeavours to deal with aspects of the Hebrew verbal system as well as questions of word order and its function/significance.

---

9. See the more detailed summary in NICCACCI. *The Syntax of the Verb*, pp. 168ff.
10. VAN DER MERWE. *An Overview*, p. 12.

Methodology/ Terminology

In his recent contribution to the 1996 Tilburg Conference[11], Niccacci outlines his methodology as follows: begin with the identification of grammatical constructions (sentence types), endeavour to understand the function of the sentence types (syntax: the relationship between different types of sentence), examine the role of the various sentence types in shaping a text. Niccacci identifies different basic types of sentence based on the model of Arabic grammarians which he finds better suited to Hebrew syntax than the generally accepted definitions: "... a verbal clause begins with a verb, a noun clause begins with a noun. A verbal clause tells us *what the subject does*, in other words, what the action is; a noun clause tells us *who the subject is*. If a noun is followed by a verb the noun clause is complex."[12] Thus Niccacci proposes three different sentence types: the *simple noun clause* which does not contain a finite verb (henceforth SNC) the *verbal clause* which does contain a verbal form (henceforth VC) and the *complex noun clause* which contains a finite verbal form but not in the first position (henceforth CNC). The present analysis of Isa 24-27 follows Niccacci's terminology in the awareness that it has not been universally accepted but in the conviction that it is of value in distinguishing sentence types and their functions and discerning how sentence types relate to one another in a larger textual corpus.

---

11. A. NICCACCI, *Basic Facts and Theory of the Biblical Hebrew Verb System in Prose*, in E. VAN WOLDE (ed.), *Narrative Syntax and the Hebrew Bible. Papers of the Tilburg Conference 1996*, Leiden, 1996, pp. 167-202.
12. NICCACCI, *The Syntax of the Verb*, p. 23. Sentence types are referred to with a variety of terminology in the literature. While it has to be admitted that Niccacci's terms (for which he is indebted to Schneider and Talstra) are sometimes applied with a degree of ambiguity in his work – the terminology employed in *The Syntax of the Verb* is conspicuously absent from his later article *Basic Facts*–, they continue to serve the purposes of the present work. An alternative and perhaps more functional set of reference terms proposed by M. Vervenne (*Hebrew Verb Form and Function. A Syntactic Case Study with Reference to a Linguistic Data Base*, in ASSOCIATION INTERNATIONALE BIBLE ET INFORMATIQUE, *Bible et informatique: méthodes, outils, résultats*, Jerusalem, 1988, pp. 605-640) which speaks of finite clauses, non-finite clauses and verbless sentences (depending on the amount of 'verb phrase structure' employed) is clearly of value for questions related to the Hebrew verbal system as a whole but lacks the option of dealing with questions concerning the position (word order) of the finite verb in the sentence and its significance. Niccacci's analysis of what he calls the *Complex Noun Clause* focuses on sentences in which a finite verb is present but does not adopt the first position in the sentence. Minor adaptation of Niccacci's terminology allows for better English: *Simple Nominal Clause / Compound Nominal Clause* (*pace* Watson).

Reception

The reception of Niccacci's *Syntax of the Verb* have been mixed. Some reviewers exhibit more general doubts as to whether the biblical writer was subject to such complex syntactical rules[13], while others lament the complexity of Niccacci's presentation as well as his "indifférence à la diachronie interne au corpus"[14]. Others still are unconvinced of his assertion that the first position in a clause is reserved for the predicate (essential to his explanation of the CNC) and lament the apparent absence of a discussion of non-finite verbal forms which Niccacci would seem to have treated as nouns[15]. A number of reviewers, in contrast, suggest that Niccacci's work is indispensable, a refreshing approach to the difficult problem of verb forms in Biblical Hebrew[16].

More substantial criticism of Niccacci's work can be found in the critical analysis offered by van der Merwe[17]. While he generously forgives Niccacci and others for their inconsistency and ambiguity with respect to terminology, putting this down to the fact that the field of study is 'still finding its feet', he objects to the suggestion that emphasis is involved with every CNC and even calls into question the very concept of emphasis in favour of "the well-defined semantic-pragmatic concept focus"[18] which can be both pre- and post-verbal. Ultimately, van der Merwe suggests that Niccacci has not achieved what he set out to achieve, namely "a method of analyzing all the elements of a sentence in the framework of the text", because he has tended to focus on Biblical Hebrew as an abstract system. For van der Merwe, in contrast, it is important that we study the "structures and formulae displayed in specific communication processes" which involve "both the conceptual and social world of all

---

13. J. SCHARBERT, review of A. NICCACCI, *The Syntax of the Verb in Classical Hebrew Prose* (JSOT SS, 86), (Sheffield, 1990), in *BZ* 38 (1994) 312-313.

14. J.-M. LÉONARD, review of A. NICCACCI, *The Syntax of the Verb in Classical Hebrew Prose* (JSOT SS, 86), (Sheffield, 1990), in *ETR* 67 (1992) 103-104.

15. A. VERHEIJ, review of A. NICCACCI, *The Syntax of the Verb in Classical Hebrew Prose* (JSOT SS, 86), (Sheffield, 1990), in *BiOr* 49 (1992) 214-217.

16. J.D.W. WATTS, review of A. NICCACCI, *The Syntax of the Verb in Classical Hebrew Prose* (JSOT SS, 86), (Sheffield, 1990), in *R&E* 88 (1991) 96; J.T.A.G.M. VAN RUITEN, review of A. NICCACCI, *The Syntax of the Verb in Classical Hebrew Prose* (JSOT SS, 86), (Sheffield, 1990), in *Bijdragen* 54 (1993) 201.

17. C.H.J. VAN DER MERWE, *A Critical Analysis of Narrative Syntactic Approaches, with Special Attention to their Relationship to Discourse Analysis*, in E. VAN WOLDE (ed.), *Narrative Syntax and the Hebrew Bible. Papers of the Tilburg Conference 1996*, Leiden, 1996, pp. 133-156.

18. W. GROSSE, *Die Satzteilfolge im Verbalsatz alttestamentlicher Prosa*, Tübingen, 1996. A. DISSE, *Informationsstrukture im Biblischen Hebräisch. Sprachwissenschaftliche Grundlagen und Exegetische Konsequenzen einer Korpus Untersuchung zu Büchern Deuteronomium, Richter und 2 Könige*, Diss. Universität Tübingen, 1996.

the participants in- and outside the text of the Old Testament. When you embark upon this approach to Biblical Hebrew you cannot escape the fact that you are in the domain of the study of language use. In other words, you are studying human communication and human communication is as complex as human beings can be."[19] In light of this, our approach will be governed by a 'controlling framework', that of the conventions of Biblical Hebrew poetry, which allows for intervention of the complexity of human creativity in the process of communication. At the same time, syntactic divisions within the textual complex will endeavour to take the participants in- and outside of the text into consideration.

Application to Poetry

A word needs to be said here concerning the application of Niccacci's prose based Hebrew syntax to the poetic text of Isa 24–27. Niccacci himself notes that, where biblical poetry is concerned, the use of verb forms probably had its own rules which differed from those of prose. For a variety of reasons, he notes, it is more difficult to present the use of verb forms in poetry than in prose. Ugaritic poetry, some archaic poetry from the Pentateuch and some of the Psalms[20] have shown that *yiqtol* forms, for example, can be regarded as ubiquitous with respect to temporal perspective, including the past even without a prefixed *waw*. In addition, it is characteristic of biblical poetry to use *yiqtol//qatal*[21] or *qatal//yiqtol*[22] for the same temporal perspective in parallel cola between verbs of the same root and verbs of different roots. If this is the case, then verb forms in Hebrew poetry must be considered fluid with respect to temporal perspective. While some have endeavoured to establish a single set of rules for both prose and poetry[23], the problem still remains that certain features of poetic style such as the desire for variety, chiastic structure, the demands of parallelism etc. ultimately 'interfere' with the prose 'rules'[24]. The poetic preference for asyndeton in Isa 24–27, for example, will create situations where the poetic text will not follow the

---

19. VAN DER MERWE, *Critical Analysis*, p. 151.
20. Gen 49; Exod 15; Num 23-24; Judg 5; Deut 32-33; Pss 18; 29; 79.
21. Hos 5,5; Ps 38,12.
22. Ps 93,3.
23. See, for example, W. GROSS, *Verbform und Funktion, wayyiqtol für die Gegenwart? Ein Beitrag zur Syntax poetischer althebräischer Texte*, St. Ottilien, 1976; ID., A. DISSE, A. MICHEL (eds.), *Die Satzteilfolge im Verbalsatz alttestamentlicher Prosa: untersucht an den Büchern Dtn, Ri und 2 Kön* (FAT, 17), Tübingen, 1996.
24. Cf. W.T.W. CLOETE, *Versification and Syntax in Jeremiah 2–25. Syntactical Constraints in Hebrew Colometry* (SBL DS, 117), Atlanta, GA, 1989. Special reference should be made to his critical survey of syntactical approaches to Hebrew verse (pp. 61-101).

rules governing prose. In this event it becomes difficult to determine the temporal perspective of an action in a poetic text. For poetry then, according to Niccacci, the temporal perspective of the verb form, "has to be determined on the basis of context and other exegetical factors"[25]. Niccacci ultimately maintains that verbs behave differently in the poetic context because of the constraints of style. He is particularly convinced, for example, that the criteria governing the word order associated with compound nominal clauses does not hold for poetry in which, he maintains, word order is governed by prosody or similar criteria[26].

A brief outline distinction between Hebrew poetry and Hebrew prose seems necessary at this point. Niccacci himself provides such an outline: (1) segmented versus linear communication; (2) parallelism of similar bits of information versus sequence of different bits of information; (3) non-detectable versus detectable verbal system[27]. Ultimately, only the first two elements of this outlined are addressed by Niccacci. He maintains that segmented communication employing parallel bits of information also has a grammatical structure. The lines of Hebrew poetry can therefore be identified according to their clause type (VC, SNC, CNC). The following considerations must be borne in mind, therefore, as one approaches the grammatical analysis of the text of Isa 24–27:

1. It seems possible, and thus reasonable, to attempt to identify clause types in poetry although we have to bear in mind that their shape may (or may not) be governed by the constraints of poetry rather than the syntactical rules of prose. Niccacci has recently written on the phenomenon of Hebrew poetry, insisting that one has to understand the relationship between the parallel lines on the basis of grammatical structure. For Niccacci, parallel poetical lines consist of grammatical units (constituting complete sentences)[28]. The present analysis thus allows the reader to compare parallel lines on the basis of their grammatical structure and to identify the poetical use of grammatical patterns. It should be noted in this context that the first line of a bicolon or tricolon frequently follows the syntax of prose while the second or third lines are more open to variation.

2. Van der Merwe insists that we focus our attention on the participants in and outside the text. Much of the division of the units in the

---

25. NICCACCI, *The Syntax of the Verb*, p. 197.
26. A. NICCACCI, *Syntactic Analysis of Ruth*, in *Liber Annuus. Studium Biblicum Franciscanum* 45 (1995) 69-106, p. 80, n. 20.
27. A. NICCACCI, *Analysing Biblical Hebrew Poetry*, in *JSOT* 74 (1997) 77-93, esp. pp. 77-78.
28. NICCACCI, *Analyzing Biblical Hebrew Poetry*, p. 93.

present analysis is based on a change of actants rather than a change of clause type.

3. As far as the verb is concerned, Niccacci is convinced that the semantic dimensions thereof, i.e. significance for translation, are primarily a function of variable forms in variable environments. The variable environment of Isa 24–27 is that of Hebrew poetry. A well informed awareness of the constraints of Hebrew poetry can, at least to a degree, allow us some access to the syntactic functioning of the text.

4. I would venture to suggest a final, common sense related argument for the efficacy, if limited, of applying a prose based syntax to a poetical text. Language, indeed every form of human communication, is not without shape and structure. While many might disagree about the detailed explanation thereof, few would argue that the Hebrew language as such exhibits no syntactical formation. Where do we begin in our approach to the syntax of a language? Given the fact that narrative is close to everyday communication it would seem appropriate that we begin here and that we focus our attention at first on the verbal system. If, along with Niccacci, however, we maintain that Hebrew poetry is a mystery, governed by the 'joy of disorder', we are almost admitting that the communication involved in a poetical text is so far removed from everyday human communication that it simply cannot be grasped. If we maintain that the syntax of language in all its forms (narrative, discursive, poetic) can be accessed (as substantially coherent) at one level, i.e. narrative prose, and not at another, i.e. poetry, we are almost suggesting that poetry is impossible to grasp (is substantially incoherent) as a means of communication. Few commentators, I believe, would be willing to subscribe to such an assertion.

Aims of the Present Analysis

What follows in this text-grammatical analysis of the poetry of Isa 24–27 is an attempt to distinguish the various syntactic units in each chapter, from the basic clause to larger units of dependant clauses, to identify the clause type[29], and to establish the hierarchy of dependence between the clauses towards the delimitation of larger units. In an effort to see what we can learn about the text, the terminology and rules determined by Niccacci for the analysis of the syntax of the verb in prose will be used where appropriate, while priority will be given to the peculiar

---

29. SNC (simple nominal clause) or so-called 'verbless sentences'; CNC (compound nominal clause) in which the verb is preceded by x, VC (verbal clause) in which the verb is in the first position.

features of Hebrew poetry in the analysis, including semantics[30]. The temporal perspectives of the verb forms, therefore, will be determined primarily, as Niccacci suggests, on the basis of their context[31].

The first part of the analysis will display each clause of the Hebrew text in four columns[32]. Column 1 will contain exclamatory particles, deictic terms etc., which do not effect the syntactical shape of the text; column 2 will contain verbal clauses (VC); column 3 will contain compound nominal clauses (CNC); column 4 will contain simple nominal clauses (SNC). Hierarchical dependence (hypotaxis) will be shown by placing dependent clause immediately below each other. Where there is a break in dependence there will be a blank line in the schema. The smallest syntactical units (single clauses or sentences), intermediate syntactical units (groups of hierarchically dependent clauses or sentences) and main syntactical units (demarcated by changes in actant, linguistic attitude etc[33].) will then become clear. *The second part* of the analysis will set about the much more complex task of determining clause or sentence type, linguistic attitude (narrative, discursive), prominence (foreground, background), and, where possible, linguistic perspective (degree zero, recovered information, anticipated information)[34] while bearing in mind the priority of the peculiarities of Hebrew poetry. H.C. Brichto points out the importance of syntactical analysis of a text: "…poetics is a study of texts for meaning(s); and one of the first problems for the literary analyst studying literature in a language not his own is that of producing a faithful translation. And the art of translation requires a grasp of the full range of the possible functions of syntactic options"[35].

S.J. Schmidt has pointed out that syntactic analysis involves two kinds of operations: a segmentation of structure assigned to the text at the

---

30. NICCACCI (*The Syntax of the Verb*, p. 163) agrees with E. TALSTRA (*Text Grammar and Hebrew Bible. I: Elements of a Theory*, in *BiOr* 35 (1978) 169-74; *Text Grammar and Hebrew Bible. II: Syntax and Semantics*, in *BiOr* 39 (1978) 26-38) that even in prose, the value of semantics has to be given its place, even if it is secondary to syntax and morphology. He notes in addition (p. 206, n. 94) that first positioning in Hebrew poetry need not imply emphasis as is often the case in prose but may be determined by other factors.
31. NICCACCI, *The Syntax of the Verb*, p. 197.
32. Framing formulae will be placed in brackets <>.
33. For a brief outline definition of the terminology used by Niccacci see *The Syntax of the Verb*, pp. 20-22.
34. NICCACCI, *The Syntax of the Verb*, pp. 168-169.
35. H.C. BRICHTO, *Toward a Grammar of Biblical Poetics. Tales of the Prophets*, New York – Oxford, 1992, pp. 17-18. Brichto's work here focuses on narrative, non-poetic texts.

level of the elementary units and a syntactic disambiguation that integrates units into syntactically coherent complexes[36]. Continuation, delimitation and coherence at the syntactic level are thus of primary importance in such an analysis and, I believe, are not inaccessible where poetry is concerned. If we have achieved these latter goals then the following pages are of value. As we noted at the outset, however, this 'text-grammar' together with the translation and Hebrew colometry are primarily a tool to assist in our discernment and reading of the metaphors in Isa 24–27.

---

36. S.J. SCHMIDT, *Some Problems of Communicative Text Theories*, in W. DRESSLER (ed.), *Current Trends in Linguistics*, Berlin, 1978, p. 57.

Clause Hierarchy

	SNC	CNC	VC		
	יְהוָה בּוֹקֵק הָאָרֶץ			הִנֵּה	24,1a
	וּבוֹלְקָהּ				b
		וְעִוָּה פָנֶיהָ			c
		וְהֵפִיץ יֹשְׁבֶיהָ			d
			וְהָיָה		2a
		כָעָם כַּכֹּהֵן			b
		כַּעֶבֶד כַּאדֹנָיו			c
		כַּשִּׁפְחָה כַּגְּבִרְתָּהּ			d
		כַּקּוֹנֶה כַּמּוֹכֵר			e
		כַּמַּלְוֶה כַּלֹּוֶה			f
		כַּנֹּשֶׁה			g
		כַּאֲשֶׁר נֹשֵׁא בוֹ			h
		הִבּוֹק תִּבּוֹק הָאָרֶץ			3a
		וְהִבּוֹז ׀ תִּבּוֹז			b
		<יְהוָה דִּבֶּר אֶת־הַדָּבָר הַזֶּה>		כִּי	
			אָבְלָה		4a
			נָבְלָה הָאָרֶץ		b
			אֻמְלְלָה		c
			נָבְלָה תֵבֵל		d
			אֻמְלָלוּ מְרוֹם עַם־הָאָרֶץ		e
	וְהָאָרֶץ חָנְפָה תַּחַת יֹשְׁבֶיהָ				5a

TEXT-GRAMMATICAL ANALYSIS

	SNC	CNC	VC	
b			כִּי־ עָבְרוּ תוֹרֹת֙	
c			חָלְפוּ חֹק	
d			הֵפֵרוּ בְּרִית עוֹלָם	
6a	עַל־כֵּן	אָלָה֙ אָכְלָה אֶ֔רֶץ		
b			וַיֶּאְשְׁמוּ יֹשְׁבֵי בָהּ	
c	עַל־כֵּן	חָרוּ יֹשְׁבֵי אֶ֔רֶץ		
d			וְנִשְׁאַר אֱנוֹשׁ מִזְעָר	
7a			אָבַל תִּיר֔וֹשׁ	
b			אֻמְלְלָה־גָפֶן	
c			נֶאֶנְחוּ כָּל־שִׂמְחֵי־לֵב	
8a			שָׁבַת֙ מְשׂוֹשׂ תֻּפִּ֔ים	
b			חָדַל שְׁאוֹן עַלִּיזִ֔ים	
c			שָׁבַת מְשׂוֹשׂ כִּנּוֹר	
9a	בַּשִּׁיר		לֹא יִשְׁתּוּ־יָ֑יִן	
b			יֵמַר שֵׁכָר לְשֹׁתָיו	
10a			נִשְׁבְּרָה קִרְיַת־תֹּ֑הוּ	
b			סֻגַּר כָּל־בַּיִת מִבּוֹא	
11a	צְוָחָה עַל־הַיַּיִן בַּחוּצוֹת			
b			עָרְבָה֙ כָּל־שִׂמְחָ֔ה	
c			גָּלָה מְשׂוֹשׂ הָאָרֶץ	

	SNC	CNC	VC	
			נִשְׁאַר בָּעִיר שַׁמָּה	12a
			וּשְׁאִיָּה יֻכַּת־שָׁעַר	b
	כִּי	כֹה יִהְיֶה בְּקֶרֶב הָאָרֶץ		13a
		בְּתוֹךְ הָעַמִּים		b
		כְּנֹקֶף זַיִת		c
		כְּעוֹלֵלֹת		d
		אִם־כָּלָה בָצִיר		e

		הֵמָּה	יִשְׂאוּ קוֹלָם	14a
			יָרֹנּוּ בִּגְאוֹן יְהוָה	b
			צָהֲלוּ מִיָּם	c
	עַל־כֵּן		בָּאֻרִים כַּבְּדוּ יְהוָה	15a
			בְּאִיֵּי הַיָּם שֵׁם יְהוָה אֱלֹהֵי יִשְׂרָאֵל	b
			מִכְּנַף הָאָרֶץ זְמִרֹת שָׁמַעְנוּ	16a
			צְבִי לַצַּדִּיק	b

			וָאֹמַר	16c
			רָזִי־לִי	d
			רָזִי־לִי	e
			אוֹי לִי	f

TEXT-GRAMMATICAL ANALYSIS

SNC	CNC	VC	
	בְּגָדִים בָּגָדוּ		g
	וּבֶגֶד בּוֹגְדִים בָּגָדוּ		h
פַּחַד וָפַחַת וָפָח			17
עָלֶיךָ יוֹשֵׁב הָאָרֶץ			
		וְהָיָה	18a
הַנָּס מִקּוֹל הַפַּחַד יִפֹּל אֶל־הַפַּחַת			b
וְהָעוֹלֶה מִתּוֹךְ הַפַּחַת יִלָּכֵד בַּפָּח			c
אֲרֻבּוֹת מִמָּרוֹם נִפְתָּחוּ		כִּי־	18d
	וַיִּרְעֲשׁוּ מוֹסְדֵי אָרֶץ		e
רֹעָה הִתְרֹעֲעָה הָאָרֶץ			19a
פּוֹר הִתְפּוֹרְרָה אֶרֶץ			b
מוֹט הִתְמוֹטְטָה אָרֶץ			c
נוֹעַ תָּנוּעַ אֶרֶץ כַּשִּׁכּוֹר			20a
וְהִתְנוֹדְדָה כַּמְּלוּנָה			b
וְכָבַד עָלֶיהָ פִּשְׁעָהּ			c
וְנָפְלָה			d
וְלֹא־תֹסִיף קוּם			e

		SNC	CNC	VC
21a		‹וְהָיָה֙ בַּיּ֣וֹם הַה֔וּא›		
b			יִפְקֹ֧ד יְהוָ֛ה עַל־צְבָ֥א הַמָּר֖וֹם בַּמָּר֑וֹם	
c			וְעַל־מַלְכֵ֥י הָאֲדָמָ֖ה עַל־הָאֲדָמָֽה	
22a			וְאֻסְּפ֨וּ אֲסֵפָ֤ה אַסִּיר֙ עַל־בּ֔וֹר	
b			וְסֻגְּר֖וּ עַל־מַסְגֵּ֑ר	
c			וּמֵרֹ֥ב יָמִ֖ים יִפָּקֵֽדוּ	
23a			וְחָֽפְרָה֙ הַלְּבָנָ֔ה	
b			וּבוֹשָׁ֖ה הַֽחַמָּ֑ה	
c	כִּֽי־		מָלַ֞ךְ יְהוָ֤ה צְבָאוֹת֙ בְּהַ֣ר צִיּ֔וֹן	
d			וּבִירוּשָׁלִַ֑ם	
e			וְנֶ֥גֶד זְקֵנָ֖יו כָּבֽוֹד	
25,1a	יְהוָ֤ה אֱלֹהַי֙ אַתָּ֔ה			
b			אֲרֽוֹמִמְךָ֙	
c			אוֹדֶ֣ה שִׁמְךָ֔	
d	כִּ֥י		עָשִׂ֖יתָ פֶּ֑לֶא עֵצ֥וֹת מֵֽרָח֖וֹק אֱמ֥וּנָה אֹֽמֶן	
2a	כִּ֣י		שַׂ֤מְתָּ מֵעִיר֙ לַגָּ֔ל קִרְיָ֥ה בְצוּרָ֖ה לְמַפֵּלָ֑ה	
b			אַרְמ֤וֹן זָרִים֙ מֵעִ֔יר	
c			לְעוֹלָ֖ם לֹ֥א יִבָּנֶֽה	

TEXT-GRAMMATICAL ANALYSIS

	SNC	CNC	VC	
3a			עַל־כֵּן יְכַבְּדוּךָ עַם־עָז	
b			קִרְיַת גּוֹיִם עָרִיצִים יִירָאוּךָ	

4a	כִּי	הָיִיתָ מָעוֹז לַדָּל	
b		מָעוֹז לָאֶבְיוֹן בַּצַּר־לוֹ	
c		מַחְסֶה מִזֶּרֶם	
d		צֵל מֵחֹרֶב	
e	כִּי		רוּחַ עָרִיצִים כְּזֶרֶם קִיר
5a			כְּחֹרֶב בְּצָיוֹן שְׁאוֹן זָרִים
b		תַּכְנִיעַ חֹרֶב בְּצֵל עָב	
c		זְמִיר עָרִיצִים יַעֲנֶה	

6a		וְעָשָׂה יְהוָה צְבָאוֹת	
		לְכָל־הָעַמִּים בָּהָר הַזֶּה	
b		מִשְׁתֵּה שְׁמָנִים מִשְׁתֵּה שְׁמָרִים	
c		שְׁמָנִים מְמֻחָיִם שְׁמָרִים מְזֻקָּקִים	
7a		וּבִלַּע בָּהָר הַזֶּה	
b		פְּנֵי־הַלּוֹט ׀ הַלּוֹט עַל־כָּל־הָעַמִּים	
c		וְהַמַּסֵּכָה הַנְּסוּכָה עַל־כָּל־הַגּוֹיִם	
8a		בִּלַּע הַמָּוֶת לָנֶצַח	
b		וּמָחָה אֲדֹנָי יְהוִה דִּמְעָה מֵעַל כָּל־פָּנִים	
c		וְחֶרְפַּת עַמּוֹ יָסִיר מֵעַל כָּל־הָאָרֶץ	
d	<כִּי יְהוָה דִּבֵּר>		

		SNC	CNC	VC
9a				‹וְאָמַר֙ בַּיּ֣וֹם הַה֔וּא›
b		הִנֵּ֨ה	אֱלֹהֵ֥ינוּ זֶ֛ה	
c				קִוִּ֥ינוּ ל֖וֹ
d				וְיוֹשִׁיעֵ֑נוּ
e		זֶ֤ה יְהוָה֙		
f				קִוִּ֣ינוּ ל֔וֹ
g				נָגִ֥ילָה
h				וְנִשְׂמְחָ֖ה בִּישׁוּעָתֽוֹ
10a	כִּֽי־			תָנ֥וּחַ יַד־יְהוָ֖ה בָּהָ֣ר הַזֶּ֑ה
b				וְנָ֤דוֹשׁ מוֹאָב֙ תַּחְתָּ֔יו
c				כְּהִדּ֥וּשׁ מַתְבֵּ֖ן בְּמֵ֥י מַדְמֵנָֽה
11a				וּפֵרַ֤שׂ יָדָיו֙ בְּקִרְבּ֔וֹ
b				כַּאֲשֶׁ֛ר יְפָרֵ֥שׂ הַשֹּׂחֶ֖ה לִשְׂח֑וֹת
c				וְהִשְׁפִּיל֙ גַּֽאֲוָת֔וֹ עִ֖ם אָרְבּ֥וֹת יָדָֽיו
12a				וּמִבְצַ֞ר מִשְׂגַּ֣ב חוֹמֹתֶ֗יךָ הֵשַׁ֧ח
b				הִשְׁפִּ֛יל
c				הִגִּ֥יעַ לָאָ֖רֶץ עַד־עָפָֽר
26,1a				‹בַּיּ֥וֹם הַה֖וּא›
b				יוּשַׁ֥ר הַשִּׁיר־הַזֶּ֖ה בְּאֶ֣רֶץ יְהוּדָ֑ה

TEXT-GRAMMATICAL ANALYSIS

	SNC	CNC	VC	
c	עִיר עָז־לָנוּ			
d	יְשׁוּעָה יָשִׁית חוֹמוֹת וָחֵל			
2a	פִּתְחוּ שְׁעָרִים			
b	וְיָבֹא גוֹי־צַדִּיק שֹׁמֵר אֱמֻנִים			
3a	יֵצֶר סָמוּךְ תִּצֹּר שָׁלוֹם ׀ שָׁלוֹם			
b	כִּי בְךָ בָּטוּחַ			
4a	בִּטְחוּ בַיהוָה עֲדֵי־עַד			
b	כִּי	בְּיָהּ יְהוָה צוּר עוֹלָמִים		
5a	כִּי	הֵשַׁח יֹשְׁבֵי מָרוֹם		
b	קִרְיָה נִשְׂגָּבָה יַשְׁפִּילֶנָּה			
c	יַשְׁפִּילָהּ עַד־אֶרֶץ			
d	יַגִּיעֶנָּה עַד־עָפָר			
6a	תִּרְמְסֶנָּה רָגֶל			
b	רַגְלֵי עָנִי			
c	פַּעֲמֵי דַלִּים			
7a	אֹרַח לַצַּדִּיק מֵישָׁרִים			
b	יָשָׁר מַעְגַּל צַדִּיק תְּפַלֵּס			
8a	אַף	אֹרַח מִשְׁפָּטֶיךָ יְהוָה קִוִּינוּךָ		
b	לְשִׁמְךָ וּלְזִכְרְךָ תַּאֲוַת־נָפֶשׁ			

	VC	CNC	SNC	
9a			נַפְשִׁי אִוִּיתִךָ בַּלַּיְלָה	
b	אַף־		רוּחִי בְקִרְבִּי אֲשַׁחֲרֶךָּ	
c	כִּי		כַּאֲשֶׁר מִשְׁפָּטֶיךָ לָאָרֶץ	
d			צֶדֶק לָמְדוּ יֹשְׁבֵי תֵבֵל	
10a			יֻחַן רָשָׁע	
b			בַּל־לָמַד צֶדֶק	
c			בְּאֶרֶץ נְכֹחוֹת יְעַוֵּל	
d			וּבַל־יִרְאֶה גֵּאוּת יְהוָה	
11a		יְהוָה	רָמָה יָדְךָ	
b			בַּל־יֶחֱזָיוּן	
c			יֶחֱזוּ	
d			וְיֵבֹשׁוּ קִנְאַת־עָם	
e	אַף־		אֵשׁ צָרֶיךָ תֹאכְלֵם	
12a		יְהוָה	תִּשְׁפֹּת שָׁלוֹם לָנוּ	
b	כִּי גַם		כָּל־מַעֲשֵׂינוּ פָּעַלְתָּ לָּנוּ	
13a		יְהוָה אֱלֹהֵינוּ	בְּעָלוּנוּ אֲדֹנִים זוּלָתֶךָ	
b			לְבַד־בְּךָ נַזְכִּיר שְׁמֶךָ	
14a			מֵתִים בַּל־יִחְיוּ	
b			רְפָאִים בַּל־יָקֻמוּ	
c	לָכֵן		פָּקַדְתָּ	
d			וַתַּשְׁמִידֵם	
e			וַתְּאַבֵּד כָּל־זֵכֶר לָמוֹ	

SNC	CNC	VC	#
		יָסַפְתָּ לַגּוֹי יְהוָה	15a
		יָסַפְתָּ לַגּוֹי	b
		נִכְבָּדְתָּ	c
		רִחַקְתָּ כָּל־קַצְוֵי־אָרֶץ	d
	בַּצַּר פְּקָדוּךָ	יְהוָה	16a
	צָקוּן לַחַשׁ		b
מוּסָרְךָ לָמוֹ			c
	כְּמוֹ הָרָה תַּקְרִיב לָלֶדֶת		17a
	תָּחִיל		b
	תִּזְעַק בַּחֲבָלֶיהָ		c
	הָיִינוּ מִפָּנֶיךָ יְהוָה	כֵּן	d
	הָרִינוּ		18a
	חַלְנוּ		b
	יָלַדְנוּ רוּחַ	כְּמוֹ	c
יְשׁוּעֹת בַּל־נַעֲשֶׂה אָרֶץ			d
וּבַל־יִפְּלוּ יֹשְׁבֵי תֵבֵל			e
	יִחְיוּ מֵתֶיךָ		19a
	נְבֵלָתִי יְקוּמוּן		b
	הָקִיצוּ		c
	וְרַנְּנוּ שֹׁכְנֵי עָפָר		d
כִּי טַל אוֹרֹת טַלֶּךָ		כִּי	e
וְאָרֶץ רְפָאִים תַּפִּיל			f

	SNC	CNC	VC	
20a			לֵךְ עַמִּי	
b			בֹּא בַחֲדָרֶיךָ	
c			וּסְגֹר דְּלָתֶיךָ [דְּלָתְךָ] בַּעֲדֶךָ	
d			חֲבִי כִמְעַט־רֶגַע	
e			עַד־יַעֲבוֹר [יַעֲבָר־] זָעַם	
21a	כִּי־הִנֵּה	יְהוָה יֹצֵא מִמְּקוֹמוֹ		
b			לִפְקֹד עֲוֹן יֹשֵׁב־הָאָרֶץ עָלָיו	
c			וְגִלְּתָה הָאָרֶץ אֶת־דָּמֶיהָ	
d			וְלֹא־תְכַסֶּה עוֹד עַל־הֲרוּגֶיהָ	
27,1a			<בַּיּוֹם הַהוּא>	
b			יִפְקֹד יְהוָה בְּחַרְבּוֹ הַקָּשָׁה וְהַגְּדוֹלָה וְהַחֲזָקָה	
c			עַל לִוְיָתָן נָחָשׁ בָּרִחַ	
d			וְעַל לִוְיָתָן נָחָשׁ עֲקַלָּתוֹן	
e			וְהָרַג אֶת־הַתַּנִּין אֲשֶׁר בַּיָּם	
2a			<בַּיּוֹם הַהוּא>	
b			כֶּרֶם חֶמֶד עַנּוּ־לָהּ	

TEXT-GRAMMATICAL ANALYSIS

SNC	CNC	VC		
אֲנִ֤י יְהוָה֙ נֹֽצְרָ֔הּ				3a
לִרְגָעִ֖ים אַשְׁקֶ֑נָּה				b
	פֶּ֚ן	יִפְקֹ֣ד עָלֶ֔יהָ		c
לַ֥יְלָה וָי֖וֹם אֶצֳּרֶֽנָּה				d
חֵמָ֖ה אֵ֣ין לִ֑י				4a
מִֽי־יִתְּנֵ֜נִי שָׁמִ֥יר שַׁ֙יִת֙ בַּמִּלְחָמָ֔ה				b
אֶפְשְׂעָ֣ה בָ֔הּ				c
אֲצִיתֶ֖נָּה יָּֽחַד				d
	א֚וֹ	יַחֲזֵ֣ק בְּמָעוּזִּ֔י		5a
יַעֲשֶׂ֥ה שָׁל֖וֹם לִ֑י				b
שָׁל֖וֹם יַֽעֲשֶׂה־לִּֽי				c
⟨הַבָּאִים⟩ יַשְׁרֵ֣שׁ יַֽעֲקֹ֔ב				6a
יָצִ֥יץ				b
וּפָרַ֖ח יִשְׂרָאֵ֑ל				c
וּמָלְא֥וּ פְנֵי־תֵבֵ֖ל תְּנוּבָֽה				d
הַכְּמַכַּ֥ת מַכֵּ֖הוּ הִכָּ֑הוּ				7a
	אִ֥ם־כְּהֶ֛רֶג הֲרֻגָ֖יו הֹרָֽג			b
בְּסַאסְּאָ֖ה				8a
בְּשַׁלְחָ֣הּ				b
תְּרִיבֶ֑נָּה				c
הָגָ֛ה בְּרוּח֥וֹ הַקָּשָׁ֖ה בְּי֥וֹם קָדִֽים				d

		SNC	CNC	VC	
9a	לָכֵ֗ן			בְּזֹאת֙ יְכֻפַּ֣ר עֲוֺֽן־יַעֲקֹ֔ב	
b				וְזֶ֕ה כָּל־פְּרִ֖י הָסִ֣ר חַטָּאת֑וֹ	
c				בְּשׂוּמ֣וֹ ׀ כָּל־אַבְנֵ֣י מִזְבֵּ֗חַ	
d				כְּאַבְנֵי־גִר֙ מְנֻפָּצ֔וֹת	
e				לֹֽא־יָקֻ֥מוּ אֲשֵׁרִ֖ים וְחַמָּנִֽים	
10a				כִּ֣י עִ֤יר בְּצוּרָה֙ בָּדָ֔ד	
b				נָוֶ֕ה מְשֻׁלָּ֥ח	
c				וְנֶעֱזָ֖ב כַּמִּדְבָּ֑ר	
d		שָׁ֣ם		יִרְעֶ֥ה עֵ֖גֶל	
e		וְשָׁ֣ם		יִרְבָּ֑ץ	
f				וְכִלָּ֖ה סְעִפֶֽיהָ	
11a				בִּיבֹ֤שׁ קְצִירָהּ֙ תִּשָּׁבַ֔רְנָה	
b				נָשִׁ֖ים בָּא֣וֹת	
c				מְאִיר֣וֹת אוֹתָ֑הּ	
d				כִּ֣י לֹ֤א עַם־בִּינוֹת֙ ה֔וּא	
e				עַל־כֵּן֙ לֹֽא־יְרַחֲמֶ֣נּוּ עֹשֵׂ֔הוּ	
f				וְיֹצְר֖וֹ לֹ֥א יְחֻנֶּֽנּוּ	
12a	⟨וְהָיָה֙ בַּיּ֣וֹם הַה֔וּא⟩				
b				יַחְבֹּ֧ט יְהוָ֛ה מִשִּׁבֹּ֥לֶת הַנָּהָ֖ר עַד־נַ֣חַל מִצְרָ֑יִם	
c				וְאַתֶּ֧ם תְּלֻקְּט֛וּ לְאַחַ֥ד אֶחָ֖ד בְּנֵ֥י יִשְׂרָאֵֽל	

	SNC	CNC	VC

13a	‹וְהָיָה בַּיּוֹם הַהוּא›			
b				יִתָּקַע בְּשׁוֹפָר גָּדוֹל
c				וּבָאוּ הָאֹבְדִים בְּאֶרֶץ אַשּׁוּר
d				וְהַנִּדָּחִים בְּאֶרֶץ מִצְרָיִם
e				וְהִשְׁתַּחֲווּ לַיהוָה בְּהַר הַקֹּדֶשׁ בִּירוּשָׁלָ͏ִם

COMMENTARY

24,1-3

1a-b SNC (pro VC): הנה clause: subject + participle + object + participle + suffix
1c-d VC: w^eqatal + object + w^eqatal + object (suffixes refer to הארץ)
2a-f VC: w^eqatal + 6x...כ ...כ construction.

3a-b VC: Infinitive absolute + *yiqtol* + subject + infinitive absolute + *yiqtol*

3c   Framing formula (subject + *qatal* + object)

Although the unit begins with what is clearly a SNC, since it constitutes the opening clause in a text linguistic unit 24,1a-b has the value of a VC. The deictic הנה opens this discursive unit (vv. 1-3), the speaker being the prophet and the actants being YHWH, the land, and the dwellers upon the land. According to Niccacci (N. 168-173), an SNC in discursive speech marks the foreground of communication and is equivalent to the present. The הנה + name + participle clause, however, also underlines the simultaneity of the action with the communication (N. 98). In relation to the w^eqatal clauses dependent upon this opening clause, however, the nuance is one of immediate future, something which is 'about to' happen[37]. In the prophetic experience, however, there is little distinction to be made between immanent future and the present. From this suggestion of immediate future in the participles in 1a-b the unit concludes with a decisive word spoken in the past (background communication, retrieved information in v.3c – *qatal*) and founding the action in a word from YHWH. The primary actant is 'the land' which begins and concludes the unit (v. 1a-d/v. 3a-b). The intervening verb forms (v. 2a, 3a,b $w^eqatals$, foreground communication, anticipated information) deal with the immanent consequences of YHWH's actions for the dwellers of the land and the land itself (i.e. the objects of the verbs) in an alternating fashion:

---

37. While a והיה clause enjoys a degree of independence, it should not be considered initial. It remains dependent on what precedes it (cf. NICCACCI, *The Syntax of the Verb*, p. 182).

24,1a-b Land/Land
1c-d   Land/Dwellers
2a-f   Dwellers (x6)
3a   Land
3b   Land

Smaller syntactic units are distinguished by the change of actant from YHWH to the dwellers of the land in v. 1a-d – v. 2a-f while vv. 3a-b break the w^e-sequence and constitute a new beginning and a smaller unit. As a framing formula, v. 3c stands outside the text-grammatical structure of the unit.

24,4-6

4a-b   VC: asyndetic *qatal* (x2) + subject
4c-d   VC: asyndetic *qatal* (x2) + subject
4e   VC: asyndetic *qatal* + subject
5a   CNC: X + *qatal* + object

5b   VC: כי + *qatal* + object
5c   VC: *qatal* + object
5d   VC: *qatal* + object

6a   CNC (pro VC): על־כן + subject + *qatal* + object
6b   VC: *wayyiqtol* + object

6c   VC: על־כן + *qatal* + subject
6d   VC: w^e*qatal* + subject

The syntactical unit Isa 24,4-6 is marked by the frequent use of asyndetic *qatal* forms. Niccacci notes that *qatal* in discourse always comes first in the sentence. He uses the term '*Qatal* for reporting'. In this sense the *qatals* here are equivalent to the present perfect in English, "a tense which belongs to the 'realm of comment'" (N. 41-43). Although v. 6a is clearly a CNC (x + *qatal*), Niccacci notes that x + *qatal*, as a construction for reporting, comprises a VC "because it corresponds to a simple QATAL. It heads the sentence and is found only in D (discourse) so differing syntactically from retrospective QATAL." Linguistic perspective is degree zero. The first position of the word אלה may also have been governed by a desire for poetic emphasis, although Niccacci would insist that syntactically no emphasis is intended (N. 189). The unit offers a discursive description of what is now happening to the primary actants, the land and its inhabitants, alternating as in the previous unit, between the two. The relative absence of narrative sequence tends to support the present aspect. Description in 4a-5a changes, as in the previous unit, to explanation in 5b-c. The reason for this present state is because the inhabitants of the land have transgressed law and covenant. V. 6a introduces a new actant 'curse', the *qatal* of report being descriptive of what is happening here and now. The four elements 'being consumed'; 'being held guilty'; 'diminishing'; 'being a mere few', each correspond to the *qatals* of the explicative clause in 5b-c. We are led, thereby, to interpret the 'devouring curse' as the consequence of breaking law and statute (i.e. the covenant). The consecutive *qatal* + *wayyiqtol* in v. 6a-b might suggest succession, i.e. as a result of the 'curse', guilt and diminishment are in the land. In any event the *wayyiqtol* in v. 6b is a "continuation *wayyiqtol* which acquires its temporal perspective from the preceding construction" (N. 178). While in prose the change in 6c-d to *qatal* + *wᵉqatal* might suggest lack of succession, in this poetic formation no shift in temporal perspective is implied and the negative consequences are continued in YHWH's further response to the broken covenant. Finally, only two terms have an attributive complement in this unit, namely [עולם] ברית and [מזער] אנוש suggesting by way of the syntax that the two are related.

24,7-13

7a	VC:	asyndetic *qatal* + subject
7b	VC:	asyndetic *qatal* + subject
7c	VC:	asyndetic *qatal* + subject
8a	VC:	asyndetic *qatal* + subject
8b	VC:	asyndetic *qatal* + subject
8c	VC:	asyndetic *qatal* + subject
9a	CNC:	X + לא *yiqtol* + object
9b	VC:	*yiqtol* + subject + ל + indirect object
10a	VC:	asyndetic *qatal* + subject
10b	VC:	asyndetic *qatal* + subject + prepositional phrase
11a	SNC:	subject + locative
11b	VC:	asyndetic *qatal* + subject
11c	VC:	asyndetic *qatal* + subject

12a   VC: asyndetic *qatal* + locative + predicate
12b   CNC: ו + X + *yiqtol* + subject.
13a-d VC: כי + כה + *yiqtol* + locative (x2) +...כ ...כ
13e   VC: *qatal* + subject

The opening of a new syntactical unit is marked by the change in actants. The land and its inhabitants fade into the background while the city of chaos, wine, joy and the other aspects of merrymaking and the city's inhabitants are brought to the fore. Once again the language is descriptive rather than narrative. The preponderance of *qatal* forms suggests 'report' type discourse and is equivalent to the present perfect which has the effect of providing a description of enduring disaster. Vv. 9a, 11a and 12b break the flow of verbal clauses focusing our attention on the transformation which has taken place. 'Song' (v. 9a) which once accompanied wine drinking is now replaced by a 'shriek' (v. 11a) brought on by lack of wine and by 'ruin' (v. 12) which broadly describes the situation in the city. As Niccacci notes, CNCs in discursive speech of the type ו + X + *yiqtol*, as we have here in v. 9a and v. 12b, are background constructions which interrupt the chain of *qatals* and have the effect of emphasising the element 'X' (N. 188-189). The SNC in 11a marks the foreground of communication and is equivalent to the present (N. 171). As in the previous units the actants move alternately in and out of focus. The syntactical unit concludes with a return to former actants 'the land' and 'people' underlined by the two locatives. From the silenced wine-drinkers and the city of chaos in the preceding verses we now turn to the broader picture. The concluding *yiqtol* (v. 13a) indicates foreground communication and anticipated information, i.e. simple future. *Yiqtol*, according to Niccacci, is the temporal perspective for speech as opposed to *wayyiqtol* which is the temporal perspective for narrative (N. 181).

24,14-16b

14a   VC: pronominal subject + *yiqtol* + object
14b   VC: *yiqtol* + object
14c   VC: *qatal* + locative.

15a   CNC (pro VC): עלי-ם + locative + imperative + object
15b   CNC: elliptical imperative + locative + object
16a   CNC: locative + object + *qatal*
16b   SNC: predicate + prepositional phrase

A new syntactical unit begins, once again, with a change of actant. The scene widens even further to include both East and West and the 'peoples' in the widest sense characterised by 'they' with those in the centre (the speakers) characterised by 'we' (v. 16) (modern 'them' and 'us'). The personal pronoun המה at the beginning of v. 14a is given a prominent position in the clause which serves to separate it from the previous unit (vv. 7-13). The deictic על־כן separates vv. 15a-16b from the previous smaller unit (v. 14a-c). V. 15a, while clearly a CNC has the equivalent status of a VC in opening a new smaller unit. Poetic technique seems to have intervened here placing the verb in the second position for the sake of parallelism with v. 15b. Again the CNC's in vv. 15b-16c function to give emphasis to the 'X' elements, the 'islands' and the 'edges of the earth'. The smaller unit vv. 15a-16b constitutes direct speech and is closed by an SNC which suggests simultaneity with what precedes and describes the content of the זמרת of v. 16a.

24,16c-18c

16c   VC: *wayyiqtol*

16d   SNC: subject + nominal predicate
16e   SNC: subject + nominal predicate
16f   SNC: subject + nominal predicate
16g   CNC: X + *qatal*
16h   CNC: X + *qatal*
17   SNC: subject (x3) + predicate (עליך) + vocative (יושב הארץ)

18a   VC: (autonomous והיה)
18b   CNC: X + locative + *yiqtol* + locative
18c   CNC: X + locative + *yiqtol* + locative

Once again a new syntactical unit is introduced by a change of primary actant. 'I' is now the point of focus, a fact hammered home by the juxtapositional ו and the repetition of the nominal clauses. The *wayyiqtol* in 16c provides succession and relationship with the previous unit while at the same time introducing direct speech which continues up to the end of v. 17 where it is closed by a vocative which identifies the addressee using a collective singular and relating them to the actants of vv. 1,5,6 (ישבי בה/ישביה). While emaciation is the lot of the speaker in v. 16d-f and he bemoans his fate (nominal clauses

[x3] with 1st person nominal predicate and double subject), he concludes, using the same syntactic structure, that the inhabitants of the land (the secondary actants) are to meet an even worse fate in v. 17 (simple nominal clause with 2nd person predicate and triple subject). V. 18 changes back to discursive speech and 'I' fades into the background thus marking a new smaller unit. The verb form והיה is autonomous in syntactic status and is analogous with *wayᵉhi*. According to Niccacci, the function of והיה "is not in the individual sentence but in the unit of discourse or narrative to which it belongs. This function consists in placing the circumstance, or rather the paragraph which follows it (...) within the main thrust of the message and of connecting this with the preceding context"(N. 182). V. 18 elaborates on the direct speech, applying it more directly to the addressees, the inhabitants on the earth. This entire unit contrasts with the previous unit in the shift from 'we' / 'they' to 'I' / 'you'. Alternation in the unit encompassing vv. 16c-18c between simple nominal and compound nominal clauses highlights the relationship between ongoing condition of v. 16c-e (emaciation, woe) and the 'cause' of that condition in the past (2x *qatal* in v. 16g-h) and the ongoing condition of v. 17 (terror, tomb, trap) and what will 'result' from that condition in the future (2x *yiqtol* of v. 18a-d). The syntax is beautifully inclusive of past, present and future.

24,18d-20

18d CNC (pro VC): כי + X + *qatal*
18e VC: *wayyiqtol* + subject

19a VC: infinitive absolute + *qatal* + subject
19b VC: infinitive absolute + *qatal* + subject
19c VC: infinitive absolute + *qatal* + subject
20a VC: infinitive absolute + *yiqtol* + subject + nominal phrase + כְּ
20b VC: *wᵉqatal* + subject (ה) + comparison

20c VC: *wᵉqatal* + object (ה) + subject
20d VC: *wᵉqatal*
20e VC: ו + negation + *yiqtol*

The asseverative כי together with the change from discursive to descriptive language in v. 18e introduce a new syntactical unit. V. 18d is clearly a CNC yet it is equivalent to a verbal clause in that it constitutes the beginning of a syntactic sequence. The CNC is explained by the chiastic parallelism in which the verbs follow one another in an **abb'a'** pattern. Succession is immediately suggested by the *qatal/wayyiqtol* combination between the two subjects. The 'foundations' tremble *because* the 'floodgates' are open. The *qatals* which dominate this unit are of the 'report' type and are equivalent to the present perfect (cf. supra). The *yiqtol* in v. 20a may have a purely stylistic function (variation) or it may function to distinguish between the more passive description of land in v. 19a-c and the more active description involved in v. 20a-b. After the series of *qatals* bearing a present perfect meaning the *wᵉqatal* verbal forms continue the present sense (J-M, §119 t).

24,21-23

21a Framing formula (autonomous והיה + temporal indicator)

21b-c VC: *yiqtol* + subject + object 1 + locative + object 2 + locative.
22a VC: *wᵉqatal* + subject + locative
22b VC: *wᵉqatal* + locative
22c CNC (pro VC): X + *yiqtol*

23a VC: *wᵉqatal* + subject
23b VC: *wᵉqatal* + subject

23c-e VC: כי + *qatal* + subject + locative (x3)

Two new groups of actants, together with YHWH, introduce this discursive syntactical unit, namely the 'army of the height' and the 'kings of the land'. Their fate is presented by a *yiqtol* in v. 22b, which denotes foreground or anticipated information, as does the string of *wᵉqatals* which follows. In v. 22c we would expect a VC rather than a CNC. Chiastic parallelism with v. 22a-b, however, seems to have intervened at this point. V. 22c, therefore, should be considered the equivalent of a VC. The smaller unit v. 23a-b features two new actants, the moon and the sun. The suffix on זקניו refers to YHWH. The introductory framing formula והיה ביום ההוא is a start signal which serves to open the syntactical unit while the explanatory statement of v. 23c-e serves to close the unit and the chapter as a whole.

25,1-5

1a SNC: Vocative + predicate + subject
1b VC: *yiqtol* + pronominal suffix (for object)
1c VC: *yiqtol* + object

1d VC: כי + *qatal* + object (x3)
2a VC: כי + *qatal* + object + apposition (x2)
2b SNC: subject + negation (מן) + predicate
2c CNC: X + negation (לא) + *yiqtol*

3a VC: על־כן + *yiqtol* + pronominal suffix (for object) + subject
3b VC: subject + *yiqtol*

4a VC: כי – *qatal* + nominal predicate + indirect object
4b (VC: ellipsis) + nominal predicate + indirect object + preposition
4c (VC: ellipsis) + nominal predicate + indirect object
4d (VC: ellipsis) + nominal predicate + indirect object

4e SNC: כי + subject + nominal predicate (nominal phrase + כ)
5a SNC: nominal predicate (nominal phrase + כ) + subject

5b VC: *yiqtol* + object + prepositional phrase
5c CNC: X + *yiqtol*

The vocative followed by a nominal clause (followed by *yiqtols*) opens this discursive syntactical unit 25,1-5. Once again we have a new set of actants in this unit: 'I', YHWH ('you'), city, a nation ('they'), the poor/needy, the violent/strangers. The alternation between *qatals* of report which signify retrieved information (present perfect) and *yiqtols* which express anticipated information (simple future) forms a quite regular pattern in the unit. A statement of present faith in the form of a SNC (v. 1a) is followed by a promise to praise in the future (v. 1b-c). What YHWH has done in the past (vv. 1d-2b) will result in a future in which 'nation' will glorify and revere him (v. 3a-b). Once again what YHWH has done in the past for the poor and needy (vv. 4a-d) he will repeat in the future (v. 5b-c). The SNC's in vv. 4e-5a governed by the כי represent a kind of aside or comment and are situated in the present. As such they may be considered syntactically distinct from the first three verses[38]. The

---

38. As is the case with the colometry and translation.

sequence of VC in v. 3a followed by CNC in v. 3b may be due to the chiastic placing of the elements of this bicolon.

25,6-8

6a-c   VC: *w^{e}qatal* + subject + indirect object + locative + object
7a-c   VC: *w^{e}qatal* + locative + object (x2)
8a   VC: *qatal* + object + adjunct

8b   VC: *w^{e}qatal* + subject + object
8c   CNC: X (object) + *yiqtol* + locative

8d   Framing formula (subject + *qatal*)

This discursive syntactic unit is marked off from what precedes it by a single subject which is stated once in the third person at the beginning of v. 6 and continues to govern through to the end of v. 8 where it is restated. The predominance of *w^{e}qatal* verbal forms also demarcates the unit and places the action firmly in the future. The *w^{e}qatal* form is mainly used for future action subsequent to a former action (J-M §119c). The *qatal* in v. 8a may be explained by the poet's preference for asyndetic forms and would be syntactically equivalent to *w^{e}qatal*. The CNC in v. 8d serves to emphasis the initial component חרפת עמו and the change of location from 'mountain' to 'all the land'.

25,9-12

9a   Framing formula (*w^{e}qatal* + temporal indicator)

9b   SNC: הנה + subject + nominal predicate
9c   VC: *qatal* + object
9d   VC: *w^{e}yiqtol*

9e   SNC: subject + nominal predicate
9f   VC: *qatal* + object
9g   VC: *yiqtol* (cohortative)
9h   VC: *w^{e}yiqtol* (cohortative) + object

10a   VC: כי + *yiqtol* + subject + locative

10b-c VC: *wᵉqatal* + subject + locative + subordinate comparative clause (inf. + subj. + prepositional phrase)
11a VC: *wᵉqatal* + object + locative
11b VC: subordinate comparative clause (כאשר + *yiqtol* + subject + prepositional phrase)
11c VC: *wᵉqatal* + object + prepositional phrase
12a CNC: object + *qatal*
12b VC: *qatal*
12c VC: *qatal* + locative + locative

The syntactical unit 25,9-12 opens with a formula introducing direct speech which continues through to the end of v. 12. 1st plural suffixes in v. 9 further constitute the indefinite subject of the opening *wᵉqatal* in v. 9a. The indefinite speaker can be assumed, therefore, to be a collective and is most probably a 'people' presented in contrast to Moab in 10b and specified further as Jerusalem by the locative בהר הזה in v. 10a. According to Niccacci, the function of הנה in an SNC of the type found in v. 9b "... is to link the past or present event very closely with the actual moment/time of discourse. Without the הנה the same event would be introduced as information with no significance for the actual moment of communication" (N. 58). In this event, the demonstrative זה (J-M, §143 a) in v. 9b would be most appropriately interpreted as 'our God is this[29] and he saves those who wait'. Here the demonstrative is proleptic and thus the predicate and 'our God' the subject. Statistically the word order in a nominal clause is for the most part Subject – Predicate. When זה is in the first slot as in v. 9e, however, it is given some prominence (J-M, §154 fb) pointing emphatically to YHWH. In this event one can interpret the demonstrative as cataleptic and thus the subject: 'this saving God is (called) YHWH. The *qatals* which follow are once again *qatals* of report. V. 10a constitutes something of a hinge in this unit. It is an explicative clause giving the grounds for the rejoicing in v. 9g-h yet at the same time setting the stage (as an explanation) for the adversative clause in 10b. The *yiqtol* of v. 10a expresses repeated or continued action in the past while the *wᵉqatal* of v. 10b expresses immanent future with the additional nuance of future action subsequent to a prior action (succession between the saving act and resting hand of YHWH and the trampling 'feet'). The unit closes with an abrupt change of subject. YHWH's indefi-

---

39. According to J-M, §143 a, זה originally had a temporal meaning 'here, now'. In any event, it is used when what it refers to can be pointed to (actually or mentally). זה can be used anaphorically (v. 9b, focusing on YHWH's salvific activity) and cataphorically (v. 9e, this saving God we call YHWH).

nite presence in v. 11 is made more explicit. The direct speech also concludes with a change from passive reference to Moab and its fate to direct address (ך). Note that in v. 12 three terms referring to 'height' are matched with three verbal clauses of 'bringing down'. The *qatals* of v. 12 are prophetic perfects.

26,1-6

1a   Framing formula (temporal indicator)

1b   VC: *yiqtol* + subject + locative

1c   SNC: subject + predicate

1d   CNC: X (object) + *yiqtol* + object predicate
2a   VC: imperative + object
2b   VC: *w^eyiqtol* + subject
3a   CNC: X + *yiqtol* + object
3b   SNC: כי + object + predicate [=participle passive]

4a   VC: imperative + object + temporal adjunct
4b   SNC: כי + subject + predicate

5a   VC: כי + *qatal* + object
5b   CNC: *casus pendens*: x (object) + *yiqtol* + suffix (refers back to x)
5c   VC: *yiqtol* + suffix (refers back to x of v. 5b)
5d   VC: *yiqtol* + suffix (refers back to x v. 5b)
6a   VC: *yiqtol* + subject
6b   (VC: ellipsis) subject
6c   (VC: ellipsis) subject

The framing formula in v. 1a and the transition from subject-matter of discourse (vv. 1-2) to explicit subject (YHWH v. 4b) together with the explicative SNC (v. 4b) serve to demarcate the opening of this syntactical unit. The same speaker and actants continue from the previous unit in the 1pl verbs and suffixes with an unnamed city in the land of Judah taking over from Moab and enduring an entirely different fate. The 'righteous/faithful nation' and the 'constant one' are presumably to be identified with the inhabitants of the unnamed city. After the introduction, the bulk of the material is discursive speech marked by two imperative clauses (2a & 4a). The attributive participial elements in v. 2b and 3a are a-temporal (J-M §121a). The complex use of parallelism in this sequence makes it difficult to comment on the syntax. The 'parallel terrace pattern', for example, which extends from v. 2 – v. 4a (and perhaps further)[40] may have interfered with the placing of verbal forms, thus making it unclear which type of clause is present and how the verb forms should be interpreted. An analysis of the text approximating to Niccacci's syntax does, however, yield some clarity. The *yiqtol* in v. 1b introduces the 'song' and represents foreground communication and anticipated information. The SNC of 1c begins the song proper. The *yiqtols* in the CNC's of 1d and 3a have the nuance of past action which continues into the present; YHWH secured and preserved and continues to do so. The two imperative clauses in v. 2a and v. 4a represent foreground communication and degree zero (present) in terms of linguistic perspective. Both are closed by SNC in v. 3b and v. 4b. After the imperative of 2a, the *yiqtol* of 2b has a jussive nuance.

The asseverative verbal clause introduces an abrupt statement concerning the 'dwellers of the height', new actants with respect to the previous unit. If we understand the *qatal* in v. 5a to be retrospective, retrieving a unique action in the recent past, then the *yiqtols* which follow would have present or near future nuance, i.e. the dwellers of the height have been brought low while the process of bringing down the town of loftiness, another new actant, is not yet complete[41]. Niccacci points out that it is difficult to distinguish between *casus pendens* and the CNC[42]. At a syntactical level, however, they function differently. "*Casus pendens* is a noun or noun equivalent freed from the position it would occupy in a normal clause and placed at the head of the sentence. It does not really occupy the first position of the clause but is placed outside it ('extra position') and reference to it is usually made by an anaphoric or resumptive pronoun. Its function is not to place the emphasis on the nominal part of the sentence now placed at the beginning but to mark off the topic to be considered. Where the CNC is concerned, the

---

40. A parallel terrace pattern is evident in the repetition of synonymous terms such as righteousness//fidelity//constancy//preserve//peace//peace//trust//trust. On the form and function of the parallel terrace see: W.G.E. WATSON, *Classical Hebrew Poetry. A Guide to Its Techniques* (JSOTSS, 26), Sheffield, 1995², pp. 209-212.

41. According to J-M §113o, however, the *qatal* places in the past the action expressed by the following *yiqtol*.

42. As far as the text is concerned the *casus pendens* is placed in the same column as the CNC. Niccacci considers the *casus pendens* to be possible in the protasis of so-called 'double sentences' of the x-*qatal* or x-*yiqtol* type. The primary distinction with CNC being the absence of emphasis.

noun taking first position in the clause is given emphasis (N. 148). At the formal level, therefore, v. 5b would appear to be *casus pendens* because of the anaphoric pronominal suffixes in v. 5cd and v. 6a. Syntactically speaking the 'trampling' of v. 6 and the 'humbling' of v. 5 are on the same level but they have different subjects, 'he' (presumably YHWH) and the 'poor/humble'. Perhaps there is a suggestion that the two should be identified.

26,7-10

7a	SNC:	subject + indirect object + predicate
7b	CNC:	X (object) + *yiqtol*
8a	CNC:	אף + X (prepositional phrase) + *qatal* + object (pronominal suffix)
8b	SNC:	predicate x2 + subject
9a	CNC:	*casus pendens* + subject + *qatal* + temporal adjunct
9b	CNC:	אף + X + *yiqtol*
9c	SNC:	כי + temporal כאשר + subject + predicate
9d	CNC:	X (object) + *qatal* + subject
10a	VC:	*yiqtol* + subject
10b	VC:	negation + *qatal* + object
10c	CNC:	X (locative) + *yiqtol*
10d	VC:	syndetic negation + *yiqtol* + object

A change of actants introduces this unit. Besides YHWH we are now in a world of 'abstract' actants: 'the righteous', 'the wicked', YHWH's 'adversaries', 'them'. YHWH is the direct addressee while the speaker remains vague: 'I', 'we'. J-M §164g suggests that the nuance of emphasis with particles such as אף is difficult to establish. Syntactically speaking this exclamatory particle does not effect the syntactical shape of the clauses to which it is appended. CNC's following אף in v. 8a and v. 9b are foreground constructions serving to emphasise the term placed in first position as they do throughout the unit. The unusual word order in v. 8a is interesting. One would expect to find the vocative in the initial slot yet it gives way to the adverbial modifiers for the sake of emphasis (J-M §155p). From a syntactical perspective, therefore, the focus is on 'the way of your judgements'. The SNC's in vv. 7a, 8b and 9c express a continuing present state rather than an individual action, i.e. the way of the righteous is always level, YHWH's judgements are always 'in the land' etc.. The *casus pendens* of v. 9a is taken up in the first person form of the verbs in v. 9a and b and in the pronominal suffixes of v. 9a and b. The use of the term נפשׁי with the first person pronominal suffix may suggest a sort of reflexive form. V. 10a-d is a conditional clause set up by simple juxtaposition of a protasis clause without any grammatical modification and three apodoses similarly unmodified. The contrast between 'I', 'we' / 'he', 'they' continues the lexical contrast between צדק and רשׁע. Both syntactical (at the level of actants) and lexical contrast provides the unit with cohesion.

26,11-15

11a   VC: Vocative + qatal + subject
11b   VC: negation + yiqtol
11c   VC: yiqtol
11d   VC: w^eyiqtol + object
11e   CNC: אף + X (subject) + yiqtol

12a   VC: vocative + yiqtol + direct object + indirect object
12b   CNC (pro VC): כי גם + X (direct object) + qatal + indirect object

13a   VC: vocative + qatal + prepositional phrase
13b   CNC (pro VC): X (prepositional phrase) + yiqtol + object
14a   CNC: X (subject) + negation + yiqtol
14b   CNC: X (subject) + negation + yiqtol
14c   VC: לכן + qatal
14d   VC: wayyiqtol
14e   VC: wayyiqtol + object

15a   VC: qatal + object + vocative
15b   VC: qatal + object
15c   VC: qatal
15d   VC: qatal + object

The jussives in v. 11c-e[43] express foreground information and degree zero (present) of linguistic perspective. They are used to express a wish/prayer from an inferior to a superior (J-M §114h). The wish/prayer is introduced by the vocative in v. 11a and continued in v. 11c-e. The

---

43. In narrative texts, yiqtol is normally follwed by w^eqatal. This suggests that we are dealing with jussives.

change of mood opens the unit as does the change from a single specific referent – the wicked – to a general plural adversary – they. The vocative introducing this discursive unit continues the prayer of the previous unit although the focus changes from YHWH's adversaries to the indefinite 'us'. There is a degree of syntactical ambiguity intorduced by the parallelism in v. 11. While we have opted to understand אש צריך as a subjective genitive, צריך might also be understood as the object of the clause which is then repeated in the pronominal suffix of the verb. The vocatives in vv. 12a and 13a have a deictic character and do not affect the sentence type. The verbal focus also shifts from a predominance of *yiqtols* to a predominance of *qatals* and *wayyiqtols*. As elsewhere in this text complex the *qatals* are 'report' *qatals* and suggest foreground communication and present perfect. Niccacci suggests (see supra) that this kind of *qatal* constitutes a VC and not a CNC (X+*qatal* [cf. vv. 12b and 13b]). The vocatives and the numerous 2ms suffixes place YHWH in the foreground as addressee. The *qatal/wayyiqtol* (x2) construction in 14cd strongly suggests succession, giving an explanation of the bold negations in 14ab. The semantic antithesis between v. 14 and v. 15 is underlined by the change from *qatal/wayyiqtol* to the series of four asyndetic *qatals*. Although the suffixal endings tend to make the object of discussion and the speaker(s) rather vague, (only the addressee is explicit), the text encourages us to identify the actants with the righteous/wicked in the previous unit. The vocative in v. 15a is clearly positioned for stylistic purposes, to establish inclusion with v. 11.

26,16-19

16a CNC (pro VC): vocative + X + *qatal*
16b VC: *qatal* + object
16c SNC: subject + predicate

17a CNC: comparative particle + X (subject) + *yiqtol* + prepositional phrase
17b VC: *yiqtol*
17c VC: *yiqtol* + prepositional phrase
17d VC: (כן marking apodosis) + *qatal* + prepositional phrase + vocative
18a VC: *qatal*
18b VC: *qatal*
18c VC: particle + *qatal* + object
18d CNC: X + negation + *yiqtol* + locative
18e VC: negation + *yiqtol* + subject

19a VC: *yiqtol* + subject
19b CNC (pro VC): X + *yiqtol*
19c VC: imperative
19d VC: ו + imperative + vocative
19e SNC: כי + predicate + subject
19f CNC: X (= subject + object) + *yiqtol*

Once again the addressee is made clearly explicit in the use of the opening vocative of this discursive unit. V. 16a is the equivalent of a VC, the word order being as it is under influence from the partly chiastic parallel structure of the verse. The *qatals* in v. 16 are 'report' *qatals* indicating foreground communication and present perfect. The SNC in v. 16c is also foreground information and represents degree zero in terms of linguistic perspective. The change of referents from 'they' to 'we' to 'they' to 'you' in the verb forms of this unit is very complex. The primary actants are the 'we' group. A gradual process of revelation of the subject is perhaps being worked out between vv. 16 and 19 of this syntactical unit. The inexplicit subject 'they' in v. 16 becomes more explicit in vv. 17c-18 'we' and is then identified in v. 19 with the 'dead' / 'corpses'. In this sense the infertile 'we' is identified with the 'dead' who will experience 'resurrection'. The semantic context of anticipated birth might have influenced the poets choice of *yiqtols* in v. 17a-c which represent anticipated information. The *qatals* of vv. 17d-18c are 'report' *qatals*. In prose, according to Niccacci (N. 77), the indicative *yiqtol* expressing simple future, as we find it here in v. 19, would never take the first position. Again the parallelism with v. 19b has introduced its own constraints. The particle כמו in v. 18c is read as a logical marker, in line with כן in v. 17d: 'thus' and is likewise placed in the first column[44]. The imperatives in v. 19c-d offer foreground information and express degree zero in linguistic perspective. The SNC in v. 19a continues this while the CNC in v. 19f serves to emphasise the 'X' components.

26,20-21

20a VC: imperative + vocative
20b VC: imperative + locative
20c VC: imperative + object + locative
20d VC: imperative + temporal adjunct
20e VC: conjunction [temporal adjunct] + *yiqtol* + subject

44. Cf. discussion in NIDOTTE IV, pp. 1029-1030.

21a   SNC: כי־הנה + subject + predicate + locative
21b   VC: infinitive of purpose + object + locative
21c   VC: $w^e qatal$ + subject + object
21d   VC: ו + negation + *yiqtol* + temporal adjunct + object

    This new syntactical unit concludes chapter 26 with a change of addressee and a change of general object of discussion. The actants are 'you', 'my people', 'the land', 'her blood/slain' and YHWH. The 4 imperatives in v. 20a-d represent foreground communication and degree zero in terms of linguistic perspective while the *yiqtol* in v. 20e suggests immanent future. As noted above with reference to 24,1 the construction הנה - name – participle, according to Niccacci, describes an action which is happening at the very moment of the communication. The $w^e qatal$ and w^e + negation + *yiqtol* which follow in v. 21c-d should be understood as analogous to the *wayyiqtols* of 'narrative discourse' which continue a *qatal*.

27,1

27,1a Framing formula (temporal indicator)

1b   VC: *yiqtol* + subject + modifier
1c   VC: (ellipsis) + object
1d   VC: (ellipsis) + object
1e   VC: $w^e qatal$ + object

    The framing formula introduces this short syntactic unit in which YHWH and Leviathan are the primary actants. The opening *yiqtol* in v 1.b expresses foreground communication and anticipated information as does the $w^e qatal$ which continues it in v. 1e.

27,2-6

2a   Framing formula (temporal indicator)

2b   *Casus pendens* (pro VC): X + imperative + prepositional object
3a   SNC: subject + apposition + predicate
3b   CNC: X + *yiqtol*
3c   Dependent VC: פן + *yiqtol* + prepositional object
3d   CNC: X + *yiqtol*

4a SNC: subject + negation + predicate
4b VC: subject (מי) + *yiqtol* + object (x2) + ind. object
4c VC: *yiqtol* + prepositional object
4d VC: *yiqtol* + adverbial phrase
5a VC: *yiqtol* (jussive) + prepositional object
5b VC: *yiqtol* + object
5c CNC (pro VC): X + *yiqtol* + indirect object

6a VC: framing formula (temporal indicator [הבאים] + *yiqtol*)
6b VC: *yiqtol*
6c VC: *w^eqatal*
6d VC: *w^eqatal*

The *casus pendens* in v. 2b is complicated by the gender of the subject (m) and the suffix gender of the retrospective pronoun (f). The noun כרם seems to be found only here with feminine retrospective pronouns. The reason is probably stylistic[45]. *Casus pendens* construction is formally similar to the CNC and as such is placed in the CNC column. One would perhaps expect a VC here in that it opens a new section and introduces the new actant, the 'fruitful vineyard'. The *casus pendens*, however, does not draw emphasis to the 'fruitful vineyard', it simply states that the 'fruitful vineyard' will be the topic of what follows. The imperative suggests foreground communication and degree zero of linguistic perspective. Normally the *yiqtol* represents anticipated information yet the introductory imperative grounds us in the present for the entirety of the song. As elsewhere, the CNCs in v. 3b and 3d serve to emphasis the X component, the temporal dimension of YHWH's protection. According to Niccacci, conditional clauses can take a variety of forms in the protasis and apodosis (N. 138). Here we have an interrogative particle + *yiqtol* in the protasis (v. 4b) and a string of *yiqtol*s in the apodosis (v. 4c-5c). The entire conditional unit stretches, therefore, from v. 4b to v. 5c and as such provides background or circumstantial information within the syntactical unit stretching from v. 2a to v. 6d. It is possible that the word order which constitutes the CNC in v. 5c has been brought about for stylistic purposes and that the phrase takes the place of a VC. The term הבאים in v. 6a is an abbreviation for הימים הבאים 'the coming days' and is used adverbially (and anaphorically) as a temporal indicator. As such, it functions as a framing formula. The *yiqtol* + *w^eqatal* forms in v. 6a-d suggests simple succession and anticipated information.

---

45. See detailed analysis of the text (chs. III-VI).

27,7-11

7a   CNC: (pro VC) X (interrogative + comparison) + *qatal*
7b   CNC: X + (conjunction + comparison)+ *qatal*

8a-c CNC: XX (prepositional phrases) + *yiqtol*
8d   VC: *qatal* + modal phrase + temporal adjunct
9a   CNC: לכן + X (prepositional phrase) + *yiqtol*
9b   SNC: predicate + subject + apposition
9c-e CNC: X (= temporal adjunct + comparative) + negation + *yiqtol* + subject

10a-b SNC: subject + predicate
10c   SNC: predicate + comparative
10d   VC: adjunct of place + *yiqtol*
10e   VC: adjunct of place + *yiqtol*
10f   VC: *wᵉqatal* + object
11a   CNC: X (prepositional phrase) + *yiqtol*
11b   SNC: subject + predicate
11c   SNC: predicate + object
11d   SNC: predicate + subject
11e   VC: על־כן + negation + *yiqtol* + subject
11f   CNC: X (subject) + negation + *yiqtol*

V. 7a opens this discursive unit with a CNC serving as VC and perhaps constrained by the highly stylised phrase of v. 7a-b. The disjunctive question constituted by the ה in the first member and אם in the second is, according to J.-M. §161e, "sometimes a mere [sic.] stylistic feature, used in cases of synonymous parallelism." Vv. 8a-c constitute a single CNC in which the 'X' components are given prominence. Similarly, the CNC in v. 9a provides emphasis to the 'X' element (anaphoric זאת) which becomes more explicit in the CNC of v. 9c-e (proleptic זה). A new smaller unit is introduced by the SNC in v. 10a-c which begins anew the description of the city and represents foreground information (present). Although Niccacci notes that it is rare (N. 181), it would seem here that the *yiqtols* of 10d-e do not represent anticipated information but rather repeated or continued action in the past. Once again the three SNCs of v. 11b-d represent foreground information equivalent to the present. The CNC concludes the unit emphasising again the 'X' element, i.e. 'he who formed'. Following on the SNCs, the *yiqtols* of v. 11e-f represent simple future. The poetic character of the text introduces a degree of ambiguity in v. 11a, allowing one to interpret קצירה as forming a construct with ביבש or as constituting the subject of the verb תשברנה[46].

27,12-13

12a Framing formula (autonomous והיה + temporal indicator)

12b VC: *yiqtol* + subject + locatives

12c VC: pronominal subject + *yiqtol* + adverbial phrase + vocative

13a Framing formula (autonomous והיה + temporal indicator)

13b VC: *yiqtol* + prepositional object
13cd VC: *wᵉqatal* + subject (x2) + locative
13e VC: *wᵉqatal* + prepositional object + locative

The final syntactical unit of the entire text complex opens with a framing formula followed by *yiqtols* (v. 12 b-c) which represent simple future. The deictic use of ואתם serves to separate v. 12c from the previous smaller unit. The framing formula is repeated in v. 13a and is followed again by *yiqtol* + *wᵉqatals* representing simple future.

---

[46]. Cf. J.N. OSWALT, *The Book of Isaiah, Chapters 1-39*, Grand Rapids, MI, 1986, pp. 496, 499; cf. also H. WILDBERGER (*Jesaja 13-27* [BKAT, 10/2], Neukirchen-Vluyn, 1978, p. 1014) who maintains Ehrich's suggestion that the subject of the verb is the 'women'. As a collective, however, קציר can also constitute the subject of the verb.

ABBREVIATIONS

Abbreviations used in this volume follow, for the most part, those proposed by *Ephemerides Theologicae Lovanienses* 66 (1990) 477-512. The remainder were found in S.M. SCHWERTNER, *Theologische Realenzyklopädie. Abkürzungsverzeichnis*, Berlin – New York, 1994². Abbreviations for older and often discontinued English language periodicals were sought in W.G. HUPPER (ed.), *An Index to Periodical Literature on the Old Testament and Ancient Near Easter Studies*, Vol I (ATLA Bibliography Series, 21), Metuchen – London, 1987, pp. xxiii-li.

AASOR	Annual of the American Schools of Oriental Research
AB	The Anchor Bible
ABD	*The Anchor Bible Dictionary* (ed. D.N. FREEDMAN)
AnBib	Analecta Biblica
AOAT	Alter Orient und Altes Testament
ASTI	Annual of the Swedish Theological Institute (Jerusalem)
ATD	Das Alte Testament Deutsch
ATANT	Abhandlungen zur Theologie des Alten und Neuen Testaments
ATSAT	Arbeiten zu Text und Sprache im Alten Testament
BAfO	Archiv für Orientforschung, Beihefte
BBB	Bonner biblische Beiträge
BETL	Bibliotheca Ephemeridum Theologicarum Lovaniensium
BHK	Biblia Hebraica (ed. R. Kittel)
BHS	Biblia Hebraica Stuttgartensia
Bib	Biblica
BiTr	Bible Translator
BibOr	Biblica et Orientalia
BiOr	Bibliotheca Orientalis
BKAT	Biblischer Kommentar Altes Testament
BOT	De Boeken van het Oude Testament
BS	Bibliotheca Sacra
BTB	Biblical Theology Bulletin
BWANT	Beiträge zur Wissenschaft vom Alten und Neuen Testament
BZAW	Beihefte zur Zeitschrift für die alttestamentliche Wissenschaft
CB	Coniectanea Biblica
CBQ	The Catholic Biblical Quarterly
COT	Commentaar op het Oude Testament
DCH	The Dictionary of Classical Hebrew
EHAT	Exegetisches Handbuch zum Alten Testament
EB	Études bibliques
EstBib	Estudios bíblicos
EstEcl	Estudios eclesiasticos
ETL	Ephemerides Theologicae Lovanienses

ETR	Études théologiques et religieuses
EvQ	The Evangelical Quarterly
ExpT	Expository Times
Explor	Explorations
FAT	Forschungen zum Alten Testament
FOTL	The Forms of Old Testament Literature
GHAT	Göttinger Handkommentar zum Alten Testament
HALOT	The Hebrew and Aramaic Lexicon of the Old Testament
HOTTP	Hebrew Old Testament Text Project
HSAT	Die heilige Schrift des Alten Testaments
HSM	Harvard Semitic Monographs
HThR	Harvard Theological Review
HUCA	Hebrew Union College Annual
ICC	The International Critical Commentary
IDB	The Interpreter's Dictionary of the Bible
Interp	Interpretation
JAAR	Journal of the American Academy of Religion
JANES	Journal of the Ancient Near Eastern Society, Columbia University
JETS	Journal of the Evangelical Theological Society
JBL	Journal of Biblical Literature
JJS	Journal of Jewish Studies
JLT	Journal of Literature and Theology
J-M	*A Grammar of Biblical Hebrew* (P. JOÜON and T. MURAOKA)
JNSL	Journal of Northwest Semitic Languages
JQR	Jewish Quarterly Review
JR	Journal of Religion
JSem	Journal of Semitics
JSOT	Journal for the Study of the Old Testament
JSOT SS	Journal for the Study of the Old Testament, Supplement Series
JTC	Journal for Theology and the Church
JTS	Journal of Theological Studies
KAT	Kommentar zum Alten Testament
KEHAT	Kurzgefaßtes exegetisches Handbuch zum Alten Testament
KHAT	Kurzer Handkommentar zum Alten Testament
LEH	*A Greek–English Lexicon of the Septuagint* (J. LUST, E. EYNIKEL, K. HAUSPIE)
MTZ	Münchener theologische Zeitschrift
MU ATSAT	Münchener Universitätsschriften. Arbeiten zu Text und Sprache im Alten Testament
NBDB	The New Brown-Driver-Briggs-Gesenius Hebrew-English Lexicon
NEchB	Die Neue Echter Bibel
NedTT	Nederlands Theologisch Tijdschrift
NICOT	The New International Commentary on the Old Testament
NIDOTTE	New International Dictionary of Old Testament Theology and Exegesis
NRSV	New Revised Standard Version

NSKAT	Neuer Stuttgarter Kommentar – Altes Testament
NTS	New Testament Studies
OBO	Orbis Biblicus et Orientalis
OTA	Old Testament Abstracts
OTL	Old Testament Library
OTM	Old Testament Message
OTS	Oudtestamentische Studiën
OTW	Proceedings of die Ou-testamentiese Werkgemeenskap in Suid-Afrika
POT	De prediking van het Oude Testament
RB	Revue biblique
R&E	Review and Expositor
RHPh	Revue d'histoire et de philosophie religieuses
RSR	Recherches de science religieuse
RTL	Revue théologique de Louvain
SB	Sources bibliques
SBL DS	Society of Biblical Literature Dissertation Series
SBL SP	Society of Biblical Literature Seminar Papers
SBM	Stuttgarter Biblische Monographien
SBS	Stuttgarter Bibelstudien
SBT	Studies in Biblical Theology
SJOT	Scandinavian Journal of the Old Testament
StT	Studia Theologica
SVT	Supplements to Vetus Testamentum
TDOT	Theological Dictionary of the Old Testament
TZ	Theologische Zeitschrift
TWAT	Theologisches Wörterbuch zum Alten Testament
TynB	Tyndale Bulletin
WBC	Word Bible Commentary
WMANT	Wissenschaftliche Monographien zum Alten und Neuen Testament
ZAH	Zeitschrift für Althebraïstik
ZAW	Zeitschrift für die alttestamentliche Wissenschaft
ZBK	Zürcher Bibelkommentare
ZMR	Zeitschrift für Missionswissenschaft und Religionswissenschaft
ZS	Zeitschrift für Semitistik
ZTK	Zeitschrift für Theologie und Kirche
ZWT	Zeitschrift für wissenschaftliche Theologie

BIBLIOGRAPHY

ADLER, E.J., *The Background for the Metaphor of Covenant as Marriage in the Hebrew Bible*, Diss. (UMI), University of California at Berkely, 1990.
ALEXANDER, J.A., *A Commentary on the Prophecies of Isaiah I*, Philadelphia, PA, 1875² (Reprinted, Grand Rapids, MI, 1976).
ALMER, A.F., *Studies in Isaiah, Chapters 24–27*, in *Augustana Quarterly* 10 (1931) 363-373.
ALONSO SCHÖKEL, *La Cancion de la viña. Isa 27:2-5*, in *EstEcl* 34 (1960) 767-774.
— and SICRE DIAZ, J.L., *Profetas I, Isaias & Jeremias* (Nueva Biblia Española, Comentario), Madrid, 1980.
— L. *Hermeneutica de la palabra. II. Interpretación literaria de textos bíblicos* (Academia christiana, 38), Madrid, 1987.
— *Isaiah*, in R. ALTER and F. KERMODE (eds.), *The Literary Guide to the Bible*, Cambridge, MA, 1987, pp. 165-183.
— *A Manual of Hebrew Poetics* (tr. A. Graffy), (Subsidia Biblica, 11), Rome, 1988.
ALSTON, W.P., *The Philosophy of Language* (Foundations of Philosophy Series) Englewood Cliffs, NJ, 1964.
ALTER, R., *The Art of Biblical Poetry*, New York, NY, 1985.
AMSLER, S., *Des visions de Zacharie à l'apocalypse d'Ésaïe 24–27*, in J. VERMEYLEN (ed.), *The Book of Isaiah – Le livre d'Isaïe* (BETL, 81), Leuven, 1989, pp. 263-273; reprinted in *Le dernier et l'avant-dernier. Études sur l'Ancien Testament*, Geneva, 1993, pp. 246-256.
ANDERSON, B.W., *The Slaying of the Fleeing, Twisting Serpent: Isaiah 27:1 in Context*, in L.M. HOPFE (ed.), *Uncovering Ancient Stones. Essays in Memory of H. Neil Richardson*, Winona Lake, IN, 1994, pp. 3-15 (= B.W. ANDERSON [ed.], *From Creation to New Creation*, Minneapolis, MN, 1994, pp. 195-206).
ANDERSON, G. A., *Isaiah 24–27 Reconsidered*, in *Congress Volume, Bonn* (SVT, 9), Leiden, 1963.
ANON., *Comparative Translation: Isaiah 26:3. A Study in Modernizing the English Bible*, in *Biblical World* 24 (1904) 283-284.
AQUINAS, Thomas, *Summa Theologiae, Latin Text and English Translation, Introduction, Notes, Appendices and Glossaries*, London, 1964.
AUBERT, L., *Une première apocalypse (Ésaïe 24–27)*, in *ETR* 11 (1936) 280-296.
AUVREY, P., *Isaïe 1–39* (SB), Paris, 1972.
AYER, A.J., *Language, Truth and Logic*, London, 1971 (first published 1936).
BACHE, C.M., *The Logic of Religious Metaphor*, Diss. (UMI), Brown University, 1978.
BACKMAN, G., *Meaning by Metaphor*, Uppsala, 1991.
BAILLIE, J., *Our Knowledge of God*, New York, NY, 1959.
BAL, M., *Metaphors He Lives By*, in *Semeia* 61 (1993) 185-207.

BALENTINE, S.E., *A Description of the Semantic Field of Hebrew Words for Hide*, in *VT* 30 (1980) 137-153.
BARANOWSKI, M., *La teologia di Sion nel libro d'Isaia. Studio esegetico-teologico. Con particolare riferimento a Is 25,6-8; 28,14-22; 54,11-17; 60*, Diss., Gregoriana, Rome, 1997.
BARBOUR, I.G., *Myths, Models and Paradigms*, London, 1974.
BARTEL, R., *Metaphors and Symbols: Forays into Language*, Urbana, IL, 1983.
BARTHÉLEMY, D. (ed.), *Critique textuelle de l'Ancien Testament. 2: Isaïe, Jérémie, Lamentations* (OBO, 50/2), Freiburg, 1986.
BARTON, J., *Isaiah 1-39* (Old Testament Guides), Sheffield, 1995.
BASCOM, R., *The Targums: Ancient Reader's Helps*, in *BiTr* 36 (1985) 301-316.
BAUMGARTNER, W.I., *Auferstehungsglaube im Alten Orient*, in *ZMR* 68 (1933) 193-214.
BEARDSLEY, M., *The Metaphorical Twist*, in *Philosophy and Phenomenological Research* 22 (1962) 293-307.
— *Metaphor*, in P. EDWARDS (ed.), *The Encyclopedia of Philosophy*. Vol. V, New York, NY, 1967, pp. 284-289.
BECKER, J., *Isaias – Der Prophet und sein Buch* (SBS, 30), Stuttgart, 1968.
BEKKER, I. (ed), *Aristotelis Rhetorica et Poetica*, Berlin, 1873.
— *Aristotelis Opera*, Berlin, 1960.
BEEK, M. A., *Ein Erdbeben wird zum prophetischen Erleben*, in *Archiv Orientální* 17 (1949) 31-40.
BEESTON, A. F. L., *The Hebrew Verb SPT*, in *VT* 8 (1958) 216-217.
BEN DAVID, Y., *Ugaritic Parallels to Isa 24:18-19* [Heb.], in *Lešonenu. Quarterly for the Study of the Hebrew Language and Cognate Subjects* 45 (1980) 55-59.
BEN YEHUDA, E., *A Complete Dictionary of Ancient and Modern Hebrew*, New York, NY, 1958-1950.
BERGES, U., *Das Buch Jesaja: Komposition und Endgestalt* (Herders biblische Studien, 16), Freiburg, 1998.
BERLIN, A., *The Dynamics of Biblical Parallelism*, Bloomington, IN, 1985.
— *On Reading Biblical Poetry: The Role of Metaphor*, in J.A. EMERTON (ed.), *Congress Volume, Cambridge, 1995*, Leiden, 1997, pp. 25-36.
BERRIGAN, D., *The Marvelous Design; Isaiah 25: A Song of Ecstasy and Truth*, in *Sojourners* 18 (1989) 24-27.
BETZ, H.D., *On the Problem of the Religio-Historical Understanding of Apocalypticism*, in *JTC* 6 (1969) 134-156.
BEUKEN, W.A.M., *The Prophet Leads the Readers into Praise. Isa. 25:1-10 in Connection with Isa. 24:14-23 Seen against the Background of Isaiah 12*, unpublished paper read at the Annual Meeting of the AAR-SBL, Orlando, FL, November, 1998.
BEVAN, E., *Symbolism and Belief*, London, 1938.
BIDDLE, M.E., *The City of Chaos and the New Jerusalem: Isaiah 24–27 in Context*, in *Perspectives in Religious Studies* 22 (1995) 5-12.
— *The Figure of Lady Jerusalem: Identification, Deification and Personification of Cities in the Ancient Near East*, in B. BATTO, W. HALLO and L. YOUNGER (eds.), *The Canon in Comparative Perspective* (Scripture in Context Series, 4), Lewiston, NY, 1995, pp. 173-187.

BINKLEY, T., *On the Truth and Probity of Metaphor*, in M. JOHNSON (ed.), *Philosophical Perspectives on Metaphor,* Minneapolis, MN, 1981, pp. 136-153.
BIRD, P., *'To play the harlot': An Inquiry into an Old Testament Metaphor*, in P.L. DAY (ed.), *Gender and Difference in Ancient Israel*, Minneapolis, MN, 1989, pp. 75-94.
BJØRNDALEN, A.J., *Untersuchungen zur allegorischen Rede der Propheten Amos und Jesaja*, Berlin, 1986.
BLACK, M., *Models and Metaphors: Studies in Language and Philosophy*, Ithaca, NY, 1962.
— *The Labyrinth of Meaning*, New York, NY, 1968.
— *How Metaphors Work: A Reply to Donald Davidson*, in S. SACKS (ed.), *On Metaphor*, Chicago, IL, 1979, pp. 181-192.
— *More about Metaphor*, in A. ORTONY (ed.), *Metaphor and Thought*, Cambridge, 1979, pp. 19-41.
BLEEK, F., *Introduction to the Old Testament* (tr. G.H. Venables), London, 1869.
BLENKINSOPP, J., *Fragments of Ancient Exegesis in an Isaian Poem*, in ZAW 93 (1981) 51-62.
BLOMMERDE, A.C.M., *Broken Construct Chain, Further Examples*, in Bib 55 (1974) 548-552.
BOADT, L., *Understanding the Mashal and its Value for the Jewish-Christian Dialogue in a Narrative Theology*, in C. THOMA and M. WYSCHOGROD (eds.), *Parable and Story in Judaism and Christianity*, Mahwah, NJ, 1986.
BOELTER, F.W., *From the Old Testament: an Isaiah Apocalypse [ch. 24–27]?*, in *Explorations* 4 (1978) 75-78.
BONS, E., *L'approche «métaphorologique» de livre d'Osée (1)*, in RSR 72 (1998) 133-155.
BÖHMER, J., *Zu Jes. 24–27*, in ZAW 22 (1902) 332-334.
BOOTH, W., *Afterthoughts on Metaphor IV: Ten Literal 'Theses'*, in S. SACKS (ed.), *On Metaphor*, Chicago, IL, 1979, pp. 173-174.
— *Metaphor as Rhetoric*, in S. SACKS (ed.), *On Metaphor*, Chicago, IL, 1979, pp. 47-70.
BOSMAN, H.J., VAN GROL, H.W.M. et al. (eds.), *Studies in Isaiah 24–27. The Isaiah Workshop* (OTS, 43), Leiden, 1999.
BOTTERWECK, G.J., RINGGREN, H., FABRY, H.-J., ANDERSON, G.W., *Theologisches Wörterbuch zum Alten Testament* [TWAT]. Vols. I-IX, Stuttgart, 1973-1997.
— *Theological Dictionary of the Old Testament* [TDOT]. Vols. I-VIII, Grand Rapids, MI, 1974-1997.
BOURGUET, D., *Des métaphores de Jérémie* (EB, 9), Paris, 1987.
BOUTFLOWER, C., *The Book of Isaiah Chapters (I-XXXIX) In the Light of the Assyrian Monuments*, London, 1930.
BOX, G.H., *Some Textual Suggestions on Two Passages in Isaiah*, in ExpT 19 (1907-08) 563-564.
BREDENKAMP, C.J., *Der Prophet Jesaja*, Erlangen, 1887.
BREGMAN, L., *Academic 'Immortality' and the Eschatological Destiny of the Dead*, in *Religion and Intellectual Life* 2 (1985) 28-36.

BRENSINGER, T.C., *Simile and Prophetic Language in the Old Testament* (Mellen Biblical Press Series, 43), Lewiston, NY, 1996.
BRETTLER, M., *God is King. Understanding an Israelite Metaphor* (JSOT SS, 76), Sheffield, 1989.
— *Images of YHWH the Warrior in Psalms*, in *Semeia* 61 (1993) 135-165.
— *Incompatible Metaphors for YHWH in Isaiah 40-66*, in *JSOT* 78 (1998) 97-120.
BRUEGGEMANN, W., *Theology of the Old Testament*, Minneapolis, MN, 1997.
BRICHTO, H.C., *Toward a Grammar of Biblical Poetics. Tales of the Prophets*, New York – Oxford, 1992.
BRIGGS, J. and MONACO, R., *Metaphor: The Logic of Poetry*, New York, NY, 1990.
BROCKHAUS, G. *Untersuchungen zu Stil und Form der sogenannten Jesaja Apokalypse*, Master's Thesis, Bonn, 1972 (typescript).
BROWN, F. (ed.), *The New Brown – Driver – Briggs – Gesenius Hebrew and English Lexicon with an Appendix Containing the Biblical Aramaic* [NBDB], Peabody, MA, 1979.
BROWN, F.B., *Transfiguration: Poetic Metaphor and the Languages of Religious Belief*, Chapel Hill, NC, 1983.
BROWN, S., *Images and Truth. Studies in the Imagery of the Bible*, Rome, 1955.
BRUNO, D.A., *Jesaja, eine rhythmische und textkritische Untersuchung*, Stockholm, 1953.
BULLINGER, E.W., *Figures of Speech in the Bible: Explained and Illustrated*, London, 1898.
BURNEY, C. K., *Old Testament Notes. III. The Three Serpents of Isaiah XXVII.1*, in *JTS* 9 (1909-10) 446-452.
BURROWS, M. (ed.), *The Dead Sea Scrolls of St Mark's Monastery, I The Isaiah Manuscript and the Habbakuk Commentary* (AASOR), New Haven, CT, 1950.
— *The Dead Sea Scrolls of the Hebrew University*, Jerusalem, 1955.
BUTTLER, C., *Isaiah* (Layman's Biblical Commentary, 10), Nashville, TN, 1982.
BUTTRICK, G.A. (ed.), *The Interpreter's Dictionary of the Bible* [IDB], New York – Nashville, TN, 1962.
CAIRD, G., *The Language and Imagery of the Bible*, London, 1980-1988.
CAMP, C., *Woman Wisdom as Root Metaphor: A Theological Consideration*, in K.G. HOGLUND et al. (eds.), *The Listening Heart. Essays in Wisdom and the Psalms in Honor of Roland E. Murphy* (JSOT SS, 58), Sheffield, 1987, pp. 45-76.
— *Metaphor in Feminist Biblical Interpretation: Theoretical Perspectives*, in *Semeia* 61 (1993) 3-36.
CAQUOT, A., *Remarques sur 'le banquet des nations' en Ésaïe 25, 6-8*, in *RHPhR* 69 (1989) 109-119.
CARLSTON, C.E., *The Parable and Allegory Revisited: An Interpretative Review*, in *CBQ* 43 (1981) 228-242.
CARMIGNAC, J., *Six passages d'Isaïe eclairés par Qumran (Isaïe 14, 11; 21, 20; 22, 5; 25. 4; 27, 3; 50, 6)*, in S. WAGNER and H. BARDTKE (eds.), *Bibel und Qumran: Beiträge zur Erforschung der Beziehungen zwischen Bibel und Qumranwissenschaft: Hans Bardtke zum 2.9.1966*, Berlin, 1968, pp. 37-46.
CEBALLOS ATIENZA, A., *La argumentación teológico-bíblica en la Biblia Parva de San Pedro Pascual*, in *EstBib* 42 (1984) 89-139.

CHEYNE, T.K., *Requests and Replies*, in *ExpT* 10 (1898-99) 444.
— *The Book of the Prophet Isaiah*, New York, NY, 1904⁵·
CHILDS, B.S., *The Enemy from the North and the Chaos Tradition*, in *JBL* 78 (1959) 187-198.
CHILTON, B., *Varieties and Tendencies of Midrash: Rabbinic Interpretations of Isaiah 24:23*, in R. FRANCE and D. WENHAM (eds.), *Studies in Midrash and Historiography* (Gospel Perspectives, 3), Sheffield, 1983, pp. 9-32.
CHISHOLM, R.B. Jr., *The 'Everlasting Covenant' and the 'City of Chaos', Intentional Ambiguity and Irony in Isaiah 24*, in *Chinese Theological Review* 6 (1993) 237-253.
CLARKE, G.H., *Religion, Reason and Revelation*, Philadelphia, PA, 1961.
CLEMENTS, R.E., *Isaiah 1–39* (New Century Biblical Commentary), Grand Rapids, MI, 1980.
CLIFFORD, R.J., *The Unity of the Book of Isaiah and Its Cosmogonic Language*, in *CBQ* 55 (1993) 1-17.
CLINES, D.J.A. (ed.), *The Dictionary of Classical Hebrew* [DCH]. Vols. I-IV, Sheffield, 1993-1998.
CLOETE, W.T.W., *Versification and Syntax in Jeremiah 2-25: Syntactical Constraints on Hebrew Poetry* (SBL DS, 117), Atlanta, GA, 1989.
COCAGNAC, M., *La Parole et son miroir. Les symboles bibliques* (Lire la Bible, 102), Paris, 1994.
COGGINS, R.J., *The Problem of Isaiah 24–27*, in *ExpT* 90 (1979) 328-333.
— *Which is the Best Commentary? Isaiah*, in *ExpT* 102 (1991) 99-102.
COHEN, C., *The Widowed City*, in *JANES* 5 (1973) 75-81.
COHEN, L.J., *The Semantics of Metaphor*, in A. ORTONY (ed.), *Metaphor and Thought*, Cambridge, 1993², pp. 58-70.
COHEN, T., *Notes on Metaphors*, in *Journal of Aesthetics and Art Criticism* 34 (1975-76) 253-255.
COLLINS, J.J., *The Expectation of the End, from Hebrew Prophets to the End of the First Century*, in J.J. COLLINS (ed.), *The Encyclopedia of Apocalypticism*. Vol. 1, New York, 1998.
CONDAMIN, A., *Le Livre d'Isaïe: Traduction critique avec notes et commentaire* (EB), Paris, 1905.
CONRAD, E. W., *Reading Isaiah*, Augsburg, 1991.
COOPER, D.E., *Metaphor*, Oxford, 1986.
COSTE, J., *Le texte grec d'Isaïe xxv 1-5*, in *RB* (1954) 67-86.
COX, S., *The Veil and Web of Death Destroyed by Christ. Isaiah xxv. 7,8*, in *The Expositor, 2nd Series* 4 (1882) 331-342.
CROSS, F.M., *New Directions in the Study of Apocalyptic*, in *JTC* 6 (1969) 157-165.
— *Cananite Myth and Hebrew Epic*, Cambridge, MA, 1973.
CRÜSEMANN, F., *Studien zur Formgeschichte von Hymnus und Danklied in Israel* (WMANT, 32), Neukirchen-Vluyn, 1969.
CUA, A.S., *Basic Metaphors and the Emergence of Root Metaphors*, in *The Journal of Mind and Behaviour* 3 (1982) 251-258.
CURTIS, J.B., *A Detached Note on hereb [Is 27:1]*, in *Proceedings, Eastern Great Lakes and Midwest Biblical Society* 4, (1984) 87-91.

DAHOOD, M., *Congruity of Metaphors*, in J. BARR et al. (eds.), *Hebräische Wortforschung. Festschrift zum 80. Geburtstag von Walter Baumgartner* (SVT, 16), Leiden, 1967, pp. 40-49.

DAICHES, S., *An Explanation of Isaiah 27:8*, in *JQR* 6 (1915-16) 399-404.

DARR, K.P., *Isaiah's Vision and the Family of God* (Literary Currents in Biblical Interpretation), Louisville, KY, 1994.

— *Two Unifying Female Images in the Book of Isaiah*, in L.M. HOPFE (ed.), *Uncovering Ancient Stones. Essays in Memory of H. Neil Richardson*, Winona Lake, IN, 1994, pp. 17-30.

DAVIDSON, D., *What Metaphors Mean*, in S. SACKS (ed.), *On Metaphor*, Chicago, IL 1979, pp. 29-46.

DAVIS, P.R. and CLINES, D.J.A. (eds.), *Among the Prophets. Language, Image and Structure in the Prophetic Writings* (JSOT SS, 144), Sheffield, 1993.

DAY, J., בל *in Is 26:19*, in *ZAW* 90 (1978) 265-269.

— *A Case of Inner Scriptural Interpretation*, in *JTS* 31 (1980) 309-319.

— *The Dependence of Isaiah 26:13-27:11 on Hosea 13:4-14:10 and its Relevance to Some Theories of the Redaction of the 'Isaiah Apocalypse'*, in C.C. BROYLES and C.A. EVANS (eds.), *Writing and Reading the Scroll of Isaiah. Studies of an Interpretive Tradition* (SVT, 70:1-2), Leiden, 1997, pp. 357-358; = revised version of *JTS* 31 (1980) 309-319.

— *Resurrection Imagery from Baal to the Book of Daniel*, in J.A. EMERTON (ed.), *Congress Volume, Cambridge, 1995* (SVT, 66), Leiden, 1997, pp. 25-36.

— *God and Leviathan in Isaiah 27:1*, in *BS* 155 (1998) 423-436.

DE GROOT, J., *Alternatieflezingen in Jesaja 24*, in *Nieuwe Theologische Studiën* 22 (1939) 153-158.

DELBECQUE, N., *Images and Metaphors in a Feminist Perspective*, in J.-P. VAN NOPPEN (ed.), *Metaphor and Religion. Theolinguistics 2* (Study Series of the Vrije Universiteit Brussel, 12), Brussels, 1983, pp. 231-250.

DEL BRASSEY, P., *Metaphor and the Incomparable God in Isaiah 40-55*, Diss. (UMI), Harvard University, 1997.

DELCOR, M., *Le festin d'immortalité sur la montagne de Sion à l'ère eschatologique en Isa 25:6-9 à la lumière de la littérature ugaritique*, in *Salmanticensis* 23 (1976) 89-98.

DELITZSCH, F., *Commentar über das Buch Jesaia* (BKAT, III-I), Leipzig, 1889[4].

— *Commentary on the Old Testament, VII: Isaiah* (tr. J. MARTIN), Edinburgh, 1875, 1910 [Reprinted, Grand Rapids, MI 1973].

DIJK-HEMMES, F. VAN, *The Metaphorization of Women in Prophetic Speech: An Analysis of Ezekiel 2*, in A. BRENNER (ed.), *A Feminist Companion to the Latter Prophets* (The Feminist Companion to the Bible, 8) Sheffield, 1995, pp. 244-255.

DILLMANN, A., *Der Prophet Jesaja* (KHAT, 5), Leipzig, 1890; 1898[2] (edited by R. KITTEL).

DIRVEN, R., and PAPROTTÉ, W. (eds.), *The Ubiquity of Metaphor: Metaphor in Language and Thought* (Amsterdam Studies in the Theory and History of Linguistic Science Series 4: Current Issues in Linguistic Theory, 29), Amsterdam – Philadelphia, 1985.

DOBBS-ALLSOPP, F.W., *Weep, O Daughter of Zion: A Study of the City-Lament Genre in the Hebrew Bible* (BibOr, 44), Rome, 1993.

DÖDERLEIN, J.C., *Esaias, ex recensione textus Hebraei*, Altsofi, 1789.
— *Esaias*, Altsofi, 1825.
DOMINGUEZ, N., Vaticinios sobre el fin del mundo, in *Ciencia tomista* 51 (1935) 125-146.
DOYLE, B., A Literary Analysis of Isaiah 25,10a, in J. VAN RUITEN and M. VERVENNE (eds.), *Studies in the Book of Isaiah. Festschrift Willem A.M. Beuken* (BETL, 132), Leuven, 1997, pp. 173-193.
DRESCHLER, M., *Der Prophet Jesaja*, Stuttgart, 1849.
DRIVER, G.R. Hebrew Notes on Prophets and Proverbs (Isa. 27:11), in *JTS* 41 (1940) 162-175.
— Hebrew Notes, in *JBL* 68 (1949) 57-59.
DRIVER, S.R., *Isaiah, His Life and Times, and the Writings Which Bear His Name*, New York, NY, 1888.
DUHM, B., *Das Buch Jesaja* (GHAT), Göttingen, 1968⁵.
DUMBRELL, W.J., The Purpose of the Book of Isaiah, in *TynB* 36 (1985) 111-128.
EICHRODT, W., *Der Heilige in Israel: Jesaja 1–12* (BKAT), Stuttgart, 1960,
— *Der Herr der Geschichte: Jesaja 13–23 und 28–39* (BKAT), Stuttgart, 1967.
EIDEVALL, G., *Grapes in the Desert. Metaphors, Models and Themes in Hosea 4-14* (CB, 43), Stockholm, 1996.
EISSFELDT, O., *Einleitung in das Alte Testament unter Einschluss der Apokryphen und Pseudepigraphen sowie der apokryphen- und pseudepigraphenartigen Qumranschriften: Entstehungsgeschichte des Alten Testaments* (Neue theologische Grundrisse), Tübingen, 1964³.
— *The Old Testament: An Introduction Including the Apocrypha and Pseudepigrapha, and also the Works of Similar Type from Qumran; the History of the Formation of the Old Testament* (tr. P.R. ACKROYD), New York, NY, 1966.
EITAN, I., A Contribution to Isaiah Exegesis (Notes and Short Studies in Biblical Philology: Isa. 24:11), in *HUCA* 12–13 (1937-38) 55-88.
ELDER, W., *A Theological-Historical Study of Isaiah 24–27*, Diss. (UMI), Baylor University, 1974.
ELLIGER, K. and RUDOLPH, W. et al. (eds.), *Biblia Hebraica Stuttgartensia* [BHS], Stuttgart, 1990⁴.
ELLINGTON, J., A Swimming Lesson (Isaiah 25:11), in *BiTr* 47 (1996) 246-247.
EMERTON, J. A., A Textual Problem in Isaiah 25:2, in *ZAW* 89 (1977) 64-73.
— Notes on Two Verses in Isaiah (26:17 and 66:17), in J. A. Emerton (ed.), *Prophecy: Essays Presented to Georg Fohrer on his 65th Birthday*, (BZAW, 150), Berlin, 1980, pp. 12-25.
ES J.J. VAN, *Spreken over God: letterlijk of figuurlijk? Analogie en metafoor in het spreken over God*, Amsterdam, 1979.
EXUM, J.C., Of Broken Pots, Fluttering Birds, and Visions in the Night: Extended Simile and Poetic Technique in Isaiah, in *CBQ* 43 (1981) 331-352.
FELDER, C.H., The Bible, Black Women and Ministry, in *Journal of the Interdenominational Theological Center* 12 (1984-85) 9-21.
FELDMANN, F., *Das Buch Isaias übersetzt und erklärt I (Kap. 1-39)* (EHAT, 14), Münster, 1926.

FENSHAM, F.C., *The Preposition B in Isaiah 27:13*, in *EvQ* 29 (1957) 157-158.
FEY, R., *Amos und Jesaja* (WMANT, 12), Neukirchen-Vluyn, 1963.
FICHTNER, J., *Prophetismus und Apokalyptik in Protojesaja*, Diss., University of Breslau, 1929.
FIELD, F., *Origenis Hexaplorum quae supersunt II*, Oxford, 1875; reprinted 1964.
FISCH, H., *The Analogy of Nature, a Note on the Structure of Old Testament Imagery*, in *JThS* 6 (1955) 161-173.
FISCHER, I., *Tora für Israel – Tora für die Völker. Das Konzept des Jesajabuches* (SBS, 164), Stuttgart, 1995.
— *Das Buch Jesaja*, in L. SCHOTTROFF and M.-T. WACKER, *Kompendium feministischer Bibelauslegung*, Gütersloh, 1998, pp. 246-257.
FITZGERALD, A. *The Mythological Background for the Presentation of Jerusalem as a Queen and False Worship as Adultery in the OT*, in *CBQ* 34 (1972) 403-416.
— *BTWLT and BT as Titles for Capital Cities*, in *CBQ* 37 (1975) 167-183.
FLOB, J. P., *Die Wortstellung des Konjugationssystem in Jes 24*, in H.-J. FABRY (ed.), *Bausteine biblischer Theologie: Festgabe für G. Johannes Botterweck zum 60. Geburtstag dargebracht von seinen Schülern* (BBB, 50), Cologne – Bonn, 1977, pp. 227-244.
FOHRER, G., *Das Buch Jesaja* (ZBK), Zurich, 3 vols., 1960-1964.
— *Der Aufbau der Apokalypse der Jesajabuchs. Jesaja 24–27*, in *CBQ* 25 (1963) 34-45; = ID., *Entstehung, Komposition und Überlieferung von Jesaja 1-39, Studien zur alttestamentlichen Prophetie* (BZAW, 99), Berlin, 1967, pp. 170-181.
— *The Origin, Composition and Tradition of Isaiah i-xxxix*, in *Annual of the Leeds University Oriental Society* 3 (1961) 3-38; = ID., *Entstehung, Komposition und Überlieferung von Jesaja 1-39, Studien zur alttestamentlichen Prophetie* (BZAW, 99), Berlin, 1967, pp. 113-147.
FOLLIS, E.R., *The Holy City as Daughter*, in ID. (ed.), *Directions in Biblical Hebrew Poetry* (JSOT SS, 40), Sheffield, 1987, pp. 173-184.
FOUTS, D. M., *A Suggestion for Isa. xxvi 16*, in *VT* 41 (1991) 472-495.
FRANCISCO, C.T., *Isaiah in the Christian Proclamation (Chaps. 24–27)*, in *R&E* 65 (1968) 471-482
FRANKE, C.H., *The Function of the Oracles against Babylon in Isaiah 14 and 27*, in *SBL SP* 32 (1993) 250-259.
— *Reversals of Fortune in the Ancient Near East: A Study of the Babylon Oracles in the Book of Isaiah*, in R.F. MELUGIN and M.A.SWEENEY (eds.), *New Visions of Isaiah* (JSOT SS, 214), Sheffield, 1996, pp. 104-123.
FREEDMAN, D.N. (ed.), *The Anchor Bible Dictionary* [ABD], New York, NY, 1992.
FROST, S.B., *Old Testament Apocalyptic: Its Origin and Growth*, London, 1952.
FRYE, N., *The Great Code*, London, 1982.
— *Words With Power: Being a Second Study on the Bible and Literature*, San Diego, CA,1990.
FRYMER-KENSKY, T., *In the Wake of the Goddesses: Women, Culture and the Biblical Transformation of the Pagan Myth*, New York, NY, 1992.
FUNK, R., *Language, Hermeneutic and the Word of God*, New York, NY, 1966.

GALAMBUSH, J., *Jerusalem in the Book of Ezekiel: The City as Yahweh's Wife* (SBL DS, 130), Atlanta, GA, 1992.
GARCÍA MARTÍNEZ, F. and WATSON, W.G.E., *The Dead Sea Scrolls Translated: the Qumran Texts in English*, Leiden, 1994; = F. GARCÍA MARTÍNEZ, *Textos de Qumran Trotta*, Madrid, 1992.
GARCÍA RECIO, J., *'La fauna de las ruinas'. Un topos literario de Isaías*, in *Est-Bib* 53 (1995) 55-96.
GARDINER, F., *On the Duplication of the Tetragrammaton in Isaiah 12:2; 26:4*, in *The Old and New Testament Student* 9 (1889) 219-223.
GERHART, M. and RUSSELL, A., *Metaphoric Process: The Creation of Scientific and Religious Understanding*, Fort Worth, TX 1984.
— HEALEY, J.P., and RUSSEL, A.M., *Sublimination of the Goddess in the Deitic Metaphor of Moses*, in *Semeia* 61 (1993) 167-182.
GERSTENBERGER, J., *Psalms, with an Introduction to Cultic Poetry* (FOTL, 14), Grand Rapids, MI, 1988.
GESENIUS, W., *Der Prophet Jesaia: übersetzt und mit einem vollständigen philologisch-kritischen und historischen Commentar begleitet*, Leipzig, 1821.
GIBSON, J.C.L., *Language and Imagery in the Old Testament*, London, 1998.
GILEADI, A., *A Holistic Structure of the Book of Isaiah*, Diss. (UMI), Brigham Young University, 1981.
— *The Apocalyptic Book of Isaiah*, Provo, UT, 1982.
GILL, J.H., *On Knowing God*, Philadelphia, PA, 1981.
GILLINGHAM, S., *Psalmody and Apocalyptic in the Hebrew Bible: Common Vision or Shared Experience?*, in J. BARTON and D.J. REIMER (eds.), *After the Exile. Essays in Honour of Rex Mason*, Macon, GA, 1996, pp. 147-169.
GILSE, J. van, *Jesaja XXIV-XXVII*, in *NedTT* 3 (1914) 167-193.
GITAY, Y., *Why Metaphors? A Study of the Texture of Isaiah*, in C.C. BROYLES and C.A. EVANS (eds.), *Writing and Reading the Scroll of Isaiah. Studies of an Interpretive Tradition* (SVT, 70: 1-2), Leiden, 1997, pp. 57-65.
GLASSON, T.F., *Theophany and Parousia*, in *NTS* 34 (1988) 259-270.
GLUCKSBERG, S. and KEYSAR, B., *How Metaphors Work*, in A. ORTONY (ed.), *Metaphor and Thought*, Cambridge 1993[2], pp. 401-424.
GOLLINGER, H., *Wenn einer stirbt, lebt er dann wieder auf (Hiob 14,14): zum alttestamentlich-jüdischen Hintergrund der Deutung der dem Kreuzestod nachfolgenden Erfahrung der Jünger mit dem Bekenntnis zur Auferweckung Jesu*, in L. OBERLINNER et al. (eds.), *Auferstehung Jesu – Auferstehung der Christen: Deutung des Osterglaubens*, Freiburg, 1986, pp. 11-38.
GOODMAN, N., *Metaphor as Moonlighting*, in S. SACKS (ed.), *On Metaphor*, Chicago, IL, 1979, pp. 175-180.
GORDON, C.H., *Leviathan: Symbol of Evil*, in A. ALTMANN (ed.), *Biblical Motifs: Origins and Transformations*, Cambridge, MA, 1966, pp. 1-9.
— *Hby, possessor of horns and tail*, in K. BERGERHOF et al. (eds.), *Ugarit-Forschungen 18*, Kevelaer, 1986, pp. 129-132.
GOSHEN-GOTTSTEIN, M.H. (ed.) *The Book of Isaiah, Part I and II. The Hebrew University Bible*, Jerusalem, 1975.
— *The Aleppo Codex* [facsimile edition], Jerusalem, 1976.

GRAY, B., *Critical Discussions. Isaiah 26; 25:1-5· 34:12-14*, in ZAW 31 (1911) 111-127.
GRAY, G.B. and PEAKE, A.S., *A Critical and Exegetical Commentary on the Book of Isaiah I-XXVII* (ICC), New York, NY, 1912.
GRÄTZ, H., *Die Auslegung und der historische Hintergrund der Weissagung in Jesaja Kap. 24–27*, in Monatschrift für Geschichte und Wissenschaft des Judenthums 25 (1886) 1-23.
GRÄTZ, S., *Der strafende Wettergott, Erwägungen zur Traditionsgeschichte des Adad-Fluchs im Alten Orient und im Alten Testament* (BBB, 114), Leipzig – Bodenheim, 1998.
GRAY, M.,*The Shaking of the Foundations – Again!*, Unpublished lecture delivered on the Feast of St Thomas of Aquinas, Faculty of Theology, KU Leuven, March 7th, 1995.
GREEN, B., *Like a Tree Planted. An Exploration of Psalms and Parables through Metaphor*, Collegeville, MI, 1997.
GREENBERG, M., *Ezekiel 1-20* (AB, 22), New York, NY, 1983.
GREGGS, G.A., *Priest, Prophet and Apocalyptic; The Authoring of Identity in the Period of Restoration*, Diss. (UMI), Yale University, 1991.
GROSS, W., *Verbform und Funktion, wayyiqtol für die Gegenwart? Ein Beitrag zur Syntax poetischer althebräischer Texte* (ATSAT, 1), St. Ottilien, 1976.
— A. DISSE, A. MICHEL (eds.), *Die Satzteilfolge im Verbalsatz alttestamentlicher Prosa: untersucht an den Büchern Dtn, Ri und 2 Kön* (FAT, 17), Tübingen, 1996.
GRYSON, R., «*Enfanter un esprit de salut*». *Histoire du texte de Isaïe 26,17.18*, in RTL 27 (1996) 25-46.
GUNKEL, H., *Jesaja 33, eine prophetische Liturgie*, in ZAW 1 (1924) 182-183.
GUTHE, H., and EISSFELDT, O., *Jesaja* (HSAT), Bonn, 1922.
HABETS, G. N. M., *Die grosse Jesaja-Apokalypse (Jes 24–27). Ein Beitrag zur Theologie des Alten Testaments*, Diss., Bonn, 1974.
HANHART, R., *Die jahwehfeindliche Stadt*, in E. DONNER (ed.), *Beiträge zur alttestamentlichen Theologie: Festschrift für Walther Zimmerli zum 70. Geburtstag*, Göttingen, 1977, pp. 152-163.
— *Die Bedeutung der Septuaginta in neutestamentlicher Zeit*, in ZTK 81 (1984) 395-416.
HANSON, P., *The Dawn of Apocalyptic. The Historical and Sociological Roots of Jewish Apocalyptic Eschatology*, Philadelphia, PA, 1975.
HARMANSON, E.A., *Recognising Hebrew Metaphors: Conceptual Metaphor Theory and Bible Translation*, in JNSL 22 (1996) 67-78.
HAUGE, M.R., *Some Aspects of the Motif 'the City Facing Death' of Ps 68:21*, in SJOT 1 (1988) 1-29.
— *Between Sheol and Temple. Motif, Structure and Function in the I-Psalms* (JSOT SS, 178), Sheffield, 1995.
HARRELSON, W., *Death and Victory in 1 Corinthians 15:51-57: The Transformation of a Prophetic Theme*, in J. CARROLL et al. (eds.), *Faith and History: Essays in Honour of Paul W. Meyer*, Atlanta, GA, 1990, pp. 149-159.
HARTSHORNE, C., *Creative Synthesis and Philosophic Method*, Lanham, MD, 1983.

HAYES, H.J., and IRVINE, S.A., *Isaiah: The 8th Century Prophet: His Times and His Preaching*, Nashville, TN, 1988.
HAYES, K.M., *'The Earth Mourns': Earth as Actor in a Prophetic Metaphor*, Diss. (UMI), The Catholic University of America, 1997.
HEINTZ, J.G.S., *Oracles et métaphores prophétiques en Israël antique: Ésaïe, Jérémie et le Second Ésaïe*, in *RHPhR* 70 (1990) 209-239.
HELFMEYER, F. J. *'Deine Toten – meine Leichen'. Heilszusage und Annahme in Jes. 26:19*, in H.-J. FABRY (ed.), *Bausteine biblischer Theologie: Festgabe für G. Johannes Botterweck zum 60. Geburtstag dargebracht von seinen Schülern* (BBB, 50), Cologne – Bonn, 1977, pp. 245-258.
HELLER, A., *200 biblische Symbole*, Stuttgart, 1962.
— *Biblische Zahlensymbolik*, Stuttgart, 1951.
HEMPEL, J., *Die Grenzen des Anthropomorphismus Jahwes im Alten Testament*, in *ZAW* 57 (1939) 82-84
HENRY, M.L., *Glaubenskrise und Glaubensbewährung in den Dichtungen der Jesaja Apokalypse* (BWANT, 86), Stuttgart, 1967.
HERBERT, A.S., *The Book of the Prophet Isaiah, Chapters 1-39* (Cambridge Biblical Commentary), Cambridge, 1973.
HERRMANN, J. R., סאסא *Jes 27:8 und* שׁאוּשׁ *Hes 39:2*, in *ZAW* 36 (1916) 243.
HESCHEL, A.J., *Die Prophetie* (Polska Akademja Umiejetnosci. Mémoires de la commission orientaliste, 22), Krakow, 1936.
— *The Prophets*, New York, NY, 1962.
HESSE, M., *The Cognitive Claims of Metaphor*, in J.P. VAN NOPPEN (ed.), *Theolinguistics. Vol. 2: Metaphor & Religion* (Study Series of the Vrije Universiteit Brussel, 12), Brussels, 1983, pp. 27-45.
HIEBERT, P.S., *'Whence Shall Help Come to Me?': The Biblical Widow*, in P.L. DAY (ed.), *Gender and Difference in Ancient Israel*, Minneapolis, MN, 1989, pp. 125-141.
HIERONYMUS [JEROME], *Commentarium in Esaiam*, Libri I-XVIII, Turnhout, 1968.
HILGENFIELD, A., *Das Judentum in dem persischen Zeitalter*, in *ZWT* 9 (1866) pp. 398-488.
HILLERS, D.R., *Treaty-Curses and Old Testament Prophecy* (BiOr, 16), Rome, 1964.
HITZIG, F., *Der Prophet Jesaja, übersetzt und ausgelegt*, Heidelberg, 1833.
HÖFFKEN, P., *Neuere Arbeiten zur Sprachgestalt alttestamentlicher Texte*, in *BibOr* 43 (1986) 647-660.
— *Das Buch Jesaja Kapitel 1-39* (NSKAT, 18-1), Stuttgart, 1993.
HØGENHAVEN, J., *Die symbolischen Namen in Jesaja 7 und 8 im Rahmen der sogenannten 'Denkschrift' des Propheten*, in J. VERMEYLEN (ed.), *The Book of Isaiah – Le livre d'Isaïe* (BETL, 81), Leuven, 1989, pp. 231-235.
HOLLADAY, W.L., *Isaiah: Scroll of a Propetic Heritage*, Grand Rapids, MI, 1978.
HORDERN, W., *Speaking of God: The Nature and Purpose of Theological Language*, New York, 1964.
HUGENBERGER, G.P., *Marriage as a Covenant. Biblical Law and Ethics as Developed from Malachi* (SVT, 52), Leiden, 1994.
HUMBERT, P., *La rosée tombe en Israël*, in *TZ* 13 (1957) 487-493.

HUTMACHER, H.A., *Symbolik der biblischen Zahlen und Zeiten*, Paderborn, 1993.
HYLMÖ, G. *De s.k. profetishka liturgiernas rytm stil och komposition* (Lunds Universitets Arsskrift N.F. Avd. 1. Bd. 25. Nr. 5), Lund, 1929.
IBN EZRA (ABRAHAM BEN MEIR), *Commentary of Ibn Ezra on Isaiah* (tr. M. FRIEDLANDER), New York, NY, 1966².
INDURKHYA, B., *Metaphor and Cognition*, Dordrecht, 1992.
IRWIN, W.H., *Syntax and Style in Isaiah 26*, in *CBQ* 41 (1979) 240-261.
— *The Punctuation of Is 24:14-16a and 25:4c-5*, in *CBQ* 46 (1984) 215-222.
— *The City of Chaos in Isa. 24,10 and the Genitive of Result*, in *Bib* (1994) 401-403.
ITOH, R., *A Literary and Linguistic Approach to Isaiah 24-27*, Diss. (UMI), Trinity Evangelical Divinity School, 1995.
JAUSS, H., *Tor der Hoffnung. Vergleichsformen und ihre Funktion in der Sprache der Psalmen* (Europäische Hochschulschriften, 23-412), Frankfurt am Main, 1991.
JACOB, E., *Du premier au deuxième chant de la vigne du prophète Ésaïe. Réflexions sur Ésaïe 27:2-5*, in H.J. STOEBE and W. EICHRODT (eds.), *Wort, Gebot, Glaube: Beiträge zur Theologie des Alten Testaments: Walther Eichrodt zum 80. Geburtstag*, Zurich, 1970, pp. 325-330.
JARVIS, P.G., *[Isa. 25,1-9...] A Good Time Coming 2*, in *ExpT* 105 (1993) 374s.
JASTROW, M., *A Dictionary of the Targumim, the Talmud Babli and Yerushalmi, and the Midrashic Literature*, New York, NY, 1982 (1st Edition 1950).
JAY, P., *L'exégèse de saint Jérôme d'après son Commentaire sur Isaïe* (Études Augustiniennes), Paris, 1985.
JENNI, E., *Eschatology of the Old Testament*, in *IDB*, 1962, pp. 126-134.
JENNINGS, F.C., *Studies in Isaiah*, Neptune, NJ, 1935.
JENSEN, J., *Isaiah 1–39* (OTM, 8), Wilmington, IN, 1984.
JOHNSON, D. G., *From Chaos to Restoration. An Integrative Reading of Is 24–27* (JSOT SS, 61), Sheffield, 1988; = revised version of *Devastation and Restoration, A Compositional Study of Isaiah 24-27*, Diss. (UMI), Princeton Theological Seminary, 1985.
JOHNSON., M., *Philosophical Perspectives on Metaphor*, Minneapolis, MN, 1985.
JONGELING, B., *L'expression my ytn dans l'AT [27:4]*, in *VT* 24 (1974) 32-40
JOÜON, P., and MURAOKA, T., *A Grammar of Biblical Hebrew* [J–M] (Subsidia Biblica, 14/I-II), Rome, 1991.
JÜNGEL, E., *Metaphorische Wahrheit. Erwägungen zur theologischen Relevanz der Metapher als Beitrag zur Hermeneutik einer narrativen Theologie*, in P. RICŒUR and E. JÜNGEL (eds.), *Metapher. Zur Hermeneutik religiöser Sprache*, Munich, 1974.
— *Thesen zur theologischen Metaphorologie*, in J.-P. VAN NOPPEN (ed.), *Erinnern, um Neues zu sagen. Die Bedeutung der Metapher für die religiöse Sprache*, Frankfurt am Main, 1988, pp. 52-67.
KAISER, O., *Der Prophet Jesaja: Kapitel 1–12, Der Prophet Jesaja: Kapitel 13-39* (ATD, 17-18), Göttingen, 1960-73.
— *Einleitung in das Alte Testament*, Gütersloh, 1969.

— *Isaiah 1–12, Isaiah 13–39* (tr. A.WILSON), (OTL), Philadelphia, PA, 1972²-1973².

KAMINKA, A., *Le développement des idées du prophète Isaïe et l'unité de son livre VIII: L'authenticité des chapîtres xxiv à xxvii*, in *Revue des études juives* 81 (1925) 23-36.

KAUFMANN, Y., *The Religion of Israel* (tr. M. GREENBERG), Chicago, IL, 1960.

KEEL, O., *Feinde und Gottesleugner* (SBM, 7), Stuttgart, 1969.

— *Die Welt der altorientalischen Bildsymbolik und das Alte Testament: am Beispiel der Psalmen*, Zurich, 1972.

— *YHWH-visionen und Siegelkunst* (SBS, 84-85), Stuttgart, 1977².

— *Deine Blicke sind Tauben: zur Metaforik des Hohen Liedes* (SBS, 114-115), Stuttgart, 1984.

KEIZER, P.K., *De profeet Jesaja*, Kampen, 1947.

KESSLER, W., *Gott geht es um das Ganze, Jes. 56-66 und Jes. 24–27* (Die Botschaft des A.T., 19), Stuttgart, 1960.

KHIOK-KHNG, Y., *Isaiah 5:2-7 and 27:2-6 – Let's Hear the Whole Song of Rejection and Restoration*, in *Jian Dao* 3 (1995) 77-94.

KILIAN, R., *Jesaja I: 1–12* (NEchB, 17), Würzburg, 1986.

— *Jesaja II: 13–39* (NEchB, 32), Würzburg, 1994.

KISSANE, E.J., *The Book of Isaiah*. 2 vols., Dublin, 1941 (Revised Edition, 1960).

KITTAY, E.F., *Metaphor: Its Cognitive Force and Linguistic Structure*, Oxford, 1987.

— and LEHRER, A., *Semantic Fields and the Structure of Metaphor*, in *Studies in Language* 5 (1981) 31-63.

KITTEL, R., KAHLE, P., BAUMGARTNER, W., *Biblia V.T. Biblia Hebraica* [BHK] Stuttgart, 1937 (Gesamtherstellung, 1973).

KJÄRGAARD, M., *Metaphor and Parable. A Systematic Analysis of the Specific Structure and Cognitive Function of the Synoptic Similes and Parables qua Metaphor* (Acta Theologica Danica, 20), Leiden, 1986.

KLINE, H., *Death, Leviathan, and Martyrs: Isaiah 24:1–27:1*, in W. KAISER, Jr. and R. YOUNGBLOOD (eds.), *A Tribute to Gleason Archer*, Chicago, IL, 1986, pp. 229-249.

KNOBEL, A.W., *Der Prophet Jesaja* (KEHAT, 5), Leipzig, 1898⁴.

KOCH, K., *Ratlos vor der Apokalyptic*, Gütersloh, 1970.

— *Was ist Formgeschichte? Methoden der Bibelexegese*, Neukirchen – Vluyn, 1974³.

KOEHLER, L., BAUMGARTNER, W., STAMM, J.J., *The Hebrew and Aramaic Lexicon of the Old Testament* [HALOT]. Vols I-III, Leiden, 1994.

— *Hebräisches und aramäisches Lexikon zum Alten Testament*, Leiden, 1995³.

KÖNIG, E., *Stilistik, Retorik und Poetik in Bezug auf die biblische Literatur*, Leipzig, 1900.

— *Das Buch Jesaja eingeleitet, übersetzt und erklärt*, Gütersloh, 1926.

KOOIJ, A. VAN DER, *The Teacher Messiah and Worldwide Peace. Some Comments on Symmachus' Version of Isaiah 25:7-8*, in *JNSL* 24 (1998) 75-82.

— *Isaiah 24–27: Text Critical Notes*, in H.J. BOSMAN, H. VAN GROL et al. (eds.), *Studies in Isaiah 24–27: The Isaiah Workshop (De Jesaja Werkplaats)* (OTS, 43), Leiden, 1999.

KORPEL, M.C.A., *A Rift in the Clouds: Ugaritic and Hebrew Descriptions of the Divine*, Münster, 1990.
— *Metaphors in Isaiah LV*, in *VT* 46 (1996) 43-55.
KOZIOL, S., *Symbolika małzenska... La symbolique matrimoniale et familiale dans les oracles prophétiques*, Diss., Lublin, 1992.
KRASOVEC, J., *Punishment of the Nations and Deliverance of Israel in the Apocalypse of Isaiah*, in *Bogoslovni Vestnik* 54 (1994) 253-268.
— *Deliverance of the Remnant from Judgement in the Prophecy of Isaiah*, in *Bogoslovni Vestnik* 54 (1994) 331-357.
KRAUS, H.-J., *Psalms 1-59*, Minneapolis, MN, 1988.
KRUGER, P.A., *The Relationship Between Yahweh and Israel as Expressed by Certain Metaphors and Similes in the Book Hosea*, Diss., University of Stellenbosch, 1983.
KUENEN, A., *The Religion of Israel to the Fall of the Jewish State* (tr. A. H. MAY), London – Edinburgh, 1874.
KUGEL, J., *The Idea of Biblical Poetry. Parallelism and Its History*, New Haven, CT, 1981.
LACK, R., *La symbolique de livre d'Isaïe. Essai sur l'image littéraire comme élément de structuration* (AnBib, 59), Rome, 1973.
LAGRANGE, M.-J., *L'apocalypse d'Isaïe (24–27)*, in *RB* 3 (1984) 200-231.
LAKOFF, G. and JOHNSON, M., *Women, Fire and Dangerous Things: What Categories Reveal about the Mind*, Chicago, 1987.
— *Metaphors We Live By*, Chicago – London, 1980.
— and TURNER, M., *More than Cool Reason. A Field Guide to Poetic Metaphor*, Chicago – London, 1989.
— *The Contemporary Theory of Metaphor*, in A. ORTONY (ed.), *Metaphor and Thought*, Cambridge, 1993², pp. 202-251.
LANDY, F., *Poetics and Parallelism. Some Comments on James Kugel's* The Idea of Biblical Poetry, in *JSOT* 28 (1984) 61-87.
— *On Metaphor, Play and Nonsense*, in *Semeia* 61 (1993) 219-237.
— *In the Wilderness of Speech: Problems of Metaphor in Hosea*, in *Biblical Interpretation* 3 (1995) 35-59.
LÉONARD, J.-M., Review of A. NICCACCI, *The Syntax of the Verb in Classical Hebrew Prose* (JSOT SS, 86), (Sheffield, 1990), in *ETR* 67 (1992) 103-104.
LESLIE, E.A., *Isaiah*, New York, NY, 1963.
LEUPOLD, H., *Exposition of Isaiah*. 2 vols., Grand Rapids, MI, 1963-1971.
LEWIS, D.J., *A Rhetorical Critical Analysis of Isaiah 24–27*, Diss. (UMI), The Southern Baptist Theological Seminary, 1985.
LEWY, J., *The Old West Semitic Sun God Hammu*, in *HUCA* 18 (1944) 436-443.
LIEBMANN, E. *Der Text zu Jesaja 24–27*, in *ZAW* 22 (1902) 285-304; 23 (1903) 209-86.
LIEBREICH, L.J., *The Compilation of the Book of Isaiah*, in *JQR* 67 (1956) 236-257.
LINDBLOM, J., *Die Jesaja-Apokalypse: Jesaja 24–27* (Lunds Universitets Årsskrift, N.F. 1, 34, 3.), Lund, 1938.
— *Die Jesaja-Apokalypse (Jes 24–27) in der neuen Jesaja-Handschrift*, in *K. Humaniska Vetenskapssamsfundets i Lund Arsberattelse* 2 (1950-51) 79-144.

— *Gibt es eine Eschatologie bei den alttestamentlichen Propheten?*, in *StT* 6 (1952) 79-114.
LIWAK, R., *Die altorientischen Grossmächte in der Metaphorik der Prophetie*, in R. LIWAK and S. WAGNER (eds.), *Prophetie und geschichtliche Wirklichkeit: Fs. S. Herrmann*, Stuttgart, 1991, pp. 206-230.
LJUNG, I., *Bildspraksanalys, sprakfilosofi och litteraturvetenskap: Kirsten Nielsen; for et trae er der hab om traeet som metafor i Jes 1-39*, in *Dansk Teologisk Tidsskrift* 49 (1986) 81-95.
LOCKE, J., *Essay Concerning Human Understanding*, Oxford, 1894; first published in 1690.
LOEWENBERG, I., *Identifying Metaphors*, in M. JOHNSON (ed.), *Philosophical Perspectives on Metaphor*, Minneapolis, MN, 1981, pp. 154-181.
LOHMANN, P., *Zu Text und Metrum einiger Stellen aus Jesaja. II. Das Lied 25: 1-5*, in *ZAW* 33 (1913) 256-262.
— *Die selbständigen lyrischen Abschnitte in Jes 24–27*, in *ZAW* 37 (1917-18) 1-58.
LONG, G.A., *Dead or Alive? Literality and God-Metaphors in the Hebrew Bible*, in *JAAR* 62 (1994) 509-537.
LORD, D.N., *A Designation and Exposition of the Figures of Isaiah Chapter XXIV*, in *Theological and Literary Journal* 6 (1853-54) 321-329.
— *A Designation and Exposition of the Figures of Isaiah Chapter XXV and XXVI*, in *Theological and Literary Journal* 6 (1853-54) 479-493.
— *A Designation and Exposition of the Figures of Isaiah Chapter XXVII*, in *Theological and Literary Journal* 7 (1854-55) 145-151.
LORENZ, H., *Heil und Wohl*, in *Evangelische Theologie* 45 (1985) 389-400.
LOWTH, R., *Isaiah: A New Translation*. 2 vols., London, 1834[10]; first edition, 1779.
LUDWIG, O., *Die Stadt in der Jesaja-Apokalypse, Zur Datierung von Jes. 24–27*, Cologne, 1967.
LURIA, B.Z., *Isaiah 25*, *Beth Mikra* 26 (1981) 313-317.
LURKER, M., *Wörterbuch biblischer Bilder und Symbole*, Munich, 1973.
LUST, J., *For I Lift Up My Hand to Heaven and Swear: Deut 32:40*, in F. GARCÍA MARTÍNEZ et al. (eds.), *Studies in Deuteronomy in Honour of C.J. Labuschagne on the Occasion of his 65th Birthday* (SVT, 53), Leiden, 1994, pp. 154-164.
— *The Raised Hand of the Lord in Deut 32:40 According to* MT, 4QDEUT^Q, *and* LXX, in *Textus* 18 (1995) 33-45.
— EYNIKEL, E., HAUSPIE, K. (eds.), *A Greek-English Lexicon of the Septuagint* [LEH]. 2 vols., Stuttgart, 1992-1996.
LUTHER, M., *Der Prophet Jesaia*, in *D. Martin Luthers Werke, Kritische Gesamtausgabe*. Vol. 25, Weimar, 1883, pp. 87-401.
— *Lectures on Isaiah chaps. 1-39* in *Luther's Works*. Vol. 16 (ed. and tr. J. PELIKAN and H.C. OSWALD), St Louis, MI 1969.
LUZZATTO, S.D., *Commentary on the Book of Isaiah* (Heb.), Tel Aviv, 1970.
MACCORMAC, E., *Metaphor and Myth in Science and Religion*, Durham, NC, 1976.
— *Religious Metaphors: Linguistic Expressions of Cognitive Processes*, in J.P. VAN NOPPEN (ed.), *Theolinguistics. Vol. 2: Metaphor & Religion*

(Study Series of the Vrije Universiteit Brussel, 12), Brussels, 1983, pp. 47-70.
— *A Cognitive Theory of Metaphor*, Cambridge, MA, 1985.
MACCRAE, A.A., *Some Principles in the Interpretation of Isaiah as Illustrated by Chapter 24 [and the nature of OT prophecy]*, in J.B. PAYNE (ed.), *New Perspectives on the Old Testament*, Waco, TX, 1970, pp. 146-159.
MACKY, P.W., *The Centrality of Metaphors to Biblical Thought. A Method for Interpreting the Bible* (Studies in the Bible and Early Christianity, 19), Lewiston – Queenston – Lampeter, 1990.
MANDELKERN, S., *Veteris Testamenti Concordantiae Hebraicae atque Chaldaicae*. Vols. I-II, Graz, 1975; first edition 1895; thoroughly revised F. Margolin, 1937.
MARCH, W., *A Study of Two Prophetic Compositions In Isaiah 24:1-27:1*, Diss. (UMI), Union Theological Seminary, 1966.
MARCONCINI, B., *La grande apocalisse. Is 24–27*, in *PSV* 28 (1993) 65-78.
MARGALIOTH (MARGULIES), R., *The Indivisible Isaiah: Evidence for the Single Authorship of the Prophetic Book*, New York, NY, 1964.
MARGALIT, B., *Ugaritic Contributions to Hebrew Lexicography*, in *ZAW* 99 (1987) 391-404.
MARTI, K., *Das Buch Jesaja* (KHAT, 10), Tübingen, 1900.
MARTIN-ACHARD, R., *Trois remarques sur la résurrection des morts dans l'Ancien Testament*, in *Cahiers de la Revue de théologie et de philosophie* 11 (1984) 170-184.
— *'Il engloutit la mort à jamais'. Remarques sur Ésaïe 25:8*, in A. CAQUOT et al. (eds.), *Mélanges bibliques et orientaux en l'honneur de M. Delcor* (AOAT, 215), Kevelaer, 1985, pp. 283-296.
MATTHEWS, V.C. and BENJAMIN, D.C., *Social World of Ancient Israel, 1250-587 BCE*, Peabody, MA, 1993.
— (eds.), *Old Testament Parallels. Laws and Stories from the Ancient Near East*, New York – Mahwah, NJ, 1997.
MAUCHLINE, J., *Isaiah 1–39* (Torch Bible Commentaries), London, 1962.
MAYER, R., *Zur Bildsprache der alttestamentlichen Propheten*, in *MTZ* (1950) 55-65.
MAYORAL, J.A., *El uso simbólico-teológico de los animales en los profetas del exilio*, in *EstBib* 53 (1995) 317-363.
MCCREESH, J.P., *Biblical Sound and Sense. Poetic Sound Patterns in Proverbs 10-29* (JSOT SS, 128), Sheffield, 1991.
MCEWAN HUMPHREY, E., *The Ladies and the Cities: Transformation and Apocalyptic Identity in Joseph and Aseneth, 4 Ezra, the Apocalypse and the Shepherd of Hermas* (JSOT SS, 17), Sheffield, 1995.
MCFAGUE, S., *Speaking in Parables. A Study in Metaphor and Theology*, Philadelphia, PA, 1975.
— *Metaphorical Theology. Models of God in Religious Language*, Philadelphia, PA, 1982.
— *Models of God. Theology for an Ecological, Nuclear Age*, Philadelphia, PA 1987.
MCGUIRE, E.M., *Yahweh and Leviathan: An Exegesis of Isaiah 27:1*, in *Restoration Quarterly* 13 (1970) 168-179.

MCINLAY, J., *Bringing the Unspeakable to Speech in Hosea*, in *Pacifica* 9 (1996) 121-134.
MCKENZIE, D.L., *Isaiah 1–39* (The Communicator's Commentary, 16A), Dallas, TX, 1993.
MCKEON, R. (ed.), *The Basic Works of Aristotle* [Poetics], New York, NY, 1941, 1457b, 6-9.
MCPHEETERS, W.M., *The Authenticity of Isaiah XXIV.–XXVII.*, in *The Presbyterian Quarterly* 10 (1896) 31-45.
MERWE, C.H.J., VAN DER, *An Overview of Hebrew Narrative Syntax*, in E. VAN WOLDE (ed.), *Narrative*, pp. 1-20.
— *A Critical Analysis of Narrative Syntactic Approaches, with Special Attention to their Relationship to Discourse*, in *Ibid.*, pp. 133-156.
MILLAR, W. R., *Isaiah 24–27 and the Origin of Apocalyptic* (HSM, 11), Missoula, MT, 1976.
MILLER, G., *Isaiah 25:6-9: God's Banquet*, in *Interp* 49 (1995) 175-179.
MILLS, M.E., *Images of God in the Old Testament*, London, 1998.
MISCALL, P. D., *Isaiah*, Sheffield, 1993.
— *Isaiah – Labyrinth of Images*, in *Semeia* 54 (1991) 103-121.
MOOIJ, J.J.A., *A Study of Metaphors* (North-Holland Linguistic Series, 27), Amsterdam – New York – Oxford, 1976.
MULDER, E. S., *Die Teologie van die Jesaja-Apokalypse. Jesaja 24–27*, Djakarta, 1954.
MÜLLER, H.-P.,*Vergleich und Metapher im Hohenlied*, Göttingen, 1984.
MUNCH, P.A., *The Expression 'Bajjom Hahu': Is It an Eschatological Terminus Technicus?* (Avhandlinger utgett av Det Norske Videnskap-Akademi i Oslo, II Hist.-Filos. Klasse), Oslo, 1936.
MUTIUS, H.G. VON, *Zwei Bibeltextvarianten bei Bachja ibn Pakuda (Jes 26:8)*, in *VT* 30 (1980) 234-236.
MOTYER, J.A., *The Prophecy of Isaiah*, Leicester, 1993.
NÄGELSBACH, C.W.E., *The Prophet Isaiah* (tr. S.T. LOWRIE and D. MOORE), Edinburgh, 1878.
NAIRN, M., *Hope [and New Zealand Society-Isa 25]*, in *East Asia Journal of Theology* 4 (1986) 29-32.
NAKAMURA, C.L., *Monarch, Mountain and Meal; The Eschatalogical Banquet of Isaiah 24:21-23; 25:6-10a*, Diss. (UMI), Princeton Theological Seminary, 1992.
NEWMARK, P., *The Translation of Metaphor*, in DIRVEN R. and W. PAPROTTÉ (eds.), *The Ubiquity of Metaphor*, Amsterdam, 1985, pp. 295-326.
NEWSOM, C.A., *A Maker of Metaphors: Ezekiel's Oracles Against Tyre*, in R.P. GORDON (ed.), *The Place is Too Small for Us: The Israelite Prophets in Recent Scholarship* (Sources for Biblical and Theological Study, 5), Winona Lake, IN, 1995, pp. 191-204.
NEVAS, J. C. M., *A Teologica da Traducao Grega dos Setenta no Libro de Isias*, Diss., Lisbon, 1973.
NICCACCI, A., *Sintassi del verbo ebraico nella prosa biblica classica* (Studium Biblicum Franciscanum Analecta, 23), Jerusalem, 1986.
— *The Syntax of the Verb in Classical Hebrew Prose* (JSOT SS, 86), Sheffield, 1990.

— *Lettura sintattica della prosa ebraico-biblica*, Jerusalem, 1991.
— *On the Hebrew Verbal System*, in R.D. BERGEN (ed.), *Biblical Hebrew and Discourse Linguistics*, Winona Lake, IN, 1994, pp. 117-137.
— *Analysis of Biblical Narrative*, in R.D. BERGEN (ed.), *Biblical Hebrew and Discourse Linguistics*, Winona Lake, IN, 1994, pp. 175-198.
— *Essential Hebrew Syntax*, in E. TALSTRA (ed.), *Narrative and Comment. Contributions Presented to Wolfgang Schneider*, Amsterdam, 1995, pp. 111-125.
— *Syntactic Analysis of Ruth*, in *Liber Annuus. Studium Biblicum Franciscanum* 45 (1995) 69-106.
— *Basic Facts and Theory of the Biblical Hebrew Verb System in Prose*, in E. VAN WOLDE (ed.), *Narrative Syntax and the Hebrew Bible. Papers of the Tilburg Conference 1996*, Leiden, 1997, pp. 167-202.
— *Analysing Biblical Hebrew Poetry*, in *JSOT* 74 (1997) 77-93.

NIEHAUS, J., *Raz-pesar in Isaiah XXIV*, in *VT* 31 (1981) 376-378.

NIELSEN, K. *Das Bild des Gerichts [Rib Pattern] in Jes. I-XII*, in *VT* 29 (1979) 309-324.
— *Reinterpretation of Metaphors – Tree Metaphors in Isa 1–39*, in M. AUGUSTIN and K.D. SCHUNK (eds.), *Wünschet Jerusalem Frieden: Collected Communications to the XIIth Congress of the International Organization for the Study of the Old Testament* (Beiträge zur Erforschung des Alten Testaments und der Antiken Judentums, 13), Jerusalem, 1986, pp. 425-429.
— *There is Hope For a Tree. The Tree as Metaphor in Isaiah* (JSOT SS, 65), Sheffield, 1991.

NOEGEL, S.B., *Dialect and Politics in Isaiah 24–27*, in *Aula Orientalis* 12 (1994) 177-192.

NOPPEN, J.P. VAN, (ed.), *Theolinguistics. Vol. 2: Metaphor & Religion* (Study Series of the Vrije Universiteit Brussel, 12), Brussels, 1983.
— et al. (eds.), *Metaphor: A Bibliography of Post-1970 Publications*, Amsterdam, 1985.
— *Erinnern, um Neues zu sagen. Die Bedeutung der Metapher für die religiöse Sprache*, Frankfurt am Main, 1988.
— *Metaphors*, in J. PETÖFI and T. OLIVI (eds.), *Von der verbalen Konstitution zur symbolischen Bedeutung – From Verbal Constitution to Symbolic Meaning* (Papiere zur Textlinguistik/Papers in Textlinguistics, 62), Hamburg, 1988.
— *Metapher und Religion*, in ID. (ed.), *Erinnern, um Neues zu sagen. Die Bedeutung der Metapher für die religiöse Sprache*, Frankfurt am Main, 1988, pp. 7-51.
— and HOLS, E. (eds.), *Metaphor II: A Classified Bibliography of Publications 1985-1990*, Amsterdam, 1990.

NOTH, M., *Das Geschichtsverständnis der alttestamentlichen Apokalyptik*, in ID., *Gesammelte Studien zum Alten Testament* (Theologische Bücherei, 6), Munich, 1960.

O'CONNELL, R.H., *Concentricity and Continuity. The Literary Structure of Isaiah* (JSOT SS, 188), Sheffield, 1994.

O'CONNOR, M.P., *The Pseudosorites: A Type of Paradox in Hebrew Verse*, in E.R. FOLLIS (ed.), *Directions in Biblical Hebrew Poetry* (JSOT SS, 40), Sheffield, 1987, pp. 161-172.

— *The Pseudo-sorites in Hebrew Verse*, in E.W. CONRAD and E.G. NEWING (eds.), *A Ready Scribe: Perspectives on Language and Text. Essays and Poems in Honor of Francis I. Andersen's Sixtieth Birthday*, Winona Lake, IN, 1987, pp. 239-251.

OLIVIER, J.P.J., *Rendering ידי as Benevolent Patron in Isa. 5:1*, in *JNSL* 22 (1996) 59-65.

ORELLI, C. VON, *The Prophecies of Isaiah* (tr. J.S. BANKS), Edinburgh, 1889.

ORFALI, M., *Anthropomorphism in the Christian Reproach of the Jews in Spain (12th-15th cent.)*, (tr. L. KESHET), in *Immanuel* 19 (1984-85) 60-73.

ORTONY, A., *Why Metaphors Are Necessary and Not Just Nice*, in *Educational Theory* 25 (1975) 45-52.

— (ed.), *Metaphor and Thought*, Cambridge, 1993².

— *The Role of Similarity in Similes and Metaphors*, in ID. (ed.), *Metaphor and Thought*, Cambridge, 1993², pp. 342-356.

OSWALT, J.N., *The Book of Isaiah, Chapters 13-39* (NICOT), Grand Rapids, MI, 1986.

— *God's Determination to Redeem his People (Isaiah 9:1-7; 11:1-11; 26:1-9; 35:1-10)*, in *R&E* 88 (1991) 153-165.

OTZEN, B., *Traditions and Structures of Isaiah 24–27*, in *VT* 24 (1974) 196-206.

PAGAN, M.A., *Apocalyptic Poetry: Isaiah 24–27*, in *BiTr* 43 (1992) 314-324.

PALMER, H., *Analogy: A Study of Qualification and Argument in Theology*, New York, NY, 1973.

PEARSON, B.W.R., *Resurrection and the Judgment of the Titans: ἡ γῆ τῶν ἀσεβῶν in LXX Isaiah 26.19*, in S.E. PORTER, M.A. HAYES & D. TOMBS (eds.), *Resurrection* (JSOT SS, 186; Roehampton Institute London Papers, 5), Sheffield, 1999, pp. 33-81.

PENNA, A., *Isaia* (La Sacra Biblia), Torino, 1958.

PETÖFI J. and OLIVI, T. (eds.), *Von der verbalen Konstitution zur symbolischen Bedeutung – From Verbal Constitution to Symbolic Meaning* (Papiere zur Textlinguistik/Papers in Textlinguistics, 62), Hamburg, 1988.

PINTO, C.O., *O uso de Isaias em Apocalipse: hermenéutica e escatologia intra-testamentàrias*, in *Vox Scripturae* 2 (1992) 35-53.

PLÖGER, O., *Theocracy and Eschatology* (tr. S. RUDMAN), Richmond, VA, 1968.

POLASKI, D.C., *Banquet Hall or Barnyard: Locating the Nations in YHWH's Empire (Isa. 24:21–25:12)*, Unpublished SBL Paper, San Francisco, 1997.

— *Reflections on a Mosaic Covenant: The Eternal Covenant (Isa. 24.5) and Intertextuality*, in *JSOT* 77 (1998) 55-73.

POLK, T., *Paradigms, Parables, and* Meshalim: *On Reading the* Mashal *in Scripture*, in *CBQ* 45 (1983) 564-83.

PREUSS, H.D., *Auferstehung in Texten alttestamentlicher Apokalyptik (Jes 26,7-19; Dan 12, 1-4)*, in U. GERBER (ed.), *Linguistische Theologie; biblische Texte, christliche Verkündiging und theologische Sprachtheorie*, Bonn, 1972, pp. 101-133.

PROCKSCH, O., *Jesaja I. Erste Hälfte: Kapitel 1-39* (KAT, IX), Leipzig, 1930.

PUTNAM, F.C., *A Cumulative Index to the Grammar and Syntax of Biblical Hebrew*, Winona Lake, IN, 1996.

QUINTILIAN, *Institutio Oratoria* (tr. H.E. BUTLER), London, 1921.

RABIN, C., *Bariah*, in *JTS* 47 (1946) 38-41.

RAD, G. VON, *Theologie des Alten Testaments* (Einführung in die Evangelische Theologie, 1), 2 Vols., Munich, 1961-1965.
— *Old Testament Theology, Vol. II, The Theology of Israel's Prophetic Traditions* (tr. D.M.G. STALKER), Edinburgh – London, 1965.
RADAY, Y.T., *The Unity of Isaiah in the Light of Statistical Linguistics*, Hildesheim, 1973.
RADLER, A., *Odædlighetstanke och uppstandelsetro*, in *Svensk Teologisk Kvartalskrift* 61 (1985) 154-163.
RAHLFS, A. (ed.), *Septuaginta II*, Stuttgart, 1935⁹.
RAURELL, F. *LXX-Is 26: La 'doxa' com a perlicipació en la vida escatalògica*, in *Revista de cultura teologica* 7 (1982) 57-89.
REDDITT, P., *Isaiah 24–27: A Form Critical Analysis*, Diss. (UMI), Vanderbilt University, 1972.
— *Once Again, the City in Isaiah 24–27*, in *Hebrew Annual Review* 10 (1986) 317-335.
REDDY, M., *The Conduit Metaphor*, in A. ORTONY (ed.), *Metaphor and Thought*, Cambridge, 1993², pp. 164-201.
RENKEMA, J., *Klaagliederen* (COT), Kampen, 1993.
RENTDORFF, R., *The Book of Isaiah: A Complex Unity: Synchronic and Diachronic Reading*, in *SBL Seminar Papers*, 1991, 8-20; = R.F. MELUGIN and. M.A. SWEENEY (eds.), *New Visions of Isaiah* (JSOT SS, 214), Sheffield 1996, pp. 32-49.
REUSS, E.W.E., *Die Geschichte der heiligen Schriften Alten Testaments*, Braunschweig, 1890.
RICHARDS, I.A., *The Philosophy of Rhetoric*, Oxford, 1936.
RICŒUR, P. *La symbolique du mal*, Paris, 1960.
— *Fatherhood: From Phantasm to Symbol*, in D. IHDE (ed.), *The Conflict in Interpretations. Essays in Hermeneutics*, Evaston, IL, 1974, pp. 468-497; = *La paternité: du phantasme au symbole*, in ID., *Conflit des interprétations*, Paris, 1969, pp. 458-86.
— *Stellung und Funktion der Metapher in der biblischen Sprache*, in ID. and E. JÜNGEL, *Metapher. Zur Hermeneutik religiöser Sprache. Mit einer Einführung von Pierre Gisel*, Munich, 1974, pp. 45-70.
— *Interpretation Theory: Discourse and the Surplus of Meaning*, Fort Worth, TX, 1976.
— *La métaphore vive*, Paris, 1975.
— *The Rule of Metaphor: Multi-Disciplinary Studies of the Creation of Meaning in Language* (tr. R. CZERNY), Toronto, 1977.
— *The Metaphorical Process as Cognition, Imagination and Feeling*, in S. SACKS (ed.), *On Metaphor*, Chicago, IL, 1979, pp. 141-157.
RIDDERBOS, J., *Het Godswoord der Profeten, 2: Jesaja*, Kampen, 1932.
— *Isaiah* (tr. J. VRIEND), Grand Rapids, MI, 1985.
RINGGREN, H., *Some Observations on Style and Structure in the Isaiah Apocalypse*, in *ASTI* 9 (1973) 107-115.
— *Die Religionen der Menschheit. Vol. XXVI: Israelitische Religion*, Stuttgart, 1963.
ROBERTS, J.J.M., *Double entendre in First Isaiah [Isa 27:12]*, in *CBQ* 54 (1992) 39-48.

ROBERTSON, E., *Isaiah XXVII 2-6*, in *ZAW* 47 (1929) 197-206.
ROBINSON, G.R., *The Book of Isaiah*, New York, NY, 1910.
ROCHAIS, G., *Les origines de l'apocalyptique*, in *Science et Esprit* 25 (1973) 36-40.
ROSENBERG, A.J., *Isaiah I. Translation of Text, Rashi and Commentary* (Miqra'ot Gedolot), New York, NY, 1982.
ROSENMÜLLER, E., *Scholia in Jesajae vaticinia in compendium redacta* (Scholia in Vetus Testamentum, II), Lipsiae, 1835.
RUDOLPH, W., *Jesaja 24-27* (BWANT IV, 10), Stuttgart, 1933.
RUITEN, J.T.A.G.M. VAN, Review of A. NICCACCI, *The Syntax of the Verb in Classical Hebrew Prose* (JSOT SS, 86), (Sheffield, 1990), in *Bijdragen* 54 (1993) 201.
RUNNING, L.G., *Syriac Variants in Isaiah 26*, in *Andrews University Seminary Studies* 5 (1967) 46-58.
RUPPERT, L., *Critica de los dioses en el libro Isaias*, in *Revista bíblica* 63 (1996) 129-159.
RUSSEL, D.S., *Apocalyptic Imagery as Political Cartoon?*, in J. BARTON and D.J. REIMER (eds.), *After the Exile. Essays in Honour of Rex Mason*, Macon, GA, 1996, pp. 191-200.
RÜTERSWÖRDEN, U., *Erwägungen zur Metaphorik des Wassers in Jes 40ff*, in *SJOT* 2 (1989) 1-22.
SACKS, S. (ed.), *On Metaphor*, Chicago, IL, 1979.
SAKENFELD, K.D., *Bread of Heaven*, in *Princeton Seminary Bulletin* 7 (1986) 20-24.
SAWYER, J.F.A., *Hebrew Words for the Resurrection of the Dead*, in *VT* 23 (1973) 218-234.
— *Isaiah*. Vol. 1 (Daily Study Bible), Philadelphia, PA, 1984.
— *Isaiah*. Vol. 2 (Daily Study Bible), Edinburgh – Philadelphia, 1986.
— *The Role of Jewish Studies in Biblical Semantics*, in H. VANSTIPHOUT et al. (eds.), *Scripta Signa Vocis: Studies About Scripts, Scriptures, Scribes and Languages in the Near East, Presented to J.H. Hospers by His Pupils, Colleagues and Friends*, Groningen, 1986, pp. 201-208.
— *'My Secret Is With Me' (Isaiah 24:16): Some Semantic Links between Isaiah 24-27 and Daniel*, in A.G. AULD (ed.), *Understanding Poets and Prophets: Essays in Honour of George Wishart Anderson* (JSOT SS, 152), Sheffield, 1994, pp. 307-317.
SCHARBERT, J., Review of A. NICCACCI, *The Syntax of the Verb in Classical Hebrew Prose* (JSOT SS, 86), (Sheffield, 1990), in *BZ* 38 (1994) 312-313.
SCHMID, H.H., *Schöpfung, Gerechtigkeit und Heil, 'Schöpfungstheologie' als Gesamthorizont biblischer Theologie*, in *ZTK* 70 (1973) 1-19.
SCHMIDT, K.L., *Jerusalem als Urbild und Abbild*, in *Eranos-Jahrbuch* (1950) 207.
SCHMIDT, S.J., *Some Problems of Communicative Text Theories*, in W. DRESSLER (ed.), *Current Trends in Linguistics*, Berlin, 1978, pp. 50-65.
SCHMIDT, T., *Das Ende der Zeit. Mythos und Metaphorik als Fundamente einer Hermeneutik biblischer Eschatologie* (BBB, 109), Bodenheim, 1996.
SCHMITT, J.J., *Isaiah and His Interpreters*, New York, NY, 1985.
— *The Motherhood of God and Zion as Mother*, in *RB* 92 (1985) 557-569.
— *Israel und Zion – Two Gendered Images: Biblical Speech Traditions and their Contemporary Neglect*, in *Horizons* 18 (1991) 18-32.

— *Gender Correctness and Biblical Metaphors: The Case of God's Relation to Israel*, in *BTB* 26 (1996) 96-106.
— *The City as Woman in Isaiah 1–39*, in C.C. BROYLES and C.A. EVANS (eds.), *Writing and Reading the Scroll of Isaiah. Studies of an Interpretive Tradition* (SVT, 70: 1-2), Leiden, 1997, pp. 95-119.
SCHOEN, D., *Invention and the Evolution of Ideas*, London, 1967.
SCHOORS, A., *Jesaja* (BOT, IX), Roermond, 1972.
SCHÜSSLER FIORENZA, E., *In Memory of Her. A Feminist Theological Reconstruction of Christian Origins*, London, 1983.
SCHWARTZ, G., *...Tau der Lichter...?*, in *ZAW* 88 (1976) 280-281.
SCOTT, R.B.Y., *Introduction and Exegesis of the Book of Isaiah, Chapters 1–39*, in G. BUTTRICK *et al.* (eds.), *Interpreter's Bible*, Vol. 5, New York – Nashville, 1956, pp. 156-381.
SEARLE, J.R., *Metaphor*, in A. ORTONY (ed.), *Metaphor and Thought*, Cambridge, 1993², pp. 83-111.
SEEBASS, G., *The Importance of Apocalyptic for the History of Protestantism*, in *Colloquium* 13 (1980) 24-35.
SEIFERT, B., *Metaphorisches Reden von Gott im Hoseabuch*, Göttingen, 1996.
SEITZ, C., *Isaiah 1-66: Making Sense of the Whole*, in ID. (ed.), *Reading and Preaching the Book of Isaiah*, Philadelphia, PA, 1988, pp. 105-126.
SHIBLES, W., *Metaphor. An Annotated Bibliography and History*, Whitewater, WI, 1971.
SIEVERS, E., *Alttestamentliche Miscellen I: Jesajas 24–27* (Verhandlungen der königl. Sachs. Ges. d. Wiss. zu Leipzig, phil. hist. Kl. B 56), Leipzig, 1904, p. 151ff..
SIMPSON, J.A. and WEINER, E.S.C., (eds.), *The Oxford English Dictionary*, Oxford, 1989².
SKINNER, J., *The Book of the Prophet Isaiah in the Revised Version* (Cambridge Biblical Commentary), Cambridge, 1963.
SKJOLDAL, N.O., *The Function of Isaiah 24–27*, in *JETS* 36 (1993) 63-67.
SMEND, R., *Anmerkungen zu Jes 24–27*, in *ZAW* 4 (1884) 161-224.
SMITH, G.A., *The Book of Isaiah* (The Expositor's Bible), 2 vols., New York, NY, 1928.
SMITH, J.Z., *Earth and Gods*, in *JR* 49 (1969) 108-127.
SNIJDERS, L.A., *Jesaja. Deel I* (POT), Nijkerk, 1969.
SODEN, W. VON, *Ist im Alten Testament schon vom Schwimmen die Rede (Jes. 25,8)?*, in *ZAH* 4 (1991) 165-170.
SOSKICE, J.M., *Metaphor and Religious Language*, Oxford, 1985-1987.
SPENCER, A.B., *'Father-Ruler, The Meaning of the Metaphor Father' for God in the Bible*, in *JETS* 39 (1996) 433-442.
SPERBER, A. (ed.), *The Bible in Aramaic. III The Latter Prophets According to Targum Jonathan*, Leiden, 1962.
SPIECKERMANN, H., *Stadtgott und Gottesstadt, Beobachtungen im Alten Orient und im Alten Testament*, in *Bib* 73 (1992) 1-31.
STACHOWIAK, L., *Das Buch Jesaja. Übersetzung, Einleitung und Kommentar*, Lublin, 1991.
STANSELL, G., *Micah and Isaiah: A Form and Tradition Historical Comparison* (SBL DS, 85), Atlanta, 1988.

STASSEN, S.L., *Marriage (and Related) Metaphors in Isaiah 54:1-17*, in *JSem* 6 (1994) 57-73.
STAUDIGEL, H., *Hermeneutische Überlegungen zu einer triumphalen Glosse in Jesaja 25,6-8*, in J. ROGGE and G. SCHILLE (eds.), *Theologische Versuche, 17*, Berlin, 1989. pp. 9-13.
STEEN, G., *Understanding Metaphor in Literature*, London, 1994.
STEINGRIMSON, S.Ö., *Gottesmahl und Lebensspende. Eine literaturwissenschaftliche Untersuchung von Jesaja 24,21-23, 25,6-10a* (MU ATSAT, 43), St. Ottilien, 1994.
STENNING, J.F. (ed. and tr.), *The Targum of Isaiah*, Oxford, 1949.
STERN, D., *The Rabbinic Parable: From Rhetoric to Poetics*, in SBL SP 25, (1986) 631-643.
STIENSTRA, N., YHWH *is the Husband of His People. Analysis of a Biblical Metaphor with Special Reference to Translation*, Kampen, 1993.
SWEENEY, M.A., *Textual Citations in Isaiah 24–27: Toward an Understanding of the Redactional Function of Chapters 24–27 in the Book of Isaiah*, in *JBL* 107 (1988) 39-52.
— *New Gleanings from an Old Vineyard: Is 27 Reconsidered*, in C.A. EVANS and W. F. STINESPRING (eds.), *Early Jewish and Christian Exegesis. Studies in Memory of W. H. Brownlee* (Homage Series,10), Atlanta, GA, 1987, pp. 33-49.
— *Isaiah 1–39 with an Introduction to Prophetic Literature* (FOTL, 16), Grand Rapids, MI, 1996.
SWINBURNE, R., *Revelation: From Metaphor to Analogy*, Oxford, 1992.
SYREENI, K., *Metaphorical Appropriation: (Post) Modern Biblical Hermeneutic and the Theory of Metaphor*, in *JLT* 9 (1995) 321-338.
TALBOT, W. C., *Misquoted Scriptures. No. IX (Isa. 26:19)*, in *History of Religions* 7 (1882-83) 293-294.
TALMON, S., *Prophetic Rhetoric and Agricultural Metaphors*, in D. GARRONE and F. ISRAEL (eds.), *Storia e tradizioni di Israele. Scritti in onore di J. Alberto Soggin*, Brescia, 1991, pp. 269-270.
TALSTRA, E., *Text Grammar and Hebrew Bible. I: Elements of a Theory*, in *BiOr* 35 (1978) 169-74.
— *Text Grammar and Hebrew Bible. II: Syntax and Semantics*, in *BiOr* 39 (1982) 26-38.
THATCHER, T., *Empty Metaphors and Apocalyptic Rhetoric*, in *JAAR* 66 (1998) 549-570.
TILLICH, P. *The Shaking of the Foundations*, London, 1962.
TITUS, H.W., *God's Gift to Man: Laws, Not Paradigms for Public Policy – A Response to R. Sider [pp.1-9]*, in *Transformation* 2 (1985) 10-12.
TODD., V.H., *Biblical Eschatology: an Overview*, in *Cumberland Seminarian* 22 (1984) 3-16.
— *Apocalyptic Eschatology*, in *Cumberland Seminarian* 25 (1987) 36-49.
TOWNER, W.S., *Tribulation and Peace: the Fate of Shalom in Jewish Apocalyptic*, in *Horizons in Biblical Theology* 6 (1984) 1-26.
TRAUGOT, E., *'Conventional' and 'Dead' Metaphors Revisited*, in R. DIRVEN and W. PAPROTTÉ (eds.), *The Ubiquity of Metaphor*, Amsterdam, 1985, pp. 17-56.

TRIBLE, P., *God and the Rhetoric of Sexuality*, Philadelphia, PA, 1976.
TROMP, N., *La métaphore engloutie. Le language métaphorique du Psaume 80*, in *Sémiotique et Bible* 47 (1987) 30-43.
TURBAYNE, C.M., *The Myth of Metaphor*, New Haven, CT, 1962.
TUR-SINAI, N.H., *Unverstandene Bibelwort, I*, in *VT* 1 (1951) 307-309.
VANGEMEREN, W.A. (ed.), *New International Dictionary of Old Testament Theology and Exegesis* [NIDOTTE]. Vols. 1-5, Grand Rapids, MI, 1997.
VAN GROL, H.W.M., *Isaiah 27,10-11: God and His Own People*, in J. VAN RUITEN and M. VERVENNE (eds.), *Studies in the Book of Isaiah. Fs. Willem A.M. Beuken* (BETL 132), Leuven, 1997, pp. 195-209.
VAN HOONACKER, A., *Het Boek Isaias*, Brugge, 1932.
VAN ZYL, A. H., *Isaiah 24-27: Their Date of Origin*, in *OTW* 5 (1962) p. 44-57.
VERHEIJ, A., Review of A. NICCACCI, *The Syntax of the Verb in Classical Hebrew Prose* (JSOT SS, 86), (Sheffield, 1990), in *BiOr* 49 (1992) 214-217.
VERHOEF, P. *Die Dag van die Here* (Exegetica, 2-3), The Hague, 1956, pp. 12-28.
VERMEYLEN, J., *La composition littéraire de l'Apocalypse d'Isaïe*, in *ETL* 50 (1974) 5-38.
— *Du prophète Isaïe à l'Apocalyptique. Isaïe, I – XXXV, miroir d'un demi-millénaire d'expérience religieuse en Israël I-II* (EB), Paris, 2 vols., 1977-1978.
— *The Book of Isaiah / Le livre d'Isaïe* (BETL, 81), Leuven, 1989.
VERVENNE, M., *Hebrew Verb Form and Function. A Syntactic Case Study with Reference to a Linguistic Data Base*, in ASSOCIATION INTERNATIONALE BIBLE ET INFORMATIQUE, *Bible et informatique: méthodes, outils, résultats*, Jerusalem, 1988, pp. 605-640.
VIA, D.O., *The Parables: Their Literary and Existential Dimension*, Philadelphia, PA, 1967.
VICENT, R., *Análisis estructural de Isaías 24-27. La imagen como elemento de estructuración*, in *EstBib* 36 (1977) 21-35.
VRIES, S.J. DE, *From Old Revelation to New. A Tradition-Historical and Redaction-Critical Study of Temporal Transitions in Prophetic Prediction*, Grand Rapids, MI, 1995.
VRIEZEN, TH.C., *Prophecy and Eschatology. Congress Volume: Copenhagen 1953* (SVT, 1), Leiden, 1953.
WAARD, J. DE, *The Interim and Final HOTTP Reports and the Translator: a Preliminary Investigation*, in G.J. NORTON and S. PISANO (eds.), *Tradition of the Text: Studies Offered to Dominique Barthélemy in Celebration of his 70th Birthday* (OBO, 109) Fribourg, 1991, pp. 277-284.
WAHL, O., *'Wir haben eine befestigte Stadt': Zur Botschaft von Jes 26,1-6*, in F. DIEDRICH and B. WILLMES (eds.), *Ich bewirke das Heil und erschaffe das Unheil (Jesaja45,7)* (Forschung zur Bibel, 88), Würzburg, 1988, pp. 459-481.
WALTKE, B. K., *Creation account in Genesis 1:1-3*, in *BS* 132 (1975) 327-342, (1976) 28-41.
WATSON, W.G.E., *Internal Parallelism in Classical Hebrew Verse*, in *Bib* 66 (1985) 365-384.
— *Traditional Techniques in Classical Hebrew Verse* (JSOT SS, 170), Sheffield, 1994, pp. 392-413.

— *Classical Hebrew Poetry, A Guide to Its Techniques* (JSOT SS, 26), Sheffield, 1995², pp. 263-272.
WATTS, J.D.W., *Isaiah 1–33* (WBC, 24), Waco, TX, 1985.
— *Isaiah 34–66* (WBC, 25), Waco, TX, 1987.
— Review of A. NICCACCI, *The Syntax of the Verb in Classical Hebrew Prose* (JSOT SS, 86), (Sheffield, 1990), in *R&E* 88 (1991), 96.
WEBB, B.G., *Zion in Transformation. A Literary Approach to Isaiah*, in D.J.A. CLINES et al. (eds.), *The Bible in Three Dimensions. Essays Celebrating Forty Years of Biblical Studies in the University of Sheffield* (JSOT SS, 87), Sheffield, 1990, pp. 65-84.
WEBER, O. (ed.), *Biblia Sacra iuxta vulgatam versionem II*, Stuttgart, 1969.
WEDER, H., *Die Gleichnisse Jesu als Metaphern: Traditions- und redaktionsgeschichtliche Analysen und Interpretationen* (FRLANT, 20), Göttingen, 1978.
— *Metapher und Gleichnis: Bemerkungen zur Reichweite des Bildes in religiöser Sprache*, in *ZTK* 90 (1993) 382-407.
WEEMS, R.J., *Gomer: Victim of Violence or Violence of Metaphor?*, in *Semeia* 47 (1989) 87-104.
WEINRICH, H., *Tempus: besprochene und erzählte Welt* (Sprache und Literatur, 16), Stuttgart, 1964.
WEISER, A., *Einleitung in das Alte Testament*, Göttingen, 1966⁶.
WEISS, M., *The Pattern of the 'Execration Texts' in the Prophetic Literature*, in *Israel Exploration Journal* 19 (1969) 150-157.
WELLHAUSEN, J., *Einleitung in das Alte Testament*, Berlin, 1878.
WELTEN, P., *Die Vernichtung des Todes und die Königherrschaft Gottes: Eine traditionsgeschichtliche Studie zu Jes 25,6-8; 24,21-23 und Ex 24,9-11*, in *TZ* 38 (1982) 129-146.
WESTERMANN, C., *The Praise of God in the Psalms*, Richmond, VA, 1965.
— *Vergleiche und Gleichnisse im Alten und Neuen Testament* (Calwer Theologische Monographien, 14), Stuttgart, 1984.
WETTE, W.M.L. DE, *Critical and Historical Introduction to the Canonical Scriptures of the Old Testament* (tr. T. PARKER), Boston, MA, 1867.
WHEELWRIGHT, P., *Metaphor and Reality*, Bloomington, IN, 1962.
WIDENGREN, G., *The King and the Tree of Life in Ancient Near Eastern Religion* (King and Saviour, IV), Uppsala, 1951.
WIDYAPRANAWA, S.H., *The Lord is Saviour: Isaiah 1–39*, Grand Rapids, MI, 1990.
WIERINGEN, A.L.H.M. VAN, *Jesaja 6-12: die Vegetationsbildsprache und die prophetische Struktur*, in J. VERMEYLEN (ed.), *The Book of Isaiah – Le livre d'Isaïe* (BETL, 81), Leuven, 1989, pp. 203-207.
WILDBERGER, H., *Das Freudenmahl auf der Zion*, in *TZ* 33 (1977) 373-384.
— *Jesaja 1–12, Jesaja 13–27, Jesaja 28–39* (BKAT, X-1,2,3), Neukirchen – Vluyn, 1972, 1978, 1982.
— *Isaiah 1–27* (tr. T.H. TRAPP), Minneapolis, MN, 1997.
WILLIAMSON, H.G.M., *The Book called Isaiah: Deutero-Isaiah's Role in Composition and Redaction*, New York, NY, 1994.
— *Sound, Sense and Language in Isaiah 24–27*, in *JJS* 46 (1995) 1-9.
WILLIS, T. M., *Yahweh's Elders (Is 24:23): Senior Officials of the Divine Court*, in *ZAW* 103 (1991) 375-386.

WILLMINGTON, H.L., Isaiah: Shakespeare of the Prophets [Is 24], in *Fundamentalist Journal* 4 (1985) 60.
WINNER, E. and GARDNER H., *Metaphor and Irony: Two Levels of Understanding*, in A. ORTONY (ed.), *Metaphor and Thought*, Cambridge, 1993², pp. 425-443.
WODECKI, B., *The Religious Universalism of the Pericope Is 25:6-9*, in K. SCHUNK and M. AUGUSTIN (eds.), *Goldene Apfel in silbern Schalen* (Beiträge zur Erforschung des Altes Testaments und des Antiken Judentums, 20), Frankfurt am Main, 1992, pp. 35-47.
WOLDE, E. VAN (ed.), *Narrative Syntax and the Hebrew Bible, Papers of the Tilburg Conference 1996*, Leiden, 1997.
WOLF, H.M., *Interpreting Isaiah: The Suffering and Glory of the Messiah*, Grand Rapids, MI, 1985.
WÜNSCHE, A., *Die Bildersprache des Alten Testaments. Ein Beitrag zur aesthetischen Würdigung des poetischen Schriftums*, Leipzig, 1906.
YEE, G.A. *By the Hand of a Woman: The Metaphor of the Woman Warrior in Judges 4*, in *Semeia* 61 (1993) 99-132.
YOUNGBLOOD, R.F., *The Book of Isaiah: An Introductory Commentary*, Grand Rapids, MI, 1995².
— *A Holistic Typology of Prophecy and Apocalyptic*, in A. GILEADI (ed.), *Israel's Apostasy and Restoration, Essays in Honour of Roland K. Harrison*, Grand Rapids, MI, 1988, pp. 213-221.
ZIEGLER, J. (ed.), *Isaias. Septuaginta* (Vetus Testamentum Graecum Auctoritate Academiae Scientiarum Gottingensis, 14), Göttingen, 1983³·
ZORELL, F., *Lexicon hebraicum et aramaicum Veteris Testamenti*, Rome, 1940,1954².

INDEXES

INDEX OF AUTHORS

AALEN, S. 313[96]
ACKROYD, P.R. 267[152] 268[155] 269[162]
ADLER, E.J. 229 230[37,38,39]
ALEXANDER, J.A. 31[123]
ALLEN, L.C. 302[64]
ALONSO SCHÖKEL, L. 50[3] 153[5] 171[50] 181[72] 184[84] 197[118] 231[40] 241[74] 252[98] 253[104] 259[116] 282[4] 310[90] 322[116] 350[43]
ALSTON, W.P. 74[103,104] 100[160] 102[165] 109 122
ALTER, R. 1[2]
ALTHANN, R. 236[60]
ANDERSON, B.W. 321[116] 322[117]
ANDERSON, G.A. 20[65] 21[72] 33 36[158] 39[176] 322[117]
ANDERSON, G.W. 317[102]
AQUINAS, T. 60 92-94 115[191] 121 124 126 157 200 201 247 287 295 327
ARISTOTLE 51[7] 53[13] 60[34] 87
ARNOLD, B.T. 172[57] 241[73]
AUGUSTIN, M. 350[41]
AUGUSTINE 60
AUVREY, P. 184[84] 259[116] 317[102] 322[116]
AVERBECK, R.E. 163[39]
AYER, A.J. 91[131] 122

BACHE, C.M. 72[98]
BAILLIE, J. 99[156]
BAL, M. 98[154] 114[187] 155[29] 226[24] 257[109] 332[148] 371[2]
BALENTINE, S.E. 325[129]
BALOIAN, B.E. 300[54]
BARR, J. 64[68]
BARTEL, R. 70[90] 72[98]
BARTH, K. 92[132]
BARTHÉLEMY, D 161[36] 182[81] 235[56] 241[73,75] 283[10] 289[19,20] 290[22] 308[78] 309[85,86] 340[2] 341[4] 353[59,60]
BATTO, B. 181[76] 225[13]
BAUMANN, A. 163[39]
BAUMGARTNER, W.I. 33[141]
BAVINCK, H. 92[132]
BEARDSLEY, M. 78[115] 133[222]
BEEK, M.A. 31[120]

BEKKER, I. 51[7]
BENJAMIN, D.C. 228[30] 303[67]
BERGMAN, J. 167[152] 268[155]
BERLIN, A. 1[1,2,5,6] 2 136 144 295[37] 328[137] 375
BETZ, H.D. 25[89]
BEUKEN, W.A.M. **182-183**[80] 187[98,99] 253[103] 259[114]
BEVAN, E. 76[112]
BIDDLE, M. 181[76] 225[13]
BINKLEY, T. 91[131]
BIRD, P. 98[154]
BJØRNDALEN, A.J. 49[3]
BLACK, M. **60-63** 64[68] 66 67 73[100] 100[160] 104[169] 106 121 122 123 125 126 132 138 139 156 157 166[44] 175 179[190] 205 246 287 294 327 347[35] 363[103]
BLEEK, F. 31[124] 32[125]
BLOCK, D. 243[80] 292[32] 312[94]
BOADT, L. 119[196]
BÖHMER, J. 322[118]
BOOTH, W. 106[172]
BOSMAN, H.J. 235[55]
BOSMAN, H.L. 172[54] 183[81]
BOTTERWECK, G.J. 245[83]
BOURGUET, D. 5[21] 49[2,3] 50 **51-58** 59[31] 61[46,47,48] 65[76] 66[77,78] 67[83] 68 69 71[94] **77-92** 106[172] 112 120 121[199] 122 123 124[206] 125[208,210] 130 132 133 134 135 137 139 153[10] 154[11] 155[15] 156[23,24] 163 166 175 179[190] 205 239 246 250 255 267[149,150] 268[160] 269 270 311 314 323 326 347 363
BOX, G.H. 25[88]
BRACKE, J.M. 357[74]
BREDENKAMP, C.J. 153[6] 180[72] 231[40] 241[73,74] 259[116] 317[102]
BRENNER, A. 98[154]
BRENSINGER, T.L. 305[72]
BRETTLER, M. 49[3] 371[1]
BRICHTO, 387[35]
BRIGGS, J. 1[4]
BROYLES, C.C. 50[3] 224[11] 299[48]
BRUEGGEMANN, W. 26[96] 375[9] 376[12]

BULLINGER, E.W. $54^{17.19}$ 57^{24} 293^{36}
BURROWS, M. 3^{12}
BUTTERWORTH, G.M. 361^{94}
BUTTRICK, G.A. 26^{96} 245^{83}

CAIRD, G.B. 57^{25} 95^{144} 155^{15} 266^{143}
CALVIN, J. 94^{132}
CAMP, C. 98^{154}
CARPENTER, E.E. 164^{39} 302^{60} 345^{27}
CARROLL, M.D. 154^{12}
CHEYNE, T.K. 33^{143} 34^{144} 317^{101}
CICERO 60^{36}
CLARK, G.H. 110^{179}
CLEMENTS, R.E. 164^{39} 305^{75} 322^{117}
CLIFFORD, R.J. 222^{3}
CLINES, D.J.A. 222^{2}
CLOETE, W.T.W. 384^{24}
COGGINS, R.J. 22^{76}
COHEN, C. $228^{31.32}$ 229^{33} 272^{171}
COHEN, L.J. 67^{82}
COHEN, T. 106^{171} 135^{236}
COLLINS, J.J. 26^{96} 357^{73} 358^{82}
CONDAMIN, A. 153^{5} 183^{82} 241^{73} 259^{116} 322^{117}
CORNELIUS, I. 343^{19} 345^{27} 362^{97}
CROSS, F.M. 27^{100} 32^{132}
CRÜSEMANN, F. 232^{41}

DAHOOD, M. 64^{69}
DARR, K.P. 106^{172} 204^{132} 222^{1} $223^{7.8}$ $224^{9.10.11.12}$ 225^{14} $226^{17.18.20.}$ 227 228^{34} 135^{97} 360^{91}
DAVIDSON, D. 92^{131}
DAY, J. 22^{79} 299^{48} 317^{102}
DAY, P.L. 98^{154} 272^{171}
DELBECQUE, N. 98^{154}
DEL BRASSEY, P. 224^{11} $371^{3.4.}$
DELITZSCH, F. 31^{123} 153^{9} 197^{117} 259^{116} 308^{79} 317^{101} 322^{116} 342^{8}
DE MOOR, J.C. 254^{107}
DE VRIES, S.J. 12^{8} 197^{117} 208^{136} 323^{122} 342^{12} 352^{57}
DILLMANN, A. 32^{131}
DIRVEN, R. 59^{28}
DISSE, A. 383^{18}
DOBBS-ALLSOPP, F.W. 224^{11}
DÖDERLEIN, J.C. 235^{55}
DOHMEN, C. 255^{108}
DOMERIS, W.R. 154^{12}
DOMMERHAUSEN, W. 175^{58}

DONNER, H. 43^{195}
DOYLE, B. 259^{114}
DRESSLER, W. 388^{36}
DRIVER, G.R. 308^{82}
DRIVER, S.R. 32^{127}
DUHM, B. 12^{2} 13^{11} 16 21 24 27 29^{108} 35^{150} 38^{164} 172^{55} 182^{78} 233^{46} 241^{73} 282^{1} 317^{101} 321^{115} 322^{116} 342^{8} 354^{62}

EIDEVALL, G. 49^{3} 142^{257}
EISSFELDT, O. 13^{20} $38^{166.167.168}$
EITAN, I. 234^{53}
ELDER, W. 178^{63} 186^{93} 198^{119} 251^{95}
ELLIGER, K. 3^{10}
ELLINGTON, J. 262^{127}
EMERTON, J.A. 1^{1} 234^{55} $235^{55.56.57}$ 317^{102}
ENGELKEN, K, 186^{15}
EVANS, C.A. 22^{77} 50^{3} 224^{11} 299^{49} 340^{1}

FABRY, H.-J. 267^{153}
FERRÉ, F. 138^{253}
FIELD, F. 3^{12}
FISCHER, J. 169^{47} 342^{7}
FITZGERALD, A. 224^{11} 226^{22}
FLEISCHER, D. 175^{58}
FOHRER, G. 13^{18} 14 15 16 21 26^{97} $33^{138.139.140}$ 197^{117} 236^{60} 237^{63} 241^{73} 252^{98}
FOLLIS, E.R. 224^{11} 226^{19}
FREDERICKS, D.C. 292^{31}
FREEDMAN, D.N. 172^{54} 245^{84}
FRETHEIM, T.E. 286^{15} 292^{33} 361^{95}
FROST, S.B. $35^{147.148}$
FRYE, N. 132 **136-137** 139
FRYMER-KENSKY, T. 224^{11} 226^{25}
FUNK, R. 119^{195}
FUTATO, M.D. 309^{87}

GALAMBUSH, J. 181^{76} 225^{16} $226^{23.24}$ $227^{27.28}$ 228^{229}
GARCÍA MARTÍNEZ, F. 3^{12} 302^{66}
GARCÍA RECIO, J. 359^{85}
GARDNER, H. 129^{215}
GARRONE, D. 362^{97}
GERHART, M. 107^{173} 159^{30} 192
GERSTENBERGER, J. 232^{41}
GESE, H. 308^{78}
GESENIUS, W. 32^{129} 42^{188} 308^{79}
GILL, J.H. 99^{156}
GITAY, Y. 50^{3}

GOODMAN, N. 91[131]
GÖRG, M. 177[59]
GOSHEN-GOTTSTEIN, M.H. 3[11]
GRABOWSKI, J.S. 230[37]
GRÄTZ, H. 31[124] 32[126]
GRÄTZ, S. 159[29]
GRAY, G.B. 152 172[55] 183[81.82] 351[50]
GRAY, M. 6[25]
GREENBERG, M. 119[197]
GREGORY OF NAZIANZEN 60
GRISANTI, M.A. 164[39] 177[55] 362[98.99]
GROSSE, W. 383[18] 384[23]
GUNKEL, H. 14[22]

HAAG, H. 172[54]
HABETS, G.N.M. 44[198]
HALLO, W.W. 131[76] 225[13]
HAMILTON, V.P. 161[36] 172[57] 293[35] 346[29]
HANHART, R. 42[195] 44[196]
HANSON, P. 17[45] 18[52] 27[100] 29[114] 32[132] 41 42[185]
HARMAN, A.M. 240[71] 358[82]
HARTSHORNE, C. 115[193] 116 131 265[140]
HAUGE, M.R. 44[200]
HAYDEN, R.E. 163[39] 312[95]
HAYES, J.H. 31[119] 42[189] 180[68] 181[73.74]
HAYES, K.M. 49[3] 165[40] 166[42] 167 168 171[50] 172[53.56] 178[62] 184[83] 187[101] 196[112] 214[138.140] 215[141.142.143] 216[144]
HEALEY, J.P. 159[30]
HEERING, H. 92[132]
HEMPEL, J. 230[39] 313[96]
HENRY, M.L. 13[15.17] 14 16[39.40.41.42] 17 32[130] 39[176] 40 233[50] 341[7]
HENTSCHKE, R. 175[58]
HIEBERT, P.S. 229[35]
HILL, A.E. 302[61]
HILLERS, D.R. 214[138]
HITZIG, F. 32[127] 38[164] 40[177] 153[7]
HÖFFKEN, P. 152[1] 162[37] 171[50.51] 180[68] 184[83] 194[109] 197[114] 231[40] 259[116]
HOGLUND, K.G. 98[154]
HOLS, E. 49[1]
HOPFE, L.M. 106[172] 315[97]
HORDERN, W. 115[190] 131 264[137]
HORSNELL, M.J.A. 308[80]
HOSTETTER, E.C. 359[89]
HOWARD, D.M. 173[57]
HUGENBERGER, G.P. 230[37]
HYLMÖ, G. 14 15[26] 16 21 308[85] 322[117]

IRVINE, S.A. 31[119] 42[189] 180[68]
IRWIN, W.H. 291[27]
ISRAEL, F. 362[97]
ITOH, R. 18[52] 321[116] 323[122] 342[12] 346[30.32] 355[66]

JACOB, E. 344[22]
JAUSS, H. 49[3]
JENNI, E. 26[96] 344[22]
JEROME 59
JOHNSON, D.G. 21[69.70.71.73.74.75] 24[87] 27[101] 36[158] 39[171.174] 42[187.188] 43[194] 44[199] 152[1] 155[17.19] 160[34] 162[37] 180[71] 194[108] 231[40] 232[42.43.44] 233[49.50] 234[52] 239 252[100] 260[118.119] 262[125] 268[156] 273[177] 282[1.5] 283[7] 290[23.24] 298[46.47] 300[54.55] 307[77] 309[85] 310[89] 319[109.111] 320[112] 321[116] 323 330[142] 340[2] 342 344[21] 345[27] 351[50.51] 352[57] 353[58] 355[63.64] 356[68.69] 362[96] 368[105.106.107] 372[2]
JOHNSON, M. 63-66 73[101] 74 75 91[131] 94 110[178] 111[180] 112[184] 121 122 123[203] 125 126[212] 157 167 191 197[117] 206 246 265[141] 294
JOÜON, P. 379[3]
JÜNGEL, E. 51[9] 132[220] 134[234] 135[238] 137-138 139

KAISER, O. 19[61] 20 21 24 28[105] 33[134] 36[153.155] 37 38[164] 43[192.193] 152[1] 155[18] 184[83.84] 187[99] 189[104] 231[40] 232[43] 233[48] 235[58] 236[60] 243[81] 310[92] 317[101] 322 17 342[8] 351[50] 354[62]
KAISER, W.C. 243[80] 292[32] 312[94]
KAMINKA, A. 31[123]
KAUFMANN, Y. 29 30[116] 31[123]
KEEL, O. 50[3] 248[91]
KEUNEN, A. 33[141]
KILIAN, R. 186[94] 194[109] 197[115] 200[125] 231[40] 252[98] 259[116] 282[4] 310[90] 321[116]
KISSANE, E.J. 29[115] 31[123] 152[1] 162[37] 180[69] 187[99] 241[74] 259[116] 317[102] 322[116] 351[50] 359[87]
KITTAY, E.F. 60[33] 65-66 121 123[203] 126
KITTEL, R. 32[131]
KJÄRGAARD, M.S. 106[172]
KNOBEL, A.W. 241[73]
KOCH, K. 25[90.91]
KONKEL, A.H. 154[12] 173[57]
KORPEL, M.C.A. 49[3] 92[132] 96 129[215] 266[145] 273[174]

KÖNIG, E. 32 54[17.19] 153[3] 187[99]
KOZIOL, S. 59[30]
KRAUS, H.-J. 232[41]
KUGEL, J. 1[2]
KUITERT, H. 92[132]

LACK, R. 50[3]
LAGRANGE, M.-J. 31[123] 322[118]
LAKOFF, G. **63-66** 73[101] 74 75 94 111[180] 112[184] 121 122 125 126[212] 157 167 191 206 246 265[141] 294 [363]
LANDY, F. 1[3] 49[2] 78[115] 98[154]
LAWSON YOUNGER, K. 225[13]
LEHRER, A. **65-66** 121 126
LÉONARD, J.-M. 383[14]
LEUPOLD, H. 31[123]
LEWIS, D.J. 18[52] 154[12] 162[37.38] 171[51.52] 180[70] 182[79] 184 185[86.89.90] 187[97] 189[104] 196[113] 197[118] 231[40] 236[60] 237[64] 238[66] 241[74.75] 252[101] 259[116] 261[124] 262[129] 291[27] 309[86] 322[116] 323[121] 343[20]
LEWY, J. 226[21]
LIEBMANN, E. 235[58] 241[73] 308[85]
LIEBREICH, L.J. 12[3]
LINDBLOM, J. 14 15[34] 16 26[96] 27[102] 29[111.112] 33[137] 36[157] 39[171.176] 40 153[5] 180[69] 182[78] 197[117] 231[40] 233[50.51] 236[60] 237[63] 252[100] 259[116] 260[120] 290[23] 317[101] 322[117] 341[7] 352[53]
LOCKE, J. 60[37]
LOEWENBERG, I. 123[203]
LOHMANN, P. 232[44] 308[85] 342[8] 354[62]
LONG, G.A. 114[189] 160[31] 240[72] 265[141] 266[147.148] 268[157.158] 286[15]
LONGMAN, T. 346[29]
LORD, D.N. 180[64] 185[92] 238[65.67] 257[110] 293[36] 302[65] 316 317[100] 329[140]
LOWTH, R. [16]033 235[55] 241[74] 308[78] 316[98] 318
LU, J.S. 359[87]
LUC, A.T. 326[132] 332[146]
LUDWIG, O. 14 16[37] 35[152] 41[184] 252[98] 322[118] 342[13]
LUNDBOM, J. 172[54]
LURKER, M. 50[3]
LUST, J. 302[66]
LUTHER, M. 94[132]

MACCORMAC, E.R. 70[88.89] 72[98] 78[115] 104[169] 111[180] 265[141] 268[159]

MACKY, P.W. 5[23] 50[6] 51 56[22] **68-77** 78[116] 92[132] **98-120** 122 123 124 125 126 **127-129** 130 131 132 133 134 135 136 137 139 143[258] 155[15.16] 156[22] 157[28] 158 159 167 168[45] 169 178 191 192 201 204[130] 247 264[136] 265 267[151] 268 269[160] 270[165] 273[178] 287[16] 295 314 327 328 374
MARCH, W.E. 14 15[29] 21 32[128] 39[171] 41[180.181.182] 160[35] 165[41] 176 179 180[69] 182[78] 184[84] 198[120] 236[60] 237[63] 241[74] 251[95] 252[100] 259[116] 260[121] 308[85] 310[91] 322[116.117.118] 323 347
MARTENS, E.A. 305[73]
MATTHEWS, V.H. 228[30] 303[67]
MAUCHLINE, J. 31
MCCREESH, J.P. 327[136]
MCEWAN HUMPHREY, E. 225[16]
MCFAGUE, S. 97[152.153] 104[169] 122
MCINLAY, J. 49[3] 114[186]
MCKEON, R. 51[7]
MERRILL, E.H. 291[29] 292[30]
MICHEL, A. 384[23]
MILLAR, W.R. 11[1] 18[52.53.54.55.56] 19 23[82] 32[132] 37[162] 38 39[172.173] 42[186] 180[70] 198[121] 239[69] 259[116] 260[121] 262[128] 321[116] 323[119] 349[38]
MISCALL, P.D. 1[7] 2 50[3] 144 222[6] 223 258[113] 259[113] 271[167]
MONACO, R. 1[4]
MOOIJ, J.J.A. 123[203]
MOSIS, R. 325[127]
MOTYER, J.A. 24[85] 30[118] 162[37] 169[47.49] 171[50] 181[72] 184[84] 187[100] 194[110] 197[116] 231[40] 235[56.58] 236[60] 237[62] 250[94] 252[97] 254[105] 259[116] 263[132.134] 269[163.164] 282[6] 284[11] 296[38] 300[52] 308[78] 309[86.97] 310[91] 317[101] 322[117] 340[2] 343[15] 346[33] 350[45] 351[50] 356[67.69] 357[76] 358[79] 361[96] 362[101]
MULDER, E.S. 13[16] 14[21] 34[146] 35 36[157] 38 39[169] 180[72] 183[82] 185[91] 186[95] 317[101]
MULDER, M.J. 248[91] 254[107]
MÜLLER, H.-P. 49[3]
MUNCH, P.A. 12[8]
MURAOKA, T. 379[3]

NÄGELSBACH, C.W.E. 31[122]
NEL, P.J. 301[59]
NEWMARK, P. 59[28]
NICCACCI, A. **379-423**
NIELSEN, K. 49[3] 248[91] 349 350[41] 351[50]

NOTH, M. 25[93]

O'CONNELL, R.H. 24[86] 164[39] 346[28] 363[101]
OLIVER, A. 163[39]
OLIVIER, J.P.J. 350[42]
ORTONY, A. 62[52] 67[82] 74[103] 114[185] 156[27]
OSWALT, J.N. 20[67] 30[118] 43[195] 171[50] 257[110] 317[101] 322[116]
OTTOSSON, M. 163[39]
OTZEN, B. 36[158] 39[176] 40[173]

PALMER, H. 115[192] 131 264[138] 265
PAPROTTÉ, W. 59[28]
PARK, S.H. 164[39]
PAUL, M.J. 326[133,135] 328[139]
PEAKE, A.S. 152[1]
PEELS, H.G.L. 301[58]
PLATO 60[35]
PLÖGER, O. 14 17 18[52] 24 27[98] 28[104] 29[113] 30 35[149] 43[190,191] 181[73] 322[117] 351[50] 352[56]
POLASKI, D.C. 373[8]
POLK, T. 119[197]
PREUß, H.D. 270[166] 272[172] 286[15]
PRICE, J.D. 324[125]
PROCKSCH, O. 13[19] 34[145] 38[164] 153[3] 183[81,82] 184[84] 187[99] 235[58] 236[60] 237[63] 241[73] 252[99] 309[95] 317[101] 322[118] 352[55]

QUINTILIAN 60[36]

RAHLFS, A. 3[12]
RAMSEY, I. 92[132]
REDDITT, P. 12[4,5,6,7,8] 14[25] 15[27,28,30,31,35] 16[38] 17[43,46,47,48,49,50] 18 23[81] 25[88,91,92] 26[94,95,96] 27[99] 33[135] 36[160] 37 162[37] 180[70] 184[84] 185[87] 232[44] 235[56,58] 236[59,60] 241[75] 252[98] 305[76] 309[85] 310[88,91] 321[115] 342[8,9] 348[37] 357[76] 372
REDDY, M.J. 101[163]
RENKEMA, J. 155[14] 181[75,76] 187[96] 207[135] 248[90,91] 249 271 272[168,169,171] 358[81,83] 373[7]
REUSS, E.W.E. 32[128]
RICHARDS, I.A. 60[40] 67[85] 73[99] 122
RICŒUR, P. 50[4] 51[9] 52 56[21,22] 62[53] 70[91] 74[105,106] 104[169] 105[170] 120 122 **132-134** 135[238] 137 139 166[43]
RINGGREN, H. 20[65] 33 36[158] 154[12] 253[104] 362[97]

ROBINSON, G.R. 31[121]
ROGERS, C.L. 357[76,77] 362[97]
RUDOLPH, W. 3[10] 14[22] 24 27[103] 29[110] 39[176] 40 180[72] 182[78] 231[40] 233[47,50] 235[55] 252[98] 290[23] 317[101] 322[118] 352[54] 354[62]
RUPPERT, L. 186[15] 358[80]
RUSSELL, A. 107[173] 159[30] 192
RYLE, G. 133[223]

SACKS, S. 92[131] 106[172]
SAWYER, J.F.A. 304[71] 305[74]
SCHARBERT, J. 383[13]
SCHMID, H.H. 298[46]
SCHMIDT, S.J. 388[36]
SCHMITT, J.C. 224[11] 227[26]
SCHNEIDER, W. 380[8] 381 382[12]
SCHOORS, A. 156[26] 162[37] 168[46] 171[50,51] 180[65] 184[84] 185[91] 231[40] 236[59] 239[70] 241[73] 252[98] 259[116] 260[121] 310[91] 317[101] 322[116] 350[43,44]
SCHUNK, K.D. 350[41]
SCHUPPHAUS, J. 254[104]
SCHÜSSLER FIORENZA, E. 97[150]
SCHWAB, M. 249[92]
SCHOVILLE, K.N. 346[28]
SEARLE, J. 67[82]
SEIFERT, B. 49[3]
SEITZ, C.R. 24[5] 42[188] 222[4,5] 356[70,71]
SELMAN, M.J. 313[96]
SEOW, C.L. 273[173]
SHIBBLES, W.A. 49[1]
SICRE DIAZ, J.L. 153[5] 171[50] 181[72] 184[84] 197[118] 231[40] 241[74] 252[98] 259[116] 282[4] 310[90] 322[116]
SIEVERS, E. 14[23]
SKINNER, J. 250[94]
SKJOLDAL, N.O. 22[78]
SMEND, R. 14[21] 28[107] 33[142] 34 38[165] 184[84]
SMITH, G.A. 32[129]
SMITH, G.V. 161[32] 293[35]
SMITH, J.Z. 320[113]
SNIJDERS, L.A. 153[2] 168[46] 180[69] 254[104] 317[102]
SOGGIN, J.A. 267[153]
SOSKICE, J. **67-68** 70[92] 74[107] 75[108] 76[111] 92[132] 94[142] 99[156] 101[162] 106[172] 122 239[68] 270[165]
SPERBER, A. 3[12]
SPIECKERMANN, H. 225[15]
STAMM, J.J. 344[22]

STENNING, J.F. 3[12]
STIENSTRA, N. 5[22] 49[2] 50[5] 51 **58-68** 69[87] 75 77 **91-98** 112 115[191] 121 122 124[207] 126 **130-131** 132 133 134 135 136 139 154[12] 155[16.20.21] 156[25] 157 167 206 265[142] 266[146] 273[175.176] 348[36] 371
STINESPRING, W.F. 22[77] 340[1]
STOEBE, H.J. 344[22]
SWEENEY, M.A. 22[77.79.80] 23 24[85] 30[118] 32[133] 39[176] 40 152[1] 153[8] 184[85] 193[106] 194[107.109] 231[40] 235[58] 236[60] 250[93] 252[98] 253[102] 258[112] 259[115.116] 260[117] 263[133] 282[1.2] 285 286[14] 290[21.23] 300[53] 308[78] 309[85.86] 310[88] 317[102] 332[145] 340[1] 343[17] 346[34] 351 355[65] 356 357[76] 358[78] 362[97]

TALMON, S. 359[84] 362[97]
TALSTRA, E. 380[5] 382[12] 387[30]
THATCHER, T. 30[118]
TILLICH, P. 6[24]
THOMA, C. 119[196]
TOMASINO, A. 163[39]
TORREY, C.C. 39[170]
TRIBBLE, 97[151]
TROPPER, J. 286[15]
TURBAYNE, C.M. 111[180.182]

VAN DAM, C. 154[12] 173[57] 357[75] 358[81] 362[97]
VAN DER KOOIJ, A. 235[55] 236[60] 241[73.75] 253[102] 283[9] 289[20]
van der MERWE, C.H.J. 379[1] 380[6] 381[10] 383[17] 384[19] 385
VAN DIJK-HEMMES, F. 98[154]
VAN ES, J.J. 92[132] 93[135] 115[191] 157
VAN GILSE, J. 35[151] 36[159]
VAN GROL, H. 235[55]
VAN NOPPEN, J.-P. 49[1] 98[154] 132[219] 137 **138-139**
VANONI, G. 177[60]
VAN PELT, M.V. 243[80] 292[32] 312[94]
VAN ROOY, H.F. 154[12]
VAN RUITEN, J.T.A.G.M. 259[114] 383[16]
VAN WOLDE, E. 379[1] 382[11] 383[17]
VAN ZYL, A.H. 31[123]
VERHEIJ, A. 383[15]
VERMEYLEN, J. 19[62] 20 184[83] 231[40] 355[63] 358[78] 362[96] 368[105]
VERVENNE, M. 259[114] 382[12]
VON ORELLI, C. 31[123]
VON RAD, G. 26[96]

VON SODEN, W. 267[152] 268[155]
VIA, D.O. 119[197]
VRIEZEN, TH.C. 26[96]

WAGNER, S. 325[128]
WAKELY, R. 164[39]
WALKER, L.L. 346[28]
WATSON, W.G.E. 3[12] 4[13.15.16] 50[3] 54[15] 140[256] 261[123] 262[130] 284[12] 355[66]
WATTS, J.D.W. 3[10] 16[36] 20[65] 23[84] 30[118] 39[175] 45[201] 152[1] 153[9] 155[19] 160[32] 165 184[84] 234[54] 235[56.58] 236[60] 257[111] 259[115.116] 269[161] 282[1] 283[9] 289[19] 290[21] 300[52.54] 308[78] 309[85.86] 310[92] 317[102] 322[117] 340[2] 350[45.46.47] 353[59] 363[102] 383[16]
WEBB, B.G. 222[2]
WEDER, H. 132 **134-136** 137
WEEMS, R.J. 98[154]
WEGNER, P. 362[99]
WEINRICH, H. 380[4]
WELLHAUSEN, J. 31[124]
WESTERMANN, C. 52[12] 232[41] 319[110.111]
WETTE, W.M.L. DE 32[129]
WHEELWRIGHT, P. 78[115]
WIDENGREN, G. 248[91]
WILDBERGER, H. 19[58.60.63] 20[64.65.66] 21 23[83] 24 28 30[117] 36[154.156.157] 37 41[183] 44[197.198] 152[1] 153[9] 155[18] 156[26] 162[37] 171[51.52] 180[66.67] 181[73] 184[83.84] 187[99] 194[109] 197[117] 214[139] 231[40] 232 233[45] 235[55.56.58] 236[60] 241[73.75.76] 251[96] 252[98] 259[116] 260[121] 262[127] 263[131] 269[161] 282[4] 283[9] 289[19.20] 290[21.22.23.24.25] 291[27] 298[44.45.46.47.48] 299[49.50] 300[52.54] 304[70] 308[78.79.80.82.84] 309[84.85.86] 310[90] 318[104.105] 319[107] 322[117] 329[141] 332 333[149] 340[2] 341[6] 342[8.10.11] 344[22.24] 349[39.40] 351[49.50] 352[57] 353[59.60] 355[65] 356[69] 362[98.100]
WILLIAMS, W.C. 341[3]
WILLIAMSON, H.G.M., 18[52] 22[79] 353[58]
WINNER, E. 129[215]
WRIGHT, C.J.H. 324[124]
WYSCHOGROD, M. 119[196]

YEE, G. 98[154]
YOUNG, E.J. 31[123]
YOUNGER, K.L. 181[76] 346[30]

ZIEGLER, J. 3[12]
ZOBEL, H.-J. 325[130]
ZÖCKLER, O. 31[123]

INDEX OF SCRIPTURE REFERENCES

GENESIS

1	326^{133}
1,2	177^{59}
1,16	201
1,16-17	202
2,6	346_{28}
2,7	362^{96}
2,10	346^{28}
2,18	358
2,20	358
3,8-10	95 121^{200} 266
6,17	292^{32}
7,1-16	329
7,11	199^{123} 200
7,23	164^{39}
8,2	199^{123}
8,4	270
8,13	164^{39}
8,21	96
8,21-22	200
9,5-6	169^{47}
9,14	200
9,16	169^{47} 214^{139}
18,1	172^{54}
18,18	301^{57}
18,20-21	95^{145} 256^{144}
22,6	267^{152}
24,22	267^{152}
31,29	267
32	96 131 266^{146}
37,34	163^{39}
38,28	267^{152}
40,11	267^{152}
41,35	267
47,18	164^{39}
47,24	267^{154}
49	384^{20}
49,24	267

EXODUS

3,8	268
3,19	267
3,20	253^{104}
6,8	267^{152}
9,3	268
9,29	262^{127}
9,33	262^{127}
10,5	163^{39}
10,12	163^{39}
10,14	270
10,15	163^{39} 164^{39}
12,23	330
13,3	268
14,31	268
15	384^{20}
15,12	268
17	285
18,18	163^{39}
19,20	109^{175} 269^{160}
20,4-5	332^{147}
22,3	267^{152}
23,3	245^{83}
24,11	252
29,18	96
29,25	96
29,41	96
30,34-37	96
32	$359^{86.88}$
33,13	301^{57}
34,9ff.	332^{147}
34,21	172^{54}

LEVITICUS

1,9	96
1,13	96
1,17	96
2,2	96
2,9	96
4,22	164^{39}
5,21	267^{152}
11,33	172^{57}
19,15	245^{83}
20,18	325
24,8	169^{47}
25,8ff	356
26,34	172^{54}
26,35	172^{54}

NUMBERS

10,36	270
11,25	270
13,20	183^{81} 187^{102}
14,40	109^{175} 269^{160}
20,20	268
22,23	267^{152}
23-24	384^{20}

DEUTERONOMY

2,15	268
3,20	272
4,6	301^{57}
6,11	345^{27}
7,8	268
7,16	163^{39}
10,17	245^{83}
10,18	$245^{83.86}$
11,10	346^{28}
12,9f.	272
17,20	253^{104}
19,12	268
22,19	357^{73}
22,29	357^{73}
23,13	267^{154}
24,1	357^{73}
24,3	357^{73}
25,19	272
28,32	267
28,63	177^{60}
28,65	272
30,9	177^{60}
32-33	384^{20}
32,4	287^{16}
32,14	340^{2}
32,15	287^{16}
32,18	287^{16}
32,39	268
32,40	302^{66}

33,13	309[87]	2 Samuel		9,28	270
				10,32	267[154]
Joshua		2,28	363[101]		
		7,14	120	Esther	
1,7	253[104]	13,10	324[126]		
2,24	268	13,31-37	163[39]	9,6	270
4,24	273	17,12	270	9,22	270
8,18	267[152]	18,16	363[101]		
8,20	267	19,44	267[154]	Job	
13,1ff.	164[39]	20,1	363[101]		
15,8	269[160]	20,19	227	3,13	270
23,7	253[104]	20,22	363[101]	3,16	270
		21,10	270	3,26	270
Judges		22,28	245[83]	4,20	172[57]
		22,46	163[39]	5,15	245[83]
2,14	268	23,3	287[16]	6,2-3	117
2,15	268	23,5	169[47]	11,13	262[127]
5	384[20]			12,10	292[32]
6,26	244[82]	1 Kings		17,3	267[152]
7,20	172[57]			18,16	359[90]
8,3	243[80]	8,38	262[127]	21,24	346[28]
9,8ff.	248[91]	18.36	268	29,19	359[90]
9,15	244[82] 269[160]			30,21	267
9,57	109[176]	2 Kings		30,30	164[39]
15,1	324[126]			34,20	267
16,9	324[126]	2,15	270	38,6	199[123]
16,12	324[126]	3,23	243[81]		
18,30	172[57]	11,8	267[152]	Psalms	
		17,23	173[57]		
Ruth				1,3	163[39]
		1 Chronicles		2	248
1,13	268			2,7	117
		4,10	268	5,12	177[60]
1 Samuel		11,23	267[152]	7,16	109[176] 269[160]
		18,3	267[154]	9,2	245[83]
2,1	177[60]	28,2	272[172]	9,7	299[50]
2,5	163[39]			10,12	245[83]
9,5	172[54]	2 Chronicles		14,4	164[39]
10,2	172[54]			14,6	244[82]
12,21	177[59]	6,29	262[127]	16,9	177[60]
15,4	267[154]	26,10	345[27]	18	384[20]
15,22	96			18,2	103 246[87] 288
17,46	268	Ezra		18,3	287[16]
21,4	267[152]			18,4-5	105
23,13	172[54]	8,22	268	18,36	267[153]
26,13	109[175] 269[160]			18,47	287[16]
20,15	268	Nehemiah		19,15	287[16]
				21,2	177[60]
		1,10	268	24,7	178[63]

24,9	178⁶⁵	89,26	267	6,17	267¹⁵²
27,1	313⁹⁶	89,27	287¹⁶	11,21	267¹⁵²
28,1	287¹⁶	92,16	287¹⁶	14,33	270
28,2	267¹⁵²	93,1	199¹²³	19,13	105
29	384²⁰	93,3	384²²	21,6	270
29,(5)6	107	94,22	287¹⁶	23,23	68⁸⁷
31,3	287¹⁶	95,1	287¹⁶	27,25	173⁵⁷
31,9	268	95,4	268	29,4	244⁸³
34,6	245⁸³	96,10	199¹²³	30,14	164³⁹
35,9	177⁶⁰	97,10	177⁶⁰	42,1	106
37,2	163³⁹	103,6	253¹⁰⁴		
37,24	268	104,13	346²⁸	QOHELET	
38,3	269	105,10	169⁴⁷		
38,12	384²¹	105,35	163³⁹	1,6	312⁹⁴
40,2	107	106,5	301⁵⁷	1,14	312⁹⁴
41,6	299⁵⁰	106,9	164³⁹	1,17	312⁹⁴
46,2	244⁸²	106,10	268	2,11	312⁹⁴
48,11	267¹⁵³	106,15	187¹⁰²	2,17	312⁹⁴
49,16	268	106,38	163³⁹	2,26	312⁹⁴
58,11	177⁶⁰	106,40	104	4,4	312⁹⁴
61,4	244⁸²	107,2	268	4,6	312⁹⁴
62,3	287¹⁶	107,41	245⁸³	4,16	312⁹⁴
62,7	287¹⁶	109,27	268	6,9	312⁹⁴
62,8	287¹⁶	119	345²⁸	7,9	268
62,9	244⁸²	119,2	345²⁸	10,4	243⁸⁰
63,9	267¹⁵³	119,17	177⁶⁰	10,6	286¹⁵
68,5	245⁸⁶	119,22	345²⁸		
68,31	359⁸⁵	119,33	345²⁸	SONG OF SONGS	
69,12	178⁶³	119,34	345²⁸		
70,5	177⁶⁰	119,115	345²⁸	1,4	324¹²⁶
71,3	287¹⁶	119,129	345²⁸	3,4	324¹²⁶
71,7	244⁸²	119,145	345²⁸	5,4	267¹⁵⁴
71,19	253¹⁰⁴	122,2	178⁶⁰	7,7	106
72,18	253¹⁰⁴	132	18⁵⁵		
73,26	287¹⁶	132,8	272¹⁷²	SIRACH	
74	245⁸³	132,14	272¹⁷²		
74,11	267¹⁵³	132,15	245⁸³	14,27	244⁸²
74,13	199¹²⁴	133,1-2	117	16,4	243⁸¹
74,17	58	133,3	310⁸⁷	33	199¹²⁴
74,23	143⁸¹	134,2	267¹⁵²	36,2	199¹²⁴
75,6	287¹⁶	138,7	267¹⁵³		
78,35	287¹⁶	139,10	267¹⁵³	ISAIAH	
79	384²⁰	139,15	361		
80,9ff.	56	146,9	245⁸³	1-4	22⁸⁰
80,11	244⁸²			1-12	12
82,6-7	299⁴⁸	PROVERBS		1-27	351⁵⁰
87,2	178⁶³			1–33	1¹⁰ 23⁸⁴ 152¹
89,14	267¹⁵³	3,20	309⁸⁷		153⁹ 160³² 184⁸⁴
89,15	313⁹⁶	4,14	106		234⁵⁴ 235⁵⁵·⁵⁸

SCRIPTURE REFERENCES

	236[60] 257[111]	4,3	305
	259[115.116] 269[161]	4,5b-6	22[79]
	282[1] 283[9] 289[19]	4,6	243[80] 244[82]
	290[21] 300[52.54]	5	349
	309[85] 310[92]	5-23	22
	317[101.102] 322[117]	5,1	340[2] 344[23] 350[42]
	350[45.46] 363[102]	5,1-4	343
1-35	184[83]	5,1-6	345[27]
1-39	13[18.19] 16[36] 24[85]	5,1-7	22[79] 342 344
	30[118] 32[133] 39[176]		349[38] 371
	42[188] 52[12] 152[1]	5,2	340[2]
	153[4.8] 155[18]	5,4	340[2]
	171[50] 183[81]	5,5-6	344
	184[84.85] 193[106]	5,5a	340[4]
	194[109] 224[11]	5,6	344 346[30]
	231[40] 232[43]	5,7	56 351
	233[48] 235[58]	5,7a	352
	236[60] 250[94]	5,13	172[57]
	252[98]	5,14	243[81]
	257[110] 259[115.116]	5,20c	214
	260[117] 263[133]	7,2	270
	282[2] 286[14]	7,8	235[57]
	290[21.23] 297[39.43]	7,19	270
	300[53] 305[75]	7,23-25	346[30]
	309[85] 310[88]	8,11	268
	317[101.102] 322[117]	9,11	268
	332[145] 340[1]	9,17	346[30]
	343[17] 346[34]	10,16	187[102]
	350[41] 356[70.71]	10,17	313[96] 346[30]
1-66	22 222	10,23	253[104]
1,7	163[39]	11,2	270
1,8	204[132]	11,4ff.	245[83]
1,21	227	11,10	272[172]
1,23	245[83]	11,10-16	22[79] 332[145]
1,25	268	11,11	268 345[28]
1,29	201[126]	11,15	268
1,30	163[39]	12	183[80]
1,31	360	12,2	283[9]
2,2	109[175] 269[160]	13	40
2,6-21	22[79]	13,1-22	41
2,9-17	22[79]	13,1-39,8	24[86]
2,10ff.	288[18]	13,3	177[60]
2,19	288	13,4	243[81]
2,11	286[15] 288[18]	13,8	22[79]
2,12	286[15]	13-23	12
2,19	288	13-27	12 19[58.60.63]
2,21	288		20[64.65.66] 23[83]
3,14	304[70]		30[117] 36[154.156.157]
4,1	255[108]		41[183] 44[197.198]

	152[1] 153[9] 155[18]
	156[26] 162[37]
	171[51.52] 180[66]
	181[73] 184[84]
	194[109] 197[117]
	214[139] 231[40]
	233[45] 235[55.56]
	236[60] 241[75]
	242[76] 251[96]
	252[98] 262[127]
	263[131] 269[161]
	282[4] 283[9]
	289[19.20]
	290[21.23.24.25]
	291[27] 297[43]
	298[44.45.46.48]
	299[49.50] 300[52.54]
	304[70]
	308[78.79.80.82]
	309[84.85.86] 310[90]
	318[104] 322[117]
	329[141] 333[149]
	341[6] 342[8.10.11]
	344[24] 349[40]
	351[49] 352[52]
	353[60] 355[66]
	356[69] 357[76]
	362[98.100]
13-39	19[61] 20[67] 28[105]
	30[118] 36[153.155]
	38[164] 155[18]
	184[83.84] 186[94]
	231[40] 235[58]
	236[60] 297[53]
	317[101] 322[117]
	342[8] 351[50] 354[62]
14,7	270
14,19	345[27]
14,31	178[63]
15,2	39[169]
17,10	285
17,17	237[62]
16,1-5	38[168]
16,7-10	38[168]
16,8	163[39]
16,13	254[107]
16,16	38[168]
17,1-9	358[78]
17,2	243[81]

17,2-11	368		348 357 367	24,5bcd	254^{104}
17,4	187^{102}		**404-405**	24,5-15	41
17,6	180 187^{102}	24,1-4	153 187 196	24,6	162 164 180
17,7	22^{79}	24,1-5	153		184^{84} 200 214
17,10	244^{82} 287^{16}	24,1-6	12^7 15 16 20		302^{61} 307
19,5	164^{39}		153 162^{37} 181	24,6a	$254^{104.105}$
19,8	163^{39}	24,1-7	13^{19} 153	24,6ab	162
19,16	268	24,1-12	152	24,6a-c	320
21,1-4	182^{80} 183^{80}	24,1-13	20^{65} 41^{179} 152	24,6bc	320
	187^{98} 214		153 162 170	24,6cd	162 169^{49}
21,1-10	40		181 182^{77} 184^{84}	24,6d	300 320
21,2	22^{79}		197 349^{38}	24,7	162 171 174
21,5	163^{35}	24,1-16a	18 349^{38}		177 202
22	194^{108}	24,1-20	15 17 21 28 41	24,7a	174
22,2	177^{60}		42 153 162^{37}	24,7a-13e	**201-203** 211
22,5	184^{84}		208^{136} 232 319		243^{81} **406-407**
22,12-14	184^{84}		320	24,7-9	171 178 356
22,13	177^{60}	24,1-23	258	24,7-11	38^{168}
23	19	24,2	153 159 163	24,7-12	16 32 38 162^{27}
23,7	177^{60}		196 213^{137} 216		171 173 181
23,11	244^{82}	24,2-3	155		320
23,12	270	24,2-13	20	24,7-13	18 164 **170-182**
23,14	244^{82}	24,3	153 159		186 188 **210-**
24	6, 7, 13^{12} 27	24,3a	320		**211** 213
	29^{108} 35 145^{216}	24,3-6	177^{59}	24,7-16aa	15 341^7
	222 223 227	24,4	11 160 197^{117}	24,7a	171
	228 232 233		202	24,8	171 177
	234 244 245	24,4-5	196	24,8-9	282
	249 254 257	24,4-5a	165	24,8a-c	174
	259 274 316	24,4a-6d	**203-206 211-**	24,8b	174 178 210
	324^{124} 330 331		**212 405-406**		243^{81}
	340^2 345^{27} 348	24,4ab	162 169^{49}	24,8-12	41
	349 352 356	24,4b-d	320	24,8-18a	13^{19}
	367	24,4b-e	320	24,9	171 174 177
24,1-25,9	262	24,4c-5a	162		284
24,1-27,1	332	24,4d	320	24,10	13 34 39^{169} 41
24,1	45 177^{59} 196	24,4-6	16 17 153 161-		43^{192} 171 177
	367		170 176 180		202 235^{58}
24,1a	320		188^{205}	24,10a	177^{59} 184^{84} 215
24,1b	305	24,4-9	367	24,10b	178
24,1d	320	24,4-13	12^7 162^{37}	24,10-11	16
24,1-2	153	24,5	11 193 196 230	24,10-12	172 178
24,1-3	16 18 **152-161**		$214^{138.139}$ 230	24,10-13	171
	162 153 165		232 284 307	24,11	171 177 178^{61}
	169 172 173^{57}		325 345^{28} 373^8	24,11-12	367
	179 130 181	24,5a	204 205 320	24,11a	175^{58} 204^{131}
	196^{115} 197 200	24,5b-6d	165	24,11a-c	172
	201 209 210	24,5bc	162 163 164	24,11b	174 178 202
	211 320 344		169 176 ^{227}		210

24,11c	300 320	24,18e-19c	199 200 210	25,1b	12^{10} 235^{57} 237 302^{66}
24,12	171 174 177 180	24,18e-20	197	25,1cd	238
24,12b	178	24,18e-23e	**195-214**	25,1d	238
24,13	$12^{7.10}$ 16 18 22^{79} 79^{121} 171 **179-181** 184 187 356 362^{97} 367	24,19-20	367	25,1-2	42 259^{116}
		24,19a-c	320	25,1-3	231^{40} 232 234-240 242
		24,20	184^{84} 193 197 198 203 205 211-212 228 367	25,1-4c	259^{116} 349^{38}
24,13a	320			25,1-5	$13^{11.19}$ 14 15 16 17 29^{109} 31 32 35 41 42 43^{192} 231^{231} 232 233 237^{64} 242 253^{103} 259^{116} 341^{7} 411-412
24,13b	180	24,20a	320		
24,13-17ff.	184^{83}	24,20c	204		
24,14	182^{78}	24,21	12^{8} 184 198 206 302^{66} 330		
24,14-16	18 38 39 181 197 213	24,21ff.	197		
24,14-16a	349^{38}	24,21a	197^{117}	25,1-8	258^{116}
24,14-16aa	16	24,21bc	212 213^{137} 214 320	25,1-10	183^{80}
24,14a-16b	**182-194** 209 **407-408**			25,1-12	231 240 258 259 282
		24,21-22	12^{7} 27 184^{84} 206 207 208 212 299		
24,14a-18d	**182-194** 206-209 212-213			25,1-15	38
		24,21-23	12^{7} 15^{35} 16 17 18 197 198 410	25,2	41 43 232 233 $235^{55.57}$
24,14-20	20				
24,14-22	197^{118}	24,21-25,10a	15	25,2a	237
24,14-23	183^{80}	24,21-26,19	322	25,2ab	238 242
24,15	12^{10} 182^{78}	24,21-26,21	17	25,2b	237 238 239 240 243^{79}
24,16	12^{9} 22^{79}	24,21-27,1	15 21 28 41 330		
24,16a	320			25,2c	237 240
24,16a-25,9	18	24,22abc	208 212	25,2cd	238
24,16ab	197	24,22c	320	25,2d	237 240
24,16ab-20	15 20	24,23	$12^{9.10}$ 18 197^{118} 231 233 236^{59} 248 259^{115}	25,2-3	232
24,16abb	16			25,3	184^{84} 233 242
24,16a-25,9	349^{38}			25,3-5	259^{116}
24,16b-18b	349^{38}	24,23ab	**201-203** 210 211 320	25,3a	237 242
24,16c-18c	**408-409**			25,3ab	237
24,16c-18d	**182-194**	24,23b	199	25,3b	237 243^{79}
24,16c-20	186	24,23cde	**206-209** 212 213	25,4	242 243 245^{83} 347
24,17	187 196 320				
24,17-18a	40 185	25	208^{136} 216 222 223 226 227 229 232 234 236 239 240 242 252 259 274 325 340^{2} 360	25,4-5	22^{79} 231^{40} 232 233 **241-251** 341^{4} 344
24,17-20	16 197				
24,18	5 45 184^{84} 187				
24,18-20	28 34			25,4a	242 245
24,18b-20	16 20			25,4ab	249
24,18b-23	13^{19}			25,4c	243
24,18c-23	349^{38}			25,4d	243
24,18cd	320	25-26	14 15	25,4de	244^{82}
24,18c-e	320	25-27	224 259	25,4e	243
24,18d-20	**409-410**	25,1	231 $253^{103.104}$ 259	25,4ef	241^{74} 243 249 250
24,18e	213				
24,18ef	213	25,1a	237 244	25,4ef-5ab	242
24,18e-9a	210	25,1ab	238	25,4f	243

ISAIAH

25,5	231 243 244[82]		257 258 259[114]	26,1-14	15
25,5a	243		260[121] 261	26,1-19	13[11]
25,5ab	241[74] 243 244[82] 249 250		262-273 300[56] 302[64] 306	26,1-27,1 26,2	323[121] 45
25,5b	243[79]			27,2-11	342[7]
25,5c	242 243	25,10-12	17[43] 39 234 239 259[116] 349[38]	26,2abc	284[13]
25,5cd	241[74] 244[82]			26,2b	287
25,5d	243[79]	25,10-26,8	349[38]	26,2c	287
25,6	12[9.10] 216 231 253[103] 260 272[170] 345[27]	25,10b	19 34 38 239 244[82] 260 262[126] 263 273[179]	26,3a 26,3abc 26,4-6	287[16] 284[13] 16 32
25,6b	252	25,10bc	238 262	26,4	284
25,6-7	252[104] 259[116]	25,10b-11	15[31]	26,4a	283[9]
25,6-8	12[7] 13[12] 14 16 18 29[108] 31 38[168] 232 233 249 **251-257** 259[1.6] 349[38] 412	25,10b-12	15[35] 17 232 234-240 259[116] 260[121] 262	26,4ab 26,4b 26,5	284[13] 285 287[16] 22[79] 41 42 43 288[18]
		25,10c	263 300[56]	26,5-6	12[9] 38 41 284 286 300[56]
25,6-9	259[1.6]	25,11	238 263		
		25,11-12	240	26,5ab	284[13] 286
25,6-10a	13[19] 15 182[77] 233 252 259[116]	25,11a 25,11ab	238[66] 239 238 262[126] 253	26,5cd 26,6	284[13] 38 42 43 259[116] 273 282 283
25,6-12	231 259 260	25,11b	239		
25,7	216 272[170] 303[67]	25,11b-12	22[79]	26,6abc	284[13]
25,7-8	309[85]	25,11b-13a	240	26,6ff.	233
25,7a	254	25,11c	237 239 240	26,6-8	257
25,7a-8a	253	25,11cd	238 262[126]	26,7	44 283
25,8	28 34 194 252 253[115] 272[170]	25,11d	237 238[66] 239	26,7b 26,7-9	289[19] 296 342[7]
25,8-9	259[116]	25,12	12[10] 13[11] 15[31] 29[109] 263	26,7-10	289-297 300 **416-417**
25,8.9-12	259[116]	25,12a	239 240 263		
25,8a	252[102] 254	25,12ab	238 262[126]	26,7-18	14 22[79] 318
25,8d	255[108]	25,12b	239 240	26,7-19	13[19] 15 16 290
25,9	12[8.9] 177[60] 252 253 259[116] 262[127] 263	26 26,1	35 274 **276-333** 12[8] 31 231 236[59] 259	26,7-21 26,8 26,8-9	15 20 332 293 20
25,9cd	263	26,1ab	282	26,8-19	321
25,9e	263	26,1b	33	26,9	286 296[38] 330
25,9-10a	18 232 233 249 252 **257-273**	26,1b-3 26,1b-4	18 284	26,9b 26,9cd	292 297[42] 293
25,9-11	13[11] 29[109]	26,1c	282	26,9-10	291
25,9-12	13 14 259[116] 260 261 262[126] 297[41] **412-414**	26,1c-6 26,1cd 26,1-4	283-289 284[13] 341[7]	26,10 26,10-11	44 291[28] 293 300 342[7]
25,10	38[168] 216 238 262 263	26,1-6	12[7.19] 14 15 16 17 41 43[192] 232 282 288[18] 414-416	26,10c 26,11	302[62] 291 299 300 301 306 320
25,10ff.	297[42]			26,11-12	182[77]
25,10a	12[7] 39 179 216 223 238[66] 239 243[80] 244[82] 252	26,1-8 26,1-9	18 349[38] 29[109]	26,11-13	20

Reference	Pages	Reference	Pages	Reference	Pages
26,11-15	**298-307 417-418**	26,18bc	312 315		367 **420-421**
26,11-19	282^1 297^{39} 310	26,18b-19d	313 315	27,2-11	15 17^{44} 322 341
26,11-27,6	18	26,18c	312	27,2-13	15 21 38
26,11a	301	26,19	11 28^{107} 33^{136} 34 228 290^{25} 300 305 307 310 311 315 316 317^{102} 318 319 323	27,2-23	28
26,11b	298^{44} 301			27,3	345^{26} 350
26,11c	303^{67}			27,3-4	344
26,11d	301			27,3-5	343 350
26,12	229 298^{47}			27,3a-d	367
26,12-15	310 333	26,19a-d	314 315	27,4	343 344 345^{26} 346
26,12a	301 303^{67}	26,19e	314	27,4a	350
26,12ab	301	26,19f	314 320	27,4b	343 350 367
26,12b	301	26,19-21	15	27,4bcd	367
26,13	256 298^{48} 301 303 307^{77} 314 320	26,20	18 44 311 322 352	27,4cd	367
				27,4-5	18
26,13a	301 303 305	26,20a	329	27,5	12^9 244^{82} 342^{13} 343^{18} 345^{26}
26,13ab	301	26,20a-d	324		
26,13b	302^{66}	26,20ff.	288	27,5bc	303^{67} 343
26,13-14	305 306 307 349^{38}	26,20-21	15 17 20 27 **419-420**	27,5c	343
				27,6	12$^{8.10.19}$ 18 182^{77} 342^{13} 343^{19} 344 345^{26} 350 351 355^{65} 367
26,13-15	349^{38}	26,20-27,1	13$^{12.19}$ 15 16 29^{108} **321-333**		
26,13-27,11	299^{48} 317^{102}	26,20-27,1b	349^{38}		
26,14	298^{48} 299 303^{67} 305 315 316	26,21	12^7 18 20^{65} 194 322 323^{122} 324^{330}	27,6ab	367
				27,6c	367
26,14ab	301 303 305	26,21ab	324	27,7	12$^{9.13}$ 340 342 354 355^{65} 358
26,14cd	301	26,21cd	324		
26,15	12^9 228 299 301 306 315 320 349^{38}	26,21-27,1	321^{116}	27,7-11	15^{31} 34 356 368 **422-423**
		27	17 22^{77} 322 **336-368**		
				27,7-13	340 **353-368**
26,15a	299 301	27,1	12$^{7.8}$ 15^{35} 17 28 31 32 34 35 321 322^{117} 323^{122} 329 332 356 420	27,7ab	366
26,15b	301 302^{62}			27,8	37 317^{102} 354 355^{66} 357 358 359 362
26,15c	301				
26,15d	301				
26,15-19	15^{35} 33^{136} 300			27,8-9	355
26,16	300 310 320	27,1a-f	324	27,8-13	355
26,16ff.	272^{170}	27,1c	349^{38}	27,8a	367
26,16-18(19)	20 **308-320** 349^{38} **418-419**	27,1cde	323^{120}	27,8ab	366 367
		27,1-6	15	27,8b	367
26,16-27,6	349^{38}	27,1-13	17 22^{79}	27,9	12$^{10.19}$ 18 26 37 194 354 357 362 363 367
26,17	310 319 320 333	27,2	12^8 323 343^{19} 344^{23} 345^{26} 352		
26,17-18	41^{179} 83^{125} 228	27,2a-6d	343 349^{38}	27,9-11	13^{13}
26,17-18a	311 313 314	27,2ff.	322	27,9ab	366 367
26,17-19	182	27,2-3	341^4 350	27,9b	367
26,17a-19f	315	27,2-4	16	27,9cde	359 360 366
26,18	305 319 330	27,2-5	13$^{13.19}$ 29^{109} 342 344^{22} 350^{43} 351	27,10	43^{192} 354 355^{63}
26,18a	320			27,10abc	366 367
26,18bff.	320	27,2-6	**340-352** 356	27,10def	359 360 366

ISAIAH – JEREMIAH   471

27,10f	359	36-39	12	59,9	313^{96}
27,10-11	31 38 41	37,5	319	60,11	178^{60}
27,10-11a	12$^{7.13}$ 18	37,18	164^{39}	60,18	178^{60}
27,10-13	355	38,13	83^{126}	60,19-20	313^{96}
27,11	44 356 360 361	38,14	83^{126}	60,21	345^{28}
	362^{95}	38,16	292^{32}	60,22	301^{57}
27,11ab	359 360 361	40-55	224^{11} 371^{3}	61,5	345^{27}
	364 366 367	40-66	371^{1}	62,4	254^{107}
27,11b	18	40,2-3	18^{56}	62,5	177^{60} 254^{107}
27,11c	366	40,17	177^{59}	65	27
27,11de	361 367	40,23	177^{59}	66,1	272^{172}
27,12	12$^{8.12}$ 349^{38} 356	41,20	267	66,2	268
	362^{97}	14,29	312^{94}	66,6	243^{81}
27,12-13	13^{19} 15 16 19	42,5	292^{32}	66,7	310^{89} 319^{110}
	29^{108} 45 322	42,6	313^{96}	66,7-9	22^{79}
	340 349^{38} 351	42,9-13	18^{56}	66,8	310^{89} 319^{110}
	355 356 365	42,15	164^{39}		
	423	44,8-9	287^{16}	**JEREMIAH**	
27,12b-d	367	44,9-20	360		
27,12d	362^{97} 367	45,1	178^{60}	1,3	173^{57}
27,12de	366	45,7	313^{96}	1,5	361^{93}
27,13	12$^{7.8.\,2}$ 18 28 34	45,12	268	1,11-12	82
	236^{59} 349^{38} 356	45,18	177^{59}	1,13-14	89
	362	47,8-9a	228	2-3	230^{37}
28	19	48,13	267^{153} 268	2-25	384^{24}
28,2	243^{80}	49,1	361^{93}	2,8	56 90
28-33	12	49,2	244^{82}	2,13	58
28-35	12	49,5	361^{93}	2,23-24	90
29,8	83^{126}	49,6	313^{96}	2,26	79^{119} 88
29,21	177^{59}	49,8	361^{73}	3,1	163^{39} 357^{73}
30,26	202^{127}	49,13	245^{83}	3,20	79^{120}
30,29	287^{16}	49,21	310^{89} 319	4,13	55 79$^{117.118}$ 90
31,3	268	51	228	4,23	177^{59}
31,4	83^{126}	51,8	228	4,23-28	215-216
31,5	83^{126}	51,9	204 326^{133}	4,28	163^{39}
31,32	304^{70}	51,9-11	18^{56}	4,31	262^{127}
32,1-2	22^{79}	51,10	228	5,3	79^{118}
32,2	244^{82}	51,17	228	5,27	79^{119}
32,13	177^{60} 346^{30}	51,18	228	6,3	267^{154}
33	14^{24}	51,16	244^{82}	6,7	79^{119}
33,1	22^{79}	51,21-22	228	7,34	214^{139}
33,9	163^{39}	52,7-8	18^{56}	8,2	90
33,11	243^{80}	54,1	254^{107} 310^{89} 319	8,7	88
34-35	12	54,2	228	8,13	163^{39}
34,10	243^{81}	54,4	228 255^{108}	9,22	90
34,11	177^{59}	54,5	254^{107}	10,5	89
34,17	268	56,5	267^{154}	10,7	79^{117} 90
36,17	345^{27}	57,8	267^{154}	11,4	80 81
36-29	12	57,10	267^{154}	11,16-17	55

11,19	55	48,2	34 39[169]	12,20	243[81]
12,2	82	48,6	79[117]	15,4	164[39]
12,4	163[39]	48,29	297[42]	15,5	164[39]
12,11	163[39]	48,43-44	38	16	95 131 230[37]
13,11	80[122] 87 88	48,43-44a	40 185	16,16	68
13,12-14	89	49,11	245[86]	16,25	109[175] 269[160]
15,5	204	49,35	172[57]	16,30	163[39]
15,8	79[118]	50-51	40	16,31	269[160]
15,9	163[39]	50,17	55	16,32	109[175]
15,16	163[39]	50,21	243[81]	16,38	301[58]
15,17	268	50,27	243[81]	16,42	301[58]
16,5	188 204	50,23	81	17	248[91]
16,9	214[139]	51,5	228	17,18	267[152]
16,21	268	51,30	172[54]	17,23	244[82]
17,3	81	51,34	326[133]	20,30	227[27]
17,6	164[39]	51,36	164[39]	21,19	109[175] 269[160]
17,17	244[82]	51,55	243[81]	21,21	109[175] 269[160]
18,6	79[117.119]			22,7	245[83]
18,9	163[39]	**LAMENTATIONS**		23	230[37]
18,14-45	88			23,25	301[58]
19,10-11	79[122]	1,1	358[81]	25,11	253[104]
19,11	80[122]	1,1bc	228	26,13	214[139]
19,11-12	80[122]	1,1-2	255[108]	31	248[91]
20,9	88	1,3	271 272	31,6	244[82]
20,17	79[117]	1,7	358[83]	31,12	244[82]
23,10	163[39]	1,9	272	31,17	244[82]
23,29	79[121]	1,10	262[127]	35,10	300[57]
24,5	79[119]	1,12	262[127]	37	28[107] 118 318
24,8	79[119]	3,1	272	37,1-14	305
25,10	214[139]	3,33	181[75]	37,5-14	292[32]
25,11	243[81]	3,47	185[88] 187[96]	42,12	269[160]
25,30	55	3,52	187[96] 207	47,12	163[39]
25,31	244[81]	3,53-54	207		
25,33	90	4,20	244[82]	**DANIEL**	
26,9	164[39] 243[81]	4,20b	248		
28,2	172[57]	5,3	272	2,22	183[81]
28,4	172[57]	5,15	214[139]	4,6	183[81]
28,11	172[57]			8,25	267
30,11	253[104]	**EZEKIEL**		11,31	244[82] 246[88]
31,10	84 88			12,12	317[102]
31,11	268	1-20	119[197]	12,13	329
32,41	177[60]	3,14	268		
34,7	164[39]	5,10	253[104]	**HOSEA**	
38,8	172[57]	5,15	253[104]		
41,8	172[54]	6,6	164[39] 243[81]	1-3	227[28] 230[37] 358
43,12	80[122]	6,9	227[17]	1-4	49[2]
46,21	84	7,12	177[59]	1,6	362[96]
46,23	79[118] 84	9,8	164[39]	2,13	214[138]
47,23	86	11,9	253[104]	2,19	120[256]

4,3	163³⁹	2,2	243⁸¹	ZECHARIAH	
4,13	109¹⁷⁵ 244⁸²	2,6	245⁸³		
	269¹⁵⁰	4,9	163³⁹	12-14	29
4,15	164³⁹	5,11	340²	12,6	163³⁹
5,5	384²²	7,2	163³⁹	14,5	31
5,15	164³⁹	7,9	164³⁹ 243⁸¹		
6,2	305			MALACHI	
9,1	177⁶⁰	OBADIAH			
10,12	164³⁹			2,15-16	292³²
10,14	243⁸¹	15	109¹⁷⁶ 269¹⁶⁰	2,16	357⁷³
12,4-5	96 131 266¹⁴⁶			4,4	26
13,4	299⁴⁸	MICAH			
13,4-14,10	299⁴⁸ 317¹⁰²			TOBIT	
13,14	317¹⁰²	2,2	245⁸³		
14,1	164³⁹	7,8	313⁹⁶	7,15	324¹²⁶
14,7[8]	305	7,8-9	313⁹⁶	7,16	324¹²⁶
14,8	244⁸² 249			8,1	324¹²⁶
		NAHUM		8,4	324¹²⁶
JOEL					
		1,2-8	215	4ᵀᴴ EZRA	
1,4	163³⁹				
1,11	345²⁷	HABAKKUK		14,45-47	27
1,12	163³⁹ 202				
1,17	202	3,14	164³⁹	MATTHEW	
2,5	163³⁹				
2,16	324¹²⁶	ZEPHANIAH		11,29-30	69⁸⁷
3,4	109¹⁷⁶ 269¹⁶⁰			23,4	119
3,18	346²⁸	2,11	187¹⁰²	23,27	119
4,16	244⁸²				
4,18	346²⁸	HAGGAI		I COR	
		1,10	310⁸⁷	9,24-27	76
AMOS		2,15-19	26		
1,1	31				

BIBLIOTHECA EPHEMERIDUM THEOLOGICARUM LOVANIENSIUM

Series I

* = Out of print

- *1. *Miscellanea dogmatica in honorem Eximii Domini J. Bittremieux*, 1947.
- *2-3. *Miscellanea moralia in honorem Eximii Domini A. Janssen*, 1948.
- *4. G. Philips, *La grâce des justes de l'Ancien Testament*, 1948.
- *5. G. Philips, *De ratione instituendi tractatum de gratia nostrae sanctificationis*, 1953.
- 6-7. *Recueil Lucien Cerfaux. Études d'exégèse et d'histoire religieuse*, 1954. 504 et 577 p. FB 1000 par tome. Cf. *infra*, n°s 18 et 71 (t. III).
- 8. G. Thils, *Histoire doctrinale du mouvement œcuménique*, 1955. Nouvelle édition, 1963. 338 p. FB 135.
- *9. *Études sur l'Immaculée Conception*, 1955.
- *10. J.A. O'Donohoe, *Tridentine Seminary Legislation*, 1957.
- *11. G. Thils, *Orientations de la théologie*, 1958.
- *12-13. J. Coppens, A. Descamps, É. Massaux (ed.), *Sacra Pagina. Miscellanea Biblica Congressus Internationalis Catholici de Re Biblica*, 1959.
- *14. *Adrien VI le premier Pape de la contre-réforme*, 1959.
- *15. F. Claeys Bouuaert, *Les déclarations et serments imposés par la loi civile aux membres du clergé belge sous le Directoire (1795-1801)*, 1960.
- *16. G. Thils, *La «Théologie œcuménique». Notion-Formes-Démarches*, 1960.
- 17. G. Thils, *Primauté pontificale et prérogatives épiscopales. «Potestas ordinaria» au Concile du Vatican*, 1961. 103 p. FB 50.
- *18. *Recueil Lucien Cerfaux*, t. III, 1962. Cf. *infra*, n° 71.
- *19. *Foi et réflexion philosophique. Mélanges F. Grégoire*, 1961.
- *20. *Mélanges G. Ryckmans*, 1963.
- 21. G. Thils, *L'infaillibilité du peuple chrétien «in credendo»*, 1963. 67 p. FB 50.
- *22. J. Férin & L. Janssens, *Progestogènes et morale conjugale*, 1963.
- *23. *Collectanea Moralia in honorem Eximii Domini A. Janssen*, 1964.
- 24. H. Cazelles (ed.), *De Mari à Qumrân. L'Ancien Testament. Son milieu. Ses écrits. Ses relectures juives* (Hommage J. Coppens, I), 1969. 158*-370 p. FB 900.
- *25. I. de la Potterie (ed.), *De Jésus aux évangiles. Tradition et rédaction dans les évangiles synoptiques* (Hommage J. Coppens, II), 1967.
- 26. G. Thils & R.E. Brown (ed.), *Exégèse et théologie* (Hommage J. Coppens, III), 1968. 328 p. FB 700.
- 27. J. Coppens (ed.), *Ecclesia a Spiritu sancto edocta. Hommage à Mgr G. Philips*, 1970. 640 p. FB 1000.
- 28. J. Coppens (ed.), *Sacerdoce et célibat. Études historiques et théologiques*, 1971. 740 p. FB 700.

29. M. DIDIER (ed.), *L'évangile selon Matthieu. Rédaction et théologie*, 1972. 432 p. FB 1000.
*30. J. KEMPENEERS, *Le Cardinal van Roey en son temps*, 1971.

SERIES II

31. F. NEIRYNCK, *Duality in Mark. Contributions to the Study of the Markan Redaction*, 1972. Revised edition with Supplementary Notes, 1988. 252 p. FB 1200.
32. F. NEIRYNCK (ed.), *L'évangile de Luc. Problèmes littéraires et théologiques*, 1973. *L'évangile de Luc – The Gospel of Luke*. Revised and enlarged edition, 1989. X-590 p. FB 2200.
33. C. BREKELMANS (ed.), *Questions disputées d'Ancien Testament. Méthode et théologie*, 1974. *Continuing Questions in Old Testament Method and Theology*. Revised and enlarged edition by M. VERVENNE, 1989. 245 p. FB 1200.
34. M. SABBE (ed.), *L'évangile selon Marc. Tradition et rédaction*, 1974. Nouvelle édition augmentée, 1988. 601 p. FB 2400.
35. B. WILLAERT (ed.), *Philosophie de la religion – Godsdienstfilosofie. Miscellanea Albert Dondeyne*, 1974. Nouvelle édition, 1987. 458 p. FB 1600.
36. G. PHILIPS, *L'union personnelle avec le Dieu vivant. Essai sur l'origine et le sens de la grâce créée*, 1974. Édition révisée, 1989. 299 p. FB 1000.
37. F. NEIRYNCK, in collaboration with T. HANSEN and F. VAN SEGBROECK, *The Minor Agreements of Matthew and Luke against Mark with a Cumulative List*, 1974. 330 p. FB 900.
38. J. COPPENS, *Le messianisme et sa relève prophétique. Les anticipations vétérotestamentaires. Leur accomplissement en Jésus*, 1974. Édition révisée, 1989. XIII-265 p. FB 1000.
39. D. SENIOR, *The Passion Narrative according to Matthew. A Redactional Study*, 1975. New impression, 1982. 440 p. FB 1000.
40. J. DUPONT (ed.), *Jésus aux origines de la christologie*, 1975. Nouvelle édition augmentée, 1989. 458 p. FB 1500.
41. J. COPPENS (ed.), *La notion biblique de Dieu*, 1976. Réimpression, 1985. 519 p. FB 1600.
42. J. LINDEMANS & H. DEMEESTER (ed.), *Liber Amicorum Monseigneur W. Onclin*, 1976. XXII-396 p. FB 1000.
43. R.E. HOECKMAN (ed.), *Pluralisme et œcuménisme en recherches théologiques. Mélanges offerts au R.P. Dockx, O.P.*, 1976. 316 p. FB 1000.
44. M. DE JONGE (ed.), *L'évangile de Jean. Sources, rédaction, théologie*, 1977. Réimpression, 1987. 416 p. FB 1500.
45. E.J.M. VAN EIJL (ed.), *Facultas S. Theologiae Lovaniensis 1432-1797. Bijdragen tot haar geschiedenis. Contributions to its History. Contributions à son histoire*, 1977. 570 p. FB 1700.
46. M. DELCOR (ed.), *Qumrân. Sa piété, sa théologie et son milieu*, 1978. 432 p. FB 1700.
47. M. CAUDRON (ed.), *Faith and Society. Foi et société. Geloof en maatschappij. Acta Congressus Internationalis Theologici Lovaniensis 1976*, 1978. 304 p. FB 1150.

48. J. KREMER (ed.), *Les Actes des Apôtres. Traditions, rédaction, théologie*, 1979. 590 p. FB 1700.
49. F. NEIRYNCK, avec la collaboration de J. DELOBEL, T. SNOY, G. VAN BELLE, F. VAN SEGBROECK, *Jean et les Synoptiques. Examen critique de l'exégèse de M.-É. Boismard*, 1979. XII-428 p. FB 1000.
50. J. COPPENS, *La relève apocalyptique du messianisme royal. I. La royauté – Le règne – Le royaume de Dieu. Cadre de la relève apocalyptique*. 1979. 325 p. FB 1500.
51. M. GILBERT (ed.), *La Sagesse de l'Ancien Testament*, 1979. Nouvelle édition mise à jour, 1990. 455 p. FB 1500.
52. B. DEHANDSCHUTTER, *Martyrium Polycarpi Een literair-kritische studie*, 1979. 296 p. FB 1000.
53. J. LAMBRECHT (ed.), *L'Apocalypse johannique et l'Apocalyptique dans le Nouveau Testament*, 1980. 458 p. FB 1400.
54. P.-M. BOGAERT (ed.), *Le livre de Jérémie. Le prophète et son milieu. Les oracles et leur transmission*, 1981. Nouvelle édition mise à jour, 1997. 448 p. FB 1800.
55. J. COPPENS, *La relève apocalyptique du messianisme royal. III. Le Fils de l'homme néotestamentaire*. Édition posthume par F. NEIRYNCK, 1981. XIV-192 p. FB 800.
56. J. VAN BAVEL & M. SCHRAMA (ed.), *Jansénius et le Jansénisme dans les Pays-Bas. Mélanges Lucien Ceyssens*, 1982. 247 p. FB 1000.
57. J.H. WALGRAVE, *Selected Writings – Thematische geschriften. Thomas Aquinas, J.H. Newman, Theologia Fundamentalis*. Edited by G. DE SCHRIJVER & J.J. KELLY, 1982. XLIII-425 p. FB 1000.
58. F. NEIRYNCK & F. VAN SEGBROECK, avec la collaboration de E. MANNING, *Ephemerides Theologicae Lovanienses 1924-1981. Tables générales*. (Bibliotheca Ephemeridum Theologicarum Lovaniensium 1947-1981), 1982. 400 p. FB 1600.
59. J. DELOBEL (ed.), *Logia. Les paroles de Jésus – The Sayings of Jesus. Mémorial Joseph Coppens*, 1982. 647 p. FB 2000.
60. F. NEIRYNCK, *Evangelica. Gospel Studies – Études d'évangile. Collected Essays*. Edited by F. VAN SEGBROECK, 1982. XIX-1036 p. FB 2000.
61. J. COPPENS, *La relève apocalyptique du messianisme royal. II. Le Fils d'homme vétéro- et intertestamentaire*. Édition posthume par J. LUST, 1983. XVII-272 p. FB 1000.
62. J.J. KELLY, *Baron Friedrich von Hügel's Philosophy of Religion*, 1983. 232 p. FB 1500.
63. G. DE SCHRIJVER, *Le merveilleux accord de l'homme et de Dieu. Étude de l'analogie de l'être chez Hans Urs von Balthasar*, 1983. 344 p. FB 1500.
64. J. GROOTAERS & J.A. SELLING, *The 1980 Synod of Bishops: «On the Role of the Family». An Exposition of the Event and an Analysis of its Texts*. Preface by Prof. emeritus L. JANSSENS, 1983. 375 p. FB 1500.
65. F. NEIRYNCK & F. VAN SEGBROECK, *New Testament Vocabulary. A Companion Volume to the Concordance*, 1984. XVI-494 p. FB 2000.
66. R.F. COLLINS, *Studies on the First Letter to the Thessalonians*, 1984. XI-415 p. FB 1500.
67. A. PLUMMER, *Conversations with Dr. Döllinger 1870-1890*. Edited with Introduction and Notes by R. BOUDENS, with the collaboration of L. KENIS, 1985. LIV-360 p. FB 1800.

68. N. Lohfink (ed.), *Das Deuteronomium. Entstehung, Gestalt und Botschaft / Deuteronomy: Origin, Form and Message*, 1985. XI-382 p. FB 2000.
69. P.F. Fransen, *Hermeneutics of the Councils and Other Studies*. Collected by H.E. Mertens & F. De Graeve, 1985. 543 p. FB 1800.
70. J. Dupont, *Études sur les Évangiles synoptiques*. Présentées par F. Neirynck, 1985. 2 tomes, XXI-IX-1210 p. FB 2800.
71. *Recueil Lucien Cerfaux*, t. III, 1962. Nouvelle édition revue et complétée, 1985. LXXX-458 p. FB 1600.
72. J. Grootaers, *Primauté et collégialité. Le dossier de Gérard Philips sur la Nota Explicativa Praevia (Lumen gentium, Chap. III)*. Présenté avec introduction historique, annotations et annexes. Préface de G. Thils, 1986. 222 p. FB 1000.
73. A. Vanhoye (ed.), *L'apôtre Paul. Personnalité, style et conception du ministère*, 1986. XIII-470 p. FB 2600.
74. J. Lust (ed.), *Ezekiel and His Book. Textual and Literary Criticism and their Interrelation*, 1986. X-387 p. FB 2700.
75. É. Massaux, *Influence de l'Évangile de saint Matthieu sur la littérature chrétienne avant saint Irénée*. Réimpression anastatique présentée par F. Neirynck. Supplément: *Bibliographie 1950-1985*, par B. Dehandschutter, 1986. XXVII-850 p. FB 2500.
76. L. Ceyssens & J.A.G. Tans, *Autour de l'Unigenitus. Recherches sur la genèse de la Constitution*, 1987. XXVI-845 p. FB 2500.
77. A. Descamps, *Jésus et l'Église. Études d'exégèse et de théologie*. Préface de Mgr A. Houssiau, 1987. XLV-641 p. FB 2500.
78. J. Duplacy, *Études de critique textuelle du Nouveau Testament*. Présentées par J. Delobel, 1987. XXVII-431 p. FB 1800.
79. E.J.M. van Eijl (ed.), *L'image de C. Jansénius jusqu'à la fin du XVIIIe siècle*, 1987. 258 p. FB 1250.
80. E. Brito, *La Création selon Schelling. Universum*, 1987. XXXV-646 p. FB 2980.
81. J. Vermeylen (ed.), *The Book of Isaiah – Le livre d'Isaïe. Les oracles et leurs relectures. Unité et complexité de l'ouvrage*, 1989. X-472 p. FB 2700.
82. G. Van Belle, *Johannine Bibliography 1966-1985. A Cumulative Bibliography on the Fourth Gospel*, 1988. XVII-563 p. FB 2700.
83. J.A. Selling (ed.), *Personalist Morals. Essays in Honor of Professor Louis Janssens*, 1988. VIII-344 p. FB 1200.
84. M.-É. Boismard, *Moïse ou Jésus. Essai de christologie johannique*, 1988. XVI-241 p. FB 1000.
84A. M.-É. Boismard, *Moses or Jesus: An Essay in Johannine Christology*. Translated by B.T. Viviano, 1993, XVI-144 p. FB 1000.
85. J.A. Dick, *The Malines Conversations Revisited*, 1989. 278 p. FB 1500.
86. J.-M. Sevrin (ed.), *The New Testament in Early Christianity – La réception des écrits néotestamentaires dans le christianisme primitif*, 1989. XVI-406 p. FB 2500.
87. R.F. Collins (ed.), *The Thessalonian Correspondence*, 1990. XV-546 p. FB 3000.
88. F. Van Segbroeck, *The Gospel of Luke. A Cumulative Bibliography 1973-1988*, 1989. 241 p. FB 1200.

89. G. THILS, *Primauté et infaillibilité du Pontife Romain à Vatican I et autres études d'ecclésiologie*, 1989. XI-422 p. FB 1850.
90. A. VERGOTE, *Explorations de l'espace théologique. Études de théologie et de philosophie de la religion*, 1990. XVI-709 p. FB 2000.
91. J.C. DE MOOR, *The Rise of Yahwism: The Roots of Israelite Monotheism*, 1990. Revised and Enlarged Edition, 1997. XV-445 p. FB 1400.
92. B. BRUNING, M. LAMBERIGTS & J. VAN HOUTEM (eds.), *Collectanea Augustiniana. Mélanges T.J. van Bavel*, 1990. 2 tomes, XXXVIII-VIII-1074 p. FB 3000.
93. A. DE HALLEUX, *Patrologie et œcuménisme. Recueil d'études*, 1990. XVI-887 p. FB 3000.
94. C. BREKELMANS & J. LUST (eds.), *Pentateuchal and Deuteronomistic Studies: Papers Read at the XIIIth IOSOT Congress Leuven 1989*, 1990. 307 p. FB 1500.
95. D.L. DUNGAN (ed.), *The Interrelations of the Gospels. A Symposium Led by M.-É. Boismard – W.R. Farmer – F. Neirynck, Jerusalem 1984*, 1990. XXXI-672 p. FB 3000.
96. G.D. KILPATRICK, *The Principles and Practice of New Testament Textual Criticism. Collected Essays*. Edited by J.K. ELLIOTT, 1990. XXXVIII-489 p. FB 3000.
97. G. ALBERIGO (ed.), *Christian Unity. The Council of Ferrara-Florence: 1438/39 – 1989*, 1991. X-681 p. FB 3000.
98. M. SABBE, *Studia Neotestamentica. Collected Essays*, 1991. XVI-573 p. FB 2000.
99. F. NEIRYNCK, *Evangelica II: 1982-1991. Collected Essays*. Edited by F. VAN SEGBROECK, 1991. XIX-874 p. FB 2800.
100. F. VAN SEGBROECK, C.M. TUCKETT, G. VAN BELLE & J. VERHEYDEN (eds.), *The Four Gospels 1992. Festschrift Frans Neirynck*, 1992. 3 volumes, XVII-X-X-2668 p. FB 5000.

SERIES III

101. A. DENAUX (ed.), *John and the Synoptics*, 1992. XXII-696 p. FB 3000.
102. F. NEIRYNCK, J. VERHEYDEN, F. VAN SEGBROECK, G. VAN OYEN & R. CORSTJENS, *The Gospel of Mark. A Cumulative Bibliography: 1950-1990*, 1992. XII-717 p. FB 2700.
103. M. SIMON, *Un catéchisme universel pour l'Église catholique. Du Concile de Trente à nos jours*, 1992. XIV-461 p. FB 2200.
104. L. CEYSSENS, *Le sort de la bulle Unigenitus. Recueil d'études offert à Lucien Ceyssens à l'occasion de son 90ᵉ anniversaire*. Présenté par M. LAMBERIGTS, 1992. XXVI-641 p. FB 2000
105. R.J. DALY (ed.), *Origeniana Quinta. Papers of the 5th International Origen Congress, Boston College, 14-18 August 1989*, 1992. XVII-635 p. FB 2700.
106. A.S. VAN DER WOUDE (ed.), *The Book of Daniel in the Light of New Findings*, 1993. XVIII-574 p. FB 3000.
107. J. FAMERÉE, *L'ecclésiologie d'Yves Congar avant Vatican II: Histoire et Église. Analyse et reprise critique*, 1992. 497 p. FB 2600.

108. C. BEGG, *Josephus' Account of the Early Divided Monarchy (AJ 8, 212-420). Rewriting the Bible*, 1993. IX-377 p. FB 2400.
109. J. BULCKENS & H. LOMBAERTS (eds.), *L'enseignement de la religion catholique à l'école secondaire. Enjeux pour la nouvelle Europe*, 1993. XII-264 p. FB 1250.
110. C. FOCANT (ed.), *The Synoptic Gospels. Source Criticism and the New Literary Criticism*, 1993. XXXIX-670 p. FB 3000.
111. M. LAMBERIGTS (ed.), avec la collaboration de L. KENIS, *L'augustinisme à l'ancienne Faculté de théologie de Louvain*, 1994. VII-455 p. FB 2400.
112. R. BIERINGER & J. LAMBRECHT, *Studies on 2 Corinthians*, 1994. XX-632 p. FB 3000.
113. E. BRITO, *La pneumatologie de Schleiermacher*, 1994. XII-649 p. FB 3000.
114. W.A.M. BEUKEN (ed.), *The Book of Job*, 1994. X-462 p. FB 2400.
115. J. LAMBRECHT, *Pauline Studies: Collected Essays*, 1994. XIV-465 p. FB 2500.
116. G. VAN BELLE, *The Signs Source in the Fourth Gospel: Historical Survey and Critical Evaluation of the Semeia Hypothesis*, 1994. XIV-503 p. FB 2500.
117. M. LAMBERIGTS & P. VAN DEUN (eds.), *Martyrium in Multidisciplinary Perspective. Memorial L. Reekmans*, 1995. X-435 p. FB 3000.
118. G. DORIVAL & A. LE BOULLUEC (eds.), *Origeniana Sexta. Origène et la Bible/Origen and the Bible. Actes du Colloquium Origenianum Sextum, Chantilly, 30 août – 3 septembre 1993*, 1995. XII-865 p. FB 3900.
119. É. GAZIAUX, *Morale de la foi et morale autonome. Confrontation entre P. Delhaye et J. Fuchs*, 1995. XXII-545 p. FB 2700.
120. T.A. SALZMAN, *Deontology and Teleology: An Investigation of the Normative Debate in Roman Catholic Moral Theology*, 1995. XVII-555 p. FB 2700.
121. G.R. EVANS & M. GOURGUES (eds.), *Communion et Réunion. Mélanges Jean-Marie Roger Tillard*, 1995. XI-431 p. FB 2400.
122. H.T. FLEDDERMANN, *Mark and Q: A Study of the Overlap Texts*. With an Assessment by F. NEIRYNCK, 1995. XI-307 p. FB 1800.
123. R. BOUDENS, *Two Cardinals: John Henry Newman, Désiré-Joseph Mercier*. Edited by L. GEVERS with the collaboration of B. DOYLE, 1995. 362 p. FB 1800.
124. A. THOMASSET, *Paul Ricœur. Une poétique de la morale. Aux fondements d'une éthique herméneutique et narrative dans une perspective chrétienne*, 1996. XVI-706 p. FB 3000.
125. R. BIERINGER (ed.), *The Corinthian Correspondence*, 1996. XXVII-793 p. FB 2400.
126. M. VERVENNE (ed.), *Studies in the Book of Exodus: Redaction – Reception – Interpretation*, 1996. XI-660 p. FB 2400.
127. A. VANNESTE, *Nature et grâce dans la théologie occidentale. Dialogue avec H. de Lubac*, 1996. 312 p. FB 1800.
128. A. CURTIS & T. RÖMER (eds.), *The Book of Jeremiah and its Reception – Le livre de Jérémie et sa réception*, 1997. 332 p. FB 2400.
129. E. LANNE, *Tradition et Communion des Églises. Recueil d'études*, 1997. XXV-703 p. FB 3000.

130. A. DENAUX & J.A. DICK (eds.), *From Malines to ARCIC. The Malines Conversations Commemorated*, 1997. IX-317 p. FB 1800.
131. C.M. TUCKETT (ed.), *The Scriptures in the Gospels*, 1997. XXIV-721 p. FB 2400.
132. J. VAN RUITEN & M. VERVENNE (eds.), *Studies in the Book of Isaiah. Festschrift Willem A.M. Beuken*, 1997. XX-540 p. FB 3000.
133. M. VERVENNE & J. LUST (eds.), *Deuteronomy and Deuteronomic Literature. Festschrift C.H.W. Brekelmans*, 1997. XI-637 p. FB 3000.
134. G. VAN BELLE (ed.), *Index Generalis ETL / BETL 1982-1997*, 1999. IX-337 p. FB 1600.
135. G. DE SCHRIJVER, *Liberation Theologies on Shifting Grounds. A Clash of Socio-Economic and Cultural Paradigms*, 1998. XI-453 p. FB 2100.
136. A. SCHOORS (ed.), *Qohelet in the Context of Wisdom*, 1998. XI-528 p. FB 2400.
137. W.A. BIENERT & U. KÜHNEWEG (eds.), *Origeniana Septima. Origenes in den Auseinandersetzungen des 4. Jahrhunderts*, 1999. XXV-848 p. FB 3800.
138. É. GAZIAUX, *L'autonomie en morale: au croisement de la philosophie et de la théologie*, 1998. XVI-739 p. FB 3000.
139. J. GROOTAERS, *Actes et acteurs à Vatican II*, 1998. XXIV-602 p. FB 3000.
140. F. NEIRYNCK, J. VERHEYDEN & R. CORSTJENS, *The Gospel of Matthew and the Sayings Source Q: A Cumulative Bibliography 1950-1995*, 1998. 2 vols., VII-1000-420* p. FB 3800.
141. E. BRITO, *Heidegger et l'hymne du sacré*, 1999. XV-800 p. FB 3600.
142. J. VERHEYDEN (ed.), *The Unity of Luke-Acts*, 1999. XXV-828 p. FB 2400.
143. N. CALDUCH-BENAGES & J. VERMEYLEN (eds.), *Treasures of Wisdom. Studies in Ben Sira and the Book of Wisdom. Festschrift M. Gilbert*, 1999. XXVII-463 p. FB 3000.
144. J.-M. AUWERS & A. WÉNIN (eds.), *Lectures et relectures de la Bible. Festschrift P.-M. Bogaert*, 1999. XLII-482 p. FB 2400.
145. C. BEGG, *Josephus' Story of the Later Monarchy (AJ 9,1–10,185)*, 2000. X-650 p. FB 3000.
146. J.M. ASGEIRSSON, K. DE TROYER & M.W. MEYER (eds.), *From Quest to Q. Festschrift James M. Robinson*, 2000. XLIV-346 p. FB 2400.
147. T. RÖMER (ed.), *The Future of Deuteronomistic History*, 2000. VIII-240p.
148. F.D. VANSINA, *Paul Ricœur: Bibliographie primaire et secondaire - Primary and Secondary Bibliography 1935-2000*, 2000. XXVI-544 p. BF 3000.
149. G.J. BROOKE & J.D. KAESTLI (eds.), *Narrativity in Biblical and Related Texts*, XIV-250 p.
150. F. NEIRYNCK
151. B. DOYLE, *The Apocalypse of Isaiah Metaphorically Speaking*, 2000.
152. T. MERRIGAN & J. HAERS (eds.), *The Myriad Christ*, 2000. XIV-605 p.
153. M. SIMON, *Le catéchisme de Jean-Paul II*, 2000. Forthcoming.
154. J. VERMEYLEN, *La loi du plus fort*, 2000. Forthcoming.

BS
1515.2
.D69
2000

PRINTED ON PERMANENT PAPER • IMPRIME SUR PAPIER PERMANENT • GEDRUKT OP DUURZAAM PAPIER - ISO 9706
ORIENTALISTE, KLEIN DALENSTRAAT 42, B-3020 HERENT